Swiss Institute for Art Research
Catalogues Raisonnés of Swiss Artists  17 / 1

WILLIAM HAUPTMAN

# CHARLES GLEYRE
## 1806–1874

I   LIFE AND WORKS

II   CATALOGUE RAISONNÉ

SWISS INSTITUTE FOR ART RESEARCH
PRINCETON UNIVERSITY PRESS
WIESE PUBLISHING LTD.

*Project Editing*
Swiss Institute for Art Research (Paul-André Jaccard), Lausanne

*Copyediting*
Princeton University Press (Elizabeth Powers, with the assistance of Terry Grabar, Elizabeth Johnson, and Carol Cates), Princeton

*Design and Layout*
Hanspeter Schmidt-Rüsch, Lausanne

*Photolithographs*
Neue Schwitter AG (Ernst Vogt), Allschwil/Basle

*Typesetting and Flashing*
Livre Total (Luce Wilquin and André Delcourt, with the assistance of Jean-François Godet-Calogeras, Cleveland), Lausanne

*Printing*
IRL-Edipresse, Imprimeries Réunies Lausanne SA, Lausanne

*Binding*
Mayer et Soutter SA, Renens/Lausanne

Princeton University Press, Princeton
ISBN 0-691-04448-1
Library of Congress Catalog Card Number 95–19298

Wiese Publishing Ltd., Basle
ISBN 3-909164-12-9

*Cover illustration*
Charles Gleyre, *Le Soir*, 1843. Oil on canvas, 156 x 238 cm
Paris, Musée du Louvre (catalogue n° 465)

# ACKNOWLEDGEMENTS

This Catalogue Raisonné has been published with the support of

The Committee of the Canton de Vaud
for the 700th Anniversary of the Birth of the Swiss Confederation
in 1991, Lausanne

and

The Swiss National Science Foundation, Berne

The Swiss Academy of Humanities and Social Sciences, Berne

The Société Académique Vaudoise, Fondation Fern Moffat, Lausanne

The Société de la Loterie de la Suisse Romande, Lausanne

The following institutions and sponsors are gratefully acknowledged for
their aid in the research phase of the project :

Swiss National Science Foundation, Berne — Canton de Vaud, Départe-
ment de l'Instruction Publique et des Cultes, Lausanne — Ville de
Lausanne, Office des Affaires Culturelles, Lausanne — Société
Académique Vaudoise, Lausanne — Association des Amis du Musée
Cantonal des Beaux-Arts, Lausanne — Swiss Foundation Pro Patria,
Zurich — Stiftung für Kunst, Kultur und Geschichte, Winterthur —
Schmidheiny-Stiftung, Zurich — Meister-Fonds, Zurich — Ernst
Göhner Stiftung, Zurich — Bankhaus Hugo Kahn & Co, Zurich —
Galerie Koller, Zurich — Hans-A. Lüthy, Egg/Zurich — And two gen-
erous friends of the SIAR who wish to remain anonymous.

FOR DAVID AND SASKIA

The artist, painter, poet, or musician, by his decoration, sublime or beautiful, satisfies the aesthetic sense; but that is akin to the sexual instinct, and shares its barbarity: he lays before you also the greatest gift of himself. To pursue his secret has something of the fascination of a detective story. It is a riddle which shares with the universe the merit of having no answer.

W. Somerset Maugham
*The Moon and Sixpence*, 1919

# TABLE OF CONTENTS

My first encounter with the compelling image of Gleyre's acknowledged masterpiece, *Le Soir*, came about in the Louvre while researching my doctoral dissertation on the iconography of melancholy in nineteenth-century painting and sculpture. Even though Gleyre's large canvas was exhibited high on a wall between two windows where incoming light obscured its form, it seemed at the time that this curious mixture of classical and romantic ideology epitomized succinctly the visual spirit of the *mal du siècle* so poignantly described in a plethora of literary sources. The artist, however, remained little known to me then, as did his nationality, and he seemed to be yet another figure of the period who was now forgotten among the luminary revolutionaries from which the general history of nineteenth-century art has been constructed. Except for this powerful evocation of the contrast of age and fleeting youth, of concrete and ethereal longing, I had little interest in his œuvre as a whole until my thesis advisor, Dr. George Mauner, presented me with a copy of the catalogue of the Gleyre retrospective exhibition held in Winterthur in 1974.

With the zealous ambition common to many graduate students anxious for a publication in a major journal, my ideas about Gleyre's *Le Soir*, now put into an artistic context as well as philosophical and literary ones, led to a paper on the iconography of the picture which by chance was published in *The Art Bulletin* at precisely the moment when the late H. W. Janson was searching for a curator to undertake the organization of a Gleyre exhibition at the Grey Art Gallery of New York University, the first showing of his work in America. When Dr. Janson called to inquire of my interest in participating in the project, I professed sincere doubts since my knowledge of Gleyre's life and work, except *Le Soir*, was limited to secondary sources and reproductions. Nevertheless, with a munificence that seems archaic in our period of perpetual financial cut backs, the Grey Art Gallery offered to send me and Nancy Scott Newhouse, who was to be responsible for Gleyre's Egyptian works, to Lausanne for several weeks to examine the rich holdings of paintings and drawings in the collection of the Musée Cantonal des Beaux-Arts. That exploration of an artistic *terra incognita*, in the company of the director at that time,

11

René Berger, and his assistant, Jacques-Edouard Berger, rapidly resolved my hesitation. I was astonished at the quantity and quality of works in the *réserves*, particularly those on paper, many of which remained unframed and stored haphazardly in large folders. Many of these drawings, incidentally, were considered of such little value then that some were insured for only five Swiss francs. Nevertheless, immersed in this sea of Gleyre's works, the decision was made on the spot to select the non-Oriental works for the exhibition.

The intention of establishing the first modern catalogue raisonné devoted to Gleyre's works, little more than a century after Charles Clément's pioneering effort, can be dated with precision to hours before the scheduled opening of that exhibition on 6 February 1980. While touring the installation of the show with several Swiss sponsors, I casually suggested to Hans A. Lüthy, then director of the Swiss Institute for Art Research in Zürich and one of the supporters of the exhibition in New York, to consider subsidizing research for a catalogue raisonné as part of the on-going series of comprehensive monographs devoted to major Swiss painters, a project that formed the core of the Institute's publishing program. Dr. Lüthy accepted the idea with alarming immediacy and work commenced in earnest six months later in Lausanne in a sparse office supplied through the generosity of the museum.

At the time, it was thought — naively, as it turned out — that three years of research and writing would probably suffice to terminate the project. This initial timetable was based on two primary suppositions: namely, that a substantial majority of Gleyre's extant works were already accounted for in the holdings of the museum or in nearby collections, and that Charles Clément's catalogue, revised with slight amendments almost a decade later, already contained the basic documentary material for the biographical aspects of his life and art. While these assumptions were well founded, it was not possible to know then that Clément was in fact selective in the documents he employed and that his cataloguing methods were at times capricious, leaving out important artistic elements he evidently thought minor or of little use in establishing Gleyre's importance for later generations. In effect, research had to begin from scratch, as though approaching new territory, this time utilizing library and archival material unknown to Clément and writers afterwards. This process inevitably led to the discovery of a spate of new sources that refined and completed the life and works and ultimately would take the better part of a decade to accumulate, digest, and finally incorporate into an impartial text.

It is justifiable to say that had it not been for Hans Lüthy's support and unshakeable enthusiasm, the publication of Gleyre's work would never have seen the light of day. He was responsible for finding considerable financial support, now spanning a period almost three times greater than originally planned; for organizing various photographic campaigns, sometimes under extremely difficult conditions; for innumerable ideas and practical suggestions; and for general guidance in a wide variety of art historical matters related to French and Swiss nineteenth-century painting. It was through his ingenuity that we were able to locate the whereabouts of Michel Clément-Grandcourt, a direct descendant of Gleyre's biographer, who in turn embraced the project and honored its author by providing information on the location of dozens of paintings, drawings, and documents scattered in his family's collection in two countries. It was equally through his zeal that we were able to discover thousands of letters to and from Clément, as well as countless notes and other writings, erratically stored in shoeboxes in the attic of his ancestor's home in Fleurier. This cache of documents provided incalculable details concerning Gleyre's life, his circle of friends, and the circumstances around which some paintings were planned and executed, information which, surprisingly, Clément never incorporated into his publication. The meeting with Michel Clément-Grandcourt opened doors and charted avenues that before seemed unimaginable, including the discovery later of seventeen sketchbooks by Gleyre which helped immeasurably to define his creative process and added dozens of unknown preliminary studies for major and minor works. To these two devoted friends I can only express deepest appreciation for their enterprise and trust.

If Hans Lüthy was in many ways responsible for creating the circumstances around which the research and writing of the catalogue could see the light of day, others were responsible for preparing the manuscript to see the printer's ink. Elizabeth Powers of the Princeton University Press, and her colleague, Terry Grabar, turned a vast, and in many ways leviathan text, conceived and typed before the dexterity made possible by the word processor, into a more tightly-knit, cohesive manuscript. No single individual, however, lead the path to publication more diligently than Paul-André Jaccard, responsible for the *Antenne Romande* of the Institute in Lausanne, who with exceptional ardor and skill undertook the painstaking practical aspects of checking data, translating edited manuscript into galleys, and ultimately seeing the process through to bound volumes. He engaged Hanspeter Schmidt as designer, a wise stroke that assured talent, lucidity, comprehension, and beauty. Mr. Jaccard's assistant, Brigitte Gendroz, was responsible for compiling the index. In addition, special thanks must be given to Hans-Jörg Heusser, the present director of the Institute, for his unflagging support of the project over the years.

In the course of the years of research required to locate and catalogue Gleyre's paintings, drawings, and watercolors, inestimable intellectual debts accumulated. Acknowledging those debts is surely the most agreeable task any author can assume. The following individuals all played a role in the creation of the catalogue raisonné for which this author was the conduit and interpreter:

In Lausanne, thanks are due to René Berger, the late Jacques-Edouard Berger, Erika Billeter, Bernard Wyder, Chantal Michetti-Prod'hom, and Catherine Lepdor, all of whom are or were associated with the Musée Cantonal des Beaux-Arts. Additional gratitude should be expressed to Jean-Claude Ducret who photographed many of the works in the collection. Colleagues at the University of Lausanne who were also helpful include Philippe Junod, Pierre Chessex, Carlo Bertelli, Michel Thévoz, and Dario Gamboni. Other associates in Lausanne who supplied documents, photographs, and information include the late Jean-Pierre Chuard, Catherine Saugy, Anne Geiser, Olivier Pavillon, Françoise Belperrin, Vérène-Françoise Kaeser, Gilbert Kaenel, Pierre Delarageaz, the late Edouard Badan, Jacques Mercier, Paul Bissegger, Jean-Pierre Chappuisat, Georges Caille, Béatrice Aubert, Vincent Garibaldi-de Cérenville, François Daulte, Philippe Thélen, Madeleine Cuendet, Gilbert Coutaz, Daniel Bovet, Pierre Knébel, the late Emile Pahud, André Cornaz, Aimery Gleyre, Pierre du Bois, Pierre Gonset, and Jean-Charles Biaudet. The respective staffs of the Bibliothèque Cantonale et Universitaire, Lausanne, and the Bibliothèque Publique et Universitaire, Geneva, were unflinchingly helpful in supplying sometimes rare and difficult to obtain documentation.

In addition, it is important to signal the sustenance of many friends who over the years inadvertently learned more than they needed or desired to know of Gleyre. Foremost is my wife, Jacqueline, who bore the stress of an author in constant fret over this detail, that illustration, or the myriad of problems that all art historians must face in the last phases of their work, concerns that seemed primary then, but happily are only remembered now.

From other Swiss sources, thanks are given to Alexandre Alioth, Peter Bovet, Olivier Cuendet, Olivier Fatio, Georg Germann, Sandor Kuthy, Pierre von Allmen, Klaus Hesse, Renée Loche, the late Jean-Louis Ormond, Cécile Perroud, Stephan Vagliano, Eric-André Klauser, Trude Fischer, Martin Fröhlich, Anne de Herdt, Pierre Gassier, H. Vogt-Kofmehl, the late Marc Sauter-Olivier, Alfred Masset-Olivier, Edmond Charrière, Mme. Jean Lecomte, the late Jean-Marc Vischer, René des Gouttes, Gustave-Olivier Epars, Jean-Marie Pilet, Alfred Schnegg, Bernard Walthard, Fritz Simon, Hugues Fontanet, Maxime Cuvit, Jean-Marc Gaudin, Jean-Daniel Candaux, H. Haeberli, Mauro Natale, Paul Lang, Urs Hobi, Olivier Fatio and Jean Courvoisier.

In France, thanks are offered to Geneviève Lacambre, Madeleine Beaufort-Fidell, Jean Bruneau, Alphonse Leduc, Marc de Langautier, Henriette Cantarel-Besson, F. Devoigne, the late Jean Adhémar, Jean Ehrmann, Albert Ehrmann, Philippe Grunchec, J.-P. Sainte-Maire, Daniel Ternois, Marie-Pierre Foissy-Aufrère, Micheline Agache, Gilles Cugnier, Jean-Jacques Anstett, Georges Brunel, the late Pierre Sabatier d'Espeyran, Bruno Foucart, Jacques Foucart, Xavier Dejean, Charles Melchior-Bonnet, Jacques Thomas, Isabella Gouy-Arens, Suzanne Peschier, Suzanne Pingoud, Claude Zuber, Paul Renaud, Alain Venturini, Pierre Georgel, Marc Latham, Monique Fuchs, François Vaudoyer, Marie-Laure Crosnier Lecomte, Jacqueline Sonolet, Jean-Marc Leri, Marie-Martin Dubreuil, Daniel Ojalvo, Louis Janvier, Gabriel Terrades, and numerous individuals who prefer to remain anonymous.

In England, recognition should be given to the following individuals who supplied material to the catalogue and answered inquiries concerning material in their possession: Col. James Edgar, Richard Ormond,

Leonée Ormond, Philip Hook, Edward Morris, Stephanie Maison, Briony Llewellyn, Ronald Searight, Mr. J. Franklin, Carl Van Dyke, Lionel Lambourne, and Ronald Parkinson.

In Boston, special acknowledgment should be given to the staff of the Egyptian Department of the Museum of Fine Arts, who generously assisted my research with the Lowell material and related areas: William Kelly Simpson, Timothy Kendall, John Herrmann, Cornelius Vermeule, Michael Padgett, and the Trustees of the Lowell family collection who permitted me access to John Lowell's journals and letters. In addition, special recognition must be cited for a volunteer in the department, whose name unfortunately I never learned, who transcribed the Lowell diaries into typescript for my use. Miriam Stewart was also helpful in locating a drawing in the Fogg Art Museum, Harvard University, and Fred Licht provided additional information concerning a Gleyre study in his possession.

Of other scholars in the United States who assisted my work, mention must be made of George Mauner, Gerald Ackerman, Albert Boime, Robert Rosenblum, Gabriel Weisberg, Norma Broude, Constance Bowen, Alice Rosenkrans, Douglas Siler, Patrick Noon, Noah Butkin, Stevan B. Baloga, John C. Weber, David B. Lawall, John Ittmann, William O'Reilly, Anthony Janson, Carol Ockman, and Jerrold Lanes.

For research into Gleyre's Tunisian portraits, I am indebted to His Excellency Heinz Langenbacher, Swiss ambassador to Tunisia, Bruno Knellwolf, the chargé d'affaires for the Embassy, and Mohamed El Aziz Ben Achour. In Helsinki, assistance was provided by Liisa Lindgren and Ali Biaudet, both of whom searched in vain for Gleyre's drawings which had been traced in the early part of this century to Finland. In Stockholm, Pontus Grate answered various requests for information on Gustave Planche. In Munich, Michael Gregor brought an important study of Gleyre to my attention. In Madrid, Manuel Gonzales and Juan J. Luna generously provided me with information from archival sources there concerning Gleyre's *Dance of the Bacchantes*. Maria Teresa Fioro in Milan answered inquiries about some of Gleyre's copies from his trip there in 1845. In Valletta, Stefano Zerafa kindly added information about sites Gleyre sketched in Malta. Efstathios J. Finopoulos in Athens resolved certain problems about nineteenth-century sites Gleyre had depicted there with Lowell.

Dozens of curators, collectors, and patrons, some who wish to remain anonymous, obliged me with various forms of assistance which I gratefully acknowledge.

Along with services rendered in scientific matters, several individuals and organizations generously supplied stipends and other financial aid that permitted research to continue through the years: the Swiss Institute for Art Research was unflinching in my (constant) demands for additional support and was the channel by which several anonymous gifts were received. To the entire staff, especially Jean-Pierre Kuhn, who photographed many of the works in Switzerland and France, special recognition should be given. A substantial part of the principal research was

15

sponsored by the Swiss National Science Foundation to which I owe a great debt, especially Danielle Ritter who sustained the project at its earliest phases and kept abreast of its progress. The offices of Marie-Claude Jéquier, director of the cultural affairs for the city of Lausanne, also supplied financial aid at various times, as did the Société Académique Vaudoise. Special thanks must also be extended to Laurette Wettstein, former head of the Département de l'Instruction Publique et des Cultes for the canton of Vaud, and Pierre Keller, now director of the Ecole Cantonale d'Art, for providing generous support for the publication through funds accumulated as a result of the festivities celebrating the 700th anniversary of the birth of the Swiss Confederation.

As these words are written — by coincidence exactly one hundred and twenty-one years to the day after Gleyre's death — I realize that research on the catalogue raisonné began when my son, David, was almost three years old; by the time its publication date approaches, my daughter, Saskia, will be the same age. It is to them and their generation of scholars that this work is dedicated.

W. H.
Lausanne, 5 May 1995

# INTRODUCTION

Gleyre est notre peintre national,
notre gloire. Il s'est donné
à nous ; à nous de l'adopter et de
nous montrer reconnaissants.

Louis Vulliemin to Juste Olivier
12 September 1858

Gleyre, the greatest painter
yet produced by Switzerland…

Strahan, 1881

In August 1843, the popular writer and dramatist Jules Sandeau published a now forgotten story entitled "Karl Henry," which, like many others of the period, both glorified and gently mocked the artistic pretensions of Parisian bohemian life. In describing one of the groups, Sandeau wrote of the extreme pride its members had in knowing "le drame que M. Hugo achève pour le théâtre français, et le tableau que M. Glaire [sic] exposera l'an prochain au Louvre." This curious coupling of Victor Hugo and Charles Gleyre demonstrates the extraordinary prestige the painter had achieved only months after exhibiting his most celebrated canvas, *Le Soir*, an enormous success by all standards and still virtually the only work by which he is known.

Sandeau's allusion stresses the special place Gleyre occupied in elite art circles at this time, since by knowing what paintings were in progress, members of the group could claim privileged insight into the work of one of the most reclusive artists of the day. Even early in his career, Gleyre was recognized as an independent painter who shunned celebrity and financial reward for introspection and austerity. Even the exhibition of his works in the forum of the official salons held no allure for him. Little could the characters in Sandeau's story know in 1843 that Gleyre would willingly submit to the salon only one more time, despite remaining in the forefront of Parisian artistic activity for another quarter of a century. His absence from public exhibitions in France drew both criticism and envy from friends and critics alike — the former because the public inevitably felt deprived of seeing the production of a painter widely admired and respected but little known, the latter because Gleyre's retreat was linked in many minds with an artistic integrity his colleagues could rarely maintain.

Gleyre's fame in his native Switzerland also assumed a level of importance that by mid-century catapulted him to the status of a national painter, as the eminent Swiss historian Louis Vulliemin aptly noted to the poet Juste Olivier after Gleyre's triumphal exhibition of his *Romans Passing under the Yoke* in Lausanne. Part of the reason for this distinction, which bordered on adulation, was the fact that Swiss painting in the middle of the century could not yet claim a painter so conspicuously esteemed beyond its frontier. It might be argued with some justification that Johann Heinrich Füssli, who died when Gleyre was almost twenty, was more daring in his art and more influential through his teaching at the Royal Academy. Similarly, it could be noted that later, Ferdinand Hodler, who was in his twenties when Gleyre died, was more visionary and more attuned to the progressive elements of contemporary painting. But between these polarities, no other Swiss painter — including Léopold Robert, François Diday, Alexandre Calame, Frank Buchser, and Arnold Böcklin — can be said to have attained the international prominence enjoyed by Gleyre. During his lifetime Swiss museums vied to exhibit his works, and numerous Swiss patrons and art societies competed to commission paintings from his studio. His historical paintings were so widely reproduced that generations of school children were saturated with his images, believing in the historical veracity of his depiction of these events. Through his extensive teaching and influence, he helped to establish many of the essential characteristics of Swiss painting in the latter half of the century, all despite his retreat from any form of publicity.

This restraint from self-promotion, at a time when artists were expected to vaunt their talents, is one of the most often cited aspects of Gleyre's artistic career. He painted most of his life in Paris, worked in a milieu that included dozens of luminaries in the art world, traveled in the company of writers, poets, journalists, and composers; he had easy access through his contacts to the highest forms of government patronage. His *soirées* in the studio were renowned events in which artistic ideas were discussed, readings of new literature given, and even plays premiered; his teaching atelier was one of the most distinguished and well-attended in the Second Empire. And yet, Gleyre never tried to benefit from these enormous assets, nor did he use his connections to enhance his livelihood, even though memories of the penury of his youth remained with him until his death. For Gleyre, to make and maintain an artistic career according to the standards of the day was nothing less than an infringement of artistic liberty. In this sense, Gleyre's pronounced individualism echoes the romantic attitude attributed to the bohemian *rapins* who preferred to live for their art and disdain traditional bourgois values.

Why then is Gleyre's art so little known today? Why have historians of nineteenth-century art neglected his œuvre? Why is Gleyre's name so often relegated to footnote status in general histories of the period whereas even the youth of such figures as Whistler, Renoir, Bazille, Sisley, or Monet is discussed? I suspect the answer lies in our customary system of values which attributes merit to the vanguard and relegates the rest to the heap of history. But history is not only a record of progressive ideas; it is also dependent on what the historian chooses to single out within the fabric of the whole. Our practice of history — thus our selection of what to chronicle — must also be attuned to changing beliefs about value, to revitalization, and to a restudy of accepted patterns. One may assert that Boime's, Weisberg's, and Ackerman's studies of Couture, Bonvin, and Gérôme — to name but three examples of monographs that surely

18

could not have been easily justified as major publications twenty-five years ago — reveal as much about nineteenth-century artistic trends as comparable monographs on Delacroix, Courbet, or Manet. The crucial question is how can we faithfully perceive the true nature of nineteenth-century French art when we almost systematically exclude from our research those artists who are no longer household names? To look no further than the titular heads of radical movements is to ignore, and thus falsify, the veritable core of what painting was all about in this diverse century.

It is ironic that Gleyre has been neglected by historians because he was frequently linked to the moribund Academy or simply classified with the staid teachers of the Ecole des Beaux-Arts. In fact Gleyre was never an Academician — his independence and open disdain for Academic ideals precluded the possibility — nor was he affiliated with the Ecole. Even his contemporaries had some difficulty in categorizing his art, since he was neither rigidly classical in outlook nor extravagantly romantic in approach. He seemed to follow no single school of painting dogmatically, nor did he blindly endorse the merits of one movement over another. It is evident from all accounts that his freedom to alter his artistic perspective, to venture into diverse camps, was for him a sine qua non of true artistic liberty and therefore the proper goal of the artist. Thus he felt free to experiment with different styles, to attempt varied and sometimes puzzling themes, and to work at his own measured pace to assure himself that his point of view was correct.

His assertion of artistic freedom, often at the cost of popular recognition and the trappings associated with it, won for Gleyre an inordinate amount of respect from divergent groups, even from those critics who might have been thought hostile to his art. The unexpected praise that he won from Edmond Duranty is a case in point. Duranty, who ardently defended the Realist movement and courageously championed Courbet and Manet, admired Gleyre's work despite the fact it never approached the Realist ideal. In an article published after Gleyre's death, Duranty, who signed the article with the initials "JI," apologized neither for Gleyre's art nor for his own admiration of it. Indeed, he noted that since Gleyre was not well known to the public because of his refusal to participate in Parisian exhibitions, it was all the more necessary to alert that same public to the works of this "grand artiste." He added, in effect, the highest form of homage by noting that Gleyre's reputation was formed by those who count most in the art world, the painters themselves. As for Gleyre's art, Duranty wrote that some pictures were indeed dated, too much echoing past tastes that had now changed, but some were also fresh, dreamy, gracious, and profound. Gleyre was capable, Duranty continued, of representing noble subjects, dramatic landscapes, and tender themes, as well as violent works with broad colors or unexpected energetic compositions. Duranty's praise is a reminder that Gleyre's art, far from being mundane or directed to specific tastes, appealed to a varied audience in the crucial decades from the 1840s to the 1870s when painting was undergoing its most radical transformation.

For almost a quarter of a century, Gleyre maintained a private atelier for teaching, which became a mecca for students of all artistic persuasions. More than five hundred students received their basic training there and learned their craft, always encouraged to pursue their individual talents and tastes rather than emulate the master. Dozens of accounts note that Gleyre, unlike the heads of other teaching studios, implanted in his students a real horror of imitation, that he advocated originality over obedience once the basic techniques had been learned. Writing in 1867 but recalling experiences from the late 1850s, the journalist Ion Perdicaris noted that Gleyre was the idol of his pupils as a painter, a philosopher, and a man, revered in fact because he respected the individuality of each student. It is no small measure of Gleyre's reputation that the atelier could, and did, accommodate students seeking instruction in the applied and decorative arts, as well as the later revolutionaries of the period. The studio was the breeding ground for such Néo-Grecs as Gérôme, Hamon, and Toulmouche, and it equally welcomed Whistler, Bazille, Renoir, Sisley, and, briefly, Monet. When the history of teaching practices in nineteenth-century Paris is written, there is no doubt that Gleyre's studio will occupy a major chapter.

## A NOTE ON SOURCES

One of the most crucial sources for research on Gleyre's life and art is a monographic study and appended catalogue raisonné, published more than a century ago, which established much of the basic data only three years after the painter's death. The author of the study was Charles Clément, Gleyre's most intimate friend, who could claim to know him fig. 1 better than any of his other associates. Clément was also the executor of Gleyre's will and the heir to the entire contents of his studio, including the surviving letters. Clément therefore had a solid documentary base from which to draw, apart from his own extensive recollections and those of other close friends. Thus, all research must begin with the data Clément gathered despite, as will be seen, the substantial flaws that inevitably exist in the methodology of a fervent admirer who wished to preserve and elevate Gleyre's reputation.

Clément was in fact well equipped to undertake the task of biography and analysis. Born in Rouen in 1821, only months earlier than his compatriot and neighbor Flaubert, Clément was educated in Geneva, Lausanne, Tübingen, and Berlin. He settled in Paris in the early 1840s, where he earned his living through private tutorial services, at the same time keeping abreast of developments in art, literature, and criticism. It was certainly through contacts he made here that he met Gleyre, although the precise circumstances seem not to be recorded. In late 1849 Clément wrote a long article on Poussin which so impressed the publisher Buloz that he sent Clément to Italy for further study of Antiquity and of the

1. Anonymous, *Charles Clément*, c. 1855. Switzerland, Private collection

Renaissance masters. After his return, Clément quickly established himself as a critic, producing a wide variety of articles on artistic and literary matters, and eventually took over the post of main art critic for the *Journal des débats*, replacing the influential Etienne Delécluze who had held the position for almost three decades.

Clément's importance as an art critic has yet to be fully appreciated or even explored. Beside his weekly tasks in journalism, Clément voraciously studied historical problems and themes, writing long articles on past masters. His monograph on the art of Leonardo, Michelangelo, and Raphael, which incidentally contained a small frontispiece portrait of the three by Gleyre, won high praise for its intelligence and erudition from various literati, including Flaubert, who complimented Clément on the work, citing its straightforward elucidation of esoteric elements of theory. Clément was also an able administrator, who organized the transfer and establishment in Paris of the Campana collection, writing as well the catalogue of the antique jewels in the collection. He was an ardent botanist who wrote a scientific treatise on cyclamens. But Clément's most significant efforts were the respective catalogues raisonnés he produced on the works of Géricault, Prud'hon, Léopold Robert, and Gleyre. It is no exaggeration to say that the very idea of this form of art historical study, documented with letters, dimensions, provenance of works, and solid biographical data based on valid records, had its essential source in Clément's work.

Clément's career, while wholly independent of Gleyre, was nevertheless intricately linked to him during more than four decades. The two saw each other several times a week except during holiday periods; so close were they that the critic Emile Montégut quipped that they were as inseparable as Damon and Pythias. Clément was one of the privileged few who had unlimited access to Gleyre's studio when he was absent, a privilege, he noted, he used rarely so as not to disturb Gleyre's privacy. Clément oversaw the production of many of Gleyre's works after mid-century; he was intimate with all of his friends and therefore privy to Gleyre's personal life and habits. But Clément's study, drawn as it is from these experiences, suffers from historical myopia. Clément frequently discusses Gleyre's art with intelligence, but rarely with pure objectivity, although he was not averse to pointing out the weaker canvases. In some cases Clément is inexact with the information available to him; the dates of some of Gleyre's pictures were known to him — as his private notes show — but they are omitted in the catalogue or simply approximated. The dimensions of the drawings are likewise not always accurate since he, or others at his behest, sometimes measured the actual page, and in other instances measured only the drawing itself. Some of the models for Gleyre's portraits are not identified although Clément or his friends knew them personally.

The art historian confronting Gleyre will be immediately struck by the paucity of his correspondence. Unlike his contemporaries, Gleyre wrote relatively few letters and preserved even fewer of those sent to him, even when his correspondents were distinguished literary figures such as

Mérimée or Flaubert, both of whom were known to have written him. One reason for Gleyre's lack of correspondence is that he literally feared disclosing his deficient Classical education or being ridiculed for his grammatical errors. By the early 1850s, Gleyre wrote almost no letters at all, instead asking a friend such as Clément or Juste Olivier to act as his secretary when necessary. Correspondence pertaining to commissions and appointments was handled almost exclusively by Clément and Olivier, a fortunate circumstance as it turns out, since many of these letters are preserved. Gleyre's early letters are often short, narrative, to the point, and indeed full of grammatical errors; they are almost always addressed to his aunt and uncle or his brother Henry — but not to his other brother, Samuel. Gleyre's lack of interest in keeping records extends as well to the private journals he kept in Italy and during his long trip to the Middle East. Both are brief and record events and ideas in fragmentary form; the Egyptian diary ends in mid-sentence.

But even if Gleyre was uninterested in preserving important details about his life for later biographers, there remain two primary sources of unpublished documentation. The first of these is Clément's own collection of correspondence to and from associates. Clément preserved his letters with the zeal of an archivist, keeping even scraps of paper with two or three words jotted here and there. This rich deposit of material, containing by my estimate about four thousand items, had been scattered among Clément's surviving family for generations before being reassembled in his summer house in Fleurier, near Neuchâtel, Switzerland. Because this material was not catalogued when my research began but was interspersed with the correspondence of his father-in-law, Fritz Berthoud, use of the material was difficult, all the more so because the owner lived elsewhere and used the house only sparingly in the summer months. This is why, when these letters are cited, there are no archival or folio numbers; rather, they are indicated only as being in the Clément Family Collection, where they are still only loosely organized. It is not certain, as I write, that all of Clément's papers have been located.

The chief importance of this collection, apart from its historical value in delineating the critic's milieu, is the large number of letters Clément received from Gleyre's friends recounting incidents and events in the painter's life. Some contain vital information on the whereabouts of paintings and drawings. But in many instances, Clément did not make use of this material, possibly because he felt it to be too trivial or unimportant for the image he wished to create. In certain cases, new information became available to him after the publication of the first edition of his study which, oddly, Clément did not include in the second, revised version. Nonetheless, precious information emerges from these letters, including little known elements of the painter's early life and his trip to the Middle East, the accounts of which in Clément's monograph are almost wholly taken from vague recollections by Gleyre himself — who provided little practical information — or incomplete data gleaned from other friends. Contained here as well are notes on ideas for paintings that Gleyre discussed with others and important documentation from after his death on the provenance of his works, all of which refine considerably Clément's published material.

The second major source of documentation on Gleyre is the large cache of correspondence to and from Juste Olivier, the preeminent Vaudois poet fig. 2 of his age, who, like Clément, knew Gleyre intimately for decades. Olivier, born in 1807, established himself in Paris after having taught history and literature in Lausanne, where, incidentally, he had invited Sainte-Beuve for a series of lectures that became the basis for his book *Histoire de Port-Royal.* It was certainly through Sainte-Beuve that Olivier met Gleyre in the autumn of 1845, before installing himself permanently in Paris. In a letter of 8 October 1845, Sainte-Beuve wrote Olivier that "Gleyre doit aller vous voir," noting that he would give Gleyre his address through Gustave Planche. In the following year Olivier played a crucial role in providing Gleyre with essential information on Major Davel, the last moments of whose life Gleyre had been commissioned to paint for Lausanne; Olivier had previously published an account of the episode, one of the first to use historical data in reconstructing the importance of this national figure. Gleyre would base his canvas largely on Olivier's research and indeed would even employ Olivier and his entourage as models.

Olivier was a prodigious correspondent, writing sometimes as many as six letters a day. When taking his annual leave in Switzerland alone or with Gleyre — his wife inevitably remained behind to look after the boarders they took in — Olivier made it a point to write at least once a day, generally numbering his letters in chronological order; his wife, Caroline, reciprocated in the same fashion with news from Paris. In this substantial correspondence, Gleyre's name appears frequently; anecdotes are shared, conversations related, Gleyre's thoughts often transmitted. Most of these letters are preserved in hundreds of dossiers in Lausanne, Bibliothèque Cantonale et Universitaire, Département des Manuscrits (BCU/DM) under the rubric IS 1905 and catalogued chronologically by year. Like the Clément letters, this correspondence provides important data on Gleyre's relationships with Olivier's circle of friends. Since Olivier, like Clément, acted as an intermediary for Gleyre with dozens of literary and political figures, particularly in the canton of Vaud, his correspondence is a major source for studying Gleyre's contacts in his native canton.

Because of his extensive interests and activities in this canton — Gleyre always considered himself to be a Vaudois and never became a French citizen despite living in Paris for almost three decades — several archival sources in Lausanne, the cantonal capital, are crucial. Besides the considerable resources of the BCU/DM, which also contains dossiers on the major political figures of the era, the most significant depository of documents is the Archives Cantonales Vaudoises (ACV). Almost all of the pertinent papers concerning the Vaudois commissions and exhibitions are housed here in the K XIII series. The Musée Historique de Lausanne and the Association du Vieux-Lausanne are also rich in photographic and iconographical material on Vaudois cultural life in Gleyre's time. The Archives du Conseil d'Etat house the minutes of meetings in which

2. Anonymous, *Juste Olivier*, c. 1870. Lausanne, Musée Historique de Lausanne

Gleyre's cantonal activities were discussed. Letters to and from Gleyre and the Conseil were seldom preserved, but their contents were recorded in the Registres des délibérations.

The Archives of the Musée Cantonal des Beaux-Arts (MCBA), formerly the Musée Arlaud for which Gleyre produced his most important Vaudois commissions, contain dozens of portfolios on the extensive holdings of Gleyre's works they acquired in 1908. Virtually all of the known correspondence is here as well. Eight unpublished volumes of copies of letters kept by Emile Bonjour, the director of the museum for four decades, are especially valuable sources for notes on acquisitions and donations, and for information about collectors who wrote to Bonjour about their holdings.

Outside of these cantonal sources, the most significant archival holdings in Switzerland concerning Gleyre's work are found in Neuchâtel. Many of Gleyre's Swiss students were from the region, including Albert de Meuron, Albert Anker, Auguste Bachelin, Edmond de Pury, and Jules Jacot-Guillarmod, all of whom corresponded frequently with family and friends about Gleyre's advice to them and reported on the development of his projects. Only the letters of Jacot-Guillarmod were not fully classified when research began. Archival sources in Basel, Bern, and Geneva also provided specific information related to Gleyre's works there.

In Paris, the archives of the Louvre include the most complete documentation regarding Gleyre's exhibition in the salons from 1833 to 1849, with a particularly rich dossier on Gleyre's success in the salon of 1843. The Archives Nationales (AN) record state commissions in France — although not for the city of Paris — and include documents on Gleyre's progress for these commissions and payment vouchers. Legal matters regarding Gleyre's will and estate, as well as the obligatory inventory of the studio after death, are contained in the AN, Minutier Central, in the dossier of his lawyer Alfred Bezanson. Gleyre's presence at the Ecole des Beaux-Arts in his student years and the records of the *concours* are documented in these archives.

Outside Europe, the most revelatory documentary source is the unpublished diary of John Lowell, Jr., deposited by the Lowell family in the Boston Museum of Fine Arts, Egyptian Department. The diary is in eight volumes but not in Lowell's hand, having been transcribed at some point in the nineteenth century. All of the essential facts of Gleyre's trip to the Middle East in Lowell's company are recorded here in precise detail. It is important to note that these journals are all the more precious in delineating this aspect of Gleyre's biography since Clément had no access to them; indeed, he never knew the identity of the American who had hired Gleyre for the trip and therefore was forced to base his entire account on secondary recollections forty years after the fact.

## A NOTE ON GLEYRE'S CHARACTER

From the wealth of archival material now available, it might be assumed that enough exists to elucidate and define Gleyre the artist and man of this time. Actually, this is not the case, since much of the documentation does not relate the intimate aspects of his life, nor does it clearly explain the sometimes contradictory elements of his personality. This is due in part to Gleyre's own desire to guard his privacy at all costs; Clément even noted in the introduction to his book that "Gleyre a caché sa vie, et autant qu'il a pu, ses œuvres." Even his letters were blatantly censored when they discussed private matters; an unknown hand, most likely that of his niece Mathilde who had possession of these after his death, systematically excised whole passages with scissors or a razor, evidently when they became intimate — no doubt out of fear of embarrassing friends still living. The large body of correspondence in the Clément and Olivier archives likewise does not generally reveal the intimate sides of Gleyre. Consequently, despite the wealth of documentation available now — much of it discovered only recently — Gleyre still remains as he evidently wished to be remembered: reclusive, enigmatic, controversial, an *être à part* whose history can only be partially reconstructed, a leading painter who cared little for, and even deliberately hindered, his future biographers.

This aspect of his character may be well illustrated through the recollections of various friends who knew him at different periods of his life and in diverse capacities. Many noted his extreme reserve and timidity, which were often thought an indication of indifference to others, while some noted his good nature, his abundant generosity, and his sociability with a select few. Monet, who was Gleyre's student only for a short while, thought Gleyre rigid, severe, and uncompromising as a teacher, offering neither encouragement nor tolerance, while his classmate Renoir found Gleyre to be benevolent and open-minded, qualities that made him revere his teacher. Bachelin and Anker were especially grateful for Gleyre's attention and his intelligent teaching methods, while Paul Milliet, another Swiss student, was struck by Gleyre's cynical mockery of some atelier students. When the caustic Goncourt brothers met Gleyre at Flaubert's apartment in 1861 for a private reading of *Salammbô*, they found him stiff, formal, ill at ease in company, and remote, seemingly uninterested in the bravura reading Flaubert provided. On the other hand, Flaubert, who had met Gleyre in 1849, found him to be erudite, sensitive to literature and even "angélique" in his reserved manner. The critic Hippolyte Taine, who knew Gleyre well in the last decade of the painter's life, thought him as severe as an Arab, excessively modest about his formidable talents, and wholly capable of removing himself from the mundane aspects of daily life, not unlike, Taine noted, a Buddhist monk who observes and absorbs and feels no need to comment.

Almost two decades after Gleyre's death, a short descriptive portrait of him was written by Edouard Grénier, the brother of the better known Jules. Grénier, clearly one of Gleyre's admirers, wrote that Gleyre was the only man he had met "qui n'ait fait de compromis avec sa conscience" either in political or artistic matters. Gleyre was, above all, stoical, proud, independent, severe on himself, and obsessed with his privacy and solitude. Grénier wrote that he spoke little and hardly corresponded; Grénier himself, after years of friendship, had received only one brief note. As for Gleyre's work habits, Grénier remarked that he painted very slowly, "à petites touches," often spending months on a single figure that other painters might have dispatched more rapidly. Gleyre's proverbially unhurried nature and limited output led Grénier to question whether Gleyre could really be considered an "artiste-peintre;" he almost thought a better term would be "un penseur, un méditatif" who also painted. In a revealing comment, Grénier said that Gleyre had only tolerated painting as a profession, but that he did not actually like producing paintings, a fact borne out, incidentally, by similar comments by friends and by Gleyre himself.

Another document in the Clément archives, curious for the time, addresses the problem of Gleyre's personality. This is an unpublished analysis of Gleyre's handwriting: neither the circumstance in which it was made nor its author can be determined. The handwriting of the analysis itself may possibly be that of Gleyre's physician and close friend, François-Auguste Veyne (1812–1875). Among the most significant traits mentioned here is Gleyre's diffidence and introspection, a sense of indecision, an acute scorn for society, a marked tendency toward pessimism, despair, and withdrawal. Gleyre, we are informed here, had no practical sense of finance, no desire to be concerned with mundane affairs, and no ambition. He was, however, moral, honest, and generous, the latter to a fault. The author found as well that Gleyre had a forceful spirit of autonomy, no urbanity or wit, but nevertheless a calm resolution despite his bouts with melancolia. To be sure, documents such as this one cannot be weighed scientifically or used with impunity: it was certainly penned by a friend whose objectivity might be questioned. Yet much of what emerges here is supported by other accounts, and while this document exaggerates Gleyre's traits, the elements outlined within it are for the most part accurate.

What is clear from all accounts is that Gleyre was fiercely, almost neurotically, determined to preserve his independence and anonymity. He cared little for public acclamation or honors, and frequently shunned them to the detriment of his career. In 1849, when his reputation was at a peak, he refused categorically to participate in salon exhibitions, although he contributed major pictures to provincial Swiss museums where exposure was much less than that in Paris. He refused lucrative commissions from Napoléon III because, it was said, he hated his politics and thought this refusal to be an effective means of protest. He even declined the Légion d'Honneur, one of the few painters of the period to have done so. He cared little for the fate of his paintings after they were completed, much to the frustration of his friends. Olivier complained to his cousin in 1863 that Gleyre "ne sait rien de ce qui arrive à ses ouvrages, de ventes et de reventes, s'il en a." This nonchalance towards his paintings was for Clément further proof of Gleyre's disinterest in worldly matters, but at the same time it baffled the critics who had difficulty locating certain works even in the painter's lifetime.

Gleyre's self-effacement is also reflected in the fact that there exist so few images of him. The only known oil portrait of Gleyre, by his oldest friend, Sébastien Cornu, delineates a still shy adolescent ill at ease in the role of a model. There are several informal portraits of Gleyre, including fig. 3 one in which, wearing the pince-nez he was forced to use when his eyes weakened, he inspects a canvas in the teaching atelier; another is by his fig. 4 pupil Bocion. It is not surprising that only three self-portraits are known fig. 5 in his œuvre. An oil of 1827, like the portrait by Cornu, is still youthful fig. 6 and as much a symbolic representation of romantic aspirations as it is a probe of personality. A small watercolor of three years later has the ap- fig. 7 pearance of a souvenir snapshot sent home to his family to reassure them of his well-being. A third example of 1841 depicts Gleyre as distant and fig. 8 already world-weary at the age of thirty-five. Only two photographs of him are known to have been taken: one in 1858 in Lausanne which shows fig. 10 a customary discomfort in confronting the lens, and another, by Etienne fig. 9 Carjat before 1871, showing Gleyre in profile, as detached from the camera as he was from the society around him.

Because of Gleyre's reticence in expressing himself verbally or in written form, we have insufficient evidence concerning his ideas about the

3. Sébastien Cornu, *Portrait of Charles Gleyre*, 1826–27. Lausanne, Musée Cantonal des Beaux-Arts

rich cultural environment in which he worked and lived. Gleyre always professed to have no formal education and therefore frequently claimed ignorance in cultural matters. This claim seems to have been another example of Gleyre's self-denigration, since friends have attested with authority to the contrary, and indeed the known facts bear this out. Gleyre was known, for example, to have read Homer and Herodotus in Greek and was sufficiently versed in Classical iconography to extract and exploit lesser known aspects for his work. In regard to contemporary literature, he personally knew such writers as Alfred de Musset, with whom he played chess, and Flaubert, with whom he kept in contact for almost twenty years, but none of Gleyre's views of their work has surfaced. Gleyre dined frequently with Maxime du Camp, Arsène Houssaye, Jules Sandeau, and their respective entourages, yet never commented upon their works. He knew Olivier intimately and even illustrated one of his poems, but there is no record of Gleyre's appreciation of his typically Vaudois verse. Gleyre met Baudelaire and Heine — he drew a most distinctive portrait of the latter — but no source tells whether he read their works or what they discussed in their meetings. We know, however, that he read widely — the inventory of his studio indicates a substantial library — and devoured Parisian newspapers: his student François Ehrmann recalled that Gleyre usually read about a dozen each day while having coffee at the Café d'Orsay. It was said that no major political event or issue in France or abroad escaped his attention.

Of Gleyre's interest in philosophy and music, even less is certain. Gleyre surely read the works of Edgar Quinet, whom he first met in Italy in 1830 and whom he saw in Switzerland after the philosopher's exile; his work can be traced as a source for some of Gleyre's images. Moreover, Gleyre absorbed the dense theological discussions of Jean Reynaud, as is clear in the unpublished diaries of the Vaudois theologian Jean-Daniel Gaudin, with whom he discussed Reynaud's recently published treatise, *Terre et Ciel*. But nothing is known of his interest in Renan or Michelet,

4. Anonymous, *Portrait of Charles Gleyre*, 1858.
Toulouse, Private collection

5. François-Louis Bocion, *Portrait of Gleyre* (?),
c. 1858. Lausanne, Musée Cantonal des Beaux-Arts

6. *Self-Portrait*, 1827. Lausanne, Musée Cantonal des Beaux-Arts (catalogue n° 7)
7. *Self-Portrait*, 1830–34. Lausanne, Musée Cantonal des Beaux-Arts (catalogue n° 50)

both of whom he met through common friends, or Carlyle, whose portrait he drew to illustrate an article on him by Emile Montégut, himself a philosopher of note and a personal friend.

References to Gleyre's enjoyment of music are also contradictory. Juste Olivier's nephew Gustave recalled that Gleyre disliked music to such an extent that during his visits to Olivier's brother Urbain, the traditional family music-making had to be curtailed in Gleyre's presence. Gleyre, however, attended La Scala in Milan where he heard the greatest basso of the day, Luigi Lablache; he also wept openly when he heard the celebrated soprano Pauline Viardot perform Gluck's *Orfeo* in a version prepared by Berlioz. Gleyre seems to have had a personal relationship with Berlioz and may have even lodged with him briefly in Rome; indeed, the composer is identified as an habitué of Gleyre's atelier. It is known as well that Gleyre had met the aged and already retired Rossini, but Olivier, who was stunned to see the two in the studio, noted in an unpublished letter only that they discussed the painting on Gleyre's easel.

More serious is the lacuna regarding Gleyre's ideas on the painting of his epoch. He once told Cornu that he found modern German painting lamentable, but at the same time he copied works by the Nazarenes in the Casino Massimo. Regarding contemporary Italian painting, which he saw during his two visits to Italy and during the Expositions Universelles of 1855 and 1867, he could say nothing positive. He found Swiss painting also lagging, particularly in the areas of history and genre, but rightfully praised the accomplishment in landscape painting where Swiss artists were strongest.

Gleyre said little concerning his contemporaries in Paris. It is known that he favored the traditional values of strong drawing and refined com-

8. *Self-Portrait*, 1841. Versailles, Musée du Château de Versailles (catalogue n° 457)

position, but at the same time he was hardly opposed to artistic trends that veered from his own principles. It is probable that Gleyre had encountered Courbet in the cafés they both frequented, or at the salon of 1849 where they both exhibited important works, but there is no hint of either esteem for or rejection of Realist ideals. Nor do we have Gleyre's notions about the Barbizon school, even though he entertained Corot and Troyon in his studio; yet his advice to his students to paint *en plein-air* suggests a certain sympathy for their goals. It would be of interest to know how Gleyre voted on the jury committees for the salons of the 1860s, to which he was repeatedly elected — what were his views on Manet's entries? — but his votes seem not to have been recorded. It would be equally enlightening to know how he reacted to the first Impressionist show, which opened only two weeks before his death, knowing as he must have that four of his former students were participants. The critic Arsène Houssaye, who had admired Gleyre's work since 1843, addressed himself to this point indirectly when he praised Renoir's contribution to the salon of 1870:

32

Gleyre, son maître, doit être bien surpris d'avoir formé un pareil enfant prodigue qui se moque de toutes les lois de la grammaire parce qu'il ose faire à sa façon. Mais Gleyre est trop grand artiste pour ne pas reconnaître l'art, quelles que soient ses expressions.

As we cannot pinpoint Gleyre's ideas on the more progressive painters of his circle, so we cannot clarify his opinions on the more conservative artists he knew. Gleyre visited the salons frequently — and indeed asked about them when he was not in Paris — but there are few concrete indications of his taste. Many painters whom Gleyre is known to have met often are never mentioned in his correspondence or in the letters of

9. Etienne Carjat, *Gleyre*, c. 1871. Paris, Bibliothèque Nationale, Cabinet des Estampes

10. Samuel Heer-Tschudi, *Gleyre*, 1858. Lausanne, Musée Historique de Lausanne

33

11. Anonymous, "Salle Gleyre" in the Musée Cantonal des Beaux-Arts, c. 1930. Lausanne, Musée Cantonal des Beaux-Arts

friends: nothing emerges regarding his ideas about Delacroix, Couture, Chassériau, or Scheffer, to name a few prominent examples. Gleyre was associated early in his career with both Vernet and Delaroche but, so far as we know, did not openly comment on their works. Gleyre knew Paul Chenavard for almost a half century, and even used him as a model in at least one important work, yet apparently never overtly expressed his thoughts on the latter's concept of "philosophical art," despite clear affinities with his own aesthetics. Similarly, he knew his compatriot Léopold Robert in Rome and was supposedly encouraged by him early on, but did not indicate his opinions on Robert's major works in the Louvre. Gleyre admired Ingres's work but was known to dislike him personally, or at least to have been bitter when Ingres destroyed or effaced murals at the Château de Dampierre that occupied Gleyre in 1840. He also esteemed Gérôme and Meissonier, even though both of them used figures from Gleyre's unfinished canvases, forcing him to alter one significantly and abandon another out of fear of accusations of plagiarism.

Gleyre's concealments and important gaps like those briefly outlined here have certainly daunted historians and kept them from delving more deeply into his art after the publication of Clément's monograph in 1878; but these lacunae do not explain the neglect that Gleyre's art suffered

34

after his death. One can attribute the decrease in interest in part to the growing value placed on the development of modern art, where Gleyre had no discernible influence except through his training of budding Impressionists. Even in the canton of Vaud, by nature conservative in outlook, where Gleyre had been proclaimed by the critic Eugène Rambert "le génie de notre pays," his celebrity waned considerably. In spite of the paucity of artists from the canton who could claim international fame — Steinlen and Vallotton come to mind — the municipal government never honored his contributions. Already in 1910 the local historian Marc Christin, writing on the origins of Lausanne street names, asked why there was no "rue Charles Gleyre." More than eight decades later, no street or public square bears the painter's name, no monument attests to the adulation the canton once gratefully offered.

This curious neglect is also evident in the lack of exhibitions in the canton devoted to Gleyre's work. While the *Major Davel* and its companion piece, *The Romans Passing under the Yoke*, assumed the extraordinary status of Vaudois icons and were prominently displayed as central historical documents, the rest of his paintings, watercolors, and drawings were hardly known. It is true that the Musée Cantonal des Beaux-Arts fig. 11–12 maintained a "Salle Gleyre" after acquiring almost four hundred works from Clément's widow in 1908, but this permanent homage was abandoned because of the growing need for space for the museum's collection. As a result, more than two generations of art historians had little opportunity to examine firsthand the majority of Gleyre's works, many of which had never been photographed, except in the confines of the museum basement. Apart from the centenary retrospective of 1974, Gleyre's works rarely hung in a coherent fashion in the very museum that so assiduously collected them. Even his *Major Davel*, the painting that established Gleyre as the paramount Swiss history painter at mid-century, was eventually demoted to an ill-lit corridor outside the museum walls, where in 1980 it was destroyed by a vandal. Ironically, only the weeping soldier from the lower right-hand corner remained intact to bear witness to one of Gleyre's best paintings.

fig. 13

fig. 14

13. *Major Davel* after the fire of 1980 (Author's photograph)

14. Fragment of *Major Davel*, 1980. Lausanne, Musée Cantonal des Beaux-Arts

36

## CHAPTER 1

# 1806–1828

## THE STUDENT YEARS

15. *Madame François Gleyre*, c. 1825. Detail of illustration 19

Clément began his biography of Gleyre cautioning the reader that much of the painter's life remained hidden and obscure, partly through the wish of Gleyre himself. Nowhere is this more evident than in the attempt to reconstruct the facts and events of his youth before 1828, when he undertook his first trip to Italy. A lack of primary documents precludes a full-scale analysis of these years, as it also impedes an exploration of his early artistic inclination and training. Clément himself must have felt frustration since he could only devote a scant five and a half pages to the period before Gleyre's decision to seek instruction in Paris at the Ecole des Beaux-Arts.[1] In the following pages, the essential details are culled from primary sources and the slim recollections of friends, most of which were unavailable to Clément when he constructed his biography.

The origin of the name Gleyre is vague; it is known in several variations and spellings in the canton of Vaud.[2] It is generally assumed by genealogists that the name goes back as far as the fifteenth century and

1. Clément, pp. 3–9.
2. Leuba 1953–55, pp. 56f., gives pertinent information on the various family branches.

was concentrated in the region of Cossonay and La Sarraz north of Lausanne. In about 1550, the village of Chevilly contained three family heads by that name, now spelled Gleyre, as opposed to Glayre, the common variant. It was probably at the same time that the village assumed its name, derived from the root "chevillier," which in old French designated a carpenter or a joiner.[3] The village itself is situated four kilometers northwest of Cossonay, the district capital, and about the same distance southwest of La Sarraz. Since the sixteenth century, the village, like almost all others in the region, had been an agricultural seat which counted a limited, almost unvarying population. In 1803, the population was recorded as 242 inhabitants, a figure that rose only slightly during the century;[4] in 1850, the census report indicated a total population of 295 inhabitants — including several who lived on the periphery — of whom 150 were male and 293 were Protestant.[5] A century later, with population movements into rural areas, the number of residents declined to 132 inhabitants.[6]

Gleyre's family lineage can be traced as far as about 1600 to Joseph Gleyre, known in family records as "l'aîné." From these roots, one can follow the family line through Samuel and Jean François Gleyre, both of whom remained in Chevilly, to Benjamin Gleyre (1708–91), who had a lifelong association with the consistory church in the parish seat of Cuarnens.[7] His son, Jean-Georges (1742–1806), married twice, producing at least two sons, Jean-François and Charles-Alexandre-Gabriel, the latter of whom would be the painter's father. Little has survived concerning him, and Gleyre himself provided Clément with scant information on his character or the events in his life. Clément noted only that Charles-Alexandre was a simple peasant, as were all the inhabitants of the village, who seemingly had an uncanny aptitude for drawing which he practiced directly on the kitchen table after the evening meal.[8] The only known memory of him apart from Gleyre's is contained in an unpublished diary maintained by one of his friends, Jean-Daniel Gaudin, an extraordinary religious thinker who was born in the neighboring village of Dizy and whom the painter would eventually meet in Lausanne in 1850.[9] Gaudin, it seems, had encountered Charles-Alexandre at the end of September 1802, when both had volunteered to fight for independence. Gaudin, who recalled that Charles-Alexandre had an extremely strong personality, was struck by his literacy; he was, in fact, one of the few in Chevilly at the time who could read and who expressed a passion for literature. Gaudin described him as an unusual peasant because of his intellectual capacities and his fabled Herculean strength. It was Gaudin who later wrote to Gleyre about these memories, a letter that, we are told, moved Gleyre significantly.[10]

In about 1800, Charles-Alexandre met Suzanne Huguenin, who lived in La Sarraz. She was the daughter of Isaac Huguenin and Louise-Marie Knébel, who had recently settled there from Neuchâtel.[11] This liason with the Knébel family would be of great use to Gleyre later in Rome, when he was able to contact members of the family there in an effort to establish links in the artistic community. Charles-Alexandre married Suzanne

3. *Dictionnaire historique, géographique et statistique…*, I, p. 430.
4. Martignier and Aymon de Crousaz 1867, p. 198.
5. *Tableaux de la population* 1851, pp. 290f.
6. See the figures for 1927–1928 in Maillefer 1927–28, p. 288, and *Dictionnaire des localités de la Suisse* 1967, V, p. 230, which provides the population figures to 1960. Mr. Martin, the syndic of the village in 1985, informed me on the population trends, as well as on other matters relating to the history of Chevilly.
7. This and the following information on the Gleyre family genealogy was provided by various nieces of Gleyre who made a genealogical tree. The chart was given to me by Mme. Suzanne Pingoud of Lausanne who knew two of the nieces personally. It was augmented by members of their families in Lyons and by Mrs. Alice Rosenkrans of Wayzata, Minnesota, a direct descendant of Gleyre's niece, Esther Filbert.
8. Clément, p. 4.
9. On Gaudin and his meetings with Gleyre, see Hauptman 1983, pp. 93f.
10. Olivier to Gaudin, 28 May 1855, cited in Perrochon 1948, pp. 204–205.
11. Agassiz 1935, pp. 360–61.

on 10 August 1801.[12] When the marriage took place, Suzanne was already about three months pregnant with her first child, christened Antoine-Samuel-Henry (in the English spelling rather than the French Henri), who was always referred to as Samuel.[13] A second son, Louis-Henry, known as Henry, followed on 12 June 1804.[14] The last child in the family, Marc-Charles-Gabriel, known as Charles, was born on 2 May 1806.[15]

Clément wrote that Charles-Alexandre died in about 1814, thus when Charles was eight years old. The records indicate, however, that the actual date of his death was 10 December 1816, when the family had already left Chevilly to take up residence in the larger village of La Sarraz.[16] Although the documents do not indicate the cause of death, Clément recounted, possibly from Gleyre's own recollection, that Charles-Alexandre had tried to disengage a hay wagon with a broken axle. Apparently the wagon fell on him and he died of his injuries shortly afterwards.[17] The event seems to have been so banal that local newspapers, which reserved space to report on happenings in the local villages, did not even mention it.

The life of the family, now in La Sarraz, with Suzanne as the sole source of support, is not recorded. Little information has filtered down in regard to Gleyre's mother, except that she had a poetic side to her and a sweet disposition that Gleyre cherished all his life. Gleyre remembered that she had a frail constitution and was sickly, but she was also optimistic. We are told that Charles was the son upon whom she doted. Gleyre would recall in September 1828, while visiting La Sarraz on his way to Italy, that he and his mother had frequently walked on the ample grounds of the château, then as now the seat of the Knébel family.[18] Clément wrote that after her husband's death, Suzanne could not carry the burden of caring for the family alone and soon succumbed. Her actual death is documented on 15 February 1818, from unknown causes.[19] She was thirty-eight years old; Charles was twelve.

It was at this point that Gleyre's uncle Jean-François, who, after having lived briefly in Geneva, had established a modest merchandising business in Lyons, took the three orphans to live with him and his wife, Esther. Gleyre regarded them as surrogate parents and made it a point to visit them often in Lyons and later in Chevilly, where they eventually resettled. Gleyre's life in Lyons after 1818 is so little documented that we can only rely on Clément's account of these years. Gleyre apparently exhibited an interest in drawing at this early age and had already copied an engraving so perfectly that his uncle was convinced that he should pursue a career in art. Gleyre himself thought of becoming a designer of fabrics, an important trade in Lyons and one that could assure him of steady income. Following this initial goal, he was enrolled in the Ecole Saint-Pierre — the date is not known, but certainly must be either 1821 or 1822 — which at that time served as the Ecole des Beaux-Arts for the city.[20] The training process there emphasized the applied arts as a service to the industrial needs of the city, although students normally followed a curriculum that included figure drawing and painting. Nude models were

12. Lausanne, ACV, Registres paroissiaux, Cuarnens, EB 41/8, p. 117. The wedding was first announced on 21 June, again on 28 June, and a third time on 5 July.
13. Ibid., EB 41/9, p. 197. The godfather here was listed as Charles-Alexandre's brother, François.
14. Ibid., p. 215.
15. Ibid., p. 231.
16. Ibid., La Sarraz, EB 70/5, p. 166.
17. Clément, p. 4.
18. Cited in Gleyre's travel notes of Italy, MCBA, GA 998, and partially cited by Clément, p. 24.
19. Lausanne, ACV, Registres paroissiaux, La Sarraz, EB 70/5, p. 173.
20. Nolot 1906, pp. 319f., provides the basic information on the background, as well as general reference to the training process at the Ecole.

only permitted in the evenings, and special courses in anatomy were given intermittently by Doctor Trolliet, a renowned physician of the region. Classes in history and aesthetics were not introduced until 1875.

Clément did not say with whom Gleyre first studied at the Ecole; either Gleyre had never mentioned it, or Clément did not feel it important enough to cite in his biography. However, it is now known that Gleyre's first teacher of figure drawing was François Fleury Richard (1777–1852), who temporarily replaced the celebrated Révoil between 1818 and 1823. Gleyre's stay with Richard is mentioned by the master himself in his short, unpublished biography: "… j'ai eu le bonheur d'avoir des élèves qui se sont distingués, tels que Messieurs Duclaux, Jacquand, Biard, Gleyre, Cornu, et quelques autres…"[21] Richard had himself studied with David in Paris; he showed regularly in the salons, became a favorite painter of the Empress Joséphine, and is often regarded as one of the chief founders of what in 1820 was called the "école lyonnaise." It was around 1820 that his career began to wane, and in 1824 he suffered from a stroke that virtually ended his painting activities. Richard was foremost a distinguished painter of historical subjects, who worked extremely slowly, gathered historical documentation for his pictures over a period of years, and remained absorbed in all forms of medieval architecture and applied arts. He was also a mystic and a philosopher interested in theological questions. His paintings were always praised for their meticulousness in execution and research.

It is difficult to assess accurately Richard's influence on Gleyre at this early stage in his education. Like his master, Gleyre would become known as a meticulous and slow painter, who based his art on literary and philosophical research. Richard was known to have imparted to his students an interest in and respect for Dutch art, particularly De Hooch and Dou, whom he copied and at times emulated. Gleyre, however, seems never to have followed the master in this direction, although we know that he admired the Dutch technique and skill. It is not clear how Richard ran the program — he never mentioned it in his autobiography — or what he especially emphasized, other than the standard exercises demanded of all art students of the period. Although it is not known for certain when Gleyre abandoned his plans for pursuing a career in the applied arts, in which he kept an interest throughout his life and about which he talked to his own students later, it may be assumed that Richard's teaching was crucial in Gleyre's decision to follow the course in the fine rather than the applied arts. But of Gleyre's experiences in Richard's studio, the only fact to come to light was his meeting with Sébastien Cornu, who had won the *prix de peinture* in 1820 at the age of sixteen. Cornu would remain one of Gleyre's closest friends, traveling with him and even briefly sharing a studio in Paris in the early 1840s.[22] It was probably in Lyons that Cornu painted the portrait of Gleyre that remains the earliest image fig. 16 we have of the painter and that clearly delineates the melancholy often remarked upon in his lifetime.[23]

While Gleyre was working with Richard, he also frequented the studio of the painter Jean-Claude Bonnefond (1796–1860).[24] Bonnefond him-

21. Lyons, Private collection, Fleury-Richard, "Mes souvenirs," p. 7. On Richard, the basic text is Chaudonneret 1980, pp. 47f., from which the following information about him is taken. My thanks to Mme. Isabelle Gouy Arens in Lyons for her help in sorting out the difficult archival sources there.
22. On Cornu, see Audin and Vial 1918, I, pp. 214–15, and Brune 1912, p. 64.
23. Lausanne, MCBA, Inv. P. 1371. There is no specific documentation on when the portrait was painted. Mme. Cornu had given the painting to Gleyre's niece Mathilde, who in turn willed it to the museum.
24. On Bonnefond, see Audin and Vial 1918, I, p. 110, and Rocher-Jauneau 1981, p. 33.

40

16. Sébastien Cornu, *Portrait of Gleyre*, 1826–27.
Lausanne, Musée Cantonal des Beaux-Arts

self was a product of the Lyonnais school; he had studied with Révoil from 1808 to 1813 and won great acclaim in Paris after 1817 when his work was patronized by the Duc de Berry. He later became a close friend of Ingres, who greatly esteemed his work.[25] Bonnefond, unlike Richard, emphasied technique over philosophical and historical matters, and it was almost certainly under him that Gleyre learned the craft of his profession. It is known that Gleyre did not stay with Bonnefond after June 1824, when the latter left Lyons to join his friend Orsel in Paris. But when Gleyre went to Rome in 1828, he saw Bonnefond often: it was probably through him that he was introduced to the German painters there.[26]

Of Gleyre's other artistic associations while in Lyons, very little is documented. There is no mention of his having met Révoil, who replaced Richard in June 1823. Nor is there any indication that he knew Révoil's students, such as Genod or Orsel, although the latter would become a close friend in Rome. Among the students at the Ecole at this time was Paul Chenavard, but there is no evidence that he and Gleyre knew each other while they were there; they would, however, become close friends shortly afterwards in Paris where they both studied in the same atelier. The only documented encounter Gleyre had with students in Lyons, other than Cornu, was with the Flandrin brothers who sketched with Gleyre in about 1821.[27] Gleyre would also have contact with them in 1840 in the course of the ill-fated commission for the decorations of the Château de Dampierre.

It was the natural course of provincial art education that students continue their studies at the Ecole des Beaux-Arts in Paris. Gleyre told Clément that he went to Paris when he was seventeen — that is, in 1823 — but Clément was correct in being cautious about the precise date being this early.[28] From documents recently examined anew, it is known that Gleyre, accompanied by Cornu, left Lyons for Paris early in 1825

25. Ingres wrote to Flandrin in 1832 praising Bonnefond's work; see Ternois 1980(b), p. 110, n. 97, which cites the letter in part.
26. Clément, pp. 36–37. As will be seen later in the section devoted to Gleyre's stay in Rome, Bonnefond also lent Gleyre some money so that he could establish his studio there.
27. Flandrin and Froidevaux-Flandrin 1984, p. 14. In the text the encounter with Gleyre is noted, but his name is spelled "Gleyze," while in the footnote for the page, his name is given as "Gleyse." From the context and from Flandrin's circle in Lyons, this must be Gleyre.
28. Clément, pp. 9 and 11, n. 1. Clément points out that perhaps Gleyre's first visit to Paris occurred in 1823, but this was certainly not when he went to study there.

for the purpose of enrolling in the Ecole. Entry into the Ecole was not automatic: the prospective student had to be presented by a master to the admission competitions. The aspirant had to have adequate documentation concerning his previous art education, and if he did not live in Paris, he was required to have an attestation of his age, domicile, and good conduct. These formalities permitted the student to compete for the limited places available — the *concours de places* — which generally took place twice a year and consisted of a life drawing in natural light and a drawing after a plaster cast. The results were judged by members of the Ecole.[29] Until the major reforms to the educational system of 1863, the Ecole did not offer specific training through a prescribed curriculum, but rather provided a supervised studio where the student could draw under the eye of a recognized master who generally came twice a week for corrections and assignments. At times there were lessons in anatomy and perspective, but most often students were left alone to perform the prescribed exercises. Many of these were designed not only to enhance a professional career, but also to give the student the necessary practice to compete successfully in the many competitions, of which the most important was the Prix de Rome.[30]

Gleyre's arrival in Paris can be dated almost certainly to February 1825. In a letter, probably the first he wrote from there, to his uncle and aunt on 20 March 1825,[31] he refers to having been there almost a month. During Gleyre's stay in Paris, he was entirely supported by the generosity of his aunt and uncle. Money was sent either directly to him or through friends from Lyons who passed through Paris — in the letter cited above, Gleyre mentions having received 170 francs from a Mr. Coutance. During the first spring, Gleyre's aunt asked him for an account of how he lived, to which Gleyre responded in a letter of 19 May,[32] which provides us with a depiction of his expenses and habits. By this time Gleyre was attending a private studio — that of Hersent about which more will be said later — and was paying a monthly rent of 31½ francs, which included 18 francs for the atelier fees, 5 francs for the model fees, 2½ francs for his chair and easel, and an additional 6 francs for heating.[33] In addition, there was the customary expenditure of the *bienvenue*, a fee paid once by an entering student to supply his comrades with beer or punch as a sign of his good will, as well as certain other one-time fees, such as 6 francs for the rental of plaster casts used in the drawing exercises. Gleyre also noted his living expenses, including furnishings for his room (80 francs), shoes (7½ francs), an umbrella (19 francs), and books (14 francs). His expenses for food, he calculated, amounted to 16½ francs for each two week period, a modest sum but in accord with the norm for students at that time, who consumed very little meat. Gleyre noted several other items such as theater tickets, twice, and a salon livret. To stress that he did not spend his time frivolously, he wrote to his aunt that he arrived at Hersent's studio at 6 A.M. — probably an exaggeration since most private studios did not open until 7 A.M. — and did not leave until 5 P.M., when he continued his studies at the Académie Suisse. After dinner, he retired to his third floor room at 21 quai des Augustins.

29. Grunchec 1983, pp. 90f.
30. Boime 1971, pp. 7–8.
31. Cited in Clément, p. 11, but dated incorrectly 24 March. All Gleyre's extant letters to his aunt and uncle are preserved in Lausanne, MCBA, GA 985.
32. Cited in Clément, pp. 12–14, but dated incorrectly 20 May 1825.
33. Clément cites these figures correctly although Gleyre had added them incorrectly in the original letter.

42

On 23 June 1825, Gleyre wrote again to his uncle and aunt, reporting dutifully on his progress in his studies.[34] One of the friends from Lyons had come by, a Mr. Villarme whom he had already seen, with a gift of food and probably money. Gleyre informed them that he was living well in Paris, even though his room, his diet, and his clothes were modest; he also assured them that he cleaned his room twice a week, took a bath once a week, and shined his shoes regularly. Except for reporting progress, Gleyre did not mention the nature of his work, but promised to send some examples as soon as he judged them of value. Gleyre also reminded them that he would need more money before 8 July when his rent, payable at three-month periods, was due. Gleyre did not fail to mention that he was in regular contact with various friends of theirs in Paris, mentioning a cousin Louis Cuat — or Cuhat, as he spelled it later — and his uncle's friend from Chevilly, Jacques Bredaz.[35]

It is not possible to evaluate fully Gleyre's financial situation in 1825 since comparative figures are not always available. But because Gleyre always remembered his student years as extremely harsh, it is worthwhile to lay out some equivalent expenses that demonstrate the extent of his poverty at this time. It has been estimated that in 1817 a modest room in Paris cost on average 20 francs a month, excluding charges for heat. In 1843, the average Parisian spent 352 francs a year for food; Gleyre's calculation of 33 francs a month is slightly higher than the average. For a student at the Ecole des Beaux-Arts, there were additional expenses for equipment such as paper, pencils, brushes — a supply of 60 brushes was normal — and, later, colors, all of which could amount to as much as 200 francs a year. Many colors could be bought for as little as 35 centimes, but some cost four times that amount, and the costliest reds and blues could run to 10 francs and more. A medium-sized canvas of mediocre quality cost about 30 francs; if even unpretentious frames were bought, the expense could be considerable. A large canvas could require the equivalent of 300 to 500 francs of paint. In general, an average tube of paint represented an expense equal to a meal.[36] Although it is not certain how much Gleyre received each month from Lyons — the figure of 170 francs has been mentioned, but it is not known whether that was a monthly allowance — it is clear that Gleyre was forced to live in marginal penury. It is no wonder that much of Gleyre's correspondence has indirect appeals for additional funds. It is equally a measure of how this poverty affected him that in 1843 he told his own students that he would forego their traditional fee so as to ease their lot.

Gleyre's first academic studies in the spring of 1825 were in the private teaching atelier of a distinguished painter, Louis Hersent (1777–1860), who was named a professor at the Ecole on 26 March 1825.[37] Hersent had been a student of Regnault and had done well in the Prix de Rome competitions of 1797 and 1798, although he did not win.[38] His style was founded on the basic tenets of the Davidian school, but with additional romantic elements, including a repertoire of North American Indian subjects. His work, often disseminated in popular prints, had a slick, academic surface and photographic finish, not unlike the work of

34. The letter is unpublished, in Lausanne, MCBA, GA 985.
35. Ibid., letter of 15 or 16 November 1825. The family name Bredaz originated in Chevilly or the region; see *Répertoire des noms de famille suisses* 1968, I, p. 261.
36. This and the information above is outlined in Lethève 1972, pp. 14f.
37. On Hersent's nomination, see Brem 1993–94, p. 28.
38. Grunchec 1983, pp. 126–27.

Richard but without the liberties in composition and proportion. Ary Scheffer's portrait of Hersent in 1830 shows him to have been a sensitive and probably romantic personality.[39]

It was through Hersent that Gleyre received instruction in figure drawing, shading, perspective, anatomy, proportion, all within the standard practice of private atelier study, the goal of which was to compete successfully for entrance into the Ecole. As a new student in the private atelier, Gleyre was surely given the most out-of-the-way spot in the atelier; the best places were reserved for advanced students and favored pupils. After copying engravings aimed at perfecting outline and shading, Gleyre probably began working on plaster casts, known as passing *à la bosse*, as was customary in the curriculum of instruction. Only after mastering this aspect of the instruction was the student permitted to work from live models, known as passing *à la nature*, a relatively advanced stage in the training process. After months and in some cases years, the student was then permitted to work in colors.

It is not certain how much of this curriculum Gleyre followed in Hersent's private studio or what benefits he derived from the master's bi-weekly visits. No documents illuminate this aspect of Gleyre's artistic education, nor did Gleyre ever discuss it with Clément, who mentions only several students Gleyre encountered in the atelier.[40] The critic Gustave Planche, whom Gleyre befriended later and who was responsible for the first critical article on Gleyre's work during his lifetime, noted that Gleyre did not particularly follow Hersent's lessons, but absorbed only the essential visual grammar.[41] However, it is known that Gleyre, like other students, augmented his studies outside of Hersent's studio, particularly in anatomy at Clamart, where in a year more than 1500 cadavers were kept for eventual study by medical and art students.[42] Gleyre also studied, as he noted in his letter of 19 May 1825, at the Académie Suisse, named after its founder and not after the country, where any student could, for a small fee, work from the model. Virtually all students of the 1820s and 1830s passed some evening hours here after the instruction in the private ateliers. In the late nineteenth century, it became an exceptionally popular studio because of its free atmosphere and inexpensive fees; in 1859 Cézanne studied there for only 10 francs a month. In addition, Gleyre made regular trips to the Louvre for copying exercises.

The first record of Gleyre having attempted to enter the Ecole is in the fall of 1825. In September, the competitive examination was held for the winter semester in the *salle des modèles*; a limit of 62 places was allotted for more than twice that number who took the examination. Gleyre's work was judged as number 63, which meant that he was the first candidate on the supplementary list.[43] In the next month, the examination was held for the *bosse*, this time with 65 places allotted. Gleyre's study was judged number 9, thus assuring his entry.[44] Gleyre officially enrolled on 19 November 1825, presented by Hersent; his inscription was recorded as number 900 and the next student to follow was Paul Chenavard.[45] Gleyre presented a document attesting to his birth date and place

39. The portrait is now in Grenoble; see Kolb 1937, pp. 13f.

40. Clément, p. 9.

41. Planche 1851, pp. 490f.

42. For general studio practices and drawing outside the confines of the official programs, see Boime 1971, p. 22 and Lethève 1972, pp. 13–27.

43. Paris, AN, Concours pour les places..., le 6 octobre 1825, AJ⁵², 7.

44. Ibid., le 19 novembre 1825. The jury listed for the examination consisted of Lethière, Regnault, and Hersent.

45. Paris, AN, Enregistrement de MM. les élèves..., AJ⁵², 234, here spelled "Gleyres."

and a letter from the judge of La Sarraz, Alexandre Gleyre, attesting to the accuracy of the document.[46] Gleyre participated in another examination for the *nature* on 6 March 1826, this time finishing number 63 out of 72 places;[47] this was noted later on his inscription of the previous November.

Hersent's classes at the Ecole, in comparison with the private studio, were relatively small and had little of the prestige of his contemporaries Regnault and Gros. From April 1825 to November 1827, a total of only 19 students, excluding Gleyre, were recorded as having been presented by Hersent to the Ecole,[48] although some students enrolled earlier in other ateliers switched later, not an uncommon practice.[49] Of Hersent's most prominent students at the Ecole at this time, who worked there while Gleyre studied, one can name Brascassat, Jules Laure, and François-Gustave Dauphin, whom Gleyre would meet later in Paris while he was working on his *Mission of the Apostles.*[50]

One of the purposes of the training process was to prepare the student to compete in the rigorous Prix de Rome contests. These competitions were held every year — although a first prize was not always awarded, as in the contest of 1828 — and were open to all French citizens under the age of thirty. Gleyre was excluded because of his Swiss citizenship, but compatriots such as Lugardon and Chaponnière were eligible since they were considered French, having come from Geneva. Gleyre in fact was one of only a few foreign students enrolled in the Ecole at this time, which contributed to the sense of isolation often expressed in his letters at this time. The records of the Ecole do not indicate any other competitions in which Gleyre participated after the placement examination.

Another part of Gleyre's Paris training needs to be examined further. Clément noted that Gleyre, beside taking classes with Hersent and making trips to Clamart and the Académie Suisse, spent some afternoons working in watercolor with the English painter Richard Parkes Bonington (1802–28).[51] Clément says no more about this remarkable fact, nor does he pursue it, despite its consequence for early influence on Gleyre. Bonington was one of the most esteemed and original watercolorists of his day and is often credited with introducing into France the idea of watercolor technique as an important medium in its own right, apart from its use in studies or sketches. A student of Gros, Bonington was a friend of the young Delacroix,[52] with whom he shared a studio from August 1825 until January 1826. A few months later Bonington took his own studio at 11 rue des Martyrs, which his friend Thomas Shotter Boys recorded in a drawing.[53] During the spring of 1826, Bonington was in Italy, returning to Paris only in late June; he then took sporadic trips to London and the French countryside until 1828 when, after a period of failing health, he died prematurely.

Several questions arise about Gleyre's encounter with Bonington. It should be noted that at no time does Gleyre mention Bonington in his letters, during his Paris years or later. Presumably Clément must have received the information about Gleyre's work with the English painter from Gleyre himself, or possibly from Cornu, the only friend of Gleyre's

46. Paris, AN, Elèves, AJ[52], 261. The judge who signed the attestation seems to have no direct relationship to Gleyre.
47. Paris, AN, Concours pour les places..., le 6 mars 1826, AJ[52], 7. The jury for this examination consisted of Hersent, Cortot, Lethière, and Gros.
48. Paris, AN, Enregistrement de MM. les élèves..., AJ[52], 234, n° 862 to 987.
49. Numerous students became affiliated with several masters who answered their specific artistic needs. Such double affiliation is often noted in the salon *livrets*, as well as in the records of the Prix de Rome contests in which studio training had to be noted.
50. Clément, p. 9, notes the presence of Dauphin, but he was unaware that the two would meet in 1845 in circumstances relating to Gleyre's painting, *The Mission of the Apostles.*
51. Ibid.
52. The few details of Bonington's meeting and subsequent friendship with Delacroix are outlined in a letter from Delacroix to Thoré on 30 November 1861, in Delacroix 1932, IV, pp. 285–89.
53. See Ingamells 1979, p. 19; Peacock 1980, p. 70; and Noon 1991, p. 73.

youth whom Clément knew personally when he wrote the biography. The notion that Gleyre worked with Bonington is at once suspect because the latter never undertook a program of teaching or training students in watercolor, which, incidentally, was not taught at the Ecole. The frequent visitors to his studio were his friends, such as Delacroix, Boys, the Baron Charles Rivet with whom he went to Italy, and Jules-Robert Auguste, the wealthy Orientalist and amateur painter who also had a studio in the same building. Gleyre is never mentioned in association with these habitués. Furthermore Bonington was present in his studio only infrequently, so that Gleyre could not have met with him regularly.

How could Gleyre have met Bonington? The likely candidate for the intermediary between the two is a mutual friend, Louis-Godefroy Jadin (1805–82).[54] Gleyre had known Jadin in Hersent's private studio — Jadin is not noted as having enrolled in the Ecole — and Jadin is known to have worked briefly with Bonington after 1826. He may have suggested to Gleyre that he see Bonington in order to learn watercolor and to see personally the extraordinary work Bonington produced, which at that time was becoming well known in Parisian circles. Unfortunately, Gleyre never mentioned Jadin in his youthful letters, nor is there any record of their having kept in contact later.

The consequences of possible meetings with Bonington, therefore, are intriguing in regard to what Gleyre may have seen and learned. Can we assume that it was Bonington who fostered Gleyre's interest in watercolor, a medium in which he would excel later, as is evidenced by the paintings done in the Near East? Could the circle of Bonington's friends at this time also have influenced Gleyre's artistic interests? Did Gleyre meet Delacroix at a time when he had already painted his *Massacre at Chios* and was at work on his *Sardanapalus*? Delacroix's journal ends abruptly in 1825 just when Gleyre arrived in Paris, and therefore offers no elucidation. Could Gleyre have encountered Mr. Auguste, who may have implanted in the young painter the desire to go to the Near East? Might Gleyre have already met Horace Vernet, who had an atelier in the same building as Bonington, thus easing his *entrée* into Vernet's circle when he was the director of the French Academy in Rome where Gleyre was openly welcomed despite never being a member of the group? These questions, important as they are in establishing the early influences on Gleyre's artistic education, must remain unanswered due to a lack of adequate documentation.

In Gleyre's few surviving letters from Paris between 1825 and 1828, there is no mention of specific works he had completed, although there are repeated references to continued progress in his studies. It is known that Gleyre, like all other students, copied intensely from engravings and selected works in public collections, notably in the Louvre. Some of his copies have survived in a notebook Gleyre kept at the time, which Clément apparently never saw or did not consider important enough to mention or discuss in the monograph.[55] Among a variety of subjects — some of which date later, since he took the notebook with him to Rome — are details from works in the Louvre, after Fra Bartolomeo, Feti,

54. Clément, p. 9, notes Jadin as one of Gleyre's friends from the atelier, but does not mention him as an acquaintance of Bonington. On Jadin, see Bénézit, VI, p. 18.
55. The notebook, now in Geneva, MAH, Inv. 1918/5, cannot be dated precisely since works executed in Paris and Rome are included. Further information on the notebook, as well as another one Gleyre kept at the same time, is provided in the catalogue section.

Holbein, and others. The most interesting copies here, however, are a dozen drawings Gleyre made after the two series of lithographs of horses produced by Géricault, one of the first examples of copies made in the 1820s.[56] There is no documentation as to when or where Gleyre had access to these works or who might have suggested them to him. In all probability, the lithograph series had circulated in the studios or at the Ecole in the late 1820s, but it is tempting to speculate that either Bonington or Jadin may have been the intermediary. The latter artist in particular was interested in animal studies and later became a respected *animalier*. Another possibility is that Gleyre had copied the Géricault prints from a set owned by Horace Vernet; Géricault had studied with Carle Vernet in 1808 and had met Horace at that time. Interestingly enough, Clément, who wrote a major study on Géricault in 1867, had no idea that Gleyre had, as a student, copied some of these lithographs.

17. Pierre-Paul Prud'hon, *Aminta*, 1800. France, Private collection

Clément noted, however, that the works Gleyre produced during his Paris years were lost after he confided them to an unnamed friend before leaving for Rome; the works were not to be found when Gleyre returned to Paris a decade later.[57] He mentioned among these lost works a portrait of Jourdain, which he thought the most interesting painting of the period. Charles Jourdain was to become an architect who worked briefly for the Bey of Tunis in 1841–43 and who may have been the link between Gleyre and the Bey for the portraits Gleyre painted of his entourage when they visited Paris in 1846.[58] Gleyre kept in touch with Jourdain even when in the Near East; he wrote Jourdain a long letter on Christmas day, 1834, from the harbor at Rhodes, in which, in an intimate fashion generally reserved for his closest friends, he described his profound despair at his meager accomplishments.[59] It was Jourdain who introduced Gleyre to the influential but feared critic Gustave Planche whom Gleyre befriended — one of the few artists to do so — and helped to support before his death in 1857.[60]

An indication of Gleyre's interests in other works of art while he was a student is a lost copy of an illustration Prud'hon made for an 1800 edition of Tasso's pastoral drama *Aminta*.[61] The scene represents the attempted violation of the wild nymph Sylvie by a satyr who has overcome her near a brook and has tied her hair to a branch. Just as the satyr starts to touch the naked nymph, he is stopped by Daphne, who calls upon Aminta and Ticis to help chase the intruder. Gleyre, Clément noted, had made an oil rendition in which the figures were about three inches high.[62] Gleyre's interest in this subject is surprising in two respects. The first is the fact that Gleyre was drawn to Prud'hon, who after his death was already considered passé and decidedly out of step with current aesthetic trends; his sentimental scenes seemed in the mid-1820s to revert to a style incompatible with the romanticism that imbued avant-garde ideas. Gleyre's attraction to Prud'hon's work must have seemed curious to his studio comrades who were more interested in emulating the works of Delacroix or Horace Vernet.

It is also surprising that Gleyre would have engaged in copying a work whose theme was so blatantly sexual. All of the literature devoted to

fig. 17

56. On the Géricault prints, see Grunchec 1978 and Eitner 1983. Important information on the dates of Géricault's lithographs is contained in Joannides 1973, pp. 666–71. There is still little information about the dissemination of these works in Paris in the 1820s.
57. Clément, p. 18.
58. On Jourdain, see Thieme-Becker, XIX, p. 195.
59. Clément, pp. 76–77. The original letter has not been found.
60. Ibid., p. 9. On Gleyre and Planche, see below.
61. The work was published by Antoine-Auguste Renouard. Prud'hon also provided a frontispiece portrait of Tasso. See Clément 1872, pp. 255–56, and Guiffrey 1924, p. 396, n° 1045.
62. Clément, pp. 18–19.

Gleyre emphasizes his prudish, timid nature in regard to sexual subjects or themes: when the female figure plays an important role in his pictures, it is the idealization of the figure that is stressed rather than the sensual elements. And yet, when compared to a brutally frank work such as the *Roman Brigands* produced only a few years later, it is not wholly out of character for Gleyre to be concerned with an iconography that is graphic and sometimes sexually explicit. As will be seen later, some of Gleyre's studies after his return from the Near East take up this theme, but in a more restrained manner. Similarly, the influence of Prud'hon, a painter later much admired by Gleyre, can be discerned in some of Gleyre's idyllic scenes of the 1860s.

Of the surviving works of this period before Gleyre's sojourn in Italy, the most significant are portraits, with one exception, a nude, which fig. 18 Gleyre painted as one of the exercises in Hersent's atelier.[63] The work clearly depicts a typical model's pose of the type common in the studios, here transplanted to an outdoor setting. The work is awkward in its proportions and in the delineation of the pose, particularly in the arch of the back and the strange foreshortening of the right arm. The shadows similarly lack nuance. Over all, the effect is one of unsureness in the depiction of the female anatomy. The work probably was painted towards the end of Gleyre's apprenticeship with Hersent, since painted model studies were generally reserved for advanced students.

If Gleyre's nude demonstrates a weakness in realizing the nude figure in paint, his portraits of the later 1820s already point to an excellence in the genre that marks his later years. Although Clément was unaware of these works, there exist three portraits of Gleyre's family, his aunt and two brothers, which from the respective ages of the sitters date within

18. *Study of a Female Nude*, 1825–28. Lausanne, Fondation de l'Hermitage (catalogue n° 4)

63. Clément., p. 389, under catalogue n° 1, but not discussed in his text.

this period. No details have come to light as to whether they were executed in Lyons before Gleyre's trip to study in Paris or when he stopped in Lyons before going to Italy; there is no documentation that any of the models went to Paris while Gleyre was there between 1825 and 1828. The portrait of his aunt, Esther Chatelan, whom Gleyre revered, is a straightforward depiction revealing her simple manner and appearance.[64] The work, although not as accomplished as other portraits of the period, does not show the same uncertainty seen in the nude; rather, it reveals Gleyre's interest in physiognomic directness. The portraits of his brothers, Samuel and Henry, are even more refined, more nuanced in regard to the character of the sitters and in the modeling of their features. Both works bear the stamp of a professionalism that is surprising in Gleyre's œuvre of this period.

As Clément mentions, one of the most successful portraits that Gleyre painted at this time was of his friend Jourdain. While it has not survived

fig. 19
fig. 15

fig. 20–21

19. *Portrait of Madame François Gleyre*, 1825(?). Geneva, Musée d'Art et d'Histoire (catalogue n° 3)
20. *Portrait of Samuel Gleyre*, 1825(?). Lyons, Private collection (catalogue n° 1)
21. *Portrait of Henry Gleyre*, 1825(?). Lausanne, Musée Cantonal des Beaux-Arts (catalogue n° 2)

64. No information about her has come down to us. From the records provided by Mme. Suzanne Pingoud, it is probable that she was born around 1760 and therefore would have been about sixty-five when Gleyre left Lyons.

22. *Bust of a Young Man*, 1825(?). Present location unknown (catalogue n° 5)
23. Sébastien Cornu, *Self-Portrait*, c. 1826. Besançon, Musée des Beaux-Arts et d'Archéologie

24. *Portrait of John-Etienne Chaponnière*, 1826. Geneva, Bibliothèque Publique et Universitaire (catalogue n° 6)

and there is no description of it, another portrait of a youth, also probably produced in the years with Hersent, does exist. Clément thought the painting feeble, so much so that he placed it among Gleyre's earliest works, done while he was still in Lyons.[65] In comparison, however, with the nude, the portrait demonstrates a certain maturity in the modeling that places it somewhat later. The identity of the youth is not known, but it must be one of his studio comrades. It is not Cornu, as can be seen in a self-portrait that he painted slightly later. It is tempting to speculate that the youth is Jourdain himself, who, in 1825, was only seventeen years old, about the age of the sitter. Gleyre never discussed this portrait, nor have any portraits of Jourdain surfaced with which to compare it.

fig. 22

fig. 23

One of the most intriguing portraits, probably produced by Gleyre in Paris, one that also was unknown to Clément, is a pencil study of the Genevan sculptor Jean-Etienne, or John, Chaponnière. Although the work has been atributed to Gleyre, there is no sure documentation to verify it.[66] Chaponnière had come to Paris in 1822 to enroll as a painting student at the Ecole, first with Petit and later with Hersent.[67] By 1824 Chaponnière's interests had developed towards sculpture — in that year, he had competed in the sculpture section of the Prix de Rome, finishing a very respectable third behind Grevenich and Duseigneur.[68] He had also met the celebrated sculptor James Pradier who took him into his atelier.[69] By 1825, when Gleyre arrived in Paris, Chaponnière divided his time between Hersent and Pradier.[70] There is no extant record that the two met at this time; Gleyre is not mentioned in the only edition of Chaponnière's correspondence.[71] Still, it would have been natural for Gleyre to seek out Chaponnière in the Swiss artistic community in the

fig. 24

65. Clément, p. 433, under catalogue n° 119.
66. The work was sold to Geneva, BPU, Cabinet des Estampes, in 1914 by an anonymous dealer in Geneva who attributed it to Gleyre but dated it erroneously, as will be seen.
67. Paris, AN, Enregistrement de MM. les élèves, AJ52, 234, n° 766.
68. Paris, AN, Concours pour le Grand Prix, AJ52, 17, le 1er avril 1824.
69. See Pradier 1984, I, pp. 341–42.
70. Gaberel 1838, pp. 51f., for other details on his life in Paris, but with no mention of Gleyre.
71. Vallette 1911, pp. 68f., for the letters of this period.

50

Portrait de Jean Etienne, ~~xxx~~ <u>Chaponnière</u>
Sculpteur Né à Genève 1801, mort à Mornex 1835

Giraud
ami des
Goncourt et de
la Princesse
Mathilde
Voir le Journal
des goncourt.

ce dessin a
été exécuté
vers 1821-1824

1941/222

Chaponnière

Auteur du bas relief de la Prise d'Alexandrie à l'Arc de triomphe
de l'Etoile. Elève de l'Ecole des Bx Arts à Paris de 1821 à 1824 et
ensuite de <u>Pradier</u> pendant 2 ans. Ce dessin peut être
attribué avec presque certitude à Ch. <u>gleyre</u>, le peintre
vaudois (1806-1874). Il provient de l'album d'Eugène Giraud (1806-1881)
ami de gleyre et de chaponnière avec lesquels il fit ses études à l'Ecole
des Bx Arts

25. *Self-Portrait*, 1827. Lausanne, Musée Cantonal des Beaux-Arts (catalogue n° 7)

early months of his Parisian sojourn, and he may have befriended him while he was with Hersent.

The dating of the portrait, however, is uncertain and can only be approximated from the known facts of Chaponnière's life at this time. It has been thought that Gleyre produced the portrait between 1821 and 1824, when he was in Lyons, but Chaponnière was then in Geneva and

52

Paris. In the summer of 1826, Chaponnière went to Naples; Gleyre did not arrive in Naples until 1832 when Chaponnière was already back in Paris. Thus, the portrait, if done by Gleyre, must be dated between 1825 and 1826. Since so few drawings by Gleyre survive from this period, the portrait cannot be compared stylistically to others.

fig. 25 The only dated work of Gleyre from the period in Paris is the self-portrait inscribed 1827. When compared with the portraits of his brothers, probably painted earlier, there is evident a marked difference in style, which here is more linear and less defined in its modeling, not unlike the nude mentioned earlier. Curiously, Clément did not include this painting in his catalogue, although he surely knew it since it was in the possession of Gleyre's niece Mathilde, who had received it after the death of her father, Gleyre's brother Henry. This fact, as well as the stylistically uncharacteristic aspects of the portrait, raised doubts as to the authenticity of the work's author, but not its model. When Mathilde died in 1918, the director of the Musée Cantonal des Beaux-Arts in Lausanne, Emile Bonjour, who had inherited the painting, seriously questioned whether Gleyre had painted the portrait and wrote to Mlle. Pape-Carpentier, Mathilde's companion and executrice of her will, for verification and a solid provenance.[72] She replied that the Gleyre family had never doubted Gleyre's authorship, but noted as well that it was painted by Gleyre when he was eighteen — thus, in 1824 when he was still in Lyons and contrary to the inscribed date. Furthermore, she wrote that Gleyre had painted the canvas in the presence of his brothers, thus verifying a pre-Paris date

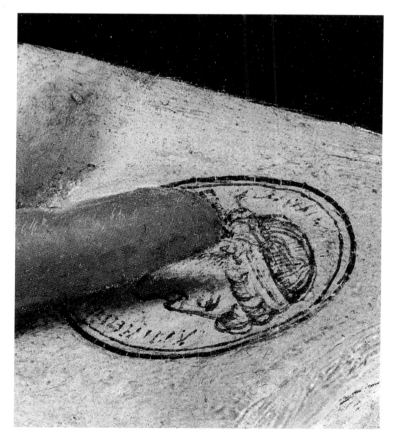

26. *Self-Portrait*, 1827. Detail of illustration 25

72. Letter of 30 January 1918 to Mme. Pape-Carpentier, in Lausanne, MCBA, Bonjour, "Copies de lettres," IV, unpaginated.

since neither Samuel nor Henry is known to have gone to Paris when Gleyre was studying there.[73]

These facts, then, disagree with the date of 1827 meticulously inscribed in gold at the right. Perhaps Mlle. Pape-Carpentier's information was faulty, although she must have had it from Mathilde herself, or perhaps Gleyre had painted the self-portrait during an unrecorded visit to Lyons in the summer months when normally the Paris ateliers were closed. The background reflects Gleyre's weakness in landscape — although during his trip to the Near East he would excel in the form — but is clearly meant to be understood as a symbolic decoration elaborating the character of the sitter. This symbolic aspect is further enhanced by the gesture of the finger pointing to a Classical medal probably representing one of the Caesars.[74] The composition should no doubt be understood as a reference to Gleyre's interest in Classical art, which he would maintain throughout his life. The landscape is clearly Italian in nature, thus implying Gleyre's artistic concerns in 1827. It is no accident that in the following year Gleyre would come into direct contact with both of these elements — antiquity and Italy — an encounter that would be decisive for Gleyre's later art.

fig. 26

73. Letter of 2 February 1918 from Mme. Pape-Carpentier to Bonjour, in Lausanne, MCBA, GA 1020.

74. Huggler and Cetto 1943, p. 45, identify the medal as such. Efforts by Mlle. Anne Geiser of the Cabinet des Médailles, Lausanne, have failed to identify the medal more specifically. Books of the type Gleyre holds in the portrait, with reproductions of coins and medals, were abundant in Paris in the 1820s.

## CHAPTER 2

# 1828–1834

ITALY AND THE OLD MASTERS

27. Copy after Michelangelo, 1828. Lausanne, Musée Cantonal des Beaux-Arts (catalogue n° 29)

A common goal of art students in Paris during the 1820s was to complete their artistic education through an extended sojourn in Italy. Since Gleyre could not compete for the Prix de Rome, the most prestigious avenue for accomplishing this ideal, he was forced to find other means for such a trip. Despite the state of penury in which he lived in Paris, Gleyre had by 1828 decided upon the necessity of an extended stay in Italy. No documents have been found that show precisely when he decided to undertake the journey or by what financial means. Once again his family offered to help defray the expenses, but as will be seen in his letters, financial worries plagued Gleyre throughout this period.

Thus, in the summer of 1828, after three full years of study in Paris, Gleyre, accompanied by Cornu, left Paris via Lyons for the Alpine crossing. They managed the first leg of the trip on foot, despite the fact that the Paris-Lyons rail line had been in operation for a year.[75] They remained in Lyons only for a short while, presumably to visit relatives, and also to pick up Nicolas-Victor Fonville (1805–56), a comrade from their student years at the Ecole St-Pierre.[76] On 3 September 1828, the three of them left Lyons for Geneva. Gleyre could hardly have imagined at this point that he would not set foot in France again for almost a decade.

The voyage from Lyons to Italy is documented by Gleyre in the form of an abbreviated diary he maintained, often in haphazard form, for the course of the trip. The journal, like the one he would keep during the trip to the Orient, is notational rather than complete, frequently omitting several weeks' events at a time. The small notebook of thirty-two pages, of which only eleven and a half are used, is written in pencil; two small sketches, probably made en route, are included. The volume, such as it is, serves as a record of Gleyre's experiences, but it is never complete in describing his ideas or his encounters along the way.[77]

The party stopped in Geneva, where they visited the yet incomplete museum holdings. Gleyre mentioned certain works that caught his attention, particularly a *David and Goliath* then attributed to Domenichino.[78] He was also struck by the rich exhibition of Dutch art, especially works by Ruysdael and Wowermans, and likewise noted the important sculpture collection.[79] Gleyre did not record whether he attempted to visit the private collections that at that time formed an important element in the Genevan artistic milieu, nor did he indicate the rest of his activities in the city. He remained in Geneva until 6 September, at which time he took the steamboat to Lausanne. Gleyre noted only that Cornu and Fonville "s'y conduisent d'une façon ridicule" and that he saw an Englishman with "son favori," meaning his dog. There is no mention of his having visited the small collection of paintings on view in Lausanne at the time.[80]

On 7 September, Gleyre made his way to La Sarraz, where his aunt and uncle received him coldly. Gleyre himself did not warm to the country environment, understandably after three years in Paris: "Je suis tout à fait dégoûté de la vie champêtre par le tableau que j'en vois ici. Quel ennui!" It might be mentioned here that despite frequent later visits to La Sarraz and Chevilly, Gleyre was always ill at ease in the country and disliked intensely the provincial mentality he encountered.[81] On this visit, he was overcome by his feelings in La Sarraz and by memories of his youth. In one of the few personal lines of the journal, he writes that he remembers how he and his mother had walked on the extensive grounds of the château. And when he saw his own house, where he had lived after moving from Chevilly, he was stunned to notice that the charm he remembered had disappeared. He noted that he was so brokenhearted that he refused at first to enter.

The next day Gleyre was again in Lausanne, but this time alone, since Cornu was ill; there is no mention of Fonville. Gleyre profited by going to visit the cathedral, which he called l'Eglise Saint-Martin.[82] He found the entrance particularly enchanting and remarked upon several sculpted figures in wood wearing costumes of the fifteenth and sixteenth centu-

75. Michel 1986, pp. 20–23.
76. Fonville had gone to the Ecole between 1820 and 1821. On his career in Lyons, see Bénézit, IV, p. 429.
77. The notebook, 11 by 9 cm., is preserved in Lausanne, MCBA, GA 998. It was given to the museum after the death of Mathilde. Clément quoted from it generously in his section on the Italian trip, pp. 22f.
78. The work has subsequently been given to Vaccaro, but at the time was one of the showpieces of the collection.
79. On the collection at this time, see Rigaud 1876 and Natale 1980. Information was also provided by the curator of the collection, Mlle. Renée Loche.
80. See Bonjour 1905, pp. 9–19, for the state of the Lausanne collection before the construction of the museum.
81. See Gleyre's views on this later, as recounted to Gaudin, in Hauptman 1983, p. 112.
82. Lausanne did not have a church dedicated to Saint Martin. The basic text on the architecture of Lausanne, particularly the churches, is Grandjean 1965 and 1979.

ries. This is surely a reference to the numerous wooden stalls which were intact until 1829 when a program was initiated for their dismantlement.[83] He also noted the words "Othon de Grandson," referring to the mausoleum of Otton of Grandson (1240–1328), which still preserves the gisant figure of him.[84]

Cornu regained his health by the 12th and they were able to leave Lausanne for Brig. They passed through Vevey, Clarens, and Chillon without stopping to inspect the monuments. They then proceeded by the traditional route to the Simplon Pass where Gleyre thought, erroneously, he caught a glimpse of the Jungfrau, and finally arrived at Isola, the first Italian customs station. They then went to Domodossola, on foot in drenching rain, carrying thirty pounds of provisions on their backs; Gleyre could only comment sarcastically, "Ah! quel plaisir d'être en voyage." From there, they were able to hire a cart, but were in constant fear of the brigands known to be in the region. Gleyre had in fact seen two of them along the way, one openly carrying a rifle. The sight of these brigands would not be forgotten and certainly played a role in the creation of his first important Roman painting three years later.

By October, the party had arrived in Milan. Gleyre's notes here are meager and scattered, indicating little of his activities or even the length of his stay. Nevertheless, he quickly recognized the oppressed nature of the Milanese, who, since 1815, had been assimilated into the Austrian Empire. Gleyre was even greeted at the entrance to the city by the horrifying sight of two hanged men, as well as Austrian soldiers manning their canons in a show of domination. As a lifelong Republican who esteemed liberty as the only viable political force, Gleyre was appalled and disgusted.

Gleyre wrote of his admiration for Italian women, commenting on their particularly well developed hips and "postérieurs."[85] He also amused himself at the opera, one of the few instances in which he recorded his interest in music: at La Scala he heard an unnamed, but mediocre work, and was enchanted by the extraordinary singer Luigi Lablache, who at the time was causing a sensation on the continent.[86]

Gleyre's primary concern in Milan was to study the collections of paintings, but his notes in this regard cover less than half a page and indicate only in summary form what he saw and admired. He recorded that the "galerie de peinture" — meaning the Brera, then still in its infancy[87] — "est riche de tableaux anciens," but he remarked upon only five works. Raphael's *Marriage of the Virgin*[88] and Bellini's *Saint Mark at Alexandria*[89] clearly impressed him greatly, but they received no commentary. "Un tableau de Bassan" that created "un effet magique" most probably refers to Bassano's painting *San Rocco and the Virgin*;[90] a canvas by Veronese, "le mieux conservé que j'ai vu," is difficult to identify, since by 1828 the Brera owned six works by the painter.[91] Gleyre was greatly impressed by the many frescoes by Luini, some of which he would copy, as will be seen shortly.

Gleyre also visited the Ambrosiana, noting that he studied several works by Michelangelo, Leonardo, Raphael, and Titian. The works of

83. Bach et al. 1944, pp. 267f. Some of the stalls were later recovered and set into place.
84. Ibid., pp. 310–11.
85. Clément, p. 30, changed Gleyre's prose slightly, indicating his appreciation of the forms of these women. It might be noted in this context that Clément edited several passages of Gleyre's original text, both here and later.
86. Luigi Lablache (1794–1858) was considered the greatest basso of his day. The son of a Frenchman and Irish mother, he made his début at La Scala in 1817; he excelled in comic roles, both as actor and singer. Such luminary composers as Donizetti and Schubert wrote for him, but he once refused to sing an aria by Wagner because it did not suit his style. On his career, see Widen 1897.
87. See Olivari 1983, p. 5, for the history of the collection at the time.
88. The work entered the Brera after 1801; see Bertelli et al. 1984.
89. Gleyre called the painting "*La Prédication de Saint Pierre à Constantinople* de Gentil Belino." The work entered the Brera in 1809.
90. The work was the only example by Bassano in the collection; see Arslan 1960(a), I, p. 171. Another painting by the artist had been in the Ambrosiana since 1618.
91. Pignatti 1976, I, pp. 132, 158, 161, 167, and 193–94.

the last two artists can be readily identified: by Raphael, a large preparatory drawing for his fresco in Rome, the *School of Athens*;[92] and the *Adoration of the Magi* by Titian, which Gleyre called the *Holy Family*, referring to the left side of the canvas.[93] He described the works by Leonardo as "un portrait sur papier de couleur, d'une grande finesse," several studies of horses, and a "Sainte Famille," in which the figure of Anne is "une figure vraiment divine." The Ambrosiana collection did not contain a Leonardo portrait, nor a *Holy Family*. It did include a Luini drawing on colored paper that could have been attributed to Leonardo, but no work known in the Ambrosiana fits the description of a *Holy Family* that might have been thought to be by Leonardo. Gleyre's reference to several studies of horses must be to the drawings in the Codex Atlanticus,[94] in which several sheets depict horses in motion, a particular interest of Gleyre's in light of his copies after Géricault's prints. The reference to a work by Michelangelo indicates "deux dessins, études pour son *Jugement dernier*." No catalogue of Michelangelo indicates that any of his drawings were in Milan; the Ambrosiana catalogues show no copies after Michelangelo's fresco. Gleyre makes no mention of having visited Leonardo's *Last Supper*, an omission that would be rectified during his second trip to Milan in 1845.

Besides studying the works mentioned above — as well as others not noted in the journal — Gleyre made copies of works that stirred him, but the extent of these is not certain. Clément mentions that a large number of copies were included in two or three small notebooks Gleyre kept, but Clément did not know whether they dated from the first trip.[95] Of the copies most assuredly done in 1828 in Milan, only two have surfaced on loose sheets — clearly from a small notebook. Both of the works illustrate details from Luini's frescoes at Santa Maria della Pace, which were removed from their site and placed in the Brera after 1805. The subjects were taken from *Apocalypsis Nova* and represent the Annunciation to Anna and Joseph returning after the marriage.

fig. 28–29

Gleyre left Milan by the route leading to Lodi. He does not record whether he stopped there to see any of the local frescoes. His journal notes only that he was shown the spot where Napoléon was almost captured by the Austrians.[96] The party then continued to Piacenza where they were blocked by a visa problem that forced them to remain several days. Gleyre was not pleased by the inconvenience and wrote that the city was "la plus triste que j'aie jamais vue." Despite a richness of churches, palaces, and a substantial public collection, Gleyre could only remark that there are "point de peintures, rien de pittoresque."

But his journal entry here also contains a brief remark that shows his erudition in fields other than art. Referring to the singularly unattractive women he saw in Piacenza, Gleyre wrote that "M. Geoffroid (sic) de St. Hilaire pourrait faire ici ample moisson de monstres du genre féminin." The reference is to the scientist Etienne Saint-Hilaire (1772–1844) who with Cuvier — who later opposed his views vehemently — organized a complex theory of harmonic balance in natural law pertaining to animal forms and structures. In 1821 he published his *Essai de classification des*

92. The cartoon had been acquired in 1626; see Knab et al. 1983, p. 589, n° 362.
93. Wethey 1969, I, pp. 64–65.
94. Cogliati Arano 1982 reproduces several studies which Gleyre may have seen.
95. Clément, p. 187.
96. Here Gleyre refers to the incident of 10 May 1796.

28. Copy after Bernardino Luini, 1828. Lausanne, Musée Cantonal des Beaux-Arts (catalogue n° 8)
29. Copy after Bernardino Luini, 1828. Switzerland, Private collection (catalogue n° 9)

*monstres*, which developed the scientific study of monstruous forms in nature.[97] His influence was widespread in France and Germany, attracting such figures as Balzac and Goethe. The importance of Gleyre's reference in the journal is that it substantiates his interest in science and philosophy, despite his repeated proclamations that he never had a formal education and was always ill at ease with contemporary literature and ideas.[98]

Gleyre found Parma, his next stop, enchanting. He visited the palace of Marie-Louise, Napoleon's second wife, who by then had married the infamous von Neipperg. Gleyre thought the palace itself "mesquin" and noted that the wedding gifts given Marie-Louise by Bonaparte, which he saw there, were covered with dust.[99] Of the husband of Marie-Louise, Gleyre wrote, "L'homme qui a remplacé l'Empereur des Français n'a pas seulement la beauté physique po..."[100]. And it is in this manner, in midword, that Gleyre finished the journal of the trip. It is not clear what else Gleyre saw in Parma or precisely where he stopped afterwards, although surely he passed by Modena and Bologna — there is a copy of the figure of the Magdalene in Raphael's painting *Saint Cecilia*, then on view in Bologna.

Gleyre probably went directly to Florence after his stay in Bologna, arriving at the beginning of October 1828. Clément noted that he stayed here, presumably still with Cornu and Fonville, for a period of about three months,[101] but it is impossible to reconstruct his visit accurately: he wrote no letters to his family until the beginning of 1829 when he was already in Rome. The only extant documentation of his artistic activities is two dozen or so copies after Florentine works of art, more of which existed, it is clear, even in Clément's time.[102]

97. On the importance of his ideas in the context of the science of his day, see Cahn 1962.
98. Clément, p. 21, notes this, but Gleyre later referred repeatedly to his lack of formal education.
99. Chastenet 1983, p. 77, recounts the history of Bonaparte's gifts and his relationship to Marie-Louise.
100. Not cited by Clément in his account.
101. Clément, p. 33.
102. Ibid.; Clément remarks upon other copies including a *Venus de Medici*, none of which were found among Gleyre's drawings left in the atelier after his death. The recent discovery of his youthful sketchbooks and loose sheet drawings from this trip elucidates more clearly what he saw and studied.

Gleyre's direct contact with the works of Renaissance art in situ formed a strong impression. His copies testify to a vivid admiration for Raphael and Michelangelo, as might well be expected, but also for the sculpture fig. 27 of Della Robbia, Donatello, and Verrocchio. His sketches from the Uffizi show an unusual interest in Mannerist art, particularly the portraits of Pontormo, Parmigianino, and Bronzino, then considered decadent and not deserving of the study afforded to the masters of the High Renaissance. Nor was Gleyre insensitive to early Italian frescoes, as can be seen in his drawings after the works in San Miniato and Santa Maria Novella, where he copied details of lesser known painters. It is important to note that Gleyre's interest in Florentine art extended to a wide variety of examples, in some cases obligatory for the art student of the period, but in some instances, unusual. His admiration for various styles of Italian art, ranging from the early to the late Renaissance, would become even more acutely articulated during his stay in Rome, and once again almost two decades later when he undertook a separate study trip to northern Italy.

Gleyre left Florence on 3 January 1829, traveling directly to Rome where he wrote his first letter to his uncle, dated 10 January, explaining that the trip from Florence was especially arduous and lasted six days because of an unexpected snow storm.[103] His stay in Rome can be reconstructed more fully than his sojourn in Florence because of his more extensive correspondence, mostly to his brother Henry. Unfortunately, many of the letters are fragmentary, having been cut wherever the information appears to approach sensitive personal matters; in some instances, the information can be adduced through the letters and memoirs of friends.

Gleyre installed himself first at the Café Greco on the Via Condotti, which often served throughout the century as a point of reference for newly arrived artists, writers, and composers. Shortly afterwards, he sought out his distant relative François Keisermann, about whom more will be said later. He also decided to rent a studio in which to work, but since he did not have enough money to pay the rent in advance as was customary, he was forced to borrow the money from his former teacher, Bonnefond, who had arrived in Rome earlier.[104] This lack of funds would plague Gleyre in Rome, as it had in Paris. We know that when he arrived in Rome, he had less than four hundred francs, which he assumed would be sufficient to establish a base from which to augment his income.[105] He learned shortly that he had barely enough to meet even his most basic requirements, and during the years 1830 to 1833, there are constant pleas to Henry for additional financial help.[106] When Henry had not written for more than three months, Gleyre wrote, "Vous êtes donc bien décidés à me prendre par famine."[107] In the summer of 1833 he wrote to Henry in desperation, saying that he had no money at all and his sources for earning even a little were rapidly drying up.[108] He even noted, in Faustian manner, that he would gladly give up ten years of his life for three thousand francs.[109]

Gleyre's correspondence from Rome was laced with expressions of his misery, poverty, and disillusionment, but he also recounted mundane

103. Ibid., p. 35.
104. Gleyre recounted this in a letter of 29 April 1829, cited partially in ibid., p. 37. On Bonnefond in Italy, see Colin 1984, pp. 213–35.
105. In an unpublished letter to Henry, 10 February 1829, in Lausanne, MCBA, GA 986.
106. Several letters in ibid., some not published by Clément.
107. In Clément, p. 43. The letter is dated only "le 26 1832."
108. Ibid., p. 50.
109. Ibid., p. 38, from a letter of 5 January 1830. Gleyre's poverty was substantial, and without any trappings of the bohemian existence that other artists in Rome professed. He had only one shirt, so frayed that at times he embellished it with paint to make it appear fresher; see Perrochon 1943, p. 23. He ate as cheaply as possible, often at the Lepri, but sometimes had to forego meals entirely.

30. Copy after Salvator Rosa, 1829–33. France, Private collection (catalogue n° 71, folio 37ʳ)

events and sometimes told Henry of his activities. On 21 April 1829, he wrote of his fascination at watching the installation of the new Pope in the Sistine Chapel.[110] In a letter of 1 May 1830, he described his daily routine — rising at 6 A.M., breakfast of coffee and water, work in the mornings, reading, walks, visits to galleries, and lonely evenings.[111] Unfortunately, Gleyre never specified in any of his Roman letters which galleries or churches he visited, except for certain obvious choices, nor which works he particularly admired. From the two sketchbooks preserved in Geneva,[112] which record not only his Roman works but also some copies evidently completed in Paris before 1828, it can be surmised that Gleyre followed the traditional course of art students in that period: there are ample copies of Michelangelo and Raphael, particularly from the Sistine Chapel and the Loggia. Yet the recently discovered sketchbooks, only one of which appears to date wholly from the Roman sojourn, demonstrate that Gleyre's interests were broader and more extensive than the previous evidence might suggest.

We know, for example, that Gleyre repeatedly visited the Capitoline museum, where he copied details of lesser known Renaissance paintings and even made a full watercolor copy of Salvator Rosa's *Soldier*.[113] It can

fig. 30

110. Clément, p. 36. Leo XII died on 10 February 1829, and was succeeded by Pius VIII on 31 March. He was followed less than a year later by Gregory XVI.
111. The letter is unpublished by Clément, but is contained in Lausanne, MCBA, GA 986.
112. Geneva, MAH, Inv. 1918–5 and 1918–6. The provenance and contents of the sketchbooks are discussed in the catalogue.
113. Lausanne, MCBA, Inv. P 92. It had already been incorporated into the collection as early as 1780. On the importance of Rosa's art in the early nineteenth century, especially his prints, see Wallace 1979, pp. 107f.

be shown as well that he sought out numerous works by Raphael and Giulio Romano in Santa Maria della Pace and the Sala di Constantino. In a particularly interesting section of the sketchbook, Gleyre's admiration for Filippino Lippi's fresco of the *Triumph of S. Tomaso* painted in the Caraffa Chapel in Santa Maria sopra Minerva is evident, since he finished three separate watercolors, on three different sheets, of details of the work.[114] One should note that the church, restored and cleaned in 1824, also contained works by Michelangelo and Bernini in which Gleyre was apparently less interested.[115]    fig. 31

Perhaps the most revealing section of this sketchbook shows Gleyre's fascination with the varied works in San Clemente, particularly the fresco cycle of Saint Catherine of Alexandria in the Branda da Castiglione chapel. Gleyre made at least two drawings and two watercolors from it, as well as two separate watercolor studies after the large Crucifixion fresco on the main wall of the chapel. These works are generally attributed to Masolino, but in the early nineteenth century they were thought to be by Masaccio.[116] Few painters in Rome in the 1820s were interested in Masaccio's work — even the Brancacci Chapel in Florence was little visited — or other frescoes dating before the mid-fifteenth century, many of which were still generally regarded as primitive, curious, even decadent, and not wholly worthy of serious study.[117] Indicative as well of Gleyre's attraction to neglected examples of art forms is another sheet from San Clemente that shows the large medieval candle holder in the Scuola Cantorum. Nor did Gleyre neglect to record the strange twisted columns in the cloister of Saint John Lateran. An even more surprising object of study is seen in a drawing Gleyre made of the sixth-century mosaic of Pope Felix IV from the extreme left side of the apse of SS. Cosmos and Damien, this at a time when early mosaics were still    fig. 33
considered objects of little artistic merit.

31. Copy after Filippino Lippi, 1829–33. France, Private collection (catalogue n° 71, folio 10ʳ)

32. Copy after Masolino, 1829–33. France, Private collection (catalogue n° 71, folio 9ʳ)

114. On Lippi's work, see Berti and Baldini 1957, who discuss the fresco in the context of the late fifteenth century, but not in the early nineteenth.
115. On the works in Santa Maria sopra Minerva, see Buchowiecki 1967, II, pp. 691f. Michelangelo's *Risen Christ* is at the left of the altar; Bernini's work consists of his monuments to Maria Raggi and Vigevano, as well as the monument to Alexander VII in the square at the entrance. It might be noted as well that Fra Angelico's tomb is here, a point of interest for Gleyre, since he also copied several figures from the painter's frescoes in the Chapel of Nicholas V in the Vatican.
116. Seroux d'Agincourt 1841, VI, pp. 217–18. On the question of attribution, see Beenken 1932, pp. 7–13, and Longhi 1975, pp. 25f., regarding the San Clemente frescoes.
117. See Haskell 1980, pp. 85f. On nineteenth-century literature on Masaccio, see Salmi 1948, pp. 134f.

33. Copy after a mosaic in SS. Cosmos and Damian, Rome, 1829–33. France, Private collection (catalogue n° 71, folio 15ʳ)
34. Copy after Schnorr von Carolsfeld, 1829–33. France, Private collection (catalogue n° 71, folio 17ʳ)

What should be understood from these examples is that even as a student, he was drawn to works of art not yet wholly appreciated by the traditional aesthetics of the period, which he nevertheless must have sensed could help in establishing an important criterion for his own studies. His liberal attitude toward unfamiliar examples of art, not very common in the period under review, would manifest itself yet more strongly during Gleyre's second trip to Italy in 1845, when his selection of works to study and copy was even more unusual and personal.

From all the documented sources available, written and drawn, precious little has come down to us regarding which contemporary works Gleyre saw, esteemed, and copied. Gleyre met a variety of French, Swiss, German, and Italian artists in Rome, but their works are hardly mentioned. In the Roman sketchbook that has recently come to light, only one contemporary work is studied: the fresco cycle in the Stanza di Ariosto in the Casino Massimo, which was completed by Schnorr von fig. 34  Carolsfeld in 1827.[118] On a separate page from another sketchbook, which is exclusively devoted to the Egyptian trip but which Gleyre evidently already possessed in Rome, he noted that among the works he desired to see were "les œuvres . . . [de] Schnorr."[119] Gleyre in fact made several drawings and a watercolor after the vaults of the Casino Massimo, each with the same intensity and fidelity seen in his copies after Michelangelo or Raphael. There are, however, no particular indications elsewhere of his regard for the art of Nazarenes, even though their works were well known in the Roman circles that Gleyre frequented. It is not improbable that Gleyre's interest in contemporary painting seen in Rome was far greater than the visual evidence suggests.

Gleyre's letters from Rome indicate that the painter was also actively involved in his own painting and drawing, apart from his studies after

118. On the cycle as a whole and Schnorr's contribution, see Susinno 1981, pp. 369–81.
119. The passage is cited in Clément, p. 19, with a note that it comes from one of the Orient sketchbooks.

older masters. Already on 21 May 1829, only a few months after arriving in Rome, he wrote his brother that he had begun some oils, but he was having difficulty with these because of the expense of hiring adequate models; he hoped nevertheless to finish two or three small pictures before Fonville was to leave for Lyons — therefore, January 1830 —so that he could consign them to him without having to incur the expense of shipment.[120] Yet, he also admitted to Henry that his work in general amounted to little because he felt himself blocked: "ce tableau que j'ai commencé ne va pas comme je voudrais." Gleyre never explained to Henry why his work seemed to go so slowly or why he felt that so much of it was a failure.

It is likely that Gleyre, like many foreign artists in Rome, made ends meet with occasional drawings and portraits aimed at the brisk tourist trade, or by giving drawing instructions to wealthy visitors and residents. In one instance, he is known to have given drawing lessons to the Empress of Russia, although no details are included in any of the correspondence.[121] Gleyre mentioned his drawings and paintings to Henry only when the projects seemed to abort, as in a letter of 1 September 1830, in which Gleyre recounts that he had begun a portrait of a Roman count and his wife who left Rome abruptly, presumably without paying his fee.[122] This incident repeated itself later when Gleyre reported in a letter of 4 April 1834, that he had drawn a portrait of an Englishman who left Rome with the portrait but without paying the six hundred francs agreed upon.[123] It is not surprising to learn that Gleyre could no longer work in oils after the summer of 1833 because of the prohibitive costs, and instead tried to sell pencil drawings for one to two hundred francs each.[124]

Gleyre's pessimism became so pronounced in Rome that even the city itself, after his initial enthusiasm, held little fascination for him.[125] He wrote frequently of his boredom even in the presence of the great masters of Renaissance. His despair took on a form of self-denigration: he was convinced of his own ugliness, and noted to Henry that his nose was becoming grotesquely long, a fact contradicted by his self-portrait.[126] Besides his constant financial worries, Gleyre noted in a letter to his uncle dated 26 February 1830 that no fewer than four of his friends had died within a month, none of them older than twenty-six.[127] It is little wonder that Gleyre could lament to his uncle in the same letter that "cette vie est détestable."

Although Gleyre's Roman period was often fraught with melancholy, extreme poverty, and even tragedy, he nevertheless took advantage of the presence of foreign artists in Italy to widen his artistic horizons. His immediate associates in Rome were painters he had already known in Lyons, and included, beside Fonville and Bonnefond, Isidore Flacheron and Victor Orsel.[128] When Gleyre went to Naples in the winter of 1832–33 — Henry had furnished five hundred francs for the trip after Gleyre's repeated demands — he met Chenavard again. Chenavard would recall the meeting a half century later in one of his few surviving letters, an undated one to Abraham Hirsch, director of the Ecole des Beaux-Arts in Lyons.[129] Chenavard remembered the enthusiasm with which he, Gleyre,

120. Not cited by Clément, but see Lausanne, MCBA, GA 986.

121. Clément, pp. 57–58, provides some details. The introduction was made through Hortense Lacroix, who would later marry Gleyre's best friend, Sébastien Cornu.

122. Lausanne, MCBA, GA 986.

123. Clément, p. 66. Clément noted that Gleyre had painted the figure *en pied* with another figure in the background holding the reins of the horse. No trace of the work has surfaced. The commission, however, was negotiated through Horace Vernet and, ironically, the failure of Gleyre to receive the fees agreed upon would be an important element in Vernet's recommendation of Gleyre for the trip to the Orient.

124. Ibid., pp. 49–50.

125. See ibid., pp. 47 and 49 for various expressions of this.

126. The work was later given to Mathilde Gleyre who thought it represented her uncle at the age of twenty-four.

127. Clément, p. 39. In the letter cited here, Gleyre noted the death of a Mr. Lugiens, who has not been identified; Mme. Lugardon, the wife of the painter, who died in childbirth; a German poet whom he does not name; and the brother of one of his friends.

128. Grégoire Isidore Flacheron (1806–73) had already known Gleyre in Lyons at the Ecole des Beaux-Arts where he studied with Révoil between 1824 and 1827. Flacheron is mentioned in several of Gleyre's letters; see Clément, pp. 45–46, as well as unpublished correspondence in Lausanne, MCBA, GA 986 and 988. Victor Orsel (1795–1850) also studied with Révoil and worked with Overbeck in Rome; Gleyre also was acquainted with Orsel's friend and biographer, Alphonse Perin (1798–1874); see Clément, p. 53, where the name is spelled "Perrin."

129. On Abraham Hirsch, see Thieme-Becker, XVII, pp. 130–31. He was also the municipal architect of Lyons and was instrumental in trying to establish a Salle Chenavard for the Pantheon sketches; see Sloane 1962, pp. 146f.

and Edgar Quinet studied the landscape of the area.[130] Chenavard had introduced Gleyre to Quinet and to Charles Nanteuil, both of whom remained lifelong friends.[131] Chenavard himself met with Gleyre when he returned to Paris and played an important role in his paintings of the 1840s. It was also through Chenavard and his other associates from Lyons that Gleyre was introduced to the German colony of painters in Rome, which included Overbeck, Cornelius, and Schnorr von Carolsfeld.[132]

Gleyre was naturally attracted to the Swiss artists in Rome and actively sought out Keisermann, the distant relative from La Sarraz who had established a successful career in Roman circles,[133] Léopold Robert, and Lugardon. Gleyre wrote in his first Roman letter of 10 January 1829, that he had seen Keisermann immediately upon his arrival. Gleyre, who had probably not met Keisermann before, took an instant dislike to him and wrote his uncle that he was "un vieux chien d'avare" who had acted improperly in regard to his adopted son, Charles-François Knébel, who was related to Gleyre's mother.[134]

Gleyre's relationship with the revered and celebrated Swiss painter Léopold Robert is more complex. According to Clément, Robert and Gleyre established a close relationship in Rome and despite a certain laziness Robert had discerned in Gleyre's work habits, the older painter praised him by saying he represented the hope of the younger artists of his circle.[135] Curiously, Gleyre makes no mention in any of his letters of his meetings with Robert, even though he knew that their relationship would have pleased and reassured his relatives. Neither does Robert mention Gleyre in his correspondence during that period.[136] We know that Robert left Rome in February 1831,[137] when Gleyre still had produced very little that might have elicited the kind of praise Clément reports. Robert may have seen some of Gleyre's copies, perhaps some portraits, or small pictures he had begun and abandoned — like those mentioned in Gleyre's letter of 21 May 1829 — but hardly more. Nevertheless, Gleyre may have used Robert's wide circle of friends to gain entrance into some ateliers and salons that otherwise might have been closed to him.

It may have been through Robert that Gleyre met the Genevan painter Jean-Léonard Lugardon, who had already established a firm reputation in Switzerland. Gleyre admired Lugardon's painting *Bonivard* when he saw it in Geneva on the first leg of his trip.[138] Apparently, Gleyre sought out Lugardon shortly after his arrival in Rome, since he wrote to Henry on 10 February 1829, "… ainsi tôt après mon arrivée à Rome, j'ai fait la connaissance de M. Lugardon, peintre d'un grand talent et de plus l'homme le plus aimable que j'ai vu depuis longtemps."[139] By this time, Lugardon, who had been in Rome since 1827, knew Robert well, and had even rented a small studio from his brother Aurèle.[140] Gleyre saw Lugardon frequently.[141] A measure of Gleyre's affection for him may be seen in the portrait he made, one of the most sensitive of his youthful renderings. The work must date to 1829 or 1830 and clearly not to 1824, as inscribed on the drawing itself, and is the only one extant of the portraits Gleyre made of his colleagues in Rome.

fig. 35

130. Bertrand 1911, p. 536.
131. Clément, p. 48. Charles Nanteuil, no relation to the more famous graphic artist Célestin, had studied briefly with Ingres. Little information on his career is available, but see the biographical entry in Bénézit, VII, p. 650. His memories of Gleyre, transmitted to Clément in letters and notes, are an important source for details. Gleyre's relationship with Edgar Quinet and his circle will be discussed later.
132. Gleyre had earlier expressed the desire to study their works, as noted in Clément, p. 19.
133. François Keisermann (1765–1833), who sometime spelled his name Kaisermann, first went to Rome in 1790 to work with his Vaudois compatriot Louis Ducros, but later, with the patronage of Prince Borghese, set up his own studio where he established a formidable career. When Gleyre met him, he lived in a large apartment at 31, Piazza di Spagna. On his life and work, see Agassiz 1930; Perrochon 1943, pp. 10f., notes his living quarters and reputation. It is probable that Gleyre asked Keisermann to help him establish himself in Rome, but he was almost certainly rebuffed. Gleyre, however, lodged briefly in Keisermann's apartment and apparently painted three portraits there, which are discussed in the catalogue section.
134. Clément, p. 35. On the affair with Knébel, see Agassiz 1935 and La Sarraz, Knébel Family, Correspondence.
135. Berthoud 1874, p. 462; Clément, p. 53; Ségal 1973, p. 199; but the critique is not mentioned in Gassier 1983.
136. Clément 1875 for the essential correspondence, augmented by Gassier 1983.
137. Gassier 1983, p. 285.
138. Clément, p. 23.
139. Not cited in Clément, but see Lausanne, MCBA, GA 986.
140. Gassier 1983, pp. 204 and 213.
141. Gleyre wrote to his uncle about Lugardon, particularly mentioning the latter's desolation after the death of his wife; see Clément 1875, p. 335, and Clément, p. 39.

35. *Portrait of Jean-Léonard Lugardon*, 1829(?). Neuchâtel, Musée d'Art et d'Histoire (catalogue n° 44)

36. *Portrait of Hortense Cornu*, c. 1832. From Emerit 1937(b), frontispiece (catalogue n° 61)
37. Sébastien Cornu, *Portrait of Madame Cornu*, c. 1835. Compiègne, Musée du Second-Empire

142. On Louis Châtelain (1805–85), see von Allmen 1985, pp. 25–26. Bachelin 1878, p. 198, is the only source that mentions the portrait, noting that it was a signed drawing by Gleyre. The portrait was last seen in the 1940s, but efforts to trace it through the heirs of the family in Neuchâtel have failed.
143. Gleyre wrote to Henry about it in very bitter terms on 19 October 1833, as noted in Clément, p. 51.
144. The portrait itself has not been located, but it is reproduced as the frontispiece to Emerit 1937(b) with no indication that it was painted by Gleyre. Clément's description of the work, however, leaves no doubt that the watercolor is indeed the same.

Gleyre also met Louis Châtelain, an architect from Neuchâtel, whom he may have already known in Paris, since Châtelain had enrolled in the Ecole des Beaux-Arts one year before Gleyre. By 1828, Châtelain was in Rome and associated with Robert's circle. Gleyre apparently drew his portrait in 1829 as there is no documentation that the two met after Gleyre's return to France or during his summer trips to Switzerland.[142]

Among Gleyre's others friends, one must mention a close attachment to an amateur painter named d'Etouilly, about whom almost nothing is known. They met frequently at the Lepri, where they took meals and talked politics. Later, in Lebanon, Gleyre witnessed his tragic death. One of the few persons Gleyre met in Rome who was not intimately associated with the foreign artistic community was Hortense Lacroix, whose godfather was Louis-Napoléon. It was she who was the intermediary between Gleyre and the Empress of Russia. In October 1833, much to Gleyre's displeasure, she married Sébastien Cornu.[143] Mme. Cornu remained a close friend of Gleyre's throughout his life and almost certainly used her political influence to help Gleyre obtain commissions later. It is possible that Gleyre made his watercolor study of Mme. Cornu in 1833 as a wedding present.[144] In many ways Gleyre's portrait is a more sensitive work than the portrait painted by her husband slightly later.

fig. 36

fig. 37

66

145. Clément, p. 53, mentions that Berlioz was one of Gleyre's friends at this time, and notes, p. 203, that he was a regular member of Gleyre's circle, even though Gleyre is not mentioned in Berlioz's letters or memoirs. Nanteuil wrote to Clément that Gleyre and Berlioz lodged together in Rome for a while, but there is no other documentation to verify this, and Nanteuil's letter was written four decades after the fact. On Mendelssohn in Rome, see Blunt 1974, pp. 88f. His letters indicate that he frequented the Vernet circle. On Berlioz in Rome, see Barzun 1969, I, pp. 199f. On Vernet's tenure in Rome, see Lapauze 1924, II, pp. 184f. and *Horace Vernet* 1980.

146. On these architects in Rome, see especially Levine 1982, pp. 66–123. There are no modern monographs on Duc and Duban, but see the discussion in Van Zanten 1987. Duc commissioned decorative motifs from Gleyre in the context of his project for the Cour d'Assise in the Palais de Justice which Gleyre sketched but never completed. The only information on this commission is in Clément, p. 453, under cat. n° 200. Félix Duban, who became chief architect of the Ecole des Beaux-Arts expansion project, defended Gleyre's decorations in the Château de Dampierre when they were menaced with destruction. On Duban's role in the Dampierre affair, see Ockman 1982.

147. The basic information on Vaudoyer's career is in Blanc 1876, pp. 225–48, and Bergdoll 1991, cat. n° 5. The only previously known reference to this portrait was in a private Parisian exhibition in 1923; see *L'art et la vie romantique* 1923, p. 31, n° 212. The work, however, disappeared until published by Bergdoll.

148. Vaudoyer's main works are in the Conservatoire des arts et métiers in Paris and the cathedral of Marseille. Vaudoyer also published articles in the *Magasin pittoresque* with Albert Lenoir on the history of architecture, surveying monuments of the nineteenth century.

There is no reliable documentation regarding Gleyre's acquaintance with other luminaries in Rome between 1829 and 1834, although Stendhal, Chateaubriand, and the poet Mickiewicz were associated with various friends of his. The composers Berlioz and Mendelssohn were indirectly part of Gleyre's circle, but there are only tenuous links to Gleyre himself.[145] If Gleyre was indeed in contact with these figures, the intermediary almost certainly would have been Horace Vernet, who, since 1829, had been director of the French Academy in the Villa Medici, where Gleyre was frequently invited. Vernet welcomed Gleyre often despite the fact that he was never officially a member of the Academy. There Gleyre met various *pensionnaires*, including Norblin, Dupré, the sculptor Dantan, and particularly the architects Labrouste, Vaudoyer, Duc, and Duban. Duc and Duban seem to have developed a lasting relationship with Gleyre, and both played minor roles in his later career.[146]

fig. 38   In 1831, his last year as a *pensionnaire*, Vaudoyer commissioned Gleyre to paint his portrait, a work that has only recently been discovered.[147] Vaudoyer had been a precocious student, entering the Ecole in 1819 when he was only sixteen. He later distinguished himself as an important architect in Paris and Marseilles, and as an astute historian of architecture.[148] After entering the Prix de Rome competition six times — he was a finalist in five — he won the prize in 1826 and set out for Rome at the end of the year. Gleyre's watercolor portrait, much more refined than might be expected from the evidence of his earlier work, is an extremely subtle portrayal of character and setting. Vaudoyer is seen in a formal pose, with drawing material in his right hand, an elegant scarf in his left, and the profile of the Villa Medici in the background. The lavish use of foliage and atmospheric surrounding is altogether surprising in Gleyre's watercolors before his trip to Egypt three years later. The painting, however, reminds us of Gleyre's undeniable facility in portraiture, which he exploited later in the depiction of selected friends.

There was another reason for Gleyre's frequent visits to the Vernet family, namely, the celebrated charms of Horace's daughter Louise.[149] She was only fifteen years old when she accompanied her father to Rome, but was even so an admired figure in Roman society. When she met Léopold Robert in 1829, he was instantly smitten by her beauty and, although more than twice her age, dared to express a certain passion for her.[150] Most of the literary and artistic figures in Vernet's circle admired Louise: Berlioz noted her particular sensitivity, beauty, and talent at the piano, which inspired him to dedicate his song *La Captive* to her.[151] Even a decade after her departure from Rome, Louise Vernet was still remembered there with particular fondness. It is no wonder that her sad beauty prompted portraits from such celebrated figures as Ingres, Géricault, and her own father.[152]

fig. 39

The nature of Gleyre's relationship with Louise is somewhat unclear, as is the whole of his attitude toward women. The tradition, established in large part by Clément, is that Gleyre was a misogynist, although there is not much evidence for this view; Clément surely based his notion on the fact that Gleyre's circle of friends were all male. Evidently Gleyre preferred the intellectual company of men, but among the letters to Henry there is one, perhaps written in 1829, in which he complained that among his Roman friends, there was not a single woman — thus suggesting a certain frustration about the lack of feminine companionship.[153] One thing is clear: throughout his life, Gleyre opposed marriage as an institution and generally considered it a form of male enslavement; he was hostile to the prospective marriages of his brothers and expressed his aversion in various letters to them.[154]

Nevertheless, if Clément's account can be trusted here, we must believe that Gleyre had actually fallen in love with Louise Vernet. Gleyre certainly felt timid about this and perhaps even somewhat ashamed of his feelings: in 1830 at the age of twenty-four, he was virtually penniless and without immediate prospects, while Louise, still an adolescent, was already accustomed to the brilliant circle of established artists that surrounded her father. Gleyre's self-consciousness about his appearance, particularly his large nose and shabby dress, must have contributed to his timidity. Clément noted that a cartoon caricature of a marriage proposal circulated to the delight of Gleyre's friends; in it, Chenavard acts as Gleyre's intermediary in asking Horace Vernet for the hand of his daughter while Louise is seated next to him, averting her eyes in a gesture of

149. Clément, p. 56. Anne-Elisabeth-Louise Vernet was born in 1814, Vernet's second daughter; his first was born two years earlier, but died shortly afterwards. Louise left a private diary of her Roman years, but it is now in a private collection in Paris and was not made available to me. For further information on her, see Ziff 1977, pp. 13f.

150. Gassier 1983, p. 213.

151. See Berlioz's letter to Hiller, 13 May 1832, in Berlioz 1879, p. 97, and his letter to Mme. Vernet, 27 July 1832, p. 101. See also *Horace Vernet* 1980, p. 82.

152. See Ernest Hébert to Paul Delaroche, 8 June 1843, in Delaroche-Vernet 1910, p. 507. Ingres's portrait of her is discussed in Naef 1979, III, pp. 208–19; Géricault painted her as a young girl, in Grunchec 1979, n° 135; and Vernet's own portrait of her, dated 1831, is reproduced in *Horace Vernet* 1980, p. 83, n° 54.

153. In a letter of 27 October, probably 1829, partially cited in Clément, p. 37.

154. See ibid., pp. 16 and 46, although there are other letters in Lausanne, MCBA, GA 986 which touch upon the subject, including one dated only 10 September which is unfortunately torn to shreds. Another curious incident about Gleyre's relationships with women in Rome was recounted by Charles Nanteuil to Clément. Nanteuil wrote that Gleyre had a model, a prostitute, who claimed that she was Gleyre's mistress, "ce qui, vous comprenez, n'allait pas du tout à notre ami." When Gleyre confronted her, she menaced or cut him with a knife. (Knife attacks on foreigners in Rome were common at the time, so much so that Vernet insisted that the artists at the Academy take arms with them when leaving the grounds.) Nanteuil's unpublished letter, probably from 1877 or 1878 when Nanteuil sent various letters with his recollections of Gleyre, is in Fleurier, CFC, dated only 28 November. It adds that Clément has the portrait of this woman in his collection.

38. *Portrait of Léon Vaudoyer*, 1831. France, Private collection (catalogue n° 51)

39. Horace Vernet, *Portrait of Louise Vernet*, 1831. Paris, Private collection

innocence.[155] In reality, Louise was attracted to the dashing and successful painter Paul Delaroche to whom she became engaged on 4 December 1834, eight months after Gleyre left Rome.

Whether Gleyre truly suffered from an unrequited love for Louise cannot be known. If Horace Vernet was aware of Gleyre's intentions toward his daughter, it is not recorded. But Vernet genuinely admired Gleyre's talents and perhaps helped him by steering clients in his direction and putting him in contact with potential sitters. It was at Vernet's recommendation that an American in Rome, John Lowell, Jr., invited Gleyre to accompany him on an extended voyage to the Near East in 1834, a trip that was to prove singularly important to the development of Gleyre's art.

Certainly Gleyre had active periods of creativity in Rome and, despite his financial worries, produced several important pictures. Beside the copies already cited, Gleyre's Roman works included several historical works not unlike those that characterize the school of Lyons, a startling contemporary scene, portraits, and, in the notebooks he kept, several

155. Clément, p. 57.

69

projects for pictures that he never painted — these studies are discussed in the catalogue section on his Roman sketchbooks. In all cases, it can be seen that even in his early years, Gleyre sought originality in his subjects as well as in the sources he utilized.

Of the Roman portraits, one of the most remarkable is the watercolor self-portrait of about 1830. Gleyre has represented himself in a regional costume, standing in a dignified and confident pose in the Roman countryside. The work is fluid in color and touch, and wholly substantiates Gleyre's reputation, already early in his career, as a particularly gifted watercolorist. It is curious to reflect upon Gleyre's misery and poverty in relation to the manner in which he depicts himself here. The portrait rather confirms Mme. Cornu's description of Gleyre during his Roman sojourn as a man of grace, irony, and intelligence, as well as an almost feminine softness of visage, all of which is portrayed in the work.[156] It will be noticed that Gleyre also represented himself with a beard. He had noted to Henry on 10 September, probably 1830, that "je suis le seul des français (car je passe pour tel) qui porte de la barbe au menton, je remettrai à (la) famille une petite portrait de moi avec ma barbe."[157] It is not known if this is the work Gleyre sent; it later turned up in the collection that Mathilde willed to the Musée Cantonal des Beaux-Arts.

In 1833 Gleyre sent his first works to the Paris salon, three watercolor portraits.[158] The salon jury for 1833 was exceptionally harsh: of 4,620 works submitted for inclusion in the salon, more than 1,700 were refused outright, particularly in the category of portrait painting.[159] The quality of the works Gleyre sent — almost certainly through his brother in Lyons — may be measured by the fact that they were accepted without difficulty. The salon *livret* lists them as portraits, but without any information as to the identity of the sitters. These works have not surfaced, nor were they bought by the state. From the information contained in the registration books in the Louvre, it is known that the watercolor portraits were unusually large, two of them measuring 48 by 38 centimeters, and the third 90 by 43 centimeters, probably with the frames included.[160] No critic remarked upon them in the reviews of the salon, nor did Clément discuss them in his work. It was the first time that the Paris public saw Gleyre's work exhibited, but they would have to wait exactly a decade before they could see another.

Of the historical works Gleyre completed during these years, only two have survived for study. From the descriptions provided by Clément, it is known that Gleyre's interests extended from the Romanticism of the Byronic hero, like Manfred, to the Troubadour historicism of *The First Kiss of Michelangelo*. His *Raphael Leaving His Father's Home*, published here for the first time, is described by Clément as a youthful work in which the mature aspects of Gleyre's art are not yet visible. Clément, whose unenthusiastic analysis of the developed sketch is meager and mostly descriptive, underestimated the importance of the painting, which already demonstrates Gleyre's search for originality in subject and treatment.

To be sure, the life of Raphael played an important role in the iconography of the Old Masters in France when such historical subjects began

fig. 40

fig. 41

40. *Self-Portrait.* 1830–34. Lausanne, Musée Cantonal des Beaux-Arts (catalogue n° 50)

156. Mme. Cornu's account is cited in ibid., p. 55.
157. Not cited in Clément; see Lausanne, MCBA, GA 986.
158. These were listed in the *livret* under the same number, 1077, with the notation "M. Gleyre, à Rome."
159. Hauptman 1985(a), p. 98.
160. Paris, AL, Enregistrement des ouvrages, 1833, n° 1824–26. When works were submitted to the jury, they were automatically measured, but not always with the frame.

70

71

to be treated more frequently.[161] The major source used by painters at the time was Quatremère de Quincy's highly popular account of the artist's life, which in itself stems from Vasari's version.[162] Gleyre's image, however, seems to rely more on Vasari, who describes how Raphael's father arranged an apprenticeship with Perugino "and took the boy with him to Perugia, his mother, who loved him tenderly, weeping bitterly at the separation."[163] In fact, it is known, and may have been known even in the nineteenth century, that Raphael actually left Urbino when he was already seventeen years old and orphaned.

Gleyre's choice of this moment, hardly the most picturesque in Raphael's life, may be due to the aspects of the scene that relate to Gleyre's own life. In the Raphael painting, the scene is not so much a recounting of Raphael's leaving Urbino as a more general scene of departure from parental supervision, a subject with which Gleyre had a certain emotional affinity. From the Roman letters, it is evident that his feelings of loss and displacement were strong, despite an active circle of friends. And, although it is barely touched in Clément's biography, there are many hints that Gleyre was psychologically scarred by the loss of his own parents, particularly his mother to whom he was especially attached. In the painting the central motif is the embrace of the mother and the child, while the two onlookers are passive observers. This emphasis on maternal concerns has many other echoes in Gleyre's later art, most notably in his last painting, *The Return of the Prodigal Son*, completed almost four decades later. It is surely not fortuitous that the latter painting is in almost all respects the precise inverse of his Roman picture in theme and composition and therefore belies Clément's notion that the Raphael painting is but an immature effort curiously isolated in Gleyre's œuvre.

The manner in which Gleyre envisioned the central motif of his Raphael painting is important. Unlike more traditionally drawn figures of the family, that of the not yet adolescent Raphael is composed with such great liberty that it defies physical reality. This form of artistic abstraction can also be seen in the school of Lyons and in some of Bonington's historical works, but the fluidity of the gestures and attitudes in Gleyre's painting suggest the pointed exaggeration of Ingres. Both mother and child — particularly the latter, with his serpentine lines and the head thrown backwards in an attitude of despair over the impending departure — add to the compositions emotional and psychological elements typical of Gleyre's expressiveness even in his developing years.

It is probable that Gleyre's lost watercolor *Francesca da Rimini*, painted according to Clément in 1831 or 1832, was similar in style to the *Raphael*, although it represented a more dynamic aspect of Gleyre's early art. Clément examined the painting in Paris while writing the biography and described it as a vivid example of Gleyre's Roman works, replete with rich details, ornaments, furnishings, and a refinement of execution that was remarked upon by Roman artistic circles.[164] As in many of his later historical works, the painter took pains to research the secondary aspects of the work so that the details accord with historical facts. In this painting, one element described by Clément verifies this observation. He notes,

161. The classic account of the renewned interest in treating the Old Masters as subjects for historical painting is Haskell 1971, pp. 55–85.
162. The *Histoire de la vie et des ouvrages de Raphaël* first appeared in 1824 and remained the standard work for almost a generation.
163. Vasari 1963, II, p. 222.
164. Clément, pp. 62–63.

41. *Raphael Leaving his Father's Home*, 1830–34.
Zürich, Private collection (catalogue n° 48)

among the details of the interior, wall hangings that bear the coat of arms
of the Malatesta family. The precise delineation of the coat of arms was
taken by Gleyre from Marc'Antonio's *L'Arte del Blasone* published in
Venice in 1756, from which he had copied in one of his Roman sketchbooks the actual motif as well as the description of its arrangement and
color, which he presumably incorporated into the watercolor.[165] The same
coat of arms is also present on a curtain in Ingres's 1819 version of the
subject and may indicate a use of the same source.[166]

 Although Clément did not survey the use of the Dante subject in other
painters' representations of the doomed lovers, it is still clear from his
description that Gleyre's approach to the theme was outside the norm.
Since Flaxman's illustration of the account from the *Inferno* (Canto V),

165. See Sketchbook, n° 248, inside cover, verso,
where the title of Marc'Antonio Ginanni's book is
noted and, similarly, folio 1ʳ where the coat of arms
and the inscription appear.
166. It appears only in the 1819 version in Angers,
where it is emblazoned on the wall directly behind
the lovers.

painters have chosen to represent the moment when the lovers first kiss, as Malatesta, hidden behind a curtain, witnesses the event. The romantic nature of the moment is implied in the illicit kiss itself, but the tragedy that ensues appears not to have been represented. Gleyre chose to paint the *fait accompli*, after Paolo and Francesca have been killed. In the central background Gleyre has placed the figure of Malatesta, seated, his hands bloodied, contemplating with horror and remorse the fact that he has slain his wife and brother. The poetic, almost innocent kiss before an open book of Arthurian romance, is replaced by the terrifying revenge and brutal punishment. Such consequences of human fault, treated by Gleyre throughout his career, form the underlying iconographic motif of many of his most accomplished works.

Clément is correct in stating that the most important work by Gleyre dating from the Roman period is his *Roman Brigands*, completed in 1831.[167] Perhaps because of the provocative nature of the subject and its underlying eroticism, the painting is hardly mentioned in Gleyre's letters and has been known almost exclusively through Clément's generalized description. Gleyre was sensitive about the picture, as he indicated in a letter to Henry on 1 May 1830 in which he described the difficulty of the execution and his desire to send the work to Lyons, but also gave the instruction — repeated twice in the same letter — not to exhibit the painting in public under any circumstances.[168] In another letter to Henry date 17 June, Gleyre wrote of the difficulties he was having with one of the models:

fig. 42

> Si je t'écris ce matin à huit heures, c'est parce que mon modelle [sic] a donné una *coltellàta*, coup de couteau, il s'est caché. Ce ——— [illegible] de *Brigands* que je fais, tu vois qu'il est fier dans sa robe…[169]

Here the letter is cut by a razor, indicating that certain intimate details about the subject or the incident were too personal. Gleyre wrote to Henry again on 26 December 1831, noting that the painting had been sent to him in Lyons.[170]

In later correspondence with his brother, Gleyre was again adamant that the painting should not be shown publicly. On 4 April 1833, when his three watercolor portraits were already en route to the salon of that year, he wrote to Henry insisting in the strongest terms that he should not include the *Brigands*.[171] Five years later, after his return from the Orient, Gleyre asked Henry to return the painting to him, and he later refused the considerable sum of 1,500 francs when a private collector offered to buy the canvas.[172]

As a result, even Gleyre's closest friends did not see the work,[173] nor was it ever discussed in his lifetime. Nowhere in Gleyre's œuvre before 1831 had he attempted to depict a scene that was so brutal or so frankly explicit. Scenes of Italian brigands were not uncommon at this time in Italy and France — chiefly in the works of Robert and Pinelli, both of whom specialized in the genre — but rarely were they as graphic as

167. Clément, p. 59. The following material on the painting is drawn largely from Hauptman 1981(a), pp. 17–34.
168. In Lausanne, MCBA, GA 986, but not cited in Clément.
169. Ibid.
170. Ibid., but other details are not known since the letter is badly cut.
171. Ibid., but it is not known if Gleyre meant the Paris salons or those in Lyons which since 1821 had been haphazardly organized by the Société des amis d'art; it was only in 1836 that the exhibitions were mounted on a regular basis. See Bleton 1906, I, p. 505. Information on the Lyons exhibitions was kindly provided by Mme. Isabelle Gouy, Lyons.
172. By this time the work was with Nanteuil who had found a prospective buyer; see letter of 11 May 1838, in Clément, pp. 131–32.
173. The only friend who saw the work was Nanteuil, but even the critic Gustave Planche, who knew virtually all of Gleyre's paintings up to the mid-1850s, seems not to have studied the work. Later critics such as Paul Mantz, who tried to write from another perspective on Gleyre's works, never made mention of the painting.

42. *Roman Brigands*, 1831. Paris, Musée du Louvre, on loan in Cleveland, The Cleveland Museum of Art (catalogue n° 52)

Gleyre's painting. In most cases the brigand was represented as a romantic hero or victim of an unjust society, whereas in reality the brigand was no more than a cruel gangster and profiteer.[174] It is rather in this light that Gleyre depicts the figures in the painting, certainly more in accord with what he had seen or heard than with the myth, as indeed he noted in his journal.[175]

The scene Gleyre represents is the aftermath of a raid on travelers, identified by Clément as English, the common victims of highway attacks.[176] The husband, tied to the tree, is forced to observe while two brigands play the game of *morra* for the favors of the young wife. A third figure surveys the scene in the center — he is undoubtedly the figure for whom the model posed as mentioned in Gleyre's letter of 17 June — while an older figure is seen at the right counting the booty. In an earlier

174. See the bibliography on brigandage in Hauptman 1981(a), pp. 23–24.
175. Clément, p. 27.
176. Ibid., p. 59.

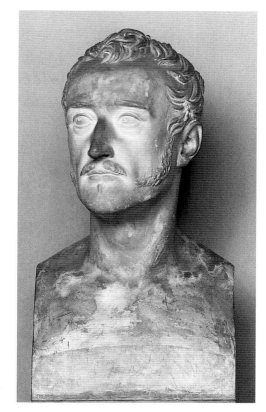

43. Bertel Thorvalsden, *Horace Vernet*, 1831. Copenhagen, Thorvalsden Museum
44. *Head of a Brigand*, 1831. Lausanne, Musée Cantonal des Beaux-Arts (catalogue n° 53)

essay, I showed that the scene as envisioned by Gleyre was based upon his own experiences with the Vernet family and surely directly related to his rejection by Louise.[177] It is clear that the features of the "husband" tied to the tree are modelled on Vernet himself although Gleyre altered the likeness somewhat so as to disguise the fact. It is probable that the young woman can be understood to represent Louise, in accord curiously with Berlioz's image of her in his song, *La Captiva*. The brigand at the left is surely modelled on Gleyre himself, his curly hair and beard resembling Gleyre's own, as indicated in a study thought to be a self-portrait.[178]

fig. 43

fig. 44

This explains why Gleyre was so hesitant to permit exhibition of the painting: not only is the subject matter imbued with eroticism, wholly unexpected in Gleyre's art, but he was certainly terrified that Vernet or his daughter might be recognized as principals. Even later Gleyre never permitted the work to be shown publicly for fear of embarrassing Louise, then Mme. Delaroche, for whom he always felt a certain respect and affection. But the painting represents an important step in the development of Gleyre's art, since it is the first major work that demonstrates the subjective originality of his mature paintings. It is in fact only a short step aesthetically from the *Brigands* to the hidden imagery in Gleyre's titular masterpiece, *Le Soir*, of 1843.

177. See Hauptman 1980, pp. 17–20, and 1983, pp. 26f.
178. The identification of the drawing as a self-portrait comes from Mathilde Gleyre through her companion, Mme. Pape-Carpentier, in a letter to Emile Bonjour, date 2 February 1918, in Lausanne, MCBA, GA 1020. The work is, incidentally, the only extant study for the painting.

## CHAPTER 3

# 1834–1838

## THE VOYAGE TO THE MIDDLE EAST

45. *View of the Ramesseum, Thebes*, 1835. Boston, Museum of Fine Arts (catalogue n° 266)

By the spring of 1834, Gleyre had already spent five years in Rome, much of it in abject poverty and artistic disappointment. While it is true he had significantly broadened his artistic experience, his efforts had proved to be less enriching than he had hoped. However, he never seriously expressed a desire to return to France any time soon in order to commence his career in Paris. Rather, being romantic in nature, he dreamed of exotics lands that could nurture his artistic tastes and at the same time free him from the constrictions of his Roman life. In a letter to Henry, dated only 4 April, but almost certainly 1833, just after his brief stay in Naples, he wrote :

> Voilà bien de temps que je ne t'ai pas écrit. Voici pourquoi. J'ai fait la connaissance d'un monsieur qui doit me faire faire un voyage en Egypte cet automne prochain.[179]

179. Lausanne, MCBA, GA 986. Clément, p. 48, only published one line of the letter in which Gleyre noted that he had received 500 francs sent by Henry. The letter can be dated to early 1833 since there is a reference to Kaisermann's recent death; he died on 4 January 1833. While Clément discusses Gleyre's disillusionment in Rome, he also plays down its importance; but see too Gleyre's other letter to Henry in GA 986.

77

The name of the man involved is not mentioned here, nor did Gleyre later discuss it with Clément. He did, however, repeat his desire to leave Rome for Africa in another undated letter.[180]

By the 1820s, continental voyagers to the Orient — which then implied the Middle East — had become numerous. The Napoleonic expeditions to Egypt, coupled with the publications of Vivant Denon, had aroused a remarkable interest in all Oriental objects and exploration, so that by this time a voyage to Egypt had become almost as popular as the Grand Tour a century before.[181] Frequently scientists and explorers engaged draftsmen to record sites, often using the drawings in guides and publications as major illustrative material. After the trip of Jules-Robert Auguste in 1815, important French painters provided firsthand views of African culture: painters such as Champmartin (1826), Montfort (1827), Decamps (1828), Dauzats (1829), Marilhat (1831), and Delacroix (1832) all profited from the experience in a variety of locales.[182] Gleyre's desire to go to Egypt, therefore, was fully in accord with the growing interest in non-European culture.

Gleyre's opportunity materialized not in autumn 1833, as he had hoped in his letter to Henry, but in the following spring. The occasion was the presence in Rome of a rich American industrialist, John Lowell, Jr., who was preparing a voyage to Egypt, India, and China. Lowell (1799–1836) had inherited an immense fortune from his father, who was responsible for the introduction of the power loom in the American textile industry. Lowell worked to augment the family business, but he was also keenly interested in art and the natural sciences, and often used his fortune to pursue these interests. In 1830–31, in the span of eighteen months, Lowell had lost his wife and two daughters in an epidemic of scarlet fever. It was under these tragic cicumstances that he decided to alleviate his grief by travel. Lowell left New York on 21 November 1832, stopping in London, Paris, and Florence, where he stayed longer than he had planned.[183]

When Lowell arrived in Rome, he continued his planning for the voyage to the East. During his stay in Rome, he apparently decided to hire an artist to accompany him, both as a companion and to record the people and sites he would encounter. Sometime during the spring of 1834, he called upon Horace Vernet in his capacity as the head of the French Academy for a recommendation. Vernet first suggested an artist, whose name we do not know, a staunch Carlist well-placed in high government circles, but the painter declined the offer. Vernet's second choice was Gleyre, whom he described as an able painter, particularly gifted in watercolor technique and quick pencil studies, talents indispensable for Lowell's needs.[184]

But Vernet's choice of Gleyre may have resulted from other considerations as well. In a previously unknown manuscript of Charles Nanteuil, who had become Gleyre's intimate friend, Nanteuil remembered distinctly that Vernet's recommendation of Gleyre was an attempt to compensate him for his recent bad fortune.[185] Apparently Vernet had acted as the intermediary in securing Gleyre's commission to paint the portrait of

180. Clément, pp. 49–50.
181. On the French interest in the Oriental experience, Carré 1956 is indispensable; see Thornton 1983, and Stevens 1984, for literature on artists in Egypt.
182. Rosenthal 1982, p. 27, and Bugler 1984, pp. 27–31.
183. On Lowell and Gleyre, see Newhouse 1980, pp. 79f. Besides the sources cited there on the Lowell family, see too Boston, BMFA, Everett, and *Harvard Alumni Bulletin*, 1949, p. 636. Lowell's stay in Florence may have been extended because of his meeting with the American sculptor Horatio Greenough from whom he commissioned a work for the Boston Atheneum, the first of many works Lowell sent to his native city during the tour. On the latter commission, see Everett as above, and Crane 1972.
184. Greenslet 1946, pp. 205–6.
185. See Nanteuil in Fleurier, CFC. Clément, however, makes no mention of this.

an English captain and his friend in a full-figure format. When the portrait was finished, the sitter took the work with him on the pretext of wanting to show it to the friend, but later, when Gleyre went to the hotel to collect his fee, he found that the captain had already left Rome. Gleyre asked the British authorities to intervene in the case, but they were unable to trace the model or secure the fee noted in the contract. Gleyre, in fact, had to borrow the equivalent sum indirectly from his brother through Chenavard, whose mother in Lyons was charged with receiving the repayment from Henry.[186] Nanteuil added that Vernet, always eager to help and encourage younger talent, felt responsible and therefore recommended Gleyre to Lowell.

One of the curious aspects of this association between Gleyre and Lowell is that Gleyre never mentioned the name of his patron in letters, nor even privately to Clément in almost three decades of friendship. When Clément tried to reconstruct this aspect of Gleyre's biography, he repeatedly asked Nanteuil for information, including the name of the American, but Nanteuil remarked in various letters that, despite having met him at least twice in Rome before the departure for the East, he could not remember his name.[187] In Clément's biography, therefore, Gleyre's patron is always referred to as "l'Américain" from Boston. The literature devoted to Gleyre's voyage is vague regarding details since the only account available for years was Clément's, in which the documentation was incomplete. Ironically, Gleyre did provide the name of his patron, but only on the last page of his Egyptian journal, after many blank pages, where he made a list of persons encountered; the first name is "Mr Lowel" [sic].[188] Clément, who had the journal in his possession for a while after Gleyre's death, seems not to have noticed this page, nor apparently to have made the connection with "l'Américain." Lowell's identity remained unnoticed in art historical circles until 1976, when his name was mentioned in this context.[189]

Lowell's arrangement with Gleyre was that he would pay all the expenses of the trip and provide a monthly salary of 200 francs, an offer that would considerably ease Gleyre's financial circumstances.[190] In turn Gleyre was to furnish Lowell with a topographical view and a "costume drawing" at each major site visited from southern Italy to China. In a letter to his brother of 5 April, the last he would write from Rome, Gleyre seemed satisfied with the arrangements and particularly eager to profit from the occasion; he estimated that the entire trip would not exceed one year.[191]

Unknown to Clément was the fact that virtually the entire trip could be reconstructed, not from Gleyre's sparse notes, but from the extensive diaries Lowell kept.[192] Between 21 November 1832, when Lowell sailed for Europe, and 29 February 1836, just before his death in Bombay on 4 March, Lowell recorded almost daily the events of this voyage, as well as weather, barometric readings, customs, philosophic musings, and general observations of nature and geology, all in accord with his varied interests. Lowell's eight volumes of writings, which have never been published, represent one of the most remarkable records known of nine-

186. Clément, p. 66.
187. Nanteuil's letters to Clément, all dating from the mid-1870s, are in Fleurier, CFC.
188. Lausanne, MCBA, GA 999, unpaginated. A substantial part of the "Journal," which passed into Mathilde Gleyre's hands after the painter's death, was published by Clément, but in many places it was severely edited. Parts of the journal are illegible and many pages are in bad physical condition.
189. Lowell's association with Gleyre was known to members of the Lowell family for generations, as well to Egyptologists in Boston, but not to art historians. The Gleyre drawings remained in the hands of the Lowell family throughout the nineteenth century and were first seen by members of the Boston Museum of Fine Arts staff on 20 June 1947, as indicated in an unpublished report from D. Dunham of the Egyptian Department to the director of the museum — the memorandum is in the BMFA files. Dunham noted a visit on that day to the estate of Ralph Lowell in Westwood, where he saw "little fewer than 200 pencil and water-color drawings" by the Swiss artist "Gabriel Gleyre." He indicated that Mrs. Lowell believed him to be the first scholar to examine the works. Dunham advised that the works be photographed and duly recorded which was apparently done. Ralph Lowell eventually lent the entire group to the BMFA on 22 March 1949, where they were housed in the Egyptian Department. Probably the first time that Gleyre is noted in print as the artist who accompanied Lowell is in the *Harvard Alumni Bulletin*, 1949, p. 636. By the time that Weeks published his history of the Lowell family (1966), Gleyre's name was already common in this context; see Weeks 1966, p. 19. Lowell's role was not mentioned, however, in the 1974 Gleyre retrospective. The first citation in art historical literature of Lowell's identity is in Weisberg 1976, p. 465.
190. See a letter to Henry, undated, reproduced in part in Clément, p. 50; the original is in Lausanne, MCBA, GA 998.
191. Clément, p. 66.
192. Lowell's diaries, in eight volumes, are owned by the Lowell family and deposited in the Egyptian Department of the BMFA, with the drawings and watercolors. Each volume measures 21.3 x 17.6 cm., but none of them is in Lowell's own hand. It may be assumed that a member of Lowell's family transcribed the journals sometime in the nineteenth century. In some instances, there are blank sections with indications that no transcription was made from the original manuscript. Several inquiries to the Lowell family reveal that the original untranscribed manuscript is not extant in their collection or in the Houghton Library, Harvard, where some of the Lowell papers were deposited. My thanks to Mr. Timothy Kendall, Acting Curator of the Egyptian Collection in Boston, for permitting me to study the manuscripts in his care. Throughout the discussion of the voyage, citations from the journal are by date.

teenth-century travel to places then rarely visited. By contrast, Gleyre's journal, on which Clément based much of his material, is, like the one he kept on his Italian voyage, random and sketchy with incomplete phrases and ideas. Furthermore, it begins only after he left Corfu on 6 July 1834 and ends in mid-sentence a year later, three years before he returned to France.[193]

Lowell's journal is at once very detailed in certain areas and sadly deficient in others where one might expect further discussion, particularly in regard to the people he encountered. He says nothing of his stay in Rome and his meeting with Vernet. The first instance in which Gleyre's name occurs comes about one month after they left Rome: "On the 30th of April and 1st and 2nd May, I went to Paestum with Mr. Gleyre by the route of Pompeii and Salerno." This kind of casual, cursory citation often occurs for others figures noted in the journal, despite the fact that such encounters were at times quite significant for the travelers' itinerary or their knowledge of local events and customs. At times, it can be shown that these meetings were responsible for extending the trip considerably.

In Athens, for example, besides being officially presented to Otto I, the Bavarian ruler of Greece since 1832, and Leo von Klenze, the architect charged with the reconstruction plans for the Parthenon,[194] Lowell and Gleyre also became acquainted with at least two other artists. One who is noted in Lowell's journal simply as "Captain Petier" was actually the accomplished French cartographer Jean-Pierre Eugène Peytier (1793–1864), charged with producing the first modern map of Greece. Peytier was also a distinguished artist and watercolorist whose views of Greece have only recently come to light.[195] As will be seen in the catalogue section, the proximity of certain views and models suggests not only that Gleyre and Peytier knew each other well, but in several instances may have collaborated on certain scenes or copied from each other.

Lowell also noted in Athens that he and Gleyre met a "M. Wolfenburg" — the same form of spelling used by Gleyre in his journal entry on the same page in which "M. Lowell" is cited — who was briefly described as a Swiss artist and a friend of Gleyre's. This is a reference to Johann Jacob Wolfensberger (1797–1850), who had been associated with Vernet's circle in Rome in 1830 where he undoubtedly had met Gleyre.[196] Like von Klenze, Wolfensberger went to Athens in 1832 to work for the Bavarian mission there, producing popular views of the city, sometimes in the context of illustrations for travel publications. Although there is no mention in Gleyre's diary that he actually saw Wolfensberger's works, Lowell noted that the examples he saw were particularly "brilliant and beautiful," and it is likely that Gleyre's watercolors of the city were influenced by them.

Lowell's and Gleyre's encounters in Egypt, as seen in the large number of names that appear in this section of Lowell's journal, were even richer and more diversified. One of the first acquaintances they made after docking in Alexandria was the American George Gliddon (1809–57) who, besides pursuing his substantial diplomatic duties, took a particular interest in archeology and was thus in a position to advise Lowell on spe-

193. Lausanne, MCBA, GA 999. Sometimes whole pages are left blank, the narrative continuing later, perhaps indicating Gleyre's intention to fill in the pages. In several instances, chronological order is not strictly followed.
194. On Leo von Klenze's project, see Lieb 1979, passim.
195. On Jean-Pierre Eugène Peytier's career and artistic interests, see Papadopoulos 1971, pp. 7–21. My thanks to the Vagliano family for permitting me to examine the Peytier works in their collection.
196. Hofmeister 1854, p. 7, briefly discusses the artist's sojourn in Rome and Athens. On Johann Jakob Wolfensberger in the context of foreign artists in Athens in the late 1830s, see Tsigakou 1981. There are no monographs on the artist and the bulk of his Athenian works have not surfaced. The Graphische Sammlung, Eidgenössische Technische Hochschule, Zürich, contains only three Athenian watercolors, while the Kunsthaus, Zürich, contains ten drawings, none of which shows any connection with Gleyre.

cific sites to visit.[197] Also in Alexandria and later in Cairo, the travelers profited from the hospitality and advice of the former French consul, Bernardino Drovetti (1775–1852). Like Gliddon, Drovetti had a keen interest in Egyptian antiquities and had amassed two major collections of art.[198] Drovetti's influence and importance in official Egyptian circles, even though by this time he was retired from service, were instrumental in facilitating Lowell's travel plans and the export of objects he bought, particularly in Thebes.

While in Cairo, Lowell and Gleyre met a large number of the French entourage there, which was mostly concerned with France's military and economic interests in the region.[199] Several references indicate meetings with Ibrahim Pasha (1789–1848), who, although known primarily as a brilliant military leader — he had recently completed a successful campaign against Syria, thus solidifying Egyptian autonomy — was also an unusually well educated man with probably the largest library in Egypt.[200] His tastes in the literature of history, travel, and the natural sciences appealed particularly to Lowell and helped to form a relationship between the two that went beyond the expected formality. Gleyre found him severe and ferocious in appearance.[201]

Curiously, Lowell makes no mention of having met Ibrahim's more illustrious father, Muhammad Ali (1769–1849), the wali of Albanian origins who was more responsible than anyone else for bringing enlightened Western progress to Egypt. However, from a section of Gleyre's journal, it is known that they had at least one audience.[202] Gleyre was impressed by "Son Altesse," whom he described in glowing terms, noting that among the topics of discussion was cotton production — Muhammad Ali was responsible, with French help, for introducing the industry into Egypt — a subject that must have particularly appealed to Lowell's interests.[203] Gleyre also noted that they discussed other industries and the introduction of a viable railroad system, and drank excellent coffee, but that no pipe was offered at the end of the audience. It is possible, as will be seen in the catalogue section, that Gleyre sketched a portrait of the ruler.

It was also in Cairo that Lowell and Gleyre first met the Père Enfantin, the socialist leader and chief advocate of the Saint-Simonian movement, while he was in residence in Soliman Pasha's quarters.[204] Gleyre must have

197. On George Gliddon, see especially Hilmy 1886–87, II, p. 263, and Dawson and Uphill 1972, p. 117. Gliddon became one of the first American writers on Egyptian antiquities and a strong advocate of historic preservation; it is certainly no coincidence that he returned to America in 1842 to work for the newly formed Lowell Institute, one of the immediate results of their close association. He delivered a highly successful series of lectures on ancient Egypt in Boston, December through February 1842–43 which he published later; the thirteen lectures ran to twelve separate editions. His appeal for the preservation of Egyptian monuments was voiced in very strong terms in 1849.
198. He donated the first collection to his native Piedmont, where it became the nucleus of the formidable collection of Egyptian artifacts in Turin, while the second he sold at a substantial profit to Charles X for the Louvre holdings. On Bernardino Drovetti's highly successful diplomatic career in the service of the French consulate, see Al-Sayyid-Marsot 1984, pp. 44f. On his collections, see Curto 1976, pp. 45–50, which stresses the first collection now in Turin.
199. These included Colonel Varin, charged with the organization of the military schools, and the elusive adventurer Joseph Sève, who had earlier fled France under curious circumstances and would become the military force behind the throne. Sève eventually converted to Islam and took the name of Soliman Pasha, as he is repeatedly cited in Lowell's and Gleyre's notes. There is no monograph on

Varin, but see Marlowe 1974, p. 25. On Sève, see particularly Al-Sayyid-Marsot 1984, p. 127, for his military activities, and p. 194, for his conversion to Islam.
200. Ibrahim Pasha made his triumphal entry into Cairo, after an absence of three years in the Syrian campaigns, on 21 January 1835; Lowell and Gleyre met him three days later in his house and gardens. The standard monograph on him is Enkiri 1948, but see also Al-Sayyid-Marsot 1984, pp. 80–85, on this phase of his career.
201. Clément, p. 90, from an entry in Gleyre's journal.
202. Ibid., p. 94. The literature on Muhammad Ali is vast, but see Cattaui 1931–36, who traced his political career through documents in the archives of the Russian consulates in Alexandria and Cairo.
203. See Owen 1969 for the importance of the introduction of cotton manufacture into the Egyptian economy in Muhammad Ali's reign. It might be noted that Lowell was the scion of a family with considerable interests in American cotton manufacture.
204. Enfantin (1796–1864) had come to Egypt with his followers in October 1833, having been forced out of France, in search of his ideal of *La Femme Messie*, and intending to pursue the possibility of piercing the Suez peninsula with a navigable waterway. The standard work on Enfantin's life and projects is Alem 1963, but see also the important contribution in Charléty 1931, pp. 205–22, on his voyage to Egypt. See too Voilquin 1978, who accompanied Enfantin to Egypt, for more detailed information on him and his milieu. On Enfantin and the arts, see Egbert 1970, pp. 124–33.

looked forward to the meeting with Enfantin, as he had openly advocated the Saint-Simonian ideal of a new social order. While in the mountains of Albania on 12 July 1834, Lowell noted that Gleyre had a long discussion on the subject with Pussin, Lowell's brother-in-law. The actual meeting with Enfantin in Cairo, however, proved to be a profound disappointment for Gleyre, as well as for Lowell, who described the enigmatic leader as a rogue and implied that he considered him a charlatan. Gleyre encountered Enfantin again several months later in Thebes, where the two visited the ruins together and discussed not only the grandeur of antiquity, but also the banal subject of cooking.[205] Despite Gleyre's discontent with Enfantin as a spiritual leader, he nevertheless produced one of the most sympathetic portraits known of him.

fig. 46

Perhaps the most important figure the two encountered in Cairo was "Mr. Lane," Edward William Lane (1801–76), who became one of the leading scholars of Arab sociology, language, and customs. Lane first traveled to Egypt in 1825, ostensibly for his delicate health, but he soon embarked on a landmark study of Egyptian society which he had just completed when he met Lowell and Gleyre.[206] Lowell and Gleyre later met Lane several times in Luxor, where he was living in a vacated tomb. Apparently Lane and Lowell became more intimate friends here, since Lane confessed that he had recently been circumcised in order to facilitate his access to sources that otherwise might have been closed to non-Muslims.

In the last portion of the trip in the isolated Nubian desert, the names that appear in Lowell's journals are almost exclusively those of local officials with whom the party had to negotiate for supplies, money transfers, and general advice on traveling conditions. On 20 October 1835, near the site of Meroe, however, Lowell and Gleyre met the celebrated Swedish naturalist Johann Hedenborg (1787–1865), who was journeying to Cairo after a long stay in Khartoum.[207] Hedenborg was collecting ornithological specimens — he gave Lowell a long discourse on how to preserve birds — as well as geological examples which he later donated to the Swedish Natural History Museum in Stockholm. The encounter was fortunate for Lowell and Gleyre, for both were suffering from various ailments, and Lowell in particular was weak with a continuing case of dysentery. Hedenborg, who was a trained physician, treated the travelers with local, natural medicines described in the journals. Lowell's condition was so severe that Hedenborg strongly advised him against continuing the trip as he had planned, especially considering the harsh conditions and poor sanitation of the cities yet to be visited. By this time, Gleyre had already decided to return to Cairo after their projected stay in Khartoum; Lowell decided to continue in his feeble state, a decision which led to his death six months later.

Lowell's journals reveal that he was particularly well prepared for the long trip through extensive reading. On Greece and Albania, Lowell had read and generally followed Byron's *Childe Harold's Pilgrimage*, Canto II, as his chief guide. The map he used in Asia Minor — the copy is still preserved among the Lowell papers — was made by J. MacDonald

205. Clément, p. 101, from Gleyre's journal ("… nous raisonnâmes cuisine"). Enfantin himself wrote no letters from this phase of his trip to Luxor; the first one he sent was on 16 June 1835, several days after Gleyre and Lowell had left; see Voilquin 1978, pp. 332–33.

206. See Lane 1836, which went through various editions in Lane's lifetime and has served as a standard text to the present. Lane eventually produced the first authoritative English translation of the *Arabian Nights* (1838–40) and would spend almost thirty years compiling an Arab-English lexicon that is still used today. The only biography of Lane, published in 1877 by his grand-nephew, lacks objectivity and makes no mention of either Lowell or Gleyre. For a portrait of him, see the sculpture by his brother, Richard James Lane, in the National Portrait Gallery, London. His manuscripts are preserved in London, BL and contain more than a hundred of his own drawings.

207. Little information is available on Hedenborg, but see the biographical notice in Larousse 1866–90, IX, part I, p. 132. Hedenborg published an account of his voyage; see Hedenborg 1843.

46. *Portrait of Père Enfantin, Cairo*, 1835. Boston, Museum of Fine Arts (catalogue n° 244)

Kinnier in 1816 and published in London the following year. It principally illustrated the marches of Xenophon, Julian, and Heraclitus, and served as the basic source for the land routes. In the Egyptian section of the journals, the direct citation of authors with descriptions and exact measurements indicates that Lowell actually carried with him certain texts pertaining to his travels. As early as the first month in Egypt, Lowell disagreed with measurements cited by no less an authority than Champollion. It is not certain which text of the celebrated archeologist Lowell had in hand, but it is clear from the context that Lowell referred to the text while he was present at the monuments. In other notes from the region of Lower Egypt, Lowell refers extensively to the writings of Giambattista Belzoni (1778–1823). Both authors, it should be noted, were considered standard guides — indeed, they were written as such — and constituted part of the normal baggage for the European traveler before Baedecker's more generalized books on Egypt a half century later.[208]

As Lowell and Gleyre went further south into the lesser known and more rarely visited areas near Nubia, they relied on more esoteric works. At Abu Simbel, Lowell mentioned the "Hayes" [sic] expedition, referring to the explorer Robert Hay who was responsible for extended excavation at the site, and no doubt saw the inscription the party made there in June 1832.[209] For the lengthy stay in the region near Meroe, Lowell took vol-

208. Several works by Champollion are possible, including *L'Egypte sous les Pharaons* (Paris, 1814) or his *Panthéon égyptien... d'après les monuments* (Paris, 1825), but not his *Monuments de l'Egypte et de la Nubie*, pertaining to his voyage of 1828–29, the first volume of which did not appear until 1835 when Lowell was already in Egypt. The reference to Belzoni must be to his *Narrative of the Operations and Recent Discoveries with the Pyramids...* (London, 1820, revised 1827), or his *Travels of Belzoni in Egypt and Nubia* (London, 1822). There were also several French and Italian editions of these that were available to Lowell.

209. On Robert Hay, see Christophe 1965, pp. 96–100. Robert Hay had cleared part of the colossal statues and the door of the entry to the large temple. This fact, incidentally, was already noted in Wilkinson 1835, p. 496, although the preface to the edition is dated 1831. Lowell also knew the writings of James Bruce, as well as the important books of George Waddington and the naturalist Wilhelm Rüppel. Bruce's *Travels to the Source of the Nile* (Edinburg and London, 1790), of which there were many translations and editions, was published in a French edition of fourteen volumes, undoubtedly too cumbersome for Lowell to take with him. See too Waddington and Hanbury 1822, recounting his voyage of 1820–21. Lowell's references to Rüppel are not clear since he often cited him in connection with Waddington. But it is possible that Lowell may have had either Rüppel 1826, or Rüppel 1829 which contains engravings and maps of important sites. No French or English translations of the works are known to have been published before Lowell's journey.

umes of Frédéric Cailliaud's works, and made several references to following his detailed maps of the region, the only ones available.[210]

The exact route of the trip has already been treated in detail elsewhere,[211] and it is documented anew in the catalogue here in connection with the works made in situ. It is useful, however, to outline the principal places Gleyre visited, some of which are not listed either in Gleyre's journal or in Lowell's. As Gleyre indicated, he and Lowell left Rome on 5 April 1834 for a three-week stay in Naples followed by visits to Pompeii and Paestum. On 8 May, they went to Sicily, where they remained until about the 27th, then departed for Malta where they stayed until 13 June — Lowell, incidentally, described nothing of their visit here, but as will be shown, this part of the trip can be documented from Gleyre's private sketches. Corfu followed and in early July they were trekking in the Albanian mountains, visiting the major cities there, eventually going south to Missolonghi to see the graves of Byron and the Greek hero Marco Botzaris, whose brother they were able to locate.[212] Later in the month they traversed the Argolian plain and in early August made their way past Mycenae; Gleyre, however, was ill with fever and produced no drawings of the region.

In late August, Lowell and Gleyre entered Athens, still under Turkish rule. They had the good fortune to witness the laying of the first stone in the reconstruction of the Parthenon, which was in ruins after centuries of abuse. Lowell noted on 10 September that he heard the architect Leo von Klenze deliver a speech in German; it was on this occasion that he was presented to the Bavarian king, Otto I, then only nineteen years old. After their stay in Athens, the party sailed for the Turkish coast, but ill winds forced them to seek refuge on the island of Syros, where Gleyre was able to make some studies of the local villagers. They eventually came to Smyrna where they spent several weeks, generally in the company of non-Greeks, although Gleyre's works indicate that several noteworthy encounters took place with the inhabitants of nearby villages. Gradually, they made their way to Constantinople, and in December set sail for Egypt. Once again unfavorable winds forced a change in plans, this time an unscheduled stop in Rhodes, where Lowell was enchanted by the architecture and decided to extend his stay so that Gleyre could have sufficient time to complete his watercolor studies. They arrived off the coast of Alexandria near Christmas — Gleyre was seasick nearly the whole time — but were forced to stay in quarantine for two weeks. It was here, while waiting for permission to disembark, that Gleyre painted a stunning portrait of his patron.

fig. 47

In the eight months of the trip thus far, Gleyre had produced about 120 works in watercolor and pencil, averaging about four per week. When these works are studied chronologically, it becomes evident that Gleyre found his artistic way very slowly. The works produced in Naples, for example, show an almost clumsy effort to delineate topography and atmosphere, and they do not yet exhibit Gleyre's personal artistic stamp. A drawing of the ruins of Pompeii demonstrates Gleyre's technique in rendering architecture and nuance precisely, not unlike his eighteenth-

47. *Portrait of John Lowell, Jr., Alexandria*, 1834. Boston, Museum of Fine Arts (catalogue n° 232)

210. See Cailliaud 1823–27.
211. See Berger 1974, Newhouse 1980, and Hauptman 1985(d), all of which rely on the same documentation, except that Berger did not have access to the Lowell journals.
212. On the importance of Marco Botzaris (c. 1870–1923) in the war of independence and his position in Romantic ideology, see Athanassoglou 1980, pp. 63f. The subject was treated by Juste Olivier in 1826 in a poem for which he received a prize. Gleyre, incidentally, noted in his journal that the burial sites of Byron and Botzaris were not marked.

48. *Study of Three Greeks*, 1834. Lausanne, Musée
Cantonal des Beaux-Arts (catalogue n° 115)

century predecessors, and his proficiency in working rapidly under uncertain conditions. But the drawings made in Sicily are already more deft
and the watercolors less rigid in their depiction of sites. By the time
Gleyre arrived in Malta, he seems to have found his own distinctive style
in the works Lowell demanded of him. Details of local atmosphere, as
well as particular elements of costume and physiognomy, all indicate a
marked advance in technique and proficiency, both of which improved
during the remainder of the trip.

Blending a delicate line and Ingresque objectivity, his study of three
Greeks made on the spot is remarkably fresh and distinctly more assured    fig. 48
than the earlier figure studies, such as his still ungainly representation of
a Maltese woman. Compared to his Roman style, the figure studies in    fig. 49

86

49. *Maltese Woman*, 1834. Boston, Museum of Fine Arts (catalogue n° 100)

Greece and Turkey seem to be by another hand. Gleyre was clearly inspired by the freshness of the people he saw and was now able to turn documentation into art. While all of the figures here were executed in situ under less than perfect conditions, none appears forced or so improvised as to lack the essentials he and Lowell wished to preserve.

During the month Gleyre spent in Athens, he produced about twenty-five works, some of which may be recognized as his finest efforts of the trip. Gleyre was enchanted by the light and the direct confrontation with Classical remains, here in a purer form than in Rome. Lowell noted on 8 September 1834 that Gleyre, whom he would later accuse of indolence, was particularly industrious in Athens, producing more than satisfactory watercolor views of monuments and costumes. The measure of Gleyre's

50. *View of the Acropolis*, 1834. Boston, Museum of Fine Arts (catalogue n° 124)

51. *Mosque at Athens*, 1834. Boston, Museum of Fine Arts (catalogue n° 140)

success can be seen in his view of the Acropolis, which at once provides a fig. 50 literal description of the site and creates the impression of the open spaces around it through careful editing of the composition. Similarly, the factual studies of the Parthenon from the east end and from the interior of the cella, showing the mosque still in place, reveal a skillful handling of a fig. 52 difficult composition that he must have attempted only infrequently in Paris or Rome. This powerful work, in its curious juxtaposition of architectural and historical styles, transcends the postcard renditions of the monument common to Gleyre's contemporaries. These watercolors, like many of the architectural views, do not contain figures to indicate scale, and are thus removed from the contemporary; the structures are por-

52. *View of the Parthenon*, 1834. Boston, Museum of Fine Arts (catalogue n° 128)

trayed as timeless, to be studied with awe. In one view of Athens in which the Acropolis is incidental, Gleyre's portrayal of the geometry of the structures is a tour de force that shows a highly advanced manner of delineating planar projections through carefully analyzed color variations, not unlike the works of Cézanne at the end of the century.

No less impressive are the watercolors Gleyre made in Rhodes in December 1834. The fact that Lowell extended their unexpected stay there so that Gleyre would have enough time to complete his studies indicates Lowell's appreciation of the quality of the work Gleyre was producing at the time. Lowell wrote on 18 December that the medieval architecture on the island was "beyond expectation," and clearly Gleyre himself was

53. *Palace of the Knights, Rhodes*, 1834. Boston, Museum of Fine Arts (catalogue n° 225)

inspired with the same enthusiasm. One of the most accomplished examples from Rhodes is Gleyre's rendition of a coffee house, one of the fig. 53 few interior views he had attempted up to this point. The work not only affords a precise definition of the distinctive architecture, but also blends the spontaneous with the formal elements through the animated figures who appear to look at the viewer as he enters.

Gleyre was so inspired by the island that he wrote a long letter to his friend Jourdain. Typically, he did not describe the monuments or report his activities; rather he indulged in philosophical musings and a melancholy longing that would characterize his thoughts again in the Egyptian desert. With the same ennui and self-doubt expressed in his letters from Rome, Gleyre told Jourdain that

> … rien de ce que j'avais osé espérer ne s'est réalisé… Voilà, j'ai parcouru une grande plaine grise semblable au désert que je crois voir sans que mes pieds y laissent la moindre trace. J'ai reconnu le néant de toutes choses sans en avoir possédé aucune.[213]

213. Clément, p. 76.

90

It is difficult to account for Gleyre's malaise in Rhodes, particularly in light of the remarkable work he produced there. No indications in the journal of either Lowell or Gleyre account for Gleyre's despair eight months after leaving Rome in ebullient spirits, yet a preoccupation with lost opportunities, the idea that he was unable to realize his goals, and an awareness of persistent emptiness seem to envelop him. These notions became *idées fixes* that expressed themselves forcefully in his later work, especially in his first salon success in 1843.

Gleyre and Lowell finally embarked on the Nile journey after their period of quarantine in January 1835. The early part of the Nile trip followed the pattern established by earlier voyagers. They stopped in Sais on 19 January where Gleyre not only made several drawings but also shot a menacing wild boar that suddenly appeared, and then continued to Cairo where they remained for about two weeks. They sailed up the Nile gradually, stopping at the ruins of Beni Hassan on 5 March, and continuing to Assyout and then to Thebes, where they camped for almost a month. Returning to Assyout once again, they took the inland desert route to the fabled oasis of Kargeh, which they visited on 25 May after a particularly arduous journey. The party then returned to Assyout and again camped in Thebes before proceeding southward to Esna on 12 June, Edfou the day after, and Gebel Silsileh on 14 June.

By this point in the journey, more than a year after leaving Rome, Lowell was becoming more and more indisposed by the harsh conditions of travel. When they visited the enchanted island of Philae on 22 June, Lowell was so much troubled by a constant stomach ailment and a recurring case of ophthalmia that he was forced to remain on the site against his wishes for about a month. He noted in his journal that since leaving Esna, he could barely see, that he had great pain from dysentery, and that at times he could neither walk nor stand upright.[214] From Philae, Gleyre took most of the supplies, one of the Arab guides, and a boat and, after stopping at Dundoor, established the next camp at Abu Simbel. By 8 July, Lowell had recovered sufficiently to join Gleyre, and by the middle of July, the two were camped in sight of the colossal figures of Abu Simbel.

fig. 54 During the journey up the Nile Gleyre worked unevenly and produced relatively few drawings for reasons neither he nor Lowell enumerated in their respective journals. The only scene executed in Alexandria was a straightforward postcard-like depiction of Pompey's Column, which decidedly lacks the imagination and creativity of the Greek and Rhodes watercolors. He did, however, record in his journal his impressions of the Egyptian peasants and their daily customs, and he included his notions on African women who shocked his Western sensibilities by their lack of hygiene and their indolence. He noted in his journal their manner of living and added:

> Je n'ai jamais vu de plus dégoûtantes femelles. Il faut que la loi de procréation soit bien impérieuse pour que les hommes consentent à s'accoupler avec des êtres semblables.

54. *Pompey's Column, Alexandria,* 1835. Boston, Museum of Fine Arts (catalogue n° 234)

214. Lowell described his symptoms with almost clinical accuracy on 19 June 1835 near Aswan. He noted too that about one third of the Egyptian population was afflicted with dysentery. Voilquin 1978, pp. 230–31, wrote upon her arrival in Alexandria that the disease was endemic to the Egyptian population because of the horrid living conditions.

91

57. *Interior of a Coptic House, Cairo*, 1835. Boston, Museum of Fine Arts (catalogue n° 237)

55. *The Pyramids*, 1835. Boston, Museum of Fine Arts (catalogue n° 243)
56. *Temple of Denderah*, 1835. Lausanne, Musée Cantonal des Beaux-Arts (catalogue n° 247)

215. On the condition of Egyptian women, see Tucker 1985, especially pp. 16–63. See also Voilquin 1978, pp. 240f., which discusses the effects of tedious labor on the physical condition of the women.
216. Clément, p. 91.

This was undoubtedly a far cry from the exotic ideal he had formed from the images in art and literature. But Gleyre was moved by the immense poverty he witnessed and the degrading daily tasks that were generally assigned to women, as he was horrified by the exploitation of the Egyptian women in Cairo and in the countryside. He found the plight of African women pitiable and sketched some of them he encountered with evident sympathy.[215] Gleyre's reaction to Cairo was mixed. While intrigued by the city as a whole, including the ancient sites as well as the picturesque Moslem architecture, he was also profoundly disappointed by the evidence of Western influences that the French in the area had already produced. He also found to his chagrin that the city contained a substantial number of European painters, none of whom he names: "On ne sait plus où aller pour éviter la société des peintres. J'en trouve ici une douzaine au moins."[216] Gleyre produced about five works in Cairo, but none of them depict the city itself. The only finished watercolor is the astonishing view of the interior of a Coptic house, replete with details and precise perspectival nuances. Even the pyramids at Giza failed to inspire Gleyre very much; he drew at Lowell's behest a flat, undistinguished touristic view, without attempting to show their immensity or grandeur. Lowell, however, examined each of the pyramids scrupulously, measuring the bases, entering the tombs, and climbing to the top of the Great Pyramid to admire the view which he described in poetic detail. There is no indication that Gleyre accompanied him.

fig. 57

fig. 55

The voyage from Cairo to Thebes proved to be so difficult that only one drawing is known to have been completed along the way, a study of the half-submerged Temple of Dendera. Neither Lowell nor Gleyre bore well the constant sandstorms and excessive heat, which Lowell recorded almost every day. Lowell also noted that he had fevers of various sorts, hallucinations at times, and intense migraines. For a period of about ten days, he was afflicted with sores on his body and noted sardonically that

fig. 56

92

58. *Ruins of the Temple of Amon, Karnak*, 1835. Boston, Museum of Fine Arts (catalogue n° 259)

the biblical plagues of ancient Egypt still exist. On 10 March, Lowell had to take ten drops of laudanum in order to sleep, the first mention of an addiction to the drug that was described often in the coming months of travel. Lowell did not indicate whether Gleyre suffered from similar afflictions at this time, but it is probable that he too was susceptible to them; this may account for his meager production during this period.

The stay in Thebes, however, turned out to be a revelation to Gleyre and a welcome respite from the harsh conditions. Gleyre completed more than twenty works, including some of the most noteworthy of the Egyptian trip. He was so awestruck by the vastness and quality of the ruins that he wrote, "la plume et le pinceau demeurent impuissants" before the extraordinary majesty of these monuments. At the ruins of Karnak, Gleyre confessed that he had never imagined anything like the monuments he saw there.[217] The same was true for Lowell, who wrote on 13 March:

> The gate at the entrance of the temple of Karnak is superb. Its magnitude and majesty make it even appear sublime. The immense ruins of the temple itself with its obelisks and its sculptured granite portico and numerous stupendous columns; some standing, some prostrate and others falling; but all half buried by the accumulated rubbish of ages, produce a great effect on the imagination.

Gleyre's views of the temples verify his sense of reverence as well as his desire to show these monuments within a specific context; nowhere in his earlier studies is there a similar sense of space and environment. The Great Ramseum on the west bank is indicated in no fewer than four sepa-

fig. 58

217. Clément, p. 96.

fig. 45 rate views from various angles so as to convey the overall disposition of the site. Lowell shared Gleyre's astonishment at even the smaller details of the architecture and sculpture; he bought certain block fragments fig. 59 which he shipped back to Boston, and these form the basis for the rich collection of Egyptian art there. Lowell's purchases at the site also included, as he noted on 1 April, a "well stuffed crocodile" almost ten feet in length for which he paid $2.50.

Although the outburst of Gleyre's creative energies at Thebes paralleled that in Athens, it was here that he produced his last watercolors for Lowell. There is no specific mention why Gleyre did no further studies in the medium, which by now he had mastered completely, but probably he could no longer maintain the rigorous pace Lowell had established earlier. After more than a year in close company, the disciplined Yankee and the self-doubting, reserved Swiss no longer had a harmonious relationship, and tempers flared repeatedly. The desert climate and fragile nerves evidently precluded a continuous production in the exacting watercolor technique. In addition, Gleyre began to show signs of ophthalmia, which weakened his eyes considerably and created a condition that continued to affect him for more than thirty years.

In the oasis of Kargeh — almost fifty hours on foot through the desert from Assyout, as Lowell noted — the strain between the two was somewhat eased. Gleyre recorded in his notes his own sense of relief and tranquility among the fountains, the famous wells, the picturesque palms, and, as he wrote, the best dates he had eaten in Egypt. The party rested here for several days, but the return to Assyout and Thebes, a necessary stop for continuing further up the Nile, rekindled the stress. Furthermore, on 22 May, Lowell noted that Gleyre was "indisposed, with an

59. *Sanctuary at Karnak*, 1835. Boston, Museum of Fine Arts (catalogue n° 264)

inflammation of the gums," a condition that worsened during the following week. On 29 May, just before sailing for Aswan, Lowell wrote:

> I think the temperature at 3PM under the tent of the 27th must have been 45. But I slept well though melting with perspiration and covered with sand, and eat well though plates, mouth and nose were filled with it. The journey agreed with me. It set me up. Not so my companion. Mr Gleyer [sic] suffered from inflammation of the gums and jaws.

The contrast between Lowell's eagerness and Gleyre's malaise was typical for the remainder of the trip. At this point, while Lowell remained optimistic, Gleyre already envisioned the possibility of breaking the contractual agreement. In the same journal entry, Lowell noted that Gleyre

> is quite discouraged [and] thinks he cannot work in hot countries, will go as far as Nubia, and then return to Cairo. No sketches of India for me.

Why Gleyre agreed to go as far as Nubia, another six months in an even more hostile, less traveled region, is not clear. Yet despite Gleyre's physical and psychological difficulties further south, he produced some of the most interesting drawings in his Egyptian corpus. Lowell, it might be noted, became increasingly ill with ophthalmia, dysentery, and severe diarrhea. Gleyre's spirits recovered somewhat in mid-July at the ruins of Abu Simbel. He was probably aware of the fact that the large temple had   fig. 60 been discovered by the Swiss explorer Burckhardt and opened by Belzoni only eighteen years before. Gleyre recorded in his journal the immense calm and peace he felt here in contrast to the boring monotony of desert horizons. But, as in Rhodes, Gleyre's exaltation was laced with despair:

> Oh! chères et douces illusions de ma jeunesse, hélas! trop tôt dissipées; vous êtes donc perdues, perdues à jamais. L'âme regimbe à cette dure triste et fatale conviction.[218]

This is the persistent melancholy that would find its greatest expression in his painting of 1843.

On leaving Abu Simbel after 17 July 1835, Gleyre and Lowell entered Upper Nubia. This last leg of the voyage for the two was the most hazardous, since it abandoned the traditional tourist routes. Indeed, before 1835 few travelers dared venture beyond the first cataract near Aswan, except to visit the island of Philae. Travel to the second cataract and beyond was still only sketchily charted; those who had attempted the voyage were explorers and adventurers rather than tourists. The Englishman Thomas Leigh had gone 900 miles up the Nile in an expedition of 1812–13, and Burckhardt had followed as far as Shendi near the sixth cataract. In 1820 a major expedition had been formed by Waddington and Hanbury, followed by the legendary French archaeologist Cailliaud — as

218. Clément, p. 109.

60. *Temple of Abu Simbel*, 1835. Boston, Museum of Fine Arts (catalogue n° 291)

was noted earlier, Lowell took their books with him for this section of the trip. Cailliaud was in fact the first scientist to record the curious monuments in Nubia, providing valuable information on the major sites, as well as a detailed map of the region. Prudhoe and Hoskins also ventured here — the former is mentioned in Lowell's journal — in 1829 and 1833 respectively. Thus, when Gleyre and Lowell entered the Nubian desert, the western tourist was still very rare; Gleyre in fact was the first major artist to record the extensive ruins here. Only the artists associated with the fabled Lepsius expedition in 1842 would record more of the region than did Gleyre.[219]

Lowell was still ill when he joined Gleyre in Wady Halfa near the second cataract; his ailments forced him to remain near the site until 10 August. Later they set out on camels and horses for Dongola near the third cataract; Gleyre by this time had already ceased writing in his journal, an indication of his weakened state and his constant fatigue. On 13 August,

219. The artists involved were Bonomi, Wedenbach, and the architect Wild. Their drawings were published in twelve folios containing 894 plates. On the travelers at the site, see especially Christophe 1965, who summarizes the work done during the early nineteenth century. On travelers in Nubia, see Budge 1907(b), pp. 1f.

61. *Temple at Semna*, 1835. Boston, Museum of Fine Arts (catalogue n° 298)

they stopped in Semna, and a week later Gleyre alone — Lowell was too ill to continue — visited the island of Sace to inspect the monumental sculpture there. They later continued to Soleb and Old Dongola, where further illness, sandstorms, and other discomforts, such as a loss of a camel's saddle, made travel a heroic task. On 12 September, Lowell recorded that they were attacked by a horde of white ants that ate through the wood in Gleyre's trunk.

fig. 61
fig. 63

Perhaps the most important site they visited in Nubia was Djebel Barkal before the fourth cataract, which they first saw on 18 September. Here they actually made some archaeological excavations among the small pyramids, and Lowell wrote a remarkably long and detailed report of the site including exact measurements. They then continued by the desert route further into Ethiopia, sometimes camping with Nubian tribesmen in the desert, and by 24 October they were in Naga. This was the last major archaeological site that they visited together, and the last monuments that Gleyre sketched. From Naga, Lowell and Gleyre slowly proceeded to Khartoum.

fig. 64

The drawings Gleyre made after Abu Simbel were mostly descriptions of the ruins, as well as hieroglyphic details that fascinated Lowell. In some cases, two sites appear on the same page. At Djebel Barkal, Gleyre made at least a dozen drawings of the temples, as well as several physiognomic studies of the Nubians of the region. The works at Naga are similar in

fig. 62

98

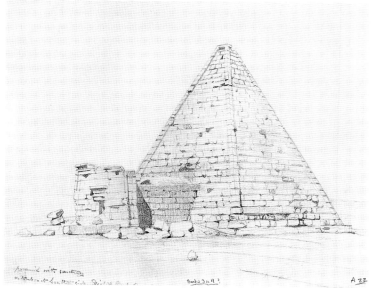

62. *Woman, Djebel Barkal*, 1835. Boston, Museum of Fine Arts (catalogue n° 312)
63. *Temple at Soleb*, 1835. Boston, Museum of Fine Arts (catalogue n° 300)
64. *Pyramid at Djebel Barkal*, 1835. Boston, Museum of Fine Arts (catalogue n° 302)

65. *Corinthian Gate at Naga*, 1835. Boston, Museum of Fine Arts (catalogue n° 324)

their simplicity and archaeological importance; in some cases, Gleyre recorded monuments that no longer exist or have been subsequently altered. But already in Naga, Gleyre had considerable difficulty in accomplishing his work, and Lowell noted with some dismay that Gleyre was hurrying so that he could quit the site as soon as possible. He also commented that Gleyre's drawings were no longer of the same quality as earlier in the journey, an observation not borne out by the drawings themselves. On 31 October, Lowell wrote that Gleyre was now in a constant state of apathy and in any case would be useless as a draftsman in later travels.

fig. 65

Lowell undoubtedly exaggerated the situation because of his fatigue, discomfort, and constant illness. His journal, however, records periodically in Nubia that Gleyre himself was ill or in fragile health, and at times was afflicted with crippling ophthalmia that prevented continued production. Lowell's unrelenting eagerness and Gleyre's increasing discomfort combined to create a friction that could only result in a rupture. After giving Gleyre the last installment of his salary, Lowell noted on 11 November 1835 in Khartoum: "Settled my accounts with Mr Gleyre. He leaves me here. He has been with me 19 months and 6 days." Despite Lowell's irritation with Gleyre, five days later he paid him an additional 2,000 piastres, the equivalent of about 1,000 francs, as severance pay.

It is difficult to reconstruct accurately the events in Gleyre's life after he left Lowell in Khartoum until he returned to Europe as Gleyre had stopped writing in his journal well before his arrival in Khartoum. We know that Lowell continued his trip alone to Bombay, after crossing the Arabian desert, and in his weakened condition succumbed to a fever five

100

months later. The last entry in his journal is dated 29 February 1836 and says only, "Very fresh NW (wind), sea breeze the last 3 hours. fair." Gleyre at the time was still in Khartoum and in Sennar, the center of the Nubian slave trade, where he remained almost a year. Gleyre recounted some aspects of his stay in a letter to Henry, written from Lebanon, on 25 May 1837, the first contact it seems he had with his brother since December 1834.[220] In the letter, Gleyre wrote briefly of his separation from "l'Américain," and indicated that he had been so severely stricken with a case of ophthalmia that he was virtually blind for a period of about ten months. Clément added, from information received later from Hortense Cornu with whom Gleyre stayed in Paris, that in Sennar, Gleyre was cared for by a young woman named Stella with whom he had fallen in love.[221] Further information on this period in Gleyre's life is provided by Nanteuil, who wrote to Clément about it, almost certainly after the publication of the first edition of Clément's monograph.[222] Nanteuil told Clément that with the money Gleyre received from his patron, he bought himself a male slave and a pet monkey; Gleyre's blindness is not mentioned, nor is the attachment to a woman who may have taken care of him. The slave Gleyre bought remained with him during his stay in Khartoum and seems to have gone with him to Cairo, where he was given his freedom. He refused to accept it, wanting instead to go with Gleyre to Paris, and the French consul had to be called in to convince the slave he could not accompany Gleyre.

Nanteuil added other information in the letter, which Clément never used and which contradicts Mme. Cornu's account. He noted that Gleyre's blindness occurred after Khartoum, during the return voyage down the Nile. Nanteuil stated that Gleyre was accompanied by a Mr. Ponnerat who later visited Gleyre in his studio, where, Nanteuil said, he also met Clément. There is no record of who this Mr. Ponnerat was, and his name is never mentioned in the correspondence of Gleyre's Parisian circle; Clément had no recollection of ever meeting him. Clément in fact wrote that Gleyre's return to Cairo was in the company of an unnamed Englishman, although there is no indication from his letters where he received his information. Gleyre reached Cairo in November 1836 — exactly one year after leaving Lowell — where, incidentally, he found a letter waiting from Henry, who had written desperately for news in February 1834.

Gleyre's immediate goal in Cairo was to find passage to Marseilles. For reasons he never explained, he instead booked a ship heading eastward to Beirut. During the voyage Gleyre's physical condition worsened considerably, and he was so ill with dysentery that at one point he was taken for dead and placed, immobile and covered with a cloth, on the top deck. The captain was preparing for a funeral at sea when, Clément noted, a small miracle occurred: Gleyre's pet monkey, christened Adam, licked the painter's eyelids, reanimating him. Gleyre arrived in Lebanon without further incident, but he was almost blind when he disembarked from the ship. When he entered the port, Gleyre was met by his colleague from Rome, the painter d'Etouilly, who eventually helped him regain his

220. Clément, pp. 117–20.
221. Ibid., p. 114. There are no letters in Fleurier, CFC from Mme. Cornu with this information, which suggests that Clément received it verbally. No other contemporary source mentions the fact.
222. The letter is not dated, but is in the series he wrote in 1877 and 1878; it is contained in Fleurier, CFC.

health.[223] The presence of d'Etouilly in Beirut may explain indirectly why Gleyre chose to go to Lebanon rather than Marseilles as he had planned, but there is no documentation of any prior contact between the two.

Precious little is known about Gleyre's stay in Beirut. From a letter written to Henry the following summer, on about 14 August 1837 — Gleyre noted that the date was only an approximation since he had no calendar and had already lost track of the days — we know that he lived in penury. For a period of almost a month, Gleyre wrote, he ate only a bit of Lebanese bread each day, enough to ward off starvation. He added that besides the persistent eye difficulties, he also had mysterious sores on his legs which severely limited his mobility.[224] A firsthand account of Gleyre's condition is preserved in an unpublished manuscript by the painter Antoine-Alphonse Montfort, a former pupil of Géricault and Vernet, whom Gleyre knew in Beirut.[225] Montfort and his friend Pierre-François Lehoux had established themselves there earlier and returned later in their respective careers, each producing uncommonly interesting paintings and watercolors of Arab life. On 6 June 1837 Montfort recorded in his journal that he had met "M. Glaire," as he is cited throughout the journal, through d'Etouilly; he noted that he was very much impressed by Gleyre's character and spiritual strength, but that he feared for his fragile health, particularly during the excessive heat of the Lebanese summer. Montfort recorded that the constant sand and blazing sun prevented Gleyre from venturing outdoors unless he took exceptional precautions.

On 10 July, Montfort wrote that now not only was Gleyre ill, but d'Etouilly as well. They both appear to have recovered sufficiently to have undertaken a drawing expedition to a nearby village where they remained for about two weeks, but both fell ill again. Montfort noted that they were lodged in a mission house, and treated by local Arab doctors, but d'Etouilly's condition deteriorated considerably, so that he had to be transported on a stretcher to Beirut where, it was hoped, he could have better care. When Montfort visited Gleyre in the mission, he was stunned to realize that Gleyre could not see who his visitor was; it was only after they greeted each other in Arabic that Gleyre recognized Montfort's voice. Gleyre remained several days longer, presumably in this blinded state, and then returned to Beirut. By this time d'Etouilly was suffering from delirium, and Montfort was certain that he could not survive. A few days later, d'Etouilly died; Gleyre was present at his funeral.[226]

The last mention of Gleyre in Montfort's journal occurs on 26 July. Montfort and Lehoux had been on a brief sketching excursion to the Lebanese hills and upon their return, they found Gleyre in a state of feverish delirium not unlike that of the unfortunate d'Etouilly.[227] After this date, there is a month-long gap in the journal. When Montfort began his journal anew on 31 August, Gleyre had already left Beirut.

From the letter written to Henry in mid-August 1837, we know that Gleyre had found passage to Marseilles and was to leave within the next few days. He later told Henry that the first leg of the trip from Beirut to Livorno took fifty-two days and that he was seasick almost the entire

223. Clément, pp. 116–17; see also Berthoud 1874, pp. 463–64.
224. Clément, pp. 121–22.
225. Antoine-Alphonse Montfort (1802–84) had been to Egypt in 1827; see Dussaud 1920, pp. 58f. He was in Lebanon in 1837 and remained there for about eighteen months. Montfort's own drawings and watercolors — about 900 of them — were donated to the Louvre after his death, but only a handful have been published. Montfort later became a regular habitué of Gleyre's atelier in Paris; see Clément, p. 203. Montfort's unpublished journal, containing 608 pages, is deposited in the Paris BN.
226. Paris, BN, Montfort, pp. 92, 94, 95. Montfort added later that Gleyre suffered from an exceptionally high fever and appeared to have no physical resistance to other ailments.
227. Ibid., p. 106.

time. He therefore must have arrived in Italy around the first week of October, but he was in quarantine for twenty-six days. While waiting to disembark, Gleyre told his brother, he was ill with fever and had a constant pain in his eyes; his condition, he said, was a thousand times worse than that of the Prodigal Son, an allusion that may have remained in Gleyre's mind when he undertook the theme as a subject for a painting in the 1840s. He told Henry that after more than eight years away from France and still only thirty-one, he felt himself to be "un homme usé au moral et au physique."[228]

Gleyre surely remained in Italy only a short while before his voyage to Marseilles. His health was apparently so precarious upon arrival that he was hospitalized. Supposedly, an unidentified Swiss in Marseilles, perhaps the consul, had heard of Gleyre's condition and provided medical attention so that he could be transferred to Lyons.[229] He was cared for by his family there for about three months near the end of 1837. By spring 1838 Gleyre was back in Paris, staying now with Cornu, but apparently not yet fully recovered. He wrote to Henry on 11 May: "Je suis arrivé ici fort malade, les bras et les jambes perclus."[230] Nevertheless, after a period of further recovery, Gleyre felt still so uncomfortable in Parisian society that he expressed the desire to return to the primitive cultures of the Near East. It was Cornu's arguments regarding Gleyre's fragile health that persuaded him from doing so.[231]

The question of what works from his travels with Lowell Gleyre had with him in Paris is difficult to answer. While he was contracted to produce watercolors for Lowell, he was also free to make his own studies when time permitted, but the extent of this private work has never been known. The works made for Lowell were naturally the American's property and designated as such in the initial contract. However, during their second stop in Luxor — after their overland trip to the oasis of Kargeh — Lowell knew already that Gleyre intended to leave him in Khartoum but made a generous provision that allowed Gleyre to make copies of these works. On 9 June 1835 Lowell recorded that upon their arrival in Luxor, the French consul "has taken charge of 69 colored designs, and 56 designs in crayon all by Mr G for Mr Glidden." The intention was to allow Gleyre or Glidden to take the works, which Gleyre himself carefully packed, back to Paris where they would be deposited with the Wells Company, Lowell's forwarding agent, "for a year for Mr G to copy them." Lowell reiterated the arrangement more formally in a letter to the Wells Company on 13 November, two days after he and Gleyre separated, noting that after the year's time in which Gleyre was to have access to these works, they should be sent directly to his family in Boston.[232]

Gleyre, of course, had no way of knowing at this time that his return to Paris would take almost three years. Nevertheless, he did attempt to retrieve the drawings. On 29 August 1838 Gleyre, now in Paris, wrote to Henry that while he was in Cairo, he had already inquired at the French consulate as to the whereabouts of the works, but with no success; he may even have feared that some had been destroyed when the consulate was pillaged. In the same letter, however, he added, "J'ai fait quelques

228. Clément, p. 124.
229. The incident is not recounted in Clément, but see *Journal de Genève*, 7 May 1874, p. 2.
230. Lausanne, MCBA, GA 986.
231. Clément, p. 129.
232. Newhouse 1980, p. 113, n. 1; Lowell noted that the portfolio contained 158 works, but the total now in the Lowell collection in Boston is, by my count, 154 works.

démarches afin de revoir le portefeuille qui est allé à Boston."[233] By this time Gleyre had certainly checked with the Wells Company and must have been told that, following Lowell's instructions in his letter of 13 November 1835, they had already forwarded the portfolio to Boston.

Gleyre's reference to his second attempt to find the portfolio was to a letter he had written the Lowell family in June 1838 requesting that the works be sent to Paris so that he could copy them, in accord with the arrangements provided by Lowell himself in Egypt.[234] Apparently there was no immediate response from the Lowell family, prompting Gleyre to make the demand again in April 1839; the portfolio finally arrived in December of that year. The Lowell family stipulated that Gleyre could make the copies he desired for a period of one year, and afterwards he was required to deposit the portfolio with the Wells Company for reshipment to Boston. During the year 1840, Nanteuil recalled having seen the portfolio in Gleyre's studio, and even remembered the seal of the American Embassy prominently affixed to the cover.[235] Gleyre sent the works back to Boston sometime at the end of 1840; they were retrieved by Lowell's cousin on 30 January 1841.

During the year that Gleyre had access to his works in Paris, he copied many, but not all of them. He selected particularly the Greek and Egyptian scenes, but none from Italy and few from Turkey. In some cases, he traced the study directly onto another page, adding the color later. Very rarely did he alter the original design, although in several examples, it is clear that he changed details or corrected the drawing. In at least three instances, he traced a watercolor in pencil without adding the colors, only indicating them in pencil or pen notes at the borders. In total, Gleyre copied only about half the Lowell works in Paris. In some instances his choice was evidently prompted by artistic merit; in others, the selection depended upon personal memories or ethnographic considerations.

To what extent Gleyre's own copies after his originals were known to his colleagues, students, or friends is unclear. Clément indicated that their very existence was barely suspected, although certainly such a close friend as Nanteuil was well aware of them since he remembered seeing the portfolio. When Gleyre moved into his permanent studio on the rue du Bac in 1845, he put his copies into a closet behind a large piece of furniture, telling Clément, "J'ai là tout mon voyage en Orient. Je vous le montrerais bien, mais il faudrait déplacer la commode." Gleyre never showed Clément these works; Clément was astonished to find them in the closet when he was required to make an inventory of the studio after the painter's death. But some knowledge of their existence circulated in Gleyre's Parisian circles. In the context of the salon of 1843, the critic Etienne Delécluze praised the exotic nature of the painter's canvas *Le Soir*, adding that "M. Gleyre… a rapporté de si beaux dessins de ses voyages en Orient."[236] And later, when the critic Gustave Planche wrote of Gleyre's work up to 1850, he hinted that Gleyre had a stock of Oriental works of which the public knew nothing.[237]

The material preserved in the Lowell family collection remained unknown a long time. This was due in part to the fact that Gleyre's Ameri-

233. Clément, pp. 132–33, cited in part from a letter in Lausanne, MCBA, GA 986 and incorrectly dated by Clément.
234. Boston, BMFA, Lowell Family Collection.
235. Clément, p. 125.
236. Delécluze 1843.
237. Planche 1851, p. 494.

can patron was not identified until recently. Even though the works were on loan to the Fogg Art Museum after 1931 and permanently deposited in the Boston Museum of Fine Arts in 1949, their existence was either unknown to or ignored by art historians until 1976. And yet, a hint of their existence apparently came to the attention of Emile Bonjour, the director of the Musée Cantonal des Beaux-Arts in Lausanne, in 1927. By this time, Bonjour had substantially increased the museum's holdings of Gleyre's works and consistently searched for more acquisitions. Bonjour's expense account record for 1927 reveals that he had written to "M. Lawrence Lowell" in Boston.[238] While Bonjour meticulously kept copies of most of his correspondence during his tenure from 1894 to 1935, unfortunately he did not retain a copy of this letter, nor did he mention in his annual report that he was in contact with the Lowell family. The archival documents for the year 1927 in Lausanne show no evidence of a reply from Boston.

Another crucial point that has escaped attention until now is the fact that the works Gleyre made for his own use during the trip are largely preserved in his recently discovered notebooks. These drawings, all pencil studies within the notebooks except for a few larger loose sheet drawings, were at one time in Clément's hands, but were never inventoried.[239] They consist of about 200 works covering almost all aspects of the voyage, except, it seems, the last part when Gleyre was in Lebanon, although some of the unidentified landscapes may belong there. More than 150 works represent Egyptian scenes, sites, physiognomic studies, and fantastical imaginative plans for projected paintings or studies, as well as caricatures. It now seems clear that several of Gleyre's Oriental compositions had their origins years before in Egypt, either in events seen there or imagined. From several of Gleyre's private drawings it is possible to reconstruct aspects of the trip not recorded by Lowell — for instance, that during their Maltese sojourn they went further inland than supposed to visit the Cathedral of Mdina. As in the case of Gleyre's copies after the Boston works, there is no evidence that these sketches were known, although it is possible that the references by Delécluze and Planche may have been to these works.

If Gleyre was reluctant to share or exploit the more than 300 works from the Orient in his possession after 1841, he nevertheless enjoyed regaling his friends with stories of his adventures for years afterwards. Many documents recount that Gleyre often sat in the traditional Arab style in the afternoons that were reserved to his friends, telling endless stories of Oriental customs and traditions, and fantastic tales. The painter Eugène Fromentin, who was not normally associated with Gleyre's immediate circle, had frequent discussions with him concerning their common interest in the Orient, where, by 1852, Fromentin had already made three trips. When he published *Un été dans le Sahara* in 1856, he sent Gleyre a copy through Clément, asking the latter to convey his thanks to the painter for his contributions.[240]

Yet more notable, Gleyre provided advice and common-sense instructions in 1849 to the prospective Egyptian travelers Gustave Flaubert and

238. Lausanne, MCBA, Bonjour, "Copies de lettres," V, p. 355. Lawrence Lowell was the President of Harvard University at the time and the chief trustee of the Lowell Foundation.
239. Clément, p. 69, makes a reference to the notebooks in regard to a view of Sicily. The provenance of the notebooks can be traced back to Clément's widow, Angèle.
240. Fromentin's letter to Clément is dated 16 February 1857 and is in CFC. Fromentin probably met Gleyre after 1845 when he wrote a review of *The Mission of the Apostles* which will be discussed later.

Maxime du Camp. The impetus for their trip came from du Camp, who had already traveled to Egypt in 1844 and had his account published in 1848, dedicated to Flaubert. Du Camp had to convince Flaubert's mother to permit the voyage, because of the young writer's health and his mother's strong attachment. Du Camp succeeded and the two had their farewell dinner with Louis Bouilhet, Louis de Cormetin, and Théophile Gautier on 29 October 1849.[241]

That very evening they took the coach to Châlon and from there the steamboat to Lyons; they planned to travel to Marseilles before taking a steamer directly to the Egyptian coast.[242] In Lyons, Flaubert and du Camp sought out Gleyre — they knew he was visiting his brother Henry — for his advice on which sites to see. Flaubert recounted that they had sent Gleyre a note requesting that he come to their rooms when it was convenient; Gleyre apparently was so anxious to see them that he arrived that very evening at eleven, when they were already in bed. Nevertheless, Gleyre began a vivid description of adventures, the desert, the fertile Nile valley, and his arduous stay in Nubia; he even demonstrated the grimaces of the wild monkeys who lifted the tent covers periodically during the encampments, a scene he had already drawn in one of his private sketchbooks.[243] Flaubert later described the memorable evening in two separate letters to his mother: in the first, written in Marseilles on 2 November, Flaubert noted that on Gleyre's counsel, he and du Camp had decided to spend more time in Egypt than originally planned,[244] while in the second letter, written from Alexandria on 17 November, Flaubert described how Gleyre had contorted his face while imitating the monkeys.[245] Later, on 14 December, when Flaubert was in Cairo, he confessed that Gleyre, "autant que j'ai pu juger, est un garçon assez froid et assez timide,"[246] a curious judgment in light of their obvious camaraderie. Nevertheless Mme. Flaubert asked to meet Gleyre in Paris, which she did before 4 December 1849, much to the concern of Flaubert who was clearly angry that the introduction had been made by Gustave Planche.[247] In the years that followed, Gleyre and Flaubert maintained a usually warm, if occasionally distant, relationship, aspects of which will be discussed later.[248]

241. For the background and the dynamics of the trip, see Flaubert 1972, pp. 9–18.
242. Du Camp 1883, I, p. 323.
243. Flaubert, "Voyages," in Œuvres, X, 1972, p. 443.
244. All references here to Flaubert's letters are from Jean Bruneau's edition of the Correspondance 1973 et seq.; this letter is I, p. 520. It seems that on Gleyre's advice, Flaubert dropped the idea of continuing to Kurdistan, which permitted about three months more in Egypt.
245. Ibid., p. 527. Here Flaubert provides the information that Gleyre remained in his rooms until 1 A.M.
246. Ibid., p. 553. The reference is in the postscript, where Flaubert informed his mother that Clot-Bey was much more discursive on the subject of Egypt than Gleyre. Antoine Clot, known as Clot-Bey (1796–1868), was a doctor from Montpellier who had established himself in Egypt in 1825. Flaubert and Du Camp met him upon their arrival.
247. Ibid., p. 546: "C'est fâcheux que ce soit Planche qui t'ait présentée à Gleyre. Si nous eussions été avertis, Maxime lui eût écrit." It is not clear why Flaubert was angry at Planche.
248. Contact was kept, particularly through du Camp, but also through other mutual friends; see Du Camp 1978, pp. 160 and 163. Gleyre was mentioned several times in Flaubert's letters and was invited to a private reading of Salammbô in Flaubert's apartment.

106

## CHAPTER 4

# 1838–1843

PARIS AND THE FIRST COMMISSIONS

66. Study for the *Entry into Jerusalem of the Queen of Sheba*, 1835. France, Private collection (catalogue n° 392, folio 6ʳ)

When Gleyre reached Paris in the spring of 1838, he stayed with Sébastien and Hortense Cornu who had lived near the rue du Bac since 1835. Slowly, Gleyre tried to regain his artistic contacts, to feel at ease in Parisian society after an absence of almost a decade, and above all to recover his health, which was still fragile. Although there is no extant correspondence from him during this period, one can well imagine that he wished to establish himself within the artistic milieu from which he must have felt estranged. Through the help of Cornu, Gleyre was able to rent his first studio in Paris at 19 rue de l'Université.

Because the Oriental experience was still vivid in Gleyre's mind, it seems only natural that his first efforts in oil in Paris centered on those recent images, aided, to be sure, by the many sketchbooks and loose studies he had brought back from his travels. Between 1838 and 1839, he was able to produce several canvases on Egyptian subjects, despite his fig. 67 proverbial slowness. Only one of these is a landscape, drawn probably after his observations in Lower Egypt where he himself noted some West-

107

67. *Landscape in Lower Egypt*, 1838. Lausanne, Musée Cantonal des Beaux-Arts (catalogue n° 395)

68. *Entry into Jerusalem of the Queen of Sheba*, 1838–39. Lausanne, Musée Cantonal des Beaux-Arts (catalogue n° 399)

69. *Harem Women*, 1838–39. Lausanne, Musée Cantonal des Beaux-Arts (catalogue n° 401)

249. Newhouse 1980, p. 107, discusses the painting and the sources from Gleyre's notes.
250. Clément, p. 127, identifies it as coming from Lower Egypt but does not specify which portion of the trip.

ern style houses with Classical features not unlike those seen in the painting.[249] The canvas is restrained and decidedly lacks the spontaneous quality of his works for Lowell. But the indefinite nature of the subject, as well as its lack of dramatic character and locale, may have induced Gleyre to leave the work unfinished.[250]

Yet other paintings of this period demonstrate that Gleyre strove to depict a more energetic Oriental imagery, less academic in appearance and substance. The most striking example is his depiction of the *Queen of Sheba* which shows his dazzling color effects and bravura brush technique. With the discovery of his private Egyptian sketchbooks, it is now known that the scene itself evolved during his travels, most likely in Nubia, the supposed origin of the queen, as is shown in the adjoining studies in the sketchbook. On one page, duly labeled "l'entrée de la reine de Saba à Jérusalem," Gleyre drew the essential elements of the composition but in an arrangement that is parallel to the picture plane. In both this pencil sketch and in his first study in color for the picture, the historical figure central to the iconography is virtually incidental to the overall spectacle of triumphal entry. In the pencil sketch, her chariot is drawn by giraffes alone, while in Paris Gleyre added elephants and

fig. 68

fig. 66

leopards to the *cortège*.[251] The landscape recalls the barren desert scenes that he so assiduously studied for Lowell, while the temple in the background is certainly a product of Gleyre's own imagination. Despite the dazzling effects in the work, Clément was hardly convinced that it represented one of Gleyre's best efforts of the period. He thought the study was "plus bizarre que belle," but he acknowledged the Romantic spirit present and felt no qualms about comparing it to the works of Delacroix and Turner.[252]

Gleyre, however, never transferred the small work onto a large canvas, nor, it seems, did he ever consider finishing it as a salon vehicle. Nonetheless, the study attracted the attention later of at least one critic, Arsène Houssaye, who openly championed Gleyre's works after 1843. Houssaye was particularly drawn to the vibrant effects and the freedom of the imagery, in which he recognized the subject itself as no more than a pretext; he noted as well that the work pleased no less visonary a poet than his friend Gérard de Nerval, who would later undertake his own voyage to the Orient.[253] It is not known under what circumstances the poet saw the painting, or the dynamics of his relationship with Gleyre. De Nerval was not only a close associate of Houssaye, but also an intimate friend of Chenavard, who must have renewed contact with Gleyre after his return.[254] However, Houssaye was correct in his poetic assertion that all Gleyre's Oriental images cast a magical spell apart from their obvious artistic importance and mastery.[255]

Similar effects are present in two other studies of the same period. *Harem Women* and *Turks and Arabs*. The former is also a study rather than a completed work and likewise attempts to render an impression of Oriental light and color. Gleyre has here deftly controlled the lighting effects filtered delicately through the palms in a manner rarely seen in other works at this time. The reclining female figure in the center, probably draws upon a similar figure Gleyre sketched from life near Philae. The scene is one of repose, calm, and sumptuousness, and appears wholly attuned to the Western notion of Oriental mood and landscape. $\qquad$ fig. 69–70

The *Turks and Arabs*, however, records a more violent scene both in image and form. As in Gleyre's study of the Queen of Sheba, the origin of the composition goes back to an idea noted in his Nubian sketchbook. fig. 71 The drawing already shows the basic concept, here envisioned in a more horizontal arrangement with the leaping horse even more dynamically represented. Gleyre rearranged this figure in the painting, simplifying as well the top section, so as to emphasize the leap itself and the shadow it produces at the right. This aspect, as well as the fluttering birds at the right, which Gleyre added only when he was working on the oil study, is a noticeable departure from the static compositions now and later. Moreover, the rich earthen tones that permeate the scene in accord with the desert locale show Gleyre's interest in color harmonies and nuances around a general scheme. Gleyre would, in fact, point to this study later, in answer to criticism of obsessive monochromatism, as an example of his delicate tonality.[256] The iconography itself is probably imaginary but in accord with the theme of Arab equestrian skills which had pervaded

251. It is probable that Gleyre refreshed his memory of these animals by studies in the Jardin des Plantes. A giraffe was given to the Jardin in 1827, the first example in Europe, and caused a veritable sensation; see Juste Olivier's impression after having seen the animal; in Olivier 1951, p. 5.
252. Clément, p. 135.
253. Houssaye 1885, I, p. 323.
254. Rioux de Maillou 1917, pp. 65f.
255. Houssaye 1843, p. 285.
256. Clément, p. 137.

70. *Turk and Arab Horsemen*, 1838–39. Lausanne, Musée Cantonal des Beaux-Arts (catalogue n° 402)
71. Study for *Turk and Arab Horsemen*, 1835. France, Private collection (catalogue n° 393, folio 36ʳ)

French Orientalism since the Napoleonic invasions. Clément himself pointed out that the painting is reminiscent of Decamps's works, and elsewhere it is argued that the chase, the dynamic features of the composition, and certain stylistic elements, recall Vernet.[257] It should also be noted that the present title of the picture seems to derive from Clément and is probably incorrect. There is no specific indication that the dress of any of the figures is Turkish; indeed, comparison with Gleyre's Nubian sketchbooks reveals that the costumes are close to those he had drawn throughout his last months in Egypt.

fig. 72    The least successful of this group of works executed immediately after Gleyre's return to Paris is the so-called *Egyptian Modesty*. The painting depicts a Nubian, who has stopped at a well to admire a young Arab girl who reveals her body while hiding her face. This work, in contrast to the other discussed above, was completed; the finished work clearly sacrifices the sense of improvisation and romantic brushwork of the studies. Few of the broad, luxurious elements of the previous works can be readily distinguished. It seems clear that Gleyre attempted to appeal to popular French tastes with both the Oriental iconography as a whole and the coquettish, sexual imagery that often accompanied it. The most notable aspect of the composition is the panoramic landscape that recalls the area near Edfu. Clément thought this painting to be one of Gleyre's minor works, which, he wrote, almost too purposefully attempted to draw upon Vernet's popular Eastern imagery.[258]

Before Gleyre left Paris in 1828, he had already developed a solid interest in Classical subjects and mythology. He continued to work in the

72. *Egyptian Modesty*, 1838. Lausanne, Musée Cantonal des Beaux-Arts (catalogue n° 394)

257. Clément, p. 136; Hauptman 1980, p. 20.
258. Clément, p. 134.

111

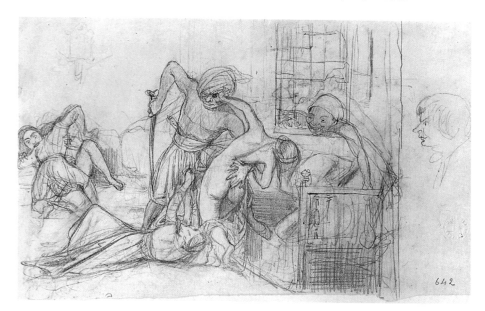

73. *Unknown Subject*, 1835. Lausanne, Musée Cantonal des Beaux-Arts (catalogue n° 387)
74. Eugène Delacroix, *Death of Sardanapalus* (detail), 1827. Paris, Musée du Louvre

75. Horace Vernet, *Judith and Holofernes*, 1829. Pau, Musée des Beaux-Arts

76. *Nero and Agrippina*, 1838–39. Lausanne, Musée Cantonal des Beaux-Arts (catalogue n° 404)

259. Hauptman 1980, I, p. 21.
260. The sources are *Vita Caesarum* and *Annalum*, respectively. The latter source is the only one that directly places Nero at his mother's side after the murder. For further details, see Hauptman 1980, pp. 21–22.

genre, but now with a broader experience and creative powers of observation gleaned from his contacts in Rome. One of the pictures that demonstrates these aspects was executed shortly after his return to Paris, the small study of *Nero and Agrippina*. Gleyre always professed that since he had no Classical education and was largely unfamiliar with Greek and Roman authors — assertions that, as will be seen, are unfounded — he was generally ill at ease in the genre.[259] This small study reveals the opposite; namely, that he was not only accomplished in depicting scenes on Classical subjects, but also adept at capturing their essential elements, even in scenes rarely depicted by his contemporaries. Gleyre found his source here in Tacitus and Suetonius, but tempered the account so as to make it accord with his romantic nature.[260] The work shows the aftermath of Nero's murder of his mother, a subject that hardly seems to fit with the body of Gleyre's work up to this time. It is, in many ways, one of his most demonic representations, and at once rivals the fury and violence of his *Pentheus* some thirty years later, in which the iconographic schema is reversed: Pentheus is killed by his mother. Already at this early date, an aspect of Gleyre's search for a middle road in the selection of subjects can be seen. Rather than relying on iconographic motifs exhibited in the salons each year, Gleyre attempted to find elements within themes which were later praised by the critics as innovative.

Gleyre was not impervious to visual sources in the conception of his subjects. In this case, several sources may be cited to show that Gleyre integrated these into a composition wholly his own. The reclining figure of Agrippina, at once tragic in her death and sexual in her attitude, suggests a similar figure Gleyre had drawn in Egypt in an imagined but brutal scene of abduction. She is likewise reminiscent of the female slave in Delacroix's *Death of Sardanapalus*, which Gleyre in all likelihood had seen in the salon of 1827 before he left Paris for Italy. However, the overall compositional elements of Gleyre's *Nero* may derive from Vernet's painting *Judith and Holophernes*, which Gleyre had first seen in Rome in 1830

fig. 76

fig. 73

fig. 74

fig. 75

112

and which after 1834 hung in Paris.[261] Gleyre inverted the positions of the male and female figures and slightly modified their gestures; Vernet's eerie light and infernal colors are retained, creating the violent effect.

One of Gleyre's first goals upon his return from the Near East must have been to procure commissions that would help alleviate his financial problems and also help establish his reputation. It is probable that he sought the help of not only Cornu and his wife, well-placed as they were in official circles, but also of Vernet, who had recently returned to Paris and whose reputation was already established. Vernet lived with Delaroche, his son-in-law, at 58 rue Saint-Lazare, and almost certainly Gleyre had asked the latter to intercede on his behalf for future commissions. Clément noted that Delaroche was ready to offer his aid, but could not provide the necessary contacts.[262] Nevertheless, Gleyre did receive a commission sometime after 1838 — the exact date is not clear — to decorate a dining room for a Mr. Lenoir.[263] Although it is not documented in the Gleyre literature, it is likely that Vernet was the prime intermediary in this commission. Lenoir and his wife, Marie-Aspasie Jousserand, were friends of Vernet and his father Carle: in 1814, Horace Vernet painted their portraits and apparently maintained a long-lasting relationship with the family.[264]

For the commission, Gleyre produced two large panels entitled *Diana* and *The Nubian*. These images were thought to represent the Classical and Oriental world, respectively, although it is not known whether this was the expressed desire of the patron. Unfortunately, the Lenoir house was destroyed and therefore we cannot see how Gleyre's images relate to the environment for which they were meant. Gleyre himself later admitted that he valued these works very little, claiming that they were no more than the means by which he earned his first fees in Paris, and his opinion in this instance was shared by Clément and Mantz.[265] Very few of his other friends had actually seen the works until after Gleyre's death when they were sold.[266] In contrast to the passionately romantic and personalized studies of the same period, these canvases are pale and diffuse, certainly intended to please his patron. In this light, it must be remembered that Lenoir was a collector of eighteenth-century miniatures and most likely wanted a sober decoration to accord with his collection.

Despite Gleyre's later negative reaction to these works, there are elements here that underscore aspects of his inventiveness. *The Nubian* in particular draws upon some of Gleyre's drawings done from life in Egypt, transformed into a more idealized form. It should be noted, however, that the details of the dress, landscape, and pose reflect a veracity not always seen in other Oriental images. The counterpart figure of *Diana* is only barely reminiscent of Classical prototypes, reflecting instead Gleyre's interest in Mannerist art. To be sure, there is a sense of the artificial, seen in the windblown hair, the posed drapery, and the stylized stance but there are also some remarkable details, particularly in the flora and the freshly killed fowl. Although these works are not yet mature examples of Gleyre's art, they nevertheless show approaches that Gleyre would explore in later variations.

fig. 77–78

261. The work was first exhibited in the Capitol in the exhibition of the Société des Amis des Arts in Rome; see Gassier 1983, p. 218. The work entered the Musée du Luxembourg in Paris after 1834. For a detailed account of the picture, see *Horace Vernet* 1980, pp. 79–80, and Comte 1977, pp. 137–39. None of the literature, however, relates the painting to Gleyre except Hauptman 1980, p. 22.

262. Clément, pp. 130–31.

263. Clément was not sure who this client was, but the critic Paul Mantz later correctly identified him as Philippe Lenoir; Mantz 1875, p. 236.

264. Both portraits are presently in the Louvre, n° RF 1938-93 and 95, respectively. On the portraits, see *Horace Vernet* 1980, pp. 38–39.

265. See Mantz 1875, pp. 235f.; Clément 1876, pp. 338–39; Clément, p. 138f.

266. Albert Anker (1831–1910), one of Gleyre's students and a close friend in Gleyre's later years, wrote his friend François Ehrmann in 1874 of his surprise at having seen these works for the first time, noting as well that none of the other students had seen them before; see Quinche-Anker 1924, p. 108. In this light, it is unlikely that the *Diana* was the direct source for Renoir's painting of the same subject, as claimed by Boime 1974, p. 122. On the sale of the works, see the entries in the catalogue section.

77. *Diana*, 1838. Lausanne, Musée Cantonal des Beaux-Arts (catalogue n° 396)
78. *The Nubian*, 1838. Lausanne, Musée Cantonal des Beaux-Arts (catalogue n° 397)

Also around 1838, Gleyre received another commission to make several portraits in the series known as *Le Plutarque français*. Clément listed these works, but made no mention of how Gleyre had received the commission or from whom. Once again it may be speculated that Vernet or Delaroche had a role, although it is equally possible that Mme. Cornu, by way of her contacts with the publishing world, had gotten the commission for Gleyre.

*Le Plutarque français* was a creation of Edouard Mennechet.[267] His idea was to issue brief but significant biographies of principal figures in French history for the public at large. He published several volumes containing twenty-four folios of biographies, accompanied in each case with a portrait of the subject. The first edition was published between 1839 and 1841 in eight volumes. Various celebrated artists participated in the project, including Vernet, Ingres, Delacroix, Cogniet, Flandrin, Scheffer, and a host of lesser figures. The enterprise proved to be such a success that an expanded version was issued in 1844 by Mennechet's assistant, Hadot.

Gleyre was contracted to produce six separate portraits as well as the frontispiece to the set. Since no documents survive concerning Gleyre's participation, it is not known who selected the subjects or whether Gleyre himself requested these portraits in particular. The choice, however, is a

267. Edouard Mennechet (1794–1845) was associated with the Duc de Duras, the chamberlain of Louis XVIII, who later named him "son lecteur," a position he also maintained under Charles X. He was a prodigious author and historian of French literature. See Thieme 1933, II, p. 2.

79. Study for *Héloïse*, 1839. Lausanne, Musée Cantonal des Beaux-Arts (catalogue n° 413)
80. *Héloïse*, 1839. Engraving from *Le Plutarque français*. Paris, Ecole des Beaux-Arts (catalogue n° 412)

268. See Clément, p. 18, and the first chapter of this study. A tracing of the drawing is contained among the unfiled papers in Fleurier, CFC, but with no annotation as to whether it is by Gleyre or traced after him by another hand.

curious one, since Gleyre executed portraits as diverse as Voltaire, General Hoche, the seventeenth century philosopher and theologian Fénelon, Abelard's lover Héloïse, Rousseau, and the painter Prud'hon. In each case, with the exception of the frontispiece and Héloïse, both of which are clearly invented, Gleyre based his drawings on well-known images of his subjects, available for the most part in public collections or in popular illustrations. The portraits themselves are traditional examples of the illustrator's talents in characterization, as would be the case later in his portrait of the poet Heinrich Heine produced in 1852, also for illustration. The preparatory drawing for Héloïse, the only one of the preparatory drawings that is extant, demonstrates Gleyre's freeflowing style and deft handling of form, but these are hidden in the engraved work. The most interesting examples are the portraits of Voltaire, for which a very preliminary study is found in the sketchbooks, and Prud'hon, where Gleyre showed the painter at his easel, on which is the completed canvas of *Psyche and Zephyr*. The work is a reminder of Gleyre's admiration for Prud'hon, which was already manifest in his student days and which would continue to Gleyre's mature years.[268]

fig. 79
fig. 80
fig. 81
fig. 82

116

81. *Voltaire*, 1839. Engraving from *Le Plutarque français*. Paris, Ecole des Beaux-Arts (catalogue n° 415)
82. *Prud'hon*. 1839. Engraving from *Le Plutarque français*. Paris, Ecole des Beaux-Arts (catalogue n° 419)

Clément was correct in noting that after Gleyre's return to Paris, it was necessary for him to overcome his natural timidity and produce a large work for the public in order to help establish his name and reputation. The Lenoir commissions were reserved for a particular patron and remained largely unknown, while the commission for the *Plutarque français* illustrations was hardly an ideal vehicle in the competitive Paris art world. It seemed natural, therefore, that Gleyre attempt a large canvas for the salon which could attract critical attention — in effect, Gleyre's first effort to show publicly in Paris since the salon of 1833, when he sent three watercolor portraits from Rome. To this end, Gleyre created a painting that derived from Christian iconography and which drew upon his experiences in the Near East, a depiction of Saint John on the isle of Patmos envisioning the coming of the Apocalypse. Clément pointed out the importance of this work in Gleyre's early œuvre,[269] but he was severely handicapped in his own analysis of the painting since he had never seen it, nor did he have any documentation with the exception of one drawing he presumed to represent the subject. For generations, the painting was assumed lost, but has resurfaced recently and is reproduced here for
fig. 83 the first time.

83. *Saint John on the Isle of Patmos*, 1839. France, Private collection (catalogue n° 405)

Gleyre probably worked on the canvas toward the end of 1838 and during most of the following year, although there is not a single document regarding the picture from this time. The painting was the largest Gleyre had conceived up to then, measuring 2,30 by 1,65 meters, substantially larger than the *Roman Brigands* of seven years earlier.[270] Gleyre did not envision showing the painting in the Paris salon first: his intention, it seems, was to exhibit the work in Lyons, which had its exhibitions at the end of the year rather than in the spring. This decision may have been prompted by practical considerations in that the painting was not finished in time for the Paris show, or perhaps he wanted to test the

269. Clément, p. 141.
270. Paris, AL, Enregistrement, Salon de 1840, n° 3982, here titled *Vision de Saint Jean*. The dimensions noted probably include the frame, although it is not specifically stated.

critical climate by exhibiting the painting first outside the capital. It is equally possible that Gleyre's decision may have been directed toward his family in Lyons who had seen only few examples of his work since his departure in 1825.

The exhibitions in Lyons were under the sponsorship of a local association, the Société des Amis des Arts, which, although formed in 1808, did not function regularly or efficiently in organizing exhibitions until its revitalisation under the prefect Rivet in 1836.[271] Nevertheless, as France's second city in population and industry, Lyons had begun to attract works by first-rate artists and its exhibitions were regularly reported in the Paris press. Major artists of the region, as well as those of Paris and Switzerland, frequently sent works there hoping for positive critical comments and sales; they profited from the fact that the exhibitions in Lyons never coincided with the Paris Salon, thus offering another avenue for public showing. Gleyre sent the picture to the Société in late 1839 — it is not known if there was a jury system to judge the entries — where it was exhibited under the title *Saint Jean l'Evangéliste.*[272]

The school of Lyons, of which Gleyre himself was a product, had always advocated an interest in religious mystical iconography and Gleyre could therefore be assured that his subject would be viewed and comprehended with some sensitivity. Critical reaction was indeed more than favorable, regarding not only Gleyre's conception of the scene but also his mastery of technique. In his extensive review of the exhibition, the critic Léon Boitel spoke harshly about most of the paintings on view, noting that few showed genuine artistic merit or even ingenuity. He signaled the importance of the efforts of the Flandrin brothers and praised the painting of Bouterwerk and de Rudder, as well as the Swiss Alexandre Calame. As to Gleyre, Boitel noted that his painting, which he never cited by title, was clearly the work of a conscientious artist, but that the canvas had flaws. He criticized especially the proportions of the saint and found the physiognomy to be too common for such an exalted personage. Moreover, he was bothered by the all too realistic depiction of the hands and feet which he felt diminished the overall effect of saintliness. The color was too monochromatic and tended to emphasize the darker hues. But despite these negative comments, Boitel acknowledged the vigorous effect of the overall composition and noted the presence of "une grande harmonie."[273]

The anonymous critic for the popular *Courrier de Lyon* was more generous in his praise.[274] He noted that Gleyre's painting was in fact the sensation of the exhibit, pointing out that the marriage between "le pinceau de M. Gleyre" and Fromenger's frame, itself "une véritable œuvre d'art," was perfectly realized. The critic, incidentally, provided the only published description of Gleyre's imagery, which he said showed the figure of the saint seated on the shore of the isle, leaning on the book that contains the revelations he has received. He praised the saint's form and especially underscored the mystical expression of the face, which truly depicted divine inspiration. But like Boitel, the critic found the hands and feet discordant elements and regretted the dark tonalities, "l'abus de

271. For the history of the Lyons salon, see Bleton 1906, I, p. 505, and Audin and Vial 1918, pp. xvi–xviii. I am also grateful to Mme. Isabelle Gouy who kindly supplied additional information on the exhibitions in Lyons during this period.
272. *Livret explicatif...* 1839, p. 22, n° 176. The elaborately carved frame, as a note in the livret indicates, was made by Fromenger, Paris.
273. Boitel 1840, pp. 78–84.
274. *Courrier de Lyon*, 31 December 1839. This reference was kindly sent to me by Mme. Gouy.

noir," evident in the somber background. He noted that the painting was nevertheless a true masterpiece, worthy of serious critical and public attention. The review also suggested that Gleyre was able to conceive this imagery of inspiration and revelation without basing his ideas on the banalities usually associated with religious painting precisely because of his harrowing and presumably enlightening experiences in the East. The implication is that Gleyre's pictorial ideas in showing the saint in this fashion, isolated from the physical world and its comfort, are a result of his own travels and suffering.

These critical remarks, which hardly neglected to expose the deficiencies of the painting, had an effect on the committee responsible for purchases. In the first round of voting, Gleyre's painting was selected as a possible acquisition; this would have meant that Gleyre's canvas would be hung in the permanent collection of the very museum in which he had made his first artistic studies. After the second round of voice votes, however, the picture was eliminated, although the minutes of the meeting do not reveal the reasons for the committee's rejection.[275] Instead the committee decided to buy paintings by Cibot, who had already won a second-class medal in Paris in 1836, by Gué, whose reputation was well known, and by Paul Flandrin, who had local support.

Perhaps because the painting found no buyer in Lyons, Gleyre decided to exhibit the picture at the forthcoming Paris Salon.[276] His decision seems to have been a hesitant one since he entered the painting on the last day permitted; indeed, it was virtually the last work to be registered.[277] It is not known whether Gleyre took the opportunity to make alterations in light of the criticism in Lyons, but the painting was accepted at first view, no easy accomplishment given the severity of the 1840 jury, which rejected almost half the works submitted. Several celebrated painters were in fact excluded that year, including Gigoux, Cabat, and Chassériau; even Delacroix's *Justice of Trajan* was at first rejected, though reinstated on a second vote. In reaction to these draconian decisions by the jury many critics pleaded for drastic reforms, a position supported by the entire artistic community, even those artists backed by the government support.[278] Gleyre's acceptance in the Salon, therefore, was nothing less than a vote of confidence that at least temporarily justified his efforts. The painting was seen by the Paris public in March 1840, although it was unfortunately hung in one of the obscure corners of the Grand Salon.[279]

The reception of the painting in Paris must have dispelled Gleyre's fears about critical comment. Although many Paris critics complained, as they usually did, of the large number of religious works shown — some, like the critic for *Le National*, noted the inevitable boredom with these works that resembled each other more and more[280] — many commented on the excellence and originality of Gleyre's painting. Prosper Haussard, who would criticize Gleyre severely in 1843, found his *Saint John* and Ferret's *Cénobite* the cornerstones of the exhibition. Haussard commented on what he perceived as the Grand Style in Gleyre's art, which recalled for the critic the feeling and monumentality of the Renaissance.[281] Similarly, the more influential critic Jules Janin emphasized the natural ele-

275. Lyons, BM, Sér. R²; Procès-verbaux, 1839–40.
276. Gleyre's letters are silent at this time on his intentions; neither salons in Paris nor in Lyons are mentioned.
277. Paris, AL, Enregistrement, Exposition de 1840. Gleyre's painting was logged as n° 3982 out of 3993 entries.
278. Hauptman 1985(a), pp. 100–101.
279. Livret n° 714. On its placement in the salon, see Janin 1840, p. 204. In another corner was de Rudder's *Saint Augustin*, n° 1458. Gleyre listed his address in the livret as "Chez M. Cornu, 11 passage Ste-Marie, Faubourg St. Germain."
280. L., St. 1840.
281. Haussard 1840. Haussard would recall the *Saint John* later in his review of Gleyre's *Le Soir* as "dans le goût de Michel-Ange;" see Haussard 1843.

ments Gleyre so aptly utilized — the same that had been found to be vulgar and undignified in Lyons — noting as well that Gleyre had fully understood the dynamics of his subject, another way of saying that Gleyre's painting avoided the banality of simply copying previous artistic solutions.[282]

Probably the most satisfying criticism, and no doubt the least expected, came from Gustave Planche. Because of his association with the *Revue des Deux-Mondes* in 1831, Planche was one of the most feared and hated critics.[283] He could be vicious, often denouncing works of friends and enemies alike, which prompted the sobriquet "Gustave le Cruel,"[284] but he was also respected as a liberal who at least had the courage of his convictions. Planche devoted only one paragraph to Gleyre's work, but in a few words he was able to crystallize the essentials of the picture, which he deemed a "succès légitime." Planche acclaimed the draftsmanship, the details — especially the head "(qui) exprime très bien l'extase dans laquelle est plongé saint Jean" — and, curiously, the color, which he said was vigorously handled. His reserve was focused, like that of the critics of Lyons, on the lack of proper idealization. Planche, however, was explicit in noting that the painting "révèle chez l'auteur un remarquable talent d'exécution," hardly faint praise.[285]

Perhaps because of this unexpected laudatory review, Gleyre immediately struck up a friendship with Planche through their common friend Jourdain. Planche left Paris for Italy later the same year and it is known that he wrote to Gleyre several times, although none of this correspondence has been found.[286] During the late 1840s and 1850s Planche remained an habitué of Gleyre's studio;[287] it was during these visits that Gleyre discreetly gave Planche money when he was in dire financial difficulties.[288] Gleyre also attempted to use his considerable influence with Planche's publisher Buloz when differences between them arose, as seemed often to be the case.[289] In return, Planche offered Gleyre practical advice on pictures in progress, advice that Gleyre took seriously even to the point of deleting a section of his painting *The Dance of the Bacchantes* of 1849 when Planche convinced him that it was weak.[290] Despite persistent counsel from many friends to abandon Planche, Gleyre never did so. Indeed, were it not for Gleyre's friendship and regular financial assistance, Planche, it was said, would have died years before he succumbed to blood poisoning in 1857.[291]

Although Gleyre's painting received none of the official prizes offered that year, he was nevertheless rewarded by additional commissions and by the sale of the picture itself. His *Saint John* was recommended, among many others, for purchase by the state.[292] This form of patronage fell within the government policy of supplying provincial churches and museums with paintings, especially in cases where local associations could not afford such purchases; from August to December 1840, no fewer than seventy-three paintings and one statue were bought for that purpose. From the available documentation, the painting, now with a frame different from the one Gleyre used in the Lyons exhibition, is known to have been sent to the church of Saint-Vulfran in Abbeville on 29 Octo-

282. Janin 1840, p. 204.
283. Grate 1959(b), pp. 278f.
284. Flanary 1980, p. 44. It was probably the critic Gustave Karr who gave Planche this epithet.
285. Planche 1840, p. 108. Planche wrote a longer analysis of the painting later — see Planche 1851, pp. 489–505 — which Clément reprinted almost verbatim in Clément, pp. 141f.
286. Regard 1955, I, p. 265. Mr. Pontus Grate kindly informed me in private correspondence that Planche's letters were either destroyed or have disappeared; none of Planche's known letters to Gleyre were found in the latter's studio after his death.
287. Clément, p. 204.
288. Flaubert noted this in a letter to his mother on 7 July 1850, in Flaubert 1973, I, pp. 649–50. See also Flaubert's letter to Louise Colet of 19 March 1854 in which he states that Planche is always in Gleyre's studio and generally in need of funds; ibid., p. 538.
289. Regard 1955, I, p. 424.
290. Clément, p. 195.
291. Nanteuil wrote this to Clément who cited it; Clément, p. 205. Gleyre was one of the last persons to see Planche alive before he succumbed on 18 September. Despite the importance of Gleyre in Planche's life and work in his last decade, no literature on the critic makes note of it.
292. Paris, AN, Demandes d'achat, 1840, F²¹, f. 485; the painting was recommended by a M. Lachaise, "et demandé par M. Alcock et Durotin par l'église de Roanne."

ber 1840.[293] Oddly, none of the extant documents that reveal the location where the painting was sent or the framing bills notes the purchase price, although from comparative pictures it appears that Gleyre must have been paid between 1,500 and 2,000 francs.[294]

With the installation of the work in Abbeville, it became virtually lost to the public and quickly forgotten. Clément noted in 1865 that the picture was in a provincial church, but he was at a loss as to which one. Clearly, Gleyre, a quarter of a century after its shipment north, had either forgotten where the painting hung or simply did not want to inform Clément.[295] In 1890, the *Saint John* was in fact listed in the inventory of the church, but Gleyre's name was not cited.[296] From this point on, the painting is not mentioned again in the literature concerned with Gleyre. It has been assumed that it was destroyed when the church was bombed in an allied attack on 20 May 1944,[297] but either it survived the attack or had been removed earlier for storage. The later history, until its recent rediscovery, is not known.

It is difficult to judge the picture now or to understand it within the context of Gleyre's early works. It bears little stylistic relationship to the paintings of the 1830s and even less to the two panels Gleyre executed for Lenoir. Yet the painting clearly confirms the critical judgment of Gleyre's technical mastery of drapery, the expressive head, and the solidity of the figure as a whole, as well as the weakness of the large hands and feet. Similarly, the criticism of the dark tonalities seems to be well founded, although from the image at hand, they can as well be said to add measureably to the sense of solitude and mysticism that imbues the subject. It is no wonder that Planche and others saw the monumentality associated with Renaissance figures — the figure itself seems to be drawn more from Baroque sources along the line of the saints of Guercino — in the manner in which Gleyre envisioned the composition as a whole. It is worth noting that the only surviving study related to the work shows the saint in a prone position, a form that Gleyre clearly rejected in favor of a more dynamic artistic structure.

After the completion and exhibition of the *Saint John*, Gleyre was occupied by two important artistic tasks. On December 1839, his Egyptian studies in the Lowell collection in Boston were sent to him so that he might make copies. He copied or traced a large proportion of these works, as well as executing several oils from studies made directly on the spot; none of these was exhibited or sold.

The second artistic activity — one that would end curiously and bitterly for Gleyre — was the commission to participate in the decoration of the restored Château de Dampierre near Paris, the seat of the Duc de

fig. 84

84. Study for *Saint John*, 1839. Lausanne, Musée Cantonal des Beaux-Arts (catalogue n° 406)

293. Ibid., F[21], f. 500; and see also *L'Artiste*, 1840, p. 166. The file also contains, piece 184, a framing bill from Mr. Souty dated 24 October 1840; it is for 90 francs, 52 centimes. See too piece 498, in which the crater Toussaint noted the completion of the packing on that date for "Un tableau par M. Gleyre à l'Eglise St. Walfrand [sic] d'Abbéville."
294. The documents in the AN, Mandats, O[4] series, list the payments made to artists for their works; the 1840 payments are in O[4], 1899–1900, but none specifies any payment to Gleyre.
295. Clément 1865, p. 216. A year later in *Le Touriste*, 1866, p. 280, it was noted that Gleyre's painting was in a provincial English church. Juste Olivier repeatedly chastised Gleyre for not knowing where his paintings were once they left the studio. Olivier noted that Gleyre simply had no interest in any of his works once they were finished. It should be noted as well that while Gleyre's lack of interest was always a curious matter, it was not unique. Chenavard also lost track of his painting *The Resurrection* in precisely the same manner; see Sloane 1962, p. 185.
296. *Inventaire général...*, *Province*, 1886–1901, III, pp. 3f., for the church in Abbeville. The inventory was made by E. Delignières and dates to 31 July 1890.
297. This information was transmitted to me by Mme. Micheline Agache of Abbeville who attempted to trace the painting earlier through local archival sources.

85. Château de Dampierre

298. Clément, pp. 144–54.
299. For biographical details of Honoré-Théodoric-Paul-Joseph d'Albert, Duc de Luynes (1806–67), see de Vogüé 1868; for aspects of his art interests, see Shedd 1986. See also Schlenoff 1956, p. 252 and Ockman 1982, pp. 65f.
300. On Jacques-Félix Duban (1797–1870), see Van Zanten 1987.
301. Lapauze 1911, p. 406.
302. Ockman 1982, p. 36. A small article in *L'Artiste*, 1841, p. 298, mentions Gleyre as a member of the team. Duban had met Gleyre in Rome. Gleyre already knew the Flandrins, and also Simart, whom he had met at the Ecole in Paris. Simart was admitted in 10 May 1824 (AN, AJ⁵², 234, n° 831) and participated in the same *concours de modèle* as did Gleyre on 6 October 1825 (AN, AJ⁵², 7).
303. Clément, p. 145; Cornu later painted a portrait of the duke, exhibited in the salon of 1869 (n° 547 of the livret), but his connection to the family in the 1840s is not known. Montégut 1878, p. 405.
304. Ockman 1982 gives the essential details from which my text is drawn. See also Ockman 1984 for a summary of the main points.

Luynes. The history of the commission and the work that occupied Gleyre [fig. 85] during 1841 still remains unclear from the available documents. Gleyre himself discussed the events very little, forcing Clément to outline the commission in the briefest possible terms.[298] The Duc de Luynes was highly placed in art circles and widely respected as an expert in antique art.[299] His erudition and knowledge of the field brought him to the attention of Charles X, who named him director of the newly created Musée des Antiquités Grecques et Egyptiennes. He published various learned treatises on ancient coins and bronzes, and later donated his substantial collection — some 7,000 items — to the Bibliothèque Impériale. He was also an avid Orientalist who traveled in Egypt in the very year the restoration project for the château began.

In 1840, he had decided to modernize the ancestral home in Dampierre, hiring Jacques-Félix Duban for the task, the same architect who had designed the Ecole des Beaux-Arts.[300] Among his assistants on the project was Alexandre Denuelle, the future father-in-law of Hippolyte Taine, who remained one of Gleyre's closest friends until his death. To head the decoration program, Duban named Vernet, Delaroche, and Ingres, as the most reputed artists of the day; eventually Ingres was chosen to head the team of decorators for an unprecedented fee of 70,000 francs.[301] The main work of smaller decorations in the various salons of the château was to be carried out by some thirty to forty painters, sculptors, and assistants, among whom were the Flandrin brothers, Rude, Simart, Duret, and Gleyre.[302] Precisely how Gleyre became involved in the project is not known for certain: Clément noted only that Gleyre was introduced to the duke by either Duban, Delaroche, or Cornu, while Montégut stated later that it was Delaroche who helped secure the commission.[303] Gleyre's work at Dampierre called for the decoration of three tiers: life-size figures in niches at the grand staircase with medallions of reclining or standing figures in the vault zones, and the ceiling area of the main salon, which was to contain a large painting of the allegory of Abundance.[304]

This commission, then, represented for Gleyre, after the triumph of his *Saint John*, yet another means of establishing his reputation in Parisian circles, now in prestigious association with such luminaries as Ingres and the Duc de Luynes. Curiously, despite its importance, Gleyre mentioned his work in Dampierre only incidentally; he barely indicated to friends the nature and progress of his decorations except in oblique references. The first letter he wrote from there was sent to Cornu in Paris on 1 January 1841, asking him to send a copy of Herodotus so that he could pass his evenings more agreeably.[305] Later that month, Gleyre again wrote to Cornu about the long hours spent in painting his figures, but also about his boredom during the hours when he could not work. He noted in the same letter that he had canceled his plans to come to Paris because he had to repaint one of his figures entirely, but he did not indicate which one or why. He told Cornu, however, that the duke, presumably back from Egypt, was scheduled to arrive shortly to inspect the progress — thus, perhaps, Gleyre's hesitancy to interrupt his work.[306]

No further news was transmitted by Gleyre until April. By this time, about half of the decoration scheme was completed and the duke pressed the painters to finish it all by July when Ingres himself was scheduled to inspect the site.[307] The pace of activity was therefore increased so that work began at six in the morning and continued with only short pauses until about six in the evening when light began to fade. About thirty painters were working simultaneously and the Flandrin brothers remarked on the noise and stifling air that made breathing difficult at times.[308] Gleyre probably reacted badly to this added pressure, which no doubt reminded him of the frenzied pace at which Lowell had made him work and which Gleyre could hardly bear. On 6 April 1841, Gleyre again wrote to Cornu:

> Je suis prisonnier et on ne me relâchera que quand mes deux
> figures seront terminées, c'est-à-dire vers le 12 ou 13 avril.[309]

He did not indicate on which figures he was working at the time, but he asked Cornu to send specific colors which were running short, as well as the latest salon reviews which he eagerly wanted to read. Gleyre now noted that he had no time to be bored: his routine consisted of painting, eating, and sleeping with virtually no other distractions.

But the results of this intense activity apparently did not altogether satisfy Gleyre. In another letter to Cornu, undated in this case but clearly from mid-April, he told him that he had just removed the scaffolding to look at his figure from a different perspective and was discontented with the effect.[310] Gleyre had no respite during the rest of the spring months and apparently had no time to inform Cornu or others of details until the end of May. On 28 May, more than a month after he had thought he would be finished, he wrote to Cornu, who had planned to see Gleyre in Dampierre, to postpone the visit because the remaining work was not progressing as he had hoped and because the duke who wanted the work finished before Ingres's inspection visit, had forbidden all guests.[311] But

305. Clément, p. 146.
306. Lausanne, MCBA, GA 988, postmarked 14 January 1841.
307. Ockman 1982, p. 36, citing a letter from Flandrin to Ernest Vinet, 15 April 1841. Ingres was in Rome until at least May of that year; see Lapauze 1911, pp. 366–67.
308. Foucart 1984, p. 91.
309. Lausanne, MCBA, GA 988.
310. Ibid.
311. Ibid., and partially cited in Clément, p. 151. The Clément citation reads "Jusqu'à ce que Ingres ait fait sa visite…" whereas the original letter adds "le petit tonton d'Ingres." The letter was written, incidentally, at 5 A.M.

86. Study for *Labor*, 1841. Lausanne, Musée Cantonal des Beaux-Arts (catalogue n° 451)

still problems continued to plague Gleyre and the completion of the decorations in question was again delayed, as he wrote to Cornu a month later on 29 June. Not only was he indisposed with a severe cold, but he also indicated to Cornu that one figure to be repainted necessitated a modeling session with one of his models, Céline, in the Paris studio which he hoped Cornu could arrange at short notice.[312] The last letter Gleyre wrote to Cornu was dated 23 August — that is, well after Ingres had already inspected the work in progress for the first time — and noted despairingly the fact that even now some of the figures were not as advanced as they should have been.[313]

Despite the lack of precise information in Gleyre's letters, it is clear that the commission was hardly a simple affair. One detail regarding his difficulties has surfaced, presumably recounted to Clément at a later date. One of the large figures in the bottom tier, which Gleyre painted directly on the wall, was meant to allegorize *Work*. It represents a blacksmith fashioning a scythe, an image seemingly in accord with the accepted iconographic scheme of the whole. The duke himself had inspected the design and even approved the work, but later changed his mind, having decided that Gleyre's conception of the figure was too realistic, not only in the clearly naturalistic facial features, but also in the abundant musculature of the laborer. Gleyre, it seems, was asked to replace the figure, which he did with a more idealistic representation of a woman spinning cloth, now fully clad and clearly more in the Classical ideal.[314] This was surely the reason why Gleyre was forced to schedule a new modeling session with the female model Céline in Paris.

fig. 86

fig. 87

The change of figure would prove to be an augury of the strange history of the entire commission. Clément wrote with some assurance that after the completion of all the decorations, the duke decided to destroy them without exception.[315] Gleyre, clearly hurt by the decision, said little about it afterwards and apparently never recounted either to Clément or to other intimate friends precisely what had happened, a suspicious lacuna at best. Clément himself investigated the incident as best he could more than three decades later, but noted sadly that the persons who had witnessed the event thought it prudent not to publish the full account at that time. The implication is that a revelation of what had actually occurred could still be sensitive with respect to individuals in powerful positions in the 1870s. Nevertheless, Clément cited a letter he had received from Nanteuil, who was not in Dampierre and seemed to have had little contact with Gleyre in early 1841, which assigned fault in the affair to Ingres. It appears that when Ingres visited Dampierre in the summer of 1841, he reacted to Gleyre's paintings by covering his eyes and turning away, demonstrating his extreme displeasure. He then asked the duke to efface the works Gleyre had executed, either, one assumes, because they were not up to the standard he expected or desired, or because he felt they would be discordant with the design scheme he had in mind for his own decorations.

Ingres's role in the effacement of Gleyre's paintings was, then, decisive, but hardly a secret even in Ingres's own lifetime. Gérôme wrote baldly

312. Lausanne, MCBA, GA 988. The name of the model is given in the letter, but there are no other indications before or after as to whether she was a regular model, or for which other pictures she posed.
313. Lausanne, MCBA, GA 988.
314. Clément, p. 150.
315. Ibid., pp. 152–53.

and assuredly that Ingres should bear the entire responsability for the destruction of Gleyre's work, a harsh statement from an acknowledged follower of Ingres's artistic ideals.[316] This view was accepted afterwards as authoritative: Hippolyte Taine stated it openly in print — albeit after Ingres's death. He received his information, he said, from an unnamed witness, most likely Alexandre Denuelle who, as we saw, was in fact present in Dampierre with Gleyre, and who at the time Taine wrote was his father-in-law.[317] Even Manet, apparently not an intimate of either Gleyre or Ingres, mentioned the fact to Arsène Houssaye in 1878 while discussing Ingres's portrait of Bertin: "M. Ingres a été un vandale quand il a fait détruire certaines peintures de Gleyre dont le voisinage lui déplaisait."[318]

Another indication of what happened to Gleyre's work at Dampierre can be found in a letter from Denuelle's brother Charles to Clément which he never used in his biography. In the letter, Charles related that the culprit in the affair was Hippolyte Flandrin who, having been given a smaller role in the decoration scheme than Gleyre, was intensely jealous. According to Charles, who presumably got his information from his brother, Flandrin, Ingres's favorite pupil at the time, had persuaded Ingres to have the works destroyed, possibly in the hope that he would be asked to replace them with his own painting.[319] Unfortunately, Charles's assertion cannot be proven: in the Flandrin letters of the period, there is no hint of jealousy or animosity toward Gleyre. In the Gleyre correspondence from Dampierre, there is only one mention of Flandrin, in a letter of 6 April when Gleyre wrote to Cornu: "Les Flandrins sont ici. Ils ne sont pas trop embêtants." None of the studies devoted to Flandrin suggests any role in the destruction of Gleyre's works. Yet when Clément began writing his biography in the mid 1870s, of the principal figures in the affair, Ingres and the three Flandrin brothers, only Paul was still alive. It may have been precisely because the Flandrins were involved that the true account was never given to Clément.

It is clear, however, that Ingres was the central instigator in having the works effaced, perhaps not because Gleyre's work was of poor quality, but the contrary, because it was of superior quality which Ingres did not want juxtaposed with his own painting. Gleyre had his defenders in the incident, the most important of whom was the architect, Duban, who pleaded strenuously with the duke to save the works. But since the entire project revolved around Ingres and in light of his imposing stature in the art world, his demands were fulfilled. The irony, however, is that Ingres's projected paintings, showing scenes of the Ages of Gold and Iron in the
fig. 89
Salon de Minerve — just below Gleyre's decorations — proved to be more difficult than anticipated. Ingres worked on them intermittently during the 1840s, but finally withdrew from the contract, much to the duke's dismay, and quite possibly to Gleyre's delight.[320]

Gleyre rarely spoke of the affair, and he made it a point to show publicly no ill will toward Ingres, whom he indeed considered a great master. But it is not certain that Gleyre himself was fully aware of the extent of the destruction of his work at Dampierre: he seems never to have made

87. Study for *Labor*, 1841. Lausanne, Musée Cantonal des Beaux-Arts (catalogue n° 453)

316. Moreau-Vauthier 1906, p. 73, citing a conversation the author had with Gérôme.

317. Taine 1903, pp. 252–53, reprinted from an article published in the *Journal des débats*, 11–12 April 1878.

318. Manet's statement is recorded in Proust 1913, p. 51. Gleyre had served on the salon juries in the 1860s when several of Manet's works were rejected. We have, however, no records of his votes in regard to Manet's paintings that were submitted to the salons.

319. Unpublished letter of 3 January 1878 now in Fleurier, CFC.

320. Lapauze 1911, pp. 414f., recounts this aspect of Ingres's work and the ongoing difficulties with the duke. These, as well as Ingres's personal problems after the death of his wife, contributed to his failure to complete the commission.

88. François Edouard Picot, Staircase decoration, after 1843. Dampierre, Château de Dampierre
89. Jean Auguste Dominique Ingres, *The Age of Gold*, 1843–50. Dampierre, Château de Dampierre

321. Berthoud 1874, p. 466.
322. François Edouard Picot (1786–1868) was a student of David and had a great success after 1820. He was awarded the Legion of Honor in 1825. On the present condition of the Dampierre murals, see Ockman 1984, pp. 111f.

the short trip there to inspect the effacement. In 1874, Fritz Berthoud — by then Clément's father-in-law — wrote that of the paintings Gleyre had executed for Dampierre, "Il n'en reste pas de trace."[321] Clément, as well, wrote that nothing was left of Gleyre's efforts, thus giving the impression that no work of Gleyre's could actually be seen in the château. Yet, recent inspections of the site reveal, astonishingly, that not everything was destroyed. Only the large life-size figures on the first level were completely effaced and later replaced by ornamental designs painted by Picot.[322] The second level and the ceiling decorations have remained virtually intact, although they show considerable reworking by another hand. Gleyre never hinted, or perhaps never knew, that almost two-thirds of his paintings were actually in place as he had designed them. fig. 88

Clément wrote that after the incident, Gleyre was disappointed and bitter for a period of almost two years. In fact, in 1842, just after the completion of the Dampierre commission, Gleyre was actively involved in another commission, this time in the decoration of the church of Saint-Vincent-de-Paul in Paris, a project that would occupy him for most of the year. Once again, the precise facts concerning his engagement and contract are not known. When Clément was writing his biography, he attempted to obtain the crucial documents concerning this commission, but he was told they had been burned during the Commune of 1871.

The church was one of the largest and most imposing structures of the period. Designed by Lepère in 1824, but ostensibly completed by his assistant, Ignace Hittorff, the decoration of the interior, begun in part in 1839, was considered one of the most important commissions from the state.[323] Several artists were considered for the major work, including Vernet, Delaroche, Scheffer, and Ingres; the latter accepted the invitation — with a fee assigned at 200,000 francs — but afterwards withdrew. Finally, in 1848, the frieze decoration and painting of the apse was given to Hippolyte Flandrin and Picot, respectively, both of whom had been involved in the Dampierre project. Flandrin painted a monumental frieze consisting of eighty-nine figures over a span of forty-two meters. The entire project was overseen by Hittorff, who was a close friend of Mme. Cornu.[324] Gleyre was commissioned to paint five medallions of papal saints in the entablature, surrounded by five busts of angels; the former were each one meter high, the latter sixty centimeters high.[325]

fig. 90

Gleyre's correspondence for the year is minimal, and no letter of his discusses the work in any detail. Only two letters survive that mention the work at all: an undated one to Cornu noting that he had not been paid for almost a year, and one of 13 September 1843, also to Cornu, where he told his friend that he had finally seen Hittorff, who approved his commission vouchers so that he could receive his fee.[326]

Clément is correct that Gleyre's decorations in the church are ordinary and without special interest either as examples of Gleyre's art or as church decoration. Gleyre probably took little trouble with them because the works were placed very high and in deep shadow. Moreover, his recent experiences in Dampierre surely diminished his interest. The project profited him little; there was no publicity which cited his works here, nor any reviews in which his name was mentioned. It was only in September 1843 that Delaunay, writing in *L'Artiste*, mentioned that some of the decorations "sont dues au talent de M. Gleyre,"[327] but by this time, Gleyre's name was recognized throughout Paris as a result of his contribution to the salon of that year.

Although nothing is known of Gleyre's sources for the medallions in Saint-Vincent-de-Paul, it is likely, from the evidence of the remaining studies, that some of the figures were derived from live models. It has been suggested that one of these was Hittorff's daughter Isabelle, who in 1842 was only ten years old.[328] It is difficult to ascertain from the meager documents whether Gleyre had any contact with the Hittorff family; only the architect himself is mentioned in Gleyre's letters, and only in the context of Gleyre's payments for his work. If indeed Gleyre used Isabelle as a model, it must have been Mme. Cornu who made the contacts, since she was a close family friend; it is equally likely that she had a hand in persuading Hittorff to hire Gleyre for the decorations.

Gleyre's work at the church was presumably finished before the end of fall 1842. By this time Gleyre had accepted two further commissions, both from the state. The first of these is not noted in either Clément's text or in his catalogue and has not been mentioned in the literature on the painter. Documentation is sparse, with almost no details regarding Gleyre's intentions or progress on the work. Sometime before 29 June 1842, Gleyre received a commission for a fee of 1,500 francs to paint a picture to be entitled *The Knights of Saint John Reestablishing Religion*.[329] There is, however, no indication that Gleyre made studies for the com-

323. The basic work on Ignace Hittorff is Schneider 1977, I, pp. 296f., which recounts his role in the construction of the church.
324. Emerit 1937(b), p. 81.
325. *Inventaire général… Ville de Paris*, 1884, III, p. 164, which gives the dimensions and their precise locations. My thanks to Georges Brunel for further information and the photographs of these works.
326. See Lausanne, MCBA, GA 988, and Clément, p. 156.
327. Delaunay 1843, p. 206.
328. Toussaint 1985, p. 127, suggests the possibility of Isabelle as a model, but without adequate documentation. She proposed as well that Gleyre's medallions later served as models for Ingres. On Ingres and Hittorff, see Naef 1964, p. 258.
329. The actual commission to Gleyre for this painting was not found in the documentation pertaining to the state's commissions at this time; however, it is noted in Paris, AL, Dossier X, 1843, "Etat des ouvrages non terminés, 31 juillet 1843."

90. *Saint Julian and Angels*, 1842. Paris, Saint-Vincent-de-Paul (catalogue n° 458)

position or began a canvas for it. By 31 July 1843, when Gleyre had already achieved considerable fame, the project was described as not yet completed. By 6 May 1845, almost three years after Gleyre received the commission, the painting in question, now titled *The Knights of Rhodes, Pierre de Sugnan and His Army of Crusaders Taking Alexandria*, was again listed as incomplete.[330] No other information has come to light on the project; it was never mentioned in Gleyre's correspondence, nor that of his friends. Clearly Gleyre lost interest in the idea or he may have been discouraged from actually painting it by Delacroix's *The Taking of Constantinople by the Crusaders*, which undoubtedly he knew from its exhibition in 1841 or its installation in Versailles. No sketch or study for the commission is known to exist.

The second commission Gleyre accepted at this time was for a religious painting for one of the provincial churches. In the 1840s, the state policy of commissioning religious paintings for poor rural churches not only provided decorations for communities that otherwise could not afford works of art, but also generated commissions for numerous painters of repute. In 1841, thirty-seven such commissions were paid for by the state, while in 1842, 130 paintings were designated for churches throughout the country.[331] The commission Gleyre received originated in a letter to the Ministère de l'Intérieur from the mayor of Goumois, a village with a population of only 200, located in the Doubs near the Swiss border.[332] The mayor explained that the village had spent almost 30,000 francs in rebuilding the church and had no funds left for any form of decoration. He asked that the state provide a painting, preferably of the Virgin, no larger than 1,70 by 2,75 meters, which would be placed at the high altar. The mayor's request was dated 12 July 1842; Gleyre received the commission officially on 23 August. The contract called for him to copy Murillo's *Assumption*, then in the Louvre — a copy was preferred to an original work since it could be made more quickly and for a smaller fee. Gleyre's contract called for a fee of 1,000 francs, half to be delivered with the contract, the other half when the painting was completed.

fig. 91

fig. 92

91. Church at Goumois, France
92. Copy of Bartolomé Estebán Murillo's *Assumption of the Virgin*, 1842–45. Goumois, France (catalogue n° 461)

330. Ibid., Dossier X, 1845, "Dossier C: Etat des travaux non terminés, 6 mai 1845."
331. Paris, AN, F²¹, 12–60, provides the essential details, but see also Angrand 1967, pp. 161f.
332. All of the documents from which the following account of the commission are taken from AN, F²¹, 33, dossier 6. Clément, p. 155, mentions the commission as "donnée à l'église de Saint-Gaumois [sic]" but provides no further information. He clearly did not think the work important enough to study or include in his catalogue.

As might be expected, Gleyre had little interest or enthusiasm in the commission: copying another artist's work was alien to his spirit, except, as we have seen, in the context of his own studies. Consequently, the completion of this commission for Goumois took longer than anyone anticipated. On 7 September 1843, more than a year after Gleyre had received the contract and accepted the first payment, the prefect for the Doubs wrote to Paris asking for a progress report, adding that the village was impatient to receive the painting in question, and received a reply that the painting "était encore en cours d'exécution," that another letter had been sent to Gleyre asking him to hurry the work, and that it was hoped it would be completed shortly.

On 27 March 1844, the department wrote to Gleyre reminding him of the commitment he had made and asking him to deliver the picture by the end of the year, now for the good reason that the church could not be properly inaugurated until the painting was set in place. For reasons that are not recorded in the documents, Gleyre was not able to finish the canvas by the end of 1844, thus prompting the prefect of the Doubs to write once again to Paris asking that Gleyre be prodded further. The letter was answered on 8 May 1845 with the despairing news that no one knew when the painting would be completed and delivered. Gleyre meanwhile wrote to Cornu on 26 June 1844, when Cornu was in Venice: "Je n'avance pas mon gueux de tableau" — probably referring to the difficulties, psychological or other, involved in the commission.[333] On 4 July 1845, almost three years after the commission was accepted, the authorities from the Doubs informed Paris that the work still had not arrived but there was reason to believe that it was in fact finished.

It was only on 5 August 1845 that Gleyre received the authority to collect the remaining 500 francs owed him for the commission. Presumably Gleyre had already delivered the picture to the Paris authorities to be shipped to Goumois. The length of time required to complete his copy would be a portent of the similar difficulties Gleyre encountered in two commissions he received from the canton of Vaud. But in the summer of 1845, Gleyre's artistic situation changed dramatically: during the time he worked on the Goumois commission, he showed two canvases in the salons that were highly regarded by critics and public alike, and, at the same time, he assumed the direction of the most prestigious private teaching studio in Paris. If before the Goumois copy Gleyre's name and art were known only to a select few, by the time that the copy was put in place, his art was known by *tout Paris*.

333. Lausanne, MCBA, GA 988. From the context of the letter, it cannot be determined to which painting Gleyre referred.

## CHAPTER 5

# 1843–1850

CELEBRITY AND A SECOND ITALIAN TRIP

93. Study for *Le Soir*, 1843. Lausanne, Musée Cantonal des Beaux-Arts (catalogue n° 468)

In late 1842, Gleyre once again considered producing a large canvas for the Salon that would help to make his name and art better known in Paris. The favorable criticism he had received earlier for the *Saint John* was largely forgotten and the painting itself completely out of view. The commission for the decorations at Saint-Vincent-de-Paul earned him little, and the commission for the church of Goumois was not yet begun. For Gleyre to undertake a large painting without the benefit of a commission was difficult because of his perennial poverty, although the fees received from his commissions must have offered a welcome, if temporary, relief. Gleyre was aware that at thirty-seven, when many of his contemporaries had already made their mark in the Salons, he had not yet fulfilled the hopes of his artistic education and diverse experiences, or the promise of the *Saint John*. It was clearly imperative that he create a solid artistic base in order to avoid living perpetually on minor commissions that would bring no recognition.

131

The Salon of 1842 was tranquil compared with those of 1840 and 1841.[334] The difficulties arising from the tumultuous conflicts between artists and juries, rekindled early in 1843 in regard to the Salon of that year, scheduled to open on 15 March. Members of the jury who were familiar with Gleyre's previous work did not actually serve: Vernet was in Russia at the time; Gleyre's teacher Hersent was ill and had to be excused; and Delaroche refused to serve because of his belief that the jury system was fundamentally corrupt. Of the painters on the jury who evaluated the works submitted, probably only Picot, who had replaced Gleyre's destroyed works at Dampierre, knew Gleyre or his work. To make matters worse, there was an unusually high number of works submitted — more than 4,000 items — before the deadline of 20 February, providing substantial competition. The jury proved to be unduly harsh, moreso than in the previous salons, and rejected more than 2,300 works by more than 950 artists, including such painters as Corot, Couture, Boulanger, Millet, Huet, Glaize, and even Hippolyte Flandrin. Gleyre could hardly have known in late 1842 when he was preparing his painting for the salon that this exhibition would be one of the most severe in his lifetime.

The painting that occupied Gleyre and wholly diverted him from completing the Goumois commission was titled *Le Soir*. Gleyre sent the work to the Louvre on 19 February, where it was registered as n° 3202.[335] Despite the exacting jury, the painting was accepted unanimously and thus for only the third time in a decade the Parisian public had the opportunity to see one of Gleyre's works. When the salon opened in March, the picture, listed as n° 512 in the livret, received an enormous amount of attention. Within days, Gleyre's painting was drawing large audiences, and his name was becoming known in the Parisian press.

fig. 94

Gleyre's painting of 1843 has been discussed by many art historians and critics, some of whom have attempted a careful examination of the imagery, which is curious, but wholly acceptable within the context of the iconographic trends of the period.[336] Clément is certainly correct in his assumption that the origin of the imagery was Gleyre's vision in Egypt, noted in his journal under 21 March 1835 when he was already in deep despair and had told Lowell that he could no longer continue.[337] However, Clément does not mention the importance of another section of the journal, the one for 9 July, written near Abu Simbel, where Gleyre referred to the "illusions de ma jeunesse… perdues à jamais" as playing an equal role in creating the despair that underlies the imagery.[338] It is no accident that Gleyre's *Le Soir* rapidly became known as *Lost Illusions*, not only reflecting Gleyre's own intentions, but also echoing the psychological malady of an age so graphically depicted in Balzac's novel of the same title published in the same year.

Yet while the pictorial ideas go back to Gleyre's Egyptian experiences, the essential elements of the painting come from a fusion of Gleyre's own melancholy and the disillusionment common to artists and writers in France in the 1840s. The work anticipates the philosophical spirit that typifies Gleyre's mature paintings: the images appear within an iconographic framework attuned to the temper of the age, but usually reflect

334. See Hauptman 1985(a), pp. 101f., for details on the problems with the juries for the years that Gleyre exhibited in Paris.

335. Paris, AL, Enregistrement des ouvrages, 1843. The size of the work was recorded as 175 x 280 cm. with frame. Gleyre gave his address as "chez Cornu" but supplied no birthdate as was customary. Cornu submitted works just after Gleyre, n° 3203 and 3204.

336. See Hauptman 1978.

337. Clément, p. 98.

338. Ibid., p. 109. Clément, however, never cited this passage in regard to the imagery of *Le Soir*.

94. *Le Soir*, 1843. Paris, Musée du Louvre (catalogue n° 465)

personal concerns in their detail and selection. Moreover, Gleyre utilized imagery that drew from Classical, Romantic, and Academic domains, all forged into an unified whole that seeks a middle ground, a *juste milieu* that could not be attacked as following a specific course or contemporary school of artistic thought. It is no wonder that Gleyre's painting appealed to the critics and to the public, since it contained elements that touched upon current ideals that were readily accessible. The celebrity of the work, in fact, had a somewhat adverse effect on Gleyre's career since he was, throughout his life, associated with this single painting almost to the exclusion of others that later better expressed his artistic philosophy. In this light, Clément is correct in stating that *Le Soir* was Gleyre's most accomplished work to date, but not his masterpiece.[339] Yet the painting opened doors for him and permitted him to produce his art in a freer, more inventive manner than was possible before.

Despite the fact that *Le Soir* has been considered Gleyre's magnum opus, it is only recently that the theme of the picture has been analyzed from the perspective of its implications for his art and life.[340] Clément saw the canvas as having a place in Gleyre's œuvre similar to *Werther* in Goethe's in the sense that the subtext has autobiographical origins, but he made no attempt to probe further into the mysterious imagery that astonished artists and critics in the 1840s.[341] The key to comprehending

339. Clément, p. 168.
340. The work is thoroughly discussed in Hauptman 1978, pp. 323f., and summarized in Rosenblum 1984, p. 170.
341. Clément, p. 169.

133

the picture lies in the old man on the river bank who watches his own life, represented by the Muse-laden boat, slip away into the crepuscular landscape. The lyre distinguishes him as a poet, but the position of the instrument at his feet indicates silence and inactivity. The iconographic elements in the composition point to a more specific subject, with which Gleyre obviously identified, namely the little known story of the Thracian bard Thamyris.[342] Thamyris was said to have boasted of his poetic prowess, which, he arrogantly announced, surpassed the beauty of the Muses. He was severely punished for this act of human blasphemy by being blinded and made mute — thus the attributes of the silenced lyre and the blind man's cane.

Gleyre had selected a story whose basic elements — human contemptuousness, artistic failure, creative impotence, and even blindness — reflected his own concerns in the early 1840s, notions that he had expressed at various times in Rome and Egypt and which would become idées fixes in his artistic career. In this sense, the painting transcends abstract poetic beauty and becomes both objective and subjective : the former because it delineates the perpetual feelings of frustration common to artists of the early nineteenth century, and the latter because it aptly portrays Gleyre's own state of mind in his previous activities as an artist, his own lost illusions as a painter. It is ironic that Gleyre's most acclaimed success was wedded to a canvas whose ultimate theme was artistic failure.

For a painting as significant as this in Gleyre's œuvre, it is astonishing that there is so little documentation regarding its creation and development. Gleyre did not mention it in a single letter, nor is there any information in the correspondence of his friends at this time. The only surviving preparatory study for the composition as a whole shows Gleyre's first idea, which is clearly in accord with the vision he had in the desert, fig. 93 especially in the right-hand side of the landscape where the Colossus of Memnon can be distinguished. Gleyre wisely modified the composition into a more poetic work in which the quiet resignation of the poet replaces the frenetic movement seen in the drawing. The barque, symbolic rather than narrative, takes on a more important role and intensifies the meaning.

The only surviving record of Gleyre's opinion of the painting was a remark he made to Clément: when he was asked, as he often was, to make copies of the painting, he generally refused because, he said, he was dissatisfied with the figure of the poet.[343] In fact, he did authorize copies fig. 95 later, as will be noted.

One important document to come to light regarding the picture in its early stage before the exhibition in the Salon is a letter addressed to "M. Glère" from Prosper Mérimée, a response to a letter Gleyre had sent earlier. Mérimée's letter to Gleyre is not dated, but must, from its contents, have been written in early 1843. By this time Mérimée was already an important figure in French letters through his fiction, historical writings, and even art criticism. From 1834, Mérimée had served as the inspector of historical monuments, a post that kept him in touch with a wide range of artists and historians. From the letter in question, it is

342. Homer, *Iliad*, II, 594f., Loeb ed., p. 95. Homer, however, does not recount the entire history of Thamyris in the form that would be best known later. See too Pausanias, *Descriptions of Greece*, IV, XXXIII, 7, Loeb ed., II, p. 357. The story of Thamyris appeared in a variety of later sources including Milton.
343. Clément, p. 168.

95. Study for *Le Soir*, 1843. Lausanne, Musée Cantonal des Beaux-Arts (catalogue n° 467)

evident that Gleyre and Mérimée had already met earlier, although there is no documentation to tell when, how, or under what circumstances. The likeliest person to have introduced the two was Gustave Planche, who had known and admired Mérimée since 1832. While it is true that Planche was in Italy from 1840 to 1845, he may have asked Gleyre in one of the lost letters to meet with the writer.

Mérimée's letter, then, is an answer to a request Gleyre had made for appropriate citations from Anacreon for "quelque pensée mélancolique." Mérimée sent two quotations from odes 8 and 46 — in Greek — and added:

> Je ne sais, Monsieur, si vous pourrez faire usage de mes cita-
> tions grecques. Soyez persuadé que votre tableau n'en a pas
> besoin pour paraître vraiment grec. Vous vous rappelez que
> nous sommes convenus ce matin que grec voulait dire beau.[344]

It is clear from the passage and in light of Gleyre's work at this time that Mérimée's reference could only be to *Le Soir*, which the writer must have seen in the studio before Gleyre sent it to the jury in February. But the question here is, why did Gleyre need a citation from Anacreon? It is

344. Mérimée 1943, III, pp. 474–75, lettre n° 878.

135

probable that Gleyre asked for one to help explain the nature of the icono-graphic disposition, which he would have included in the Salon livret; if so, that might date the letter to after the acceptance of the painting by the jury. It was customary at the option of the artist to include a citation in the livret to explain the source of his image or to add to its meaning through a literary quotation. Often a few lines from the Bible or a his-torical text were printed in the livret as a point of reference for the viewer.[345] Gleyre, however, did not use either of Mérimée's proposals, per-haps because they were in Greek or perhaps, as Mérimée suggested, it was not necessary. The livret listed only the title of the work, and Gleyre's address as "11, passage Sainte-Marie, rue du Bac, chez M. Cornu."

The literary quality of *Le Soir* struck a visual nerve that was immedi-ately noted by the major critics. The most admiring review, by the re-spected critic Arsène Houssaye, was published only eleven days after the opening of the Salon. Gleyre's work was the first Houssaye discussed in his review — "la première toile qui vous frappe et vous saisisse, le tab-leau le plus poétique" — despite the fact that it was badly hung and not directly visible upon entry into the salon. Houssaye correctly judged that Gleyre had intended to represent not a poetic evocation of Evening, but rather "le soir de la vie," in which the old man at the right reflects upon his life, now fading away. Houssaye devoted two large paragraphs to a description of the work, stressing at the same time that the painting is not meant to be a literal image of the Egyptian landscape, but rather a timeless depiction of despair, applicable to the malaise of contemporary life. Houssaye paid the picture the highest compliment in noting that "tous les peintres, ceux qui sont de bonne foi et ceux qui sont de mauvaise foi, aiment *Le Soir*," a sentiment quickly echoed by the public at large. It was also in this review that Houssaye referred to the work as representing "les illusions perdues," a title that persisted and by which the painting was known afterwards.[346]

Other critics wrote in admiring tones, often referring to the painting as one of the finest in the salon. In fact, so popular had the painting become while on exhibit that it was removed from its initial position and placed at the entrance to the salon, perhaps to entice visitors inside.[347] Only one reviewer wrote a negative review of the painting — Prosper Haussard, who had earlier encouraged Gleyre with his critique of the *Saint John* and who would later praise Gleyre's works in 1845 and 1849. Haussard remarked that he had seen the picture twice, precisely because it had already achieved a certain notoriety, but still thought the idea of the painting too vague. He also objected to the pale colors and mono-tone, although he noted that despite these weaknesses, it was clear that Gleyre had considerable talent.[348]

In view of the fame the painting achieved, it became inevitable that Gleyre was considered for one of the annual prizes offered by the state to reward effort and to encourage further work. In 1843, no fewer than sixty-five medals were given: twelve first-place gold medals, twenty-one second-place, and thirty-two third-place medals. Gleyre was awarded a second-place medal in the genre category on 18 May 1843, no small

345. Vernet seems to hold the record for the length of citation, having printed no less than six pages of text to explain his huge canvas *The Taking of Smahla* in 1845 (n° 1628 in the salon livret).
346. Houssaye 1843, pp. 285–87.
347. Delécluze 1843.
348. Haussard 1843.

achievement considering the competition, which included works by Cogniet and Papety, both of which also achieved wide popularity among the critics and the public.[349] The medal Gleyre received was valued at 200 francs; he proudly sent it to his uncle François with the note, "C'est à vous qu'elle revient, car c'est à vous que je la dois."[350]

It was usual, when paintings were decorated and publicly acknowledged for their excellence, that offers of purchase for the work would come to the painter either from the public or through the government.[351] It seems that no offers of purchase for *Le Soir* were made before the painting was decorated in May, and when this fact came to the attention of Houssaye, he offered to buy it himself.[352] Henry Houssaye told Clément that his father had indeed bought the work from Gleyre for 1,500 francs, but that a few days later, after the purchase had been concluded, the government expressed an interest in buying it.[353] According to Henry, Gleyre went to Houssaye for his opinion on the matter, stating that he preferred to have the picture in the Musée du Luxembourg where it could be seen by the public. Houssaye agreed and returned the painting, which then was purchased by the state for a fee double that of Houssaye. This sum, the most Gleyre had earned up to that point for one of his paintings, was not excessive for a work so revered in the public's estimation.[354]

As a result of the acclaim Gleyre received in 1843, his fame was firmly established in both critical and public circles. *Le Soir* was admired for two generations in the Musée du Luxembourg until December 1865, when it was transferred to the Galerie du Corps législatif for a period of two years.[355] But by 1879 the work had been relegated to an obscure corner of the Luxembourg, where it attracted little attention or interest. The curator at that time, Etienne Arago, brother of the celebrated scientist, suggested moving the work to a more important location and discussed the matter with the eminent publisher Hetzel, one of Gleyre's friends. Arago thought to place the picture in the Louvre, in the so-called *galerie française*; the fact that Gleyre was Swiss should not hinder this effort, he explained to Hetzel, since paintings by other foreigners, including Bonington and Léopold Robert, were already represented.[356] Through the efforts of these two, *Le Soir,* now almost universally known as *Lost Illusions*, was finally admitted to the Louvre on 1 December 1879, the only painting by Gleyre to hang there.[357]

349. Paris, AL, Dossier X, 1843, "Rapport… état des médailles."

350. Clément, p. 164. Gleyre received a reply from his uncle later, as recounted in an undated letter to Cornu in Lausanne, MCBA, GA 988.

351. In Paris, AL, Dossier X, 1843, a report by Caillieux indicates that the government allotted 45,500 francs for the purchases of works that year from the salon; the document is signed 18 May 1843.

352. Villarceaux 1874, p. 447, noted incorrectly that Houssaye offered 2,000 francs for the work. The facts are elucidated in an unpublished letter from Houssaye's son Henry to Clément, dated 19 October 1877, which Clément did not use in his biography; in Fleurier, CFC.

353. In Paris, AL, Dossier X, 1843, "Acquisitions ordonnées," signed 22 May, *Le Soir* is noted with a price of "2,000 à 2,500 francs" in pencil at the right margin. In a later document in the same dossier, "Propositions à revoir," with recommendations to the minister, but undated, *Le Soir* appears with the figure 2,800 francs.

354. The figure is confirmed in Paris, AN, O⁴, 2118, "Mandat de paiement, numéro 6563, 25 juillet 1843, ordonnance n° 1357." The price of 3,000 francs was approved, but Gleyre did not sign the mandate until 16 October 1843. The price paid for a painting often was in proportion to the reputation of the artist rather than to the work bought. From the mandates of payment in the O⁴ series of the AN, we see that Ingres received 8,000 francs for

his portrait of the Duc d'Orléans (n° 7653) while Paul Flandrin received only 400 francs for his copy of Ingres's portrait of Cherubini (n° 5628). From the records Paris, AL, Dossier X, 1843, it seems that 2,000 to 2,500 francs was the average price paid by the state at this time.

355. *Notice*… 1866, n° 15.

356. Letter from Arago to Clément, 14 November 1879, in Fleurier, CFC. Etienne Arago (1803–92) was also a well-known writer, a one-time director of the Vaudeville, mayor of Paris, and in 1879, director of the Musée du Luxembourg.

357. Lacambre 1974, p. 90.

One measure of the success achieved by the provocative imagery of Gleyre's painting is its afterlife in art and literature. Already in 1845, a minor painter, Frédéric Chevalier, profited from the celebrity of Gleyre's painting by exhibiting in the Salon of that year a drawing — now lost — copied after it.[358] Thirty years later, Mlle. Augusta-Julia Granier exhibited a painted porcelain of the painting in the salon of 1875.[359] In the same year, Vincent Van Gogh, then twenty-two years old and working in Goupil's in Paris, noted in a letter to his brother Theo that Gleyre's painting was one of his preferred works, an opinion reiterated in another letter several months later.[360] Nor was the image forgotten in literary accounts: Count Eugène Melchior de Vogüé described a scene in the Orient very close to the image in Gleyre's painting and at the end of the account acknowledged its source.[361]

Similarly, the painting was so popular among art students throughout much of the nineteenth century that countless copies have come to light. Although the records from the Louvre archives are incomplete, it is known that from 1893 to 1914, no fewer than seventy-eight requests to copy the painting were filed and presumably granted.[362] Photographic copies and engravings likewise abounded in Gleyre's lifetime: even the painter Gérôme, who had studied with Gleyre, wrote Gleyre personally requesting permission to have the painting photographed when the copyright was still with the painter.[363]

So successful in fact was Gleyre's canvas that he often received requests to furnish copies himself, or at least reductions for private collectors, a common practice during the nineteenth century for especially celebrated works from which painters generally profited since it afforded a brisk business.[364] Gleyre was always reluctant to accept these commissions, or even to authorize reduced versions, during the 1840s and 1850s, partially because he was never fully satisfied with the figure of the bard.[365] Gleyre must have taken seriously the criticism of Delécluze who, while admiring the work, thought that the weakest element in the painting was precisely the old man.[366] It was only in 1865 that Gleyre consented to copy the work when he was commissioned for a reduction of the canvas by the Baltimore industrialist William Walters, who negotiated the transaction through Goupil and George Lucas, his agent in Paris.[367] Although the initial sketch was made by Gleyre's pupil Léon Dussart, Gleyre himself reworked the canvas entirely, finding it much more difficult and time-consuming than he had imagined. He did not deliver the reduction to Lucas until 1867; it is, in all likelihood, the only copy of the canvas to have come from Gleyre's hand.[368]

In the summer of 1843, Gleyre was offered a position, the most important in his career, that provided him with an important base to launch his long career as teacher.[369] At this time, Paul Delaroche had abandoned his private teaching studio, the most admired of the Restoration, and asked his students to continue their education with Gleyre. About twenty students, including Gérôme and Hamon, formed the nucleus of the teaching studio under Gleyre's supervision. Gleyre agreed to offer his advice, but refused to accept the usual fees because, he told his students,

358. Livret n° 1744. On the artist, see Bénézit, II, p. 718.

359. Livret n° 2346. There is some doubt who the artist was since Bénézit, V, p. 167, lists two artists, both painters on porcelain, named Augusta and Julia, respectively. The livret lists the artist's name as spelled here in the text. Probably, Bénézit has confused the artist's name and assumed two different identities. Her work is presently in Sèvres, Musée National de Céramique.

360. See Van Gogh 1960, letter n° 31, dated 15 July 1875, and letter n° 42, dated 11 October 1875. Van Gogh saw the picture in the Luxembourg.

361. See Vogüé 1901, first published 1877, pp. 89–90. He should not be confused with the Marquis Charles-Jean Melchior de Vogüé, an archaeologist and diplomat who replaced the Duc de Luynes at the Académie des Inscriptions et Belles-Lettres in 1868.

362. Paris, AL, Registre des copies, 1893–1914. The earlier registers were missing from the archives but must certainly reflect the figures recorded here. In 1900 alone, almost one permission to copy the painting was filed each month.

363. On 10 October 1856 Gérôme wrote directly to Gleyre requesting the necessary permission. Gleyre authorized the reproduction and the photograph was made on 17 October; see Paris, AL, Dossier Gleyre, P³⁰.

364. See, for example, the case of Landelle's Fellah, a hugely successful work of the salon of 1866; Charles Zacharie Landelle (1812–1908) made at least twenty copies of the painting, charging from 800 to 10,000 francs depending on the size commissioned; Stryienski 1911, p. 79.

365. Clément, p. 168.

366. Delécluze 1843.

367. Johnston 1982, p. 96.

368. Léon Dussart (born in 1824) also spelled his name "Dussard" (see Thieme-Becker, X, p. 229 and Bénézit, III, p. 451); Dussart also made the sketch for Gleyre's copy of The Flood. On Gleyre's difficulties in executing the copy, see Lucas 1979, II, pp. 203f. Two other copies are also thought to have been done by Gleyre. One, in Liverpool, Walker Art Gallery, Inv. 2876, is signed by Gleyre with the date 1851, but the signature looks doubtful; see Audley 1923, p. 22. The other version, now in Winterthur, Kunstmuseum, Inv. 1004, is signed and dated 1866, but is also dubious. This work comes from the collection of Frida Amman-Haab and was exhibited briefly in Lausanne in 1874 when Louis Ruchonnet borrowed it from Mr. Amman in Constance. But already then, the work was thought to be a poor copy; see X., 1874.

369. A full discussion of Gleyre's teaching activities is contained in Hauptman 1985(e).

96. Gleyre's students, *Collective Portraits*, c. 1862–63. Paris, Musée du Petit Palais

97. *Cleonis and Cydippe*, 1842–43. Boston, Private collection (catalogue n° 462)

he vividly remembered his own extreme poverty while a student with Hersent, and he did not wish to inflict the same hardship on those who desired his counsel. For more than a quarter of a century, Gleyre maintained the teaching studio in three different locations, overseeing the primary artistic instruction of more than 500 students.[370] This aspect of Gleyre's career, difficult to summarize because of the varied activities over the period in question, will be discussed more fully in a chapter at the end of this text. Gleyre's studio became one of the most enlightened in Paris, open to the ideas of the academic and vanguard students alike, many of whom are shown in a curious group portrait that hung in the studio. Virtually an entire generation of Swiss students trained there, as did a substantial number of decorative artists, who certainly benefited from Gleyre's interest in the genre since his youth in Lyons. It is no accident that in 1863, the year of the major reforms in the teaching curriculum of the Ecole des Beaux-Arts, Gleyre's studio accommodated such titular heads of the modern school as Sisley, Bazille, Renoir, and, briefly, Monet.[371]

Gleyre's activities immediately after the celebrity of *Le Soir* centered not only in establishing his teaching studio, where he began to supervise students' works twice a week, but also in completing paintings previously begun. The most intriguing of these is known now by the enigmatic title *Cleonis and Cydippe*. Clément was especially vague about the sources for the work and speculated that the imagery resulted from Gleyre's second Italian trip in 1845.[372] However, while the painting has a decidedly Italianate air, it can now be shown that it was begun well be-

fig. 96

fig. 97

370. Staiger-Gayler 1974 provides the essential list of students, but it is not complete.
371. Boime 1971 discusses the importance of these reforms.
372. Clément, p. 188.

139

fore his trip, and indeed before he completed *Le Soir*. In the letter that Henry Houssaye, Arsène's son, wrote to Clément noting that his father returned *Le Soir* to Gleyre, he also mentioned that Gleyre sent him the *Cleonis* as a gift a week later in appreciation of his kindness.[373] The title and subject of the work have escaped interpretation, since no known mythology or Classical narrative bears the names of the two principal figures.[374] In fact, this title first appears only in 1862 when the painting was reproduced in an engraving; Houssaye earlier, in 1851, referred to it as *Leucothoé et Alcimédon*.[375] In all probability the image was meant as no more than a scene of seduction, "la scène de Joseph et Mme Potiphar reportée du monde biblique au monde olympien."[376] It should be regarded as a playful Arcadian idyll, in the style of Prud'hon, perhaps suited to Houssaye's sometimes esoteric poetic tastes. The work, however, offers yet another instance in which Gleyre flirted with a sexual subject when the painting was destined for a private audience.

Gleyre associated more and more with critics, writers, and playwrights at this time, most notably with François Ponsard, who in 1843 had a huge success at the Odéon.[377] Ponsard, like Gleyre, spent his youth in Lyons and had enormous difficulties in establishing his reputation in Paris. His first literary effort, a verse translation of Byron's *Manfred*, sold only three copies in six months. But his play *Lucrèce*, starring the tempestuous actress Marie Dorval, was, like Gleyre's *Le Soir*, so warmly received by the critics in 1843 that his name was instantly catapulted into the ranks of such figures as Hugo. A wide range of critics from Sainte-Beuve to Jules Sandeau praised the play as nothing short of revolutionary.[378]

Gleyre made several studies of scenes from the drama, none of them completed on a large canvas.[379] Only one of these has come to light, and even Clément remarked that while he had seen others, he did not know what Gleyre had done with them. These studies were probably made in collaboration with Ponsard himself and are the only examples known of Gleyre's illustrations for contemporary literature. Ponsard remained a close friend of Gleyre's even when his fortunes began to decline, and it was in Gleyre's studio in 1846 that Ponsard gave the first public reading of his new play, *Agnès de Méranie* which, however, failed to inspire the same critical adulation of his earlier success.

fig. 98

If Gleyre never transferred any of the scenes from *Lucrèce*, it may be because he was preparing a large work for the Salon of 1845. Unlike the Salon of 1843, that of 1845 was relatively free from protests of faulty judgment. There were 4,146 works submitted, of which 2,348 were accepted without difficulty. Because of the success of his painting in 1843 and the second-place medal, Gleyre had no fear that his new painting would not be accepted by the jury. Gleyre submitted the work with the title *Départ des apôtres allant prêcher l'Evangile* (*The Apostles Dispersing to Preach the Gospel*) on 2 March 1845, numbered 3,433 in the list of entries. As with *Le Soir*, the jury accepted the painting unanimously. When the Salon opened on 15 March, Gleyre's painting was hung — along with sixty others — in the first room, the most prestigious location, which virtually assured the picture a ready audience.[380]

fig. 99

373. The undated letter is in Fleurier, CFC, as is another of 16 April 1875 from Hetzel to Clément, in which the painting is noted as a gift from Gleyre to Houssaye. Hetzel was in fact puzzled why, under these circumstances, Houssaye wanted to sell the work, which he did the same year. The fact that the painting was a gift to Houssaye is likewise mentioned in Villarceaux 1874, p. 477.

374. See the discussion in Hauptman 1980, pp. 27–28.

375. Houssaye 1851, p. 29. When Houssaye sold the painting, it was titled *Faune et Bacchante*.

376. Villarceaux 1874, p. 447. Clément, p. 188, also refers to it as a form of the Potiphar story translated into Greek, as does the dealer Soullié, who sold the work in 1932.

377. On François Ponsard (born in 1788), see Mirecourt 1856, pp. 14f., but there is no mention of his association with Gleyre. Ponsard was a close friend of Arsène Houssaye, who may have introduced him to Gleyre.

378. Sainte-Beuve 1876, pp. 25f.; Sandeau 1843(a), pp. 371–78. See also a review of the criticism in Aubert 1843, pp. 560f.

379. Clément, p. 204.

380. Paris, AL, Dossier X, 1845: "Enregistrement;" "Procès-verbaux du jury," under n° 3433; and "Rapport d'emplacement." The work was listed as n° 729 in the livret and cited a passage from the Acts of the Apostles 10 : 42. Gleyre did not list his address in the livret.

98. Scene from Ponsard's *Lucrèce*, 1843–44. Lausanne, Musée Cantonal des Beaux-Arts (catalogue n° 476)

Given the choice of the placement of the painting and its religious subject matter, it seemed certain that Gleyre could expect another substantial success. Indeed, with the imagery of *Le Soir* still fresh, the critics followed with positive reviews, many of them commenting on the originality of the iconography and the graceful interplay of the gestures.[381] Gleyre was particularly praised for selecting a religious subject that departed from that normally seen in the salons; even Prosper Haussard, who disliked *Le Soir*, wrote enthusiastically of this painting.[382] Two critics noted the philosophical content of the work and referred to Gleyre as a "peintre-philosophe."[383] The work also attracted young critics who were writing their first reviews, including the painter Eugène Fromentin, who became acquainted with Gleyre later, and the young Charles Baudelaire. Fromentin was highly enthusiastic about Gleyre's painting, ranking it among the most significant of the salon; the latter denounced Gleyre's painting precisely because the religious iconography seemed to Baudelaire to be out of tune with the direction of art at that time.[384]

Gleyre was awarded another medal for his work on 31 May in the category of history painting where religious works were normally placed.[385] The award ceremony was set on 26 July at the house of the Intendant Général de la Liste Civile at 9 Place Vendôme, where Gleyre, always reticent to participate in public ceremonies, presumably appeared nonetheless to accept the prize.[386] However, there is no record of whether Gleyre indeed kept the medal; he did not send it to his uncle as he had previously with his medal of 1843, nor was it found after his death among his studio belongings.

Like *Le Soir*, Gleyre's *Apostles* was acquired by the state, but the history of the purchase is difficult to elucidate because of conflicting documentary evidence. Clément noted only that the painting was bought by the

381. P[ILLET] 1845, p. 777; Mantz 1845, p. 194; Delécluze 1845, among others.
382. Haussard 1843.
383. Gautier 1845, and Bergounioux 1845, p. 479.
384. Fromentin 1909, pp. 138–40; Baudelaire 1923, pp. 33–34.
385. Paris, AL, Dossier X, 1845, "Rapport des récompenses." Among the other winners were Sébastien Cornu, and Auguste-Barthélemy Glaize, whose name caused some confusion because of its similarity to Gleyre's. In the report cited, Glaize signed his name in Gleyre's spot and vice versa.
386. Paris, AL, Dossier Gleyre, P[30], which contains the invitation to Gleyre to accept the award.

government on 15 April 1846 — that is, a full year after its exhibition in the Salon — for the price of 3,000 francs and later deposited in the church of Montargis.[387] However, the Louvre records verify that the picture was actually bought on 19 May 1845, well before it was awarded the medal that would have made it a natural candidate for governmental purchase.[388] The history of the acquisition is further complicated by another commission which seemingly had nothing to do with Gleyre's creation of this painting and which Clément does not mention. Following a request to the state by the chapel of the college of Bergerac in Bordeaux for a painting to decorate the interior, the Minister of the Interior wrote on 18 December 1845 to the painter François-Gustave Dauphin, the same painter Gleyre had met in Hersent's studio in the 1820s, commissioning him to execute the painting for the chapel.[389] The subject was designated as *The Last Moments of Christ* and the fee of 3,000 francs was established. The documents do not indicate whether Dauphin began the work, but on 24 July 1846, the "section des Beaux-Arts" wrote to Gleyre:

> J'ai l'honneur de vous annoncer que, par décision du 15 avril 1846, M. le ministre vous a chargé d'exécuter (pour) une somme de trois mille francs, un tableau qui devra représenter les derniers moments du Christ.

It is not known why the commission was transferred to Gleyre; perhaps because of the success of his religious painting in 1845, Dauphin simply suggested that Gleyre be given the commission. Apparently Gleyre agreed to do the work, although no other details appear at this time in his correspondence.

In September 1846, the Baron de Salles, deputy of the Loiret, wrote to the minister in Paris reminding him that the king himself had authorized the commission of a work to decorate the church of Montargis. The minister responded with a proclamation to that effect on 29 September. On 2 February 1847, the minister drafted a note to the maître des requêtes, authorizing him to pay Gleyre 1,500 francs, "vu le degré d'avancement d'un tableau représentant les derniers moments du Christ, dont l'exécution a été confiée à M. Gleyre." A small note was attached that Gleyre could pick up the payment at his convenience. There is no explanation as to how these two commissions — for Bordeaux and Montargis — are related or perhaps confused in the documentation.

It seems that at this point, early in 1847, Gleyre must have begun work in earnest on the painting for Montargis, or that it may have already been in an advanced state. On 19 February 1847, almost two years after Gleyre's painting of the *Apostles* was sent to the salon, the minister wrote to the king in regard to the request made earlier for the painting destined to Montargis; he proposed

> d'accorder pour cette destination un tableau représentant *Le départ des Apôtres*, exécuté par M. Gleyre et qui est sans destination.

387. Clément, p. 179.
388. Paris, AL, Dossier X, 1845, "Acquisitions ordonnées," where under Gleyre's name is penciled the word "VENDU."
389. All the information here comes from the documents in Paris, AN, F²¹, 33, dossier 7.

There is no explanation as to why the painting Gleyre had apparently begun, showing the last moments of Christ, was now abandoned or why the *Apostles* was suggested as a replacement. On the same day a note was sent to Gleyre telling him that he was authorized to take the remaining 1,500 francs of the commission, "alloué par décision du 15 avril 1846."

By this time, Gleyre's *Apostles* was on view publicly in the galleries of Goupil. On 24 February 1847 the Baron de Salles wrote to the minister that he had seen the painting there and agreed that it could be used to fulfill the request made for a decorative work at the altar of the church of Montargis, despite the important fact that the work differed significantly in dimensions from those indicated by the parish priest as necessary for the site. The painting, however, remained at Goupil's until July 1847 — at which time it was listed for sale by Goupil — and the minister sent a note asking for its immediate return. Presumably, the painting was sent shortly afterwards to Montargis, where it remained until its transfer in 1875 to the municipality and then to the Musée Girodet.

99. *The Mission of the Apostles*, 1845. Montargis, Musée Girodet (catalogue n° 477)

143

This curious history leaves many questions unanswered. There is no trace of the painting for Montargis showing the last moments of Christ, and there appears to be no extant studies that might be associated with this iconography. Moreover, there is no indication whether Gleyre had simply abandoned the work in progress and replaced it by the *Apostles,* or whether the decision had been made by another party. There is likewise no indication of why the original commission for Bordeaux of 15 April 1846 — the same date Clément noted as the date for the purchase of the *Apostles* — was abandoned or preempted by the request for Montargis. There is a discrepancy in the dimensions of the *Apostles* between its exhibition in 1845 and its installation in Montargis two years later — a difference in dimensions of 55 by 77 centimeters, according to the documents of registration in 1845 and the measurements of the work later.[390] Is it possible that the canvas was cut between February and July 1847, when it was with Goupil, to conform to the dimensions necessary for its placement in the church? The compositional relationship of the final work to the sketch suggests no alterations of this form and magnitude. Gleyre never referred to the matter with his friends, nor did he voice displeasure over the fact that the painting was without destination, as the records state, after its success in 1845.

There is yet another unpublished chapter that further encourages doubt on the documentation regarding the *Apostles.* In the summer of 1880, Gleyre's former pupil and close friend, Albert Anker, wrote to Clément about an experience he had while in Montargis studying the painting.[391] It is probable that Anker had not seen the work before — he arrived in Paris from Switzerland only in 1854 — but in the last decades of Gleyre's life no student of Gleyre's knew his style better than Anker. He went to the museum specifically to examine Gleyre's painting. The curator directed Anker to where it was hung, very high it seems, but told him at the same time that the work was not the original. Anker was informed that the original canvas, the one exhibited in the salon, had been inadvertantly burned in Neuilly in1848. Anker requested a ladder so that he could examine the canvas at close range and noted to Clément that it seemed to him to lack Gleyre's customary brush work. Anker asked Clément if he was aware of this substitution, since he had not mentioned it in his biography or catalogue, noting that "toute cette affaire m'a semblé bizarre." There is no record of Clément's reply to Anker, nor is there any alteration in the second edition of his biography, published years after Anker's letter. Furthermore, there is no mention in Gleyre's correspondence of 1848 that his painting was destroyed, nor is there any record of it in the Louvre documentation. It is possible that a replacement canvas, if indeed it is a copy, might account for the large differences in the measurements of the work, but since there is nothing to substantiate the curator's account, it must be assumed that it is spurious. A recent examination of the work does not indicate another hand in the painting or that the canvas is anything but Gleyre's original work.

After completing the *Apostles,* Gleyre decided to travel again to northern Italy upon the advice of Sébastien Cornu, who had recently toured

390. When the painting was registered in the salon of 1845, it bore the dimensions of 250 x 350 cm., probably including the frame. The present measurements are 195 x 273 cm. without a frame.
391. Albert Anker to Clément, 10 June 1880, now in Fleurier, CFC.

Milan and Venice. Clément noted that his goal was to study the works of the great Venetian masters for their secrets of color — it will be recalled that Gleyre had not gone to Venice on his first trip — in response to criticism of his own tendency to the monochromatic.[392] In fact, Gleyre's interests went well beyond this, and the evidence from the trip reveals yet another important element of Gleyre's creativity and invention. The trip has never been fully documented, although Clément possessed enough evidence to reconstruct its itinerary and its importance for the artist. The recent discovery of the sketchbooks, which Clément mentioned several times in passing in his text but which he had not inventoried, not only permits us to retrace Gleyre's steps, but also provides key evidence about his tastes and aims.[393]

A cursory study of these sketchbooks shows that Gleyre copied more than a hundred works of art, in virtually all media, in seven principal cities during the two months he traveled. The significance of these sketches, particularly at this point in Gleyre's life, cannot be overstressed. In Gleyre's student years in Paris and Rome, he, like all other students, copied extensively as part of the formal process of art education, but in the fall of 1845 when Gleyre embarked on this journey, he was already thirty-nine years old; he had traveled widely; he had had two major successes in the salons; and he was the master of a teaching studio. Thus the object was not to develop a sound basis in drawing and composition, but rather to refresh and refurbish his skills through intensive study of works otherwise not available to him. In a sense, then, these copies represent another phase of Gleyre's intent to constantly renew his ideas through considered examination and even experimentation. This notion will be borne out by the discussion of these works in the catalogue section, especially in regard to the works Gleyre selected to study and copy, some of which are highly unusual for the period.

The value of careful and discerning copying had been embedded in the French academic system since Colbert and was particularly emphasized in the nineteenth century, even to the point of officially establishing a Musée des Copies.[394] What has not been adequately stressed is the fact that in the nineteenth century, copying after interesting and not always officially sanctioned choices was seen as a method of providing the artist with a greater sense of originality based on traditional values. Sincere application to long analysis of the timeless secrets of different Masters was viewed by the Academy in 1858 as a means of acquiring a more specific outlook of one's own.[395] It was because of this that such diverse painters as Ingres, Fantin-Latour, Degas, and Van Gogh continued to copy other works of art throughout their careers. Although Gleyre was probably not aware of Cennino Cennini's *Il Libro dell'Arte*, he nevertheless followed his advice that the artist draw every day and when possible from varied sources in museums and churches.[396] The trip to northern Italy can be seen as an unconscious demonstration of the ideal expressed in Cennini for the enrichment of the artist.

Gleyre left Paris in early October 1845, this time traveling directly eastward to Strasbourg rather than taking the traditional route south

392. Clément, pp. 184–85.
393. Ibid., pp. 32, 69, 186, in which various notebooks are mentioned.
394. On the project, proposed by Thiers in 1834, see Boime 1964, pp. 237–47.
395. The notion is expressed in the article "La Copie" in *Dictionnaire…* 1858, pp. 262–65.
396. It is possible that Gleyre may have seen an edition while he was in Rome; the manuscript was discovered only in 1820 and published the year after. The first French edition did not appear until 1858 in a translation by Victor Mottaz, a student of Ingres. In an edition of 1911, Renoir, a student of Gleyre, added a foreword in which he noted that the apprenticeship of the artist had not changed radically since the Renaissance and thus Cennini's advice was still applicable. Cennini's notions of the importance of the copy is in section XXVII f.

100. Copy after Hans Holbein, 1845. France, Private collection (catalogue n° 489, folio 13ʳ)

through Lyons.[397] Only one copy appears to have been made in Strasbourg, among drawings of local Alsatians, and it already indicates Gleyre's taste for the primitive, in this case specifically for the Gothic. The sheet contains four separate studies of the cathedral façade, including a representation of the famed statue of Ecclesia.[398] Gleyre's drawing, like those he would make throughout the trip, is clear and exact, easily capturing not only the essential outlines of the statues, but also their sweeping Gothic spirit; Delacroix would do likewise with one of the same statues a decade later.[399] When Gleyre produced his study, however, detailed analysis of Gothic sculpture was still in its infancy; it was more often seen as a historical curiosity than as art.[400] Gleyre's decision to stop in Strasbourg may have been precisely to study these statues; at this time, Gleyre had no friends from the region.

Gleyre continued southward to Basel, which apparently he had never visited before. As in Strasbourg, his sketchbook pages indicate his continuing interest in Gothic sculpture — as is seen in several drawings of details from the cathedral façade — and also an interest in the works of Holbein. Indeed, while in Basel, Gleyre made no fewer than eight separate studies after Holbein's works, the most important of which are the copies he executed after Holbein's drawings. Copies of Old Master drawings are exceedingly rare in the nineteenth century, and Gleyre's studies, which are discussed in the catalogue section, demonstrate further the wide range of his interests. It could be noted briefly that Holbein's work was not unknown in France during this period: the Louvre possessed and exhibited five portraits,[401] and Gleyre had already copied the celebrated portrait of Erasmus in Paris. But no copies of the drawings are known in France; in fact, the vast holdings of Holbein's drawings in Basel were not published until the early twentieth century.[402] It is unlikely that the drawings in question were on exhibit when Gleyre was there, nor was the *Dance of Death* series from which he also drew. These had to be requested, which indicates that Gleyre sometimes sought out specific works, or a

fig. 100

397. An unsigned notice in *L'Artiste*, 5 October 1845, p. 23, reported that Gleyre had just left for Venice.
398. On the statuary, see Recht 1971, pp. 70f.
399. He copied one of the Virtues Conquering Vice from the left side of the west portal; Delacroix's drawing is in the Louvre, Inv. RF 9503: see Sérullaz 1984, II, n° 1373.
400. See, for example, Seroux d'Agincourt 1841, whose history of art still refers to the medieval period as one of decadence, even in the 1841 edition.
401. Brejon de Lavergnée and Thiebault 1981, II, p. 28, Inv. n° 1343–48. These were portraits of Nicolas Kratzer, William Warham, Erasmus, Henry Wyatt, and Anne of Cleves. In another sketchbook, Gleyre had sketched a portrait of Wyatt, as well as a portrait by Provost, thought at the time to have been painted by Holbein.
402. Ganz 1921, although the project dates earlier, to 1909. The Windsor Castle holdings, however, were engraved by Bartolozzi between 1792 and 1800.

specific genre of works, apart from the more easily accessible examples on view in public museums.

Gleyre took the traditional route through Switzerland, passing through Zürich, where he apparently made no studies, stopping instead in Chur, which he would revisit twenty-seven years later with Clément and his father-in-law, Fritz Berthoud. Gleyre only produced three drawings here, but the most striking sheet shows one of the medieval columns in front of the cathedral, another example of Gleyre's interest in the primitive. The drawing also has historical importance in that it is one of very few that show the odd disposition of the statuary before its dismantlement at the end of the century.[403]

It is not certain which route Gleyre followed in traversing the Alps, but it is likely that from Chur he passed through Bellinzona and Lugano before reaching Milan by the end of October 1845. As he had done seventeen years earlier, Gleyre again went to the Brera, where he copied extensively, but he noted that the genuine masterpieces were hidden by modern Italian works that he thought "pitoyable."[404] He also indicated in a letter to Cornu that he went to the Ambrosiana, where, as the sketchbooks show, he copied a detail from an altarpiece by the then little-known painter, Zenale.[405] Gleyre visited Santa Maria della Grazie, which he had not done before as Clément noted. He sought out the Crucifixion fresco by Gaudenzio Ferrari in the Santa Corona chapel, not surprising considering the artist's uncommon celebrity at the time and the fact that Gleyre had already copied examples of Ferrari's work in the Brera.[406] But clearly Gleyre's primary object here was to examine Leonardo's fresco, whose principal figures he diligently copied on a large sheet separate from the sketchbooks. The critic Gustave Planche saw these studies in Gleyre's studio before 1851 and admired their precision and sensitivity, which he thought captured the spirit of Leonardo's work even more faithfully than the highly praised prints by Morghen.[407] Gleyre also permitted other friends to examine these copies, as Juste Olivier did in 1863, when he strongly advised his daughter Thérèse to study them before her own trip to Milan.[408]

Gleyre's admiration for Leonardo's work went beyond the *Last Supper*. While visiting Santa Maria della Grazie, he also saw the collection of Giocomotto della Tela in the Corso Magenta, which contained numerous fresco lunettes of portraits of the Sforza family, then attributed to Leonardo.[409] Gleyre copied seven of these and may in fact have been one of the first nineteenth-century artists to have particularly sought out these works in the collection.

fig. 101   Gleyre's interest in Luini goes back to his first journey to Milan, when in his travel notes he remarked upon the "fresques de Luini," referring no doubt to those of Santa Maria della Pace, which he had copied then.[410] This time, however, Gleyre significantly augmented his own study of Luini's works through extensive visits to San Maurizio,[411] where he made six drawings, and sought out other works by the artist in the Oratorio de Greco and Santa Maria di Brera. Interest in France at this time in Luini's work was hardly unusual — indeed, he was considered the worthy suc-

101. Copy after Bernardino Luini, 1845. France, Private collection (catalogue n° 489, folio 8ʳ)

403. See Poeschel 1948, p. 91, and Gandy 1921, I, pls. 76–77, for late nineteenth-century photographs of the column with the lion on the lintel as Gleyre represented it.
404. Letter to Cornu, in Lausanne, MCBA, GA 988.
405. Natale 1982, p. 19, on Zenale's art as understood in the nineteenth century, when he was often confused with Leonardo. The first authoritative work on Zenale is in Crowe and Cavacaselle 1871, II, pp. 38f.
406. Monographs on Ferrari had appeared in 1821 and 1835, the latter with engravings of his work. In France, he was greatly admired by Blanc and the biography in the Larousse noted that he merited an enormous place in the history of art. On Ferrari, see Mallé 1969, especially pp. 18f. Gleyre may have already known the painter's *Saint Paul in Meditation*, which was taken by the French troops in Milan and deposited in the Louvre in 1797.
407. Planche 1851, p. 492. Planche's reference is to the highly regarded prints of the painting by Rafaello Morghen (1758–1833), who was an assistant to the famed engraver Volpato.
408. See Olivier's letter to his daughter Thérèse, Lausanne, BCU/DM, Fonds Olivier, IS 1905/43, dossier 1863; Thérèse went to Milan in the fall of 1863.
409. Fioro and Garberi 1987, p. 90. These works were also noted as by Leonardo in Caselli 1827, p. 162, and Cassina 1840. The frescoes entered the Castello Sforzesco collection only in 1902, where they were ascribed to Bernardino Luini and his circle.
410. Clément, p. 31.
411. Della Chiesa 1982.

cessor of Leonardesque charm, sentimentality, and technique — but rarely had artists studied his works as assiduously as did Gleyre.[412] Even as late as 1872, Gleyre did not miss the opportunity to provide a lecture on Luini's fresco in Lugano for his fellow travelers, Clément and Berthoud.[413]

In describing the voyage of 1845, Clément noted the importance of his stay in Milan and provided detailed information on Gleyre's impressions of Venice, but he was totally silent on other aspects of the trip, including the full itinerary. From the evidence of the sketchbooks, it is now clear that after Milan, Gleyre stopped for several days in Verona. In the nineteenth century, stops in Verona were usual because of its link to the route to Venice and because of the romanticism attached to the city through Shakespeare, but relatively few French artists sought out the artistic treasures in the city. Knowledge of the works found here had already been made available in France through the publication in 1751 of Cochin's guide — which catalogued more than a hundred works of art by thirty artists in the city collections as well as those in the celebrated private collections of the Bevilacqua and Maffei families — and later in the early nineteenth century through various other guides.[414] But evidently few artists found these works worthy of extensive study.

Gleyre, like many other French travelers, probably stayed in the Auberge des Deux-Tours near the church of Sant'Anastasia. As before, he wished to examine the rich tradition of Gothic sculpture and painting, particularly in the church itself. Many writers — including Mme. Vigée-Lebrun[415] — had noted the charms and bizarre antique quality of the works in the church, but few were able at this point in the nineteenth century to grasp the importance of the pre-Giottesque frescoes here. Even John Ruskin, who had a refined sense of the Gothic when it was still considered decadent, as late as 1872 noted that Sant'Anastasia "contains nothing which deserves extraordinary praise," adding that the church offers "a quarter of an hour's attention."[416]

Gleyre's few studies from the frescoes in the church demonstrate anew his interest in early Italian painting at a time when such admiration was still uncommon.[417] It is unlikely that Gleyre was aware that some of the frescoes were by Altichiero or Martino da Verona; many of the works were identified as either by followers of Giotto or simply by anonymous hands, and many were not mentioned even by the most discerning guidebooks to the region.[418] Gleyre also made studies in the even less frequented church of San Fermo, where he copied some figures from the fourteenth-century Crucifixion by Turone, as well a sixteenth-century painting by Caroto.[419] This diversity, which becomes more evident in the last leg of the trip, supports Planche's view that Gleyre's interest in Italian art encompassed styles and artists not yet fully recognized by the painter's contemporaries.[420]

Gleyre continued eastward after his stay in Verona, stopping briefly in Vicenza. The few works produced here also indicate Gleyre's varied interests, but in another context. In 1845, there was no official city museum — the Museo Civico was inaugurated a decade later — but the ar-

412. See especially Chiara 1975. It should be noted that Luini was amply praised in Lanzi's *Storia*, but the first French study of his works was Gauthiez 1905, from four articles published in the *Gazette des Beaux-Arts*, 1899–1900.

413. Berthoud 1898, p. 126.

414. See Poli 1984, p. 90, for a discussion of the importance of Cochin's trip and his introduction to private collections in Verona. Charles-Nicolas Cochin (1715–90) was himself a well-known draftsman and engraver, and his *Voyage en Italie*, 1751, was subtitled "Un recueil de notes sur les ouvrages de peinture et de sculpture qu'on voit dans les principales villes d'Italie." For nineteenth-century guides, see Poli 1984, pp. 163f.

415. Vigée-Lebrun 1835–37, I, p. 255.

416. For Ruskin's views on Verona, see Ruskin 1972 and Hewison 1978.

417. See Seroux d'Agincourt 1841, and Haskell 1980, pp. 85f.

418. See Mellini 1965 on the subject of the nineteenth-century view of these frescoes; see Poli for various guidebooks which describe the church.

419. The basic study of the church is still Lisca 1909. A detailed description of the church also appeared in Bennassuti 1831, pp. 51f.

420. Planche 1851, p. 491.

tistic works belonging to the commune were generally exhibited in the Salone della Confraternità de Rossi on the upper floor of the Oratorio de San Cristoforo.[421] The collection on view was limited to fifteenth- and sixteenth-century works by artists of the region. Gleyre copied paintings by Cima and Buonconsiglio with the same care and attention as the primitive frescoes in Verona. He seemed uninterested, however, in the many examples of Palladian architecture in the city, and indeed during the trip limited his architectural views — a genre which suited his temperament, as the Egyptian sketches show — to pre-Renaissance examples.

If Gleyre's interest in the frescoes of the fourteenth century was aroused by his stay in Verona, it was heightened by his visit to Padua, where he stopped twice in November.[422] Dozens of works attest to his enlightened study of the frescoes in the Eremitani, the Oratorio di San Giorgio, and even the Palazzo della Ragione.[423] It is clear that the abundant works of Altichiero in Padua fascinated Gleyre, as can be seen in five separate sheets reproducing figures from various works by the artist. The name Altichiero was not altogether unknown at the time, but it was not generally associated with the frescoes in Padua. Indeed, in Jules Lecomte's guide to the area, the works in the Eremitani, which he highly recommended to the traveler, were attributed to Giotto.[424] In Moschini's guide to Padua, the frescoes in the Oratorio di San Giorgio and the Eremitani were correctly attributed to Avanzi and "Aldighieri."[425] Maria Graham, the indefatigable traveler and connoisseur, referred to the works in Padua as by Altichiero and added that they had a certain "dignity amounting to grandeur."[426] Thus, it is not unlikely that Gleyre in this instance recognized these frescoes not as works by Giotto or his followers, but by the lesser known master, and that he nevertheless thought they deserved admiration and artistic attention. Although many French artists passed through Padua on their way to Venice, including such rigid Academicians as the Flandrin brothers in 1837, there is no substantial evidence to suggest that any of them were particularly interested in examining Altichiero's frescoes, except as a tourist curiosity.[427]

Planche remarked in 1851 that while he himself was in Padua, he had often admired "une petite église dont les murailles tout entières sont décorées par Giotto."[428] In reviewing Gleyre's drawings from Padua, Planche noted that even the Arena Chapel frescoes had been copied in their entirety with such fidelity that "je me croyais encore à Padoue." This statement is curious, since the only study directly from the chapel found in Gleyre's sketchbooks is the single drawing of Giotto's figure of Despair at the bottom level of the decoration cycle, but Clément noted as well that Gleyre had sixteen pages "où il a reproduit la plus grande partie des compositions de Giotto à l'*Arena* de Padoue."[429] Except for the aforementioned drawing, no other copies of these works by Gleyre have been found, indicating either that another sketchbook existed, or that Gleyre copied the frescoes on separate sheets, as he did Leonardo's *Last Supper* in Milan, which subsequently have disappeared. There is no reason to doubt Planche's assertion nor Clément's remark, since by the time he wrote the biography, the Arena Chapel frescoes were well documented.

fig. 102

102. Copy after Giotto, 1845. France, Private collection (catalogue n° 490, folio 28ʳ)

421. See Fasolo 1940 and Ballarin 1982 for the prehistory of the museum. The collection in Gleyre's time was set forth in Barbieri 1962.
422. Clément, p. 186, where a letter from Gleyre to Cornu is cited in which he says "je m'arrêterai encore à Padoue."
423. See Mor et al. 1963, for the history of the Palazzo in the nineteenth century.
424. Lecomte 1844, p. 364. Studies on Altichiero were published by Moschini in 1826, but the first monographic work on him was Schubring 1898; the first article in French did not appear until 1910. Mellini 1965 gives the basic bibliographical studies on the artist in the nineteenth century.
425. Moschini 1817, pp. 44f.
426. Cited in Haskell 1980, p. 92, from her *Essays Towards the History of Painting* (London, 1836), published under her married name of Lady Callcott.
427. On the Flandrins' stay here, see Foucart 1984–85, p. 271, and n° 179 of the catalogue for one example of the drawings Hippolyte made in Padua.
428. Planche 1851, p. 492.
429. Clément, p. 32.

Considering Gleyre's esteem for fourteenth-century Italian art, it is hardly surprising that he was attracted to the Arena Chapel, although none of his letters makes mention of it. In 1845 Giotto's decorations were not yet a common focus for artistic study by visiting French artists. The opinion expressed in Brandolese's guide to the art of Padua, published fifty years before Gleyre's visit, in which the frescoes are seen as a "bizarra invenzione," more curious than artistically valuable, still prevailed in the early nineteenth century.[430] Some visiting artists were pleasantly surprised by, but hardly prepared for, the dramatic impact of the frescoes, as happened with the English painter William Hilton in 1825 or David Wilke the following year.[431] When Maria Graham visited Padua in 1827, she too was stunned by the works, as she had been by the grandeur of Altichiero's frescoes, and with her husband Augustus Callcott produced, in 1835, the first published illustrations of Giotto's cycle.[432] The Flandrin brothers, too, thought the chapel a jewel, exquisite in its harmonies, but their adulation was not yet typical, as can be measured from Jules Lecomte's guide of 1844.[433] Even the perceptive Ruskin, who was in Padua less than one month before Gleyre, apparently did not take the time to see the chapel during this visit.[434] Two decades later Gleyre recommended the Arena Chapel as an important monument of study to at least one favored student. He even played a minor role in the effort to acquire the chapel for the Louvre at a time when it was still in private hands and for sale.[435]

In early November, Gleyre finally reached Venice. He complained of the grey, the uncommon chill, the fact that he seemed to get lost constantly in the labyrinthine streets. He was, nevertheless, charmed by the city as a whole and noted in a letter to Cornu that the treasures there were truly remarkable. Unlike Ruskin, who was in Venice at virtually the same time, Gleyre made no comments about the blatant neglect of the works of art or the difficulty of analyzing them at ease. During this second trip to the city, Ruskin was deeply disappointed to see that much of the enchantment was destroyed by such frivolities as the widespread installation of gas lights, which reminded him too much of Liverpool, and the insensitive manner in which the present restoration of the facade of San Marco ignored the delicate state of the statuary.[436] Gleyre's sketchbooks reveal that he was highly active here, producing almost half of his entire output from the trip during the two weeks he spent in Venice.

As might be expected from what has already been written about his tastes, Gleyre particularly searched out early works of art, and he paid much attention to the Byzantine mosaics of San Marco, as at least six separate sheets in the sketchbooks attest. Again, Gleyre's interest in these works was unusual for the period. In contrast, William Hilton, who arrived in Venice on 27 September 1825, wrote that the mosaics were "curious" and not particularly "fine specimens."[437] Louis Simond, a professional traveler and sensitive author of guidebooks, remarked on the mixture of styles in San Marco as evidence of the bad taste of the Middle Ages and did not even mention the mosaics inside.[438] Similarly, Jules Lecomte wrote in 1844 that the reliefs on the exterior of San Marco were

430. Brandolese 1795, p. 213.
431. Hilton wrote of his surprise and pleasure in the Arena Chapel in a letter of 22 October 1825; see Pointon 1972, p. 346. See too Hazlitt 1826, p. 205. The latter, however, thought Giotto's works imperfect, "like the attempts of a deformed person at grace."
432. [Callcott] 1835. The text contains only nineteen pages; the six plates by AWC, Augustus Wall Callcott, are "to be looked upon as recollections rather than facsimiles." D'Hancarville's illustrations of three scenes from the chapel for Selvatico 1836 are the first illustrations that reproduce the actual frescoes, including fourteen Virtues and Vices. On the importance of Selvatico's work on Giotto and maintaining the chapel, see Bernabei 1974.
433. On Flandrin's opinion, see Hippolyte's letter to Eugène Robert, 10 October 1837, in Flandrin 1902, p. 69; and see Lecomte 1844, p. 364, for his view of the chapel.
434. Ruskin visited Padua on 14 and 15 October 1845, having already spent almost a month in Venice. He wrote two letters to his father from Padua; see Ruskin 1972, pp. 224–25; see also, p. 227, a letter from Simplon in which he noted that he was slightly ill while in Padua. Ruskin did not keep a journal of his 1845 journey — his diary ends in October 1844 and resumes on 4 January 1846.
435. On the history of the chapel in the nineteenth century, see Spiazzi 1982, pp. 13–58. Gleyre's role in the proposed purchase of the chapel will be discussed in a later chapter.
436. Clément, p. 185, reproduces a fragment of Gleyre's letter to Cornu; the full document is in Lausanne, MCBA, GA 988. See letters of 10 and 14 September 1845 in Ruskin 1972, pp. 198–99 and 201–202. Ruskin noted as well that there was scaffolding on many of the major buildings.
437. F. 82ᵛ of his notebook, cited in Pointon 1972, p. 346, contains his reaction when he first saw the mosaics on 27 September 1825.
438. Simond 1828, p. 41.

simply "bizarre" and the mosaics on the interior admirable but not worthy of lengthy examination.[439] In an undated letter to Cornu,[440] Gleyre revealed that he studied the mosaics with great care, even under conditions that were less than ideal. He complained that the mosaics were so high and so inadequately lit that he was forced to look at them for a long time in order to discern a clear image. The letter demonstrates Gleyre's understanding of the mosaics as unusually refined: he noted that he could "reconnaître le principe de la couleur vénitienne dans ces vieilles images." If Clément is correct that Gleyre's initial purpose in undertaking the trip was to study further the effects of color in Venetian painting, then it seems ironic that he found the Byzantine mosaics more revealing than the works of Titian or Veronese.

Gleyre's engagement with Byzantine art — he had already seen some examples in Sicily and Asia Minor with Lowell — extended beyond the San Marco frescoes. One drawing provides evidence of a visit to Torcello, where he copied one figure, despite Lecomte's view that these works were "affreux," an evaluation that must have typified the taste of the period.[441] We know as well that Gleyre copied portions of the Pala d'Oro, which Lecomte thought to be "plein de grandeur" and of inestimable value.[442] Lecomte had noted that the altar was not wholly visible in 1844 and was confined to a special, closed room behind the basilica, but when Gleyre sketched the altar, it was recently restored and in pristine condition.

Gleyre's interests in Venice were not confined to the Byzantine period, and dozens of sketches made in the Accademia show his attention to the works of Titian, Carpaccio, Bellini, and many lesser-known figures. Similarly, several studies after Classical statues, some from the celebrated Grimani collection, demonstrate Gleyre's zeal for the antique art that he saw in the archaeological museum, then housed in the Ducal Palace.[443] We know as well that Gleyre intended to visit the Museo Correr, but the recent death of the curator prevented access.[444]

Of special interest among Gleyre's Venetian sketches is a sheet in the sketchbook that shows four separate copies on the same page. These copies provide further evidence of the originality of Gleyre's taste, his diligence in exploring obscure and rarely visited collections, and also document little known details of two of the works.

The copy at the bottom left of the sketchbook page is of Titian's *Tityus*, long thought to represent Prometheus because of the similarity of their attributes.[445] Gleyre had already copied Titian's *Saint Jerome* in Milan and would study his *Madonna and Child* in Spain during a trip there, for which we have no dates. The *Tityus* was commissioned in 1548, as part of a series of four works, by Mary of Hungary, sister of Charles V, for her château near Brussels. After the invasion of the French, she sought exile in Spain, where she died in 1558; the painting was listed then in her inventory. The canvas remained in Madrid, escaping a fire in 1734 that claimed another one of the series, and eventually entered the Prado where it has since remained. Yet, the drawing of the *Tityus* on the sheet among other copies of paintings seen in situ suggests that Gleyre saw the painting itself and not a print of it, and clearly not in Madrid, since the sheet

fig. 103

439. See Lecomte 1844, p. 46, for comments on the bas-reliefs, and p. 85 on the mosaics.
440. Clément, p. 185.
441. Lecomte 1844, pp. 580–83.
442. Ibid., pp. 593–94. In contrast, Simond did not mention the altar in his description of the interior.
443. On the prehistory of the museum, see Traversari 1973 and 1986.
444. For the history of the museum, opened to the public only nine years before Gleyre's visit, see Romanelli 1984, p. 7. At the time of Gleyre's visit, the museum was in fact only open on Wednesdays and Saturdays. The director must have been D'Agarotti, who in fact died just before Gleyre's visit.
445. On the iconographic elements of the picture, see Panofsky 1969, pp. 147f. The following information on the drawing in question is developed further in Hauptman 1994(a), pp. 79–82.

151

103. Copies after Giorgione, Titian, and Alvise Vivarini, 1845. France, Private collection (catalogue n° 490, folio 14ʳ)

is bound in the Venetian sketchbook. Only one solution can logically emerge from this curious circumstance: namely, that Gleyre saw and drew Titian's own copy of his painting, which in 1845 was in the private collection of the Barbarigo della Terrazza family. This painting, then called *Prometheus,* was sold by the family in 1850 to the Tsar of Russia and has subsequently disappeared.[446] Thus, Gleyre's drawing, which shows small but nevertheless discernible differences from the original in the Prado, is the only extant study of Titian's copy.

In order to inform himself about which collections to see in the limited time available to him, Gleyre probably relied on specialized guidebooks, perhaps Quadri's guide to Venice, which was particularly informative on private collections. The Palazzo Barbarigo is described as particularly attractive, with its facade facing the Rio di San Paolo, and various notable works by Canova and "une galerie de tableaux précieux particulièrement de Titien."[447] Moreover, in Paoletti's study, the Barbarigo collection is also highly recommended, but more for its holdings of Canova than the other works.[448]

The second work on the sheet of Gleyre's sketchbook that is especially significant is his copy of Giorgione's *Tempest* on the upper right. Giorgione's art was little known in the early nineteenth century; his artistic fame rested almost solely on hearsay and on his *Concert champêtre* which had been in the Louvre since the seventeenth century. Giorgione's reputation was more firmly established among nineteenth-century romantic writers than among painters because of undocumented notions about his eccentric life. It is this myth of Giorgione that inspires the numerous references in French writings before 1850, especially in the works of Chateaubriand, Stendhal, Balzac, Gautier, de Musset, and others.[449] Similarly, Giorgione's image appears in the stream of paintings depicting the lives of past masters, such as Henri Bacon's canvas of 1844

446. Levi 1900, p. 287.
447. Quadri 1828, pp. 169f. Quadri's guide was first published in Italian in 1821–22 and by 1828 it was already in its fourth Italian and second French editions. Both were republished once again in 1840. On the history of the Titian collection in the Palazzo Barbarigo, see Siebenhüner 1981, p. 30 for the *Tityus.*
448. Paoletti 1840, III, p. 114, for his discussion of Canova's *Dedalus* in the collection, but see as well pp. 194–95.
449. Very little was known about Giorgione's life before the end of the nineteenth century. See Chastel 1981, pp. 565f.; and Dédéyan 1981, pp. 659f.

that portrays him in the act of painting a portrait of Gaston de Foix.[450] Gleyre's awareness of Giorgione and his art before he left Paris was therefore limited at best.

Regarding the *Tempest* more specifically, it is surprising to us today that before the middle of the century, the painting is hardly mentioned in the documents and only in connection with the sixteenth-century inventories of the Vendramin collection. In 1855 the Swiss historian Jacob Burckhardt recognized the work in the Manfrin collection in Venice and thus "discovered" the lost masterpiece.[451] The earliest study devoted exclusively to the painting was by Reinhardt in 1866; it also contained the first engraved copy of the painting. But still the work was hardly famous or highly regarded: in Walter Pater's essay of 1877 on the school of Giorgione, the *Tempest* is not directly examined in the context of Giorgione's work.[452] Thus, Gleyre's copy of the work, duly labeled as a Giorgione although the name is misspelled, came a full decade before its notice by Burckhardt and suggests that Gleyre instinctively recognized its intrinsic artistic value and mystery.[453]

It must be assumed that Gleyre had come across the work by accident, as Burckhardt did, although he was certainly aware of the rich holdings of the Manfrin collection. Quadri's guide spends three and a half pages describing the collection, but it actually provides few details on the works themselves since each of the ten picture galleries were said to have a small catalogue to instruct visitors about the paintings. Among the works Quadri noted as being exceptionally interesting — paintings by Bellini, Titian, Carracci, Mantegna, Reni, and "Barthelemi Moriglio, peintre espagnol, dont les ouvrages sont très rares en Italie" — only two are labeled as being by Giorgione: "Une femme qui pince la guitare," displayed in the first salon near Battoni's *Triumph of Venus*, and "les Trois portraits" in the second salon near Titian's portrait of Ariosto.[454] Nor does Paoletti's guide indicate the existence of the *Tempest* in the same collection, even as the work of another artist.[455]

On 25 October 1845 while Gleyre was in Venice, the Conseil d'Etat in Lausanne decided to offer Gleyre the directorship of the new museum, as well as a post as the drawing teacher. The letter offering the position, written by the radical politician Henri Druey, noted that Gleyre was chosen because of his artistic reputation, which was already known in Switzerland and did honor to his origins.[456] Druey stipulated that normally the combined post of director and drawing teacher paid an annual salary of 1,750 Swiss francs — about 2,500 French francs at this time; the teaching duties were twelve hours per week except for major holidays. However, in light of Gleyre's celebrity and reputation that figure could be increased to 2,000 or 2,400 francs per year, a sum, Druey wrote, fully in accord with the cost of living in Lausanne. Gleyre was urged to accept the offer and was told that he could take up the position at his convenience when his affairs in Paris permitted.

Druey's letter was sent to the Swiss Minister of Affairs in Paris, Georges de Tschann, who was not aware that Gleyre was in Italy at the time; on 5 November he left the letter with Gleyre's concierge in Paris.[457] Gleyre

450. In the salon of 1844, livret n° 68.
451. Burckhardt 1978, p. 313. Haskell 1980, pp. 21–22, asserts that between 1530 and 1855 the painting had all but disappeared from public view, but see n. 453 below.
452. On Pater and Giorgione, see Sutton 1979, pp. 339–42.
453. The drawing is more fully discussed in Hauptman 1994(a), pp. 78–82. While Gleyre's copy verifies that he saw the painting before Burckhardt, this citation of the work is hardly unique; my article discusses various writers and critics who in fact saw the painting well before Burckhardt's discovery.
454. Quardi 1828, p. 187.
455. Paoletti 1840, III, pp. 40–41.
456. The original letter is in Lausanne, MCBA, GA 996 and a draft is in Lausanne, BCU/DM, Fonds Druey, IS 3442. On Druey, see Lasserre 1970, who makes no mention of his relationship to Gleyre.
457. Lausanne, ACE, Conseil d'Etat, Lettres à l'extérieur du canton, p. 17, n° 46, and p. 21, n° 59. This information is also to be found in Lausanne, ACV, Conseil d'Etat, Registres des délibérations, n° 138, session of 5 November 1845, p. 344, item 23.

104. *The Virgin with the Two Children*, 1846. Switzerland, Private collection (catalogue n° 496)

105. *The Nymph Echo*, 1846. Solothurn, Collection Dr. H. Vogt-Kofmehl (catalogue n° 504)

458. Bonjour 1905, p. 44.
459. Clément, p. 186, takes this information from a letter to Cornu in which Gleyre writes that after the second stop in Padua, "je file droit sur Lausanne." Gleyre's arrival in Paris is mentioned in a letter from Sainte-Beuve to Olivier of 8 December 1845; see too Albert de Meuron's letter to his father of 10 December 1845 in Neuchâtel, AE, Fonds de Meuron, dossier 68¹.
460. Clément, p. 242; Montégut 1878, p. 414.
461. Clément, pp. 189f.
462. Planche 1851, p. 502.

was no doubt surprised by Druey's offer and surely must have considered the advantage of having a steady financial income after years of poverty. But he declined the invitation, perhaps because he thought Lausanne, which then was a provincial city with little cultural base, was too much removed from Paris where he had strong professional and personal ties. When Gleyre refused the offer — his letter to Druey is not extant — the position went to Jean-Samson Guignard, a local painter who eventually served for four years.[458]

Gleyre returned to Paris in December 1845, passing this time through Lausanne.[459] Gleyre's immediate interest after his return was in translating his Italian experiences into paintings. In early 1846, he began a series of works influenced by the Venetian light and color, a response to critics such as Delécluze who had remarked on his monochromatic palette. Among the works Gleyre began was a Virgin with Child that Clément called *La Vierge de Venise,* which wholly reflected his study of Raphael and Corregio.[460] Several other religious canvases were also begun at this time, but his most significant painting influenced by the Italian trip was *The Nymph Echo.*

fig. 104

fig. 105

Clément rightly thought the work a masterpiece of grace and elegance heretofore unknown in Gleyre's painting.[461] Actually, the composition and the main figure may be said to derive from a study of the allegory of Agriculture — one of the studies Gleyre made for the commission of Dampierre. But the bright, rich Venetian colors reveal the influence of Italian prototypes. This view was shared by Planche, who likewise hailed the work, noting a new vibrancy in Gleyre's art.[462] Planche, however, was the only Paris critic to see the work. On 2 September, Gleyre wrote to Mme. Cornu that the painting was already packed to be sent to Cologne

106. *Portrait of Achmad Bey*, 1846–47. Tunis, Collection Bardo (catalogue n° 512)
107. *Portrait of Benayet*, 1846–47. Present location unknown (catalogue n° 514)
108. *Portrait of Baron Raffo*, 1846–47. Tunis, Institut National d'Archéologie et d'Art (catalogue n° 517)

to a banker, Mr. Herstatt, who had bought it.[463] Because Gleyre informed Mme. Cornu of this and because he later gave her the study for the painting, it may be assumed that she had negotiated the sale of the work.

In late 1846 Gleyre was involved in a commission for a group of portraits of Tunisian officials. Clément listed the paintings in his catalogue but did not discuss them in his text. Moreover, he never saw the actual works, except in engravings, and by the mid-1870s was not certain where they were. The portraits are of Achmad Bey, the ruler of Tunisia, and his two ministers, Benayet and Raffo. There are no documents in the Paris archives to explain how the commission came to Gleyre; efforts to locate information in Tunis have failed.[464] It may be assumed that the intermediary between Gleyre and the royal party was Gleyre's old friend Jourdain, who had worked in Tunis from 1841 to 1843. In 1840, the Bey of Tunis gave France a parcel of land near La Goulette where Saint Louis was said to have died in 1270. It was decided that a special chapel should be erected on the site in commemoration of the event, and Jourdain was the architect charged with the commission.[465] Jourdain knew the Bey personally and had even made a portrait of him in a pseudo-Arab style.

Achmad Bey was born in Tunisia — his mother was Christian, however — in 1806.[466] He succeeded to the throne in 1837 and devoted his life to modernizing his still backward country; in 1841, in an extremely bold step for North Africa, he abolished slavery and began extensive land reforms. He was widely regarded in France as a wise ruler and deliberate statesman, one of the few in Africa who was respected in Europe; he was awarded the Legion of Honor in 1845.[467] He went to France, however, only once, in November and December 1846. He landed in Toulon on

fig. 106
fig. 107–108

fig. 109

463. Clément, p. 191, gives the destination of the painting as Mr. Herstatt, while the original letter indicates Mme. Herstatt, who in all likelihood was a friend of Mme. Cornu.
464. Efforts on my behalf by the Swiss ambassador to Tunis, Mr. Heinz Langenbacher, and his chargé d'affaires, Mr. Bruno Knellwolf, to locate pertinent information were unsuccessful. I owe the present photographs to them, however.
465. *L'Illustration*, 23 September 1843, p. 55.
466. For his biography, the essential sources is Brown 1974. See Guizot's opinion of his statecraft in Guizot 1858–66, VII, pp. 239f.
467. Mallon 1931, p. 170.

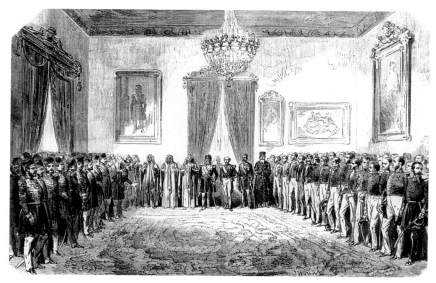

fig. 110   8 November, an event widely reported in the journals of the day, and went to Paris a few days later. As his party stopped along the way, he often gave sizable sums in charity: he offered 1,200 francs to the poor of Moulin, 2,500 francs to the poor of Lyons, and 50,000 francs to the victims of a devastating flood that inundated Roanne in mid-October of that year.[468]

He arrived in Paris on 23 November with his entourage, including his minister of Finance, Benayet, and his minister of Foreign Affairs, the Italian Baron Giuseppe Raffo. His activities in Paris were reported in the press almost daily with minute precision. It was never noted, however, that Gleyre was engaged to paint the portrait of the Bey and his ministers. In fact, the only commission noted in the press was the one given to La Rivière, a pupil of Gros and Girodet, for a portrait of the Bey to be hung in Versailles.[469] Yet it must be supposed that Gleyre painted the portraits at this time, since the Bey never returned to France, nor did Gleyre ever visit Tunisia. Apparently Gleyre's portrait of the Bey was taken or later sent to Tunisia where it hung in one of the main salons of the palace, as indicated in a print of 1858 where the portrait can be seen at

fig. 111   the left.

109. Charles Jourdain, *Achmad Bey*. From *L'Illustration*, 7 November 1846, p. 153
110. Anonymous, *Arrival of the Bey of Tunis in Toulon*. From *L'Illustration*, 21 November 1846, p. 192
111. Anonymous, *Proclamation of Reforms by the Bey of Tunis*. From *L'Illustration*, 30 January 1858, p. 72

468. For the gift to Lyons, see *Le Moniteur universel*, 17 November 1846; to Moulin, see 23 November. The gift to Roanne is described in *Journal des débats*, 23 November; for the flood itself, see *L'Illustration*, 7 November 1846.
469. This was reported in *Le Moniteur universel* on 2 December 1846. The painter was rewarded by the Bey with the order of Nichan, and was given a snuff box in gold and diamonds with the arms of the Bey encrusted on it; see *Journal des débats*, 16 December 1846.

The three portraits Gleyre executed are formal ones, in accord with the dignity of the respective models. Each costume is ornate, prompting Gleyre to use rich detail so as to bring out the textural qualities. The portraits of Benayet and Raffo have landscape backgrounds showing the port of Tunis, which Gleyre must have made after prints or from material provided by Jourdain. The only studies known for each of the portraits are drawings for the hands, which Clément did not catalogue properly since he did not have the actual portraits available to him.

In the years that followed Gleyre's second Italian trip, his life became more regular and established in the studio in the rue du Bac. Clément, among others, recounted aspects of his routine during this period.[470] His studio was frequented by painters, writers, and critics, among whom were friends such as Nanteuil, Denuelle, Chenavard, Quinet, Cornu, and, by this time, Clément himself and the celebrated Vaudois poet Juste Olivier, with whom Gleyre would shortly be in very close contact. All of these friends were aware that Gleyre was disturbed by frequent guests and therefore they instigated a "mot de passe" when his door was locked: it consisted of three soft but insistent knocks on the door, the signal that the visitor was indeed a close friend. During these years, Planche in fact used the studio as a base of operations; Planche's friends considered the rue du Bac to be his permanent address. Planche in turn introduced Gleyre to important publishers, including Buloz and Hetzel whose portrait Gleyre drew around 1848. Another frequent visitor was the famous black model Joseph, who had posed for Géricault's *Raft of the Medusa* and who often regaled invited guests with anecdotes about artists for whom he had sat.[471] Joseph was now too old to pose and in difficult financial straits, and Gleyre, with his usual generosity, hired him to clean his palettes and brushes. Montfort and Lehoux, who had cared for Gleyre in Lebanon, were also frequent guests for afternoon tea, presented in Arab style with everyone sitting on the floor.

Gleyre's studio was also filled with a variety of pets, including the monkey Adam, sometimes called Jack, the same that he had brought with him from Egypt, as well as cats and dogs, exotic birds, and even a favored pigeon. These animals generally caused havoc in the studio: Adam was known to amuse himself by tearing drawings Gleyre had left on the table, and once he urinated on one of Gleyre's paintings. When Gleyre was absent from Paris, the menagerie was looked after by the Oliviers; at times, the monkey stayed in the Olivier apartment in the elegant Place des Vosges, much to the disgust of Mme. Olivier, who had enormous affection for Gleyre but not, apparently, for the monkey.[472]

Gleyre was an habitué of the Parisian cafés and could often be found at the Café d'Orsay near his studio, or at the Café Caron, where he liked to dine. It was at the former that Gleyre was known to spend afternoons reading all of the newspapers of the day. In the evenings, he went frequently to the Taverne Anglaise on the rue Saint-Marc, usually in the company of Clément, or to the celebrated Divan Lepeltier where he seems to have been a regular client. He also stopped often at the Café de la Régence to play a game of chess with Alfred de Musset.[473] Gleyre and de

470. Clément, pp. 204f.
471. On the colorful career of Joseph, see Bédollière 1858, I, p. 370. On his role in the *Medusa* of Géricault, see Eitner 1972, p. 32.
472. See various references to Mme. Olivier having to take care of the animals in Lausanne, BCU/DM, IS 1905/43, dossier 1848.
473. Gleyre almost certainly met de Musset at Olivier's rooms around 1846; see Perrochon 1948, p. 203, and Musset 1877, p. 347.

Musset, we are told, walked the streets afterwards, discussing art and poetry.[474]

Gleyre preferred to work on his canvases only when he was assured a full day without significant interruption. Otherwise he would stand before his unfinished works, studying them from various perspectives, a form of creative idleness. He worked directly from models, usually quickly so that he could capture the essential elements of the pose or gesture before transfer to the canvas. He always painted in a standing position, wearing his working glasses, and generally worked most efficiently in the morning when the light was best. He permitted only Clément and Olivier to enter when he was absent — they were authorized to get the key from the concierge — but, as both admitted later, it was a privilege that they used only rarely.[475]

Gleyre's major project after 1846 was the completion of a commission given him by the canton of Vaud, about which more will be said later. Apart from that work, the most significant painting begun and completed in the period under discussion was a large representation of *The Dance of* fig. 112 *the Bacchantes*. The work follows the pattern of Classical imagery of *Le Soir* and reiterates Gleyre's interest in Classical iconography after the second Italian sojourn.

112. *The Dance of the Bacchantes*, 1849. Lausanne, Musée Cantonal des Beaux-Arts (catalogue n° 529)

474. Clément, p. 215.
475. Olivier noted it in a letter in Lausanne, BCU/DM, Fonds Olivier, IS 1905/43, dossier 1848; Clément, p. 213.

159

113. Anonymous, *Don Francisco d'Asis de Borbon.* From *L'Illustration*, 26 September 1846, p. 52

114. *The Dance of the Bacchantes*, 1849. Detail of illustration 112

476. Letter of 23 March 1848 in Fleurier, CFC.
477. Letter of 2 May 1848 in Fleurier, CFC.
478. Clément, p. 218.
479. The letter is not dated, but cannot have been written much later than the summer of 1848; the original is in Fleurier, CFC.
480. Clément, p. 195.
481. Letter in Fleurier, CFC. As will be seen in the catalogue section, the price Mme. Olivier cited is not correct.
482. After the Spanish Revolution of 1868, Francisco fled to Paris where he was protected by Napoléon III. In 1870, he was officially separated from his wife who nevertheless continued to provide him with a generous allowance.
483. Clément, p. 196.
484. Livret, n° 1364, bearing the title *Danse des Bacchantes.* Nothing is known about the artist; in the livret, the name is given as in the text, but in dictionaries, the name is Alexandre-Marie Longuet and the only information given is that the painter died in 1850 or 1851. The painting was not well received by the critics; Courtois 1849 noted that the women were too active and unrealistic, so that "la danse doit être un pénible exercice."
485. Clément, p. 196.

Very little information has come down about the origin and development of the painting. It was begun sometime after 1846, but Gleyre did not refer to it in any of his letters for that year. The first mention of the work is in the spring of 1848 when Clément, then in London in the service of the Comte Duchâtel as a tutor to his son, wrote to Mme. Olivier asking if the painting was finished and sold.[476] Later in May, Clément, still in London, asked Juste Olivier for a progress report, adding that he would like to buy the work himself even though he had seen the picture only in an oil study.[477] Presumably, Gleyre gave Clément news of the progress in person when, in the summer of 1848, he accompanied Cornu to London: Clément wrote that he and Gleyre had visited some of the collections together, including the one at Hampton Court.[478] The actual length of Gleyre's visit is uncertain, but in an unpublished letter to Mme. Olivier, Clément regretted that Gleyre was in England only for a few days.[479]

Although the genesis of the painting is not known from the documentation, we do know that the composition went through several stages of alteration. One example is noted by Clément, who had seen the work in an advanced study before leaving for London in March 1848. Gleyre had introduced a tiger into the composition, most probably in the foreground, tearing at the drapery of one of the frenzied dancers. This detail, we are told, was widely admired by some of Gleyre's friends, but Planche argued that it was too realistic, disturbing the classical balance of the work. Planche convinced Gleyre that the detail detracted from the overall effect; consequently, Gleyre redid this section of the composition, thus delaying the completion of the painting significantly.[480]

On 29 February 1849 Mme. Olivier wrote Clément that Gleyre was working furiously to finish the painting because "il a vendu ses Bacchantes en Espagne pour 4,000 francs."[481] What she meant was that Gleyre had sold the picture, before it was completed, to a buyer who was Spanish and would subsequently take the painting to Spain. Although she did not specify the buyer, he was none other than Francisco de Asis de Borbón, the titular king of Spain. In 1846, he had married his cousin fig. 113 Isabella II, queen of Spain, and thus assumed the title, but he had no official duties or political functions.[482] It is not known under what circumstances Gleyre had made the sale, but probably the intermediary was the Spanish ambassador in Paris, who knew well the king's artistic tastes. When news of the sale spread to Gleyre's friends, they celebrated in impromptu fashion by dancing "une sarabande furibonde" around the painting.[483]

In the same letter of February 1849, Mme. Olivier openly lamented that Gleyre did not intend to exhibit the painting in the Salon of 1849, "avant de l'exiler au-delà des Pyrénées." Yet, the painting was in fact exhibited in the Salon, along with a second work bearing the same title — the other painting was a large canvas by Marie-Alexandre Longuet.[484] Clément remarked that the decision to exhibit was the Spanish ambassador's and that it was counter to Gleyre's own desire.[485] The painting, which was not subject to jury assessment because Gleyre had won a first prize in

161

1845, was registered a few days before the opening of the salon, held that year in the Tuileries from 15 June.[486] Clément claimed that as soon as Gleyre was informed that the painting was exhibited, he had it removed immediately. If this is so, the painting was on view only a few days.[487] In fact, the documents reveal a different story: Gleyre's request to remove the painting from the Salon was not given to the exhibition officials until mid-July, and coincided with the closing of the Salon between 16 and 19 July when the works there were rearranged and rehung.[488] Gleyre's request was hardly unusual in 1849: between 10 July and 30 August, a total of sixty-nine painters and sculptors asked for the removal of ninety-one works from the Salon for a variety of reasons. Gleyre's *Bacchantes* was actually on public view for about a month and was seen by all the major critics.

Gleyre again received a plethora of positive reviews from such eminent critics as Théophile Gautier, who compared the picture to Poussin and thought it to be one of the finest in the exhibition, and Etienne Delécluze, who saw the painting as further evidence of Gleyre's growing talent, in effect the fulfillment of the promise he had shown earlier in the decade.[489] Only Galimard and the critic who signed his name D. in *L'Illustration* — where incidentally the painting was reproduced in a poor engraving — published negative critiques: the former thought the work too refined for the subject and advised Gleyre to abandon Bacchic subjects, while the latter remarked that the painting was dull, even too calm, but nevertheless regretted that the painting could no longer be seen in the Salon.[490] Presumably, the painting was sent to Madrid sometime in the late summer of 1849 and was hung in the Palais Royal, and later in the king's private chambers. Thus the work, like Gleyre's *Saint John*, remained out of view, exiled, as Mme. Olivier feared; it was seen only briefly, and still privately, in Paris in 1876 when the Spanish king installed himself there after his break with his wife.[491] The fate of the *Bacchantes* was typical for many other works of Gleyre; their location was either lost or forgotten, effectively removing them from public scrutiny. It is difficult to determine whether the imagery of the *Bacchantes* had an influence on later painting. It is tempting, however, to assume that the figure lying down at the left of the composition played a role in the development of Courbet's *Woman with a Parrot*: Courbet also exhibited in the Salon of 1849 and surely saw Gleyre's work at that time, however alien he may have found it to his developing interest in Realist iconography.

fig. 115

The exhibition of Gleyre's painting in Paris in 1849 was the last time he willingly showed a major work in this forum. His decision to abstain from the Salon system was a controversial one which was often discussed and publicly lamented.[492] Gleyre never fully explained the decision to his friends, nor did he discuss it in any of his correspondence. As a winner of a first-prize medal, he was no longer subject to the capricious decisions of the jury and could in fact exhibit at will. His decision not to participate, although curious at this time, was neither unique nor remarkable within the context of nineteenth-century art: such artists as Ingres, Cogniet, Delaroche, Scheffer, among others, refused at times to include

486. Paris, AL, Enregistrement, 1849, under n° 3736. The dimensions of the painting were then registered as 269 x 180 cm. with frame.

487. But see Clément, p. 196, who reports the painting was admired by the public, information repeated by Berthoud 1874, p. 471, and Taine 1903, p. 214.

488. Paris, AL, Dossier X, 1849, "Etats des ouvrages retirés pendant l'exposition."

489. Gautier 1849; Delécluze 1849.

490. Galimard 1849, and D[U PAYS] 1849, p. 340. The illustration was published in the latter article, p. 341.

491. The painting was listed as n° 422 in the inventory of the King's cabinet and noted as such in a letter from the Swiss vice-consul in Madrid, Bugnot, to Paul Cérésole on 7 September 1874, in answer to a request for information; both letters are in Lausanne, MCBA, GA 997. See too the letter dated 25 February 1876 from the Duc de Banos, the King's *chargé d'affaires*, to Kern, noting the presence of the painting in Paris, in ibid.; the Duke indicated that Fritz Berthoud had seen the painting privately in a recent visit.

492. See, for one example among many, *La Revue suisse* 1857, p. 474: "C'est un regret maxime que [Gleyre] ne veuille plus exposer." The author, although anonymous, is probably Juste Olivier.

115. Gustave Courbet, *Woman with a Parrot*, 1866. New York, Metropolitan Museum of Art. Bequest of Mrs. H.O. Havemeyer, 1929. The H.O. Havemeyer Collection

their work in the Salons.[493] But Gleyre's refusal, literally at the height of his celebrity, intrigued his friends; many thought that the reason was his low opinion of the jury system as a whole, although there is no record that he ever said as much, and, indeed, later he would participate in several Salon juries.[494] Others, like Taine, thought that Gleyre was very timid and wished simply to avoid publicity. Fritz Berthoud's explanation was more banal: that Gleyre no longer needed to exhibit since his fame was already established. Clément shared this view, adding that Gleyre felt that the Salon system as it operated in the 1840s was corrupt, geared to the hopes of publicity and sales of paintings; it became, in Gleyre's view, a competitive circus in which younger artists attempted to outdo each other in the hope of achieving good notices, with the overall effect that the Salon was a mediocre affair.[495]

Such considerations certainly contributed to Gleyre's decision to abandon public exhibitions in Paris. But an additional reason is contained in a letter of the American art dealer Samuel Avery, who had many contacts with Gleyre in the 1860s and 1870s, in which he said that Gleyre had told him that he refused to exhibit in the salons because he hated Louis Bonaparte and did not wish to participate in exhibitions controlled by his government.[496] It is true that Gleyre's political views were always republican, that he later refused a commission from Napoléon III, and that on 19 July 1849 — just when he withdrew his painting from the salon — he wrote his brother that he feared a coup d'état which would be disastrous for the state of liberty in France.[497] But one wonders whether the American's assertion is somewhat exaggerated, particularly since participation in the Salons implied no agreement with the government; and furthermore, even if Gleyre's politics were anti-royalist, he had just sold a picture to the King of Spain. Still, he did refuse to send his work to the Salons, and he would later refuse to send paintings to Vienna and Munich

493. See Tabarant 1942, p. 96. Clément, reviewing the salon of 1865, likewise noted that the poor quality of the salon was due to the fact that the great artists of the day no longer used it as a showplace for their major works.
494. Dubosc de Pesquidoux 1874, p. 159; Stranahan 1888, p. 287.
495. Taine 1874; Berthoud 1874, p. 472; Clément, p. 197.
496. The letter was published in the *New York Evening Post*, 18 May 1874 in response to a previous obituary notice; see Hauptman 1980, p. 14.
497. Clément, p. 222.

for political reasons stemming from the aftermath of the Franco-Prussian War. Even the arguments of such close friends as Olivier failed to persuade Gleyre that he could serve the interest of art by exhibiting his work; Olivier wrote to his friend, the Genevan publisher Jacques Adert:

> Dites [to the painter Alfred van Muyden] que j'ai fait tout ce que j'ai pu avec Gleyre, soit indirectement par d'autres, soit directement... Tout a été inutile. Il ne veut pas se départir de son principe de ne pas exposer.[498]

Although Gleyre would not send his works to the French Salons, he nevertheless accepted an invitation to participate in an important exhibition of modern art in Lausanne in 1850. With this exhibition, Gleyre began a long artistic collaboration with the canton of Vaud which extended to the last years of his life. He produced at least two large historical paintings, a genre as yet untried by him, and found an adoring Swiss public that would proclaim him in the years to come their "peintre national."

498. The letter is dated 27 January 1867 and is in Lausanne, BCU/DM, Juste Olivier, "Correspondance à Jacques Adert," IS 40.

## CHAPTER 6

# 1850

## THE FIRST SWISS COMMISSION: "MAJOR DAVEL"

116. *Major Davel* after its destruction in 1980

In the summer of 1850, after having struggled for almost four years, Gleyre sent a painting to the small museum in Lausanne; it depicted the last moments of a Vaudois hero, Major Davel, who was intrumental in liberating the canton from its subjection to Bern. The work won instant success of a kind that was rarely equaled in Switzerland or in Paris. Because the subject matter touched the Vaudois historical consciousness, the painting became a national icon, reproduced in virtually every medium, and the event was even reenacted publicly in various *tableaux vivants*. Although the painting was executed in its entirety in Gleyre's studio in Paris, it was never seen by the Parisian public. Almost one hundred and thirty years after its triumphant exhibition in Lausanne, it was destroyed by an unknown hand; ironically only the figure of a weeping fig. 116 soldier remained as a witness of the events Gleyre depicted and the destruction of the work.[499]

Clément's brief account of the genesis of this work gives only the barest essentials of the commission and the difficulties involved in its execution.[500] Recent research into unpublished letters and archival documents unavailable to Clément clarifies the situation and at the same time offers valuable insight into Gleyre's approach to the historical genre, which he had never before attempted on a large scale.

In 1821 the city of Lausanne decided to form a museum within the context of the already existing *Ecole de dessin*, and a small program of acquisitions and commissions was begun.[501] The director, who assumed his duties in December 1822, was the Vaudois painter Marc-Louis Arlaud (1772–1845), a former pupil of David in Paris.[502] The cantonal govern- fig. 117 ment took no specific action in the years that immediately followed, and in 1834, Arlaud himself offered the enormous sum of 34,000 Swiss francs toward the construction of a permanent museum structure at the Place de la Madeleine below the cathedral.[503] The architect Louis Wenger was chosen for the task, and the site was changed to the Place de la Riponne which offered a more central location.[504] After more than three years of fig. 118 construction and substantial increases in building costs, the museum was officially opened on 1 January 1841. The first exhibition contained thirty-

117. Marc-Louis Arlaud, *Self-Portrait*, c. 1837. Lausanne, Musée Cantonal des Beaux-Arts

499. The painting was set on fire during the night of 24 August 1980 while it hung in a hallway near the museum entrance in the Palais de Rumine. It was never established whether the destruction was political in nature or the act of a madman. The vandal was never identified.

500. Clément, pp. 223f.

501. The basic documentary history of the museum foundation is preserved in Lausanne, MCBA, Museum Archives, A 1821/2 and 4. Essential information is contained in Hugli 1983, pp. 21f.

502. Bonjour 1905, pp. 14f. On Marc-Louis Arlaud's career, see Brun 1905–17, I, pp. 50–51. Arlaud studied with David in 1798; he even posed for the figure of Tatius in the master's canvas of the Sabines.

503. See Bonjour 1905, p. 14, and Hugli 1983, pp. 39f.

504. Louis Wenger (1809–61) became a well-known architect in Lausanne and was responsible for numerous projects in the area. He also played an important role in Vaudois politics later in his life. It is interesting to speculate that perhaps he had already met Gleyre in Paris when he studied there, at the Ecole des Beaux-Arts, from 1827 to 1830. On Wenger, see Brun 1905–17, III, p. 476; his building activities in Lausanne are studied in Grandjean 1965, I, pp. 275–76.

six oil paintings, four of which were donated by Arlaud himself, nineteen watercolors, all by Abraham-Louis Ducros (1784–1810), and fourteen plaster casts of antique sculpture that had been used for drawing exercises in the school.

It had been Arlaud's aim from the start not only to house a permanent collection, but also to promote contemporary Swiss art, a wholly unique enterprise in the canton at that time. To this end, Arlaud began, in 1841, to acquire and commission works for the museum, which now bore his name. The first major purchase was a large canvas by the landscape artist François Diday, which had already been exhibited in Paris and Geneva, and had been destined for purchase by the French government.[505] In 1842, Arlaud commissioned a landscape from Diday's student Alexandre Calame, which was finished and on view in Lausanne in the spring of the next year.[506] A third work was requested of the young painter Alfred van Muyden, but it was not delivered until after Arlaud's death.[507]

Because of Arlaud's ardent nationalism and his desire to include works of the finest Swiss painters of the day, it was inevitable that he would desire a work by Gleyre, who by 1843 was becoming known in the canton. It is unlikely that Arlaud and Gleyre had met: there is no mention of it in Gleyre's correspondence, nor in his travel notes when he stopped in Lausanne during his first Italian trip; nor is there any record that Arlaud went to Paris at this time. However, Arlaud was aware of Gleyre's reputation in Paris and probably read the notice in *Le Courrier suisse* in 1844 that *Le Soir* was hanging in the Musée du Luxembourg, only the second work by a Swiss painter to have this honor.[508] Arlaud's interest in

118. Friedrich von Martens, *Place de la Riponne, Lausanne*, c. 1845. Lausanne, Musée Historique de Lausanne

505. The history of the work is recounted in Bonjour 1905, pp. 28–29. Arlaud paid Diday the sum of 3,000 francs for the work, which is now in Lausanne, MCBA, Inv. 1079. Diday's canvas was shown in the salon of 1841, livret n° 578. It might be added that the MCBA loaned the work to the Exposition Universelle of 1855.
506. Ibid., pp. 29–30. The work is also in Lausanne, MCBA, Inv. 589. For the correspondence, see MCBA, Museum Archives, A 1843.
507. The documentation is contained in ibid., A 1846/3, and in Lausanne, ACV, Musée Arlaud, K XIII/65, p. 64. The work, representing Joseph and his brothers, was commissioned in 1844 from funds given by Mr. Mayor. The painting, now in the MCBA, Inv. 560, arrived on 13 May 1846. It might be noted that Arlaud was influential in persuading Alfred Van Muyden to pursue a career in painting rather than law as his family wished; see Van Muyden 1950(a), p. 13.
508. *Le Courrier suisse*, 3 May 1844, pp. 3–4. It seems to be the first notice of Gleyre's activities in a Vaudois publication. The first Swiss work to enter the Musée du Luxembourg was Grosclaude's *Toast à la vendange de 1834*, purchased in 1835 by the state and exhibited in the Luxembourg in 1841 or 1842. See Lacambre 1874, p. 92, n° 108, and Hauptman 1983, pp. 117–18.

167

Gleyre is confirmed in an unpublished letter of 17 October 1844 to the young Swiss painter Emile David, then in Paris after having briefly studied with Barthélemy Menn in Geneva. The letter notes that were he in better health, Arlaud would make the voyage to Paris "pour faire la connaissance de M. Glaire [sic]. Je suis tout fier de penser qu'il est vaudois."[509] Later in the letter, Arlaud asked David if he would use his influence to persuade Gleyre to paint a work for Lausanne. Arlaud specified that the subject and size could be left to the painter's discretion. He suggested to David a convincing argument to present to Gleyre — namely, to have such a work in Lausanne would establish Gleyre's reputation in his native canton, as well as enhance the growing tourist trade. Arlaud proposed a sum between 2,000 and 3,000 francs as a possible fee for the work, roughly the same amount offered by Druey for each year of Gleyre's teaching activities in Lausanne. The sum was not negligible, since at the time in Lausanne a salary of more than 1,000 francs a year was considered privileged.[510] Arlaud added that he had talked with Auguste Jacquet,[511] who had recently visited Gleyre's studio and who attested to the artist's talents. Jacquet's testimony was important as none of Gleyre's works had ever been seen in the canton.

In 1844, Gleyre was involved in completing his *Apostles* and had yet to finish the Goumois copy, but it seems unlikely that he would have refused to consider Arlaud's request, particularly in light of the source. It is probable, therefore, that some form of communication between Arlaud and Gleyre occurred between 1844 and 1845. A specific provision in Arlaud's will — Arlaud died on 1 May 1845 — amended his testament   fig. 119 of three years earlier so that the revised will includes a section, the seventh, which states:

> Je lègue au gouvernement deux mille cinq cents francs pour être employés à l'achat d'un tableau, qui sera commandé au peintre vaudois Gleyre actuellement à Paris. Ce tableau devra reproduire un des traits les plus saillants et caractéristiques de l'histoire du Major Davel et de la tentative qu'il fit pour l'affranchissement du pays de Vaud.[512]

Arlaud's specification here that Gleyre's painting must represent the history of Major Davel suggests that he already had Gleyre's agreement to undertake the work. This may have been accomplished through the intermediary of the young painter and theologian, Henri Euler, who was close to Gleyre and Arlaud.[513]

On 28 May 1845, Arlaud's nephew, G.H. Combe of Morges, wrote to the president of the Conseil d'Etat that the funds allotted for the commission would be deposited in the government coffers shortly; the sum, however, was not available until 19 June.[514] The documentation does not indicate that any action was taken by the council immediately, but by 9 September, it was already public knowledge that Arlaud had left a sizable sum for the commission of the work by Gleyre; it was even known that the subject was the history of Major Davel. It was, however, not

509. See Lausanne, BCU/DM, David, IS 4540, which contains photocopies of some of David's correspondence. The originals of this and other letters are in Lausanne, Private collection. On David, see Bovet-David 1943.

510. On the typical salaries in Lausanne in the nineteenth-century, see Biaudet 1982, p. 286, who notes that in the middle of the century, a clergyman earned between 1,000 and 2,000 francs per year, a judge about 1,600 francs, and a professor, about 1,800 francs. For the average worker, one franc was equal to about six days of work. From this scale, it is possible to see the immense fortune Arlaud provided when he gave more than 30,000 francs for the establishment of the museum.

511. Auguste Jacquet (1802–1845) was *Conseiller d'Etat*, despite his French origins, from 1832 until his death. See Montet 1877–78, II, p. 8.

512. The will is preserved in Lausanne, ACV, Testaments, K XIX, 1845, n° 57. My thanks to Mr. Paul Bissegger for finding the document.

513. Clément, p. 223, suggests the importance of Euler but is in doubt whether he played a significant role in the commission. On Euler's relationship to Gleyre, see Hauptman 1983, pp. 100f. Euler was an important friend of Arlaud, who left to him the disposition of his paintings and drawings in the amended will. There is no correspondence extant between Arlaud and David on the subject of the commission except the letter of 1844 cited above; see note 509.

514. The funds were deposited into the *Caisse de l'Etat* by Bugnion on that date and verified by Mr. Fischer of the Department of Finances in a letter of 24 September 1850; see Lausanne, ACV, Département de l'Instruction publique, Lettres, K XIII/63. The allotment of funds was also recorded by Druey in the minutes of the council meeting on 30 May, in Lausanne, ACV, Conseil d'Etat, Registres des délibérations, bk. 137, p. 390, under that date.

noted that Arlaud's gift of 2,500 francs was precisely 1,000 francs more than the entire yearly budget for the museum.[515]

The records do not indicate how Gleyre received the official commission from the Conseil d'Etat after the price and subject matter had been set. Research into the documents of the museum and the Conseil d'Etat reveal that no correspondence between the Vaudois officials and Gleyre occurred at this time, with the exception of Druey's letter asking Gleyre to become the director of the museum. This lacuna suggests that the commission may have been transmitted orally, possibly in Lausanne when Gleyre returned from the second Italian visit in December 1845, at which time the money Arlaud had left was available. The first mention of the work in Gleyre's correspondence is an undated letter of 1846 to his brother; the actual letter has not been found, but was seen by Emile Bonjour, the director of the Musée Arlaud a half-century later, when he visited one of Gleyre's nieces, probably Mathilde:

> Tu sais que (je) fais un sujet commandé par le canton de Vaud,
> il est fort difficile et ingrat, il faudra pourtant en venir à bout.
> Je suis engagé tout de bon.[516]

119. Marc-Louis Arlaud, "Last Will and Testament", 1845. Lausanne, Archives Cantonales Vaudoises

The letter indicates that Gleyre must have begun work on the painting sometime in 1846 while he was also painting the *Echo*, the *Bacchantes*, and *The Flood*; the work on the latter painting would drag on for years. In all probability, Gleyre had already created his first studies for the composition and had envisioned the essential elements of the scene. Gleyre's indication to Henry that the work was difficult can be readily understood since, as will be seen shortly, no specific pictorial prototypes existed, so that Gleyre was forced to invent the scene, but within an accurate historical context. What is not so easily comprehensible is why Gleyre told Henry that the commission was thankless. The fee allotted for the picture represented a sum equivalent to that paid for his work of 1843 and 1845. Perhaps Gleyre thought at first that the work would not be seen in Paris but relegated to a museum with neither reputation nor a large collection. Clément noted that Gleyre actually had misgivings about taking on the task and even drafted a letter to the Conseil d'Etat expressing his unwillingness to accept the work. The letter, however, was not found among Gleyre's correspondence after his death, nor is there a record in the archives of the Conseil d'Etat that Gleyre ever expressed a reluctance to undertake the painting.

As with *Le Soir*, there is very little documentation regarding the progress of this important work, although as Clément remarked, the painting went through various alterations, including a major one, when Gleyre had already put the *esquisse* on the final canvas.[517] On 1 September 1847 — that is, about two years after Gleyre had received the commission — Guignard, the director of the Musée Arlaud who had taken the post when Gleyre refused it, wrote to "M. Glayre, peintre à Paris," asking for information on the progress of the work and noting politely that the museum was impatient to know when it would arrive in

515. See Lausanne, ACV, Département de l'Instruction publique, Lettres, K XIII/63 for various documents concerning the budget problems of the museum.

516. The letter is cited in Lausanne, MCBA, Bonjour, "Copies de lettres," IV, 5 April 1922 to Maurice Barbey who at the time was conducting research for his own study of the *Davel* painting. I have not been able to locate the original letter which appears not to be in any of the archival material in Lausanne.

517. Clément, p. 231.

Lausanne. There is no evidence of a reply from Gleyre, and Guignard wrote again on 1 February 1848, this time giving the letter to Euler to deliver personally:

> La Commission du Musée Arlaud est fort impatiente de savoir à quoi s'en tenir… elle désire ardemment pouvoir donner au Conseil d'Etat quelques renseignements sur l'époque où vous pensez pouvoir lui remettre le tableau qu'elle vous a commandé et dont vous avez bien voulu vous charger.[518]

Guignard added as well that the Conseil d'Etat had repeatedly written to Gleyre for information, but always without a reply. It was hoped that the direct contact with Euler would push Gleyre into replying and finishing the work as soon as possible.[519]

There is no record of a reply, although in this case, Gleyre probably sent a message to the Vaudois officials through Euler. Two months after Guignard's letter, we know that Gleyre was hard at work on the painting, which was becoming more and more difficult. On 24 March 1848, Juste Olivier wrote his friend Melegari that

> Gleyre est tout à son tableau. Plus il y travaille, plus il y trouve à travailler… son tableau a beaucoup gagné. Il s'est clos et ne reçoit plus personne, même Planche.[520]

A month later Gleyre wrote Henry, excusing himself for not going to the baptism of his niece — Henry's last child, Emire — noting that he had neither the time nor the money since a commission he had counted on had been withdrawn by the city of Paris.[521] But he told Henry that he had to finish quickly the work he had already begun, "celui de la mort du Major Davel." It is not possible to ascertain how much of the canvas was already done; as will be seen shortly, the documentary evidence is contradictory.

As Gleyre noted here, he was once again embarrassed by financial difficulties. Thus, on 5 May 1848 the Conseil d'Etat reported in the session for that day that a letter was received from Gleyre — actually the first letter from him since the commission was given almost three years earlier — requesting an advance on his fee. The council agreed, noting that Gleyre was reputed to be an honorable man, as well as a Vaudois, and authorized a sum of 1,200 francs to be sent.[522] Apparently, this permitted Gleyre to continue his work tranquilly; he wrote to Henry on 29 June: "Je travaille à ce tableau pour la Suisse."[523]

But at this stage in the development of the canvas, a curious document raises questions about Gleyre's progress. Juste Olivier wrote to his friend Charles Eynard in Geneva on 4 August 1848, noting that

> Gleyre… paraît décidé à faire son tableau de Davel. Il lui est imposé par un legs de M. Arlaud à ce sujet, et une commande positive du Conseil d'Etat.[524]

120. *Major Davel*, 1850. Formerly Lausanne, Musée Cantonal des Beaux-Arts (catalogue n° 545)

518. Lausanne, ACV, Musée Arlaud, K XIII/65, pp. 73–76. There are no records of letters from the Conseil d'Etat in the archives.
519. In 1847, Euler was frequently in Paris. Albert de Meuron wrote to his mother on 28 August 1847 that he went to Gleyre's studio where he met Euler, who, he said, was a frequent visitor; see Neuchâtel, AE, Fonds de Meuron, dossier 69. See also de Meuron's letters for October of that year. In 1848, Euler went to Italy.
520. Lausanne, BCU/DM, Fonds Olivier, IS 1905/42, dossier 1848, and cited in Barbey 1923, p. 264, in part. Louis-Amadée Melegari (1807–81) was a professor of political science and economics at the University of Lausanne between 1840 and 1845; he settled there after 1834, having escaped a death sentence in Italy. He had known Olivier since 1837 and certainly met Gleyre several times in the 1840s; Gleyre sent him a print of *Le Soir*. In 1867, Melegari became the Italian ambassador to Switzerland.
521. See Lausanne, MCBA, GA 986, a letter dated 25 April 1848 and cited in part in Clément, pp. 216–17, but incorrectly dated two days later. Bonjour also cited the letter in his correspondence with Barbey, as noted in n. 516 above.
522. Lausanne, ACV, Conseil d'Etat, Registres des délibérations, 5 May 1848, bk. 144, p. 409, item 60.
523. Lausanne, MCBA, GA 986; Clément cites the letter on pp. 217–18, but not this section of it.
524. The letter is cited in Barbey 1923, pp. 264–65; I have not located the original. Charles Eynard (1808–76) was the nephew of the more famous banker and historian Jean-Gabriel Eynard; see Perrochon 1931, p. 1. He apparently met Olivier as early as 1831, as noted in Lausanne, BCU/DM, Urbain Olivier, "Extraits", IS 1905/60, p. 10.

170

The letter also indicates that Olivier had been charged by Gleyre to ask various friends for details of costume, particularly their color: "L'habit, était-il bleu ou gris de fer?" Olivier noted that Gleyre was especially anxious to create the exact historical milieu for the picture because he feared that his historical research would come under scrutiny. We do not have Eynard's reply, but on 8 September 1848 Olivier again wrote to him, thanking him for his letter and for the material he had sent directly to Gleyre.[525]

If, as the letter implies, Gleyre only began to research the historical details of the iconography in the summer of 1848, what work had he accomplished earlier? No substantial information has come down to us regarding the state of the canvas from early 1846, when he began, to mid-1848, when he requested historical details. It must be assumed that he had already worked out the idea, the composition, perhaps some specific details, but without being certain of others. Olivier's notion that the work was "imposed," as he wrote to Eynard, was certainly not true — although the subject was imposed by Arlaud's will — but it may have reflected Gleyre's feeling that he had no freedom in the conception of the painting; this may also explain why he thought of it as a thankless job. It is also possible that Gleyre, with his habitual slowness, advanced but little on the composition until mid-1848, at which time he received half the commission fee, thus wholly cementing the commission in his mind.

During the summer of 1848, Gleyre and Cornu had gone to London, where they saw Clément. Exactly when Gleyre returned to Paris is not known, but on 29 August 1848 Mme. Olivier wrote to her husband, then on holiday with his brother Urbain in Givrins, that "M. Gleyre désire beaucoup ton retour et en a besoin pour son Davel."[526] Gleyre then continued to work on the canvas through the fall of 1848, but could not seem to finish it. On 14 August 1849 Olivier wrote to Fritz Berthoud that Gleyre was continuing his work on the *Davel*, but often he also worked on other projects, "qui sont plus de son goût."[527]

No further letters illuminate Gleyre's progress on the *Davel*. Nor are his movements and activities noted for 1849, except those already recounted in regard to the completion of the *Bacchantes*, and an important encounter in October of that year with Flaubert and du Camp. The painting of *Davel*, however, was not finished before the early summer of 1850. On 5 May Auguste Bachelin, one of Gleyre's earliest Swiss students, wrote his friend Edouard Perrochet that he had seen the finished *Davel* in Gleyre's studio.[528] Shortly afterwards, Gleyre had it shipped to Lausanne for exhibition.

Although the available documentation does not fully explain why Gleyre had so many difficulties with the painting, one reason was surely the nature of the subject matter. While Davel has become the Vaudois national hero — partly, as it turns out, as a result of Gleyre's painting — the historical figure was still relatively little known in the canton and unknown ouside the canton when Gleyre received the commission.[529] In the early nineteenth century, literature devoted to Davel's life and exploits was meager: histories of Switzerland such as those by Zschokke in

525. Barbey 1923, p. 265.
526. Lausanne, BCU/DM, Fonds Olivier, IS 1905/42, dossier 1848.
527. Ibid., and cited in Courvoisier 1905, p. 40.
528. Neuchâtel, AE, Fonds Bachelin, 1791, dossier 1. On the importance of Bachelin to Gleyre, particularly in regard to the correspondence that records various visits, see Hauptman 1985(e), pp. 82f.
529. Clément, p. 255.

1822 and Levade in 1824 made no mention of his contributions.[530] Even the centenary of his death in 1823 went virtually unnoticed. The Revolution of 1830 brought on a new awareness in the canton of his significance in the struggle for independence, but it was only in 1837 that he was praised as an important revolutionary; credit for this must be given to Juste Olivier, who included an account of Davel's achievement in his history of the canton.[531]

Since the nineteenth century, a huge bibliography has accumulated on Davel's life and his contribution to Vaudois liberty.[532] Jean-Daniel-Abraham Davel was born in Morrens in 1670 — not 1667 as Clément noted[533] — to a family of Protestant ministers. Even as a child, Davel was prone to visions, excessive religious piety, and frequent divine consultations. He entered the military in 1688 and had a distinguished career, achieving the rank of major. At the time, the Vaudois region was governed by Bern with absolute authority. Davel took it upon himself to "deliver" his compatriots from this state of benign bondage, an act precipitated more by religious convictions than by political considerations, not unlike the mission of Joan of Arc whom, it was said, he greatly admired. On 31 March 1723 Davel and his company marched to the Hôtel de Ville of Lausanne in the hopes of arousing the population to rise up against their governors. Instead, Davel was imprisoned for treason and tortured for weeks until he was condemned to death by decapitation on 21 April. Three days later, Davel, accompanied by three ministers, was led to the execution site in Vidy. In his last speech, he claimed that "c'est ici le plus beau jour de ma vie" and spoke of the inner joy he felt at sacrificing his life for the cause of the liberty. After a speech by Louis-César de Saussure, the venerable minister of Lausanne, Davel was decapitated with one stroke of the executioner's blade. His body was placed in a shroud, his head nailed to the gallows.

Gleyre had almost certainly heard the story of Davel's heroism while a boy in Chevilly, but in the 1840s there was only one major source available that recounted in detail his biography and his heroism of 1723. This was Juste Olivier's long study of Davel, published in Lausanne in 1842 as part of Olivier's study of national figures. More than any earlier work, Olivier's text of 140 pages was based on scrupulous research, the first on Davel using the extant documents.[534] Olivier paid tribute to him not only as a champion of Vaudois liberty, but also as an exceptional man who was part soldier and part saint, the Swiss equivalent of Joan of Arc. Olivier's study was full of remarkable details — some documented, others based on stories — which, for the first time, made Davel a legendary figure whose inner voices and saintly personality emphasized the particularly Vaudois characteristics of the man and his history.[535]

It was because of Olivier's book that he and Gleyre met for the first time. Olivier had been in touch with David and Euler in Paris and had heard from them about the Arlaud will, with the commission for a painting depicting Major Davel. Olivier noted for Clément in 1874, in a manuscript only partially used by Clément for the biography, that he decided to send Gleyre a copy of the book as a way of providing informa-

fig. 121

530. But see Biaudet 1960, pp. 120f., for an important historical citation on Davel's life in the early nineteenth century.
531. Olivier 1837.
532. See in particular Barbey 1923. The most recent work of note on Davel is Mercier-Campiche 1970.
533. Clément, p. 255.
534. Olivier's principal source was the dossier in Lausanne, ACV, containing more than a thousand items.
535. When he tried to publish his account in France, with the backing of Sainte-Beuve, he was told by his publisher, Buloz (who incidentally was of Swiss origin), that no one in France would understand either the man or the folly of attempting to liberate his people in the way Davel chose; see Rambert 1879, p. LXXXVI.

173

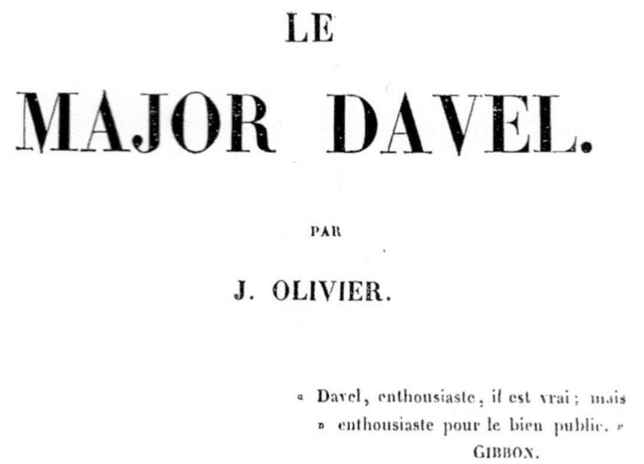

# LE
# MAJOR DAVEL.

PAR

## J. OLIVIER.

« Davel, enthousiaste, il est vrai ; mais
» enthousiaste pour le bien public. »
GIBBON.

tion and as a way of meeting his fellow Vaudois. According to Olivier the date was about 1846.[536] Gleyre seems never to have mentioned the circumstances under which he met Olivier, with whom he remained friends for three decades.

Gleyre used Olivier's work as the basic literary source for the imagery he needed to create. The earliest study depicts in a straightforward manner the scene at the scaffold, with Davel in the center on a raised platform, flanked by two ministers on one side and the executioner and his assistant on the other. In the foreground, two soldiers balance the composition and act as intermediary figures between the viewer and the central motif. The background depicts the huge crowd against the landscape of mountain and lake appropriate to Vidy. The composition follows the description in Olivier's account even in regard to the detail of a child raised on his father's shoulder so as to have a better view on the proceedings.[537] In the first effort, of uncertain date, Gleyre achieved a Renaissance-inspired composition, even using two Classical columns to balance the central figure.

While Olivier's account is rich in details, Gleyre felt the need in 1848 to request additional historical information, as evidenced in Olivier's letter to Eynard on 4 August. On 8 September, Olivier wrote to his wife, Caroline, that Eynard had sent some information to Gleyre regarding the costumes, as well as "plusieurs dessins d'après des portraits déterrés en Argovie."[538] Eynard, it was later learned, had consulted with the famous historian Frédéric de Gingins of La Sarraz who supplied the drawings that were sent to Paris.[539] Olivier and Gleyre must have been satisfied with these drawings — they have never been identified or found — since in Olivier's letter to Eynard, he wrote that Gleyre "a maintenant, je crois, tout ce qu'on pourra jamais déterrer sur ce sujet." In fact, it was determined later that the costumes Gleyre used in the painting were inaccurate for the period and the region, as Gleyre could not have known at the time.[540]

Gleyre had also asked for details on the type of sword used in executions in eighteenth-century Switzerland, and even had inquired whether the actual sword used to execute Davel was still in existence; Olivier's account does not describe the sword at all, nor does he mention whether

fig. 122

536. Lausanne, Private collection, Olivier 1874, "Notes," p. 3.
537. Olivier 1842, pp. 127f.
538. Lausanne, BCU/DM, Fonds Olivier, IS 1905/42, dossier 1848.
539. Frédéric de Gingins (1790–1863), who had known the Gleyre family when they lived in La Sarraz, was a well-known historian who later assumed the chair of history at the university; see de Montet 1877–78, I, pp. 361f. The information that de Gingins was involved in helping Gleyre comes from a letter of Jean Olivier, Juste's grandson, to Barbey on 24 October 1922, a copy of which was given to me by Mme. Sauter, Geneva.
540. See Le Conteur vaudois, 1 January 1898, p. 3, where the discrepancy is noted.

122. Study for *Major Davel*, 1847–48. Geneva, Private collection (catalogue n° 548)

123. Letter from Henri Euler to Juste Olivier, 7 January 1849. Lausanne, Bibliothèque Cantonale et Universitaire, Département des Manuscrits, IS 1905/42

the weapon was preserved. The exact date of Gleyre's request is not known, but must have coincided with his letter to Eynard. This time, however, Olivier forwarded Gleyre's request to Henri Euler who at the time was in Cossonay. Euler replied on 7 January 1849:

> Quant au glaive qui a tranché la noble tête de Davel, je pense qu'il est défunt lui-même, mais je vous dirai quelle est la mine de celui…

fig. 123 whereupon Euler drew a sword that he thought was typical of the canton in executions of the eighteenth century.[541] Euler explained that it was the type known as the "glaive gladius, c'est-à-dire une lame large, droite, à deux tranchants, avec une poignée qu'on saisit à deux mains."

541. Lausanne, BCU/DM, Fonds Olivier, IS 1905/42, dossier 1849.

175

The weapon drawn by Euler is precisely the type Gleyre employed in the second sketch for the composition, where the sword is broader and larger than the one used in the first sketch, which was a common type used in battle rather than executions. No doubt he based his drawing on actual eighteenth-century weapons. As Euler noted, he doubted whether the sword that actually beheaded Davel was then still extant, although in the bicentennial exhibition of 1923 held in Lausanne, a sword was shown that was purported to be the veritable one used in the execution.[542]

fig. 126

fig. 124

fig. 125

On 23 February 1847 Olivier wrote to his friend Eusèbe-Henri Gaullieur, thanking him for the prints and portraits he had sent for Gleyre's use in the creation of his *Davel*.[543] Gaullieur's position as editor and historian would have placed him in contact with figures who could provide important material, although none of Gaullieur's or Olivier's documents reveals the nature of the material Gaullieur sent, nor is there any hint in Gleyre's letters that he made use of it.

In Olivier's description of the execution, two ministers are mentioned as having accompanied Davel to the execution site, "Bergier et Bionens" [sic].[544] A third, de Saussure, was also present when Davel arrived; it was

126. Study for *Major Davel*, 1848–50. Lausanne, Musée Cantonal des Beaux-Arts (catalogue n° 547)

124. Execution Sword, 18th century. Lausanne, Musée d'Archéologie et d'Histoire
125. Davel Exhibition at Lausanne, Musée Historiographique, 1923. Lausanne, Musée de l'Elysée

542. In 1875 two executioner's swords of the eighteenth century were donated to the Musée Historique, Lausanne, Inv. n° 8782 and 8783. The second was for a long time believed to be the actual sword used by executioner to behead Davel; see *Le Conteur vaudois*, 18 December 1897, p. 1. Although it turned out not to be that sword, it was the type used in the exections of the period. It corresponds exactly to the one drawn by Euler in his letter and used by Gleyre in his painting.
543. Lausanne, BCU/DM, Fonds Gaullieur, IS 142/105. Eusèbe-Henri Gaullieur (1808–59) was a publisher and writer who collaborated with Olivier on *La Revue Suisse*. From 1837 to 1845 he was also editor of the radical newspaper *Nouvelliste vaudois*. After 1848, he taught history and law in Geneva.
544. Jean-Pierre Bergier de Pont (1685–1743) and Théodore Crinsoz de Bionnens (1690–1766); Olivier 1842, p. 127. See also Bridel 1921, pp. 97f., and Barbey 1923, p. 170. A portrait of the former minister was found in 1920 and is reproduced in Bridel 1921, p. 104.

the latter who pronounced the last prayer before the beheading.[545] Gleyre chose to represent only two ministers, probably to simplify the composition and to create a more harmonious unit around the central figure. In the first study, the ministers stand impassively next to Davel, while in the revised sketch, one of them takes Davel's hand in an emotive gesture, thus blending two scenes described by Olivier: after de Saussure gave his last prayer, Davel "parla de nouveau au peuple," then he bade a last farewell to the ministers who accompanied him, as suggested by the gesture of taking the hand. Gleyre chose not to paint the execution itself — as an anonymous painter would later — but to represent the spirituality of Davel's heroism in his final moments of life.

fig. 127

Olivier did not describe the ministers, and it appears that Gleyre relied on general types, although he may have utilized some costume designs sent by Gaullieur or other friends in the canton.[546] The only information to have come to light about the creation of these figures is contained in a letter from Olivier to Clément of 21 July 1874 in which Olivier reminisced briefly about Gleyre's painting.[547] In the letter Olivier wrote that the "jeune ministre" — that is, the one behind Davel with his hands clasped together — "est le portrait très ressemblant d'un de nos pensionnaires d'alors M. de Muttach [sic] de Berne." The reference is to one of the three sons of Arnold von Mutach who stayed with the Oliviers when in Paris — Mme. Olivier occupied herself in the education of young men and women whom she boarded — but it is not known which son it was.[548] Possibly it was Karl Friedrich Alfred, who was himself a painter and later a friend of Albert Anker, although he is not mentioned in any of the art historical literature or in Anker's or Olivier's correspondence. In 1848, he was seventeen years old, which would fit with the youthful physiognomy of the minister in the painting. The irony of having a Bernese model for the minister who accompanied Davel would not have escaped either Gleyre or Olivier.

Another historical element of the execution indicated by Gleyre follows Olivier's account. At the right side of the canvas, a stool is placed between the executioner and his assistant in conformity with the fact that decapitations in the canton at this time — and until 1868 — were performed while the prisoner was seated.[549] The executioner usually separated the head from the shoulders in a rapid step movement while the assistant held the hair of the prisoner so that the head would remain upright.[550] Davel's executioner came from Moudon, the ancient capital of the canton, as Olivier noted; he was later discovered to be Maître Bernhard.[551] The brooding expression of the executioner in Gleyre's painting contrasts remarkably to the inner peace projected by Davel, as though anticipating the violent encounter in the instant that follows.

As can be seen in the two studies Gleyre painted, the right-hand section of the finished canvas was changed radically. While in the first version the executioner inspects the sword, in the second version the sword is hidden, except for the handle, beneath the robes. From a psychological point of view, the second version is more effective since the instrument of death is no longer visible: this increases the dramatic suspense and, at

545. Olivier 1842, p. 131. Incidentally, Olivier had an original copy of de Saussure's speech, given to him in 1840 or 1841, by a Mr. W. C.; see Lausanne, BCU/DM, Fonds Olivier, IS 1905/51.

546. It is not known whether Olivier or Gleyre had attempted to research the facial features of the ministers. Later research form eyewitness accounts not available to Olivier described the main figures in the execution scene.

547. Now in Fleurier, CFC. Clément did not publish this letter in his biography of Gleyre.

548. On the Mutach family of Bern, see *Dictionnaire historique et biographique...* 1930, V, pp. 67–68. The three sons in question are Eduard Friedrich (1827–81) who served in the military in Sicily; Vincenz Arnold (1829–1911), an engineer; and Karl Friedrich (1831–1914), a painter. My thanks to Mr. Georg Germann of the Historisches Museum, Bern, for further information.

549. The last execution in the canton occurred on 10 January 1868 when Héli Freymond was executed for murder in Moudon. The execution was performed in precisely the same manner as described for Davel.

550. Olivier 1842, p. 132. Several eyewitness accounts verify the methods employed; see Borgeaud 1930, p. 281.

551. This fact was only discovered in 1853; it is recounted in *Le Conteur vaudois*, 1889, p. 3.

127. Anonymous, *The Execution of Davel*, c. 1850.
London, Victoria and Albert Museum. Townshend
Bequest

the same time, creates an allusion to Christ by recalling the sign of the
Cross. In light of Davel's faith, the symbolic representation of the sword
adds another dimension to the scene, placing it in the iconographic
schema of universal martyrs who perish for their faith. Yet, the alteration
was forced upon Gleyre: it seems that after he had already sketched the
scene from the first study on the canvas, Gleyre visited the Salon and was
stunned to see a figure so similar to the executioner he had drawn that he
feared a charge of plagiarism.[552] Clément, who recounted the incident,
did not give the year of the Salon, nor did he name the painting Gleyre
saw. The facts came to light in a letter from Nanteuil to Clément dated
12 December 1877 in which the former reflected upon the "bourreau de
Davel auquel le vol de Meissonier le fit renoncer."[553]

Nanteuil's reference is to the celebrated painter Ernest Meissonier, but
the context is curious. From the chronology established earlier of Gleyre's
progress on the painting, Clément's statement could only refer to the
Salon of 1848 or 1849, when Gleyre was actively involved in completing
the work; Meissonier showed four works, three of which by their subjects seem to preclude such a figure; the fourth work, entitled *Soldats* in
the livret, may be the one that had a figure similar to Gleyre's, but no
trace of the painting has come to light.[554] It is also possible that Nanteuil's
memory after thirty years was faulty, but it is certain that Meissonier
knew Gleyre and had visited his studio with Chenavard to see some drawings, including one for *The Prodigal Son* — the earliest version of the
work that Gleyre made in 1848, just when he was also working on the

552. Clément, p. 232. Clément noted that the figure was then well advanced on Gleyre's canvas.
553. Fleurier, CFC.
554. The painting was listed as n° 3252 in the salon livret. The other works Meissonier exhibited in
1848 were *Trois amis, Une partie de boules*, and three
portraits.

179

*Davel*.[555] Therefore, Nanteuil's claim that Meissonier had in fact "stolen" the figure may be accurate.

With respect to the imagery Gleyre devised for the painting, no question was more important to later scholars or more debated in the canton than the question whether Gleyre had a portrait likeness of Davel on which he based his own figure. Despite his intensive research on the Davel affair, Olivier gave no description of Davel's physical appearance in his work of 1842. Nor was there, before Gleyre began the work, a model for Davel that was used in the pictorial arts. When Gleyre began the painting and was researching the history of the affair, Olivier had written to Eynard in his letter of 14 August 1848 that he had found many important details, "sauf un portrait, portrait introuvable." It has been thought that a medallion of Davel existed and was in the possession of Mlle. Marie de Langin, the last survivor of the Davel family, who lived until 1891. This medallion was supposedly given to Gleyre by Mlle. de Langin, but the account is almost certainly spurious.[556] During the bicentenary of Davel's death, more extensive research on the matter concluded that no likeness had ever been made.[557] Furthermore, the name of Mlle. de Langin never appears in any of the correspondence of Gleyre, Olivier, or any of Olivier's friends who wrote to him while he was seeking historical information.

The suggestion has persisted that Juste Olivier himself posed for the image of Davel, precisely because no likeness of Davel was known. This was first mentioned in print in the review of the painting in 1850, while it was on view at the Musée Arlaud. The review was signed H.E. — actually Henri Euler, who was in a position to know certain details. He wrote:

> Le peintre alla s'inspirer chez le poète [that is, Olivier] et même emprunta quelques-uns de ses traits pour la tête de Davel.[558]

Within a short period of time this was accepted as fact. Eugène Rambert in his long essay on Olivier just after his death, even stressed the physical likeness between Olivier and Gleyre's image of Davel, a resemblance borne out by one of Gleyre's portraits of Olivier done about the same time he was working on the *Davel*.[559]

fig. 128

Yet the question whether Gleyre had indeed used a model for Davel was raised again later and elicited a response from Olivier's daughter, Thérèse Bertrand:

> Il me souvient d'avoir souvent entendu dire par mon père qu'il avait posé pour le Davel et j'ai toujours compris que c'était pour la figure principale... On m'a dit une fois que mon père avait posé non pour le personnage de Davel, mais pour un des soldats.[560]

Doubts as to whether Olivier had posed for the central figure were also raised by Olivier's grandson Jean.[561] Even so, in 1948 the historian Henri Perrochon stated categorically that *Davel* is the portrait of Olivier with-

555. See Gréard 1890, pp. 30 and 154 where the visit to Gleyre's studio is recalled. In the first citation, he noted the date of 1839, but this is surely incorrect.
556. See the letter from Cornaz, the Conseil d'Etat of Neuchâtel, to an unknown addressee, in Lausanne, BCU/DM, Fonds Bridel, IS 2070/VI⁵.
557. Barbey 1923, pp. 259f.
558. E[uler], 11 September 1850, p. 2.
559. Rambert 1879, p. LXXX.
560. *Le Conteur vaudois*, 1902, p. 2.
561. In a letter to Barbey, 24 October 1922, as cited in note 539 above.

out his beard.[562] In one instance, a radio play by Cécile Delhorbe, Olivier's principal biographer, places Olivier in Gleyre's studio posing for the figure of Davel.[563]

The answer to this vexing question can be found in two separate documents, one of which was known to Clément but not used by him. In the letter Olivier wrote to Clément on 21 July 1874, the one in which he mentioned the name of the model for the young minister, he also informed Clément that "pour la tête [de Davel], Gleyre me fit poser en perruque et se servit aussi du portrait de mon père." Gleyre's possession of a portrait of Olivier's father is verified by notes Olivier made for lectures

128. *Portrait of Juste Olivier*, 1848(?). Geneva, Private collection (catalogue n° 527)

562. Perrochon 1948, p. 203.
563. See Lausanne, BCU/DM, Delhorbe, IS 1905/51.

on Gleyre after his death; under the heading for the *Major Davel*, Olivier noted simply "portrait de mon père."[564] That Gleyre used Juste Olivier as a model seems wholly reasonable; it also explains Caroline Olivier's letter to her husband on 29 August 1848, cited above, that "M. Gleyre désire beaucoup ton retour et en a besoin pour son Davel."[565] But that he relied also on Olivier's father for physiognomic features of Davel is more puzzling. From various descriptions, we know Jean-Michel Olivier (1778–1850) was, like Gleyre's own father, an exceptional man, a Vaudois peasant who spent almost his entire life in Leysin and Gryon in the Vaudois Alps. He was an ardent patriot who, despite a lack of formal education, was highly cultured and remarkably well read. He was described as exceptionally vigorous, even in old age, and full of inner vitality.[566]

fig. 129

Why then did Gleyre feel the need to incorporate Jean-Michel's features in the central figure of the painting? One reason certainly was that, in the absence of an actual portrait, Gleyre wanted to embody the Vaudois physiognomy in the person of Davel, to make it more easily recognizable to Swiss viewers. Moreover, Gleyre did not wish to use the precise features of Juste Olivier, since he was too well known in the canton, so he sought a blend of the realistic with the timeless qualities that were at the core of Gleyre's style. It is unlikely that Jean-Michel went to Paris to pose; rather, Gleyre made use of the portrait which Juste Olivier had. This portrait was painted by Charles Eynard — with whom Olivier corresponded about the costume colors — between 1838 and 1839, when Jean-Michel was about sixty years old, only slightly older than Davel when he was executed.[567]

fig. 130

One last element must be mentioned concerning the models Gleyre used in the work. The figure of the young boy held up on the shoulders of his father is a detail, as we saw, that derives directly from Olivier's text

129. Juste Olivier, "Notes sur Gleyre." Lausanne, Bibliothèque Cantonale et Universitaire, Département des Manuscrits, IS 1088, p. 17

130. Charles Eynard, *Portrait of Jean-Michel Olivier*, c. 1840. Geneva, Private collection

564. Lausanne, BCU/DM, Olivier, "Notes," IS 1088, p. 17.
565. Lausanne, BCU/DM, Fonds Olivier, IS 1905/42, dossier 1848.
566. Information on Olivier's father is noted in an unpublished memoir by Jean Olivier after notes made by Urbain Olivier in Lausanne, BCU/DM, Jean Olivier, "Histoire," IS 1905/60, "La mort de Jean-Louis Olivier." It is generally thought that description of the character Michel Dombre in Urbain Olivier's novel, *L'Ouvrier*, is based on his father.
567. The history of the portrait is recounted in letters from Urbain Olivier to Eynard in Lausanne, BCU/DM, Olivier, Letters, IS 1905/81, dossier II. The portrait itself was made after a daguerreotype, but it is known that Olivier *père* saw Eynard in Rolle after 15 December 1838, perhaps to verify the finishing touches.

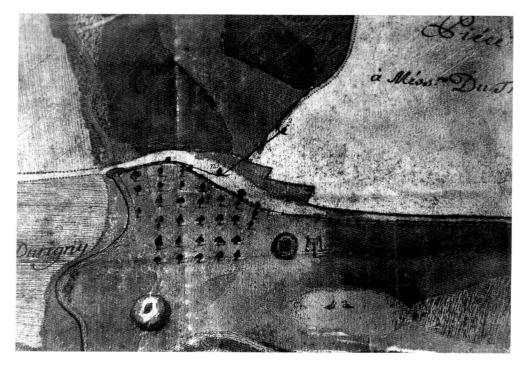

131. Anonymous, *Execution Site at Vidy*, 18th century. Lausanne, Musée Historique de Lausanne

of 1842.[568] Olivier noted that the model, named Cassat, had related the incident to his son, who in turn passed it on to his son, who told it to Olivier. Gleyre included the detail in his earliest sketch and in the final canvas as a sign of a living history, a witness to the actual event. Olivier informed Clément in his letter of recollections of 21 July 1874 that "l'enfant juché dans la foule sur les épaules de son père, c'est hélas notre pauvre Aloys." Olivier's reference was to his own son, who was born in 1836 and thus was eleven or twelve years old when Gleyre included him in the composition. He was in constant difficulty throughout his life, in effect the black sheep of the family. After a series of misadventures he went to America in 1858. In 1861, at the outbreak of the Civil War, he wrote to his father that he was enlisting in the Union Army. It was the last news Juste Olivier ever had from Aloys, despite years of effort to find him.[569] Gleyre made a portrait of him before he left for America, and used it as a model for another painting later.

Gleyre's composition is in the classic tradition which puts the central figures in direct communication with the viewer. Davel raises his eyes to heaven, in an attitude reminiscent of Christian martyrdom, and at the same time addresses the crowd in a gesture of oratory — the pose of the *ad locutio* for which there is a strong and direct tradition.[570] Gleyre knew perfectly well from Olivier's description of the execution site at Vidy that it was circular — the remains can still be seen — but Gleyre chose to bisect the plan so that the viewer is pulled into the composition in a direct confrontation with Davel. Thus the eighteenth-century Vaudois audience, like the viewer today, was forced to participate in the scene and witness the last discourse of Davel before his death.

While concentrating on the historical aspects of the Davel affair, Gleyre's painting also includes several allusions that place the work in a

fig. 131

568. Olivier 1842, p. 129.
569. The pertinent documents on him are in Lausanne, BCU/DM, Dossier Aloys Olivier, IS 1905/59.
570. On the type, see Hager 1977, pp. 135f.

183

132. Study for *Major Davel*, 1847–49. Lausanne, Musée Cantonal des Beaux-Arts (catalogue n° 554)

universal context. The most striking of these are the references to Christian iconography. In all accounts of Davel the man, there is a special emphasis on his Christ-like nature, which was noted even by his enemies. Olivier makes the point repeatedly in his text, so that in later accounts the transformation of Davel into a modern Christ became integral to the myth: in 1845, the very year in which Gleyre received the commission, Adolphe Lèbre's small article on Davel described his physical appearance and spiritual nature as like those of Christ.[571] It is therefore hardly an accident that the features and the pose selected by Gleyre for his Davel resemble those of Christ in his painting of *The Last Supper*. Moreover, the composition of the painting is a tripartite one that suggests, perhaps unconsciously, the manner in which the Crucifixion is traditionally depicted. Davel like Christ is in the center, with the equivalent of the Good Thief and Repentant Thief at either side in the pastors and the executioner. Also reminiscent of the Crucifixion is the division of the two soldiers in the foreground, and as noted earlier, the sword, hidden in the robes of the executioner, takes the form of the Cross.

Gleyre suggested the timeless nature of Davel's audacious act by drawing on yet another prototypical figure. Olivier had compared Davel in his bravery and courage of conviction to Socrates and had even made several parallels between the two.[572] It is no accident that Davel's gesture in addressing the crowd recalls the similar attitude in David's famous painting of Socrates' death that was on view in Paris in 1846.[573] This

fig. 132
fig. 133

fig. 134

571. Lèbre 1845, p. 310, and Hauptman 1980, pp. 34f., for further details.
572. Olivier 1842, p. 46.
573. The work was shown in Paris, Bazar de Bonne-Nouvelle, where Baudelaire reviewed it.

133. *The Last Supper*, 1847–48. Lausanne, Musée Cantonal des Beaux-Arts (catalogue n° 522)

134. Jacques-Louis David, *The Death of Socrates*, 1787. New York, Metropolitan Museum of Art. Wolfe Fund, 1931

reference to the *exemplum virtutis* as seen in Classical heroes did not escape reviewers in 1850, who drew upon the story of Socrates when describing Davel's martyrdom.[574]

Gleyre similarly drew upon the iconography of Joan of Arc while conceiving the pictorial elements of his *Davel*. The theologian and philosopher Alexandre Vinet, a close friend of Olivier, had made the analogy explicitly in 1842 when he noted that Davel was the Vaudois equivalent.[575] Olivier likewise twice referred to Davel as Joan of Arc incarnate.[576] Gleyre did not incorporate the typical iconography of the female saint,

574. See *Nouvelliste vaudois*, 3 September 1850, p. 2.
575. See Vinet 1947–49, III, p. 260, letter 143 of 15 March 1842 to Emile Souvestre.
576. Olivier 1842, pp. 45 and 91. See also Adamina 1923(a), pp. 2–7.

185

135. François Bonnet, *The Arrest of Davel*, 1850.
Lausanne, Musée Cantonal des Beaux-Arts

577. E[uler], 11 September 1850, p. 2.
578. See Lausanne, ACV, Commission des musées, "Copies de lettres," K XIII/55, n° 174, 13 August 1850; see also Commission des musées, Procès-verbaux des séances, K XIII/54¹, 21 August 1850, item 6. A further note of the arrival date is in MCBA, GA 1004.
579. They were Gleyre, Grosclaude, Morel-Fatio, and Martens, all in Paris, and Embde in Cassel. See *Catalogue des ouvrages...* 1850 under the individual listings. Gleyre's painting was listed as n° 83.
580. The work was by François Bonnet (1811–94), about whom more will be said later. His painting was n° 15 of the livret.
581. His report is contained in Lausanne, MCBA, Museum Archives, A 1850/24. The *Indicateur général* 1850, listed the population of the city as 15,711 (p. 37) and of the canton as 196,595 (p. 40). It might be noted that the museum hours were normally from 11 to 3 o'clock on Sunday, Wednesday, and Saturday, but for the exhibition, it was open each day, except Friday, from 9 to 12 o'clock and again from 3 to 5 o'clock. Sunday special hours were from 11 to 1 o'clock and from 3 to 5 o'clock.

but rather suggested in Davel's appearance his listening to inner voices, which Euler noticed in his critique of the painting in 1850.[577] It is no accident that Gleyre later became fascinated by Joan and devoted much time to creating a large painting of her listening to the angelic voices; he never succeeded in producing the image he desired.

After almost four years of work, Gleyre sent his painting of Davel to Lausanne on 31 July 1850; the work, then unframed, arrived on 17 August.[578] Five days later, a small wooden-strip frame was made so that the picture could be exhibited in the Musée Arlaud on 5 September 1850 at the first major exhibition of the museum. The three rooms devoted to the exhibition crowded in no fewer than 222 works, mostly by Vaudois painters: only five of the painters represented were living outside Switzerland.[579] Clearly Gleyre's work, by virtue of its size, its subject, and the reputation of the artist, was the focal point, although, oddly, another painting also represented the same history, showing Davel's arrest in the Place de la Palud.[580]

It is difficult to describe the immense success of Gleyre's work. In his report on the exhibition, the president of the museum commission, Louis Pflüger, wrote that the entire population of the canton had seen the picture and that the incessant crowds forced the museum officials to prolong the exhibition an additional two weeks.[581] The newspaper accounts verify that masses of people appeared each day before the Musée Arlaud, and when the museum doors closed between noon and 3 P.M., there were no free tables at any restaurant; hotel rooms were booked solid, and walking in the Place de la Riponne in front of the museum was literally im-

fig. 135

186

LE MAJOR DAVEL.

(D'après le tableau de Gleyre qui se trouve au Musée Arlaud, à Lausanne.)

136. Jacob (?) Sibert, *Le Major Davel*, 1850. Lausanne, Musée Historique de Lausanne

possible because of waiting crowds.[582] The critical reviews, led by the glowing critique of Euler, were rhapsodic, even in the Geneva press.[583] When an anonymous "amateur Vaudois" dared write that the painting left him cold, that it was lacking in expression and too monotonic, he was roundly chastised in the press as unpatriotic.[584]

Furthermore, in order that the public comprehend more clearly the nature of Gleyre's imagery — since Davel was not yet the heroic figure for the Vaudois that he would become later — the cantonal authorities authorized the publication of two explanatory brochures. The first was by the historian Frédéric Lecomte, who outlined Davel's career and military accomplishments, with Davel's last speech.[585] The second brochure, by Rodolphe Blanchet, also recounted Davel's life, but with more emphasis on his role in the drive for independence in the canton. Blanchet described Gleyre's painting thoroughly, and included the prehistory of the work as it stemmed from the Arlaud legacy.[586] In addition, Blanchet's work contained the first known reproduction of Gleyre's painting, a sim-

fig. 136   plified, and probably rushed, woodcut by the printer Sibert from Payerne. Blanchet offered to donate the profits from the sale of the brochure to the museum to enlarge the collection by purchasing works in the exhibition of 1850. On 17 December 1850, Blanchet presented the Musée Arlaud with two paintings bought with these profits: Bonnet's *Davel* and Albert-Durade's *The Undecided Voter*.[587]

Just before Gleyre's painting arrived in Lausanne, the Société Artistique Vaudoise fostered a project to make a souvenir of the painting in the form of an engraving to be sold in a limited edition. The society com-

582. See, for example, *Gazette de Lausanne*, 3 October 1850.
583. See *Journal de Genève*, 8 October 1850, p. 1, although the reviewer raised some trivial points concerning the position of Davel's left arm.
584. *Nouvelliste vaudois*, 7 September 1850, p. 1.
585. Lecomte 1850. His pamphlet met with great success and went through four separate editions before 1891. Frédéric Lecomte (1826–99) was also a career military man. He had fought in the American Civil War and later became the cantonal librarian.
586. Blanchet 1850. The documentation on the publication of the brochure is in Lausanne, MCBA, GA 1001 and 1002. Rodolphe Blanchet (1807–64) was curator of the Musée Botanique and the Cabinet des médailles in Lausanne, and also vice-president of the Département de l'Instruction publique. He was a good friend of the painter Bocion and was depicted by him in a painting, *Druey in the cellar of the Abbey of Payerne*, 1845, now in Lausanne, MCBA, Inv. 139.
587. See the letter from the Conseil d'Etat in Lausanne, ACV, Département de l'Instruction publique, Lettres, K XIII/63, dossier 1, and Lausanne, MCBA, GA 1002.

137. François Bonnet, *The Last Moments of Major Davel*, 1850. Lausanne, Musée de l'Elysée
138. Bozzoli, *Davel*. From *24 Heures*, 20 July 1978

588. On the print by Bonnet, see Lausanne, MCBA, Museum Archives, A 1850/6 and 1850/24, as well as ACV, Conseil d'Etat, Lettres, K XIII/68¹ which lists the works bought, at prices ranging from 375 francs (for a landscape by Duval) to 25 francs (for a watercolor by Grevort).
589. *Revue historique vaudoise*, 1894, p. 189, and Lausanne, MCBA, Museum Archives, A 1895/17, which reviews the commission.
590. In *Concours…* 1895, as reported in May/June 1895.

missioned the same Bonnet to make the engraving which was ready while the painting was still on view. The profits from its sale were to be used for additional purchases for the museum. The work proved to be a success; more than 500 copies were sold in several months, permitting the purchase of fifteen additional works that had been on view.[588]  fig. 137

Gleyre could hardly have envisioned that his image of Davel would become a symbol in the canton for more than a century. Gleyre's painting was copied in prints, medals, commercial art, including comic strips,  fig. 138 so that Gleyre's conception became *the* representation of the hero and the event itself. When in 1893 it was decided to erect a monument to Davel at the Château Saint-Maire — the site where Davel was interrogated and tortured — the directions set forth by the arts committee in charge specified that "pour les traits du visage, les concurrents s'en tiendront au type adopté par Gleyre…"[589] Of the nineteen projects submitted for the statue, the jury selected the one by Maurice Reymond precisely because his image of Davel "est bien dans le caractère de celle du Davel de Gleyre."[590]

Moreover, so important had the image of Davel become for the citizens of Lausanne that on the evening of 31 December 1850, a public recreation of the painting in the form of a *tableau vivant* was staged by a local dramatic society.[591] The events of Davel's death as Gleyre had envisioned them inspired two writers, Gaullieur and Hurt-Binet, to create a play based on the Davel story. At the moment of the execution in the last act, the stage directions read: "Tous les acteurs se disposent de manière à représenter le tableau connu…"[592] Similarly, in the poetic drama of Virgile Rossel, written in 1898, the poet directs his actors to take the poses of the Gleyre painting as the curtain falls.[593] For the bicentenary of Davel's death in 1923, yet another play, by Maurice Constançon, proposed the same idea with a slight variation.[594]

fig. 140

Gleyre's own thoughts on the remarkable reception of his work are not recorded. It is known that he accepted an invitation from Louis Pflüger to come to the exhibition in Lausanne to see the painting in its place in the Musée Arlaud; Gleyre had, in fact, expressed the desire to make the trip two years earlier.[595] Gleyre arrived in the first week of September, and presumably he attended the opening ceremonies of the exhibition on 5 September. The only surviving document of note concerning this visit is the journal of Jean-Daniel Gaudin.[596] They met at least twice, on 15 and 16 September, and discussed a variety of things, including Gaudin's memories of Gleyre's father. They did not discuss the painting itself, which Gaudin saw — he even clipped Euler's review for his journal — but Gaudin remarked that the work was worth three times the sum Arlaud had proposed in his will. This notion that the commission for the canton was drastically underpaid would recur later.

fig. 139

Of Gleyre's other activities in Switzerland at this time, it is known that he met with Olivier both in Lausanne and Geneva on 23 September, but what they discussed or whom they saw is not known.[597] Shortly afterwards, Olivier and Gleyre went to Urbain Olivier's home in Givrins for a rest.[598] There Gleyre regaled his host with stories of his adventures in the

139. Anonymous, *Jean-Daniel Gaudin*, c. 1850. Lausanne, Musée Historique de Lausanne, Archives Bridel, 6580⁴

140. Anonymous, *Davel*. From *L'Illustré*, 14 April 1923, p. 170

591. In *La Revue suisse*, 1863, p. 264.
592. Act V, scene v, p. 149. The play, which opened in 1852, had numerous productions in the canton and was revived in 1874 and 1921. The role of Davel was considered especially difficult since it had no fewer than 1200 lines of monologue. Gaullieur was the friend of Olivier who helped in the iconographic research for the painting while Hurt-Binet was a minor French writer who had ancestral roots in the canton.
593. Rossel 1898, p. 111.
594. See Constançon 1923. See also the reviews in *L'Illustré* 1923, p. 170. Similar examples of places where Gleyre's painting is used as a model can be found in Morax 1923, and Serex 1923; see Adamina 1922, passim.
595. See the letter of 29 June 1848 in Lausanne, MCBA, GA 986, cited in part in Clément: "mon intention est de le porter moi-même (à Lausanne)." The letter of invitation is known only in draft form, dated 7 August 1850; see Lausanne, MCBA, Museum Archives, A 1850/8.
596. See Lausanne, BCU/DM, Fonds Olivier, IS 1905/42, dossier 1850. The painter Léon Berthoud wrote to Clément on 14 September 1850 that Gleyre and Olivier had met in Lausanne; the letter is in Fleurier, CFC.
597. See the letter from Olivier to his wife in Lausanne, BCU/DM, Fonds Olivier, IS 1905/42, dossier 1850.
598. See the letter Juste Olivier wrote to his mother from Givrins, 28 September 1850, in ibid.

Orient and also drew a portrait of the novelist, which Urbain disliked, as fig. 141 he said privately.[599] In memory of the visit, Gleyre sent Urbain a large print of *Le Soir* in 1851.[600]

The Conseil d'Etat was evidently very pleased with Gleyre's painting of Davel and its reception, and on 2 October 1850 Gleyre received the remaining sum owed him from the commission — 1371 Swiss francs, 40 centimes. Echoing Gaudin's view, some felt that the original sum proposed five years earlier was not sufficient, and accordingly a supplement of 500 francs was requested from the state treasury.[601] The proposal did not carry the Conseil d'Etat, but it was suggested that another commission be awarded Gleyre to produce a pendant for his *Davel*; the fee allotted for the work was 3,000 francs. The Conseil d'Etat expressed the hope that the work could be done quickly and specified a period of two years as sufficient time for its completion.[602] When Gleyre received word of the commission in Paris on 19 October 1850, he celebrated his good fortune with Olivier, who noted Gleyre's obvious pleasure.[603] Gleyre accepted the commission quickly, writing to the councilor Briatte of his gratitude.[604] But Gleyre's optimism was short-lived: rather than beginning the canvas immediately, as perhaps he had intended, Gleyre began work on other projects, some of them of less difficulty and importance. The painting that the canton commissioned would not be on view in the Musée Arlaud until the fall of 1858.

141. *Portrait of Urbain Olivier*, 1850. Present location unknown (catalogue n° 562)

599. See the letter of 28 May 1851, cited in Lausanne, BCU/DM, E. Olivier, "Ma maison", II, IS 1905/136.
600. This is mentioned in Urbain's letters of 7 and 12 February 1850, to his son Gustave, in Lausanne, BCU/DM, U. Olivier, Correspondence, IS 1905/112, dossier I, 1849–52.
601. See Lausanne, ACV, Département de l'Instruction publique, Lettres, K XIII/63 which also reports the later payments to Gleyre for the shippings charges.
602. Lausanne, ACV, Conseil d'Etat, Registres des délibérations, bk. 148, pp. 492–93, item 41, for the session of 4 October 1850, chaired by Briatte.
603. Lausanne, BCU/DM, Fonds Olivier, IS 1905/42, dossier 1850. Bonjour 1905, p. 47, cites the letter from Briatte to Gleyre giving him the commission, but the original letter or the usual archival copies have not surfaced.
604. Lausanne, ACV, Conseil d'Etat, Registres des délibérations, bk. 149, p. 162, item 242 for the session of 29 October 1850.

## CHAPTER 7

# 1850–1858

GLEYRE, PEINTRE-PHILOSOPHE

142. *The Last Supper*, 1847–48. Detail of illustration 158

When Gleyre returned to Paris after his sojourn in Lausanne, he had every reason to be gratified. In less than a decade, he had had three critical successes in the Paris Salons; he had become the recognized master of an important teaching studio in Paris; he had scored a resounding triumph in his native canton; and he had a substantial commission for yet another large work, a pendant to *Major Davel*. Yet, Gleyre sank into a state of lethargy and despair, similar to that he had experienced earlier in Rome and Egypt. He felt, oddly and unjustifiably, that at the age of forty-six he had not yet accomplished much and seemed to have little hope of fulfilling his artistic goals. Gleyre also was distressed by his tenuous financial situation, which he felt would hamper his ability to live independently. In addition, what few resources he had were drained by the needs

191

of his brothers in Lyons, who were at this time having difficulties with their business ventures.

On 3 January 1851 Juste Olivier, who was now in contact with Gleyre almost daily, wrote to Clément — then in Florence en route to Rome — that "Gleyre a été dans un état lamentable, je vous le dis parce que vous l'avez vu, et cet état est loin d'être terminé." Olivier added that Gleyre's mental state was so critical that he could no longer work as he had before and that even the act of painting exhausted him physically.[605] Olivier was never prone to exaggeration, and his report on Gleyre's condition is confirmed in a letter from Gleyre to his brother Henry two days later in which he wrote that "la peinture me fait horreur." Gleyre also experienced a severe emotional crisis that in retrospect reminds us of his habitual melancholy disposition even during his moments of success:

> … en regardant en arrière, je ne vois rien dont je suis satisfait…
> il me semble que tout est fini, et je n'ai pas vécu. Rien en arrière,
> rien en avant.[606]

There are no specific passages in any of the correspondence to suggest why Gleyre found himself in such an acute case of despondency or why he felt that he had accomplished so little. Two weeks later, he again wrote to his brother expressing similar thoughts; he even added this time that the honors he had received from his art were of little value to him. When Henry reminded him of the pride he and his uncle felt in the recent triumph of his *Davel*, Gleyre could only reply that he was happy with their reactions, but that they should not see too much significance in these mundane matters.[607]

At this time, Gleyre's crisis was heightened by serious medical problems, although these should not be seen as the only cause of his dejection. Clément described his physical problems only in their bare essentials. We know that Gleyre suffered from a severe inflammation of the facial nerves that almost paralyzed his mouth and cheeks, and affected his weak eyes so that he could focus on objects only from the side. For weeks at a time, he could barely see and was forced to remain immobile in a chair without speaking, and naturally without working. Gleyre was treated by three doctors who were called in by Clément and Olivier: the famous nerve specialist François Valleix, who tried to relieve the pain through a form of acupuncture;[608] Alexandre Thierry, then director of the Parisian hospitals and a renowned specialist in various nerve disorders[609] — both of them would later sit for their portraits, probably in appreciation for their efforts — and François Veyne, a friend of Olivier who had treated Arnold Olivier for an eye disorder and who would remain in Gleyre's close circle of friends throughout his life.[610] Despite this impressive medical team, Gleyre's sufferings continued, although they abated somewhat for a period of almost eighteen months; he could neither complete ongoing work, nor begin the second Vaudois commission.

While Gleyre remained relatively inactive, his friend Gustave Planche was preparing a long article on him and his work for the prestigious *Revue*

605. The letter is in Fleurier, CFC, and in it Olivier writes that he feared for Gleyre's life to the point that he insisted on checking on him each day.

606. Clément, pp. 236–37. Gleyre asked Henry to burn the letter afterwards.

607. Ibid., pp. 238–39.

608. François-Louis-Isidore Valleix (1807–55), whose name is constantly misspelled in Clément's biography, made his reputation in the 1840s with his *Traité des névralgies ou affection douloureuse des nerfs*; see Larousse 1866–90, XV, p. 748. On 4 May 1878 Nanteuil described to Clément how Valleix had tried to alleviate Gleyre's pain by sticking needles into the nerve centers of the face; the letter is in Fleurier, CFC.

609. Alexandre Thierry (1803–58) was one of the most distinguished physicians in Paris and the personal doctor of Louis-Philippe; see Larousse 1866–90, XV, p. 125. He was also a frequent visitor to Gleyre's atelier; see Clément, p. 204. Thierry was distantly related to Nanteuil.

610. François Veyne (1813–75) had studied with Claude Bernard and maintained a lifelong friendship with Sainte-Beuve. He was an admirer of Parisian bohemian life and counted among his friends Champfleury, Gavarni, Courbet, Nadar, Murger, and the Goncourts; see Goncourt 1956, XXII, p. 292, and passim. Veyne had treated Olivier's son Arnold for a severe eye problem; see catalogue n° 568 under Gleyre's portrait of Arnold.

*des Deux-Mondes* in their series of profiles of contemporary artists. The article, published in November 1851, is the only one printed in Gleyre's lifetime that was entirely devoted to him, and it thus deserves to be considered in some detail.[611] It is clear at the beginning of the article that Planche wanted to examine an artist who in 1851 had already achieved some acclaim among critics, but who was still unknown to the public at large. He noted the "charmant tableau" in the Luxembourg — *Le Soir*, then known as *Lost Illusions* — as an example of a work that the public continually admired, even without knowing anything about the painter. Planche explained that in fact Gleyre produced little precisely because he belonged to a class of artists much prized by the critic, "qui médite longtemps avant de produire" and therefore painted essentially for connoisseurs rather than for general audiences. He stressed that Gleyre conceived his art "dans sa plus haute acceptation, et ne l'a jamais confondu avec l'industrie," a quality that for Planche — as for Baudelaire — was the mark of the true artist. Planche noted Gleyre's extraordinary knowledge of art and aesthetics, which, he wrote, did not assure popular acceptance, but which was to be preferred to immediate success, almost always forgotten by the next salon. In introducing Gleyre's work Planche emphasized that because of the esoteric nature of his themes and subjects, it was essential to study his works deeply and from a philosophic point of view, recognizing that there is more in the paintings than meets the eye in a cursory examination.

Planche then provided some information on Gleyre's development as a painter in Paris with Hersent. While he had little enthusiasm for Hersent's work in general, with the exception of his 1819 canvas *The Abdication of Gustave Wasa,* which had already been destroyed by fire in 1848, Planche noted that there was still much to learn from his works and his teaching, particularly "des procédés matériels qui sont la grammaire de l'art." But Planche stressed Gleyre's independent nature, noting that he, Gleyre, preferred to follow his own inclinations, which were not always in accord with standard practices and indeed in many ways contrary to them. Planche then discussed the importance of the trips to Italy and the Near East and Gleyre's first major canvas, the *Saint John* of 1840, which he had already praised in his Salon review, a review that Clément used as the basis of his own description of the work. Planche devoted more than three pages to the painting, which had been outside of Paris for a decade and had been completely forgotten by the public and by other critics. With remarkable insight, he compared the monumentality of the central figure to the works of Masaccio and Masolino and the inward spirituality of the scene to Byzantine mosaics. Both of these comparisons must have seemed curious to Planche's readers, since neither Masaccio nor Byzantine frescoes were yet considered important for the history of art, as they later came to be. Planche himself clearly understood their importance as Gleyre's sources because of the drawings he had seen from Gleyre's two Italian voyages.

Significantly, Planche discussed Gleyre's paintings of the 1840s, which reveals the critic's acumen and sensitivity. He found *Le Soir* a particularly

611. Planche 1851, pp. 489–505.

successul example of contemporary allegory, despite his own aversion to the genre because he felt that too often "la pensée" implicit in this form impedes "l'animation" of the figures. Yet he thought that Gleyre had avoided the banality of allegory through his inherent elegance, artistic purity, and sensitivity to the philosophic elements of the subject, which together compensated for the lack of movement and dynamism. Similar remarks appear in regard to the gestures and attitudes in *The Mission of the Apostles* as examples of religious iconography that elevate the work above the many paintings of biblical subjects that were perennially shown in the salons. Planche also pointed out that the ideal and simple beauty of *The Nymph Echo* invites access for the viewer, similar to the manner employed in antiquity which "a guidé sa main sans enchaîner sa pensée."

Planche was especially enthusiastic about *The Dance of the Bacchantes* which he witnessed into creation, even advising Gleyre on certain aesthetic and iconographic details. He was quick to point out to the reader that the painting expressed less of the spirit of Virgil or Euripides than the memories of the frenetic dances Gleyre had observed in the Near East. Planche was careful not to diminish the poetic quality of the work by removing it spiritually from antiquity; rather, he wanted to make the reader aware that the episode had a contemporary counterpart and therefore was invested with a universal substance sometimes absent in other paintings depicting Classical scenes. This is not to say that Gleyre was not inspired by Classical prototypes in the conception of the imagery: Planche notes that Gleyre's paintings embody Greek and Italian works studied on the spot, as well as Etruscan vase painting, although none of these sources is obvious. This point was essential for Planche as he stressed the seamless blending of sources so that the spiritual aspects of the models are sensed by the viewers, a form of originality that binds the tradition of art. He reproached those responsible — either Gleyre himself or indirectly the French government — for permitting the canvas, which he considered a major work, to leave France.

Planche was particularly eloquent in his discussion of the *Major Davel*. He stated at the beginning that in the pictorial tradition of history painting, Gleyre knew very well how to compose a picture "plein… de grandeur." Planche informed his readers, who were presumed to know nothing about the Davel story or its importance in Swiss history, that the central figure embodied the "caractère mystique" and internal serenity of the martyr; he explained how Gleyre had infused the religious aesthetic into the depiction of the historical event. It is to Planche's credit that he was able to analyze precisely the elements of a painting whose iconographic and historical structure was alien to him. He even praised Gleyre for having associated himself in the creation of the work "à la pensée de Lausanne" — that is, to have created an image that harmonized the vision of the artist and the capacity of the audience.

These paragraphs discussing the major paintings Planche himself had seen, either in the studio or in exhibitions, were meant to clarify aspects of Gleyre's art that the public was not acquainted with or was unable to discern. The critic is not attempting to glorify the art of a friend; the discussion is overtly objective. The importance of Planche's comments on Gleyre's copies from Italy can be more readily appreciated now that Gleyre's sketchbooks can be examined. Planche clearly comprehended the significance of these copies in the formation of Gleyre's artistic insight and his paintings. He stressed the immense variety of the works Gleyre selected to study and copy — the "caractère encyclopédique de ses études" — as well as the fidelity to their sources. They were examples of Gleyre's erudition and originality — the latter, Planche explained, evidenced in the impartiality of the choices. This "impartialité qui ne se rencontre pas fréquemment chez les artistes de nos jours" was, for Planche, Gleyre's attempt not only to glean what he could from well-known examples from the history of art, but also to study the broader history of culture.

Planche gave several examples to prove his point, including studies of Giotto, who "n'est pas copié avec moins de fidélité que Raphaël," works from San Miniato and frescoes of Fra Angelico. Planche implies that this early discrimination in his choice of what to study helps to account for Gleyre's originality as a painter. Planche concludes that the artistic originality that sets Gleyre above his contemporaries is manifest in the scrupulous blend of carefully selected subject matter and impeccable technique, both refined through a knowledge of culture that was self-taught and self-maintained. Rarely was Planche so eloquent or so convincing in his criticism of contemporary art; from the perspective of more than a century, one can only admire his artistic judgment.[612]

It was probably through Planche that Gleyre came into contact with Buloz, the respected publisher of the *Revue des Deux-Mondes*, from whom he received commissions to illustrate three articles. These were the first illustrations Gleyre had attempted since 1838 when he was commissioned for portraits to accompany sections of *Le Plutarque français*. The first work was a portrait of the poet Heinrich Heine meant to supplement an article on him by the critic Saint-René Taillandier, scheduled to appear in the spring of 1852. Heine was a revered figure in Paris, especially at this time, because of his infirmity and failing health; he had been paralyzed since 1847 by a spinal disease and confined to his spare quarters in the rue d'Amsterdam.[613]

fig. 144    Although Clément did not mention it in his text, Gleyre made the portrait of the poet from life. The modeling sessions were arranged for September 1851; on 16 September Gleyre was forced to cancel, possibly because of his own medical difficulties.[614] One week later, Gleyre arrived at Heine's apartment to begin the work: on that day, 23 September, Heine wrote to his friend Julius Campe that he could not continue his letter because someone was waiting to see him.[615] The painter found Heine propped on his bed, as was customary for him when receiving guests, his hand holding his head upright, as may be seen in Kietz's portrait of him,

fig. 143    executed a few months earlier. It is exactly in this posture that Gleyre made his first sketch of Heine, ill but exhibiting determination and dignity in his suffering, a condition to which Gleyre must have been especially sensitive. The portrait is romantic in its conception, but it is also a moving representation of a dying poet.

612. On Planche's other criticism, see Grate 1959(b).
613. See Pailleron 1930(b), p. 326, and Mende 1970, p. 271.
614. Heine 1975, p. 320, letter 918.
615. Heine 1972, pp. 126–27, letter 1355.

143. Ernst Kietz, *Heine*, 1851. From Butler 1956, p. 228

144. *Portrait of Heinrich Heine*, 1851. Paris, Private collection (catalogue n° 566)

616. Heine 1975, p. 205, letter 1426.
617. Heine 1972, p. 249, letter 1493, and p. 288, letter 1504.
618. Emile Montégut (1826–95) also wrote an important article on Gleyre later. On his importance in nineteenth-century criticism, see Wellek 1965, pp. 86f.
619. See Wilson 1927, p. 464. Montégut had already introduced Carlyle to the French in a long article.
620. The letter is cited in Pailleron 1924, p. 170. The engraving in question was generously supplied by Col. J. R. Edgar, curator of the Carlyle House, London.

Heine thought the portrait too realistic, showing him as a pitiable figure in a state of emaciation — not unlike the image of a dying Christ, as he described the work to Théophile Gautier.[616] Although Heine seems to have had little regard for any of his portraits, he must have admired Gleyre's, since he suggested its use to his friend Christian Konrad Schad as an illustration for a German article on him and also remarked that his friends considered the Gleyre portrait to be the best one of him.[617]

While the piece on Heine was in press, Gleyre was asked by Buloz to illustrate another article, this time by the eminent critic Emile Montégut on Thomas Carlyle.[618] Montégut, along with Hippolyte Taine, was one of the few French critics to appreciate American and English letters: he greatly admired Lamb, Pope, and Hawthorne, and is credited with introducing the philosophy of Carlyle on the Continent.[619] For the Carlyle article, it was not possible for Gleyre to draw a portrait from life since Carlyle was in London and had no plans to come to Paris. Buloz therefore wrote to Carlyle asking if he had an image of himself that could be used as the basis for a portrait to accompany the article. Carlyle responded on 11 February 1852, sending an engraving made after a photograph which he thought to be of the highest quality.[620] Montégut's article appeared on 1 July 1852 with the engraving drawn by Gleyre but clearly based on the one Carlyle sent from London. It is not certain whether Gleyre simply copied the engraving, without making a new drawing. The

fig. 145

fig. 146

question also intrigued Clément, who wrote to the *Revue* in 1875 for further information; he was told that Gleyre supervised the engraving, but there are no details as to whether he actually had a hand in its production.[621]

The third illustration Gleyre provided Buloz was a portrait of the popular poet known as Jasmin for an article on him by de Mazade. Jasmin was the pseudonym of Jacques Boë (1798–1864), who had made a considerable reputation reciting his work, often in provincial dialect, from town to town — the modern equivalent, as Saint-Beuve described him, of the medieval minstrel.[622] His most famous work was the long poem "Abulgo de Castel-Culié," which was often reprinted and even translated into English by Longfellow in 379 verses. Again, it is not certain what role Gleyre had in the production of the portrait; in the letter cited above from the *Revue* to Clément, it is noted that Gleyre supervised this work also, although in this case, there is an extant drawing by Gleyre from which the engraving was made. There is no record that Gleyre had met Jasmin or that he drew his portrait from life, although Cornu had done so in 1842.[623] Gleyre's portrait was published on 1 January 1854; it was the last work Gleyre executed for Buloz, even though the publisher often asked Gleyre to write an article on his adventures in the Orient.[624]

Gleyre continued to produce drawings intended for illustration of literary works. Among these is a portrait of Juste Olivier designed as the frontispiece for the second edition of the poet's anthology, *Les Chansons lointaines*. Gleyre made several studies for the portrait in 1854, along with a portrait of Caroline Olivier — for reasons that are unknown, Clément never saw these — and proofs for the engraving were ready at the end of the year; in October, Juste showed them to his wife.[625] Both Oliviers were pleased with the results, although some friends expressed misgivings. Olivier's cousin, Jules Hébert, himself a painter, remarked that the engraving did not adequately show the subtlety of Gleyre's drawing.[626]

fig. 147

fig. 148

145. J. H. Lynch, *Portrait of Carlyle*, c. 1850. London, National Portrait Gallery
146. *Portrait of Thomas Carlyle*, 1852. Paris, Bibliothèque Nationale, Cabinet des Estampes (catalogue n° 567)
147. *Portrait of Jasmin*, 1853. Lausanne, Musée Cantonal des Beaux-Arts (catalogue n° 581)

621. Clément received a letter from the *Revue*, but the signature is illegible; it is in Fleurier, CFC.
622. On Jasmin, see Mariéton n.d., pp. 55–56.
623. See Audin and Vial 1918, I, p. 214. The portrait by Cornu was executed on 13 March 1842 during a single sitting with the poet.
624. Villarceaux 1874, p. 448, notes that Buloz pleaded for years with Gleyre for such an article but apparently Gleyre always refused.
625. Lausanne, BCU/DM, Fonds Olivier, IS 1905/60. Clément dated the portraits to c. 1855, which was the date of publication.
626. Ibid.

148. *Portrait of Juste Olivier*, 1854. Gryon, Private collection (catalogue n° 654)

Gleyre also participated in the collective project of illustrating various poems in the collection, along with such friends of Olivier as Gustave Roux, Staal, Hébert, and Fritz Berthoud. Gleyre was asked to provide an illustration for a poem entitled "Le Sommeil du Loup" (The Sleeping Wolf), which Olivier had written in 1843. Gleyre's drawing illustrates the scene in the third stanza:

fig. 149

> Il rêve qu'une fille
> Passe le long des bois,
> Et qu'un chamois
> Sur le gazon sautille.

Gleyre clearly took liberties with the verse, so that the young girl becomes a nearly nude nymph who feeds the animal. Olivier approved Gleyre's image despite its transformation, but difficulties later arose in regard to the Swiss edition of the poems precisely because it was feared that the nudity in this context was too suggestive. Eugène Rambert wrote

149. *Le Sommeil du Loup*, 1854. Geneva, Private collection (catalogue n° 657)
150. *Young Woman with a Goat*, c. 1858. Switzerland, Private collection (catalogue n° 747)

627. Godet 1906, p. 84.

to Olivier on 21 April 1868 that the examples of the print seen in the current edition — that is, the fourth to have been published — were censored; Rambert, who was hardly surprised by this, reminded Olivier of the natural conservatism of the Swiss, which Olivier might have forgotten after decades in Paris.[627] The small controversy over the image did not subside; as late as 1876, it was noted that at the publisher's bookshop in Bern, the offensive print had been removed from the more than

198

151. *Venus Pandemos*, 1852–53. Present location unknown (catalogue n° 571)
152. *Aphrodite Pandemos*, Hellenistic bronze. Paris, Musée du Louvre
153. Charles Simart, *Marine Venus*, c. 1842. Dampierre, Château de Dampierre

100 copies in stock.[628] Gleyre, however, had a special fondness for the poetic image he had created and used it later as the basis for the painting

fig. 150 *Young Woman with Goat*, which he completed in 1858.

Despite the medical problems that hampered his activities, Gleyre not only worked on these illustrations, but at the same time set out to finish several paintings that he had begun earlier. None of these are of the artistic force and dimension of the works produced in the 1840s; only one, the curious and dramatic *Flood*, which was painted over a span of almost a decade, bears the comparison. Probably the most important work of

fig. 151 this period is the so-called *Venus Pandemos*, completed between 1852 and 1853. The painting, one of the rare examples of Gleyre's use of tondo form, recalls the color, spirit, and classicism of his work immediately after his trip to Venice. Clément thought the canvas one of Gleyre's most admirable, although from our perspective and in light of later achievements, it is difficult to share his enthusiasm.[629]

As to the origins of the image or why Gleyre chose the subject, Clément could say little; he noted that the painting remained in Gleyre's studio for a period of almost two years, thus indicating that the work was not a commissioned one. Gleyre had no doubt derived the imagery from Clas-

fig. 152 sical prototypes such as a Greek mirror encasement he had seen in the Louvre, or a relief bearing almost the same scene by Simart for the deco-

fig. 153 ration scheme of the Château de Dampierre, which too has its origins in ancient prototypes.[630]

628. *Gazette de Lausanne*, 24 January 1876, p. 1.
629. Clément, pp. 259–61. There is very little information about the work. Clément, however, recounted a small anecdote which, in light of Gleyre's penchant for keeping animals in the atelier, may not have been a unique occurrence. One day Clément and Gleyre, entering the studio, saw one of Gleyre's monkeys performing acrobatic feats near the painting and noticed that the animal had inadvertently urinated on the figure of Venus. They quickly found sponges and washed the area "et je crois que l'incongruité du gentil petit animal n'a pas laissé de traces." Clément recounted as well that when the monkeys occasionally tore up drawings it apparently did not particularly disturb the painter who always dismissed these incidents with humor.
630. I owe this information to Carol Ockman who published Simart's relief.

154. Medal awarded to Gleyre, obverse, 1854.
Lausanne, Private collection
155. Reverse

When the painting was bought, Gleyre had some difficulty in affixing a specific title. His subject clearly is the opposition of Sacred and Profane Love, and he thought of calling the picture by that title. Gleyre knew well the painting by Titian that bears the same legend, and just as he had consulted Mérimée about an inscription for *Le Soir* to be included in the Salon livret, he now asked friends, especially Planche, to suggest a title. Planche provided the poetic epithet *pandemos*, which in Greek signifies "of all people," thus changing radically the sense of the iconography.

The *Venus Pandemos* was illustrated several times in Gleyre's lifetime and was even copied on porcelain and exhibited in that medium in the Salon of 1859.[631] The painting itself, however, was never seen publicly in Paris and was exhibited only once, in the Musée Rath in Geneva from mid-August to the end of September 1854, the first painting by Gleyre to be shown in that city.[632] At that time, the title of the painting was simply *La Bacchante*. What especially struck the local critics was the painting's Raphaelesque qualities, which, as one critic remarked, outdid even those of Ingres in the purity of form and color.[633] It is also evident that most critics were favorably disposed to the painting because of the paucity of Classical or historical scenes in the Geneva exhibitions, where landscapes almost always dominated. Gleyre's painting was extremely popular among artists and public alike, even eliciting a rhapsodic poem by the Swiss writer Gustave Roux.[634] Gleyre was awarded a first prize, a gold medal of substantial weight and value that he kept throughout his life.[635]

While working on the *Venus*, Gleyre was also occupied with another commission taken on earlier which, it turned out, created substantial artistic problems that were never fully resolved. The commission, from the city of Paris, was for a large canvas intended to decorate the church of Sainte-Marguerite near the monument to the fall of the Bastille. Crucial documents concerning the history of the commission were destroyed in the 1871 fire at the Hôtel de Ville, but from other sources it can be ascertained that Gleyre had received the commission sometime before 1848 — that is, when he was already heavily involved in finishing his painting of Davel.[636] During the political unrest of 1848, the commission seems to have been withdrawn — as Gleyre himself indicated in a letter to Henry of 27 April 1848 without specifically noting the reasons — but then reinstated on 30 August 1849, with a fee established at 4,000 francs.[637]

fig. 154–155

631. The first publication of the painting was in an engraved form in *L'Illustration*, 1854, p. 221. The porcelain was painted by the Genevan painter Jean-Marc Baud (1828–70) and exhibited in the salon, livret n° 160, as *La Vénus impudique*.
632. On the exhibition, see Geneva, ASBA, Commission, 1854. My thanks to Mr. Jean-Daniel Candaux for permitting me access to these archives.
633. See especially Gaullieur 1854, pp. 579–80.
634. The poem is unpublished and contained in a letter from Roux to Juste Olivier, 27 December 1874, now in Lausanne, BCU/DM, Fonds Olivier, IS 1905/47. Gustave Roux (1828–85) was himself an illustrator who had participated in Olivier's *Les chansons lointaines*. In 1851 he married Eugène

Rambert's sister and maintained a house in Paris where the Swiss colony, including Olivier and Gleyre, gathered regularly.
635. See Geneva, ASBA, Commission, 1854. The other winners of medals in the category of "Histoire et genre" were Van Muyden, Simon — a student of Gleyre's — and Albert Lugardon, Jean-Léonard's son. The medal was in Gleyre's studio when he died and is presently in a private collection, Lausanne.
636. Clément, p. 246, presumably from information taken from Gleyre himself. In his letter to Henry, Gleyre excused himself from traveling to Lyons for the baptism of his niece noting that "Nous autres peintres avons les vivres coupées tout d'un coup: Un tableau pour la ville de Paris décom-

mandé..." It is in this letter that Gleyre informed Henry that he must finish the *Davel* which he had already begun.
637. Clément, p. 216. Clément's information comes from a letter he received, dated 11 November 1876, from the Préfecture du Département de la Seine, now in Fleurier, CFC. The letter was in response to Clément's search for documentation concerning the commission; the prefecture informed Clément that the records had in fact perished in the fire. Concerning the fee for the commission, it is noted in *Inventaire général..., Edifices religieux*, 1884, III, pp. 186–87, that it was only 2,500 francs rather than 4,000 francs.

156. *Christ among the Doctors*, 1847–48. Lausanne, Musée Cantonal des Beaux-Arts (catalogue n° 521)

157. Giotto, *Christ among the Doctors*, 1305. Padua, Arena Chapel

Clément was not certain how or when Gleyre evolved the subject for the commission. It was assuredly not designated in the contract, since the theme underwent various changes in the course of the painting. Gleyre may have thought of using a composition he had sketched earlier, *The Prodigal Son,* which he must have felt would be appropriate. He actually used that theme in another context, which will be discussed in the section devoted to Gleyre's last years when the sketch was in fact further developed, with significant modifications, for a large canvas. In any event, he probably began active work on the Sainte-Marguerite commission in 1849, when his *Davel* was nearing completion. Olivier remarked that Gleyre worked on other canvases while completing the Vaudois commission. Clément presumed that the first actual idea for the Paris work was

fig. 156 his painted study of *Christ with the Doctors*, although he readily admitted his own doubts regarding the matter.[638] It is not impossible, however, that this study had in fact been completed earlier, in the fervor of religious work after Gleyre's return from Venice; it bears a compositional

fig. 157 similarity to Giotto's fresco of the subject, which we know Gleyre had seen. If Gleyre did consider using this study for the commission, he must have quickly given it up due to the fact that Ingres was painting the same subject at the same time for another commission.[639] In light of their previous conflicts at Dampierre, Gleyre might well have wanted to avoid further confrontation.

For whatever reason, Gleyre decided to proceed with the subject of the

fig. 158 Last Supper, which he sketched into a finely, delicately finished study. As is inevitable, the work recalls Leonardo's fresco, although there are sig-

638. Clément, pp. 246–48.
639. Hauptman 1981(b), pp. 55f.

201

nificant variations in the handling of the gestures and attitudes. Clément and Montégut were correct in praising Gleyre's use of varied physiognomic types and restrained gestures not unlike those seen in his *Mission of the Apostles*.[640] And indeed, it is certain that Gleyre did not intend to portray the scene with the same unity and drama as had Leonardo, but rather to concentrate on the philosophic nature of the theme. This is precisely what the Swiss critic Eugène Rambert noted and even thought could be proven, since when he asked Gleyre to point out the figures of Matthew, Thomas, and John, the painter was at a complete loss as to how to distinguish them; he told Rambert that their precise identification was of little importance.[641]

In Clément's catalogue not one preparatory drawing is listed in the section devoted to the painting. The discovery of Gleyre's sketchbooks shows that apparently all of the existing studies for the painting, almost twenty of them, were in one sketchbook, which, incidentally, had been given to Gleyre by Nanteuil with a poem inscribed on the first page. The sketchbook contains numerous studies for the *Prodigal Son* and the *Davel* and is one of the few sketchbooks that appears to contain works of only one period. These studies reveal Gleyre's careful method of evolving gesture and appropriate details, using various models in accord with his idea that the Apostles should represent a cross section of humanity. Some of the drawings correspond perfectly to the painted study of the subject, while others show early ideas that seemingly were transformed into the figures finally used. The studies also reveal that Gleyre had in some cases employed the same models for *The Last Supper* and *The Pentecost*, which was the subject that Gleyre eventually painted for the Sainte-Marguerite commission.

One of the models for these figures was Gleyre's friend Chenavard. A drawing for the hooded figure at the right of the painting is clearly anno- fig. 142 tated in Gleyre's hand as a portrait of his friend. From the clearly drawn physiognomic elements here, it can be seen that Chenavard in fact also posed for other figures in the composition, although Gleyre did not wholly incorporate his actual features in the final painted study. As in the development of his *Major Davel*, Gleyre was hardly averse to using friends and acquaintances as models, particularly when the model embodied physically or spiritually the personage he wished to paint. Thus, the presence of Chenavard in *The Last Supper* may have special significance, since it is not the first time that Gleyre made use of him in a religious painting: Chenavard, according to Clément, had posed for one of the figures in the *Mission of the Apostles*, but the drawing seems to have disappeared.[642]

Because of Chenavard's evident relationship with Gleyre at this important juncture in their careers, and especially in light of the fact that very rarely in the art historical literature are the two artists mentioned together, it is important to examine the context of their art in the late 1840s. It will be recalled that Chenavard and Gleyre had known each other in Paris when they studied under Hersent in 1825 and had met again in Naples in 1832–33. Chenavard was intensely involved in philo-

640. Clément, p. 250; Montégut 1878, pp. 423–24.
641. Rambert 1890, p. 332.
642. Clément, p. 462, n° 242. Clément listed the drawing as being in the collection of Louis Peisse, the noted critic and a friend of Chenavard.

sophic matters; he knew Quinet and the German colony around Overbeck in Rome; he had even met Hegel.[643] Chenavard introduced Gleyre to a philosophic approach to art, and through him Gleyre met Quinet and the German circle. While Gleyre remained in Rome, Chenavard returned to Paris and began his long quest for a new form of historical painting influenced by his contacts and his constant reading of historical and philosophic texts. He had already experienced failure in the genre of history painting in 1831, with his study of *Mirabeau and the Marquis de Dreux-Brezé*, which was warmly received by Gros and Delacroix, but ultimately excluded by Louis-Philippe for political reasons from the Salon of 1832.[644] This failure, coupled with his new experiences in Italy, led Chenavard to explore a more metaphysical approach incorporating universal themes replete with science, mythology, and theology, all in the effort to define a new theory of art based upon the great themes of history. But his obscure iconography and abstruse ideas won little praise when translated into pictorial terms: his canvas *Dante's Hell* of 1846 was greeted with reserve by such eminent critics as Baudelaire, Thoré, and Champfleury and left the public and the press baffled and unconvinced.[645]

Chenavard and Gleyre shared common characteristics and artistic goals, albeit not always of the same intensity. Both painters were from Lyons, and both were melancholy by nature and meditative, sometimes to excess, about their art; both were also cynical and nihilistic: Chenavard

158. *The Last Supper*, 1847–48. Lausanne, Musée Cantonal des Beaux-Arts (catalogue n° 522)

643. Bertrand 1911, p. 535. See also Sloane 1962, p. 23, where the same reference is incorrectly given.
644. See ibid., p. 17.
645. See Baudelaire 1923, p. 935; Thoré, "Salon de 1846" in Thoré 1868, p. 189; Champfleury 1894, p. 19. The work was listed in the livret as n° 363 and is now preserved in the Musée Fabre, Montpellier.

destroyed a great deal of his own production and Gleyre had no specific notion of preserving or promoting his. Moreover, the two painters shared common friends, including Planche, although Chenavard, by virtue of his greater sociability, had a wider circle of friends, which included Delacroix, Baudelaire, Charles Blanc, Courbet, Rossini, and members of elite Parisian society. Chenavard and Gleyre both had an interest in Eastern philosophy and mythology, as well as Saint-Simonian idealism; both were ardent Republicans, although Chenavard felt no scruples about dining with Napoléon III, while Gleyre refused commissions and public exhibitions under his régime.

In April 1848, Chenavard and his friend Charles Blanc met with the Minister of the Interior, Ledru-Rollin, to seek the ill-fated commission for the decoration of the Panthéon in which he intended to demonstrate visually his notions of history, society, and art.[646] Gleyre must have been aware of Chenavard's grandiose scheme and may have seen sketches prepared for the projects, although none of Gleyre's letters of the period or those of his friends mentions the project, or indeed includes the name of Chenavard. It was an impressive enterprise that in its completed state would have encompassed more than sixty scenes recounting human history to the present day, in effect, establishing an iconography of History to replace the iconography of Religion dictated by pictorial and philosophic tradition.[647] In this sense, Chenavard saw himself as the priest of this new art — much as Enfantin saw himself as the father of the New Society — which would replace a decadent art that failed to treat adequately the great concepts of humanity. Gleyre may well have approved. Might he have shown his sympathy with this approach by using Chenavard, in the role of the new priest of art, as a model for two separate representations of the Apostles?

Further evidence of their association can be seen in Gleyre's paintings of the period, where the influence of Chenavard's views appears in both overt and latent forms. It is probably no accident that Gleyre chose the relatively rare subject of *The Mission of the Apostles* after Chenavard himself had treated the same theme.[648] Chenavard also included the iconography as part of the overall scheme of history in the Panthéon cycle.[649] Again, both painters envisioned *The Flood* in an unusual manner and, in the topmost section of Chenavard's version, one figure makes the same gesture that Peter does in Gleyre's *Apostles*. More importantly, one wonders whether, in *The Romans Passing under the Yoke,* begun in the early 1850s, the central motif of two severed heads on lances may derive from a similar detail in Chenavard's sketch for Attila and Pope Leo. These parallels, as well as a shared artistic ideology, imply that the relationship between Gleyre and Chenavard was closer than has been suspected, and may in some measure account for various aspects of Gleyre's themes in the 1840s.

It is not certain when Gleyre actually finished the painted study for *The Last Supper.* He apparently presented the painting to the municipal council for approval before producing the final canvas. Praise for the forms and the imagery appears to have been universal, but Gleyre, we are

646. Sloane 1951, passim; Sloane 1962, pp. 24f.; Grunewald 1977, pp. 1f.
647. Sloane 1962, pp. 66f., discusses this aspect of Chenavard's vision of history.
648. The work itself is lost, but it was executed in 1837 and is mentioned in a letter from Chenavard to Thoré in Paris, BN, Chenavard, "Correspondance."
649. Sloane 1962, p. 199, n° 37; Chenavard never executed the designs for the work but it was included in his own list of the elements of the cycle, now preserved in Paris, Bibliothèque Doucet.

told, was stunned to learn that the horizontal format of the canvas was wholly unsuitable for the site the council had in mind — a narrow section of piers between the column and the architrave. Since the actual contract is lost, it is not known if the site or the format was mentioned there; Clément noted, perhaps in Gleyre's defense, that he had not gone to the church himself to see where his painting was to go, a curious omission for a painter who had already had experience in this type of decoration. Clearly the iconography of the Last Supper, which could not easily be translated into a vertical format, was an unsuitable subject for this commission. Gleyre was greatly disappointed but had no choice but to abandon the work in this context. He nevertheless kept the study in the studio and rarely failed to show it to interested visitors.[650] Some two decades later, he hoped once again to translate it into a large canvas to fulfill yet another commission from the canton of Vaud, but various circumstances prevented the realization of this hope.

fig. 159    Gleyre was thus forced to change the subject of the commission a third time. Finally, in 1851, he selected the theme of the Pentecost, which was more appropriate for the vertical arrangement, and subsequently began a series of studies for the work. By the end of the year, he had made a painted study and had plans to complete the painting as quickly as possible.[651] He had evidently lost interest in the commission, perhaps because of the difficulties involved, and finished the canvas hastily, since the painting is no more than a literal translation of the theme. Clément considered the work mundane, Gleyre's least inspired effort, which he attributed to the painter's obligation to complete the commission since he had, in fact, already accepted partial payment.[652] It is also true that *The Pentecost* was painted for the most part when Gleyre was ill and under pressure to complete other works — notably the Lausanne commission, for which he had not yet begun to make studies. Gleyre therefore produced a work which unfortunately corroborated earlier criticism of his penchant for monochrome, creating, as Clément noted, a disagreeable visual effect. Only Montégut thought the painting a success, remarking upon the mystical light that helps to create the religious aura of the event described.[653]

It is not certain how long the work remained in Gleyre's studio before he sent it to Sainte-Marguerite. Clément thought the picture was not finished until 1854 or 1855, but Gleyre's student Auguste Bachelin saw it in an almost finished state in February of 1852, mentioning in a letter that he thought Gleyre might send it to the salon of that year; the implication is that it could be ready for the salon exhibition within a month.[654] Nonetheless Gleyre did not exhibit the painting, partly because of his decision not to participate in French exhibitions, and almost certainly because he did not consider the work to be of the highest quality. The painting, however, was hung in the church sometime before 1855 where it seems to have been rarely seen; Mantz wrote that it was relegated to an exceptionally somber corner so that it was barely visible in the available light.[655] In 1856, a pendant painting by Gigoux, *The Israelites in the Desert*, was hung next to it.[656]

159. *The Pentecost*, 1851–54. Paris, Ville de Paris, on deposit in the Musée du Petit Palais (catalogue n° 582)

650. Clément, pp. 250–51.
651. Ibid., p. 250. Clément mentions that Gleyre began work on it in 1852, but Planche 1851, p. 495, notes that Gleyre began work as early as November 1851.
652. As none of the payment records are extant, the information probably came from Gleyre himself.
653. Montégut 1878, p. 424.
654. Neuchâtel, AE, Fonds Bachelin, MS 1747, a letter to his parents of 11 February 1852. This letter, incidentally, supports Planche's view — see note 651 above — that the painting was in progress in November 1851.
655. Mantz 1875, p. 405.
656. *Inventaire général…, Edifices religieux*, 1884, III, 351. Gigoux was paid 4,000 francs for the picture which is roughly the same size as Gleyre's, supporting the claim by Clément — see note 637 above — that the sum was 4,000 francs rather than 2,500 francs.

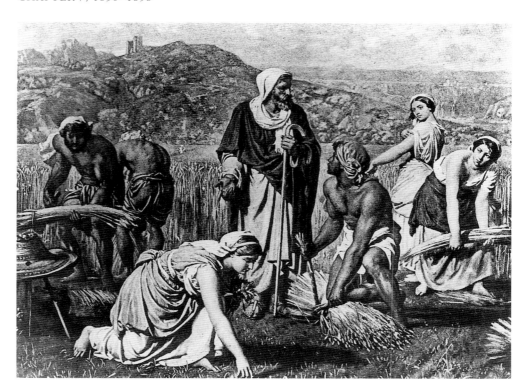

160. *Ruth and Boaz*, 1853–54. Paris, Private collection (catalogue n° 612)

657. Clément, p. 413, under the catalogue description for his catalogue n° 75.
658. Bernard 1854, pp. 2–3, and Brevans 1854, p. 222, provide information and relevant descriptions.
659. Burnier 1907, p. 71, letter of 10 February 1858.
660. In a recently discovered letter from Ernest Duplan to Clément, dated 23 October 1877, Louis de Clercq (1836–1901) is identified as the deputy from the Pas-de-Calais, then living at 5 rue Masseran in Paris, undoubtedly the place Olivier had in mind when he wrote Vulliemin. The Duplan-Clément letter is in a private collection in France, having been inherited from one of Clément's descendants.
661. See the letter of 23 April 1875 from Gaston Braun, charged with the photography, to Clément, now in Fleurier, CFC. In a photograph of the *Ruth* by Braun, preserved in the Doucet library in Paris, there is the inscription "Mme de Clercq, Paris" perhaps indicating where the painting was to be returned after the photographic session.
662. Bonjour recounts these efforts in Lausanne, MCBA, Bonjour, "Copies de lettres," I, pp. 356 and 371. The works were to be sold in Paris in 1903 and the dealer Soullié was asked to find them, but to no avail.

During the work on the *Pentecost*, Gleyre was also producing two pendant paintings, *Ruth and Boaz* and *Ulysses and Nausicaa*. Clément provides very little information on these works, which he probably saw when Gleyre was completing them in the studio, but almost certainly not when he was writing the biography. Clément wrote that these paintings were commissioned by the same person — for the price of 2,500 francs each — but he did not, or could not, name the person.[657] The fact that the first painting was exhibited in Geneva in the fall of 1854, suggests that the owner was probably Swiss, since exhibitions at the Musée Rath were largely reserved for members of the Société des Amis des Arts, which frequently showed newly purchased works in rotation.[658]

fig. 160–161

None of the correspondence of Gleyre or his inner circle gives the slightest indication who commissioned the works, if indeed there was a commission, or who first purchased them. In 1858 Olivier complained to Louis Vulliemin that both paintings were already secluded in a rich Parisian home and thus could not be seen by the public or connoisseurs of Gleyre's art.[659] Olivier must have been referring to the eventual owners, Mr. and Mme. de Clercq, who, we know from Clément, purchased the paintings for between 7,000 and 8,000 francs. The identity of Louis de Clercq, who owned the *Venus Pandemos*, which he had also bought from its original owner, has escaped attention until now.[660] By 1875, the paintings were apparently in the Pas-de-Calais, since when Clément asked Braun to have the works photographed, the paintings had to be shipped to Paris, not without some difficulty.[661] Efforts by the Musée Arlaud director Emile Bonjour to locate the paintings in 1903, when apparently they, or one of them, was to be sold, yielded no result.[662] No trace of the paintings has surfaced since; de Clercq had no descendants.

161. *Ulysses and Nausicaa*, 1853–54. Paris, Private collection (catalogue n° 631)

It is not known whether Gleyre himself selected the subjects treated in these two paintings, which, although neither Clément nor other critics ever mentioned it, represent images of the same motif seen from biblical and Classical perspectives. The use of the subjects together as an ensemble constitutes a pendant pairing unknown before Gleyre and substantiates the idea of Gleyre's philosophic base.[663] Probably Gleyre's contemporaries were hardly aware of this element in these paintings, since they seem to have been discussed as independent works.

The story of Ruth, the Moabite who returned to Bethlehem after the death of her husband to be with her mother-in-law, Naomi, had been treated frequently in art. The iconography most often represented is Ruth gleaning the grain left by the reapers when she goes to the fields of Boaz with his permission and encouragement. Gleyre chose to depict instead the moment when Boaz beseeches his laborers to permit Ruth to gather her grain without interference or restraint. The equally familiar story of Ulysses and Nausicaa, taken from Book VI of the *Odyssey*, represents the events following Ulysses' seven-year detention by Calypso. Ulysses was shipwrecked near Phaeacia, and Nausicaa, who had gone to the beach under Minerva's guidance to wash and play ball, discovered the unconscious man. Nausicaa, with the same generosity as Boaz, offers food, clothing, and shelter to the stranger. Gleyre depicted the moment when Nausicaa shows herself as Ulysses' protectress.

Both stories tell of wanderers, outcasts rescued by strangers — here seen in male and female counterparts — who belong to a privileged class: Boaz is a rich landowner; Nausicaa is the daughter of a king. That Gleyre recognized the inherent parallels in these accounts from such divergent sources indicates the thoughtfulness of careful iconographic selection.

663. Hauptman 1980, pp. 43–45.

162. Nicolas Poussin, *Summer*, 1660–64. Paris, Musée du Louvre
163. Michelangelo, *The Last Judgment* (detail), 1536–41. Rome, Sistine Chapel

The pairing of these themes provides another example of his interest in content and subtlety not common among the painter's more celebrated contemporaries.

Gleyre must have completed both works quickly since no reference to either picture is known before 1852 and both works were finished sometime in 1854. As was his custom, he made a large number of studies for the compositions, more than Clément identifies in his catalogue. In one drawing, Gleyre indicated the name of the model used for several female figures in the *Ulysses* canvas.[664] He also made several changes in these compositions as evidenced in a comparison between the studies and the final works. We do not know whether Gleyre relied upon visual sources for either work: the subject of Ruth had been treated by many painters, including Gleyre's teacher, Hersent, and we know that Gleyre was particularly drawn to the subject since he later recommended it for his students.[665] It is likely that he had studied Poussin's famous canvas of Ruth  fig. 162 in the Louvre; certain figures bear a resemblance. Similarly, the bending figure at the left of Gleyre's *Ruth* may have been drawn from Michelangelo's *Last Judgment*, where a similar pose appears. It is not impossible  fig. 163 that Gleyre was familiar with Lugardon's 1852 canvas of the same subject, which shows other similarities.[666] As for the *Ulysses*, the subject appears less frequently in nineteenth-century painting and almost never in the form of a large work as seen here. Usually the subject is a pretext for compositions of figures in a landscape, such as those in the Ecole des Beaux-Arts landscape competitions.

The *Ulysses* was yet another of Gleyre's major paintings that was never exhibited in public, but its pendant was shown in Geneva at the Musée Rath in the fall of 1854, when Gleyre also exhibited his *Venus Pandemos*. While the latter picture was universally praised for its delicate forms and colors, *Ruth* received oddly mixed reviews. One of its most ardent cham-

664. The name of the model is given as "Mlle Geanerette" but should probably be Jeanerette, a more popular name — we recall Gleyre's frequent spelling errors — who lived at 19 rue du Val Ste. Catherine.
665. See the letter from Albert Darier to Paul Milliet, 22 March 1863, in Milliet 1915, p. 236. Darier and Milliet were both students of Gleyre at the time.
666. The work was n° 858 in the livret and reproduced in *L'Illustration*, 1855, p. 397, when it was again shown in the Exposition Universelle.

164. *Portrait of Jean-Jacques Marquis,* 1855. Switzerland, Private collection (catalogue n° 659)

pions was Eusèbe-Henri Gaullieur, who through Olivier had sent Gleyre iconographic motifs for the *Davel,* and who now was enraptured by the Raphaelesque beauty of this composition. He was emphatic that in the painting "on trouve… les belles qualités de Poussin"; he called the canvas a true masterpiece.[667] On the other hand, a critic who signed his review "A.P." found the work a graceless effort hardly worthy of Gleyre's celebrity and found almost no positive value in the image or the manner in which Gleyre had conceived and executed the subject. He thought that the women appeared too bronzed — providing too much contrast with the rest of the canvas — and did not have the Semitic features he expected in such a biblical scene, noting instead that the traits of these women too much resembled "nos belles compatriotes de l'Oberland." He found the figure of Boaz overdressed for the season, and the wheat not abundant enough. Only the drapery of the figures elicited a positive response.[668]

When these works were completed in 1854, Gleyre had still not begun work on the outstanding commission for the Musée Arlaud given to him some four years earlier. His activities in 1855 are not especially well documented, but it is known that he executed several portraits, including that

fig. 164 of the celebrated Vaudois pastor Jean-Jacques Marquis, who had known

667. Gaullieur 1854, p. 579.
668. See P., A. 1855, p. 146.

209

Juste Olivier since 1841 and who frequently acted as his host during summer holidays in Switzerland.[669] Marquis had married one of the daughters of the rich industrialist Vincent Dubochet, whom Gleyre met later and whose portrait, along with his nephew's, Gleyre painted in 1869.

The portrait of Marquis was painted in the spring of 1855, when the model had come to Paris for the Exposition Universelle which opened that year on 1 May. At Olivier's request Gleyre may have served as a guide for Marquis at the painting exhibition,[670] which included works by the Swiss painters Calame, Diday, and Lugardon, among others, but contained nothing by Gleyre himself.[671] It would have been interesting to have Gleyre's views on these works — as well as on the more than a dozen proto-Realist examples shown by the Swiss painter Grosclaude — but nothing of the sort is mentioned in Olivier's large correspondence for the year. The portrait of Marquis was probably painted either in Gleyre's studio or in Olivier's apartment in the Place des Vosges, where Marquis stayed. At the left in the painting, Gleyre placed two books, the titles of which can be read. One is Vinet, referring to the works of the theologian, who was particularly close to Marquis; the other is *Chansons lointaines*, Olivier's recently published collection of poetry.[672] Olivier later noted that he thought this portrait to be one of Gleyre's finest, as it surely is.[673]

The painting that most haunted Gleyre and occupied much of his time was his wholly original version of *The Flood*, which he had begun as early fig. 165 as 1844, when he was still in the rue de l'Université. The painting, one of the most enigmatic in his œuvre, represents not the Flood itself, but the moment afterwards, when life begins to regenerate. Gleyre worked on the picture sporadically at various times when he was also involved in other works and commissions: various writers discuss the fact that it was seen on the easel between 1844 and the mid-1850s.[674] The precise date of completion, however, remains uncertain. An article of March 1853 refers to the painting as completed and already bought by an unnamed French museum, while the editor of *Le Conteur vaudois*, Louis Montet, remembered seeing the painting in 1854.[675] Olivier noted that as late as August 1856 Gleyre was still working on the canvas, even though it had been bought for a collection in England.[676]

In the context of Gleyre's other work during those ten or twelve years, the subject and manner of representing the Flood appear an anomaly. As we have seen, Gleyre's subjects were often drawn from biblical works in which figures play an important role, or Classical works that contain elements of conflict or universal despair; the Davel commission is the major exception. *The Flood* is the only work that concentrates on a landscape depiction and the only painting to revert wholly to romantic imagery. It has been often noted that the subject was frequently treated in the late eighteenth century and had a particularly receptive audience in the salons.[677] Yet, Gleyre's method of defining the subject is almost unique; there are no figures except the angelic forms that float over the landscape itself. These figures deliberately resemble those of Justice and Vengeance in Prud'hon's famous painting, which had hung in the Louvre

669. On Jean-Jacques Marquis (1799–1863), see Cart 1870–80, VI, pp. 45f. On Olivier's contacts with Marquis, see especially the letters in Lausanne, BCU/DM, Fonds Olivier, IS 1905/43 for several meetings between them. On 14 August 1847, when he made out his first will, Olivier stipulated that Marquis should take charge of his children in case of death; see BCU/DM, IS 1905/42, dossier 1847. Incidentally, Marquis sometimes signed his name as "Marquis Dubochet" as he did when he registered at the Hotel Gibbon, Lausanne on 17 October 1862; see Lausanne, AVL, Livre des étrangers.
670. Juste Olivier too wrote to Caroline while she was in Switzerland on 25 May 1855 — in Lausanne, BCU/DM, Fonds Olivier, IS 1905/43, dossier 1855 — that he was fully occupied with Marquis and mentioned having gone to the exhibition; later he informed his wife that they had all dined with Gleyre. On 8 June, Olivier recounted to his mother the visit of Marquis, noting that its duration was five weeks.
671. It was noted in the Swiss journals that Gleyre "a été vainement sollicité d'exposer; il n'aime point les expositions, qui, dit-il, dégoûtent de la peinture." It is probable the anonymous author of the article is Olivier himself. See *La Revue suisse*, 1855, pp. 451–52.
672. Alexandre Vinet (1797–1847) was also a celebrated independent religious thinker, a leader of the Eglise Libre, and a close friend of Marquis. On Vinet, see Rambert 1912. Olivier's poetry was published in 1855.
673. See Lausanne, BCU/DM, Olivier, "Notes," IS 1088.
674. Clément himself is not clear of the date: on p. 223 he mentions that Gleyre began the work while still in the old studio, while on p. 232 he mentions the possibility that it was begun in 1845, thus after he was already in the new studio on the rue du Bac. See also Berthoud 1874, p. 470, and Rambert 1890, p. 320.
675. The Chronique of *La Revue suisse*, 1853, pp. 264–65; and [Montet] 1865, pp. 1-2.
676. Olivier wrote this to Caroline on 15 August 1856, in Lausanne, BCU/DM, Fonds Olivier, IS 1905/43, dossier 1856. Actually, the painting did find its way to England, but it is not certain how or even whether it was bought by an English patron. In Clément's second edition, p. 408, n° 60, the owner is given as Philip Calderon, information Clément had received after the first edition was published; for Calderon, see catalogue n° 670.
677. See Levitine 1952, and Verdi 1981, pp. 389f., for details of the iconographic tradition from Poussin onwards. The images of the Flood in the eighteenth and the first half of the nineteenth centuries are traced in Wuhrmann 1991.

165. *The Flood*, 1856. Lausanne, Musée Cantonal des Beaux-Arts (catalogue n° 670)

since 1826; the idea that it is to these forces that the Flood can be attributed was certainly in Gleyre's mind and is at the center of the image he wished to create.

Gleyre depicted the moment when the waters recede and the regeneration of life commences in the form of the blossoming tree stump in the center of the composition. Here the essential basis of the iconography is pronounced: the natural emergence of life despite the command of God for its total destruction. This idea of natural regrowth, or historical palingenesis, is fully in accord with contemporary philosophical ideas revolving artistically around the figure of Chenavard.[678] Clément was convinced that *The Flood* should be seen in relation to *Le Soir*, probably because of a chronological sequence rather than a philosophical association between the two works.[679] But a more viable understanding of what Gleyre attempted in the painting would be to see it in relation to *The Mission of the Apostles*. These two works form a delicate balance almost like pendant works. In the canvas of 1845, regeneration is seen in a Christian context, in which the new order of man is expressed through the spreading of the Gospel to the four corners of the globe. In *The Flood*, Gleyre illustrated the natural creation of the new order after the destruction ordered by the Divine. Both paintings are inherently concerned with Judaic and Christian prologues to the rehabilitation of a natural order by which man can be guided.[680]

Gleyre's blending of the historical and the religious in these paintings demonstrates clearly the philosophical aspects of his art during this crucial period of its development. For one thing, both works reflect directly and indirectly substantial elements of a historical controversy that was

678. Sloane 1962 best describes these ideas and their origins.
679. Clément, p. 234.
680. See Hauptman 1980, pp. 26–27, for further discussion of the relationship between these works.

211

much debated in the nineteenth century, that is, the true nature of history and its relationship to biblical exegesis. A key to Gleyre's comprehension of the polarities represented by the historical and theological conflicts rests in the philosophy of Edgar Quinet. For Quinet, religion and history were inseparable phenomena, coexisting in the cosmographic picture of man, each affecting the other in diverse ways. Nowhere is this more apparent or more clearly demonstrated than in his epic poem *Ahasvérus*, written in 1833 just before Gleyre met him in Naples.[681] Quinet's poem, an important source also for Chenavard's theories of the universal past, is at once a summary of history, mythology, and religion in the broadest sense, and at the same time a manifest of the decline of Christianity as a central focus for modern man. Quinet begins with a description of the Creation, containing only the Ocean, the serpent Leviathan, a bird, and a fish, all symbolic of the new deities who will rule. Later in the poem the place of Christianity is questioned by a choir who express the religious doubt of Quinet's time: why did Christ delude later generations of mankind into believing that history revolves around Him for their salvation?[682]

Gleyre's *Flood* attempts to come to terms with this reevaluation of historical and mythological thought in which a ready-made answer is not necessarily to be found in Christian dogma. Gleyre, like Quinet and other liberal philosophers and historians, tried to find another historical basis to address the quandary of modern man, who could no longer accept biblical exegesis blindly in the light of modern science. Gleyre reverted, as did Quinet, to the origins of the Flood in an effort to reach a more primary source. This can be seen in a study Gleyre made at the same time that he was working on his *Flood*, an oil sketch generally entitled the *Elephants*, which clearly attempts to depict history before the Flood. fig. 166 The study may be understood as representing a kind of terrestrial paradise, a theme Gleyre would return to later, when man has already emerged and seems to be in harmony with the still savage nature around him. Here there is no need for the creation of a new order; the theme Gleyre treats in the study recalls similar explorations into the nature of primal origins in the works of Leconte de Lisle or Flaubert's friend Louis Bouilhet, to name but two examples.[683] Gleyre never finished the study, but he told Eugène Rambert that he attached a great importance to the image he had created.[684]

The most striking feature of Gleyre's *Flood* is the presence of a pterodactyl. The form itself recalls the large birds Gleyre had observed in the Egyptian desert.[685] Surprisingly, the actual forms of these prehistoric creatures were already well known in the 1840s, and courses taught in natural history by Blaineville at the Sorbonne discussed the anatomic features in regard to the relationship between reptilic and ornithological stuctures.[686] Gleyre included the pterodactyl in the painting to show the changing forms within the natural process of evolution; the implication is that the presence of the pterodactyl demonstrates a natural order in the process of its own formation between two forms of life.[687] In effect, it contradicts the idea of the creation of all living forms by a single Being. In this light,

681. Gleyre first met Quinet in Naples and had participated in discussions with him and Chenavard. On the importance of the poem in nineteenth-century epic poetry, the main source is Hunt 1941.
682. Quinet 1857, pp. 67–72 and 264.
683. See Hauptman 1980, pp. 27f.
684. Rambert 1890, p. 321.
685. Clément, p. 88.
686. These are described in *L'Illustration*, 29 April 1843, pp. 130–31.
687. This too is implied in a lithograph by Destouches (?) after Emy, called Telory, *Le Déluge*, of 1865, which likewise shows elephants and a pterodactyl in a primitive setting; see Wuhrmann 1991, p. XXIX, n° 184. The print was probably made in connection with the drama *Déluge universel* by Nicolaïe and Siraudin presented at the Théâtre du Châtelet on 29 July 1865.

212

it is worthwhile to point out that in Chenavard's version of *The Flood* for the Panthéon cycle, there is a triceratops that serves to recall the same philosophical and scientific ideas.

It can now be seen why Gleyre took so long to evolve the wonderful imagery of *The Flood*. The goal was not to represent the traditional scene from the Bible, but to explore pictorially the intricate relationship between biblical and historical fact in accordance with current scientific thought. Because of the obscure nature of the subject and his profound philosophic context, Gleyre struggled to find a style appropriate to its visualization. His solution is to be found in the color and texture, as well as in the primeval forms that dominate the composition. An examination of the surface reveals that Gleyre reworked it several times. At the last stage in its creation, he covered the entire surface with a layer of pastel, accenting thereby the freshness of the new work. The result is a jagged, lively surface, more like later nineteenth-century painting than the smooth academic surfaces common at the time, even in Gleyre's own works. Nowhere else in his art are surface textures of the painting so intimately wed to the essence of its content.

Gleyre never returned to this form of imagery or to this type of visual experimentation. But with the completion of *The Flood,* he concluded a cycle of paintings that would have a faint echo in his later works. If we examine the works discussed here in light of their thematic relationships, but in reverse order, the meaning of the cycle becomes more manifest. In fig. 167 his *Elephants* and the quickly made study that precedes it, Gleyre represented the prediluvian worlds when life forms were in the process of evolution and development.[688] *The Flood* represents the results of the natural

166. *Elephants,* 1856(?). Lausanne, Musée Cantonal des Beaux-Arts (catalogue n° 675)

688. The work is discussed in this context in Hauptman 1980, p. 27; see also the catalogue entry.

167. *Antidiluvian Landscape*, 1856(?). Lausanne, Musée Cantonal des Beaux-Arts (catalogue n° 676)

degeneration of these forms that, in accord with the then current scientific thought, necessitated cosmic mutation and a new order. Yet this new order that reconstitutes out of the annihilation of the Flood is once again impaired, since ultimately — here religion and history blend as in Quinet's thought — man is imperfect. Therefore there remains a search for spiritual rehabilitation in the form of Christianity, which is inherently the subject of Gleyre's 1845 canvas, *The Mission to the Apostles*. The ultimate inadequacy of even that new direction to consummate man's spiritual need was one of the most vital philosophic concerns of the period. In attempting to come to terms with it, Gleyre showed himself to be a *peintre-philosophe*.

## CHAPTER 8

# 1858

## THE SECOND SWISS COMMISSION:
## "THE ROMANS PASSING UNDER THE YOKE"

168. Studies for *The Romans*, 1854–58. Lausanne, Musée Cantonal des Beaux-Arts (catalogue n° 732)

When Gleyre received the second Vaudois commission in October 1850, he was delighted with the prospect, as Olivier recounted to his wife Caroline.[689] The contract offered by the canton provided a sum of 3,000 Swiss francs and left the subject to the discretion of the painter, while expressing the hope that the iconography would be drawn from an event in the history of the country so as to make a proper pendant to the *Davel*.[690] Gleyre immediately thought of two possible subjects. The first was the story of "La Reine Berthe," which like that of Davel, was rooted in local history and was relatively uncommon in France. Berthe was a Burgundian queen of the tenth century, the wife of Rodolphe II, the direct ruler of the Helvetian lands before the formation of the Confederation in 1291. According to legend, in the absence of her husband she defended the country against invasions, instigated significant land reform measures, and helped to instill a sense of national unity. She also

689. See the letter of 19 October 1850, in Lausanne, BCU/DM, Fonds Olivier, IS 1905/42, dossier 1850.
690. Lausanne, ACV, Conseil d'Etat, Registres des délibérations, bk. 148, n° 41, session of 4 October 1850, pp. 492–93.

215

169. *The Romans Passing under the Yoke*, 1858. Lausanne, Musée Cantonal des Beaux-Arts (catalogue n° 680)

founded churches and monasteries and was widely known as *humilis regina*. She is represented iconographically in the act of spinning because she is said to have often spun her own cloth in public, to show her sympathy with her poor subjects. By the early nineteenth century, she had become as important as the Virgin, Joan of Arc, Nausicaa and other heroines.[691] Like all Vaudois school children, Gleyre had learned the expression still used today in the canton, "du temps que Berthe filait," referring to the period of calm and peace during her rule.

The second subject Gleyre discussed with Olivier was an episode in the history of William Tell. Unlike the stories of Davel and Berthe, the legend of Tell had assumed immense importance in France after the Revolution of 1789. The Swiss hero, adopted by the French as an instance of the *exemplum virtutis* in the service of liberty and sacrifice, had taken on a significant role in the pantheon of prototypical revolutionary heros.[692] The story of William Tell was widespread in art and literature, partially through the enormous influence of Schiller's play of 1804, and Paris audiences attended numerous plays based on the hero's life as well as popular operas by Grétry (1791) and Rossini (1829). Rossini's opera, especially, was instrumental in disseminating the mythic aspects of the tale.[693]

In the end Gleyre chose neither subject for the commission, telling Olivier that the episode of Berthe was "trop romancé," meaning in this context too sentimental; although unstated, it is evident that he thought the subject would be a poor counterpart to the dynamic heroism of Davel. As for Tell, Olivier noted that Gleyre disliked the subject, probably finding the story too celebrated, already too much a part of the Swiss tradition. It had already been depicted in every imaginable genre and form before Gleyre considered it for the commission. As was typical of Gleyre's sensitivity in the choice of subject, he sought a new or little-used theme. Clearly, he wanted to reproduce an aspect of national history that would touch the same audiences that had acclaimed his *Davel* years earlier.

We do not know when Gleyre came upon the subject he finally selected, an episode from antiquity that developed into the painting he delivered to Lausanne, *The Romans Passing under the Yoke*. The primary source for the scene is Livy, but the subject is known from other ancient writers as well.[694] It concerns a battle in Gallo-Roman history which took place in 107 B.C. when the Helvetian forces under their leader Divico defeated the Roman legions. Caesar had commanded his lieutenants, Lucius Cassius, Piso, and Publius, to drive the Helvetian army from the shores of Lake Geneva. Greatly outnumbered and badly equipped, Divico devised a plan of entrapment to encircle the Romans. In the ensuing battle, the Roman chiefs were slain and their heads displayed on stakes. Divico permitted the Roman army to surrender their arms and return to Rome, but on the condition that they first pass like cattle under the yoke of humiliation.

In Swiss historical writings, the "Bataille du Léman," as the episode was known in popular legend, became another example of the Swiss love of liberty, a mythic prototype of heroic struggle to preserve independence. It was adopted as part of the Vaudois historical consciousness by writers

fig. 169

691. See Muret 1897, pp. 284f., for aspects of the legend in Switzerland. Kaenel 1982, p. 404, reviews the importance of the story for French-speaking Switzerland.

692. Rosenblum 1967, p. 80, and Ernst 1979 recount the popularity of the Tell image during the period.

693. There is a vast literature associated with the diffusion of the Tell myth; see in particular Stunzi 1973, for the most recent bibliography. On Rossini's opera, see Weinstock 1968, pp. 161f.

694. Caesar, *Gallic Wars*, I, 12–13, Loeb ed., pp. 194f.; Appian, *Gallic History*, I, 2, Loeb ed., p. 101; Livy, *Summaries*, LXV, Loeb ed., pp. 77–79. See too Paschoud 1995. These sources were known in several French translations, although Gleyre could have read parts in the original language. In spite of the fact that he claimed he could not read Latin, in fact he did with some proficiency.

217

such as von Müller, Mallet, Mommessen, and by Olivier himself.[695] Although it was never certain that the battle was actually fought on Vaudois soil, in Gleyre's time it was accepted as indisputable fact; only later was it determined through archaeological evidence that the battle was actually fought near Agen in France.[696]

Gleyre was already thinking about the site for the background of his painting as early as October 1852, when, as with his *Davel*, he asked Olivier to provide historical documentation through his contacts in the canton. Olivier wrote to his cousin, the painter Jules Hébert, on 4 October 1852:

> Vous n'auriez ou ne connaîtriez pas une vue du rocher de St-Tryphon [sic], et surtout de l'encadrement des Alpes qui le dominent, chaîne de la Dent du Midi? M. Gleyre en aurait besoin pour le fond d'un tableau dont la scène serait à peu près au pied du rocher de St-Tryphon [sic], entre le rocher et les montagnes d'Ollon...[697]

Olivier's reference in the letter is to the landscape of the Rhone valley at the extreme southeast corner of the canton: Saint-Triphon is three kilometers southeast of Aigle, and the mountain range known as the Dent-du-Midi comprises the Alpine pillars that surround Saint-Maurice, forming the background landscape of the city of Villeneuve, near the spot where it was thought the battle had occurred.

Hébert apparently acted quickly on Olivier's request, since on 10 October the poet thanked him for the package he had received containing the "calques pour M. Gleyre," which, he remarked, were precisely what the painter needed for his picture. In the same letter, Olivier informed Hébert that he had also received

> de M. Naeff [sic] deux croquis, l'un entre de la chaîne de Morcles, lequel vient ainsi compléter ce que vous m'envoyez de la Dent du Midi.[698]

The painter Samuel Naef, who had worked with Gérard and David briefly in Paris before settling in Lausanne in 1807, was widely regarded as a specialist in Alpine views whose accurate geological formations were often noticed.[699] Neither Naef's drawings nor those of Hébert were found in Gleyre's studio after his death; nor are they among the works left by Olivier. It is probable, however, that Gleyre incorporated these views into the landscape portion of his painting. Even so, his treatment of the Dent-du-Midi was criticized by Eugène Rambert for its inaccurate pictorial definition from the point of view selected; Rambert noted, however, that the other mountains to the right of the composition "sont d'une grande vérité."[700]

Thus, by late 1852, Gleyre already had some important visual documentation for the setting of the scene. Whether he began immediately the actual composition or the costume studies is not known. At this time,

695. On this, see especially Hauptman 1980, p. 39.
696. Clément knew this when he wrote his monograph and noted the inaccuracy in his text, p. 265.
697. The letter is in Lausanne, Private collection.
698. Ibid.
699. Samuel Naef (1778–1856) left hundreds of views of the area near Lausanne, now in various collections. On Naef, see Brun 1905–17, II, pp. 465–66.
700. Rambert 1890, pp. 321–22.

of course, Gleyre was involved in finishing other works, including the *Ruth* and *Ulysses* pair as well as *The Flood*, and therefore probably did not devote much time to *The Romans*. None of the letters of Olivier or Clément for the period in question indicate that Gleyre was working on it. In fact, there is no further comment on the work until almost three years later.

We hear about the commission again, although obliquely in 1855. On 30 August of that year, Olivier took his holiday in Switzerland, as was his custom, first visiting his brother in Givrins, and then going on to Lausanne where on 20 September he went to see Jean-Daniel Gaudin. Gaudin and Gleyre had been in correspondence after their meeting on the occasion of Gleyre's visit to Lausanne for the exhibition of the *Davel*. Gaudin recorded that meeting in his journal and also mentioned that he intended to correspond with Gleyre; none of his letters were found among Gleyre's belongings in his Paris atelier, but one of Olivier's replies to Gaudin on Gleyre's behalf, dated 28 May 1855, mentions that Gleyre had been much moved by Gaudin's letter.[701] When Olivier saw Gaudin in September, he informed him that Gleyre was about to visit Lausanne.[702] At that time, Gleyre was still in Paris, but Caroline Olivier wrote to her husband on 23 September that Gleyre planned to leave the next day for Givrins and to go to Lausanne afterwards; Olivier in turn wrote to Caroline on 1 October that he planned to see Gleyre in Lausanne in a few days.[703]

The purpose of Gleyre's visit may have been to take a vacation and to visit his uncle François in Chevilly, but possibly he intended to profit from his stay by discussing the matter of the commission, which was now five years old. There may be a clue in the fact that on 12 October Olivier wrote to his daughter Thérèse that Gleyre had had a meeting with Rodolphe Blanchet, a member of the Département de l'Instruction publique under whose aegis the commission fell; Olivier indicated as well that Gleyre "a dû dîner avec le gouvernement," implying a discussion of official matters, probably the commission for *The Romans*.[704] The archives do not reveal whom Gleyre saw apart from Blanchet, or what they discussed; presumably Gleyre explained his progress on the canvas.

On 6 October Gleyre made his visit to Gaudin as he had promised.[705] Gaudin recorded in some detail the nature of their conversation, but Gleyre's second Vaudois commission is not mentioned. Nevertheless, the conversation is of some interest since it illuminates an aspect of Gleyre that is rarely documented. Gaudin again noted Gleyre's modest and timid nature, which he explained as being characteristically Vaudois. He asked Gleyre whether he had considered returning to Switzerland, possibly Chevilly, when he grew tired of Paris. Gleyre was emphatic that while he greatly admired the Swiss and had great respect for the peasants, the idea of settling permanently in Chevilly was impossible for him because of the closed minds of its countrymen and the lack of intellectual stimuli. Gaudin argued that one of the tasks of an intellectual was to "amener ces âmes [that is, of the peasants] à la connaissance de la vérité et au salut éternel," which the intellectual was more capable of achieving because of his more open attitude and learning. Gleyre told Gaudin that this was

701. The letter was first published by Porret 1904, p. 1, and then again by Perrochon 1948, pp. 202f. Perrochon seemingly did not know that it was already published. A copy of the letter is in Lausanne, BCU/DM, Fonds Develey, B[15].
702. Lausanne, Private collection, Gaudin, III, p. 255.
703. Lausanne, BCU/DM, Fonds Olivier, IS 1905/43, dossier 1855.
704. Ibid. Blanchet was the same who had published the brochure on the *Davel* and who later would ask Gleyre's advice regarding the restoration of a stained glass window in his collection that he would offer to the Cathedral of Lausanne.
705. Lausanne, Private collection, Gaudin, III, pp. 228–29.

also his conviction, one that had been reinforced by a recent reading of Jean Reynaud's highly controversial book, *Terre et Ciel*.

This latter reference documents Gleyre's interest in philosophic and theological ideas that he rarely discussed with intimates but had expressed in such works as *The Flood*. Jean Reynaud (1806–63) was a brilliant theologian and philosopher who, like Gleyre, had been seduced by the ideas of Saint-Simon, but not necessarily as they were interpreted by le Père Enfantin.[706] After a brief career in the Service des Mines — he was also trained as a mining engineer in Germany — Reynaud decided to devote his life to social reform, particularly the spiritual and moral life of mankind. In fact, Reynaud's ideas were much too complex and dense to be read by the masses or too impractical to be followed by them; his blend of Western philosophy and Eastern mysticism was baffling to the uninitiated and sometimes understood as poetic rather than philosophical in nature. The work to which Gleyre referred, *Terre et Ciel*, which was published in a modest edition of 1,500 copies in the summer of 1854, expounds the essence of his theories. While it is often a rambling, somewhat esoteric exposition, Reynaud attempted, sometimes in the form of a Platonic dialogue, to explain the nature of life on earth and his answer to the problem of evil. For Reynaud, as for many of his contemporaries, including Quinet, the explanations afforded by biblical exegesis were no longer sufficient or even plausible because the Bible itself was not credible. Reynaud postulated, for example, that the earth could not have been created in only six days — scientific evidence already seemed to eliminate the notion except as a myth — but rather that the earth was created slowly by a process of cosmic evolution that might have taken thousands if not million of years. While seemingly schismatic ideas such as these were debated, rarely in the nineteenth century were they so unequivocally presented in print before Darwin's study, which was published five years later.

Reynaud wrote at length on a variety of related issues including the notion of evil in a world said to be governed by the All-Good. He explored the idea of multiple reincarnations, the meaning of Heaven and Hell, the notion of human destiny, and other topics that developed from his arguments. He defined Paradise as a mystical concept rather than a place, but eternal bliss was still attainable if one could through good works and conscious awareness expiate the sins of one's life on earth. It is no wonder that the book was banned, though briefly. Its freshness and originality made it the topic of frequent debate, and Reynaud was in turn thought to be a lunatic or a genius. One can understand why Gaudin was attracted to Reynaud's ideas, since they independently confirmed his own, but Gleyre's reading of the book and his capacity to discuss the abstruse language and allusions are surprising. His discussion of Reynaud demonstrates what often emerges in the letters of his intimate friends — namely, that he was keenly interested in a wide variety of issues and could and did discuss them in private. It is also clear from a more profound reading of his paintings that his intellectual curiosity often found expression in them, as is the case again in the commission for *The Romans*.

706. On Jean Reynaud, see Griffiths 1965, who best recounts his enigmatic ideas. The discussion below concerning Reynaud's *Terre et Ciel* is based on the seventh edition, which bears no date of publication.

After a Swiss sojourn of about three weeks, Gleyre returned to Paris, and it is likely that he began further work on the canvas. Documentation of his activities during the winter and spring of the following year is almost totally lacking, but it is known that he continued to see friends and visitors in his studio, in some cases well-known figures whose visits attest to the celebrity he had achieved by this time. For example, on 25 April 1856 Olivier wrote to his daughter Thérèse, then on a visit to Givrins, that he had stopped by Gleyre's studio and found the celebrated composer Gioacchino Rossini admiring the painting on the easel.[707]

On 19 June, Olivier wrote that he had indeed seen the *Divicon*, as he called the painting, already in a state of advanced progress.[708] He noted that the principal figures, numbering about two dozen, were sketched and about half of these were already in a final form. Olivier was convinced by this time that this painting would be a masterpiece and lamented the fact that Gleyre would receive so little compensation for it. He reflected that the sum accorded by the canton would barely cover Gleyre's expenses for materials and the time required to finish the huge work. As will be seen later, Olivier began a hidden campaign through his highly placed friends in the canton to find a discreet way to increase Gleyre's fees.

On 15 August 1856 Olivier told Caroline that Gleyre was so actively involved in the painting that he would forego his summer holiday.[709] What Olivier refrained from telling his wife was that their son Aloys was at the moment serving as one of Gleyre's models for the picture. On 22 August Olivier wrote to Thérèse, who was with her mother in Givrins, that Aloys went frequently to Gleyre's studio and that he was posing for a figure draped in the headdress of a wild boar — that is, the figure hidden by the sword of the hero Divico at the far left of the composition. Olivier added that Gleyre had found Aloys too much a "joli garçon" to portray the ferocious nature of a primitive Helvetian,[710] although it is likely that Aloys modeled for other figures in the canvas as well.

By February 1857, *The Romans Passing under the Yoke* seems to have advanced rapidly, in part because Gleyre's other projects, including *The Flood*, were already finished. One of Gleyre's students from Neuchâtel, Albert de Meuron, wrote to his father on 15 February that he had seen *The Romans* in the studio and that it was remarkable, particularly in the details; yet de Meuron reserved a final judgment because, as he noted, the composition was not finished.[711] Gleyre continued to work on the canvas throughout the spring so that by the summer it was virtually complete. During the summer months, two reports on it were published. The first of these was an unsigned article in *La Revue suisse*.[712] The author — probably Olivier — deeply regretted Gleyre's decision not to show the work in Paris, especially because he considered the picture one of his finest and thought its exhibition in the salon would add greatly to Gleyre's fame. He then described the main elements of the composition, as well as the superb details, but without explaining the subject matter. The writer predicted that the work would be finished by the end of the year and concluded that he was proud that it would be permanently housed in a Swiss museum.

707. The episode is recounted in Lausanne, BCU/DM, Jean Olivier, "Histoire," IS 1905/60, p. 87, citing the letter from Juste Olivier to Thérèse. Rossini had been in Paris since early 1855, living at 32 rue Basse-du-Rempart, only several doors away from Lenoir, who owned Gleyre's *Diana* and *The Nubian*. It is probable that the intermediary between Gleyre and Rossini was Chenavard who was one of the composer's close friends and a regular at Rossini's musical soirées; see Rioux de Maillou 1917, pp. 194f.; and Weinstock 1968, p. 467. Another possibility is Mme Cornu; it was she who arranged a visit for Rossini to the Musée Napoléon in March 1862, instructing Clément to be certain to provide a wheelchair so as to make the visit more agreeable; see her letter to Clément of 18 March 1862 in Fleurier, CFC.
708. The letter is not addressed; see Lausanne, BCU/DM, Fonds Olivier, 1905/43, dossier 1856.
709. Ibid.
710. The actual letter has not surfaced, but is recounted in Lausanne, BCU/DM, Jean Olivier, "Histoire," IS 1905/60, p. 89. The fact that Aloys went often to Gleyre's studio is also recalled in an undated letter from Caroline to Juste in Lausanne, BCU/DM, Fonds Olivier, IS 1905/43, dossier 1856. It will be recalled that Gleyre had used Aloys as a model for the *Davel*.
711. Neuchâtel, AE, Fonds de Meuron, dossier 68[III].
712. *La Revue suisse*, 1857, pp. 474–75. The short article was republished verbatim in the *Gazette de Lausanne*, 1857, p. 2.

The second review was written on 8 August 1857 by William Reymond, a well-known critic in Geneva.[713] Reymond told his readers that he had only spent one hour in Gleyre's studio, but it was sufficent time to be impressed by the imagery of *The Romans*. For Reymond, Gleyre's painting represented the highest attainment of history painting in which truth and imagined history blend in a vast panorama of visual representation. He reconstructed the scene and the event itself for his readers, noting even that one could recognize the actual site of the battle near Villeneuve, "où se trouve actuellement l'hôtel Byron." The details were a source of marvel for him, especially the costumes and the archaeological artifacts Gleyre had included. Reymond concluded that one need not be Swiss or Vaudois to appreciate fully the subject depicted; like Olivier, he predicted that the finished work would be hailed as Gleyre's masterpiece.

These reviews tend to create the impression that Gleyre's canvas was in such an advanced state that its completion was imminent. But Gleyre continued to work on it through the summer and fall of 1857. On 13 November, the canton responded to a request evidently made earlier — for which there is no documentation — for an advance on the fee, notifying Gleyre that they had authorized a payment of 2,200 francs, presumably to cover his expenses and to insure that he would have enough funds to complete the work.[714] A month later, Albert de Meuron wrote to his father that Gleyre was still working on the canvas, which had changed considerably since the summer before. This time de Meuron wrote of his admiration for the work as a whole and marveled that Gleyre would spend all the time he did on a painting so rich in figures when the canton would have been satisfied with a much simpler composition. De Meuron admired Gleyre's resolve to perfect the idea he had in mind even if it complicated the task considerably; he was, as de Meuron admitted, true to his ideals rather than to expedient.[715]

Olivier was also concerned with the amount of time Gleyre devoted to the commission, particularly in light of the small financial reward. On 29 December 1857, he wrote to Hébert: "Quant à M. Gleyre, c'est lui qui continue de se payer à lui-même son tableau que notre gouvernement ne lui payera jamais assez."[716] It was at this point that Olivier began to write to his influential friends in the canton to seek out a way to increase the sum offered by the government. Gleyre, needless to say, was unaware of Olivier's efforts and almost certainly would not have approved them. On 10 February 1858, when the canvas was not yet considered finished, Olivier enlisted the help of the historian Louis Vulliemin. He told him that Gleyre's expenses for the picture were going to run to almost double the commission fee, most certainly an exaggeration on Olivier's part to dramatize the situation. Olivier told Vulliemin that he was certain the canton would not increase the sum they had provided in the contract — he may have remembered the attempt to add 500 francs to the *Davel* commission — and thought it would be better to insist on yet another commission for the Musée Arlaud. Olivier added that the choice of subject should be left to the artist and not specified to be from national

713. See Reymond 1857. William Reymond (1823–80) was the cantonal librarian from 1852 to 1855 and the editor of several journals. In 1873, he became a professor of aesthetics in Lausanne and Geneva.
714. Lausanne, ACV, Conseil d'Etat, Registres des délibérations, bk. 159, p. 422, item 62. The letter to Gleyre authorizing the sum of the advance is in Lausanne, ACE, Conseil d'Etat, Lettres à l'extérieur du canton, bk. 20, item 142, for the same date.
715. Neuchâtel, AE, Fonds de Meuron, dossier 68[III].
716. Lausanne, Private collection, Olivier, Letters.

history.[717] Clearly Olivier feared stereotyping Gleyre's major works as Swiss subjects intended for Swiss museums. He undoubtedly hoped as well that if the subject were left free for Gleyre to choose, he would select one that was easier for him to paint.

Gleyre continued to add more elements to *The Romans* through the winter months, now almost seven and a half years after the commission was given to him. On 15 April 1858 Albert de Meuron returned to Gleyre's studio, this time with Albert Anker, and reported to his father that the canvas was still not quite completed.[718] Yet, by the summer, it seems that *The Romans* was so far complete that it had already been photographed, as Olivier told his readers in his anonymous review. Olivier added that many influential critics had received information by word of mouth on the canvas and had begun to flock to the studio to see the painting. The influential art dealer Goupil, who had reproduced and sold prints of Gleyre's earlier work, was so moved by the power of *The Romans* that he asked Gleyre if he would sell him his future works still in the form of oil studies. Olivier wrote that Goupil's offer, which would have alleviated Gleyre's perpetual financial distress, did not interest him.[719]

Olivier's statement that the painting was much admired by the French critics is substantiated by several notices that appeared in the press. Of those critics who saw the last stages of the work — Planche certainly did before his death in 1857 — the most notable review was by Théophile Gautier. Writing in May 1858, Gautier gave his readers in *L'Artiste* a full description of the work and marveled at the rich archaeological details. Gautier, however, had reservations about the density of the composition, a valid criticism, but still hailed the work as a major one, which he lamented would not be seen by the French public.[720] Similarly, Arsène Houssaye wrote in the summer of 1858 that he saw the painting in the studio and admired the vigorous representation of the event.[721] It was only in October 1858, when the first engraving of the work was published, that the Paris audiences could have a visual sense of the scene.[722]

Gleyre's development of the composition is difficult to trace, particularly since he wrote so few letter in the 1850s, even to his brother Henry. As we have seen, Olivier had become Gleyre's unofficial secretary, answering his correspondence. Nanteuil later remarked that Gleyre had always had a horror of writing and a pathological fear of making grammatical mistakes.[723] Consequently, there are no letters extant from Gleyre describing his progress or even mentioning his work on the composition. That there were changes in the composition is clear from de Meuron's letters to his father in 1857. Gleyre studied the composition and the details in this canvas more than any other; about 150 pencil studies of figures, gestures and details are extant, as well as several oil studies.[724]

fig. 171 Some of the compositional changes may be seen in the first oil study Gleyre made. The essential aspects of the narrative are already in place, as are elements of the poses, gestures, and light. The yoke under which the Romans will pass is here no more than a crude barrier constructed by the spears, in accord, incidentally, with the ancient custom.[725] The landscape is less distinguished but indeed suggests the site near Villeneuve,

717. Burnier 1907, p. 69.
718. Neuchâtel, AE, Fonds de Meuron, dossier 68[III].
719. See *La Revue suisse*, 1858, pp. 558–59.
720. Gautier 1858, p. 19.
721. Houssaye 1858, pp. 31–32.
722. It was published in *L'Illustration*, 1858, p. 241.
723. See the letter of 18 April 1878 in Fleurier, CFC.
724. Clément, p. 273, remarked that three times that number had been executed, but many were lost.
725. The way in which Gleyre represented the yoke in the first sketch is historically accurate as taken from the description; see for example the humiliation of the Romans in the battle with the Samnites in 321 B.C. where the yoke is described.

170. Théodore Chassériau, Study for *The Defense of the Gauls*, 1855. Clermont-Ferrand, Musée des Beaux-Arts

171. Study for *The Romans Passing under the Yoke*, 1856–58. Lausanne, Musée Cantonal des Beaux-Arts (catalogue n° 681)

726. Rambert 1890, p. 298, notes the importance of this point, as well as the fact that no description of Divico's appearance has survived in the myths. See also Berthoud 1874, p. 609.
727. Clément, p. 203. Henri Martin (1810–83) was one of the most respected historians of the period, but his connection to the Gleyre cénacle is not clear.
728. Ibid., p. 264.
729. On the project, which Mérimée never published, see Raitt 1970, pp. 234f.
730. Clément, p. 264. These works were not found in Gleyre's studio after his death. Raitt 1970, p. 321, notes Mérimée's talents in drawing and painting.
731. Clément, p. 273.
732. Fleurier, CFC; Nanteuil noted that the sculptor had fashioned the image of the dog in *The Prodigal Son*, which will be discussed later.
733. Fleurier, CFC contains various letters from Dubucand to Clément, none of which, however, mentions Gleyre. On Dubucand, see Lami 1914–21, II, pp. 231f.
734. See Bénédite [1931], II, pp. 465f., and Sandoz 1974, p. 400, n° 252. The painting was seen in the Exposition Universelle of 1855, which Gleyre had visited in the company of Olivier and Marquis.

more clearly than the finished painting. The most interesting element is the manner in which Gleyre depicted the hero Divico, here seen at the left on his horse. Unlike *Davel*, this composition does not focus on a single, heroic figure, but rather places the vanquished Romans at the center of the attention, thus relegating Divico to a secondary role. While Gleyre must have felt uneasy with this arrangement since there is still too much concentration on the conquered and too little on the victors, he resourcefully created a subtle balance between the two figures at the right. During the process of tranferring the study to the large canvas, Gleyre wisely preferred to hide Divico's features behind his raised arm so that all the emphasis is directed to the Romans' bowing gesture of submission, thus making the hero virtually an invisible force.[726]

As was pointed out above, Gleyre took especially keen interest in the multiple details of the work, a fact noted by almost all the critics. Clément remarked that besides the aid received from Naef and Hébert through Olivier, information was also sent to Gleyre by Prosper Mérimée and the historian Henri Martin, both of whom were habitués of Gleyre's studio.[727] Although it is not recorded in what capacity either had assisted Gleyre, it can be supposed that Martin had supplied general information about historical facts and perhaps the physiognomy of the ancient Romans. Martin had in fact already written the first volume of his history of France in which this very battle is described when Gleyre was evolving the imagery for the painting.[728] As for Mérimée, he was in a particularly good position to advise Gleyre about iconographical details — as he had done a decade earlier for *Le Soir* — since for years he had studied the life of Caesar.[729] Moreover, Clément remembered seeing, presumably in Gleyre's studio, several oil studies of Gallic attributes and ornaments.[730]

Another anecdote of interest here is recounted by Clément. Gleyre had ardently desired the use of a live horse as a model for the one on which Divico sits. Because he could not accommodate such a large animal in the studio, which was already filled with his small bestiary of pets, Gleyre himself, we are told, modeled one in wax specifically for the painting.[731] This anecdote, remarkable in its own right, must be regarded as apocryphal since there is no other evidence or record that Gleyre ever practised sculpture. More to the point is a remark by Nanteuil in a letter to Clément, dated only 28 November but probably 1878, in which he noted that on some occasions — he does not cite this work in particular — the sculptor Dubucand fashioned animals for the painter to use as models.[732] The animal sculptor Alfred Dubucand, who studied with Barye, had no known relationship to Gleyre at this time, but was later a close friend of Clément — as various letters from him to Clément indicate — and was responsible for producing Gleyre's death mask in 1874.[733]

fig. 249

In regard to the iconography of Divico, no sources in French or Swiss art existed before Gleyre began work on the canvas, but similar motifs were available, one of which may have been consciously used by Gleyre for the basic elements of the scene — Chassériau's large canvas known as *The Defense of the Gauls*. This work was painted in 1855, just when Gleyre was producing the essential elements of his composition.[734] Chassériau's

fig. 170

172. Léopold Robert, *The Return of the Pilgrims*,
1827. Paris, Musée du Louvre

173. Léopold Robert, *The Arrival of the Harvesters*,
1830. Paris, Musée du Louvre

painting parallels Gleyre's in subject: the Gallic forces under the hero
Vercingetorix repulse the Roman legions while their wives urge them on
to battle, an episode taken from Caesar's *Commentaries*, one of the sources
Gleyre himself used for *The Romans*. Gleyre, like Chassériau, envisioned
the scene from a telescopic viewpoint in which the central elements push
their way outward into the spectator's picture space. The women at the
right of Chassériau's canvas, with their vigorous gestures of encouragement, are so similar to the same section in Gleyre's work that it seems
unlikely that Gleyre's figures emerged in this form independently.

Gleyre may also have been indirectly influenced by two paintings of
Léopold Robert, *The Return of the Pilgrims* of 1827 and *The Arrival of the* fig. 172
*Harvesters* of 1830, both of which were in the Louvre.[735] In the former fig. 173
painting, the dancing figure at the right center bears a strong resemblance
to the dancing child in Gleyre's canvas, while in the latter work, a similar
composition and central focus on the yoke may be observed. The dancing figures here might also be compared to those in Gleyre's canvas.

735. See Gassier 1983, pp. 178f.

226

174. *Chimera*, c. 350 B.C. Florence, Museo Archeologico

More individual borrowings can be seen in the figures themselves; various pencil studies attest to the fact that Gleyre made use of Roman marbles for the facial features of his Romans. The clearest example is the use of the so-called Capitoline Brutus, which Gleyre had seen in Rome and a copy of which had been in Paris since at least 1800.[736] Gleyre altered the features slightly in the painting — he is the figure immediately below the severed head at the left — but the source and the allusion are unmistakable. A further example of this type of borrowing is the dog at the lower left which owes its source to the celebrated *Chimera* in Florence.

It should not be surprising, particularly in light of the obscure iconography of the subjects he chose to paint, that Gleyre adapted ideas and forms from other works of art, ancient and modern. While it is true that he had a horror of imitation as he often told his students,[737] it was still not unusual for him to borrow discreetly from other works of art, as his contemporaries did, especially in history painting. In the complex and rich symbolic and historical intentions of his *Davel*, for instance, various motifs find their realization in the painting, including an apt use of the pose of David's *Socrates*, which further distinguishes the heroic personality of the central character. Similarly, the importance of historical documentation was for Gleyre a sine qua non of all history painting, which, it might be added, was a feature of Swiss art that he would later describe as weak.

In the intricate imagery of *The Romans*, it was natural for Gleyre to document equally well the historical details of the event and the archaeological details that enliven the scene considerably and which all the critics admired. We have already seen that he made use of information from Henri Martin and Prosper Mérimée, and with the recent discovery of his sketchbooks, it is also possible to see that Gleyre extended his research into the specifically Swiss context of the subject. Several pages of one of the sketchbooks attest to a direct study of artifacts discovered in the canton during the years he was preparing the canvas. His awareness of recent excavations in the canton of Vaud came from Frédéric-Louis Troyon

fig. 168

fig. 174

736. See Herbert 1973, p. 31; dozens of engravings and other copies of the image were available to Gleyre. From the evidence of the extant sketchbooks, he did not, however, copy the statue directly in Rome.
737. Claretie 1882–84, I, p. 64; Hoffman 1903, p. 55, among others, notes this. On studio practice and imitation in Gleyre's atelier, see Hauptman 1985(e), pp. 86–87.

227

175. Anonymous, *Frédéric-Louis Troyon*, c. 1855. Lausanne, Musée Historique de Lausanne

176. Frédéric-Louis Troyon, *Archeological studies*, 1847. Lausanne, Musée d'Archéologie et d'Histoire

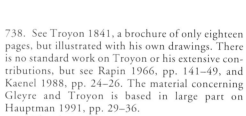

738. See Troyon 1841, a brochure of only eighteen pages, but illustrated with his own drawings. There is no standard work on Troyon or his extensive contributions, but see Rapin 1966, pp. 141–49, and Kaenel 1988, pp. 24–26. The material concerning Gleyre and Troyon is based in large part on Hauptman 1991, pp. 29–36.

739. The plate is from Lausanne, MCAH, Troyon, "Album," I, fol. 23. These three unpublished albums contain a total of 193 drawings and watercolors of artifacts seen during his travel as well as objects excavated in various finds in the canton. All date from the late 1830s to the late 1850s. The studies are all labeled in Troyon's precise hand, using an individual cataloguing system which corresponds to notes he kept describing the objects and their excavations. Both the "Albums" and the corresponding catalogues were donated by Troyon's niece, Mme. Vouga, on 3 June 1897. My thanks to Mr. Gilbert Kaenel for permission to study the Troyon's works and for his advice regarding aspects of Gleyre's own archaeological interests.

740. The shield is now in the MCAH, Lausanne, Inv. ct. 1176. Troyon noted that it was excavated in Avenches in December 1847.

(1815–66), who is considered the founder of Vaudois archaeology. Although trained in theology, Troyon became interested in archaeology in March 1838 when 162 prehistoric graves were discovered on his family property near Cheseaux. He participated in the subsequent excavations, making copious notes and drawings, and finally presented his results in 1841 before the Société d'Histoire de la Suisse Romande, which was presided over by Louis Vulliemin.[738] In 1843, Troyon realized that the center of archaeological studies of early European civilizations was to be found in the Scandinavian countries, and therefore spent three years in Sweden, Denmark, and Norway, where he studied various finds and helped to establish local archaeological museums. During his travels, which extended into Russia, Troyon constantly made sketches of works he saw, which he kept in his own private albums of reference. His meticulous watercolor renderings of archaeological finds, often done with astonishing facility and in remarkable detail, had no parallel in Swiss circles. They are well exemplified in a page of finds from Avenches in 1847, showing at the top a fragment of a shield as well as a variety of daggers and pins.[739] One can further appreciate Troyon's skills when comparing his watercolor to the shield fragment itself, which he later donated to the museum.[740] It is clear that Gleyre had seen and copied from Troyon's albums rather than the objects themselves, as can be seen in a page from his notebook that shows three items in the same manner and in the same positions with respect to each other as those in Troyon's watercolor image.

fig. 175

fig. 176

fig. 177

fig. 178

228

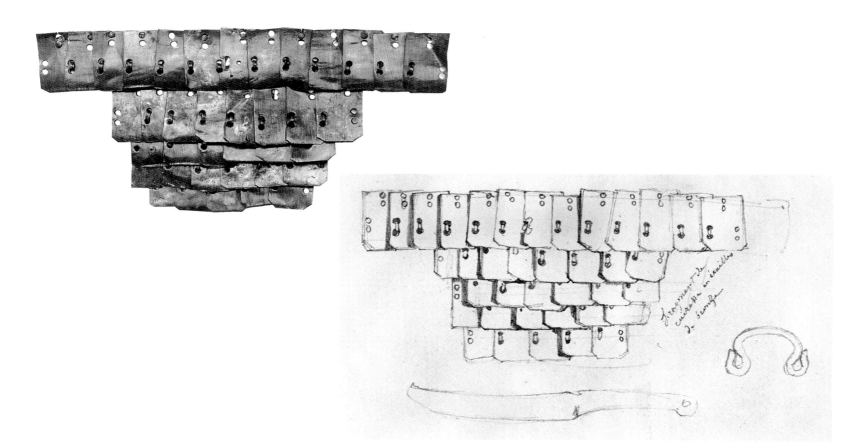

177. Roman Shield from Avenches, c. 100 B.C. Lausanne, Musée d'Archéologie et d'Histoire
178. Studies after Troyon's *Albums*, c. 1856. France, Private collection (catalogue n° 744, folio 15ʳ)

We do not know under what circumstances or when Gleyre and Troyon met, although, as will be seen shortly, internal evidence suggests that there was a meeting. Because of Troyon's celebrity both in the canton and beyond, it is not unlikely that a member of Gleyre's entourage might have suggested a meeting with the idea of providing further details for the Swiss aspects of the iconography for *The Romans*. Juste Olivier, himself a recognized historian well-versed in cantonal archaeology albeit from an amateur standpoint, could well have encouraged Gleyre to consult with Troyon. Similarly, Gaudin, who was also interested in archaeological matters, might have proposed a meeting; Troyon's name, however, does not figure in Gaudin's diary. Vulliemin himself, who knew both Troyon and Gleyre well, could have served as an intermediary, since we know from Vulliemin's letters to Olivier that he actively followed Gleyre's progress; or perhaps Rodolphe Blanchet, under whose department Troyon's functions fell, suggested such a meeting with Gleyre when he saw Troyon in Lausanne.

What is clear is that Gleyre made several studies after the Troyon albums specifically to document further the details in *The Romans*. Several pages in Gleyre's sketchbooks indicate that he faithfully copied selected artifacts known to be of the period, surely under Troyon's guidance. This surprising source is not hinted at in the letters of Gleyre's friends, nor did Gleyre himself allude to it.[741] Gleyre's sketches show a variety of Helvetian daggers and dagger handles from excavations in Vidy and Oleyres, both near Lausanne, which he in fact incorporated into the

741. Only a handful of Troyon's letters have been located in Neuchâtel, Bibliothèque de la Ville, but none of these mentions Gleyre or a meeting with him.

canvas. The studies also show an interest in other Celtic objects, including sword handles and musical horns, which Troyon had observed and copied in Oslo (then Christiana) and which Gleyre also included, slightly transformed, in the canvas. Apparently Gleyre subscribed to Troyon's theory that the Celts and the Helvetii were in fact related races.

The strongest evidence that Gleyre directly followed Troyon's watercolors is a group of drawings of an archaeological find made by Troyon between 15 and 18 July 1856. Troyon described the site of Vernand de Blonay in a long letter to the press in August of that year after he had catalogued some of the rich finds.[742] He recounted the discovery of the tumulus with four graves that contained various bronze objects he tentatively identified as Helvetian from the period of the Roman occupation. These artifacts included bracelets, brooches, small terracotta beads, pins, and fibulae, as well as amulets, all of them similar in certain respects to those he had studied in Denmark. Gleyre copied at least nine of these items directly from Troyon's albums and used them in his canvas. At no time in Gleyre's lifetime had any of these objects been reproduced or published elsewhere: the artifacts themselves remained in Troyon's own collection in Cheseaux until he donated them to the museum almost a decade after Gleyre had completed his *Romans*.

Gleyre's use of Troyon's watercolors suggests a possible date for their meeting. The available documents of Gleyre's activities during the years he worked on the canvas do not record a trip to Lausanne after 1855 and before 1858, when he attended the first exhibition of *The Romans* in the Musée Arlaud. Olivier had written to his wife in August 1856 that Gleyre would forego his annual Swiss holiday that year, as the modeling sessions with Aloys Olivier confirm.[743] It is unlikely that Troyon went to Paris with the albums, nor is it probable that he sent them for Gleyre's use. We can assume therefore that Gleyre undertook the journey, perhaps with the express purpose of seeing the artifacts themselves, in the late summer of 1857, a period in which his activities are little commented on by his associates. This might well explain de Meuron's mention, in December 1857, that the painting changed significantly since the previous summer.

Gleyre's studies after local archaeological finds near Lausanne demonstrate his concern for historical accuracy. One may compare his historical awareness here with that of a decade before when he was developing the imagery of his *Davel*. That earlier work was situated historically in a period that was only a little more than a century before and sustained in public memory through the writings of Olivier and others. Because of this, there was perhaps greater need to depict the event as exactly as possible. But *The Romans* fell under the category of ancient history which, like biblical narrative, could have been treated in a generalized form without incurring critical comment about its historical veracity. Yet Gleyre opted to include details that were specifically Swiss in origin which added significantly to the local historical consciousness that imbues the imagery. Besides attesting to Gleyre's attention to historical accuracy, this effort is a measure of his patriotic ardor in creating a Swiss historical paint-

742. See Troyon 1856. The site in question was known as Vernand de Blonay in Troyon's time and was located in the Bois Genoud about ten kilometers from Lausanne.

743. Incidentally, Gleyre missed the opportunity to visit with his brother Henry who was in Lausanne from the beginning of the year. Henry Gleyre's visit is noted in the visa records, Lausanne, AVL, Permis de séjour. Henry's request for a permit was logged as n° 503 and dated 25 January 1856. It is not known how long he stayed. Charles Gleyre's name, however, does not appear in these records, indicating perhaps that his status exempted him from having to obtain a visa.

ing designated for the Swiss public. Perhaps he already understood that *The Romans* was destined to become a national icon.

Even though the canton expected the painting two years after the commission was made — thus in 1852 — they showed no particular impatience when its delivery was substantially delayed. It was only on 14 August 1858 that Gleyre sent the canvas, rolled for protection, by rail to Lausanne. He warned the director of the Comité des Beaux-Arts to be especially cautious in installing the large canvas so that the lower section with the children would not be inadvertently cut by the frame.[744] The work arrived in Lausanne in the first week of September,[745] and the freight charges amounted to ninety-five francs twenty centimes with the customs charge assessed at seventy-two francs.[746] The rolled canvas was left in Ouchy after its transport from Geneva and was carted to the Musée Arlaud by the concierge, Mme. Delessert.[747]

Gleyre was once again invited to come to Lausanne for the exhibition. The invitation came from the radical politician Louis-Henri Delarageaz, a friend of Prud'hon and a distant disciple of Cabet and Fournier, who at the time was serving as the president of the Conseil d'Etat.[748] Gleyre responded on 4 September thanking Delarageaz for the news that the canvas had arrived safely, but informing him that he could not undertake the trip to Lausanne at that time because of other commitments. He noted that he would be free for the journey only in October and looked forward to breathing "un instant l'air *libre* dans notre heureux pays." As for the care of the painting until he arrived, Gleyre recommended that the unpacking and framing be supervised by François Bocion, who would be competent to undertake the task.[749] Bocion, who had studied with Gleyre in Paris in 1848, had just resettled in Lausanne and had recently delivered to the Musée Arlaud his painting *The Religious Dispute in the Cathedral of Lausanne*.[750]

Curiously, Gleyre was apparently asked to write a historical note about the painting to be included in the museum catalogue for the first showing, although there are no surviving documents that indicate who asked Gleyre to write the description or when the request was made.[751] Clément makes no mention of it in his text, nor does Olivier note it in his correspondence. Gleyre included the note with his letter of 14 August 1858 cited above, with the following indication:

> Voici la note historique sur le sujet du tableau que j'ai expédié… Si vous le jugiez à propos, elle pourra être imprimée dans le livret du muséum [sic].

On 28 August 1858, before Gleyre's painting actually arrived in Lausanne, a local newspaper published an excerpt of the text so as to give its reader an idea of the work.[752]

With the text in hand, the museum was not certain how to employ it since at the time there was a checklist of the museum holdings, but no catalogue as such. On 8 September, the committee decided to print a large number of pamphlets to be sold for a nominal fee during the weeks

744. The letter is in Lausanne, ACV, Département de l'Instruction publique, Lettres, K XIII/63, dated only August 1858.

745. *Nouvelliste vaudois*, 4 September 1858, p. 2; *Journal de Genève*, 1858, p. 2. See also a letter from Vulliemin to Olivier in Burnier 1907, p. 72, incorrectly dated 12 September, saying that the work arrived that day; the date must surely be 2 September. See also Lausanne, ACV, Commission des musées, Procès-verbaux, K XIII/54², 8 September 1858, n° 21, item 1.

746. Lausanne, ACV, Conseil d'Etat, Registres des délibérations, bk. 160, p. 452, n° 11; the bill for these charges was paid by the Commission du Musée, session of 29 September 1858, in the Procès-verbaux for that date. The customs charge, however, was paid by a Mr. Davel, as recorded in MCBA, GA 1004.

747. Lausanne, ACV, Commission des musées, Procès-verbaux, K XIII/54², session of 14 October 1858, item 14, and Commission des musées, "Copies de lettres," n° 2084, in K XIII/55¹ which authorized the reimbursement of the transportation charges from Ouchy — 2 francs, 50 centimes.

748. Louis-Henri Delarageaz (1807–91) was instrumental in establishing a liberal faction in Vaudois politics and therefore was surely admired by Gleyre. See Arlettaz 1890, passim, on his political career.

749. Lausanne, BCU/DM, Fonds Delarageaz, IS 3681/F¹⁷⁰.

750. See Aubert-Lecoultre 1977, pp. 11f. Bocion had returned to Paris in 1855 where he again had contact with Gleyre.

751. The history of this anecdote is outlined in Hauptman 1985(c), from which the following material is taken.

752. *Nouvelliste vaudois*, 28 August 1858, p. 3.

of the exhibition of the canvas. Two weeks later, the commission had an estimated cost for printing 2,000 copies and approved the project on 29 September.[753] The Conseil d'Etat added its approval on 14 October. By 10 November, the printers had finished the brochure and delivered the copies to the Musée Arlaud.[754]

fig. 184

The brochures sold for five centimes, the profits of which were to go to the concierge because of the additional work she was forced to do to accommodate the crowds at the exhibition.[755] Apparently, Mme. Delessert sold all the copies given to her and by the end of the year the brochure with Gleyre's text was all but forgotten. When Emile Bonjour, the director of the Musée Arlaud in 1905, began to chronicle the history of the museum up to this time, he wanted to mention the brochure. He was astonished that he was unable to locate a copy of it in either the cantonal library, or the cantonal archives, or the federal library in Bern. During the spring of 1905, he sent a series of letters to collectors and bibliophiles asking if a copy had been preserved in private hands;[756] he even wrote to Clément's son Frédéric asking if a copy could be located among his father's papers. Bonjour received no positive replies and lamented in his text on the Musée Arlaud that no examples were preserved.[757]

What was not known at the time was that a copy of Gleyre's manuscript, not in his hand, was in fact in the archives; apparently, this was the copy that had been transcribed for the printers.[758] As for the printed brochure, in 1941 a copy was found among the papers of Antoine Baron, the cantonal archivist from 1838 to 1864. In a recent search through this material, an additional copy was located.[759] Gleyre's text, written almost certainly with the help of friends such as Olivier and probably Mérimée and Martin, can now be read in its entirety and is reproduced in the appendix to this chapter.

Gleyre's *Romans* went on view in the main hall of the Musée Arlaud on 6 September 1858.[760] Almost immediately, the Lausanne press presented their critical views of the work: on 10 September the *Gazette de Lausanne* summed up critical optimism by pronouncing the work "un chef-d'œuvre historique."[761] On 14 September, Eugène Rambert, then a young professor of French literature at the university, wrote what was probably the most sensitive and balanced review of the painting. Rambert remarked first on the great pride the Vaudois took in possessing the two recognized masterpieces of history painting in Gleyre's œuvre. He described the realistic way Gleyre had depicted the Roman world pitted against the still barbarian Helvetii, but added that the real subject of the work was the universal struggle of slaves against their masters. Rambert also remarked upon the stylistic elements, the dignity, and the poetic quality of the imagery which he likened to the verse of André Chénier.[762]

The crowds during the first month were huge, as they had been for the exhibition of the *Davel* almost exactly eight years earlier. The *Journal de Genève* reported that everyone reacted with awe and surprise.[763] So celebrated did the canvas become during its exhibition in Lausanne that efforts were made by the Société des Amis des Beaux-Arts in Geneva to exhibit the work there. As early as 28 August 1858, even before the paint-

753. Lausanne, ACV, Département de l'Instruction publique, Procès-verbaux, K XIII/54², 8 September 1858, item 1, and 29 September 1858, item 6. See too ACV, Commission des musées, Lettres, K XIII/55¹, n° 2083. MCBA, Museum Archives, A 1858/3 contains an estimate from the printers Corbaz and Rouiller.

754. The Conseil d'Etat received the request on 2 October, Lausanne, ACV, Conseil d'Etat, Registres des délibérations, bk. 160, item 25, p. 515. The authorization came on 14 October; see Procès-verbaux for that date, item 11, and for 10 November, item 4.

755. Lausanne, ACV, Conseil d'Etat, Registres des délibérations, bk. 161, 13 November, item 99, p. 31.

756. Lausanne, MCBA, Bonjour, "Copies de lettres," II, under the letters written in March and April 1905.

757. Bonjour 1905, pp. 49–50.

758. Lausanne, ACV, Département de l'Instruction publique, Lettres, K XIII/63.

759. The discovery of the first copy was made by Alfred Roulin, then director of the Bibliothèque Cantonale. He wrote to Bonjour about it on 19 June 1941; the letter is in Lausanne, BCU/DM, IS 2228², and the copy is located in BCU/DM, Dossier Baron, F¹⁸, II, n° 183. The second copy, kept by Baron in another dossier of clippings and brochures, and signed by him on 14 October 1863, is now in Lausanne, MCAH.

760. *Nouvelliste vaudois*, 6 September 1858, pp. 2–3.

761. *Gazette de Lausanne*, 10 September 1858, p. 4.

762. Rambert 1858, pp. 3f.

763. *Journal de Genève*, 18 September 1858, p. 2.

179. Samuel Heer-Tschudi, *Charles Gleyre*, 1858.
Lausanne, Musée Historique de Lausanne

ing arrived in Switzerland, its fame had made its way there, possibly through the efforts of William Reymond's notice published in Geneva: the president of the society, Turretini, wrote an official letter to the Vaudois Conseil d'Etat asking that the painting be lent to Geneva where Gleyre had exhibited two works in 1854. He noted in his request that Gleyre himself had promised the society that he would permit the exhibition of the work in Geneva.[764] The commission of the Musée Arlaud refused the request without an explanation; clearly it wanted to reap the rewards of the large crowds and to enjoy the public attention the presence of the work afforded.[765] Turretini's requests for the loan of the picture on 2 October 1858 and 19 August 1864 were likewise refused.[766]

As Gleyre had promised in his letter of 4 September to Delarageaz, he left Paris for Lausanne in October, in the company of Juste Olivier.[767] They stayed with Urbain Olivier in Givrins and went to Lausanne shortly afterwards. Gleyre was forced despite himself to participate in various celebrations organized for him. One of the most interesting documents to survive from this occasion is the first known photograph of Gleyre, taken in the studio of the Lausanne photographer Samuel Heer-Tschudi.[768] Like Balzac, Gleyre disliked being photographed; he sat only one other time for a photographer, for Carjat, under circumstances that are not recorded.[769]

One of the unexpected delights of this trip to Lausanne was a meeting with Edgar Quinet. Quinet, who as an ardent Republican had openly

fig. 179

764. Lausanne, MCBA, GA 1009, and recorded in ACV, Conseil d'Etat, Registres des délibérations, session of 1 September 1858, bk. 160, p. 449. The records of the society show no evidence that it was in contact with Gleyre at this time.

765. Lausanne, ACV, Commission des musées, Procès-verbaux, K XIII/54², 8 September 1858, item 9, and ACV, Commission des musées, Lettres, K XIII/55¹, n° 2072.

766. For his request of October 1858, see Lausanne, MCBA, GA 1009; a letter in ACV, K XIII/63, notes the request of 1864 as well as the cantonal refusal. The painting in fact left the Musée Arlaud for the first time only in 1974, and it was never exhibited in Geneva.

767. See the letter of 8 October 1858, from Juste Olivier to Caroline in Lausanne, BCU/DM, Urbain Olivier, IS 1905/60. Olivier and Gleyre took the train together as far as Geneva.

768. The daguerreotype is Lausanne, Musée Historique de Lausanne, Inv. XLII/31 and reproduced, but cropped, in Breguet 1981, p. 15. Samuel Heer-Tschudi was the preeminent photographer in Lausanne after having settled there in 1848. He also photographed Gleyre's *Romans* immediately before its entry into the Musée Arlaud; the photograph is also in Musée Historique de Lausanne, Inv. XLII/32. Both photographs were surely made in his studio on the rue du Pont, only a few doors from where Gleyre would establish his makeshift studio in 1870 when he fled the fighting in Paris.

769. On the photograph as well as Gleyre's self-portraits, see Hauptman 1990, pp. 310f.

voiced his discontent with Louis Napoléon, had exiled himself from France in late 1851 — he was officially expelled by decree on 9 January 1852 — taking refuge, like many of his colleagues, in Brussels. There are no extant documents indicating that Quinet was in touch with Gleyre at this time although it is likely that some correspondence had passed between them. After the amnesty of August 1858, Quinet refused to resettle in France, opting instead for further exile in Switzerland. In October 1858, Mme. Quinet noted Gleyre's presence in Lausanne, probably ascertained from newspaper accounts, and Quinet, then in transit at Evian, sent Gleyre a brief note asking to see him. Gleyre took the first boat from Ouchy to cross the lake, but was told in Evian that Quinet had just left for Montreux.[770] Gleyre recrossed the lake to Montreux where, after a separation of seven years, he greeted his friend.

Mme. Quinet recorded the reunion in her notes: Quinet, in tears, and Gleyre embraced warmly. They reminisced about their time in Naples and discussed the political situation in France, which Gleyre described as horrible, advising Quinet to remain in Switzerland as long as possible. Quinet expressed his desire to stay but told Gleyre that he was not certain he could, since he required a special permit. It was almost certainly upon Gleyre's recommendation that Quinet later wrote to Delarageaz requesting the necessary documents. In his letter, Quinet told the Conseil d'Etat that Gleyre could serve as a reference.[771] The permission was granted and the Quinets took up residence in Veytaux, where they stayed until 1870.[772] Mme. Quinet recorded, some nine years after this meeting with Gleyre, that she had asked the painter to do a portrait of her husband.[773] Unfortunately, no such portrait has survived, nor do we know whether Gleyre ever began the work.

Gleyre's visit with Quinet in Montreux in October 1858 did not escape the attention of the Conseil d'Etat. On 12 October, Delarageaz wrote Gleyre there asking him to participate in a banquet in his honor, scheduled for the 15th of the month at the Hôtel du Faucon in Lausanne.[774] Olivier was also in Montreux at the same time — he did not note whom he saw, but probably he stayed with Marquis; he did not mention seeing Quinet — and wrote to Caroline on 14 October that he had met Gleyre in Montreux just before he was to leave for Lausanne.[775] They went as far as Vevey together; Olivier stayed there, while Gleyre continued to Lausanne, where he was to dine with Vulliemin the day before the banquet. The newspapers reported the banquet honoring Gleyre and suggested that it would be a special honor for the painter if some of the population of the city could meet in front of the hotel to show their appreciation for the paintings that enriched the museum collection. A torchlight parade was planned from the Musée Arlaud past the cathedral to the hotel; clear and crisp weather was promised.[776]

The banquet took place in the late afternoon at the hotel. Despite the fact that it was an official function, there is no record of what transpired; Olivier seems not to have been present since he makes no mention of it in his letters to Caroline. The press, however, reported the public manifestation that took place afterwards, an event unparalleled in Lausanne,

770. Mme. Quinet 1869–70, pp. 188–89, 210. The Quinets intended to reside in the area, as had been suggested by their friend Michelet; see the latter's *Journal*, 1959, II, pp. 425 and 433.

771. Lausanne, BCU/DM, Fonds Delarageaz, IS 3681/F¹⁷⁴, 1 November 1858. In fact, it is not certain that Quinet was required to have such a permit or a recommendation since his grandparents were Swiss; see Valès 1936, p. 247.

772. Veytaux is only several kilometers from Montreux; in 1860 it had a population of 287. See *Dictionnaire historique, géographique...* 1921, III, p. 764.

773. See Paris BN, Mme. Quinet, "Mémorial," X, 3 September 1867, in which she recalled having asked Gleyre to do the portrait nine years earlier. There is no other mention of it.

774. Lausanne, ACE, Conseil d'Etat, Lettres à l'intérieur, bk. 96, n° 1167.

775. Lausanne, BCU/DM, J. Olivier, "Histoire...," IS 1905/60, p. 125.

776. *Nouvelliste vaudois*, 14 October 1858, p. 4.

for a painter now celebrated as a national hero. At eight o'clock that evening a large number of students, artists, and other citizens, in the company of a military band, marched in front of the hotel entrance singing patriotic songs. When Gleyre emerged, there was a huge ovation. The leader of the student faction was a young law student and political radical, Louis Ruchonnet, who later became one of the most prominent political personages in the canton and served as a crucial link with the government in the acquisition of other works by Gleyre for the museum.[777] Ruchonnet took it upon himself to address the painter on behalf of the crowd, thanking him for his important part in glorifying their common historical background. Gleyre responded with "quelques paroles bien senties," and there were cries of "Vive Gleyre!" from the crowd. The ceremonies ended with a small display of fireworks.[778] Gleyre's friends in Paris had the opportunity to read about the event as it was proudly reported in the French press.[779]

Like the iconic image of Davel, that of the victory of the Swiss over the more powerful Romans very quickly became central to the Vaudois historical consciousness. As early as the first exhibition of the work in the Musée Arlaud, writers began to regard the work as the masterpiece that best illustrated the struggle for liberty. On 13 October 1858, the writer and explorer Henri Renou placed the image and the painter in a nationalistic framework:

> Elle est chère à nos cœurs cette toile immortelle
> Que nous admirons tous… car elle nous rappelle
> D'héroïques efforts, par le ciel couronnés,
> D'un peuple pour ses dieux et pour ses libertés.
> Le nom de Divicon comme celui de Gleyre
> Pour nous Suisses, Vaudois, deviendra populaire.
> Et tous deux, bien plus tard, à nos petits neveux
> Parleront de chefs-d'œuvre et de faits glorieux.[780]

Renou's prediction came true; the painting was reproduced in various forms for generations, and hardly a Swiss textbook on the history of the Roman invasions was printed without including it to illustrate the glorious victory. Like the *Davel*, the painting became the subject of a *tableau vivant* in the streets of Lausanne. A society called La Vigie, which often performed popular theatrical events out of doors, decided on 1 January 1867 to reenact the scene Gleyre represented, complete with the costumes modeled after those in the picture; more than 260 actors participated in bringing the scene to life not far from where the painting itself hung.[781] The newspapers reported that an unusually large crowd watched the event and that no detail in Gleyre's painting was omitted from the spectacle.[782] Similarly, the same scene of Divico's victory and the Roman humiliation was the subject of more professional performances, the most important of which was probably the verse drama by Adolphe Ribaux of 1908. The play with music, employing more than 200 participants, was performed in an open-air theater in Bevaix, near Neuchâtel. The scene

777. On Louis Ruchonnet, see Bonjour 1936, as well as his personal papers, preserved in Lausanne, BCU/DM, Fonds Ruchonnet. Ruchonnet was not only a political rebel then, but also a free spirit; on 5 August 1858, he was fined six francs for insulting the police during a demonstration.
778. *Nouvelliste vaudois*, 16 October 1858, pp. 3–4; *Gazette de Lausanne*, 16 October 1858, p. 2.
779. Dax 1858, pp. 126–27.
780. Renou 1858, pp. 3–4. The poem is signed Yverdon, October 1850, but this is clearly a misprint. Henri Renou (1837–72) was responsible, along with Louis Montet, for the establishment of *Le Conteur vaudois*.
781. *Le Conteur vaudois*, 1866, p. 1.
782. *Gazette de Lausanne*, 2 January 1867, p. 3; Michod 1867, p. 1. The event was organized and designed by a Mr. Lacaze who had already organized various festivals in Vevey.

180. Performance of *Divico* at Bevaix, 25 July 1908. From *La Patrie Suisse*, 5 August 1908, p. 191

Gleyre had painted formed the climax of the last act; here the author specified in the script "En ce moment, la scène reproduit le tableau de Gleyre."[783]

fig. 180

From the public manifestations and outward expressions of patriotic fervor that Gleyre's work precipitated, one might assume that its imagery would have exerted a pictorial influence on other artists. And yet this is hardly the case, perhaps because painters — particularly Swiss painters familiar from childhood with its imagery — thought of it as iconic, and like the *Davel*, Gleyre's painting was considered the definitive version of the subject. Certain echoes were felt elsewhere. Albert Boime claims that some of these echoes are visible in the work of Edward Poynter, one of Gleyre's English students, particularly in his spectacular painting of 1867, *Israel in Egypt*.[784] While it is true that Poynter almost certainly knew Gleyre's painting at least through reproduction, it seems that the parallels — especially in the dionysiac group at the right — are fortuitous, simply a common element of the gestural iconography of rejoicing.

fig. 181

In fact, only one work appears unabashedly to utilize Gleyre's painting as source: a plaster relief by the Swiss sculptor Anton Aloys Brandenberg depicting precisely the same moment as Gleyre's *Romans*.[785] The work was completed before 1892, most probably as a project for the decoration of the Bundeshaus in Bern, but it was not accepted as such and was never executed in marble. It is evident from the facial types of the Helvetii and the Romans, the gestures here reduced for the simpler composition, and even the detail of the snarling dog, that Gleyre's image was the direct model for the sculptor. Brandenberg replaced the oxen yoke with the historically more accurate spear yoke, possibly after reading Conrad Ferdinand Meyer's poem on the subject published in 1882.[786]

fig. 182

783. Ribaux 1908, p. 114; D. 1908, pp. 190f.
784. Boime 1974, p. 114.
785. No monographs exist on the artist but see the brief biographical notice in Brun 1905–17, I, pp. 197–98. The relief is presently in the Kunsthaus, Zug, Inv. n° 144. It was on view during the second Nationale Kunstausstellung in Bern in 1892, n° 364. My thanks to Paul Lang for bringing the sculpture to my attention. It might be added that Brandenberg undertook the project while he was in Rome, thus adding a certain irony to the very choice of this subject — the modern Helvete who portrays the Roman defeat while himself on Roman territory.
786. For Meyer's poem, see Zelger 1974, p. 97.

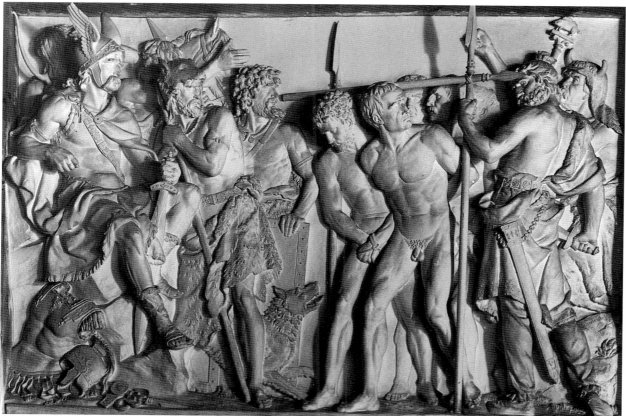

It will be recalled that already in February 1858, well before the painting was finished, Olivier and Vulliemin were secretly urging the Vaudois government to increase Gleyre's fee above the commissioned price. Neither Olivier nor Vulliemin was successful in altering the contract, but Vulliemin was certainly instrumental in the government's decision to order yet another painting from Gleyre, as Olivier had hoped. The new commissions were recorded on 12 October 1858 in the same session in which the banquet in Gleyre's honor was announced. The second and

181. Edward Poynter, *Israel in Egypt*, 1867. London, Guildhall Art Gallery
182. Anton Aloys Brandenberg, *The Romans Passing under the Yoke*, 1891. Chur, Bünder Kunstmuseum

237

third paragraphs of the session note that the council decided "de lui commander le portrait de M. le Général Jomini pour le Musée [Arlaud]," and "de lui commander un nouveau tableau, en lui laissant le choix du sujet libre et le prix à sa disposition." Further, the council thought a sum of 10,000 to 15,000 francs appropriate for the projects.[787] Gleyre received the news shortly afterwards and, as will be seen, began the portrait of Jomini as soon as he could arrange a sitting with the general. Despite his free choice of subject, the second part of the commission gave Gleyre problems until his death. Despite interventions and pleas from various figures in Vaudois art and politics, the painting was never delivered; Gleyre, it was said, added some colors to the canvas on the very day he died. fig. 183

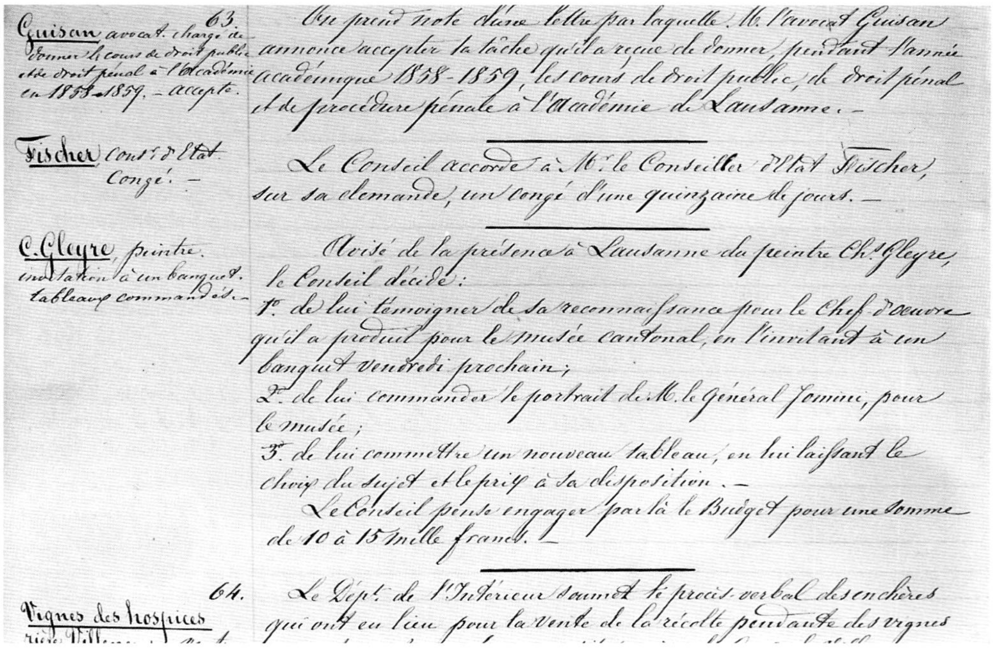

Guisan avocat. chargé de donner les cours de droit public et de droit pénal à l'Académie en 1858-1859. – accepte. 63.

On prend note d'une lettre par laquelle M. l'avocat Guisan annonce accepter la tâche qu'il a reçue de donner, pendant l'année académique 1858-1859, les cours de droit public, de droit pénal et de procédure pénale à l'Académie de Lausanne. –

Fischer Consr. d'Etat. Congé. –

Le Conseil accorde à Mr. le Conseiller d'Etat Fischer, sur sa demande, un congé d'une quinzaine de jours. –

C. Gleyre, peintre. invitation à un banquet. tableaux commandés. –

Avisé de la présence à Lausanne du peintre Chs. Gleyre, le Conseil décide:
1°. de lui témoigner de sa reconnaissance pour le Chef-d'oeuvre qu'il a produit pour le musée cantonal, en l'invitant à un banquet vendredi prochain;
2°. de lui commander le portrait de M. le Général Jomini, pour le musée;
3°. de lui commettre un nouveau tableau, en lui laissant le choix du sujet et le prix à sa disposition. –
Le Conseil pense engager par là le Budget pour une somme de 10 à 15 mille francs. –

Vignes des hospices 64.

Le Dépt. de l'Intérieur soumet le procès-verbal des enchères qui ont eu lieu pour la vente de la récolte pendante des vignes

183. Vaudois government session note, 12 October 1858. Lausanne, Archives Cantonales Vaudoises

787. Lausanne, ACV, Conseil d'Etat, Registres des délibérations, bk. 60, item 63, p. 528; a draft of the letter to Gleyre is in Lausanne, MCBA, GA 1006.

## LA
# BATAILLE DU LÉMAN

OU

## LES HELVÉTIENS

FAISANT PASSER LES ROMAINS SOUS LE JOUG

◦◦◦

Tableau peint par **M. GLEYRE** pour le Musée de Lausanne.

C'est Jules-César lui-même qui, en deux endroits de ses Commentaires, rappelle ce souvenir de la défaite d'une armée romaine par les Helvétiens. « *Du temps de nos pères,* » dit-il, (savoir environ cinquante ans avant lui), « *ils avaient vaincu* » *le consul Cassius, l'avaient tué, ainsi que son lieutenant* » *Pison, et avaient fait passer son armée sous le joug.* » César ajoute que ce Pison, tué avec Cassius, était « *l'aïeul de son beau-père.* » Il devait donc être bien informé de cet exploit d'un petit peuple indépendant et belliqueux, qui osa longtemps tenir tête à Rome, et dont Cicéron, dans ses discours et ses lettres, parle aussi comme de voisins redoutables et redoutés.

Par l'action qui forme le sujet de ce tableau, les Helvétiens avaient marqué, en effet, dans le vaste mouvement connu

2

sous le nom de *Guerre des Cimbres*, qui, 106 ans avant l'ère chrétienne, préludait déjà alors au flot d'invasions sans cesse renouvelées sous lesquelles l'Empire devait enfin succomber. Placés à l'avant-garde du monde barbare, ils n'avaient pas craint de se joindre à cette première tentative des peuples encore libres pour anéantir la domination romaine, devenue de plus en plus menaçante et insupportable à tous. Plus heureux même que leurs alliés les Cimbres, exterminés par Marius, ils détruisent aux portes de leurs Alpes une armée consulaire, et, presque seuls à pouvoir se vanter d'une telle gloire, ils lui rendent cet opprobre que les Romains avaient coutume de faire subir aux vaincus, sceau de servitude auquel la plus grande partie du monde occidental avait déjà dû se résigner. Ainsi que le *Paysan du Danube,* ces paysans des sources du Rhin et du Rhône auraient donc pu dire aux Romains, et le dire même comme d'une chose un moment par eux réalisée :

Craignez, Romains, craignez que le Ciel quelque jour
Ne transporte chez vous les pleurs et la misère,
Et mettant en nos mains, par un juste retour,
Les armes dont se sert sa vengeance sévère,
 Il ne vous fasse, en sa colère,
 Nos esclaves à votre tour.

Tel est, au fond, le sens de cet épisode, unique en son genre, d'une lutte héroïque qui ne faisait alors que de commencer, qui devait durer des siècles avec des chances variées, mais pour aboutir enfin à la transformation providentielle du monde romain en un monde nouveau : soit par là, soit surtout comme protestation contre la tyrannie, ce fait obscur et glorieux de l'histoire de nos ancêtres appartient

184. The text reproduced here is taken from the copy preserved in the personal archives of Antoine Baron, now in Lausanne, BCU/DM, Dossier Baron, F[18], II, n° 183

THE BATTLE OF LAKE LÉMAN

or

The Helvetii
Forcing the Romans to Pass under the Yoke

It was Julius Caesar himself who, in two places in his *Commentaries,* reminds us of the defeat of a Roman army by the Helvetii. "In the time of our fathers," he says (that is, about fifty years earlier), "they conquered the consul Cassius, and killed him, along with his lieutenant Piso, and made his army pass under the yoke." Caesar adds that Piso, killed with Cassius, was "the grandfather of his father-in-law." He thus must have been well informed about this exploit of a small warlike and independent people who dared to stand up against Rome, and of whom Cicero, in his discourses and letters, speaks also as formidable and dreaded neighbors.

By the action that is the subject of this painting, the Helvetii in effect left their mark on the vast movement known as the War of the Cimbri, which, 106 years before the Christian era, began the series of invasions, endlessly renewed, to which the Empire would finally succumb. Placed in the forefront of the barbarian world, they were not afraid to join in the first attempt of free peoples to abolish Roman domination, which had become more and more menacing and unbearable for all. Even more fortunate than their allies, the Cimbri, who were exterminated by Marius, destroyed a consular army at the gates of their Alps, and, almost the only ones to be able to brag of such glory, they made the Romans undergo the opprobrium that it was the Roman custom to inflict on their conquered enemies, that mark of servitude to which most of the western world had already had to resign itself. Like the *Peasant of the Danube*, these countrymen of the headwaters of the Rhine and the Rhône could thus say to the Romans, and say it even as a thing accomplished by themselves:

Fear, Romans, fear that Heaven one day
Will bring you misery and tears,
That fortune then will put into our hands
The weapons that harsh vengeance wields,
And Heaven will give you, in its ire,
Your turn to be our slaves.

This is really the meaning of the episode, unique of its kind, a heroic struggle that was only beginning then, which was to endure for centuries with varied fortunes but finally to end in the providential transformation of the Roman world into a new world: it is for this reason, especially as a protest against tyranny, this obscure and glorious fact of the history of our ancestors belongs to the great moral progression of the history of humanity. The Romans would still be able to join Gaul to their empire under Caesar, and, along with Gaul, the Helvetii, who appears to have been aroused by them and then betrayed and sacrificed; but in taking liberty from the world instead of giving it, Rome at the same time lost its own; it declined, and passed slowly over the centuries under its own yoke until other Divicos, coming again from their forests and their mountains, replaced that yoke by their own, and made them pass under it and disappear forever.

Caesar, as rapid in his narrative as in his military marches, does not say where the Helvetii were so bold as to mark the forehead of the Queen of the World with this first stain that announced her destiny and the final punishment of her pride; but in the normal course of circumstances, and from remarks by other authors, one can believe that this battle (otherwise perfectly attested) was joined in the neighborhood of the Rhône and, according to the generally accepted tradition, not far from where it empties into the magnificent basin where the torrential son of the Helvetian Alps calms and purifies his stream.

The painter thus could choose this spot, and use for the background of his picture Lake Geneva and

donc au grand courant moral de celle de l'humanité. Les Romains pourront joindre encore, sous César, la Gaule à leur empire, et avec la Gaule les Helvétiens, qui paraissent avoir été excités par elle, puis trahis et sacrifiés; mais en achevant d'ôter la liberté au monde au lieu de la lui donner, Rome en même temps perd la sienne, elle décline et défile lentement à travers les siècles sous son propre joug, jusqu'à ce que d'autres Divicons, sortis de nouveau de leurs forêts et de leurs montagnes, viennent remplacer son joug par le leur, et l'y faire passer et disparaître pour jamais.

César, dans sa narration rapide comme ses marches militaires, ne dit pas où les Helvétiens eurent l'audace de marquer au front de la reine du monde de cette première flétrissure qui lui annonçait son destin et la punition finale de son orgueil; mais d'après la nature des choses et quelques circonstances mentionnées par d'autres auteurs, on a lieu de croire que cette bataille (d'ailleurs parfaitement constatée, on le voit), fut livrée dans le voisinage du Rhône et, selon la tradition généralement adoptée, non loin de son embouchure dans le magnifique bassin où ce fils torrentueux des Alpes helvétiques apaise et épure ses flots.

Le peintre a donc pu choisir cet emplacement, et donner pour fond à son tableau le lac Léman et les rocs escarpés d'Arvel au dessus de Villeneuve, les glaciers de la Dent-du-Midi et les montagnes qui l'avoisinent.

Les Romains captifs, parmi lesquels on reconnaît des types divers de leur race, le type déjà amolli par les délices de la conquête et le type ancien et sévère, arrivent en colonnes serrées, pressés et poussés par les bandes joyeuses des vainqueurs. Au pied d'un grand chêne, l'arbre sacré des Gaulois et l'emblème de la force et de la liberté, ils rencontrent le

joug rustique sous lequel ils doivent se courber. Des piques portent les têtes du consul et de son lieutenant. À droite et à gauche sont deux chars grossièrement sculptés : à droite pour le spectateur, celui des Druides et des prêtresses, maudissant les vaincus ou rendant grâce au ciel de cette délivrance; à gauche, celui des dépouilles, avec Divicon et les autres chefs helvétiens qui ordonnent aux Romains de franchir l'ignominieux défilé; des enfants viennent leur offrir une quenouille au passage, et Divicon, à cheval et l'épée nue à la main, semble dire par un geste énergique, que voilà donc enfin ces fiers Romains, ces maîtres et ces tyrans du monde, abaissés aussi à leur tour.

Lausanne. — Imprimerie CORBAZ et ROUILLER fils.

the rock cliffs of Arvel above Villeneuve, the glaciers of the Dent-du-Midi and the neighboring mountains.

The captive Romans among whom one recognizes the different types of their race — the type already softened by the delights of conquest, and the old, severe type — arrive in close columns, pressed on by the joyous bands of conquerors. At the foot of a great oak, the sacred tree of the Gauls and the emblem of the power of liberty, they meet the rustic yoke under which they must bend themselves. The lances hold the heads of the consul and his lieutenant. At the right and left are two rudely sculpted chariots; at the spectator's right, that of the Druids and the priestesses, cursing the defeated or giving thanks to the heavens for this deliverance; at the left, that carrying the spoils, with Divico and the other Helvetian chieftains who order the Romans to cross the ignominious strait; some children come to offer a distaff to them as they pass, and Divico, on horseback with his bare sword in his hand, seems to say by his energetic gesture that here finally are the proud Romans, these masters, these tyrants of the world, brought low also in their turn.

## CHAPTER 9

# 1859–1865

## PORTRAITS AND CLASSICAL INVENTIONS

185. *The Mother of Tobias*, 1860. Detail of illustration 203

When Gleyre returned to Paris in late 1858, he was not beset by the same despair and frustration he had felt after the exhibition of the *Davel* eight years earlier. By this time, his reputation in Paris and Switzerland was established, his place in the development of art at mid-century was more certain, and he seemed to be free from the lingering fear of poverty that haunted his earlier years. Even when he suffered a recurrence of eye problems from 1859 to 1861, it did not prevent him from completing a major painting and beginning yet another one. It was in a positive and optimistic spirit that Gleyre began work on the commission he had just received from the canton for the portrait of the General Jomini.

Antoine-Henri Jomini (1779–1869) was one of Switzerland's most prominent military men, although his entire career was pursued outside the Swiss borders.[788] After service under Napoléon and then in the Rus-

788. A thorough account of the life of Jomini is contained in the biography by his friend Lecomte 1860. For recent material, see Perrochon, ed. 1969.

241

sian army, he retired from active service in 1848 but came out of retirement during the Crimean War to serve as an advisor to the Czar. By 1858, at the age of seventy-nine, Jomini was again in Paris, having achieved the status of a living legend.

On 22 June 1858, Jomini went to Lausanne to confer with his friend Ferdinand Lecomte on the details of his biography, which was to be published shortly. Because of the general's presence in the canton, it was decided to offer a banquet in his honor, since, ironically, his contributions had never before been fully acknowledged by the Swiss government. On 26 June, the head of the Conseil d'Etat, Delarageaz, informed Jomini that the banquet would be held on the 30th of the month at the Hôtel du Faucon.[789] At this time, there is no indication that the governement wished to honor him further by commissioning a portrait, even though none existed in the canton.[790] The acquisition of an official portrait seems to have been under consideration when Gleyre came to Lausanne two months later, and may have been the result of Vulliemin's pressure to aid Gleyre in light of the meager remuneration he received for *The Romans*.

While the commission was actually given to Gleyre in the decree of 12 October 1858, the painter did not have official word from the Conseil d'Etat until 6 November:

> Désirant conserver les traits de M. le Baron Général Jomini, actuellement domicilié à Paris, le Conseil d'Etat vous prie de bien vouloir vous charger de faire le portrait…[791]

On the same day, le Conseil d'Etat also wrote to Jomini in Paris, 6 rue d'Aumale, asking him to consent to having his portrait painted; it was noted that Gleyre was chosen not only because he was an eminent painter, but because he was a Vaudois. Jomini was also told that the portrait would hang either in the Musée Arlaud or in the cantonal library.[792] Jomini wrote to Delarageaz on 10 November that he would agree to sit.[793]

Gleyre accepted the commission although there is no correspondence from him on the matter. In fact, the idea of representing a general, albeit one of the best-known and most celebrated Vaudois of the nineteenth century,[794] repelled Gleyre, who had always had a horror of the military.[795] Furthermore, because the general had served with Napoléon, even his allegiance was contrary to Gleyre's republican beliefs. Yet, under the circumstances in which he was given the commission, Gleyre could hardly refuse the honor. He invited Jomini to the studio for the preliminary sittings and by 3 January 1859 had already made a sketch from life. He had not as yet begun the actual portrait, much to the indignation of the general who, given his age and frail health, feared that Gleyre's well-known slowness would prevent its completion.[796]

There are no documents that elucidate the progress of the portrait. Presumably, Jomini selected the uniform in which he posed, one that would exalt his high position: that of a lieutenant general in the Russian army, his last military rank.[797] The medals include those given by the Czar, as well as the Legion of Honor and the Cross of Saint Louis pre-

789. See Chuard 1979, p. 3, which provides essential background on the general in Lausanne at that time, as well as pertinent information on the Gleyre portrait.

790. Several early portraits are known to have existed, but none was available for commemorative purposes in the canton. See Perrochon, ed. 1969.

791. Lausanne, ACE, Conseil d'Etat, Lettres à l'extérieur, 6 November 1858, bk. 20, letter 133, as well as ACV, Conseil d'Etat, Registres des délibérations, bk. 161, p. 15, item 34².

792. Lausanne, ACE, Conseil d'Etat, Lettres à l'extérieur, letter 132.

793. The letter is recorded in Lausanne, ACV, Conseil d'Etat, Registres des délibérations, bk. 161, p. 27, item 79.

794. See Perrochon, ed. 1969, p. 25.

795. Rambert 1890, p. 295.

796. Letter from Jomini to Lecomte is published in Chuard 1979, p. 5.

797. The actual uniform is still preserved in Payerne; see Perrochon, ed. 1969, p. 68, n° 194.

sented by Louis XVIII for his services on behalf the French cause in the peace negotiations of 1815. It is certain that Gleyre detested this ostentatious display.[798] But he worked rapidly on the portrait: when Louis Vulliemin went to see him in Paris in late February or early March, he wrote to his friend Henri Calame that Gleyre "a presque achevé le portrait du Général Jomini."[799]

fig. 186

Gleyre's opinion of the final work is not recorded, but that of the sitter is. Jomini, as well as his close friends and associates, thought the portrait unsuccessful: the general's stately elegance had not been fully captured from the initial sittings and the result was stiff and awkward.[800] The general himself, it seems, preferred one of the studies Gleyre made prior to 3 January (the study has disappeared) and therefore decided to have it lithographed at his own expense. This pencil portrait was then distributed to his friends after March 1861. Jomini gave Lecomte four copies, with a note that "malgré l'habileté de son pinceau, tout le monde a trouvé ici que son crayon avait bien la supériorité."[801]

Jomini's displeasure with the final result may have stemmed from Gleyre's "petite vengeance," as Rambert called it, at having to depict a figure replete with military pomp. Gleyre told Rambert that while he admired Jomini the man, he did not appreciate the general's desire to be represented in full regalia, and that if the general wished to be represented in that fashion, then "je ne lui passerai pas une ride."[802] Nevertheless, Gleyre flattered the model to some degree, since Gleyre's portrait

fig. 187

depicts the sitter as more youthful than a photograph of the eighty-year-old Jomini taken at about the same time. Gleyre never spoke of the portrait afterwards, nor did Clément discuss it in his monograph.

798. See *Le Général Jomini et les mémoires*, 1893, p. 34.
799. Cited in Vulliemin 1892, p. 230.
800. See Chuard 1979, p. 6.
801. The letter is in the collection of Mme. Jean Lecomte, Geneva, who kindly allowed me to study the Jomini material in her possession. The lithographs were sent by Jomini's daughter; one example, signed by Jomini and Gleyre, is in Mme. Lecomte's collection.
802. Rambert 1890, p. 295. Rambert wrote this in 1875 in the context of discussing Gleyre's veracity in portraiture.

It appears that Jomini's dissatisfaction did not persist. Several years later he received a request for an image of himself to adorn the main hall of the Nicolas Academy of the General Staff in Saint Petersburg, an institution he had helped to found while in service to the Czar. The request came in the spring of 1864 from D. A. Miliutin, the Minister of War under Alexander II. Jomini responded favorably on 20 April, charging his son to make the necessary arrangements. At the time, Jomini was in his eighty-sixth year and living in retirement in Passy, in ill health and also financially pressed, therefore no doubt reluctant to provide funds for a new portrait. He decided to have a copy of Gleyre's painting made — not by Gleyre, although it is not known who made it. The copy was completed quickly and sent to Russia at the end of the year.[803] It was the second work by Gleyre to be sent to Russia, the first being the watercolor, *The First Kiss of Michelangelo*, executed in Rome in 1832 and bought by the Empress, probably through Mme. Cornu.

Gleyre's original portrait of Jomini was sent to Lausanne on 28 May 1859;[804] it arrived by rail on 3 June, as noted in a letter to Gleyre acknowledging its safe delivery.[805] On the same day, the Conseil d'Etat ordered reimbursement funds for Gleyre's shipping expenses — eighty-one francs, seventy centimes.[806] It seems that Gleyre's fee for the commission had not been fixed in the contract of 6 November 1858, but the head of the Conseil d'Etat, Delarageaz, deemed the amount of 1,500 francs sufficient and Gleyre was sent that sum on 2 July 1859.[807]

While Gleyre was still working on Jomini's portrait, he had already begun the portrait of one of the most distinguished English émigrés in Lausanne, William Haldimand.[808] The Haldimand family had Swiss roots in Yverdon, only a few kilometers north of Lausanne, but in the late eighteenth century, the family had established itself in London and Canada. After a distinguished career in the family banking concern, William Haldimand, who was always in precarious health, decided to liquidate his affairs and settle in the more temperate climate of Lausanne. In 1828 he purchased an estate in Ouchy, Le Denantou, where he remained until his death in 1862. Far from isolating himself there, he actively participated in political functions and many other events, and even opened his spacious house and garden on Sundays for public strolls and picnics. Haldimand actively contributed to liberal causes — upon the advice of his friend Eynard, he gave large sums to the Greek cause in the War of Independence — and even established a literary prize for the most distinguished essay on the subject of political liberty. Haldimand maintained a lifelong interest in the arts and often received celebrated men of letters at Le Denantou. Olivier visited him during his summer holidays, and Charles Dickens did so at various times after 1846. Haldimand was one of the founding members of the Société Artistique Vaudoise and was instrumental in promoting the first major exhibition at the Musée Arlaud in 1850 where Gleyre triumphed with his *Davel*. He not only contributed funds to meet the exhibition deficits but also purchased several pictures from the exhibition for his personal collection.[809] It is most likely that Gleyre met Haldimand in 1850 when he was in Lausanne. Gleyre

fig. 188

fig. 189

803. The history of the request to Jomini is documented in a series of letters between Miliutin and Jomini in London, BL, Egerton Papers, Ms 3166, ff. 91–93. Jomini's reply accepting the honor is Egerton Ms 3168, f. 36, dated in his hand 20 April 1864. I owe this information to Carl Van Dyke who kindly supplied me with the photocopies of the essential letters.

804. Lausanne, ACV, Conseil d'Etat, Registres des délibérations, bk. 161, 31 May 1858, p. 481, item 311⁵, records a letter from Gleyre announcing that he sent the portrait on that date.

805. Lausanne, ACE, Conseil d'Etat, Lettres à l'extérieur, bk. 20, item 72.

806. Lausanne, ACV, Conseil d'Etat, Registres des délibérations, bk. 161, p. 481, item 48.

807. Ibid., bk. 162, p. 6, item 289. A letter was sent to Gleyre on 8 or 9 July informing him of this; see Lausanne, ACE, Conseil d'Etat, Lettres à l'extérieur, bk. 20, item 99.

808. Little information is available on William Haldimand (1784–1862), but see basic biographical data in Polla 1981, pp. 128–29, as well as [Rive] 1863, which has many lacunae and emphasizes his philanthropic works in the canton. Because of his fragile health, Haldimand was particularly sensitive to matters of medicine and hygiene, and in 1843, he helped to establish the first eye hospital in Lausanne. In 1854, he created from his personal funds the first public baths in the city, this at a time when a lack of facilities prevented the population from bathing more than two or three times a year; see Heller 1979, p. 58.

809. It is not known which works he purchased. Haldimand's involvement in the exhibition of 1850 is noted in Lausanne, MCBA, Museum Archives, A 1850/8, as well as in various documents in the archives of the society and in Lausanne, AVL, under the dossier "Beaux-Arts."

would have naturally been attracted to this type of aristocrat because of his liberal views and unusual generosity.

It is not known when or how Gleyre received the commission to paint the portrait. Although Haldimand had been named Bourgeois d'Honneur of Lausanne for his services to the canton and the city — one of only three individuals so distinguished in Lausanne in the nineteenth century — no official portrait of him had been commissioned by the municipality to honor his contributions.[810] In 1859 a street was named after him, not inappropriately adjacent to the Musée Arlaud. Probably Gleyre and Haldimand met again in 1858 when Gleyre was again in Lausanne; Haldimand may have asked him to paint his portrait at that time, perhaps on the suggestion of Vulliemin, who was a regular visitor to Le Denantou. It is equally probable that Gleyre made several studies of the model then since Haldimand was not fit enough to travel to Paris for regular sittings.

The only extant document which notes Gleyre's work on the portrait is Vulliemin's letter, cited earlier in regard to the portrait of Jomini.[811] Vulliemin wrote that the portrait of Haldimand, which he saw in Gleyre's studio early in March 1859, "est excellent; il reste à arranger quelque chose à la bouche, mais bien peu, et il sera parfait." Gleyre, however, told Vulliemin that he was not totally satisfied with the portrait, precisely because the subject had not been present to model. Gleyre represented Haldimand in a dignified, almost melancholy pose, masking to a large extent the sitter's age — then seventy-five — and his frail health. A photograph of Haldimand taken just three years later shows him near death. The finished portrait was sent to Lausanne in the same package as that of

fig. 190

188. *Portrait of William Haldimand*, 1859. Lausanne, Musée Cantonal des Beaux-Arts (catalogue n° 751)
189. Friedrich von Martens, *Le Denantou*, c. 1850. Lausanne, Musée Historique de Lausanne
190. Anonymous, *William Haldimand*. 1862. Lausanne, Musée Historique de Lausanne

810. The first so honored was the Count Capo d'Istria from Corfu, who received the title in 1816. Haldimand was next in 1843, followed by Catherine de Rumine in 1862. Gleyre did a portrait of the latter's son in 1856; see the catalogue entry.
811. Vulliemin 1892, p. 230.

245

Jomini and was donated to the Musée Arlaud.[812] A reduced version, perhaps by Gleyre himself, was later donated to the eye hospital that Haldimand founded.[813]

Gleyre also painted a portrait of a third celebrated Vaudois at the same time, Louis Vulliemin.[814] He was, along with Olivier, one of the most respected historians in the canton. In 1825, he had gone to Paris where he was associated with the historian Adolphe Thiers and became his disciple. Later he met Vinet and Henri Druey and extended his interests to philosophy, theology, and politics. As discussed earlier, he had probably met Gleyre in 1850 through Olivier and was present when Gleyre first met with Gaudin.[815] It may be because of Vulliemin's efforts to increase Gleyre's remuneration for *The Romans* that the painter decided to undertake his portrait.

On 24 January 1859 Olivier wrote to Vulliemin that he had seen Gleyre, who agreed to do the painting as soon as possible. Olivier explained that it would be best if Gleyre could begin work before the summer of 1859 since afterwards he would be committed to other projects, none of which he specified. Olivier advised Vulliemin that he should count on a week to two weeks for sittings, alterations, and a preliminary drying of the canvas. He suggested March as the most convenient time to begin. Olivier ended his letter by reaffirming that Gleyre no longer wrote letters himself and that Olivier's correspondence could be considered a formal contract between the painter and the sitter.[816]

Vulliemin accordingly left Lausanne for Paris sometime after 22 February, as he confided in a letter to his friend Henri Calame. When he began sitting for Gleyre, Vulliemin wrote regularly to his family informing them of the progress. In a letter written in the first week of March, he noted that the canvas was ready in Gleyre's studio and that the painter promised to work quickly on the portrait so that Vulliemin could return to Lausanne.[817] But on the first day, Gleyre and Vulliemin did no more than spend the time in conversation, Gleyre's method for better understanding the character of the person he intended to capture. Vulliemin would soon find, however, that sitting for Gleyre was not as easy as he had imagined it would be. Vulliemin was forced to sit all day until four in the afternoon with his hand over the side of the chair, a pose that numbed his fingers. Eventually Gleyre placed a book in the sitter's hand — Vulliemin said it was a copy of the Koran — to better balance the lower section of the composition. Vulliemin's stoicism was rewarded by a three-day rest period during which Gleyre worked on the hand and other details, particularly the coat. When these were finished, Gleyre recalled Vulliemin for another sitting that lasted several hours. There was a further session for additional details that lasted all day, and by this time the painting was virtually finished.

Gleyre almost certainly sent the portrait directly to Lausanne at about the same time as he dispatched the portraits of Jomini and Haldimand. Vulliemin's letters do not record his opinion of the work, but he did note that Gleyre was pleased with the results. Once again Gleyre flattered the sitter considerably by giving him a more youthful appearance, as can be

fig. 191

fig. 192

812. Lausanne, ACV, Conseil d'Etat, Registres des délibérations, bk. 161, 31 May 1859, p. 481, item 311[5].
813. There is no record of Gleyre having actually made the reduction, but the work is probably by his hand; see the catalogue entry.
814. On Vulliemin's life, see Polla 1981, pp. 99–100, and the introduction to his letters in Vulliemin 1892, pp. 8f.
815. Hauptman 1983, p. 104. Vulliemin was with Gleyre and Gaudin on 16 September 1850.
816. Burnier 1907, p. 74.
817. Vulliemin 1892, p. 230. The following material on the portrait is taken from the two letters the historian wrote to his family while Gleyre was painting the portrait.

191. *Portrait of Louis Vulliemin*, 1859. Lausanne, Musée Cantonal des Beaux-Arts (catalogue n° 753)

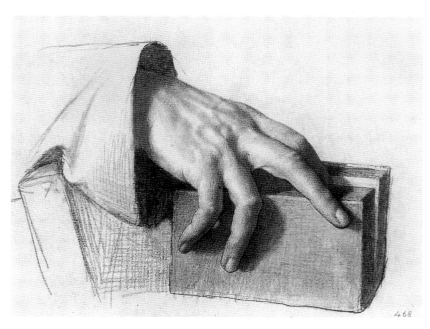

468

192. Study for the *Portrait of Louis Vulliemin*, 1859. Lausanne, Musée Cantonal des Beaux-Arts (catalogue n° 755)
193. Samuel Heer-Tschudi, *Louis Vulliemin*, c. 1860. Lausanne, Musée Historique de Lausanne

fig. 193

seen by comparing a photograph of the historian taken at about the same time.

While Gleyre was engaged in completing these portraits of eminent Vaudois personalities, he also kept up his contacts with friends in the canton, some of whom wrote to him for advice on artistic matters. In one instance, Gleyre's opinion was solicited about the restoration of a stained glass window for the cathedral of Lausanne, as we know from Gleyre's response in an unpublished and undated letter addressed only to

247

194. *Phryne before the Judges*, 1859–61. Lausanne, Musée Cantonal des Beaux-Arts (catalogue n° 785)

818. The letter, in Gleyre's hand, was kindly transmitted to me by Mr. Knébel of La Sarraz who found it in his family collection.
819. For a discussion of these windows offered by Blanchet and executed by the firm of Gérente, Paris, see Dubois 1930, pp. 201–6. The documents concerning Blanchet's wishes and the subsequent action by the cantonal authorities are contained in a dossier, Lausanne, ACV, Département des Travaux publics, K IX, 1217/9; the information was transmitted by Paul Bissegger.
820. Wissowa 1894 et seq., XX, pp. 893–907, provides a full account as well as ample variants on the subject.
821. Clément, pp. 279–80.

"Mon cher Monsieur."[818] Gleyre, who reserved this form of greeting for intimate acquaintances, informed his correspondent that "Votre idée sur la restauration des vitraux me paraît excellente." That the letter is in fact addressed to a friend in Lausanne is attested by the postscript in which he asks that his greetings be sent to Mr. Haldimand. This also gives us a terminus date for the letter, since Haldimand died in 1862.

In fact, the letter must have been written well before that. From other documentary sources it can be ascertained that his correspondent in this case was Rodolphe Blanchet, the head of the Département de l'Instruction publique et des cultes whom Gleyre knew well. On 18 May 1861 Blanchet informed the members of the Conseil d'Etat of his desire to donate a thirteenth-century stained glass from Westphalia that he had had restored. Blanchet must have shown the work to Gleyre during one of his visits and then asked his advice on whether it should be restored or not. Gleyre also suggested various firms in Paris that specialized in this type of work. The actual restoration was indeed finished in 1861; the window was later installed in the cathedral along with five others that Blanchet had had made, all in heraldic design recalling aspects of the region before it came a canton.[819]

While he was working on the Vaudois portraits, Gleyre returned to planning a large canvas on a Classical motif, Phryne before the judges. fig. 194 The story derives in its essential form from the *Deipnosophistai* of Atheneaus which was available in numerous translations in the nineteenth century.[820] Phryne, the celebrated courtesan who was adored for her beauty and talents, supposedly served as a model for Apelles and Praxiteles, whose mistress she later became. The painting shows Phryne's acquittal after her blasphemy against the gods, a crime punishable by death. She was defended in the proceedings by Hyperides, a disciple of Socrates and Plato, who, when he sensed the decision would go against his client, tore her dress from her; the jury, moved by her stunning beauty, found her innocent of the crime.

Gleyre made several studies for the central figure, exploring poses ranging from those seen in Classical works to those invented in the studio. fig. 195 He placed the scene, as a large charcoal study indicates, at the foot of the Acropolis where at the right a scribe records the event while at the left a large statue of Minerva overlooks the proceedings. Hyperides has just removed the dress as the jury looks on. The scene thus was fully worked out, but Gleyre never completed it, although he is known to have advanced the central figure into its final stage on the canvas.

Why he never finished the work is still unclear despite the account by Clément who noted that Gleyre had seen a painting on the same subject in the salon of 1861, which resembled his own picture too much. Fearing accusations of plagiarism, Gleyre solemnly turned the canvas to the wall and never returned to it again.[821] This account reminds us of the difficulties Gleyre had more than a decade earlier with the imagery of *Davel*, which he altered after he saw in the Salon of 1849 a figure similar to the one he was painting. But there are aspects of the later anecdote that are difficult to accept. In the Salon of 1861, the only painting de-

195. Study for *Phryne before the Judges*, 1859–61. Lausanne, Musée Cantonal des Beaux-Arts (catalogue n° 786)

196. Victor-Louis Mottez, *Phryne*, 1859. Dijon, Musée des Beaux-Arts

picting the subject was a canvas by Gérôme which indeed won immediate success.[822] When compared with the studies Gleyre made, however, the similarities between the works seem too incidental to warrant Gleyre's drastic response. The scene as envisioned by Gérôme takes place indoors, and the poses of the central figure and the jurors show marked differences from those in Gleyre's studies. In fact, the attitude in Gérôme's canvas bears a stronger resemblance to those seen in Gleyre's *Christ with the Doctors* of a decade earlier.

Could Clément, writing more than fifteen years after the fact, have confused the occasions and the Salon in question? Such an error seems likely since Clément himself noted that most of the studies for the Phryne canvas were already done in 1858 and 1859.[823] Furthermore, in 1859, Victor-Louis Mottez had shown a painting of the subject that likewise had drawn positive critical reaction.[824] The scene represented by Mottez is closer in conception to Gleyre's: both take place outdoors, both represent the Acropolis with the Parthenon clearly visible, and both have statues of Minerva at the left. The attitudes of the jurors also resemble those seen in Gleyre's studies, but the gestures of Phryne and her lawyer are

fig. 196

822. See von Waldegg 1972, pp. 122f., for the history of the work, but there is no mention of Gleyre in the context of the painting.
823. Clément, p. 417, under catalogue n° 83.
824. N° 2215 of the salon livret; the work is now in Dijon.

wholly different and less dramatic in Mottez's work. The subject of Phryne was an extremely popular one in the nineteenth century — important examples were shown in the salons of 1845, 1846, and 1852[825] — and thus similar attributes and attitudes were not unexpected. Furthermore, in the early 1860s Gleyre's fame in Paris was such that he could hardly have feared charges of plagiarism in a subject that was so well known and so frequently seen in the salons.

The reason why Gleyre abandoned the subject may be that he was not wholly satisfied with the way he envisioned the scene; his search for originality was a strong force in his artistic philosophy and may have prevented him from completing a painting that revealed no new aspects of the iconography. Yet another reason may be found in the iconographic motif itself: the essence of the subject is blasphemy against the gods, an accusation for which Phryne won acquittal by guile and sexuality rather than by penitence. Gleyre was attracted by the theme of blasphemy already in *Le Soir* of 1843, and he would return to the subject at least twice in the 1860s, but always with the idea that crimes against the eternal forces are met with immediate and harsh reprisals. That Phryne escapes punishment because of her sexuality is completely alien to Gleyre's philosophic principles.

Another aspect of this affair that might have inhibited Gleyre was the fact that the painting was reserved for the Prince Napoléon,[826] possibly through the mediation of Mme. Cornu who was close to the royal family. Because of Gleyre's fierce republicanism and his hatred of the monarchy, he may have abandoned the project — possibly under the pretext that his figures had already appeared in another canvas — so as not to have direct dealings with the prince. Nonetheless, the idea persisted that the cause was Gérôme's villainy in borrowing Gleyre's figures which he had seen in the course of his many visits to the atelier; Nanteuil even remarked to Clément later that Gérôme, like Meissonier, had stolen Gleyre's design.[827] Gleyre, however, never discussed the issue, nor did he exclude Gérôme from his circle of friends.

The year 1860 proved to be a very busy one for Gleyre, which may be another reason why Olivier had asked Vulliemin to come to Paris as soon as possible to sit for his portrait. During the year, Gleyre produced at least four oil studies and possibly two more, as well as several other important studies; he also began a major painting. He continued to draw and paint portraits of friends, including one of Thérèse Olivier, who was seventeen years old at the time. Thérèse found the sessions to be of particular interest because of "la conversation fine et originale du maître."[828] Gleyre's likeness of her was always considered by the family the best one ever made.[829] Thérèse, it might be added, enjoyed a special relationship with Gleyre, whom she considered more a favored uncle than a friend of the family. When possible, Gleyre and Thérèse traveled together during the summer holidays,[830] and when she married Edouard Bertrand in 1866, Gleyre acted as one of the witnesses.[831]

The four oil studies Gleyre executed during the year were certainly painted for himself and outside of any known commission. Of these stud-

fig. 197

197. *Portrait of Thérèse Olivier*, 1860. Geneva, Collection René des Gouttes (catalogue n° 757)

825. Respectively, Tabar, n° 1172 of the livret; Robert, n° 1539; and Pradier, n° 1159.
826. Clément, p. 417, under catalogue n° 83.
827. Letter to Clément of 18 April 1878, now in Fleurier, CFC.
828. Lausanne, BCU/DM, G. Olivier, "Souvenirs," IS 1905/117, p. 324.
829. Lausanne, BCU/DM, J. Olivier, "Histoire," IS 1905/60, p. 36.
830. For example in 1863, as noted in an undated letter of that year from Thérèse to her parents in Lausanne, BCU/DM, Fonds Olivier, IS 1905/43, dossier 1863. Several other instances are noted in the Fonds Olivier.
831. Letter from Caroline Olivier to Blanchet of 11 April 1866, in Lausanne, BCU/DM, Fonds Olivier, IS 1905/44, dossier 1866. The other witness was Caroline's father, Louis Ruchet.

198. *Amor and the Fates*, c. 1860. Lausanne, Musée Cantonal des Beaux-Arts (catalogue n° 762)
199. *The Bathers*, c. 1860. Lausanne, Musée Cantonal des Beaux-Arts (catalogue n° 768)

ies, only one is in the traditional rectangular form; the others are either round or oval in format. None, it seems, was completed, although in one case Gleyre returned to it later. The most curious of the group is a painting entitled *Amor and the Fates*. Clément thought that the work had fig. 198 promise and praised its elegance and finesse. The subject is a strange one that appears to have no basis in mythology and is not derived from a specific Classical episode. Gleyre worked on the canvas repeatedly, changing the image of the Fates several times so as to create a more timeless aspect. At one point, he overworked the study so much that he asked Nanteuil to take it out of the studio so that he could retouch it no more.[832] He was never fully satisfied with the results; as late as 1874, he tried to improve the composition, sketching it onto a larger canvas in a slightly different form.[833] However unsuccessful the painting is, it nevertheless points to a decided lightness of subject and color that is virtually absent in his work of the previous two decades. In spirit, the study recalls the works of his students who were labeled the Néo-Grecs, while at the same time, it recalls the earlier works Gleyre painted under the influence of Prud'hon's·sentimentalism.

The same may be said of his study *The Bathers*, also in tondo form, fig. 199 upon which he worked sporadically along with the *Amor*. It too shows a lighter vein, free from the philosophic content that marks Gleyre's major efforts. The composition reflects his desire, frequently expressed to Clément, to use the nude as the sole basis for a composition. This effervescent study formed the basis for another painting on the theme, *Innocence*, which according to Clément was meant to depict the freshness and fig. 200 naivety of youth.[834] Gleyre wanted to compose a large work around the

832. Clément, pp. 314f. It was rare for Gleyre to overwork a picture or its details, but this occurred again later with his *Pentheus*.
833. Ibid. The canvas, however, was not found in Gleyre's atelier after his death.
834. Ibid., p. 320.

200. *Innocence*, 1860. Lausanne, Musée Cantonal des Beaux-Arts (catalogue n° 759)

201. *Young Woman Reading*, c. 1860. Lausanne, Musée Cantonal des Beaux-Arts (catalogue n° 772)

figure but was unable to continue after his model stopped coming; supposedly, he never found another who incarnated the spirit he wished to capture.

fig. 201     Another composition upon which Gleyre worked in the same year was *Young Woman Reading*. The oil study, recalling the colors he used after his Venetian trip of 1845, also reflects this new, lighter feeling, an idyllic mood that returned at intervals in the last decade of his life. This canvas was also reworked several times with the main figure seen alone or in the company of other figures. The Italianate aspects of the composition are evident in the colors, in the forest setting, and even in the sleeping figure, which recalls the sleeping Joachim from the Arena Chapel frescoes.[835] If this study, like the others executed at the same time, was never fully developed in its own right, it nevertheless became the germ for his painting of *Minerva* five years later.

fig. 202     Probably the most successful work of this period was his *Daphnis and Chloe*. The subject of this pastoral with its idyllic lovers was enormously popular in French art and literature; besides countless examples in the salons, the subject appeared in almost all forms from the late eighteenth century onwards. Gleyre was certainly familiar with the examples by Cortot and Gérard, both in the Louvre, as well as variations on the theme including those by his teacher Hersent. Gleyre himself had already shown interest in the subject in 1852 when he represented another aspect of the story in an oil study.[836]

Gleyre's eagerness to finish this work — in direct contrast to the others discussed above — is attested in a letter from Juste Olivier to Jules Hébert, in which he noted that Gleyre had some difficulty with the colors and tones of the nudes, "mais il veut absolument en venir à bout."[837] The work is Ingresque, much in accord with Gleyre's own desire, as Olivier wrote to Hébert.[838] Gleyre worked on the canvas through the first half of 1861, interrupting his efforts in the summer to pay a visit to his uncle François in Chevilly.[839] When he returned to Paris three weeks later, he realized that he needed laurel branches for the background and asked Cornu to contact Clément, then in Rome negotiating the transport of the Campana collection, to send some examples as soon as he could.[840]

835. Hauptman 1980, p. 136.
836. Clément, pp. 280–81.
837. The letter, now in a private collection, Lausanne, is not dated, but was probably written in the summer of 1861.
838. Ibid., J. Olivier to Hébert, May 1861.
839. Cornu wrote to Clément, then in Rome, that Gleyre left Paris for Chevilly on 7 September 1861; the letter is in Fleurier, CFC.
840. Letter of 31 October 1861, in Fleurier, CFC.

202. *Daphnis and Chloe*, 1860–62. New York, Private collection (catalogue n° 793)

Clément, with his professional interest in botany, was a natural source for such appeals: later he also provided cyclamen plants for the *Minerva*.

Both Clément and Olivier thought the final result a highly evocative realization of the poetic side of Gleyre's art — in fact, a relief from the lofty themes that occupied him normally. The *Daphnis and Chloe*, with its bright Venetian colors and simple gestures, reflects Gleyre's interest in the decorative side of art, aligned with the work produced by artists such as his pupils Hamon and Alma-Tadema, as yet little known in France. The work is a natural conclusion to the studies Gleyre made in which the nude figure becomes the raison d'être of the work. There is no attempt here, as there is so often with Gleyre, to reveal the deeper side of the subject he selected to paint. But Gleyre must have realized that, successful as the painting was, it was not the kind of work in which he most fully expressed himself through exploring the psychology of the subject.

But to say that Gleyre abandoned this more thoughtful aspect of his art in the early 1860s for more visually pleasing work is incorrect. At times, these cross-currents acted side by side, as a work from this period vividly shows — a drawing which stands by itself as a completed work,

254

one that reverts to the earlier subjective nature of his art. The drawing is titled *The Mother of Tobias*, and although Clément recognized its importance, he nevertheless devoted little attention to it.[841] Gleyre thought of producing a large canvas on the subject later for a commission he received from Geneva, but the project never advanced to that point. Only one letter has surfaced that provides information on the drawing; in the letter Olivier wrote to Hébert on 30 December 1860, he noted that the drawing was well advanced and predicted that it would be a masterpiece.[842] Olivier's comment, incidentally, confirms the date of the work as 1860, which Clément thought to be only approximate.[843]

A large number of painters have been attracted to the subject, including Rembrandt who produced more than fifty works based on the fourteen short chapters of the book of Tobit.[844] In the nineteenth century, paintings derived from this source were less frequent, but nonetheless were seen in the salons.[845] The themes embodied in the iconography appealed to painters precisely because they provided ample scope for interpretation, from the romantic to the purely academic. Typically Gleyre selected an aspect of it that was little known, one that would demonstrate a personal element.

Gleyre chose the scene from the tenth chapter of the book, when Tobit's son Tobias has already been asked by his father to collect a debt from a man in Media. Tobias found a traveling companion who was in reality an angel; the father asked him to look after his son during the trip, offering him a reward for his safe homecoming. But the trip took longer than expected, and the parents became worried over the long delay, fearing

203. *The Mother of Tobias*, 1860. Lausanne, Musée Cantonal des Beaux-Arts (catalogue n° 761)

841. Clément, p. 311.
842. Lausanne, Private collection.
843. Clément, p. 453, under catalogue n° 196. Clément wrote that Gleyre gave him the drawing, but unsigned, to have it photographed in 1870; Clément thought it prudent to have the painter sign and date the work while at the photographer's. Gleyre, thus, put in the date 1860.
844. See Held 1964, pp. 7f., for Rembrandt's interest in the theme.
845. See Pigler 1974, I, pp. 185f. Among the nineteenth-century artists who worked on the subject were Cabat, Troyon, Delacroix, Duval de Camus, and Henri Lehmann who showed two examples, painted a decade earlier, in the Exposition Universelle of 1855 — n° 3346 and 3347.

that something had happened to the travelers. In the seventh verse of the chapter, the mother, Anna, goes out each day to look for her son; the father meanwhile has lost his sight. Gleyre has depicted the scene in which Anna scans the horizon near Nineveh and glimpses her son in the dis- fig. 185 tance, a scene hardly current in the nineteenth-century iconographic tradition. Clément is correct to direct attention to the Michelangelesque grandeur of the figure, shown against a vast, rough, deserted landscape that itself reflects the loneliness and desperation the parents feel at the loss of their son. It is one of the rare instances — along with *The Flood* — in which Gleyre's landscape reflects the psychological drama of the subject itself. One can well imagine Olivier's enthusiasm when he saw the drawing in the studio.

The central theme of the story is the Romantic wanderer, a subject that inherently attracted Gleyre and which he had already treated in his youthful canvas *Manfred*, or, obliquely, in his *Apostles* about to spread the Word to the four corners of the globe. Yet Gleyre chose to focus on the image of the mother so as to delineate the wrenching human longing in her desperate search for a lost son. The iconography once again indicates Gleyre's search for originality within traditional components. Gleyre had in fact already explored this emotion in a closely related subject, the Prodigal Son, which, while sketched in 1848, would not be completed until a year before his death.

Another aspect of the subject may have also enticed Gleyre; namely, the blindness that is inflicted upon the father and is miraculously cured by the returning son. The choice of the Tobit story probably reflects Gleyre's concerns about his persistent eye difficulties, which in 1859 had again flared up. In this instance, the problem was not only the ophthalmia contracted in Egypt that continually caused discomfort, but also an inflammation and subsequent congestion of the blood vessels near the optic nerve.[846] Gleyre had resisted treatment — he dreaded doctors — but was finally convinced by his closest friends that if he left the condition untreated, he might eventually become blind. In the same letter of 30 December from Olivier to Hébert cited earlier, the poet informed Hébert that Gleyre's right eye was especially affected, causing him such pain that at times all of his activities were severely limited.[847] Olivier gave no further details, but Gleyre must have been in a semi-disabled state for months.

Furthermore, in the Salon of 1857, Bouguereau exhibited his version of *The Return of Tobias* which shows Tobias embracing his parents.[848] The painting had a certain success in the exhibition, which prompted Bouguereau to paint a pendant picture of Tobias saying goodbye to his blind father, which he had completed by 1861.[849] Gleyre, always wishing to produce works that demonstrated his own originality and sensitive to possible accusations of plagiarism, may have dropped the painting at this time because there were at least two contemporary pictures representing the same theme, albeit in a totally different manner. Nevertheless, the idea of producing a painting based on the drawing remained in Gleyre's mind and, in fact, he considered the project again almost a decade later.

846. Clément, pp. 283–84.
847. Lausanne, Private collection.
848. N° 320 in the salon livret. The painting was sent to the Musée des Beaux-Arts in Dijon, where it is presently housed.
849. The painting is in the Hermitage, Saint Petersburg.

Whether or not Gleyre's eye problems interfered with his work, it seems that they did not long keep him from accepting social invitations. One of the most significant of these was a special request by Flaubert in May 1861 to visit him in his apartment at 42 boulevard du Temple. Gleyre responded to Flaubert's note himself, this time not relying on Olivier: "Comment pouvez-vous supposer que j'hésite à me rendre à l'invitation trois fois aimable, que vous avez bien voulu me faire?"[850] The invitation to Gleyre at this time is somewhat curious in light of the absence of documentation concerning the painter's relationship to Flaubert in the years after his return from Egypt. It may be assumed that they kept in touch through mutual friends, particularly Maxime du Camp and Jules Duplan. The former noted in several letters of 1852 and 1853 that he dined frequently with Gleyre,[851] while from the correspondence between Flaubert and Duplan we learn that Flaubert kept abreast of Gleyre's activities and general health.[852]

204. *Raphael, Leonardo, Michelangelo*, 1860. Engraving. From Clément, *Michel-Ange, Léonard de Vinci, Raphaël*, 1860, frontispiece (catalogue n° 760)

The reason for Flaubert's invitation to Gleyre at this time was a special event that has been almost wholly overlooked in both the Gleyre and Flaubert literature: Flaubert asked Gleyre to be present at the first reading of *Salammbô*, which was still not finished and would not be published until November 1862. The only other invited guests were the Goncourt brothers, who left a brief account of the gathering on 6 May:

> A quatre heures, nous sommes chez Flaubert qui nous a invités à une grande lecture de *Salammbô*, avec un peintre que nous trouvons là, Gleyre, un monsieur en bois, l'air d'un mauvais ouvrier, l'intelligence d'un peintre gris, l'esprit terne et ennuyeux.[853]

It is not certain if there was a special reason, apart from friendship, for Flaubert's invitation. Gleyre had few connections with the literary circles of either the Goncourts or Flaubert; from the unflattering description offered by the Goncourts, it is clear that it was the first time they had met. It is unlikely that Gleyre was involved in advising Flaubert on the exotic details in the novel — Flaubert's extensive work notes do not suggest it. Nevertheless, the party continued until two in the morning and one can assume that everyone debated the merits of Flaubert's work. The Goncourts wrote of their disappointment, but Gleyre's opinion seems not to have been recorded. Indeed, the meeting was not mentioned in any of the correspondence of Gleyre's friends. Of Gleyre's inner circle, it seems that only Clément had contact with Flaubert; several years later, Clément sent Flaubert a copy of his book *Michel-Ange, Raphaël et*
fig. 204 *Léonard*, which contained a frontispiece designed by Gleyre. Flaubert wrote to Clément, telling him that he thought his analysis of the High Renaissance masters was of the highest quality.[854]

After the soirée on 6 May 1861, Flaubert heard about Gleyre through Jules Duplan whom Gleyre apparently saw frequently and to whom he had given a drawing of the *Venus Pandemos*.[855] Flaubert asked Duplan in the summer of 1861 to pass on his best regards to "l'angélique Gleyre,"

850. The letter is undated but from its context must have been written on 4 May 1861. It is now in Paris, IF, Fonds Franklin-Grout, B III, ff. 264–65. This was kindly drawn to my attention by Mr. Jean Bruneau.
851. See Du Camp 1978, pp. 160f.; various entries and letters for 1851 and afterwards note Gleyre's frequent visits.
852. See Flaubert 1926–33, IV, pp. 179–80, letter 533, and Flaubert 1973, II, p. 715 — in the latter reference, p. 1375, Gleyre is incorrectly identified as a sculptor. Additional citations in Flaubert's correspondence are found in the Conard edition, IV, p. 187, letter 535; IV, p. 201, letter 543; IV, p. 226, letter 557, as well as in the Bruneau edition, II, pp. 721, 742, and 764.
853. Goncourt 1956, IV, p. 189, entry for 6 May 1861.
854. Clément's book was first published in 1861, but the undated letter from Flaubert to Clément thanking him for the copy was probably in reference to the second, somewhat revised edition which was published on 15 December 1866. This deduction, by Bruneau, is based upon the return address which was Croisset; in 1861 and 1862, Flaubert remained in Paris. The letter is now in Fleurier, CFC and was published for the first time in Flaubert 1973 et seq., III, pp. 580–81. Flaubert told Clément, "Voilà au moins un ouvrage de critique qui apprend quelque chose (qualité rarissime)."
855. The drawing is now known only from a photograph by Bingham where the inscription "à mon ami Jules Duplan" is clearly visible; see the catalogue entry for further information. The relationship between Gleyre and Duplan still needs to be thoroughly investigated; the latter's personal papers remain unpublished and inaccessible in the Institut de France.

257

205. *Joan of Arc*, c. 1860. Lausanne, Musée Cantonal des Beaux-Arts (catalogue n° 778)

206. *Hercules and Omphale*, 1862. Neuchâtel, Musée d'Art et d'Histoire (catalogue n° 808)

856. Flaubert 1926–33, suppl. I, p. 270, letter 164, dated 1 August 1861; see too p. 267, letter 167, 25 September 1861, where Flaubert asks Duplan to present his "amitiés et souvenirs à Gleyre."
857. Flaubert 1926–33, V, p. 5, letter 704; and suppl. I, p. 280, letter 173 of 18 January 1862.
858. Quinche-Anker 1924, pp. 74–75, letter of 28 February 1862. On the relationship of Ehrmann to Gleyre, see Vaisse 1976, pp. 341–61, and Hauptman 1985(e), passim.
859. Paris, BN, Mme. Quinet, "Mémorial," IV, 23 September 1862, records the visit of Gleyre with J. Dubochet's daughter.
860. Clément, pp. 311–12.
861. Paris, BN, Mme. Quinet, "Mémorial," VII, 5 September 1865.
862. Lucas 1979, II, pp. 328 and 364.
863. Clément, p. 288, n. 1.

thus indicating the warmth of his friendship for the painter.[856] By early 1862, Flaubert was seriously worried about Gleyre's recurring health problems and asked Duplan to keep him informed. On 2 January he wrote to Duplan expressing his relief that Gleyre was doing better; two weeks later he again wrote to Duplan asking if Gleyre was totally cured.[857] Actually, Gleyre's health deteriorated again in February. Albert Anker wrote to his friend François Ehrmann, who was the student head of Gleyre's teaching atelier, that he had learned from Albert de Meuron that Gleyre could no longer focus on objects in front of him.[858] But his condition cleared up considerably after treatment, so that by the summer of 1862 he could visit Quinet in Veytaux without difficulty: the Quinets, in fact, made no mention of Gleyre's problem, which suggests that he was again well.[859]

Among the studies Gleyre made at this time, working sporadically because of his health, was one depicting Joan of Arc. The origins of this idea go as far back as 1860, since a simple sketch for the figure appears on the verso of one of the portraits of Vulliemin. Clément greatly admired the subject as well as Gleyre's conception of it, which he thought the equivalent of his study *The Mother of Tobias*.[860] The subject had an extraordinary currency in nineteenth-century France, which makes us wonder why Gleyre even considered the theme. It is not impossible that he may have thought about it for the third Vaudois commission, since the subject was not as well known in Switzerland, and in a philosophical sense, as we noted before, a version of the theme could very well have acted as a counterpart for his *Davel*.

Gleyre conceived a simplistic image of the figure in the traditional guise of a shepherd hearing the voices in the forest. He altered the pose and fig. 205 gestures several times over the next few years but never made a painted study. During a visit to Quinet on 5 September 1865, this time in the company of Etienne Arago, Gleyre discussed the drawing as well as his desire to transfer the work onto a large canvas.[861] Even in the 1870s, Gleyre had hopes of undertaking the painting when he accepted a contract from the American art dealer and agent George Lucas, but by then his health prevented it.[862]

Thus, the bulk of Gleyre's work in the early 1860s, beside the three portraits, was in the various studies and sketches that he never developed into large canvases. If these full realizations were blocked by problems of composition or aesthetics or health, he was able nevertheless to complete before 1865 two significant works that demonstrated his full artistic powers and imagination. Both of these return to Classical subjects, but go beyond the common iconography.

The first represented the subject of Hercules and Omphale. Gleyre's fig. 206 interest in the iconography goes back at least to 1859 when, as Clément noted, Gleyre gave him a large pencil sketch which delineated the basic elements of the finished composition.[863] Very little documentation has survived of Gleyre's development of the canvas. Olivier's letter to Hébert of 30 December 1860 already noted that Gleyre's work on the painting had advanced considerably. But his eye difficulties prevented additional

259

work at this time, and Olivier wrote to Hébert a year later that Gleyre could work very little on the composition, much to the regret of the poet since "son grand tableau d'Omphale venait si bien."[864] Gleyre was able to devote his full efforts to the work during 1862 so that by the end of the year, it was virtually finished, as a letter from François Ehrmann attests.[865] Clément noted the date of completion as 1863, but by January 1863, the canvas was already exhibited in Goupil's gallery.[866]

In light of Gleyre's usual practice of selecting subjects that were infrequently represented, his choice of Hercules seems curious. The subject had attracted a large number of artists of all schools from the Renaissance onwards.[867] In 1859 alone, when Gleyre evidently began to envision the scene, no fewer than three examples were shown in the Salon.[868] And in 1861, Gustave Boulanger produced a prototypical representation of the iconography that was remarked upon by the major critics.

The reason why Gleyre might have wished in this instance to add another version of an image that was already known to the public in dozens of examples lies, no doubt, in his ongoing interest in exploring themes of virtue and atonement for sinful deeds. After Hercules killed Iphitus, a scene Gleyre had already drawn, the gods ordered him to do penance by selling himself into servitude for a period of three years, with half his earnings going to the father of the victim. Hercules was given by Mercury to Omphale, the recently widowed queen of Lydia, who shamed the hero by forcing him to wear women's clothes and perform banal household duties.[869] This tale has always been regarded as an example of male humiliation, even in the patristic literature where it was used as a warning against the fall of Man.[870] Echoes of this idea were still evident in Hugo's poem "Le Rouet d'Omphale" of 1856.

fig. 207

Thus, Omphale is generally regarded as dominating Hercules physically — as, for example, in Boulanger's painting where she teases the hero — or psychologically, because she forces him to do tasks that are antithetical to his prowess and skills. Yet Gleyre's painting seems remarkably void of the male/female tension that so often marks the iconography. Omphale is not represented as the conniving female who delights in her supremacy and Hercules' shame. Rather, Gleyre has represented the scene as a simple domestic one, in which the theme of humiliation is virtually ignored visually. He has in fact concentrated on the underlying theme, that is, Hercules' need for punishment and expiation for acknowledged crimes. Hercules is depicted as a hero in the sense that he willingly accepts the punishment; his humiliation at the hands of Omphale is the way he atones for his sins.

Gleyre's presentation of the subject in this form may be compared to his artistic attitude two decades earlier. Just as the blind poet in *Le Soir* accepts punishment for his insolence against the gods, so here Hercules shows his truly heroic nature by accepting his fate. Hercules takes charge of his own destiny and thus his salvation, in the same way as Davel — by his courage and strength in accepting the consequences of his acts, thus assuring his redemption.[871] Unlike *The Romans Passing under the Yoke*, in which humiliation is also the central subject, Hercules' punishment be-

864. Lausanne, Private collection.
865. Letter of 13 December 1862, in Champs-sur-Marne; Gleyre had invited Ehrmann to the studio where he saw the painting.
866. Olivier wrote to Adert on 1 August 1862, Lausanne, BCU/DM, Juste Olivier, "Correspondance à Jacques Adert," IS 40, that Goupil had already bought the painting. On the public exhibition of the work at Goupil's, see Dax 1863, and a letter from Albert de Meuron to his father, 1 March 1863, in Neuchâtel, AE, Fonds de Meuron, 68¹¹¹.
867. Pigler 1974, II, pp. 119f.
868. By Eude, n° 3220 of the livret; Vauthier-Galle, n° 3504; and Crauk, n° 3160.
869. See in particular Ovid, *Heroides*, IX, 53f.
870. See, for example, St. Augustine's *Sermons* in Migne 1844–65, XXXVIII, pp. 166 and 1249.
871. This aspect is also stressed in Michelet's account of the story, first published in 1864; see Michelet 1885–88, XXXVI, pp. 173–79.

183

207. *Hercules and Iphitus*, 1858–65. Lausanne, Musée Cantonal des Beaux-Arts (catalogue n° 845)

comes the source of his virtue and true strength. The transformation of the subject again reveals the philosophical side of Gleyre's art, even with the framework of iconography that had centuries of prototypical examples.

While this painting was never seen in the Salon, its exposure at Goupil's permitted the Paris public to examine a major work by Gleyre for the first time since the *Bacchantes* in 1849. And further, the public could read a full account of the painting in an article by Clément requested by Buloz and published in February 1863.[872] Clément began his analysis in the same way that Planche had begun his article a decade earlier, by explaining why Gleyre no longer wished to exhibit in the salons. Clément noted here that the Salon was basically a vehicle for younger painters who needed to publicize their efforts — this was not completely true — or established artists who used the forum as a way to increase their fame;

872. In a letter of 21 January 1863, Buloz suggested the idea to Clément because, he said, the work was exceptional; the letter is in Fleurier, CFC. Clément wrote the article very quickly: it was published in the *Revue des Deux-Mondes* on 15 February, pp. 1008–16.

261

since Gleyre was in neither group, he could abstain from the Salons altogether. In regard to the *Hercules*, Clément told his readers that Gleyre had had the courage to transform the scene into one of virtue and duty, which he considered to be the basis for the iconographic schema Gleyre had selected. He noted as well the physical beauty of the canvas, and made his readers aware of the archaeological details.

For Clément, the more important figure here was Omphale. He found her neither innocent nor threatening, neither a source of charm nor a cause of humiliation; she was, rather, an ideal type in accord with the iconography, but modified so as to reflect Hercules' redemption. Indeed, the fact that Gleyre too considered the figure of Omphale crucial is revealed in the number of studies devoted to her, as though he had struggled to find the appropriate gesture and facial type. It would be the image of Omphale that was most memorable, in part because one of Gleyre's drawings of her was lithographed by Bargue and widely sold by Goupil. The drawing was seen in almost all art schools and was copied by generations as a type of "ideal woman"; even in Mexico city in 1898, the twelve-year-old Diego Rivera assiduously drew the image in one of his first studies for the Academia de San Carlos.[873]

fig. 208

While Gleyre was working on the *Hercules* in 1862, the issue of his unfulfilled commission for the canton of Vaud, given along with the Jomini portrait, was again raised. The matter was broached by Jules Eytel, then the head of the Département de l'Instruction publique, who wrote to Gleyre about it, perhaps because the completion of the canvas was expected at that time. Gleyre replied on 16 May that "mon intention est toujours de faire ce tableau," that is, the commissioned painting; he promised to discuss the subject fully during his forthcoming vacation.

208. Diego Rivera, *Study of Omphale*, 1898. Mexico City, Universidad Nacional Autónoma de Mexico, Escuela Nacional de Bellas Artes

873. Rivera 1951, p. 437, n° 21.

Gleyre and Eytel did meet during the summer months, but their conversation was not reported in official documents.[874]

Apparently Gleyre was able to reassure cantonal authorities of his intentions, but two years later the subject arose once more, this time directly in connection with the *Hercules*. As mentioned above, the painting was purchased by Goupil before its completion; he in turn sold it to a Viennese "amateur d'art" who, in a curious and complicated affair, resold it to Goupil in the fall of 1865.[875] At this point, hoping to sell it once again, Goupil sent the painting to the Musée Arlaud in mid-October with the idea of offering it to the canton for the same price he had paid. It is not unlikely, given Goupil's relationship with Gleyre and his circle, that he was well aware of Gleyre's long outstanding commission from Lausanne. If so, he may have harbored hopes that his *Hercules* would be bought in lieu of a commissioned work that was not yet begun, seven years after the agreement had been made. Eytel's successor, Pierre-Isaac Joly, wrote to Gleyre while the *Hercules* was still on view, asking in acerbic terms "pour quelle époque vous pensez pouvoir nous livrer ce tableau." Joly added that the cantonal officials were obviously irritated that no new acquisitions for the museum were possible because of the financial commitment to pay Gleyre's fees, and the Conseil d'Etat could hardly consider spending the 18,000 francs Goupil desired for the *Hercules* "à cause de son engagement envers vous."[876]

Gleyre's reply was both defensive and hopeful. He wrote to Joly on 30 October 1865 that he was well aware of his commitment, but in his meeting with Eytel, more than two years earlier, he had been led to believe that neither a subject for the commission nor a specific date of completion had been specified. Moreover, he told Joly that he was informed that the canton had other pressing financial needs, which in effect precluded his working on the painting at this time. He advised Joly that the museum could in all conscience purchase the *Hercules*, should it wish to, thus in effect indirectly fulfilling the agreement made in 1858. He nevertheless reiterated his desire to complete a painting specifically for the museum, "mais je suis si lent que je ne pourrais pas m'engager pour une époque précise."[877] The canton chose not to buy the *Hercules* — it was purchased later by Fritz Berthoud, Clément's future father-in-law — preferring a painting executed expressly for Lausanne. Unfortunately, Gleyre never painted the commissioned picture.

While Gleyre was working on *Hercules and Omphale*, he began a canvas in which he explored another theme of sin and disobedience against the gods, this time through the story of Pentheus. The myth centers on the swift and cruel punishment inflicted on Pentheus because of his blasphemy and arrogance — a subject again related to *Le Soir*. Gleyre was already drawn to this myth in the late 1840s when he had prepared several studies on the subject, but he never developed any of these.[878]

The story of Pentheus is recounted in Euripides and Ovid, both of whom provide terrifying details of the gruesome punishment.[879] Pentheus, the son of Agave and Echion, was through them pretender to the throne of Thebes. When Dionysus came to Thebes to establish his cult, Pentheus

874. Eytel's letter has not been found, but Gleyre's response is in MCBA, GA, unclassified documents. We know that Gleyre was in Switzerland during the late summer of 1862, since he visited the Quinets in Veytaux.

875. Very little information is available on the matter, but Olivier, in a letter of 28 October 1865 to an unknown friend, remarked on Goupil's "échanges et de combinaisons qu'il lui est revenu, combinaisons, ou *micmacs*, si vous aimez mieux…," all of which seemed to Olivier of doubtful legality. Olivier also noted that the information was received from Gleyre himself who in turn had the confidence of Goupil. The letter itself has not been located, but is reproduced in Bonjour 1905, pp. 54–55.

876. Ibid., p. 53.

877. Ibid., p. 54.

878. Clément, p. 297, mentions only two studies, but there were actually four studies from this period; see n. 881 below.

879. *The Bacchae* and *Metamorphosis* III, respectively. On the theme in literature, see Curtius 1929.

263

refused to permit his worship, thus in effect denying his divinity. Although Pentheus was repeatedly warned, he persisted in banning all Dionysiac activity, which nevertheless attracted many women, including Pentheus' own mother. Intrigued by the rites, which took place outside the city limits, Pentheus spied on the ritual — despite the pointed advice of the blind soothsayer Tiresias — by disguising himself as a woman.[880] During the frenzied ceremony, his presence was discovered by his mother, who in her drunken state mistook him for a wild boar and rallied the women to capture the fleeing hero. They dismembered him and brought his head back to the temple.

When viewed in the light of the other themes Gleyre treated during this period, the violent aspects of the Pentheus story seem out of character with Gleyre's pictures of lyrical lovers, idyllic bathers, and pastoral landscape. Nowhere during the early 1860s did Gleyre approach a subject so rife with fury and brutality as his *Pentheus*. And yet, the very theme fig. 209 has its parallels in earlier ideas and reflects a certain continuity in Gleyre's work. One can perceive its counterparts not only in such paintings as *Nero and Agrippina*, with its theme of matricide — the inverse of the Pentheus idea — and *Le Soir*, but also in the *Davel* and *The Romans*. While the latter paintings are historical and moralistic in their imagery and approach, they are also inherently concerned with brutal events. It should not be forgotten that, like Pentheus, Davel is decapitated, and the motif reappears in *The Romans*. This violent strain, while often sublimated, is nevertheless too much in evidence in Gleyre's work to be considered coincidental. It is difficult, and perhaps even dangerous, to resort to a psychological framework to explain the frequent appearance of these elements, but they point to an important aspect of Gleyre's character.

When Gleyre prepared his studies on the theme of Pentheus in the late fig. 210 1840s, he envisioned four possible episodes.[881] The opportunity to translate one of these pictorially presented itself only in 1859 in the form of a commission from the city of Basel.[882] On 3 December of that year, it was noted in a report of the museum commission that they intended to ask Gleyre, in view of his reputation, his Swiss origins, and the recent success of his *Romans* in Lausanne, to fulfill a commission for a large work.[883] Up to that point, Gleyre's work had not been seen in the German part of Switzerland. The committee set aside a fee of 10,000 francs — it was not specified whether the fee was in Swiss or French currency, but it was considerably more than the second Vaudois commission — budgeted through the legacy of the local painter Samuel Birmann.[884] The only stipulation was that the work be large and dramatic; although the actual subject was left to the artist's discretion, it was hoped that Gleyre would produce an historical painting similar in scope and sweep to *The Romans*.[885]

Gleyre was enthusiastic about the commission, as Albert de Meuron noted in a letter to his sister on 13 April 1860.[886] Yet Gleyre did not officially accept the commission until 29 May, when he indicated that he intended to create a work on the Pentheus theme rather than an historical subject. By 17 November 1860, he had even sent the Basel officials a preliminary sketch of his idea, probably to assure them of the quality of

880. This element appears only in Euripides' version which Gleyre certainly read in Artaud's translation of 1857.

881. This information comes from a letter of Charles Denuelle, Alexander's brother, to Clément dated 3 January 1878, in Fleurier, CFC. The studies showed Pentheus hidden, Pentheus discovered by the women, Pentheus pursued, and Pentheus lacerated.

882. The circumstances surrounding the commission and its execution are outlined in Hauptman 1986(b).

883. Basel, KB, Protokoll, I, 83.

884. On Samuel Birmann (1793–1847), see Brun 1905–17, I, pp. 137–38.

885. Basel, SKB, Erziehungsakten, DD/7b.

886. Neuchâtel, AE, Fonds de Meuron, 69iv.

209. *Pentheus Pursued by the Maenads*, 1865. Basel, Öffentliche Kunstsammlung Basel, Kunstmusem (catalogue n° 850)

210. *Pentheus Surprising the Maenads*, 1859(?). Lausanne, Musée Cantonal des Beaux-Arts (catalogue n° 867)

211. John Flaxman, *Ulysses Terrified by the Ghosts*, 1805. New Haven, Yale Center for British Art

212. Raphael. *The Expulsion of Heliodoros*, detail, 1512. Rome, Vatican, Stanza d'Eliodoro

887. Basel, KB, Protokoll, I, 89 and 96.
888. Neuchâtel, AE, Fonds de Meuron, 68[iii].
889. The letter, dated 16 March 1863, is in a private collection, Lausanne.
890. *La Patrie*, 1863, p. 2.
891. Clément, p. 299.
892. Neuchâtel, AE, Fonds de Pury, unnumbered dossier, as of this writing; the dossiers were to be classified at some future date. My thanks to the de Pury family for permission to study these files.
893. Basel, BK, Protokoll, I, 180.

the work and to forestall their possible disappointement later.[887] It is not known which study Gleyre sent, as no description of it survives in the Basel records. The day afterwards, de Meuron wrote his father that Gleyre, certain that he would encounter no difficulties, would begin the work shortly.[888] His eye problems, however, prevented his undertaking the project immediately. In the Basel commission report for 19 January 1861, it was noted that Gleyre had not actually begun work in earnest; in fact, during 1861 and the following year, his attention was concentrated on completing his *Hercules*, and thus it would not be until early 1863 that he was free to begin the Pentheus canvas.

By spring, Gleyre was fully occupied with the Basel commission, as indicated in a letter from Olivier to Hébert, written in March 1863, in which Gleyre is described as actively preparing his "Panthée" [sic].[889] In October a Swiss journal reported that Gleyre had virtually finished the painting.[890] The report proved to be overly optimistic: Gleyre had great difficulty in realizing certain sections of the canvas, especially the landscape which he had to repaint several times.[891] He thus continued work on the project during the early months of 1864, and in June, his student from Neuchâtel, Edmond de Pury, wrote to his parents that he had seen the finished canvas on the easel.[892] He added that the painting was, in his opinion, superior to Gleyre's early works, which de Pury especially admired; he thought it worth far more than the fee offered by the city of Basel. Even if the canvas appeared finished when de Pury saw it, Gleyre did not deliver it immediately, preferring instead to refine the details and the surface finish of the picture. The painting did not arrive in Basel until 4 February 1865.[893]

Since the iconography of the *Pentheus* seems to be unique in nineteenth-century painting, Gleyre relied on pure invention as he had for the *Davel* two decades earlier, but without the benefit of historical documents. However, he did use artistic sources that were similar in theme —

266

fig. 211  among them, an illustration by Flaxman, *Ulysses Terrified by the Ghosts*.[894] There is no documentary proof that Gleyre had seen the plate, but Flaxman's influence in Europe was such at the time that it is unlikely that Gleyre would not have known of it, particularly in light of his appetite for nontraditional source material.[895] Of special interest is the similarity between the floating movements of the ghosts in the print and the fleeing figures of the frenzied women in the painting, both defying laws of gravity. Another source for Gleyre's imagery is the fleeing figure in

fig. 212  Raphael's Vatican fresco, *The Expulsion of Heliodorus*, which Gleyre transformed into Pentheus. Gleyre had always maintained a lively interest in Raphael's works, even the less well known ones in the Loggia, which he copied in his Roman sketchbooks. He must have been attracted to this figure, precisely because of its sweeping movement which already looks forward to the Baroque. Transplanted and slightly altered as it is in Gleyre's canvas, the figure becomes at once a focal point of the picture and also the perfect embodiment of the fear that is at the heart of the subject.

Yet another possible influence in the conception of the picture is

fig. 213  Bouguereau's *The Remorse of Orestes* which Gleyre saw in the salon of 1863.[896] There are no formal similarities, but the theme of vengeance, the intense psychological focus, and the somber tonalities that create the infernal atmosphere may have contributed to the way Gleyre devised the essential components of the scene. So close in fact were the two subjects of Orestes and Pentheus in the minds of later critics that even such a distinguished connoisseur of Gleyre's work as Samuel Avery confused the two.[897]

213. William Bouguereau, *The Remorse of Orestes*, 1862. Norfolk, The Chrysler Museum. Gift of Walter P. Chrysler, Jr., 1971

894. The illustration is of lines 779f. in Book XI of Pope's translation of the *Odyssey*.
895. See Symmons 1974, pp. 152f., for the Flaxman influence in European art of the nineteenth century.
896. Livret n° 227 of the salon; see Walker and D'Argencourt 1984, pp. 161–63.
897. See [Avery] 1874.

It is particularly unfortunate that the painting was never seen in Paris. There is no evidence that critics went to Gleyre's studio specifically to study his newest creation, although slightly later, a poor reproduction that deflated the dramatic, expressive elements of the painting was available. Only the critic Paul Mantz wrote about the painting from firsthand experience, noting that it was without doubt one of Gleyre's most interesting works, surpassing those of his youth; Mantz correctly saw the center of the composition, aesthetically as well as compositionally, as "la blanche silhouette de la Peur qui vole dans la nuit."[898] Clément too praised the picture as one of Gleyre's finest, but he was somewhat puzzled by its fury in comparison with the works that preceded and followed it. For the progressive historian Richard Muther, it was this element, among others, that elevated the *Pentheus* above the pseudo-idealism and sentimentality that had marked earlier work. It is to Muther's credit that he selected this example of Gleyre's work to demonstrate the painter's inventiveness and modernity.[899]

898. Mantz 1875, pp. 410–11.
899. Muther 1907, I, p. 364, but here the work is entitled *Orpheus Torn by the Bacchantes*.

## CHAPTER 10

# 1865–1870

## THE LATER WORKS

214. Study of Animals for *Minerva and the Three Graces*, 1865. Lausanne, Musée Cantonal des Beaux-Arts (catalogue n° 875)

The last decade of Gleyre's life centered artistically on subjects that suited the more temperate, even sensual side of his nature. These works have none of the horror and stunning violence of his *Pentheus* nor the despair of his *Le Soir*. Clément is certainly correct in attributing the change to the mellowing process of age and Gleyre's love for Classical imagery and composition.[900] In four pictures conceived and completed before 1870, the central subject is the female form in a Classical setting, a theme Gleyre attempted in his youth and in various studies later, not always successfully. If his *Pentheus* revives the baroque aspects of his art, the paintings after 1865 reveal a return to the Renaissance spirit and ideal found in his art after his trip to Venice two decades earlier.

Before turning to these works, it is important to trace another of his activities at this time that has gone virtually unnoticed in the literature; namely, his participation in the salon juries. After 1849, Gleyre had had no direct relationship with the French Salon system, a fact lamented by

900. Clément, pp. 331f.

269

friends, critics, and the public alike. The reasons for his decisions were personal; never did he advocate that his many students follow his example in this regard because he knew that without such public exhibitions, the beginner would not have the possibility of establishing his name and reputation. During the late 1850s and early 1860s, the process for selecting the juries was restructured several times with the goal of producing a system that would function better both for the artists and for the public at large. The state tried to find a way to improve the quality of the works exhibited and, at the same time, to bridge the gap between exhibitors and jury that had existed since the early nineteenth century. The major reform policies of 1863 designated that a certain percentage of the jury would be elected by the artists themselves, thus helping to eliminate the perpetual complaints of favoritism.[901] As a result of these reforms, Gleyre was named to the jury in 1864, along with such other painters as Meissonier and Cogniet, to serve in an unspecified supplementary role.[902] When Ingres, Picot, and Cogniet abstained from service, as was their right, one that Ingres, incidentally, exercised often in his long career, Gleyre was named as the first supplementary jurist. Presumably, he was supposed to serve should one of the regular jury members become ill or be unable to deliberate. The fact that Gleyre did not withdraw from this or other juries to which he was appointed indicates his willingness to offer judgment and advice, as he did in his teaching atelier. Gleyre's opinion, it seems, was always respected, not only because of his sound artistic judgment, but also because of his impartiality. He never permitted himself to favor his own students' works, unlike other jury members, nor did he oppose the exhibition of paintings that contradicted his own style or artistic philosophy.[903]

Gleyre also served in 1865 as a supplementary jurist, having received 41 votes — Cabanel, in contrast, received 167 votes of the 202 that were cast by colleagues.[904] But in 1866 Gleyre's reputation had risen to the point that he received 140 votes of the 198 cast and was therefore elected to the permanent jury for that year.[905] His presence on the jury was noted by Emile Zola who, writing his first Salon review, noted that Gleyre was an artist "si digne et si honorable" that he was a particularly trustworthy voice in the jury deliberations, which Zola otherwise criticized as not being on the highest artistic level.[906] After a consideration of the votes cast for the jury, the Minister of Fine Arts, the powerful and often feared Nieuwerkerke, announced the final composition of the jury for 1866 with Robert-Fleury as president, and Théophile Gautier and Gleyre as joint vice-presidents. The jury records do not indicate Gleyre's role in the actual voting for admissions and refusals and therefore it is not certain how he used his power in this capacity. But the livret indicates that a substantial number of Realists and young landscape artists showed their works, including Courbet, Ribot, Bonvin, Monet, Millet, Daubigny, Rousseau, and Degas, although Manet's *The Fifer* was refused. From the list of artists rewarded afterwards with medals, it is clear that Gleyre exercised no favoritism to friends or students: of the thirty-nine awards given in the salon, only three went to Gleyre's students.[907] Gleyre continued to par-

901. Hauptman 1985(a), pp. 107–108.
902. *Explication* 1864, xcv, which lists the jury and the voting of the committees.
903. Milliet 1915, p. 250.
904. *Explication* 1865, LXVII; see also *Journal des débats*, 30 March 1865, p. 1.
905. *Explication* 1865, LXXV.
906. Zola 1959, p. 56. The article first appeared in *L'Evénement*, 30 April 1866.
907. *Le Moniteur universel*, 15 August 1866, notes the awards: the three students of Gleyre were Anker, Lecomte du Nouy, and Nazon.

ticipate in the Salon juries through 1869,[908] but poor health and the advent of the Franco-Prussian war prevented such activities afterwards.

During 1867, beside his duties for the Salon jury, Gleyre also contributed indirectly to the selection of works for the Exposition Universelle in Paris. The exposition itself was a remarkable showpiece for all aspects of international achievement and offered the huge crowds — almost eleven million attended, twice the number of the last exposition in Paris in 1855[909] — an unprecedented retrospective of contemporary art. Gleyre was asked to head the final jury for the Swiss section of fine arts in four of the five categories, including painting, drawing, the graphic arts, and sculpture, but not architectural plans and models.[910] The task proved to be an enormous one, since after the final judgments, the Swiss participation included 201 works exhibited by 101 artists.[911] The smallest contribution was in the sculpture section with only fourteen works by nine artists; the graphic arts contained sixteen works by four artists, including the Girardet brothers who alone accounted for ten of the works exhibited.

Gleyre's activities in organizing the Swiss exhibition are fully outlined in a report he submitted after the completion of the show.[912] In the opening paragraph, he noted the general mediocrity of the works shown, a curious and remarkable apologia which must have stunned the Swiss authorities. He explained that there were in fact two juries that chose the works: the first had made the initial selection in Geneva, while the second reviewed them in Paris. Gleyre, in conjunction with the international committee charged with the responsibility of the art sections, found these works without particular distinction and on the whole inadequate. He wanted to strengthen the representation by eliminating those works he deemed particularly weak, but was asked not to do so because the space given to the Swiss section was far greater than had been expected and works were needed to fill the space. Thus Gleyre accepted submissions that otherwise he might have rejected, but noted for the authorities that despite this lamentable circumstance, the Swiss representation was dignified and distinguished among its rivals.

One of the most interesting aspects of Gleyre's report is an explanation of why Swiss history painting in the exhibition was so feeble. Gleyre spoke not only as an artist familiar with conditions in his native country, but also as an educator whose task was to prepare students to understand the importance of the genre for their art and their careers. Gleyre was particularly severe on the inadequate system of art education in Switzerland, which he thought did not provide the necessary resources to develop this form of art in either painting or sculpture. He noted in particular the lack of first-rate museums or private collections open to students, and, surprisingly, the reticence of the Swiss to use live nude models in their training. He also pointed out the near absence of private palaces and public sculpture, both of which foster the conditions for history painting and both of which were readily available in all other major European countries. Furthermore, Gleyre condemned the minimal support from the state, noting that generally commissions for projects

908. See *Explication* 1867, LXXX; *Explication* 1868, LXII; and *Explication* 1869, XCVII.
909. See Bouin and Chanut 1980, pp. 75f., and Ory 1982, p. 153.
910. The information is contained in outline form in Gleyre 1868, pp. 294f.
911. *Exposition Universelle* 1867, pp. 146f.
912. The original report submitted by Gleyre has not been located, but seems to have been published verbatim in Gleyre 1868.

271

were in the hands of private individuals or societies. This form of private patronage favored smaller pictures as individual showpieces or sculpture on a modest scale, which in effect failed to provide the grand forums necessary for history painting and sculpture. Gleyre was wholly correct in his view that the system under which the Swiss student was trained and worked favored genre scenes and landscape painting.

Despite these valid arguments about the lack of a national tradition in history painting, Gleyre could nevertheless point to four examples in the section that he judged exemplary. A painting of Adam and Eve by his student Albert Darier received generous praise despite the fact that the picture created "peu d'effet."[913] Arnold Böcklin's painting of *Daphnis and Amaryllis* was distinguished, according to Gleyre, by its color which was "brillante et solide."[914] As for August Weckesser's *The Duchess of Glocester,* Gleyre found it somewhat cold, but still well studied and carefully executed.[915] Gleyre had the most praise for Albert Landerer's *The Wedding of the Last of the Ramstein,* where the local color was remarkably observed and admirably captured.[916]

For Gleyre, the true strength of the exhibition was in the genre category. He singled out in particular the two works by the Vaudois painter Benjamin Vautier, *Agents and Peasants,* which belonged to the Kunstmuseum in Basel, and *The Crossing of Lake Brienz.*[917] Gleyre was correct to see these works as part of a tradition of sentimental and mannered painting, in accord with the artist's training in Düsseldorf, but he pointed out that Vautier knew the difference between sentiment and sentimentality, thus elevating his art above the banal. He was especially fond of the figure carrying the child in the former painting, which amply demonstrated the artist's merits. Gleyre was certainly influential in Vautier's receiving a second-class medal. Gleyre also noted the importance of Albert Anker's *The New Baby,*[918] but regretted that the painter had not submitted earlier examples of his work that had already won acclaim in the Paris Salons. He also admired the efforts of his student Jules Jacot-Guillarmod, but found the technique in his *Departure of the Procession* weak and ineffectual.[919] He preferred the latter's animal studies, as well as those of Rudolf Koller, which he described as full of vivacity, even though he had doubts about the aspects of the compositions.[920]

The largest group of Swiss works exhibited were landscapes. In Gleyre's view, a distinct change had occurred in the outlook of Swiss painters in this genre. The younger artists were less concerned with the grandiose, sublime aspects of the landscape that had marked the earlier tradition, and were now more interested in producing intimate works on a modest scale. He attributed this to a trend toward study in France and Italy, where the same phenomenon was perceived. Gleyre noted particularly the fine efforts of his friend Léon Berthoud,[921] where he perceived an exemplary use of site, lighting effects, and natural poetry. He also remarked upon the works of Etienne Duval,[922] who showed a strong Italian influence, as well as Edmond Favre, whose landscapes created a powerful impact.[923] The three works of Bocion[924] were something of a revelation for Gleyre in the way that the color expressed the essence of Lake Geneva, whose

913. *Exposition Universelle de 1867*, n° 28. Darier had enrolled in Gleyre's teaching studio in 1863; see Hauptman 1985(e), p. 100.

914. N° 21. On the work, see Andrée 1977, p. 295, n° 186. The work is actually entitled *Die Klage des Hirtens.*

915. N° 106. The scene represented is from Shakespeare's *Henry VI.* On August Weckesser (1821–99), see Brun 1905–17, III, pp. 443–48. The work was owned, incidentally, by Henri Moser, who later purchased Gleyre's painting *The Prodigal Son.*

916. N° 71. On Albert Landerer (1816–93), see Brun 1905–17, II, p. 220. The scene depicts an episode in the history of Basel.

917. N° 101 and 102. On Benjamin Vautier (1829–89), see Brun 1905–17, III, pp. 364–67.

918. N° 1. On the history of the painting, see Kuthy and Lüthy 1990, p. 63.

919. N° 56–59. Jules-Jacques Jacot-Guillarmod (1828–89) had studied with Gleyre in early 1851. On him, see Brun 1905–17, II, pp. 112–13. His personal papers are in Neuchâtel, AE.

920. N° 62–66. On Rudolf Koller (1828–1905), see Brun 1905–17, II, pp. 185–88.

921. N° 11–15. On Léon Berthoud (1822–92), see Brun 1905–17, I, pp. 117–18. Gleyre had already championed Berthoud's work in 1865, suggesting through Clément that the Musée Arlaud buy one of his landscapes; see the correspondence between Clément and M. Gay in Fleurier, CFC.

922. N° 38–40. On Etienne Duval (1824–1923), see Brun 1905–17, I, pp. 404–405.

923. N° 41–42. On François Favre (1812–80), see Brun 1905–17, I, p. 444; Clément probably knew this artist's work since there is some correspondence with a "M. Favre."

924. N° 16–18. As in the case of Berthoud, Gleyre often championed Bocion's work; he later made a pencil portrait of him in Lausanne.

atmosphere he knew so well. Gleyre similarly praised the paintings of Albert de Meuron, which he described as especially airy and picturesque in the best sense of the word.[925] He had nothing to say about François Diday's only contribution.

Of the other categories, Gleyre's description is minimal and clearly shows his discomfort. He admired the sculpture of Emanuele Caroni[926] and Heinrich-Max Imhof,[927] who at seventy-two was probably the oldest participant. Gleyre noted the importance of the contribution of Juliette Hébert,[928] as well as the work of the engraver Friedrich Weber, whose engraving of the *Empress Eugénie*[929] he considered a masterpiece of the art. He likewise singled out Paul Girardet's print of Vernet's *Mass in Kabylie* which displayed a masterly touch and exemplary use of the graded grey tones.[930]

Beside acting as judge and promoter of the Swiss contribution to the exhibition, Gleyre tried to utilize his considerable influence in the fair distribution of the prizes. He openly admitted in his report that he was considerably dissatisfied with the results. While some artists like Vautier and Caroni were given second-class medals, not a single first-class medal was awarded to any Swiss participant. A minimum of fourteen votes from the grand jury was necessary, but only Léon Berthoud and de Meuron came close with twelve and nine votes respectively. The request to augment the number of prizes awarded — as was done in the Industry section — was refused. However, Gleyre noted that in comparison with other small countries, the Swiss contributors distinguished themselves. Between the lines of Gleyre's report, however, one can read his condemnation of a still provincial system that was neither wholly supported nor appreciated by the federal authorities.

In Gleyre's capacity as judge, he never addressed himself to federal architectural projects which were on the whole funded by the state more generously than the other arts. One of these projects, however, affected Gleyre indirectly — the major renovation and enlargement of the Palais Fédéral in Bern.[931] For a number of years, there had been rumors that Gleyre, by virtue of his reputation at this time as the most important Swiss artist, would be asked to contribute to the interior decoration of one of the main chambers, possibly the Salle du Conseil National. Very few details have ever come to light. It is not known who initiated the idea or asked for Gleyre's participation, but while Gleyre had few contacts with Bern, he nevertheless had important political friends there.

When the idea was presented to Gleyre, he was, surprisingly, enthusiastic about the project. Various documents from his friends indicate that Gleyre took the notion seriously. Olivier noted to his friend Adert in a letter dated only 1867 that "Gleyre avait tout à fait… l'idée de faire les peintures pour le palais fédéral. Il avait même déjà son sujet."[932] This is also confirmed by Eugène Rambert who seems to have discussed the project with Gleyre. Rambert noted that the very idea of applying his artistry to such a national cause was one of the painter's secret ambitions. Gleyre even went so far as to make some studies for the decoration scheme, but the project never materialized. Rambert suggested several

925. N° 81–86. On Gleyre's help in the development of de Meuron's work, see Hauptman 1985(e), pp. 86f.
926. N° 3–5 in class 3. On Emanuele Caroni (born in 1826), see Brun 1905–17, I, pp. 273–74.
927. N° 7–8 in class 3. On Heinrich-Max Imhof (1795–1869), see Brun 1905–17, II, pp. 126–29.
928. N° 25–32 in class 2. On Juliette Hébert (1837–1924), see Brun 1905–17, Suppl. p. 208; she was the daughter of Olivier's cousin, Jules Hébert.
929. N° 6 in class 5. On Friedrich Weber (1813–82), see Brun 1905–17, III, pp. 434–39.
930. N° 4 in class 5. On Paul Girardet (1821–93), see Grellet 1920.
931. See Hofer 1947, pp. 64f.
932. The letter is in Lausanne, BCU/DM, Juste Olivier, "Correspondance à Adert," IS 40.

possible reasons, including Gleyre's timidity, as well as the fact that his friends in high government positions did not push his ideas energetically before the responsible administrators. But Rambert added that Gleyre's participation was, in fact, unlikely, since he was still too little known in the German part of Switzerland. The result, Rambert noted with some irony, was that "la Suisse a perdu une occasion unique de s'enrichir d'un premier et grand monument de peinture nationale."[933]

The only hint of what Gleyre actually had in mind for these decorations comes from Fritz Berthoud, to whom Gleyre apparently showed some of his drawings. Berthoud described a grandiose scheme, a parliamentary debate in which all of the great Swiss politicians take part. None of these drawings was found in the studio after Gleyre's death, nor is it known why the project never developed. One can presume that the vastness of the work necessary for the interior space may have been beyond Gleyre's capacities in the late 1860s. Moreover, it should be recalled that Gleyre had not been involved in any form of interior decoration since his limited experience at Saint-Vincent-de-Paul in 1842. Perhaps too the amount of time necessary to realize such an ambitious project prevented him from committing himself to the project. At one point it was suggested that Gleyre prepare the designs which could be carried out by assistants under his supervision, but even this was never pursued.[934] It is not known how long Gleyre harbored this secret ambition, as Rambert called it, but in 1872 when he planned a trip to the Engadine with Fritz Berthoud and Clément, he insisted on stopping in Bern to witness the assembly in session. Gleyre, however, was noticeably disappointed by what he saw and, it seems, confused by the politicians speaking in all of the three national languages, sometimes simultaneously.[935]

Gleyre's most important commission after his *Pentheus* was a private one for the Vaudois industrialist Vincent Dubochet. Gleyre and Dubochet were almost surely introduced by their mutual friend, Juste Olivier. Already in the 1840s, Olivier had met Dubochet through Vinet and Marquis, who was a close friend and neighbor. By 1855, Olivier was visiting Dubochet regularly during his holidays in Switzerland.[936] Moreover, Dubochet was intimate with many of Gleyre's circle, including the Quinets who lived nearby and who were often invited for political and literary discussions.[937]

Vincent Dubochet, who started life as a poor boy near Montreux, had come to Paris in 1813. He became the president of the Compagnie du Gaz de Paris and, with the approval of Hausmann, maintained a monopoly on gas distribution which netted him a sizable fortune. In addition, he speculated in railroads, establishing the Paris-Strasbourg line and helped to develop the Swiss railroad system and the Simplon Pass project. He was for the French and the Swiss a symbol of the self-made man; it was not uncommon to hear the phrase "riche comme Dubochet" to describe a large fortune.[938]

Dubochet never forgot his Swiss origins, proclaiming himself, like Gleyre, a lifelong Republican, and actively supporting dozens of liberal causes.[939] Beside Quinet, he entertained figures such as Gambetta,

933. Rambert 1890, pp. 358–59. Rambert, however, wrote these lines in 1875 and hinted strongly that his information came directly from Gleyre himself.

934. Berthoud 1874, p. 618.

935. Berthoud 1898, p. 454.

936. See, for example, Olivier's letter of 26 January 1855, in Lausanne, BCU/DM, Fonds Olivier, IS 1905/43, dossier 1855, although there are many other references to stays with Dubochet.

937. See Paris, BN, Quinet, "Correspondance," XIX, letters 401–35, as well as Mme. Quinet, "Mémorial," X, 1867–68. See also Du Pasquier 1959, pp. 119f., on the relationship between the two.

938. There is no standard biography on Dubochet, but see the obituary note in *Gazette de Lausanne*, 1877, pp. 2–3.

939. See Reymond 1867, p. 1050.

215. The Château des Crêtes, near Vevey

whom he at times supported financially, Michelet, and the Republican senator Arnaud, who later became his son-in-law.[940] Many French exiles in 1871–72, including Courbet, found shelter and encouragement with Dubochet.[941] With his liberal political leanings, it was inevitable that he would meet Gleyre. In a letter to her husband, Caroline Olivier gives the earliest record of their meeting, in summer 1863, when both Gleyre and Dubochet were in Lausanne,[942] but it is probable that they had known each other earlier in Paris. At the time, Dubochet was constructing a huge villa at Clarens with no fewer than fifteen guest rooms to accommodate the constant stream of visitors; the interior decoration was supervised by Gleyre's friend Alexandre Denuelle.[943] It was almost surely at this point and probably through Denuelle that Gleyre was asked to provide a large painting to be permanently installed in the main salon where Dubochet entertained his guests.

Gleyre chose a subject appropriate for decorative purposes, *Minerva and the Three Graces,* which he had sketched earlier and which had remained unused.[944] According to Clément, the scene represented Minerva not in her usual association with Mars but engaged in a competition with the Graces. Minerva is in the center, playing a transverse, singled-keyed flute, in accord with the ancient tradition. Seated at the right is Aglaia, the personification of Radiance, pointing to the mirror-like water seemingly to show Minerva the unharmonious grimace she is forced to make in order to produce music. Euphrosyne, personifying Joy, is at the right in the background, while Thalia, personifying Bloom, is at the left playing the double flute. The Arcadian landscape with the doe drinking from the spring provides the necessary natural setting. The composition itself follows the rules of Classical harmony, in accord with the subject, and is conceived wholly within an academic framework.

Gleyre reworked the original study he had made by February 1865, adding pastels to harmonize the color arrangements, an important consideration in this case.[945] He apparently worked quickly on the composi-

fig. 215

fig. 216

fig. 214

940. On Léon Gambetta (1838–82), see J.P.T. Bury 1973, as well as Gambetta's letters, many of which were written from Dubochet's villa. See Michelet 1959–76, III, p. 298. See Du Pasquier 1959, p. 120, for the mention of Arnaud.
941. Hauptman 1985(b), pp. 25–26.
942. Letter of 30 August 1863, in Lausanne, BCU/DM, Fonds Olivier, IS 1905/43, dossier 1863.
943. Rambert et al. 1877, p. 100. The villa, known as the Château des Crêtes, was completed in 1864.
944. Clément, pp. 330–31.
945. Ibid., p. 425, under catalogue n° 102.

216. *Minerva and the Three Graces*, 1866. Lausanne, Musée Cantonal des Beaux-Arts (catalogue n° 872)

tion, completing most of the canvas during the spring and summer months. He noted that he recognized at some point that a compositional void existed in the lower center of the arrangement and asked Clément, who apparently agreed, to supply a suitable plant that he could incorporate near the rocks in the foreground. Clément suggested a cyclamen — he thought it to be the preferred plant of Leonardo — of which he had several specimens in Paris that he had brought back from Rome in 1863. He gave Gleyre one of the type known as *cyclamen repandum,* a flower distinguished by its particularly rosy petals and thus congruous with the overall color scheme. Gleyre in fact kept the plant in his studio until 1870 when the political conditions in Paris forced him to seek safety in Lausanne.[946] The cyclamen, incidentally, was one of Clément's favored plants; he was considered an expert on the species and later even published a scientific treatise on it.[947]

By the end of the year, Gleyre had ostensibly finished the painting, as was noted by a Parisian critic who lamented the fact that Gleyre refused to exhibit works in the Salons, a situation all the more tragic because of the exceptional beauty of his art at this time.[948] Word of the completion of yet another important painting by Gleyre also reached Lausanne in May 1866, and Mr. Gay of the Société des Beaux-Arts attempted to have the work shown in the Musée Arlaud before its permanent installation at the Dubochet mansion.[949] In a letter to the Conseil d'Etat, Gay indicated that this was in fact Gleyre's desire and that he had agreed to the arrangement — actually there are no records to indicate contact between Gay and Gleyre at this time, but the agreement may have been oral — depending upon final approval from Dubochet himself. The Conseil sent an official request to Dubochet the next day; he agreed to lend the painting for a short time.

Gleyre shipped the painting from Paris in June 1866, but not directly to Lausanne.[950] Rather, it was sent to Geneva, where, under circumstances that were not recorded or are not extant, the painting was exhibited in the "permanente" exhibition organized by the Société des Amis des Arts.[951] By July, the painting was hung on an appropriately prominent wall and the newspapers urged their readers to visit the exhibition early, reminding them of the large crowds that came in November 1865 to see Gleyre's *Hercules*.[952] Gleyre's student Paul Milliet saw the painting in Geneva before his departure for studies in Florence and wrote to his mother on 29 July that as fine as the painting was, it seemed to confuse Geneva audiences because Gleyre, or the proper authorities, had not provided a title or label identifying the scene.[953] Nevertheless, despite the confusion over the curious iconography, there were large crowds throughout the exhibition.

After Geneva, the painting was sent to Lausanne before 16 August where, surprisingly, it was scheduled to be shown for only ten days.[954] By 25 August, such large crowds thronged the Musée Arlaud that the exhibition was extended, presumably with Dubochet's permission. The next day, it was reported that Gleyre and Dubochet visited the museum together to inspect the painting.[955] Later it was noted, certainly to

946. Clément, pp. 336–37.
947. Clément, "Le genre Cyclamen," first published in the *Moniteur d'horticulture* in three installments in 1887 and reprinted in its entirety in 1888.
948. Dax 1865, p. 282.
949. Gay sent a letter to the Conseil d'Etat on 30 May 1866 requesting that a formal letter of request be sent for the loan of the picture; in Lausanne, ACV, Département de l'Instruction publique, Lettres, K XIII/63.
950. Clément, p. 336.
951. On the "permanente," see Neuweiler 1945, p. 227, and Jaccard 1986.
952. *Tribune de Genève*, 31 July 1866.
953. Milliet 1915, pp. 262–63.
954. *Nouvelliste vaudois*, 17 August 1866, p. 3. See also the documentation in Lausanne, MCBA, Museum Archives, A 1866/3.
955. *Nouvelliste vaudois*, 25 August 1866, p. 3.

exaggerate the importance of the work and its reception in the canton, that virtually the entire population of Lausanne had filed past the painting while it was on exhibit. Not all the critical comments were favorable nor were the Lausannois less confused by the imagery than the Genevans; many noted that the unusually light colors were a departure from Gleyre's dense tones, and that the proportions of the figures were hardly ideal. One journal reported that the painting was hung too low and was ill lit.[956] By mid-September, Gleyre's painting was installed in the main salon of Dubochet's villa.[957]

Most critical objections to the painting centered on three elements: the strange, unharmonious grimace of Minerva, the proportions of her right leg, and the oddly lightened palette Gleyre employed. Clément defended the grimace, pointing out that Gleyre had properly studied the formation of the lips and cheeks a flutist must make in order to produce a tone; as ungainly as it appeared in the canvas, for Clément this confirmed Gleyre's fidelity to observed fact. This was also the case regarding the proportions of Minerva's right leg. Clément noted that Gleyre himself was aware that the leg as it was positioned and drawn in the composition seemed incorrect and thus he had the model take the pose again so as to verify the accuracy of his initial drawing. He found that he had indeed drawn the leg as he had observed it, but its foreshortening made it appear curiously ill-proportioned.[958] Clément did not attempt to explain the uncommonly light colors and perhaps was not aware of the fact that Gleyre purposely introduced this unusual palette for a specific reason. The lighter tones were dictated by the interior design that Denuelle had conceived for the main salon and, if we are to believe Eugène Rambert, Gleyre himself contributed to the decoration scheme and so was perfectly aware of how to best integrate the canvas into an existing color harmony.[959] Gleyre certainly knew also that the painting was to be hung with only a small hall window as the main source of light, which would suggest the use of a particularly light-color scheme; it may also explain why Gleyre used pastels earlier to change the tonal values of the sketch. Hung in a museum, the painting seems singularly out of place, and indeed wholly incongruous with Gleyre's other works, earlier and later.

Yet, it is important to place this painting properly in Gleyre's output of the mid-1860s. Coming as it does after the violence of his *Pentheus,* the subject and style of the *Minerva* mark a classicizing phase in which subject and technique look forward to the mellower, more harmonious work of Gleyre's last period. The Graces themselves represent joy, charm, and beauty; they are the embodiments of the spring of life, the precise opposite of the despair of *Le Soir.* If Clément is correct that the work represents a competition with the gods, then here they react with benevolence rather than punishment. There is no indication of revenge or brutality as in the earlier works where the subject of divine competition was treated. Rather, the painting is an idyllic pastoral of a type that might recall Prud'hon's influence, an example of the Néo-Grec school which Gleyre was said to have influenced if not to have formed.

217. *Portrait of Madame Audiffred,* 1867. Troyes, Musée d'Art et d'Archéologie (catalogue n° 900)

956. Molins, 14 September 1866, pp. 1–2.
957. Fritz Berthoud wrote to Juste Olivier on 6 September 1866 that he had recently seen Jacques-Julien Dubochet, Vincent's nephew, who informed him that the work would be installed in about a week. The letter is noted, but not actually found, in Fleurier, CFC.
958. Clément, pp. 335–36.
959. Rambert 1890, p. 307. The present owner of the château, who wishes to remain anonymous, did not permit me to inspect the interior of the salon for which Gleyre's painting was designed. She affirmed that the original decoration scheme by Denuelle, which was significantly altered at the turn of the century, was in fact almost rococo in its light, pastel colors.

218. *Portrait of Madame Eulalie Carrié*, 1867 (?).
Montpellier, Musée Fabre (catalogue n° 906)

While working on both major and minor projects, Gleyre also continued to paint portraits of friends and accept commissions for portraits of others. During 1867, two such commissions are known that bear mention because of their absence from Clément's biography. Available documents do not show how Gleyre received the commission to paint the portrait of Mme. Audiffred. She is not mentioned in any of the correspondence of Gleyre's circle; she does not seem to have been a friend of Gleyre, Clément, or Olivier. She was born Mlle. Jouannique and married F. J. Audiffred, a lawyer and businessman greatly interested in the arts and philanthropy.[960] Stylistically, the portrait, in a sadly damaged state, reflects the formal side of Gleyre's art in this genre in that it has a certain stiffness, not unlike Ingres's portrait of Mme. Moitessier. The same may be said for Gleyre's portrait of Eulalie Carrié, painted almost certainly at the same time.[961] She has no known connection with the Gleyre's circle, nor is anything known about her. Verification that the work is in fact by Gleyre is found in a preparatory drawing in Gleyre's hand, not identified by Clément but published in a photograph by Braun.

fig. 217

fig. 218

960. The information was supplied by J.-P. Sainte-Maire, curator of the Musée de Troyes. See also Balteau et al. 1929, IV, fasc. XIX, pp. 382f., for his philanthropic activities.
961. Thanks to Xavier Dejean of the Musée Fabre for information about the portrait. See the documentation regarding the work in Montpellier, AM, Séries R 2/3, dossier 6, 1902.

fig. 219

The second important commission in this period was a small painting generally titled *Sappho.* Gleyre himself had no specific intention of creating an image depicting the poetess; rather he wanted to paint a small, antique genre scene in which the female nude is the pretext for the subject. He had thought to title the picture simply *Poetess,* but for some unexplained reason he found the title "affreux."[962] Clément recounted briefly the genesis of the work. When in the summer of 1866, he and Gleyre were alone in the studio, a young girl, clearly poor and in need of employment, came asking whether she could pose for the master. Gleyre told her that he did not need a model at that time, but she insisted, and Gleyre asked her to disrobe. When he saw her take a pose, Gleyre was so moved by her fragile, youthful beauty that he began to weep. Clément was so amazed that he dared not say a word. As he noted later, in his friendship with Gleyre, which then had lasted more than two decades, he saw Gleyre weep only twice: the first time was in 1859 or 1860 when the two attended a celebrated performance of Gluck's opera *Orphée,* in a version prepared by Berlioz and sung by Pauline Viardot;[963] the second time was when this young girl took a pose in the studio.

Gleyre proceeded to make several studies of the girl and sought an appropriate subject for her. Later he realized that her head and face reflected the girl's youthful innocence, but perhaps because of her poverty and deprivation, her body seemed to be that of a much older woman. He eventually used another model for the lower part of the body and combined the two to form the figure in the canvas. Gleyre completed the painting very quickly, so that by 24 December 1867 it was already in place in the salon of the publisher Charpentier, who proudly showed it to Michelet that day.[964] Ironically, Michelet wrote that it was the lower part of the body that he found objectionable, disharmonious with the rest, because it was too large.

Clément however had no such objections. He thought the painting one of Gleyre's finest in the genre and placed its artistic merits above those of the *Pentheus.* This view was, on the whole, shared by Mantz.[965] Gleyre too thought it one of his most poetic evocations of the female form — although he never mentioned it in his correspondence — and even supervised the engraving of the image by Flamenq in 1869.[966] The public reaction, particularly in Switzerland later, is interesting to note here, because the nudity of the image provoked a form of censorship not unlike that surrounding Gleyre's engraving of *The Sleeping Wolf.* When the painting was available for sale in 1874, the Musée Arlaud considered buying it on the recommendation of Louis Ruchonnet; the head of the Conseil, however, rejected the proposition because he feared that the image was inappropriate for a small provincial museum.[967] Even as late as 1911, Gleyre's niece Mathilde refused to give permission to the museum — which, in any case, had inherited the work in 1909 — to make a postcard of the painting, fearing that the nude figure was too risqué to be sent in the mail.[968]

Gleyre continued to explore the use of the nude figure as the essential subject of a painting. In 1868, he selected the single figure of Thalia

219. *Sappho,* 1867. Lausanne, Musée Cantonal des Beaux-Arts (catalogue n° 908)

962. Clément, pp. 340–42.
963. Pauline Viardot, née Garcia (1821–1910), was the most famous mezzo-soprano of her generation. She first studied piano with Liszt and began singing when the extraordinary beauty of her voice became known. She was the first non-Russian singer to take on the Russian repertoire in Moscow where she met Turgenev, who became her lover and remained a friend throughout his life. The summit of her career was the role of Orpheus at the Paris opera in 1859 which she sang in over 150 performances in three years. She also helped launch the careers of Gounod, Massenet, and Fauré; see Fitzlyon 1964.
964. Michelet 1959–76, III, p. 535. This verifies that Clément's dating of the work to March 1868 is incorrect; see Clément, p. 344. Charpentier was the famous publisher whose small-format paperback books sold for one franc each.
965. See Clément, p. 343, and Mantz 1875, p. 412.
966. See the letter from Hetzel to Clément of 23 August 1869, in Fleurier, CFC. Flamenq exhibited the engraving in the salon of 1870, livret n° 5188, which was well received; see Burty 1870, p. 141.
967. Lausanne, MCBA, GA 1012.
968. Ibid., 1017.

220. *The Charmer*, 1868. Basel, Öffentliche Kunstsammlung Basel, Kunstmuseum (catalogue n° 914)

from his *Minerva* for a separate canvas. The work became known as *The Charmer* — even though, as with the *Sappho,* the title sprang from sources other than Gleyre — and would provide the image engraved later on Gleyre's gravestone.[969] The painting was done quickly and finished by August 1868, when Milliet saw it in Gleyre's studio.[970] Gleyre explained to Milliet that the figure in fact represented the idea of youth and innocence, reiterated in symbolic form by the birds in the tree. Milliet, however, suspected that Gleyre's true subject, hidden as it may have been, was the loss of that youth, thus making the painting a kind of counterpoint to *Le Soir.* As such, the work may be seen as echoing the iconography of "la douce mélancolie" frequently seen in eighteenth-century painting.[971]

Clément was rapturous about the poetic quality of the image, especially as it is conveyed through the spring-like harmony of the colors. He noted that Gleyre had purposely prepared the palette so as to keep the impression of harmony even when the colors faded in time; he painted the lighter sections in a clearer tonality so that they would maintain their relationship to the darker areas.[972] As with the *Sappho,* the figure was criticized, most notably by Clément himself, in regard to the proportions of the lower part of the body. Gleyre told Clément that he had actually studied these proportions carefully and assured him that they were correct for the age of the model. Gleyre discoursed at length on the subtle but perceptible changes that occur in female models over twenty, noting in particular the differences apparent in the thighs, hips, and ankles.[973] Gleyre did not mention the name of the model — here the original one who had posed for the figure in the *Minerva* — but it is known that Gleyre made use of the same model in another work he completed shortly afterwards.[974]

The painting was well received by the critics who had seen it in the window of Goupil's. Mantz, like Clément, thought the painting superior to the *Sappho,* and doubly meriting its title.[975] Eugène Rambert, who had praised *The Romans* in Lausanne in 1858, also had a particular fondness for the image and even kept a photograph of it on his writing table after 1874.[976] It seems that Gleyre's friend Hetzel was also charmed by the painting, so much so that in 1869 Gleyre gave him the study for the work.[977] This work was one of the few that was scrutinized by critics outside of Gleyre's usual audiences in Paris and Switzerland. In 1873, it was sent by Goupil, not Gleyre, to the Exposition Universelle in Vienna, where it was received with much attention and great acclaim.[978]

Virtually simultaneously with *The Charmer,* Gleyre worked on a canvas entitled *The Bath,* which continues the unofficial series of works begun with the *Minerva.* The work was commissioned of Gleyre by no less important a patron than the American John Taylor Johnston, the head of the most important railroad in America and the first president of the

fig. 220

fig. 221–222

969. The image was sculpted by Raphaël Lugeon (1862–1943) who was also a native of Chevilly. But the idea was conceived earlier, just after Gleyre's death. Gleyre's student Alfred Strohl designed a monument for his master while in Rome, which he hoped to build in Switzerland; the image of *The Charmer* was the central design. See Wagnière 1944, p. 261.
970. Milliet 1915, p. 349, in a letter to his sister Louise who would shortly become one of Gleyre's students.
971. On the concept of "la douce mélancolie," see Hauptman 1975, pp. 134–68.
972. Clément, pp. 338–39.
973. Ibid., p. 339.
974. B[achelin] 1898, p. 307. The writer is Gleyre's student Auguste Bachelin.
975. Mantz 1875, p. 412.
976. Godet 1906, p. 109, in a letter of 16 May 1874. See also Caroline Olivier's letter to her husband of 24 May 1874 in Lausanne, BCU/DM, Fonds Olivier, IS 1905/47, dossier 1874.
977. See the letter from Hetzel to Clément, 23 August 1869, in Fleurier, CFC: "Il m'a donné ma petite flatteuse il y a trois jours... c'est une adorable petite page — un bijou."
978. See Ménard 1873, p. 206. The work was in the Swiss section, n° 76. Berthoud 1874, p. 473, probably mistook the study which Gleyre had given to Hetzel for the work, since he noted the extremely small dimensions of the work. But that the painting exhibited was this work is verified in the fact that it was bought directly from Goupil by the Basel art dealer Lang who resold it to the museum in December 1873.

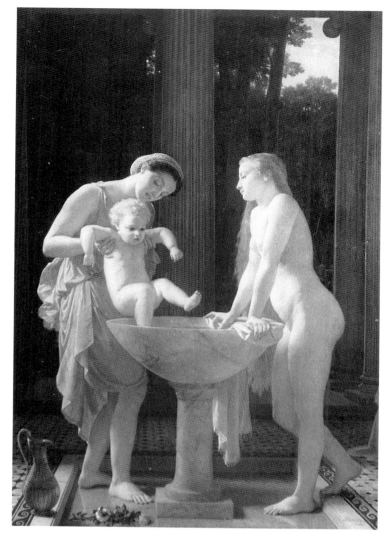

221. *The Bath*, 1868. Norfolk, The Chrysler Museum of Art. Gift of Walter P. Chrysler, Jr., 1971 (catalogue n° 920)
222. *The Bath*, 1868. Detail of illustration 221

Metropolitan Museum of Art in New York.[979] Johnston had arranged the details of the commission through his Paris agent, George Lucas, although it is not certain when or how these arrangements were made. The fact that Johnston took an interest in Gleyre's work at this time attests to his growing reputation. It is not known how Gleyre devised the iconographic scheme, although it derives certainly from a work in the Campana collection, then installed in the Louvre, but he worked on the canvas with uncommon rapidity. By the fall of 1868, the painting was completed and had already been inspected by Lucas in Gleyre's studio.[980] On 12 October, Johnston himself was able to view the work he had commissioned:

> In the afternoon, my wife, Emily, and I... went to the studio of Charles Gleyre, a Swiss artist of great ability, who had been executing a picture for me. I was delighted to find that it was really a remarkable picture of great power and sweetness, and such as I am perfectly satisfied to take. Subject, a lovely female figure standing by and leaning her hands on a marble basin in which another female is putting a child.[981]

979. On Johnston, see Baetjer 1981, pp. 410–11, who discusses his art collection, once considered one of the finest in America.
980. Lucas 1979, II, p. 278, for 7 October 1868.
981. Cited in Baetjer 1981, p. 414. Lucas also noted Johnston's satisfaction with the work in Lucas 1979, II, p. 279, for 12 October 1868.

Although the work was photographed by Goupil, Gleyre apparently showed it in its finished state to virtually none of his usual acquaintances and it was never displayed publicly in Paris. On 31 October 1868, Gleyre sent the painting directly to Johnston in New York.[982] It was the first painting of Gleyre's seen in America — although a copy of his *Le Soir,* sketched by Dussart but with substantial repainting by Gleyre himself, was already in the Walters collection in Baltimore a year earlier[983] — and was received with almost unreserved acclaim and admiration. The important critic Edward Strahan remarked that "it is such an achieved bit of perfection as a teacher leaves but once or twice in his career," and pronounced the painting "one of the most remarkable in the country." As for Gleyre, Strahan unequivocally designated him "the greatest painter yet produced by Switzerland." Strahan explained that he was struck by the hushed quality of the scene which he thought better and more poetic than examples by David or Ingres; he even perceived the child as reminiscent of the infant Buddha on the lotus.[984] Only one reviewer remarked upon the undue thinness of Gleyre's colors and the pallid tones, but despite minor reservations, nevertheless thought Gleyre to be "a fine artist."[985]

According to Clément, Gleyre's immediate pictorial source for the image was a small, antique terra-cotta in the Campana collection, although the actual sculpture was not identified.[986] Gleyre had intimate knowledge of this fine reserve of antique art, then incorporated into the Louvre, through his closest friends: Clément, Cornu, and Denuelle were all associated with the transport, preparation, exhibition, and cataloguing phases of the collection in the 1860s.[987] It was precisely this inspiration from antique art that formed for Clément the captivating charm and physical beauty of the work. He even noted that if *Le Soir* of 1843 was to be considered a kind of confessional Werther, then *The Bath* could be aptly described as Gleyre's *Mona Lisa,* that is to say, a work that aspired to a higher aesthetic ideal.[988] Although the comparison with Leonardo's masterpiece is too strong, it is nevertheless Clément's method of describing Gleyre's changing ideology which, removed from the subjective context, now aimed for the purely artistic.

In late 1868 and 1869, Gleyre worked almost exclusively in portraiture and did not occupy himself with commissions on a large scale, except for *The Prodigal Son,* about which more will be said in the next chapter. Despite the death of his beloved uncle, François, in 1868 and his brother Samuel in 1869 — his favorite brother Henry had already died in 1863 — there is no hint in the correspondence of his friends that Gleyre experienced his old despairing melancholy. Nor is there any indication that Gleyre contemplated working on the Vaudois commission that had been given to him after *The Romans* a decade earlier. In all likelihood, he considered the matter closed and forgotten, as indeed there is no extant correspondence from the cantonal authorities to Gleyre at this time concerning the project. It was only in December 1869 that Léon de la Cressonnière, the new director of the Musée Arlaud, questioned Gleyre about it during a visit to the painter's studio. De la Cressonnière wrote of this meeting to Louis Ruchonnet, who had praised Gleyre during the

982. Baetjer 1981, p. 280.
983. Johnston 1982, p. 96, gives the background for the work, as well as citations from the diaries of William Walters, who commissioned it.
984. Strahan 1879–82, II, p. 88.
985. *Putnam's Magazine,* 1870, p. 82.
986. Clément, p. 344, and Amaya 1978, p. 262.
987. Paris, AN, Musée Campana, "Etat des mémoires," F²¹, f. 486. Fleurier, CFC also contains a large dossier on Clément's work on the collection at this time.
988. Clément, p. 345. For the reference to *Le Soir* as an embodiment of the Werther idea, see p. 169.

banquet given him after the reception of his *Romans* in 1858, noting that Gleyre did not seem to consider the commission seriously at this time, but he did not entirely reject the possibility. Gleyre had even suggested that perhaps he could complete his study of *The Last Supper,* which he had originally executed for the Sainte-Marguerite project more than two decades earlier and which he particularly esteemed. Gleyre and de la Cressonnière, however, both had doubts about fulfilling the commission with a religious work, which, it was decided, would not be wholly appropriate for a still provincial museum in a Protestant canton.[989] Gleyre promised once again to consider the question; Ruchonnet later would pursue the matter further.

On 17 August 1868 Clément wrote to an unidentified friend that he had received a letter from Juste Olivier announcing his and Gleyre's imminent arrival in Fleurier, where by this time Clément had begun to spend his summer holidays.[990] The reason for his friends' visit now was Clément's decision, at the age of forty-seven, to marry Angèle Lemoine-Brétel, the adopted daughter of the banker and artist Fritz Berthoud, whom Gleyre had known for decades and who by now owned the *Hercules and Omphale.* From various accounts, it seems that Angèle possessed a special charm and sensitivity that made her a favorite in the Gleyre circle; Olivier had even composed a poem about her when she was fourteen years old.[991] Angèle had met Clément through Olivier and Berthoud in 1854 — Clément was thirty-three years old, Angèle only nineteen — and quickly developed a close relationship that was maintained during fourteen years of active correspondence. During much of this time, Clément, who was usually in Paris, was too timid to suggest an even closer liaison, and it was Angèle herself, in a bold move for the period, who actually proposed the marriage, much to the dismay of the painter Léon Berthoud who had been secretly in love with her but dared not express his feelings.[992] The wedding took place on 21 August 1868, with Gleyre acting as Clément's best man and witness. Only a short time earlier, Gleyre had also participated in Paris in the wedding of Thérèse Denuelle, Alexander's daughter, to Hippolyte Taine. He openly opposed the marriage of some of his friends, but if he felt a certain trepidation in regard to that of Clément, he seems never to have voiced it openly or privately. During the next few years, until Gleyre's death, his relationship to Clément remained close; Gleyre also accepted the presence of Angèle without the slightest reserve.

During Gleyre's brief stay in Fleurier, he took the opportunity of making a pencil sketch of Clément's bride. Clément noted in his catalogue that the drawing was "exécuté en 1868"; one can assume that it was made as a wedding present. The drawing itself seems not have survived; it was neither in the large Clément sale of Gleyre's work in 1908, nor is it among Gleyre's works still in the hands of Clément's heirs. There is no indication that the drawing was intended as a study for a painting; Gleyre knew full well that several paintings of Angèle existed already, including those by her father, Fritz, and the Orientalist Léon Belly. Nor is it certain that Gleyre remained in Switzerland for more than a short time.

989. See the letter from de la Cressonnière to Ruchonnet, 7 December 1869 in Lausanne, ACV, Département de l'Instruction publique, Lettres, K XIII/63, dossier 1.
990. In Fleurier, CFC; from the context, it is possible that Clément was writing to one of the Biaudets.
991. "Quatorze ans," in Olivier 1879, pp. 128–29.
992. This information was transmitted by Michel Clément-Grandcourt from material in Fleurier, CFC. Several letters hint at the fact, but never state it unequivocally.

223. *Portrait of Jacques-Julien Dubochet*, 1869. Vevey, Musée Jenisch (catalogue n° 937)
224. Franck (pseud. of François Gobinet de Ville-cholle), *Jacques-Julien Dubochet*, c. 1862. Lausanne, Musée de l'Elysée

In 1869, Gleyre, back in Paris, began an important portrait of Vincent Dubochet's nephew, Jacques-Julien. Like his more illustrious name-sake, Jacques was born near Vevey and went to Paris as a youth to study law. By 1830, he had already made a sizable reputation among the leading literati as an ardent defender of the rights of the press after the government instituted censorship policies following the revolution of that year. Beside advocating individual freedom and rights, the younger Dubochet also founded the popular journal *L'Illustration* in Paris; although he was revered for his political views, he was personally despised as an exceptionally miserly employer.[993] Dubochet counted among his friends both Clément and Olivier,[994] as well as countless other writers and painters; he was especially intimate with Sainte-Beuve.[995] It was therefore inevitable that he was introduced to Gleyre, although the date is not recorded; nor are Dubochet's views on his art. Dubochet died abruptly on 5 September 1868 while on a journey to Munich; Olivier, in Lausanne at the time — he went there just after Clément's wedding — heard the news three days later.[996]

The primary documents do not reveal who commissioned the portrait of Jacques-Julien Dubochet, but in all likelihood it was his uncle, Vincent, who was himself posing for Gleyre at about the same time. The only reference to the portrait comes from Clément's diary, in which he noted under the date 16 April 1869 that "Gleyre commence le portrait de J. Dubochet."[997] Clearly, Gleyre's portrait had to be made from a photograph of the model which was no doubt supplied by Vincent. Gleyre did

fig. 223

fig. 224

993. See Rossignol 1868, pp. 33–34.
994. Noted in Olivier Clément's random notes from information gleaned from Fleurier, CFC. For Olivier's connection with Dubochet, see Godet 1904, p. 60 : they were already close friends as early as 1842.
995. Sainte-Beuve 1935, IV, p. 228, n. 1 to letter n° 1308.
996. Olivier transmitted the news to Clément in a letter in Fleurier, CFC.
997. France, Private Collection, Clément, *Journal*, unpaginated.

286

225. *Portrait of Madame Raffalovich*, 1868–69. London, Private collection (catalogue n° 941)

not translate the photograph literally; rather, he altered sections of it, reversing the gestures, and adding a landscape of Lake Geneva, an appropriate attribute to indicate the sitter's Swiss origins.

At about the same time, Gleyre also finished one of his most enchanting and sympathetic portraits of a female model, that of Mme. Raffalovich, known as Madame R. The precise date of the portrait is not clear from the extant documentation: in Clément's journal pages, he wrote under the date July 1866 that "il [Gleyre] travaille au portrait de Mme Raffalowitz [sic]," but later, in references to the date 1869, he implied that the portrait was not finished then.[998] Mme. Raffalovich had an enormous circle of admirers and friends; she cultivated all of the major literary and philosophical stars of Parisian society and could discourse easily with the likes of Michelet and Renan on a variety of historical and theological issues.[999] The most important association for which she is known was her long and close friendship with the clinical scientist and

fig. 225

998. Ibid. Marie-Sarah Raffalovich was born into an aristocratic Russian family in Odessa in 1833, married her cousin Hermann, a prominent banker, when she was only sixteen years old, and with him established herself in Paris. She bore him three children, including a daughter, Sophie, who married the Irish poet William O'Brien, and a son, Marc-André, who became an intimate friend of Oscar Wilde, Aubrey Beardsley, and Henry James. Madame R, as she was called by her numerous friends, was a remarkably gifted linguist who spoke five languages fluently and read eight.
Marc-André Raffalovich (1864–1934) is often mentioned in regard to Wilde's circle; on his friendship with Beardsley, see Weintraub 1967, pp. 178–79f. Henry James frequently saw Raffalovich after 1914, as is noted in Edel and Powers 1978, pp. 391f. Raffalovich was a strong advocate of homosexuality; he defended Wilde in a pamphlet, *L'Affaire d'Oscar Wilde* (Lyons, 1895), and published the daring study *Annales de l'unisexualité* (Lyons, 1897). Although there is no biography of Mme. Raffalovich, essential material is contained in Halpern's study of Claude Bernard's letters to Madame R; see note 1000. I am also grateful to Mme. Jacqueline Sonolet who kindly passed on additional information she found in private collections in France.
999. See Michelet 1959–76, III, p. 530, especially the entry for 12 November 1867 and afterwards where several dinner parties are mentioned at which Madame R was a guest. See also Renan 1961, pp. 177f., under 7 August 1876, letter 509.

physician Claude Bernard.[1000] It was certainly through her that Bernard came to regard Gleyre, along with Regnault, as the most important contemporary painters in Paris.[1001]

Madame R's introduction into Gleyre's circle must have come about through his friends in Switzerland, particularly Edgar Quinet, whom she met about 1866. By March 1867 Quinet had already begun a substantial correspondence with her,[1002] and Mme. Quinet noted privately in her notebooks that same summer that Madame R paid almost daily visits to Veytaux while she was staying at the Hotel des Alpes in nearby Territet.[1003] It was often Madame R who accompanied the Quinets to the numerous receptions at the Dubochet villa in Clarens where her company was much prized.[1004] Although Quinet never mentioned it outright, it seems clear from the language and tone of his letters that he had in fact fallen in love with Madame R: in 1868 when she left Switzerland for Ostende, Quinet could not help but retrace his steps to Territet, much to the anguish of his wife who suspected her husband's infatuation.

The only known documentation regarding Gleyre's portrait of Madame R, other than Clément's cryptic notes, comes from the *Souvenirs* of her daughter, Sophie O'Brien.[1005] Sophie greatly admired Gleyre's portrait — more so than the others painted by celebrated artists such as Jean-Jacques Henner — because, she said, the painter was able to capture not only her mother's physical beauty, but also her philosophical nature. For the portrait sittings, Gleyre made her comb her hair back into a bun to accentuate her Russian features. She seems to have insisted upon posing in an elaborate vest with gold embroidery that her father had brought back from Russia when she was still a child. It is probable as well that Gleyre arranged the position of her hands to help suggest the elegance and refinement that characterized her person; the position is wholly different and more sensitive than the arrangements Gleyre chose for his more mundane portraits of Mme. Audiffred or Mme. Carrié. Rarely had Gleyre worked so hard to capture the essentials of his female sitter as he did here — a fact sustained by the many preliminary studies of the model — as can be especially appreciated in the uncommon details of the brocade, the lace of the sleeves, and the delicate earrings.

During the early months of 1870, when the portrait was certainly finished, Gleyre worked on two other projects which he had begun earlier, but apparently he still did not begin the third Vaudois commission, now outstanding for more than a decade. Gleyre had no immediate plans to return to Lausanne or to Chevilly, now that his uncle François had died. On 19 July, the French government declared war on the Prussian Empire and Gleyre, despite his hatred of the Napoleonic regime, sided with the French cause. After the debacle of Sedan in September, when a strike at Paris seemed imminent, Gleyre volunteered to serve in the defense of the city. He was told by the mayor of the sixth arrondissement that at the age of sixty-four he was too old to serve.[1006] Soon thereafter he was persuaded by various friends, especially Clément, that remaining in Paris might be dangerous. Carrying only a study of a work in progress, he decided to go to Switzerland. He would return a year later.

1000. They met in 1869 when she attended his public lectures at the Sorbonne. Bernard had just lost his wife and was in a state of personal emotional crisis; Madame R befriended him and developed a relationship that was largely platonic. She doted on him to meet his comforts, and he used her language abilities for summary translations of articles and books, a task for which she displayed uncommon energy and efficiency. Bernard wrote her no fewer than 488 letters; she responded to all of them faithfully, no matter where she was, but requested at his death that her letters be destroyed. These letters, some of which have been published, are presently in Paris, IF, Raffalovich. See Halpern 1974, pp. 177f., and Olmstead 1952, pp. 161f., on the dimensions of the relationship with Bernard.
1001. Olmstead 1952, p. 197.
1002. Quinet 1885–86, III, pp. 219f.
1003. See Paris, BN, Mme. Quinet, "Mémorial," X, 1867, for repeated references to Madame R and her husband.
1004. Du Pasquier 1959, pp. 166f.
1005. Cited in Bernard 1974, p. 150, n. 80.
1006. Clément, pp. 354–55.

## CHAPTER 11

# 1871–1874

THE LAST YEARS

226. *Double Portrait of Louis-Francis Ormond*, 1870. London, Collection of Richard Ormond (catalogue n° 952)

fig. 227

Gleyre left Paris sometime during the late summer of 1870, going directly to Fleurier, where Clément had settled with Angèle and Fritz Berthoud. He arrived in early September with apparently no precise idea of how he would spend his time, nor how long he would be forced to remain away from his Paris studio. Few records remain of Gleyre's sojourn there; he may have simply profited from the events in France to spend a holiday. Neither Clément nor Berthoud reveals the nature of Gleyre's activities, nor do they record conversations with him. Gleyre, however, was not wholly idle during this time: he drew a small, poignant portrait of Clément's first child, Frédéric, born almost exactly a year before.[1007] The work was clearly sketched rapidly and was presented to Clément as a gift commemorating the birth. It reveals Gleyre's accurate rendering of facial features and likeness, even without the ideal conditions offered by a studio.

1007. Frédéric Clément married Aline Secrétan in 1899 in Lausanne, where he had established himself as a journalist for the *Gazette de Lausanne*. In 1908 Frédéric helped negotiate the transfer of his father's large holdings of Gleyre's work to Lausanne. He was lost during the First World War in the Argonne on 28 February 1915; his body was never recovered. See the notes and documents in Fleurier, CFC.

227. *Portrait of Frédéric Clément*, 1870. Switzerland, Private collection (catalogue n° 947)

1008. The letter from Clément to Anker is in Neuchâtel, BV, Collection Lidia Brefin, Ms 2124, fols. 136/7. Anker's letter to Clément is not extant but is noted in a letter from Clément dated 25 October 1870 in Fleurier, CFC.

1009. Much valuable information on Louis Ormond and his career comes from the documents in the hands of the Ormond family, Vevey, made available to me through the generosity of the late Jean-Louis Ormond and Richard Ormond.

1010. This is particularly noted by Hippolyte Taine in a letter to his mother on 11 January 1871; in Taine 1902, III, p. 42.

Gleyre stayed in Fleurier for a period of about two months, as Clément noted to Albert Anker, who had written to Clément out of concern for Gleyre's welfare.[1008] Clément also informed Anker that Gleyre had just left Fleurier with the idea of going to Lausanne after a stop in Clarens, evidently to visit friends such as Dubochet, to renew contacts, and also to commence the portraits of Louis Ormond and his wife. Ormond, like fig. 228–229 his neighbor Dubochet, was a well known, liberal businessman, who had made a fortune in tobacco, railroads, and gas speculation in Vevey. And like Dubochet, Ormond had a passion for the arts: he not only knew and admired Gleyre, but he also promoted the careers of Anker and Bocion, and welcomed Courbet during his exile. He also frequently hosted Gambetta, Rambert, Taine, and Juste Olivier, who made it a point to visit him during his holidays in Switzerland.[1009] During the Franco-Prussian War, Ormond used his many business connections in Paris as a pretext for constant travel, taking advantage of his Swiss passport for liberal access across the border. In many instances, he acted as a courier between the French exiles in Switzerland and their contacts in Paris.[1010]

290

228. *Portrait of Madame Ormond*, 1870–71. Vevey, Musée Jenisch (catalogue n° 950)
229. *Portrait of Louis Ormond*, 1870–71. Vevey, Musée Jenisch (catalogue n° 948)

The commission to paint the portraits came through Gleyre's old friend and former student Emile David, who had acted in the same capacity between Arlaud and Gleyre for the *Major Davel* twenty-five years earlier. On 29 September 1870, Ormond wrote to David thanking him for his activities on his behalf and assured him that the price agreed upon by Gleyre was "un vrai prix d'ami."[1011] Gleyre worked first on the portrait of Ormond's wife, the former Marie-Marguerite Renet. Born in Versailles in 1847, she had married Ormond in 1865 when she was only eighteen; at twenty, her husband had commissioned a portrait of her from Albert Anker. Gleyre had already begun his work by 30 October, as Gleyre's niece Mathilde noted in a letter to Angèle Clément.[1012] Ormond's portrait followed. It is unlikely, however, that either portrait was actually painted at their villa in Clarens. Probably Gleyre made detailed studies upon which he relied when he worked on the canvases in his makeshift studio in Lausanne, where in fact he was able to set up an easel and work in relative calm. Gleyre returned to Clarens twice that fall and winter — on 20 November and again on 29 December — probably to check the colors and to make additional studies of the landscape background, which in the painting is precisely that seen from the terrace of the villa.[1013] Ormond would recall later in a letter to Clément that Gleyre took about two months to finish the works; they were sent to Clarens and installed before February 1871.[1014]

During one of the visits to the Ormond family, Gleyre also took the occasion to draw a small study of Ormond's son, Louis-Francis (spelled in the English fashion in accord with the Ormond's British background, rather than "François" as is sometimes seen), born in November 1866.[1015] fig. 226 Like Gleyre's portrait of Frédéric Clément, this portrait demonstrates

1011. A copy of the letter is in Lausanne, BCU/DM, David, "Correspondance," IS 4540, and the original is in a private collection in Lausanne. Nowhere is the price of the commission mentioned.
1012. In Fleurier, CFC. For the portrait by Anker, see Huggler 1962, n° 428; the portrait, for which Anker received 500 francs as he noted in his sales notebook, was finished by May 1867. The genealogy of the Ormond family was provided by the late Jean-Louis Ormond.
1013. Fleurier, CFC.
1014. See the letter from Ormond to Clément, dated probably 5 July 1877, in Fleurier, CFC, in which he noted that Gleyre had always come to their house in Clarens for the portrait sittings, rather than having Ormond come to the makeshift studio in Lausanne. Olivier referred to the portraits as completed and sent before February in a letter of 25 February 1871 to Adert, in Lausanne, BCU/DM, Juste Olivier, "Correspondance à Adert," IS 40.
1015. Information received directly from the Ormond family.

Gleyre's uncanny ability to capture pose and likeness on the spot, here probably from a perpetually moving model. It is worth remembering Rambert's amazement at Gleyre's capacity for recalling and capturing on paper the sitter's features even when the model was no longer present.[1016] There are no extant documents from Louis-Francis concerning this portrait, but it is worthwhile noting that he maintained a long-standing interest in art after his sister married John Singer Sargent whose works he assiduously collected.[1017]

When Gleyre established his makeshift studio in Lausanne in the fall of 1870 in a room at the Hôtel du Grand-Pont off the Place Saint-François, it seems that he had no immediate projects in mind beyond the Ormond portraits. Nor did he have the facilities here for working on the uncompleted projects left in Paris. Local art students made use of the master's presence in Lausanne to show him their portfolios and get his judgment on their efforts, as, for example, did the Swiss painter Eugène Burnand who saw Gleyre on 7 April 1871.[1018] Olivier, who was also there, promoted Gleyre in Lausanne like an admiring impresario, informing many of his friends and colleagues that it would be the best opportunity to have their portraits done. But he did not have much success: he confided to his Geneva friend Adert that

> Pour quelqu'un qui a une jolie fille ou femme, c'était une occasion unique d'en avoir un portrait de Gleyre — pendant qu'il est ici. Je l'ai dit à droite et à gauche ; mais on n'a pas profité.[1019]

If Olivier's friends did not profit from the occasion immediately, the Conseil d'Etat did, upon the urging of Louis Ruchonnet, then the head of the Département de l'Instruction publique under which the Musée Arlaud functioned. On 11 February 1871, Ruchonnet wrote to the Conseil asking whether they could commission Gleyre to paint the portrait of Victor Ruffy.[1020] The Conseil, under the leadership of Estoppey, fig. 230 approved the idea the same day; on 12 February Ruchonnet wrote to his friend Jules Melley, deputy to the Grand Conseil, to ask whether he knew precisely where Gleyre was staying in Lausanne so as to transmit the commission directly. Melley traced Gleyre to the Hôtel de Grand-Pont — he had to contact Olivier first — and on 13 February Ruchonnet wrote to Gleyre directly to give him the commission.

Isaac-Victor-Charles Ruffy (1823–69) was a lifelong politician who had been elected to the presidency of the Confederation, but who had died three days before assuming power for the year 1869. Gleyre was provided with a photograph of him that had been made by the photographer Gorgerat and began the work almost immediately. On 25 February fig. 231 Olivier wrote to Adert that Gleyre was busy with the portrait, and was working on others at the same time.[1021]

When Eugène Burnand visited Gleyre's studio in April, he also remarked upon the fact that Gleyre was immersed in the work, which he considered finely done, but beneath Gleyre's talents. Gleyre himself never indicated whether he felt the task demeaning, nor are there hints in

1016. Rambert 1890, p. 294.
1017. Vevey, Ormond Family Collection.
1018. Burnand 1949, p. 104. Gleyre advised the young painter to continue his studies in Paris and offered to help him establish himself in a studio there. Eventually, Burnand worked with Gérôme.
1019. 25 February 1871, in Lausanne, BCU/DM, Juste Olivier, "Correspondance à Adert," IS 40.
1020. See Lausanne, ACV, Commission des musées, K XIII/66 for the information that follows. There is no monograph devoted to Victor Ruffy, but see Polla 1981, p. 134, for short biographical details.
1021. Lausanne, BCU/DM, Juste Olivier, "Correspondance à Adert," IS 40.

292

230. *Portrait of Victor Ruffy*, 1871. Lausanne, Musée Cantonal des Beaux-Arts (catalogue n° 953)

231. Frédéric Gorgerat, *Victor Ruffy*, c. 1868. Lausanne, Musée de l'Elysée

Olivier's correspondence. The portrait, however, was quickly finished before the summer of 1871.

It seems that when Ruchonnet commissioned the portrait, he did not indicate to Gleyre the fee involved. Gleyre, under financial pressure at the time, took up the matter discreetly with the director of the museum, Léon de la Cressonnière, who in turn contacted Ruchonnet on 23 June 1871. He noted that Gleyre would have liked to donate the work to the canton, but his financial situation, given his undetermined sojourn in Lausanne, did not permit it. De la Cressonnière suggested that the fee be based on the payment that Gleyre had received for the portrait of Jomini two decades earlier.[1022] This was reported to Estoppey who noted that Gleyre had been paid 1,500 francs; with Ruchonnet's approval, he designated an equal sum. The funds were forwarded to Gleyre on 7 July, and by later that year the portrait of Ruffy was hung in the Musée Arlaud, where it was widely appreciated.[1023]

Olivier had indicated that while occupied with the portrait of Ruffy, Gleyre also worked on other portraits. Although he never identified these, fig. 232 it is probable that one was of the industrialist Jean-Jacques Mercier.[1024]

1022. Lausanne, MCBA, GA 1008.
1023. Noted in de la Cressonnière's report of 4 January 1872 to Ruchonnet in Lausanne, ACV, Commission des musées, K XIII/66, and MCBA, GA 1880/2.
1024. Mercier was known as Jean-Jacques II because it was the family tradition to give all male children the same first name; see Pelet 1953, p. 136; and *Le Conteur vaudois*, 1904, pp. 1–2. Jean-Jacques Mercier was born in 1789 and followed his father's footsteps in the tanning business which he took over in 1827, expanding the family interests into railroads and other profitable markets. He was eventually elected to the Grand Conseil and served his constituents with particular distinction.

232. *Portrait of Jean-Jacques Mercier*, 1870–71. Lausanne, Fondation Mercier, on deposit in the Musée Historique de Lausanne (catalogue n° 967)
233. *Portrait of Edouard Fehr*, 1870–71. Lausanne, Musée Cantonal des Beaux-Arts (catalogue n° 969)
234. Oswald Welti, *Edouard Fehr*, c. 1873. Lausanne, Musée de l'Elysée

1025. None of these photographs has come to light in public or private collections.
1026. Polla 1981, p. 153.
1027. Fehr himself judged it Ingresque, and wrote so to Clément on 2 August 1875; he sent a tracing of the drawing five days later so that Clément could judge for himself; see the letters in Fleurier, CFC. See also Lausanne, MCBA, GA 1047.
1028. See Lausanne, BCU/DM, Juste Olivier, "Notes," IS 1088.

Like Ruffy, Mercier had died before the portrait was commissionned, and once again Gleyre was forced to work from an existing photograph supplied by the family.[1025] Although no documents have come to light describing the circumstances of the commission, it is likely that Emile David again played an important role, since in 1858 he had married Mercier's daughter Louise. The portrait is a respectful homage to a much loved industrial leader, the face and hands particularly well delineated. In this painting, there is none of the stiffness found in Gleyre's portrait of Ruffy: the portrait looks as though it was painted from life. The background, as is typical of Gleyre's portraits of eminent Vaudois, represents a view from the family estate at 25 rue du Pré, where the Merciers lived until 1872.[1026]

Despite Olivier's remarks in the letter to Adert cited earlier, Gleyre did several studies from life in this period, generally accomplished in a few brief sittings. These are very much in the direct, Ingresque tradition, as, for example, the pencil sketch of the editor of the *Gazette de Lausanne,* Edouard Fehr.[1027] Fehr recalled later that two or three sittings were sufficient for Gleyre. Olivier, who knew Fehr well, thought the drawing an extremely accurate likeness,[1028] a fact borne out by a photograph of the sitter taken slightly later.

fig. 233

fig. 234

294

235. *Portrait of Madame Gustave Olivier*, 1871. Geneva, Private collection (catalogue n° 959)

One of the most poignant portraits Gleyre executed during his sojourn in Lausanne was that of Julie de Speyer, who in 1867 married Urbain Olivier's son Gustave.[1029] Gleyre had certainly met her before and was smitten by her beauty and simple charm. He repeatedly asked Gustave if he could draw his wife, but the opportunity did not present itself until July 1871 — not 1870 as Clément noted[1030] — when it was decided to profit from Gleyre's stay. Julie recounted in a letter to her sister in Basel that they had gone to Gleyre's room immediately after their breakfast. Gleyre chatted with his sitter as was his custom, finally deciding that a profile would be best. During the sitting for that day, Gleyre talked incessantly about all sorts of things. By lunch the portrait was finished and presented to the model.[1031]

fig. 235

1029. On her and her relationship to the Oliviers, see Lausanne, BCU/DM, Mme. Urbain Olivier, IS 1905/119 and 139.
1030. Clément, p. 505, under catalogue n° 480.
1031. The account of the sitting is contained in a letter of 15 July 1871 in Lausanne, BCU/DM, Mme. Urbain Olivier, IS 1905/119, dossier 1 (1867–71). See also in BCU/DM, E. Olivier, "Maison," II, IS 1905/136, in which Edouard Olivier also cites the letter above and corrects the date noted in Clément.

236. *Portrait of Jean-Jacques Larguier des Bancels*, 1871. Lausanne, Musée Historique de Lausanne (catalogue n° 957)
237. *Portrait of Jean-Jacques Larguier des Bancels*, 1871. Lausanne, Private collection (catalogue n° 958)

1032. Jean-Jacques Larguier des Bancels was born in Vevey in 1844. He went to Paris in 1864 for his medical studies which he completed with distinction in 1871. With the outbreak of the war, he served in the ambulance corps. Larguier had a long-lasting interest in art — he had made drawings and watercolors in his youth and sketched his impressions of the war in several notebooks — and always kept in close contact with Bocion, who had painted his portrait when he was ten years old. See Blanc 1905; there are also unpublished documents in Saint-Prex.
1033. Note in a letter from Larguier to Clément of 18 August 1875 or 1876 — the date itself is not clearly indicated — in Fleurier, CFC.
1034. On this aspect of Bocion's career, see Aubert-Lecoultre 1977.
1035. See the letter from Gleyre to Delarageaz, 2 September 1858 in Lausanne, BCU/DM, Fonds Delarageaz, IS 3681/F[170].
1036. Bocion recounted the anecdote in a letter to Clément of 13 June 1877, in Fleurier, CFC.
1037. See the letter from Léon Berthoud to Clément of 19 May 1871, in Fleurier, CFC. Berthoud was in Lausanne at the time, while Clément was in Fleurier.

It was also during his stay in Lausanne that Gleyre produced two portraits of Jean-Jacques Larguier des Bancels.[1032] It is not known why Gleyre made two portraits, although one was given to the sitter while the second one was taken with Gleyre to Paris where it remained until his death.[1033] Gleyre and Larguier kept in contact when Gleyre left Lausanne, and Larguier considered himself one of the painter's most intimate friends: when Gleyre's remains were transferred to Lausanne in 1896, Larguier requested the right to be the first speaker at the service.

fig. 236–237

When possible Gleyre sought out friends and colleagues in Lausanne and the region. In particular, he met often with Emile David and with Bocion, who by now had established a remarkable reputation in his own right with his sparkling depictions of Lake Geneva.[1034] Gleyre had always remained in contact with Bocion; he had recommended the painter's services for the uncrating of *The Romans* in 1858 and had praised his work highly in the Swiss section of the Exposition Universelle of 1867.[1035] In 1871, probably during the summer months, Gleyre had scheduled a modeling session with an unnamed model, who seems not to have inspired him. Consequently, Gleyre went to Ouchy to visit with Bocion and decided on the spot, so as not to lose his interest in drawing for the day, to do the landscape painter's portrait.[1036] Often reproduced, the work remains one of the finest Gleyre drew from life; Bocion himself was amazed at the quickness and sureness with which Gleyre accomplished the work.

fig. 238

Gleyre also made frequent trips to Chevilly, where he had inherited the house owned by his late uncle. In May 1871, while in nearby La Sarraz where he had spent a part of his youth, Gleyre fell ill with a chest congestion. Emile David went to La Sarraz to take care of him, and he seemed to recover rapidly,[1037] although the condition recurred in a more severe form months later. The summer passed without further incident, but Gleyre did very little work and seemed to be bored by the stay. Fi-

238. *Portrait of François-Louis Bocion*, 1871. Lausanne, Musée Cantonal des Beaux-Arts (catalogue n° 960)

nally, a few months later, with the situation much improved in Paris, Gleyre decided that it was the time to return. Before leaving, he called on the Ormonds and the Dubochets, and even made a surprise visit to Olivier's rustic chalet in Gryon;[1038] the Quinets had left for Paris the year before. By late September, Gleyre was again in his studio on the rue du Bac. He was much relieved to find the studio had not been harmed, although there was debris from the intense Prussian bombing still visible in the neighborhood.

Clément did not record Gleyre's immediate activities upon his return, but it is certain that he began another portrait, this time of the Swiss statesman Johann Konrad Kern. The commission came from Thurgovie, Kern's native canton, which wanted to hang the work in the Hôtel de

fig. 239

1038. See the letter from Olivier to Adert of 25 September 1871, in Lausanne, BCU/DM, Juste Olivier, "Correspondance à Adert," IS 40.

297

239. *Portrait of Johann Konrad Kern,* 1872.
Frauenfeld, Rathaus (catalogue n° 970)

Ville of Frauenfeld, where Kern had earlier presided and where he began his long career. No documents have survived indicating how Gleyre received the commission, although it is possible that Kern himself arranged it. It was as the Swiss ambassador in Paris, a post he held from 1857 to 1883, that Kern achieved his most lasting fame, and there he frequently came into contact with Gleyre and his circle in both official and unofficial capacities.[1039] Clearly Kern greatly admired Gleyre's work, which he later promoted in Paris and Switzerland. Gleyre's portrait of him, drawn from life in Paris, is a straightforward depiction of the model, not unlike the official portrait of Ruffy, and strangely reminiscent, in spirit if not form, of the earlier Tunisian portraits. Gleyre did not complete the work quickly because another illness interrupted his efforts; the work was not sent to the canton until a year later.

Gleyre's malady, diagnosed in February 1872 as a severe case of whooping cough, almost completely incapacitated him for more than a month. He coughed so violently that he could not recline, but was forced to sleep upright in a chair each night. The condition improved in March, but in April Gleyre suffered from severe chest pains and muscle spasms. His condition became so precarious that one night he was forced to summon Clément. During the following days, Clément and two former students, Ehrmann and Hirsch, took turns staying with Gleyre until he regained his strength.[1040] By the late spring Gleyre recovered sufficiently that no signs of his illness were in evidence.

Gleyre's illness prevented him from completing one of his most curious and original works, one that had been already in sketch form some seven years earlier. Gleyre had produced more than a dozen sketches for the work and had even transferred the final study to a canvas, indicating his satisfaction with the design. Clément traced the origins of the work, representing the history of Pandora, to 1865, when Gleyre was engaged in completing the *Minerva* for Dubochet's villa.[1041] One of Gleyre's regular models had brought her young sister with her to the modeling sessions and eventually asked if the painter would like to have the sister pose for him. For a period of three months, Gleyre did not permit any visitors in the studio while he sketched this model — this to insure privacy for the timid girl whom Gleyre clearly liked and admired for her beauty. Gleyre made dozens of studies of her, including a frontal nude drawing which he saw as the germ for the Pandora he had in mind.

The story of Pandora derives in its essential form from Hesiod's *Theogony,* although the version known today in its popular form owes its transformation to Erasmus.[1042] The essence of the story — defiance of the gods, and their vengeance — is very much in accord with themes in Gleyre's works from *Le Soir* to the *Pentheus.* After Prometheus challenged the gods by stealing fire and presenting it to the human race, Zeus, enraged, asked Hephaestus to fashion the image of a beautiful woman from clay and earth; she would be the vehicle for his revenge in that she would carry with her the evils and miseries destined for mankind. Because all the gods bestowed their gifts on the woman, she was known as Pandora, the all-gifted. Prometheus refused her when she was sent to him, and

1039. See Kern 1887, and Schoop 1968, II, on this aspect of his career.
1040. Clément, pp. 355–56.
1041. Ibid., pp. 325–26.
1042. Panofsky 1962 relates the history of the subject, but makes no mention of Gleyre's work.

240. *Michelangelo and Pandora*, 1872. Lausanne, Musée Cantonal des Beaux-Arts (catalogue n° 973)

warned his brother not to accept any gifts from Zeus, but his brother disregarded the warning and married Pandora when she was again presented, thus unleashing all the miseries on mankind. The subject held enormous possibilities for painters and sculptors and found ample expression in the nineteenth century, but usually in the form of a single figure: after Pradier's famous statue of 1850, more than half a dozen examples were seen in the salons while Gleyre was pondering the possibilities.[1043]

Clément noted on 25 February 1865 that Gleyre had already done a study showing Pandora being presented to Prometheus by Mercury.[1044] Clément's note indicates that Gleyre had envisioned an account in accord with the myth as drawn from the Greek sources, probably not unlike Allaux's representation of Pandora and Mercury descending from the heavens in a painting executed in 1824.[1045] But while Gleyre was evolving his imagery, he consciously transformed the traditional way of representing Prometheus into a figure bearing the likeness of Michelangelo. This transformation is highly significant, as it demonstrates Gleyre's uncommonly learned interpretation of the myth.

fig. 240

Gleyre's vision of Prometheus illustrates another aspect of the figure, for Prometheus is not only the one who stole the fire, but he is also responsible in mythic literature for the gift of inventiveness and the creative skills. In Ovid, he is presented as the molder of man and animals, thus a divine artist credited with the supreme act of creation.[1046] In this

1043. Pigler 1974, II, pp. 203–4, gives dozens of examples of pre-nineteenth-century works, and a review of the salon livrets indicates the wide use of the theme until 1864–65.
1044. Clément, p. 325.
1045. Livret n° 16; the work had been commissioned by the state.
1046. *Metamorphosis*, I, 82–83; see also Horace, *Odes*, I, 16,14.

299

role, he is a benevolent figure, creator rather than thief, a symbol of individual freedom from the powers of the gods. Gleyre was clearly aware of this dual nature, which must have been reinforced for him through his contacts with Quinet. For, in effect, Quinet also revised the image of Prometheus in his verse drama of 1838, "Prométhée,"[1047] a source which plays an important psychological role in the development of Gleyre's imagery.

Quinet's long poem is a meditation on individuality and revolt against the forces of the Divine. Already in the opening scene, when the earth is still in its primeval state after the Flood, Prometheus is introduced as the creator of mankind. Around him are various examples of men still in an incomplete or fragmented state; he is working on the image of a giant. His creation will be a human being who is free, but imperfect:

> Libre dans l'univers, esclave de toi-même,
> Entre le ciel et moi, l'autel et le blasphème,
> Tu choisiras tes dieux: tu le peux, tu le dois;
> Et de la volonté tu porteras le poids.[1048]

It is precisely in this spirit that Gleyre's imagery blends Michelangelo with Prometheus: creator, individualist, defier of the standards. In the nineteenth century, Michelangelo attained this Promethean position, as one who, like his mythological predecessor, breathed life into inanimate clay, just as Quinet's Prometheus created an independent spirit that brought the figures to life and gave them the power to choose their gods and their world. The association, therefore, was natural, but none the less inventive on the part of Gleyre. His Prometheus as creator is pitted against the gift of the gods in the form of Pandora: creation and destruction form the foci of the painting he had in mind. The Pandora idea is thereby taken from the mythological realm and placed in the mythic. It may be no accident that when Gleyre began work on the canvas, Clément published a long study on Michelangelo.[1049]

That Gleyre never finished the work he intended may be partially explained by his poor health during the spring of 1872. But this cannot be the only reason, since in the summer he was well enough to travel extensively; it must be assumed that after several years of effort, Gleyre simply lost interest in the study. It is equally possible that the complexity of the theme and subject was not completely to Gleyre's liking because it would have been difficult for the viewer to interpret. In this light, it must be recalled that Gleyre never chose a theme that was not "readable," even if the subject was not well known to the public at large, as in the case of the *Pentheus*.

In late August 1872, Gleyre went to Tréport to visit Nanteuil who was vacationing there; they returned to Paris together a week later.[1050] Then Gleyre left immediately for Fleurier to visit Clément and Berthoud. The three of them decided to take a long trip to the Engadine in eastern Switzerland, a trip that Berthoud recorded in its entirety later from notes he took at the time.[1051] The suggestion to make the excursion came from

1047. Quinet 1857, VIII, pp. 25–33.
1048. Ibid., pp. 31–32.
1049. Clément 1864.
1050. Gleyre recounted the visit briefly in a letter to his niece Mathilde, in Lausanne, MCBA, GA 987.
1051. Berthoud 1898, pp. 449f.

Berthoud, who, at sixty, complained that he traveled little. They went from Fleurier to Bern, where, as was noted earlier, Gleyre saw the General Assembly in session, and then proceeded to Chur. There he admired the landscape, but was mostly taciturn, reserved, and clearly uncomfortable; it seems he regretted being away from the studio with his unfinished projects still on their easels. Afterwards, the party went to St. Moritz where Gleyre again meditated on the Alpine landscape and regretted out loud that he was incapable of transferring the image onto a canvas. Gleyre produced hardly any true landscapes on canvas, but he was always keenly interested in the genre, as can be seen from his Egyptian works, his countless landscape studies in the private sketchbooks, and his critique of the Swiss pictures in the Exposition Universelle of 1867. After a brief stay in St. Moritz, the travelers headed south and were surprised to be stopped by a customs guard who, although they had not thought to bring passports, let the party cross the Italian border all the same.

Once in Italy, Gleyre, we are told, became more expansive and open, recalling his previous travels in the region. The party continued westward along the Adda River to Lake Como, making their way to Porlezza on the eastern shore of Lake Lugano, and finally reentered Switzerland at Lugano. Here they went to the chapel of Santa Maria degli Angioli to see the Passion frescoes of Luini, painted in 1521; since Gleyre's first trip to Italy forty-five years earlier, he had maintained a lively interest in Luini's work. Gleyre treated Clément and Berthoud to an improvised lecture that lasted all morning on Luini's merits, but Berthoud could not recall precisely what Gleyre had said when he wrote down his recollections later. The party crossed the mountains through the Gotthard Pass and slowly made their way back to Fleurier. Soon afterwards, Gleyre returned to his Paris studio.

He began work on a canvas which had been in his mind for almost a quarter of a century and which he seems to have proposed at least twice for a specific commission. The painting, the last he would complete, was entitled fig. 242 *The Return of the Prodigal Son*. The idea for the subject and the earliest painted study date back to the late 1840s when he received the commission fig. 241 for the church of Sainte-Marguerite,[1052] for which he had produced a quick oil study of the subject. That study had never been transferred to a large canvas and it was given to Juste Olivier before 1855, after Gleyre had made a minor adjustment to the gesture of the father on the left of the composition.[1053] Gleyre apparently did not touch the work again until the mid 1860s when he received a commission from the Fine Arts Society in Bern. The history of this commission has never been published and still remains incomplete because of the absence of documentation.

The commission came about as a result of the unusual success of the Swiss National Exhibition held in the Bundesrathaus from mid-June 1864.[1054] On 19 July 1864, the Bernische Gesellschaft met to consider whether they would utilize the profits from the exhibition to buy works shown in it or to commission a work for their collection. The members of the committee were not enthusiastic about a direct purchase, but rather followed the suggestion of the president, Christian Brunner, to commis-

1052. Clément, p. 353.
1053. It was noted in a letter from Olivier to his daughter Thérèse on 23 November 1855, in Lausanne, BCU/DM, Fonds Olivier, IS 1905/43, dossier 1855. See also his lecture notes in BCU/DM, Olivier, "Notes," IS 1088 in which Gleyre's adjustment is also mentioned.
1054. The exhibition was open from 19 June to 20 August 1864 and was housed in the capitol building because no permanent exhibition structure existed in Bern at the time. The show comprised 328 works, as listed in the livret, by 153 artists, as noted in Jaccard 1986, p. 441. On these exhibitions in general and their importance for Swiss art in the nineteenth century, see Jaccard 1986, pp. 436f.

241. Study for *The Prodigal Son*, 1847–48. Geneva, Private collection (catalogue n° 524)

242. *The Return of the Prodigal Son*, 1873. Lausanne, Musée Cantonal des Beaux-Arts (catalogue n° 989)

sion a new work, and proposed asking Gleyre — spelled "Glaire" in the report — if he could undertake it.[1055] Although Gleyre had not participated in the Bern exhibition and had little or no direct contact with the city, it was nevertheless natural to propose his name because of the success he had had in Lausanne and because he was then completing his commission for Basel. It was decided that the intermediary in the affair would be Albert Anker, who was considered the most important artist of the region and who still maintained close ties to Gleyre.

On 5 January 1865 — that is, when the *Pentheus* was substantially finished; it would be delivered exactly a month later — the Bern commission reported that Anker had replied to their inquiry and that Gleyre agreed in principle to accept a commission if the society would indicate the dimensions and the subject desired. The society decided to allot a sum of 4,000 francs as the payment for the work, a sum that, incidentally, was less than half what Gleyre received from Basel for the *Pentheus,* but they left the dimensions and the choice of subject to the painter. This information was given to Anker in Paris to communicate directly to Gleyre. There appears to have been no further communication until 8 October when Gleyre wrote a letter to Brunner and Christian Bühler.[1056] He noted that he had indeed received the request for a painting as early as 25 January, but did not officially reply earlier because of ill health and a journey, which he did not specify, undertaken afterwards; Clément, however, made no mention of either in his biography, nor are there any indications in letters of friends that Gleyre had been ill or out of Paris at the time. Gleyre reaffirmed that he had accepted the commission, but he informed the committee that he did not wish to have a time constraint imposed upon him, explaining that he had other commissions to complete first and that he was by nature a very slow worker. The tone of the letter, however, is decidedly enthusiastic.

The society met again on 5 December when Gleyre's letter was read aloud. It was emphasized that although they could not count on having a firm date for delivery, they could nevertheless consider the commitment on Gleyre's part to be firm. It was noted at this time as well that a letter had arrived from Anker on 2 December with the additional information that the subject Gleyre had selected for the commission was the story of the Prodigal Son. Anker assured the members of the society that he would try to persuade Gleyre to apply his energies and full artistic capacities to the work, noting that as a Bernese, he was particularly interested in having one of the master's works in the permanent collection.

Unfortunately, the documentation on the affair ends abruptly here. The matter seems never to have been brought up again at the society meetings and there are no records indicating whether the commission was followed by members of the committee or by Anker himself. The most curious aspect of the history of the commission is that Clément stated with certainty that Gleyre in fact received the commission for the *Prodigal Son* in July 1867 when he had already sketched the work in charcoal on canvas.[1057] The commission at this time came from Johann Heinrich Moser, an industrialist who had made a fortune in watchmaking and

1055. Christian Brunner was president of the society from 1852 to 1870, but no other information on him has come to light. The material here comes from Bern, Kunstmuseum, Bernische Kunstgesellschaft, Protokolle, and was transmitted by Sandor Kuthy.
1056. Christian Bühler (1825–98) was himself a painter of miniatures and a designer of heraldry. He was also, after 1854, the curator of the collections of the canton of Bern and served in 1865–66 as the secretary of the Kunstgesellschaft.
1057. Clément, pp. 353 and 430, under catalogue n° 112.

303

who had recently constructed a lavish estate on the Rhine near Schaffhausen.[1058] No information has come to light on the nature of the commission, how Moser had come into contact with Gleyre, or why the commission for the painting was accepted when the Bern agreement was seemingly still outstanding. As will be seen shortly, this curious situation had a parallel in the case of another work commissioned by Geneva, which likewise would ultimately find another destination altogether.

Gleyre apparently began work on the *Prodigal Son* in earnest in the summer of 1867, while he was completing the *Sappho* and beginning *The Bath*. He was interrupted several times, but by all accounts the early work on the painting went more rapidly than the painter had led others to believe, partially because much of the composition was adapted from an existing design. Gleyre, however, was blocked in the execution of the canvas on several occasions; in one instance, the model for the mother, a Mlle. Fernande, could not hold the pose required for the figure, that is, with the arms and hands outstretched.[1059] Gleyre was forced to ask his sculptor friend Alfred Dubucand to fashion a model of the figure in wax — as he had for other paintings earlier — so that he could have the precise attitude and gesture necessary for the work.[1060] The face of the mother was done from life but made older by the painter as the sketches progressed chronologically, to conform to the age of the mother in the canvas. By January 1870, Gleyre had prepared all of the sketches and had begun to transfer the design to the final canvas. At this point Gleyre experimented with a technique he had not tried before, but which was recommended by one of his students. He prepared the canvas with a gesso paste; upon the surface, he began to sketch the essentials of the design in watercolor and tones of gray. Afterwards, he put in light touches of oil to bring out the basic elements of the tonality. He was, however, not satisfied with the results and abandoned the technique half way through.[1061]

Gleyre was then interrupted by the outbreak of the Franco-Prussian War and again by the illness of 1872. By the time he returned to the work in the summer, his interest in the canvas had waned: his niece Mathilde, now very close to her uncle, wrote to Angèle Clément on 12 June 1872 that the canvas was progressing very slowly and that less than half of the surface was covered, all because of Gleyre's lack of enthusiasm for the subject.[1062] By late July, Mathilde had taken rooms at 86 rue du Bac to take care of her uncle and was thus able to see the painting in progress. She wrote to Angèle that her uncle was discouraged over the way in which the painting was developing, and that he had doubts as to whether the results would be worth the considerable effort he had already made.[1063] This view, however, is completely antithetical to other eyewitness accounts, particularly that of Etienne Arago, who thought the painting was progressing very well and indeed had the potential to be one of Gleyre's finest.[1064] Similarly, after a visit to Gleyre's studio on 3 July 1872, the American dealer Samuel P. Avery wrote to his patron John Taylor Johnston — who already owned *The Bath* — that the present work would indeed be "very fine," even though Gleyre was physically weak and worked only intermittently.[1065]

1058. On Henri Moser Charlottenfels, see Balsiger and Kläy 1992. Moser's collection was inventoried by his second wife, Fanny, née von Sulzerwart, in a handwritten document preserved in Schaffhausen, Stadtbibliothek, Moser Papers, Gs 73.453, where Gleyre's painting is recorded as having been purchased for 25,000 francs.

1059. She is noted as the model for the figure on a sketch Gleyre made, Clément n° 678.

1060. Clément, p. 354. It was almost certainly the sculptor Dubucand who provided the service, since later Nanteuil recalled to Clément, on 28 November, but with no indication of the year, that the sculptor had indeed modeled several figures for Gleyre's use, including the dog in the present painting. It will be recalled that he may also have fashioned the horse in the *Romans*. On Dubucand, see Lami 1914–21, III, pp. 231f. Although it is not noted here, he made Gleyre's death mask.

1061. Clément, p. 345.

1062. The letter is in Fleurier, CFC.

1063. Ibid., in a letter of 26 July 1872.

1064. The letter, in Fleurier, CFC, is undated.

1065. See Avery 1979, p. 49. The original letter is in the Archives of the Metropolitan Museum of Art, New York. Avery, as will be seen shortly, was discussing a commission with Gleyre.

Even later, there seems to have been no consensus either on whether the work had progressed as Gleyre expected or on whether the painting was a successful work. Gleyre's ideas were recorded by Mme. Milliet, the mother of his pupil Paul Milliet, who transmitted them to her son, then in Rome. Mme. Milliet referred several times to Gleyre's disillusionment over the painting itself, quoting him as saying: "C'est un tableau manqué, je n'ai rien rendu de ce que je voulais faire... je ne fais plus rien de bien."[1066] Yet, Clément, writing the very next day to Olivier, did not mention Gleyre's discontent; in fact, he told Olivier that all was well and that the painting was advancing considerably, even though at a slower pace than expected.[1067] In late April 1873 Milliet's sister Louise, who was taking private lessons from Gleyre in his studio, told her brother that the work was virtually finished, but the results were not as brilliant as she had hoped. She criticized the abundance of details and what she perceived to be the awkward, stiff gesture of the mother who, she said, had clearly been modeled on a studio mannequin.[1068] She did not indicate whether Gleyre shared this view, but the implication in the letter is that she had discussed it with him.

Gleyre worked on the last details of the painting during the spring of 1873, completing the work during the summer months. When Samuel P. Avery again visited the studio on 27 June 1873,[1069] the canvas was still on the easel, but in July Gleyre sent it to its purchaser, Heinrich Moser,[1070] just before going for a brief visit to La Sarraz with Mathilde.[1071] The only mention of the work by a contemporary Paris critic was in a small note by Pierre Dax that although Gleyre had received an offer for the painting from an American collector — one presumes Johnston, although it is not stated — he was particularly pleased that the canvas would remain in Swiss hands.[1072] Neither Dax nor any other critic of the period reviewed or criticized the painting, nor it seems was there any comment from Bern on the fact that eight years earlier there had been a possibility of having the work there.

Gleyre's conception of the traditional iconography, drawn in essence from the Book of Luke, is unusual in its focus on the relationship between the son and his mother. In most instances, in both literature and painting, it was the relationship between father and son that was stressed, even in nineteenth-century versions.[1073] In the actual parable, neither the mother nor the sister is in fact mentioned, but it was not uncommon to include female figures, especially servants, to suggest the return to the household.[1074] In Gleyre's realization, however, the mother assumes the crucial role in the iconography, since the forgiveness of the father has already occurred, as Gleyre himself indicates by placing the father's hands on the son's shoulder and wrist, thus in effect leading him into the family house. It is now the mother who offers her pardon with outstretched arms demonstrating her tacit acceptance of her son's return to the moral and physical structure of the family. Later critics commented on this unusual detail: Montégut went so far as to say that the real theme of the painting was the nature of true forgiveness, which in this circumstance could only come through maternal love.[1075] Rambert too underlined the

1066. Letter of 21 April 1873, in Milliet 1913, p. 96. On the relationship of Gleyre and Paul Milliet at this time and especially the painter's defense of him when he was condemned in absentia, see Hauptman 1985(e), p. 103.
1067. Letter of 22 April 1873, in Fleurier, CFC.
1068. Milliet 1913, p. 98, in a letter of 28 April 1873.
1069. Avery 1979, p. 174.
1070. Clément, p. 430, under catalogue n° 112 — not in 1872 as Clément states in his text, p. 360.
1071. Clément mentioned the fact to Olivier in a letter of 12 August 1873, in Fleurier, CFC.
1072. Dax 1874, p. 137.
1073. Boime 1980, pp. 95–96, discusses the importance of the iconography in the context of the nineteenth century, citing many examples also from literature, including Balzac, Murger, Sand.
1074. See, for example, the works of Puvis in 1854–55, Tissot in 1863, or Dubuffe in 1866.
1075. Montégut 1878, pp. 414–15. See also C. Berthoud 1880(b), p. 14, and Cook 1888, I, p. 12, who express similar notions.

243. *Young Girl Distracted by Amor*, 1874. Lausanne, Musée Cantonal des Beaux-Arts (catalogue n° 1018)

same notion, adding that the picture was best understood with the biblical content removed, that is, when the painting was regarded as the return of *a* prodigal son rather than *the* Prodigal Son.[1076]

The female figure here, then, signifies repentance and redemption. In this way, Gleyre heightened the idea already expressed in 1862 in his *Hercules,* where the female figure, Omphale, is the vehicle through which atonement and mercy can be found. Similarly, in Gleyre's version of the story of Tobit, the emphasis is placed on the mother figure who courageously seeks and finds her lost son in the wilderness, a point not lost on many critics who made the connection. In both subjects, the female provides the source of compassion and ultimate deliverance, a theme that now, in his last completed canvas, finds its grandest expression. This new treatment demonstrates a remarkable shift in Gleyre's philosophical and psychological attitude toward women from the works in which the female is portrayed as a brutal, savage force from whom a ferocious antagonism toward the male emanates: the iconography of *Nero and Agrippina* or that of *Pentheus,* to choose two different artistic poles in Gleyre's career, illustrates the point.

While Gleyre was completing the *Prodigal Son,* he received numerous visits from Samuel Avery, who continually pressed him for another commission for his American clients. On 4 July 1872 Avery noted in his diary that he had engaged Gleyre to paint a "Joan of Arc 1 meter high at 8,000 also Cupid Whispering to a young girl two figures about 2 feet high at 10,000."[1077]

Although Gleyre had already sketched the first scene some years earlier, he seems not to have begun the *Joan of Arc* at all, but instead worked slowly on the *Young Girl Distracted by Amor,* which he never completed, fig. 243 but which exists as a finished oil study. Clément compared its style and

1076. Rambert 1890, p. 326.
1077. Avery 1979, p. 109.

244. Study for *The Earthly Paradise*, 1869–74. Lausanne, Musée Cantonal des Beaux-Arts (catalogue n° 1023)

intention to Prud'hon, but correctly judged that the work, charming as it is, is not one of Gleyre's most brilliant conceptions.[1078] It is at best a return to the idyllic works he had attempted in the 1860s, quite different from the denser philosophic subjects of his more important paintings. Avery perhaps felt too that in the end the work, still in the form of a painted study when he saw it in Gleyre's studio after his death, was not of the highest quality: his friend Lucas wrote to Clément renouncing Avery's claim on the painting at that time.[1079]

A work of this period about which Gleyre was very positive was titled *The Earthly Paradise.* He had worked on it from time to time since the late 1840s but never finished the painting, although the final oil study provides us with what he had in mind. After the completion of *Le Soir* in 1843, Gleyre wanted to produce a pendant painting to be called *Le Matin,*

fig. 244

1078. Clément, p. 361.
1079. In a letter from Lucas to Clément of 20 June 1874, in Fleurier, CFC.

245. *Glory*, 1843–44. Lausanne, Musée Cantonal des Beaux-Arts (catalogue n° 475)

the subject of which would illustrate a scene that anticipates the despair represented in the work of 1843. By 1849, he had produced a large sketch of his first idea for the subject, as Olivier had written to Fritz Berthoud:

> Il en a une [étude], *Le Matin,* qui ferait pendant au *Soir,* sans lui ressembler. L'idée m'en paraît très heureuse et de son meilleur genre.[1080]

Olivier's reference was to a large allegory in which the central figure is a young man leaving his home in order to pursue Fame who is represented as a winged figure waiting in a chariot.[1081] Gleyre did not develop the study beyond this initial idea, no doubt sensing that the imagery was too complicated in relation to the lyrical poetry of its pendant, *Le Soir.* Later, although it is not certain when, Gleyre simplified the idea of *Morning* into only two figures, Adam and Eve, thus representing the notion of morning as a philosophical one, literally the beginning. By 1867 Gleyre included a charcoal sketch of Adam and Eve in a study for *Morning.* At this time, it was Gleyre's intention to bring the painting to its completion, although by now it had lost its meaning as a pendant for *Le Soir.* A rough study of the figures of Adam and Eve was in Gleyre's baggage when he left for Lausanne in 1871.[1082]

fig. 245

fig. 246

1080. Letter of 14 August 1849, in Courvoisier 1905, p. 40.
1081. Clément, p. 170.
1082. Ibid., p. 355.

246. Study for *The Earthly Paradise*, 1869–74. Lausanne, Musée Cantonal des Beaux-Arts (catalogue n° 1025)

While Gleyre was painting the *Prodigal Son,* he was also sporadically working on *The Earthly Paradise.* By the fall of 1872, the painted study was virtually completed, as Louise Milliet noted in a letter to her brother Paul, who was still in Rome. She referred to the graceful, charming aspects of the composition, as well as the unusually bright colors Gleyre employed, which surprised Louise since they were antithetical to the taciturn nature Gleyre displayed in public.[1083] Toward the end of 1873, Gleyre had transferred the basic elements of the design in pencil onto a large canvas, indicating his satisfaction with the work as it was. Shortly afterwards, he fell ill again, preventing further work at that time. During the spring of 1874, Gleyre was well enough to see Nanteuil in Lieusaint near Fontainebleau, where he made additional studies of the spring flowers, which he intended to incorporate into the canvas.[1084] When he returned to Paris, he planned further work on the painting, and, indeed, added additional touches to the canvas on the very day of his death.

Gleyre's conception of this earthly paradise follows the essential ideal of Arcadia, a sacred grove in which all elements of nature interact harmoniously. It is in a sense an escapist iconography that, not surprisingly, had some currency in the nineteenth century; the prototypical example of Ingres's *The Golden Age,* planned for the Château de Dampierre, may be cited as one of the works upon which Gleyre may have modeled his

1083. Milliet 1913, pp. 37–38, letter of 12 October 1872.
1084. Nanteuil related the visit and Gleyre's desire to make studies of the spring flowers in a letter to Clément of 18 April 1878, in Fleurier, CFC; see also Clément, p. 364. The illness is referred to in a letter of 8 April 1874 from Olivier to Clément, in Fleurier, CFC.

309

version. The work demonstrates, as Louise Milliet rightly noted, a side of Gleyre's artistic personality that was not always evident even to his best friends: a humane and often humanizing element is apparent here, as it is in the *Prodigal Son.* Although Gleyre may have appeared harsh and taciturn, as the Goncourt brothers noted several years earlier, it is nevertheless true that the tender and mellow aspects of his nature were visually expressed in his late pictures. And if Louise Milliet was surprised by the vivid colors in the study for *The Earthly Paradise,* it is because they are unexpected in his canvases; few works from his earlier years can be cited in which there is such color and radiance as in this one, done, not insignificantly, at a time when the Impressionists were planning their first public exhibition.

An important question that may be asked about this sketch is whether Gleyre considered the work for the canton de Vaud. This aspect of the history of the 1858 commission and this work is confusing and not adequately documented. Already in May 1862 Gleyre wrote of his intention to fulfill the commission and promised to give some details later in the year.[1085] No further records are known until 1865, when he informed the canton that it would be possible to buy the *Hercules and Omphale,* which was then unsold in Goupil's and available to fulfill the commission.[1086] By December 1869, as we noted earlier, de la Cressonnière had seen Gleyre in Paris to remind him of the commission; it was then that Gleyre thought of the possibility of using *The Last Supper,* although he had reservations about employing a religious iconography for this purpose.[1087] The matter remained unresolved until 30 December 1873 when Juste Olivier, then in Geneva, met with Louis Ruchonnet to attempt to reactivate the commission. Olivier told Ruchonnet that in his view the commission would never be fulfilled unless the canton restated the offer in an official manner; he also suggested the extraordinary sum of 30,000 to 35,000 francs for the commission, a sum almost fifteen times what Gleyre had been paid for the *Major Davel.* When Olivier wrote to Clément of his efforts, he told him that the sum was not a problem and that "l'Adam et Eve lui (Ruchonnet) irait très bien."[1088]

This matter, however, became even more complex because of another commission Gleyre received in about 1869 or 1870 from the Société des Beaux-Arts in Geneva. The details of this commission have not come to the light, but Gleyre had been an "associé honoré" since 1862, and it would have been natural for the society to want a work of his, particularly since at the time there were none in Geneva.[1089] Clément noted that Gleyre considered providing his *Tobit* for this commission, and in fact had Clément make a photograph of the drawing to send to Geneva for approval, but it seems that the authorities there did not think the work adequate for the commission.[1090] Gleyre then thought of the possibility of using *The Earthly Paradise* for the commission, but apparently hesitated even to suggest it because the Vaudois commission had come first and was still outstanding.

This fact was noted by the Conseil d'Etat in Lausanne, who had evidently sent the painter several reminders. Taking into account the slow-

1085. In Lausanne, MCBA, GA 990, in a letter to Eytel of the Département de l'Instruction publique.
1086. Ibid., letter of 30 October 1865.
1087. Lausanne, ACV, Département de l'Instruction publique, Lettres, K XIII/63, 7 December 1869.
1088. The letter, undated, is in Fleurier, CFC.
1089. The matter is treated briefly in Clément, p. 432, under catalogue n° 118. See D., M., 1874, pp. 2f., where it is noted that a group of art lovers had given the commission a number of years earlier — that is to say, in the late 1860s or early 1870s — and that the subject was thought to be Adam and Eve. The records of the society, however, provide no further information on the nature and date of the commission. On Gleyre's election to the society, see Geneva, ASBA, Société des Beaux-Arts 1862, p. 241. Other artists previously elected as honorary associates include David in 1831 and Ingres in 1851; the critic Charles Blanc was elected in 1869.
1090. No documents pertaining to this have come to light in the records of the society or in the archives of the Musée Rath, Geneva. In a report after Gleyre's death, it was noted that a work was commissioned of him by some art lovers in Geneva, but with no further details. See Geneva, ASBA, Société des Beaux-Arts 1874, p. 350.

ness with which the other commissions had been fulfilled, as well as Gleyre's advanced age, the Conseil, clearly worried that this might be the last moment to acquire a painting from Gleyre, decided to ask him not to work on a new painting, but to finish one of the works he already had in study form.[1091] Therefore, Louis Ormond and the industrialist Adrien Mercier — the cousin of Jean-Jacques Mercier whom Gleyre had painted earlier — went to Paris to negotiate with Gleyre in person, hoping that a personal meeting would be more effective in persuading the painter to complete the promised commission. Gleyre now suggested anew the possibility of painting *The Last Supper,* but did not mention the other painting which he had apparently planned for Geneva.[1092] There appears to be no further documentation on the matter in the letters of Gleyre's friends or associates. Yet later, after Gleyre's death, Clément wrote to Albert de Meuron that he thought *The Earthly Paradise* was clearly destined for Lausanne and not Geneva,[1093] and accordingly, offered the study to the Musée Arlaud, much to the chagrin of the art lovers of Geneva.

Very little information is available about Gleyre's activities in early 1874. From secondary sources we know that he continued to see his close friends periodically, generally at coffee either in the morning or in the afternoon. A banquet was given in his honor by several Swiss students in Paris on 26 February 1874, but no information has come to light regarding the specific reasons for the honor. Present at the dinner were Alfred Henri Berthoud, Théophile Bischoff, a student of Gleyre's who showed two pictures in the Salon that year, Eugène Burnand, whom Gleyre had advised in Lausanne two years earlier, Charles-Edouard Du Bois, another student, as well as Eugène Girardet, Henri von Rodt, a Bernese dilettante, Walter von Vigier, and Léo-Paul Robert, the son of Aurèle Robert. Léo-Paul produced an allegorical portrait of Gleyre, and Gleyre apparently accepted it as an homage, but several months after his death, it was returned to the artist by Clément.[1094]

fig. 247

As mentioned earlier, Gleyre had gone to Lieusaint to visit Nanteuil in April 1874, returning to Paris in May. Various documents survive describing Gleyre's activities during that week, the last of his life. Sometime during that week he received a visit from a certain Mr. Burloit who asked him to examine a painting said to be by Van Dyck; Gleyre expressed some interest in the canvas and promised to study it at his leisure, offering to give his opinion on its authenticity later.[1095] We do not know how Gleyre celebrated his birthday on 2 May. On 4 May he was in particularly fine spirits and in the late afternoon paid a visit to his friend, the photographer Martens, who lived nearby at 84 rue Bonaparte.[1096] Later in the evening, Gleyre and Mathilde were invited to dine with the Ormonds in their Paris apartment.[1097]

On the morning of Tuesday, 5 May, Gleyre, as was his habit, began work early — in this instance adding some touches to *The Earthly Paradise* — and afterwards wrote a short note to Eugène Rambert in Lausanne.[1098] Towards late morning, he went to the Café d'Orsay nearby for his coffee and the usual round of reading the daily newspapers. There he chatted expansively with friends, including Fritz Berthoud and Jules

1091. Lausanne, ACV, Conseil d'Etat, Registres des délibérations, bk. 182, session of 6 February 1874, pp. 402–403, item 40. The same notion was expressed on 9 February by the Commission des musées, in ACV, K XIII/66.

1092. In a letter from Olivier to Clément of 16 June 1874, in Fleurier, CFC.

1093. Clément to de Meuron, 16 September 1874, in Neuchâtel, AE, Fonds de Meuron, dossier 75[VI].

1094. The only information on the banquet itself and its participants is from the inscription on the back of the portrait. Robert noted as well that he had given the portrait to Gleyre with the date inscribed afterwards. The portrait, in charcoal, ink, or watercolor, measures 106.3 x 73.5 cm. and is now in the Musée des Beaux-Arts, La Chaux-de-Fonds, to which it was bequeathed in 1891 after the death of the owner at that time, Louis Huguenin-Virchaux. My thanks to Mr. Edmond Charrière, director of the museum, for this information.

1095. Noted in a letter from Burloit to Clément on 17 June 1874, now in Fleurier, CFC. Nothing more is known about Burloit.

1096. Martens informed Clément of the visit in a letter to him written on 7 May 1874, now in Fleurier, CFC.

1097. See the letter from Ormond to an unknown friend dated 6 May 1874, in Lausanne, MCBA, GA 1013.

1098. Rambert 1890, p. 291, notes that it was certainly the last letter Gleyre wrote, but he does not indicate its contents; the letter itself was not found among Rambert's papers.

247. Léo-Paul Robert, *Allegorical Portrait of Gleyre*, 1874. La Chaux-de-Fonds, Musée des Beaux-Arts

Grénier.[1099] Just before noon, he expressed the desire to see an exhibition at the Palais Bourbon, a unique event organized by the Comte d'Haussonville for the benefit of Alsatians who wanted to colonize Algeria. The exhibition, open since 23 April, was a remarkable display of almost 600 paintings, mostly from private collections, including diverse works from Cranach and Clouet to Bonington and Delacroix.[1100]

At 12:30 Gleyre was in room 16 of the exhibition admiring either a Greuze or an Ingres — the accounts vary and it cannot be determined which works he saw since there were several by the former and no fewer than eighteen by the latter — when suddenly he grew pale and collapsed without a sound. By chance, two doctors were present — Dr. Galand, an army officer assigned to the 110th regiment, and a Dr. Chrétien — both of whom rushed to his aid, massaging his chest, but Gleyre was already dead.[1101] One of Gleyre's students, Alfred Lenglet, was also present and the first of the painter's entourage to be informed that he had died of a ruptured aorta.[1102] Lenglet in turn ran to inform Clément, Mathilde, and Denuelle, all of whom lived nearby. Gleyre's body was taken to the basement area of the Palais Bourbon. Several hours later, a death certificate was made out at the *Mairie* of the 7th *arrondissement,* written by the officer in charge, Auguste-François Dargent, and countersigned by Denuelle and François Ehrmann.[1103] Soon afterwards, Denuelle's son-in-law, Hippolyte Taine, arranged for the transfer of Gleyre's body to his studio.[1104]

1099. See Berthoud 1874, p. 454, and Clément, p. 365.
1100. Timbal 1874, p. 444. The catalogue noted 568 paintings; in addition there were 120 drawings. A supplement was printed, with additional items, on 22 June. See *Explication* 1874.
1101. See *Le XIX^e Siècle*, 1874, unpaginated; *Chronique des Arts*, 1874, p. 187; and the *Gazette de Lausanne*, 1874, pp. 2–3, for the various accounts of the incident including the names of the doctors. The *Chronique* remarked that Gleyre collapsed in front of a work by Greuze, while Villarceaux 1874, p. 448, noted that the painting Gleyre was admiring at the time was by Prud'hon — of which there were four in the exhibition.
1102. Clément, p. 365.
1103. Paris, Mairie, Registre des actes de décès, 1874.
1104. Taine 1902, III, p. 244.

News of Gleyre's death was sent to Lausanne the next day at 8:13 in the morning by Louis Ormond: "Enterrement de Gleyre notre grand peintre aura lieu jeudi après-midi ou vendredi matin."[1105] The news was quickly dispatched to the Conseil d'Etat, who asked that the canton be represented at the funeral services by the ambassador, Johann Kern.[1106] Juste Olivier, who was in his chalet at Gryon on 6 May, heard the news on that day and immediately left for Paris.[1107] Quinet, in Paris, probably heard the news of the death through friends or the press: he noted in his diary on 7 May 1874, Gleyre "mort avant-hier... devant un tableau."[1108]

The funeral was scheduled for 8 May at four in the afternoon. Earlier that afternoon, some of Gleyre's most intimate friends including Olivier and Clément gathered in the studio for a private farewell,[1109] before joining a cortège from the studio to the cemetery at Montparnasse. Despite Gleyre's desire not to have a public ceremony, often expressed to friends, a large crowd formed at the cemetery, including students, colleagues, and representatives of the art establishment.[1110] The presiding clergyman was a Mr. Hollard-Bernus, whose discourse was badly received because he stated that he could not in good conscience deliver sincere words of consolation for a man who had never truly believed in Christianity.[1111] The ambassador was not present because of ill health, but was replaced by his aide, Mr. Roquin, who made a short speech on behalf of the Swiss government — neither particularly moving, nor acknowledging Gleyre's influence on the state of painting in Switzerland.[1112] The service then ended abruptly because of a steady rain.

Even before the burial in Paris, plans were made to have the body transferred afterwards to an undesignated site in the canton of Vaud. The principal moving force here was Ormond, with the approval of Kern, who vowed to help in his capacity as ambassador. Ormond took it upon himself to request the necessary permission from Mathilde Gleyre, and from Clément who was named the executor of Gleyre's estate.[1113] Kern used his official position in Paris to speed up the administrative procedures with the French government.[1114] The Vaudois government acted quickly as well to form a committee responsible for transporting Gleyre's body; the committee included Ruchonnet, Bocion, de la Cressonnière, and Adrien Mercier as its principal members.[1115] The Conseil meanwhile decided that Gleyre's body should be buried in the cemetery of Pierre du Plan in the northern section of Lausanne, but the family objected, arguing that Gleyre should by law be buried in his native village of Chevilly.[1116] Kern had convinced the French to speed the process of transferal — usually one had to wait in the order of exhumation number — and succeeded in having Gleyre's body released two weeks earlier than expected.[1117] Thus Gleyre's body arrived in Lausanne by special train, draped in black, on Sunday, 17 May, at 1:15 P.M.; it was accompanied by a member of the French mortuary group in Montparnasse.[1118]

Whereas the adverse weather in Paris two weeks earlier had decreased the number of well wishers, in Lausanne the sun was shining and the temperature agreeable. When the train arrived, between 1,000 and 1,200 people were waiting at the station.[1119] The body was placed in an-

1105. Telegram n° 36820, received in Lausanne at 9:32 A.M. by E. Rossat, in Lausanne, ACV, Commission des musées, K XIII/66.
1106. Lausanne, ACV, Conseil d'Etat, Registres des délibérations, session 6 May 1874, bk. 183, p. 13, item 56.
1107. Noted in a letter from Caroline Olivier to an unidentified friend, 6 May 1874, in Lausanne, BCU/DM, IS 1905/47, dossier 1874. Caroline, however, noted her intention of staying in Gryon because of poor health.
1108. See Paris, BN, Mme. Quinet, "Journal," pp. 69ᵛ–70.
1109. Olivier noted the fact to his son Edouard, then in Geneva, in a letter on 9 May 1874, in Lausanne, BCU/DM, Fonds Olivier, IS 1905/47, dossier 1874.
1110. Gleyre's desire was recorded in Moreau-Vauthier 1906, p. 75, but without any indication of a source: "Je ne veux personne à mon enterrement."
1111. This was commented upon by one of the witnesses at the funeral, Gleyre's Alsatian student Henri Zuber, in a letter to his mother of 11 May 1874, in Paris, Private Collection. The minister's disrespect was noted in L'Estafette on 14 May 1874, p. 6, citing a report from a journalist working for the Union Libérale of Neuchâtel.
1112. Kern had cabled the authorities in Lausanne that he was indisposed and had designated Roquin to take his place at the ceremony; see Lausanne, ACV, Conseil d'Etat, Registres des délibérations, bk. 183, session 8 May 1874, p. 14, item 50. Ernest Roquin was the first secretary of the Embassy in Paris.
1113. Ormond had telegraphed the news to the Conseil d'Etat in the session of 8 May 1874. On Clément as executor of the Gleyre estate, see chapter 12.
1114. L'Estafette, 9 May 1874, p. 6.
1115. Lausanne, ACV, Conseil d'Etat, Registres des délibérations, bk. 183, session 8 May 1874, p. 16, item 68.
1116. Ibid., session 12 May 1874, bk. 29, item 125. The objection came essentially from Gleyre's niece Mathilde who was acting, she said, on behalf of her sisters in Lyons and America.
1117. L'Estafette, 16 May 1874, p. 6.
1118. Lausanne, ACV, Conseil d'Etat, Registres des délibérations, bk. 183, session 15 May 1874, p. 38, item 179², and p. 41, item 192. The accompanying member of the French mortuary home presented the canton with a bill for the transport of the body — a sum of 1,160 francs — which the Conseil paid with a supplement of 50 francs because of the good service rendered. See the session for 6 June 1874, p. 88, item 45, for a detailed accounting of the burial costs.
1119. L'Estafette, 18 May 1874, p. 3.

other special train to La Sarraz, where a group awaited it for the final trip to Chevilly, in accord with the desires of the family. Announcements had been posted throughout Lausanne noting that anyone wishing to pay homage to the painter would be given free transportation to La Sarraz so that they could participate in the final rites. The train arrived at 2 P.M. and the procession, led by members of the family, walked the three kilometers to the village; the coffin was covered with spring flowers. In Chevilly, all activity stopped as the procession passed on its way to the cemetery. There two wreaths were placed on the coffin; a choir sang a *Hymne à Gleyre,* a modified version of the popular *Hymne à la Nuit,* as well as songs adapted for the occasion by a Mr. Vulliemoz.[1120]

The pastor of the village, Mr. Hautier, gave a speech recalling Gleyre's patriotism, his liberal political beliefs, and his charity. Then Ruchonnet took the podium to remind the crowd that Gleyre disliked public manifestations; that he was a private man in his life and his art. Ruchonnet spoke eloquently of Gleyre's humble roots, of his birth only 100 yards from where he spoke. De la Cressonnière then discussed at length Gleyre's important contributions in the field of art, both in Paris and in the canton, while Paul Cérésole, the Conseiller Fédéral, gave a last eulogy. The ceremony was closed by the judge of the district, himself a Mr. Gleyre, who pledged that the painter's remains would be treated with respect and dignity by the people of the village.[1121] Gleyre was then laid to rest a second time, in a plot adjacent to that of his beloved uncle François, who had died eight years earlier. The only known visual record of the actual burial site is a drawing by Anker in one of his sketchbooks.[1122] Anker fig. 248 himself had inadvertently missed the burial ceremony because "un Vaudois" visiting him in Anet had given him the wrong date for the interment.[1123] However, Anker was able to go to Chevilly in September after spending two weeks in Fleurier with Clément. In a letter to François Ehrmann, Anker briefly described going to Gleyre's house in Chevilly, then uninhabited, and to the grave itself; he sent Ehrmann a handful of earth taken from the grave as a souvenir.[1124]

248. Albert Anker, *Tomb of Gleyre,* 1874. Switzerland, Private collection

1120. *Gazette de Lausanne,* 18 May 1874, p. 3.
1121. Ibid., 19 May 1874, pp. 2–3, and *Nouvelliste vaudois,* 18 May 1874, p. 3.
1122. The sketchbook is unpublished and was sold at Sotheby's Zürich, on 5 June 1991 (lot 43) to a private collector, Zürich. It measures 7.7 x 11.7 cm. I am grateful to Paul Müller who provided information on the book and the photograph.
1123. Anker wrote this to François Ehrmann on 1 June 1874, in a letter reproduced in Quinche-Anker 1924, p. 107.
1124. Ibid., p. 108; the letter is dated only "été 1874."

POSTLUDE

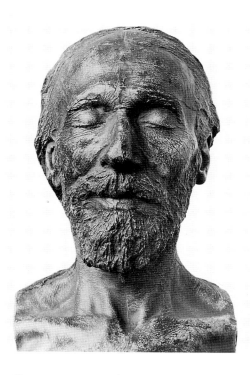

249. Alfred Dubucand, *Death Mask of Gleyre*, 1874. Minneapolis, Private collection.

The day after Gleyre's death, his will, written on 4 May 1870, was officially read by his lawyer, Alfred Bezanson.[1125] It stipulated that Gleyre's financial holdings and personal possessions, excluding works of art, were to be divided among his nieces. Clément was named the executor of the will and in turn was given the artistic contents of the studio with a significant proviso: "pour en disposer comme il entendra, à la condition bien expresse qu'il ne fera ni vente, ni exposition publique de peintures ou dessins." Gleyre gave Clément the authority to distribute as he saw fit various examples of his works, as tokens of friendship to select friends, naming in particular Cornu, Nanteuil, Denuelle, Olivier, Veyne, and de Fontenay. This Clément did in the following months after the inheritance taxes were paid and the works in question were temporarily catalogued before their distribution.

1125. See Bezanson's report filed in Paris, AS, Registre de Recette, Déclarations des mutations par décès, 29 January 1875, pp. 77–78. The original testament is contained in Paris, AN, Maître Bezanson, Minutier central. A transcribed copy of the will is also contained in a private collection in France, signed by Gleyre — surely his copy. Although Gleyre officially made out his will in May 1870, he had already told Clément on 18 January 1869 that he intended to leave the contents of his studio to him. See too France, Private collection, Clément, *Journal*, where there is a note for the above date that "Gleyre m'a dit aujourd'hui qu'il [me laissera] tout son atelier."

On 8 June 1874, Bezanson, in the company of Clément, made a cursory inventory of the studio to determine the possessions to be shared by the nieces, only two of whom resided in Paris.[1126] The bulk of Gleyre's financial holdings was in three stock certificates for French and Spanish railroads and an Italian tobacco concern, probably acquired through such friends as Dubochet and Ormond, both of whom were well placed to advise Gleyre on these matters. His bank account at the Société Générale in Paris amounted to 2,540.50 francs, while an additional sum of 180 francs in cash was in a drawer in the studio. With the furnishings in his living quarters, the total of Gleyre's fortune was estimated at 62,285.50 francs, on which Mathilde was required to pay an inheritance tax of 5,442.13 francs. Gleyre also owned the house in Chevilly, which was under the jurisdiction of Swiss law. In sum, the figure constituting Gleyre's wealth was quite large, but still well below the initial estimate offered by Olivier who thought the actual sum to be almost double.[1127]

On the same day, Bezanson began a full inventory of Gleyre's studio which took two days to complete and provided a detailed account in his official legal report.[1128] Gleyre's personal living quarters were in a small room to the right upon entering and contained an iron bed, pillows, an old wardrobe, and a small writing desk. In the wardrobe were two winter coats, one suit, two jackets, four vests, fifteen shirts, twelve pairs of socks, and a silk top hat, probably the one seen in the 1858 photograph of him in Lausanne. His night table held his entire stock of jewelry — two gold watches, numbered in series, with appropriate fobs, and a silver spoon and fork. In addition, Bezanson noted twenty-one small plaster statuettes and reliefs and nine engravings ("sujets antiques"). In the corner was a small bookcase with ninety-five paper-covered volumes of modern literature, as well as some volumes of Homer and Plato.

The studio itself was relatively modest. There was a large chest "en marqueterie" in one corner, presumably where Gleyre kept his Egyptian studies. There was also a large sofa in another corner, two large chairs, and a smaller sofa covered in red leather, where he often sat to smoke, two large tables, a small work table on which he mixed colors, a large ladder, various stools, and a plethora of pillows, surely for entertaining and drinking tea on the floor in Arab style. Gleyre used two large easels and had seven smaller ones scattered about. In addition there were ninety plaster statuettes, as well as 180 volumes, none of which were identified in the report.

Bezanson classified the works of art remaining in the studio, with Clément's help, into five separate categories. Fourteen works, all unframed, of figures, landscapes, and still lifes, were designated as "copies d'après des maîtres anciens par divers artistes inconnus"; these were surely by Gleyre's pupils and friends and probably works that he himself had collected — none were ever mentioned again and there is no trace of them after the inventory. There were also thirty-five canvases of projects that were barely begun, rough sketches and studies, presumably by Gleyre himself, although none are specified as such. Bezanson noted forty-seven canvases clearly by Gleyre, some of which he tried to sort by subject,

1126. Gleyre had six nieces, the daughters of his two brothers: one niece, Sophie, born when Samuel was sixty-two years old, died in 1870. Samuel's living daughters were Marguerite (1840), Louise (1846), and Suzanne (1855); Henry's were Mathilde (1842), Esther (1845), and Emire (1848). Only Mathilde and Suzanne were in Paris when Gleyre died; the others were in Lyons, except for Esther, who had married an American and settled in Minneapolis.

1127. See the letter from Caroline of 10 May 1874 to an unknown friend, in Lausanne, BCU/DM, Fonds Olivier, IS 1905/47, and a letter from Juste to Gustave Olivier of 12 May 1874, in BCU/DM, IS 1905/116bis.

1128. Paris, AN, Maître Bezanson, "Inventaire après le décès de M. Gleyre," 8 June 1874.

again with Clément's aid. An intriguing aspect of the report is the listing of eight portfolios with about 400 engravings, lithographs, and photographs; no trace of these has ever come to light, nor is there any information in the correspondence of Clément as to their contents; it is likely that Gleyre used these for teaching purposes. In addition, there were twelve separate portfolios with about 500 pencil studies, watercolors, and other studies for compositions — all presumably in Gleyre's hand. Bezanson noted that in Gleyre's attic, he found five additional engravings after Poussin, a collection of butterflies, and a substantial wardrobe of costumes, probably used by his models. All of these were temporarily assigned to Gleyre's concierge, Mlle. Foretay, for safekeeping until Clément could take possession, which he did shortly afterwards.

## COMMEMORATIVE EXHIBITION AND BUST

Gleyre's death elicited no particular commemorative initiatives on the part of the French authorities who rightfully considered the painter to be Swiss. But in the canton of Vaud, plans were already under way to honor the painter with an exhibition, a veritable retrospective that would permit Swiss audiences to view the bulk of his artistic activity.[1129] Efforts to organize the exhibition began in June, with Emile David and François Bocion as the chief coordinators. On 23 June 1874, permission was requested from the authorities to use the main exhibition room in the Musée Arlaud for the purpose; the request was quickly granted for a period of one month beginning on 15 August.[1130] It was hoped that a large number of Gleyre's major canvases could be borrowed from various public and private collections in Switzerland and elsewhere, but the organizers ran into substantial problems in locating these works and then in borrowing them. Even a request by Paul Cérésole through Kern in Paris for *Le Soir*, then in the Musée du Luxembourg, proved futile.[1131] Consequently, the organizing committee decided that the exhibition would contain only works of Gleyre in Swiss collections, particularly those in private hands.

The committee began sending requests for loans in late June. In Neuchâtel, which had recently acquired the *Hercules and Omphale* from Fritz Berthoud, Albert de Meuron, then the head of the local Société des Amis des Beaux-Arts, consented to send the picture, despite the fact that lending pictures even to other Swiss museums was prohibited by its charter.[1132] Eventually his personal intervention with the Conseil d'Etat permitted the museum to bypass the regulation for this exceptional purpose.[1133] The museum in Basel, however, proved to be adamantly against the loan of their two works, the *Pentheus* and *The Charmer*, the latter of which had been acquired only a few months before. Citing the same regulations forbidding loans altogether, the museum authorities refused on several occasions to approve the request for the special purpose indicated. It was only through intervention at the highest political levels in

1129. See the documentation dispersed in Lausanne, MCBA, GA 1011, and Lausanne, ACV, Commission des musées, Procès-verbaux, K XIII/ 66.
1130. Lausanne, ACV, Conseil d'Etat, Registres des délibérations, bk. 183, 23 June 1874, p. 130, item 224².
1131. The efforts to procure the paintings were recounted by Cérésole in a letter to Clément of 27 June 1874, now in Fleurier, CFC.
1132. See Neuchâtel, MAH, Procès-verbaux, 5 June 1874, p. 47.
1133. In a letter from Albert de Meuron to de la Cressonnière, Lausanne, MCBA, GA 1011. De Meuron indicated that there was some resistance to the loan.

Lausanne, Basel, and Bern, that the loans were approved, virtually at the last possible moment.[1134]

Henri Moser agreed to send the *Prodigal Son*, but only under unduly severe conditions; finally Cérésole acted as an intermediary to negotiate the loan.[1135] Many private collectors, however, lent their works willingly. Vulliemin made his portrait available, the first time it was seen in public,[1136] but such intimates of Gleyre as Clément and Fritz Berthoud were unable to contribute works in their respective collections because they were apparently already in storage in Paris.[1137] Clément noted that the works he had recently acquired under Gleyre's will, which were available, were prohibited from exhibition through the will's stipulation. Curiously, there is no correspondence between the exhibition organizers and the Oliviers in regard to their works, then for the most part in their chalet in Gryon. It was only on 29 August, almost two weeks after the exhibition opened, that Berthoud and Clément went to Gryon to pick up the studies for the *Prodigal Son* and the portrait of Thérèse for the exhibition.[1138] One week earlier, Ruchonnet had found a copy of *Le Soir* in Lucerne in the collection of a Mr. Aman, which was thought to be by Gleyre himself, but when it was exhibited the authenticity was seriously questioned by numerous authorities.[1139] Also at the last minute, three works owned by Adrien Mercier were included,[1140] but certain important paintings in local collections were conspicuously absent, including the portrait of Mme. Ormond, as Mathilde noted when she visited the exhibition.[1141] No paintings from the collections of Denuelle or Cornu were exhibited.

When the memorial exhibition opened, it proved finally to be an unassuming affair, containing only ten major oils and several portraits.[1142] The lacunae were filled by several prints, mostly from those issued by Goupil, and various photographs. No catalogue had been planned; the committee had hoped to use Fritz Berthoud's recent article on Gleyre in the *Bibliothèque universelle*, but the editor, Tallichet, refused to grant the rights to reprint the article without a substantial fee, which the committee refused to pay.[1143] Nevertheless, the exhibition was a huge success with the critics and the public alike, although Eugène Rambert pointed out that some works, especially the portraits, were hung and lit badly.[1144] The receipts from the admission fee for the month of the exhibition amounted to the sum of 12,726.50 francs.[1145]

1134. A full account is documented in Hauptman 1986(b), pp. 223–24.

1135. Cérésole recounted the affair to Clément on 27 June 1874, in a letter now in Fleurier, CFC.

1136. Vulliemin gladly accepted the invitation of Emile David to lend the picture; see his letter to David of 5 August 1874, in Lausanne, BCU/DM, David, "Correspondance," IS 4540.

1137. Berthoud explained the situation to de la Cressonnière in a letter, undated, in Lausanne, MCBA, GA 1011.

1138. Olivier described the circumstances in a letter to an unidentified friend on 29 August 1874, in Lausanne, BCU/DM, Fonds Olivier, IS 1905/47. There is no indication why Olivier had not lent the works earlier.

1139. *Gazette de Lausanne*, 9 September 1874. The work was later donated to the Kunstmuseum, Winterthur, Inv. n° 1004.

1140. These included *The Nubian* and the *Diana* which Mercier had bought only a short while before. On his last-minute inclusion of the works, see Lausanne, Institut suisse pour l'étude de l'art, Société vaudoise des Beaux-Arts, Procès-verbaux, ISEA 101, session of 27 September 1874.

1141. See the letter from Mathilde to Angèle Clément, 17 August 1874, in Fleurier, CFC. The portrait of Louis Ormond was included after the exhibition opened — as indicated in *La Suisse illustrée*, August 1874, p. 429 — but not the portrait of his wife. The portrait of Kern arrived at the same time.

1142. These were *The Nubian* and the *Diana*, here titled *L'Egypte* and *La Grèce* respectively; *Major Davel*; *The Romans Passing under the Yoke*, here

called *La Bataille du Léman*; *The Charmer*; *Hercules and Omphale*; *Sappho*; *Minerva and the Three Graces*; the *Prodigal Son*; and *Pentheus*. All these are listed on a publicity poster printed for the event, a copy of which is in the author's collection, Lausanne. At the bottom is mention of "portraits divers," which, from other reports, we know were those of Haldimand, Jomini, Vulliemin, Mercier, Ormond, and Kern. See *Gazette de Lausanne*, 9 September 1874; and a letter from Paul Cérésole to Clément of 20 July 1874, now in Fleurier, CFC, in which the author recounted the progress of acquiring loans up to that time.

1143. See the letter from Berthoud to Tallichet, undated, in Lausanne, BCU/DM, Tallichet, "Correspondance," IS 193. Berthoud's article ap-

peared in the 1874 volume of the *Bibliothèque universelle et Revue suisse*, L, in two parts, pp. 454–76 and pp. 604–27, and was written rapidly just after Gleyre's death. At the time of the exhibition, only the first part had been published.

1144. Rambert 1890, p. 293. Rambert also lamented that crucial aspects of Gleyre's art were not represented, thus creating a vastly inferior image of his career.

1145. The exceptional fee charged for entrance to the exhibition was two francs, except for Thursdays (five francs) and Sundays (one franc); the opening-day admission charge was five francs. The receipts were carefully noted in a letter from de la Cressonnière to Clément on 19 October 1874, now in Fleurier, CFC.

250. Henri Chapu, *Bust of Gleyre*, 1876. Paris, Private collection

In addition to the exhibition to honor Gleyre, the committee wished to have a more permanent memorial to the painter in the form of a portrait bust, the commission fee for the sculptor to be provided by the receipts of the exhibition.[1146] The commission for the bust went to the celebrated sculptor Henri Chapu, who may never have met Gleyre, but who had gained a considerable reputation as a portrait artist.[1147] On 9 December 1874, Chapu and several distinguished residents of Lausanne — only Emile David is identified — went to the studio of the photographer Martens to select an appropriate photograph upon which to base the memorial bust. Martens had suggested a profile of the artist, but this was rejected, presumably by Chapu, because it would have been inadequate for the purpose; the group selected instead a full-face portrait which Martens reproduced in large format for the sculptor.[1148] Chapu worked on the bust throughout 1875, selecting a white Paros marble, and finished it by the autumn of the following year, when it was sent to the Musée Arlaud.[1149]

fig. 250

1146. De la Cressonnière noted this intention in a letter to the Conseil d'Etat, 25 June 1874, in Lausanne, ACV, Commission des musées, K XIII/66.
1147. There is no documentary record indicating any connection between Gleyre and Chapu. On Henri Chapu, see Lami 1914–21, II, pp. 328f.; the bust of Gleyre is noted on p. 336. Chapu had received the highest distinction in the salon of 1875, the medal of honor.
1148. Martens noted this to Clément on 9 December 1874; see Fleurier, CFC.
1149. *Nouvelliste vaudois*, 13 October 1876, p. 3.

On 21 November 1876, the bust, officially donated by the society, was unveiled in the museum for the first time. The ceremony was headed by de la Cressonnière, who first provided a brief history of the commission and then dramatically pulled the cord of the curtain concealing the work while the audience gasped. Chapu was present for the occasion and received the applause of the spectators. Other speakers included Cérésole, Boiceau of the Conseil d'Etat, and Fritz Berthoud, who improvised a speech on Gleyre's character and artistic merits. The event was followed by a banquet in Chapu's honor.[1150]

Chapu was asked as well to provide thirty-five reduced copies of the portrait, made through Barbedienne and Sons, which were meant for various friends of Gleyre. This version of the bust was to be sold in the limited edition for twenty-two francs.[1151] De la Cressonnière, the promoter of the project and the head of the society that had commissioned the bust, gave several of these away, including one to the museum in Neuchâtel which permitted the loan of the *Hercules*, but apparently not to the museum in Basel.[1152] Most of Gleyre's close friends in the canton bought the smaller version of the bust, including Clément, who kept his on the work table in Fleurier, and Rambert, who kept his in the study as a muse of inspiration. Juste Olivier, however, had died on 7 January 1876, before the bust was dedicated.

## THE MUSÉE ARLAUD

Readers of the catalogue section of this study will note that the major collection of Gleyre's works is to be found in the Musée Cantonal des Beaux-Arts, Lausanne. It is important therefore to trace how the museum acquired its vast holdings of Gleyre's works. The process began ten days after Gleyre's death through the initiative of Clément himself, who had ties to the canton of Vaud, even though he lived in Paris and Fleurier. Although Clément had become the sole owner of Gleyre's works left in the studio, he was restrained, as noted above, from either selling them or lending them for exhibitions. But he decided to make an exception and sell various works to the Musée Arlaud for two reasons. First, he was well aware that Gleyre had never finished the commission he had received from the canton in 1858, but had hoped to be able to provide the painting during his last years. Second, Clément knew from his contacts with Mathilde that she was in difficult financial straits, despite the generous inheritance she had received from her uncle.[1153] Clément therefore decided to resolve both problems at once: to sell various painted studies of Gleyre's to the Musée Arlaud, thus indirectly fulfilling the commission, and to give the fees to Mathilde. Clément was convinced that in this way he was not thwarting the intention of Gleyre's will, but rather helping the museum and his niece as he thought Gleyre would have done were he alive. Nevertheless, he feared some legal action on the part of the other nieces if his intentions became known too quickly and thus decided to

1150. *Gazette de Lausanne*, 22 November 1876, p. 3; *Chronique des arts et de la curiosité*, 1876, p. 339.
1151. De la Cressonnière in a letter to Delarageaz, 23 February 1877, Lausanne, BCU/DM, Fonds Delarageaz, IS 3681/I, 365.
1152. Neuchâtel, MAH, Procès-verbaux, session of 1 October 1877, pp. 62–63.
1153. There are various letters from Clément to friends in Fleurier, CFC, in which he recounted aspects of Mathilde's difficulties as well as his desire to help her. See too Juste Olivier's letter to Caroline, 15 May 1874, Lausanne, BCU/DM, Fonds Olivier, IS 1905/116$^{bis}$, where the poet praised Clément's efforts. Nowhere, however, is it fully explained why Mathilde found herself in a difficult financial situation.

act clandestinely with the cantonal officials, later directing the proceeds to Mathilde's account. Clément asked the advice of various friends, including Alexandre Denuelle, who concluded that Clément's actions were not disrespectful of the painter's intentions and advised him to proceed in the matter, but delicately.[1154]

The idea of buying some of Gleyre's works to fulfill the promise Gleyre had made for a commission was pursued in Lausanne by Louis Ruchonnet. On 19 June 1874, he wrote to the Conseil d'Etat, then Boiceau, urging him to negotiate with Clément, using the argument that this sale would fulfill the commission of 1858 for which funds had already been allocated. Ruchonnet had previously seen Clément about this in Paris, selecting four works for the sale: the unfinished study for *The Earthly Paradise*, the study for *The Last Supper*, which Gleyre himself had once thought of using for the commission, a large pencil study for the definitive design of the *Hercules and Omphale*, and the study for the *Young Girl Distracted by Amor* that Gleyre had made for Samuel Avery. In Ruchonnet's argument to Boiceau, he remarked that Clément would not profit from the sale, that all remuneration would go to Mathilde — thus remaining in the Gleyre family — and that the canton must move swiftly since rumors abounded that Geneva was also interested in negotiating with Clément because it too had a claim on an unfinished commission. Ruchonnet wrote in conclusion that 20,000 to 30,000 francs would be necessary to conclude the transaction.[1155]

The Conseil deliberated the question on 23 June 1874[1156] but did not agree to negotiate with Clément until 12 August. Two days later, de la Cressonnière wired Clément that the canton would seriously consider the offer and that 30,000 francs was tentatively available if the *Amor* was included, but only 20,000 francs if not.[1157] On 15 August he also informed Ruchonnet that negotiations were under way, and that Emile David had offered to use his influence in the matter; Boiceau wrote to Clément asking him to come to Lausanne to discuss the matter in person.[1158] Ruchonnet already feared obstacles and wrote to Fritz Berthoud, who served as a Conseil in Neuchâtel, asking him to enlist friends in support of the sale while he, Ruchonnet, would do the same through friends in Bern. At the same time, Clément could no longer be involved secretly and decided to let Mathilde know of the sale, telling her that the full sum of the venture, 30,000 francs, would be available for her personal use since her uncle would have surely provided as much had he known that she was in a difficult financial circumstances.[1159]

The approval for the sale was signed on 15 August.[1160] Ten days later a formal contract was drafted between the canton and Clément with the price for the purchase established at 30,000 francs.[1161] Apparently Clément was not in a position to cede the *Amor* at this time — the reason is not known since Avery, who had commissioned the painting, had already renounced his claim to it on 20 June — and instead substituted the study for *The Mission of the Apostles*, an unexpected prize because Clément considered the work more powerful than Gleyre's finished painting; he dispatched the picture to Lausanne on 28 September as a gesture

1154. Denuelle to Clément, 15 May 1874, in CFC.
1155. The document is in MCBA, GA 1012.
1156. Lausanne, ACV, Conseil d'Etat, Registres des délibérations, bk. 183, pp. 129–30, item 224.
1157. The agreement came directly from Ruchonnet, letter n° 2056, in Lausanne, MCBA, GA 1012. The question still remained whether Avery would later claim the *Amor* for his American client. He renounced his claim in a letter through his friend, George Lucas.
1158. Boiceau wrote directly to Clément, letter n° 2099, now in Fleurier, CFC. There is no record of a reply from Clément, nor is it certain that he came to Lausanne directly, as Boiceau desired.
1159. It is not known whether Clément sent the letter; it exists in draft form in Fleurier, CFC, but was not found among Mathilde's papers after her death. It is, however, clear from other letters to various friends that Clément was not then on the friendliest terms with Mathilde, for reasons that are not known. Clément later was angry at her for her lack of gratitude in the affair.
1160. Lausanne, ACV, Conseil d'Etat, Registres des délibérations, bk. 183, p. 265, item 224.
1161. The original contract is found in Fleurier, CFC, while a draft copy is contained in Lausanne, MCBA, GA 1012.

of his good will.[1162] De la Cressonnière was elated by the substitution and wanted to exhibit it immediately. On 19 October, he wrote to Clément asking when the other three paintings would arrive, to which Clément responded on 29 October that they had already been sent.[1163] They actually arrived in Lausanne on 2 November.[1164]

Despite the earlier cantonal authorization, a problem arose concerning the price agreed upon for the four works. The documents do not elucidate at what point or why this problem developed, but seemingly a member of the council asked that this expense be justified. Accordingly, de la Cressonnière wrote a report on 16 November outlining previous expenditures by the canton for purchases and commissions for the museum. De la Cressonnière argued that in the past the canton had in fact spent very little for the purchase of art; he calculated that between 1842 and 1872, the total purchases for the Musée Arlaud amounted to 47,272 francs, an average of only 1,432 francs per year. Some of this, he added, was donated from private funds, as for example the commission for the *Davel*, which came entirely from Arlaud. Ironically, these figures support Gleyre's own claims in his report on the Exposition Universelle of 1867 that the Swiss government did not do enough to encourage younger artists. De la Cressonnière argued finally that since the Musée Arlaud had spent so little in the past, there was all the more reason to take advantage of this unique opportunity, particularly since the money would go directly to a descendant of the Gleyre family.[1165]

Meanwhile word of the canton's reluctance to proceed in the matter had spread; Juste Olivier, then in retirement in Gryon, heard about it and wrote to ask his friend Adrien Mercier to intervene. Apparently, the canton wanted to spend only 20,000 francs for the purchase, while the Société des Beaux-Arts was ready to add an additional 5,000 francs. In late November, Mercier, now acting as an intermediary, wired Clément in Paris asking if he would accept the lesser sum; the implication is that the canton was unwilling to pay the 30,000 francs agreed upon and that the situation was at an impasse.[1166] Clément was forced to accept the conditions and a new contract between the canton and the seller was ratified on 3 December; the sum of 25,000 francs was transferred to Clément's account in the Berthoud bank in Neuchâtel on 18 December.[1167] Clément afterwards telegraphed Ruchonnet in Bern expressing his disappointment.[1168]

Yet, despite this deception, Clément showed his own magnanimity in the affair by providing the museum with some additional works as a gift. By November, when the four works he had sold the museum were already in Lausanne, Clément informed Olivier that the gift consisted of six additional works because, he wrote, Gleyre had had a particular attachment to the canton.[1169] On 20 January 1875, Boiceau sent Clément a letter thanking him for the gift.[1170] Thus, less than one year after Gleyre's death, the Musée Arlaud could count a total of fifteen canvases and sketches by the artist in its permanent collection.

During the next three decades, the Gleyre holdings in Lausanne grew only minimally. The most dramatic expansion came in 1907 when the

1162. De la Cressonnière informed Boiceau of the gift on that date in a letter in Lausanne, MCBA, GA 1012.

1163. De la Cressonnière's letter to Clément is in Fleurier, CFC; Clément's reply is in Lausanne, MCBA, GA 1012.

1164. De la Cressonnière informed Clément of their safe arrival on the day after; the letter is in Fleurier, CFC.

1165. The report is directed to Boiceau and is in Lausanne, MCBA, GA 1012.

1166. This is recounted in a letter from Olivier to his wife, undated, but clearly late November, in Lausanne, BCU/DM, Fonds Olivier, IS 1905/47.

1167. Lausanne, MCBA, GA 1012.

1168. Ibid.

1169. Clément to Olivier, 7 or 9 November 1874, in Fleurier, CFC. Olivier had discussed the gift with Clément and wrote to his nephew Gustave that he did not believe the gift would violate Gleyre's intentions; see the letter in Lausanne, BCU/DM, Fonds Olivier, IS 1905/116[bis].

1170. Lausanne, MCBA, GA 1024.

director of the museum, Emile Bonjour, began negotiations with Mme. Clément — Charles had died in 1888 — for the sale of her collection, housed in Garches, near Paris.[1171] Angèle had kept the bulk of her husband's legacy from the 1870 will, although several works had been given to friends or donated to museums in France and Switzerland. Bonjour noted that about 370 works by Gleyre were in Angèle's possession and that it might be possible to acquire these. On 22 September 1907, Bonjour requested permission from the politician Edouard Secretan to enter into negotiation with Mme. Clément and her son Frédéric, then a lawyer in Paris. Bonjour also requested an expert judgment on the value and conditions of the collection, suggesting Eugène Grasset as the best person for the task.[1172]

Bonjour went to Garches with the Conseil d'Etat Decoppet in November 1907 — one month later than planned because of Decoppet's unexpected military obligation — to inspect the collection at first hand. On 8 January 1908, he made a preliminary report indicating that the collection contained 378 paintings, drawings, watercolors, studies, and other items he did not detail at this time. By 11 February, Frédéric Clément wrote to Bonjour informing him that a formal inventory was almost finished in Garches and that all that remained was to work out the details of packing, transport, insurance, and the final price. On 20 March, after reconciling disagreements, a contract was drawn up between the canton and Frédéric, representing Angèle, with the following stipulations:

1. that Mme. Charles Clément agrees to sell the works of the collection to the Musée Cantonal des Beaux-Arts in Lausanne;
2. that she accepts the offered price of 115,000 francs payable to her;
3. that the canton pays the packing costs and transportation fees up to 3,000 francs, the rest payable by Mme. Clément;
4. that all frames are included in the sale price;
5. that the collection must be delivered to Lausanne by 1 June 1908, with any delay penalized at 4% of the price per year.[1173]

These conditions were not approved by the Grand Conseil until 15 May 1908, two weeks before the deadline,[1174] and a check was drawn to Mme. Clément's name. One week later, Bonjour again went to Garches to supervise personally the packing and transport. The removal of the works from the house began on 25 May. The following day, the entire collection was crated in six large wooden containers and sent to Lausanne, arriving there on 31 May, the day before the penalty deadline. Shortly afterwards, an inventory was taken, showing a total of 368 works — ten short of the first inventory.[1175] The average price per work was therefore 312 francs.

This enormous deposit of Gleyre's works was augmented further by three additional gifts, this time from Mathilde Gleyre's own private collection. The first of these was made in 1911 on the initiative of Mathilde herself, who was then almost seventy years old and in ill health.[1176] Her

1171. The basic information on the negotiations and subsequent sale is taken from various reports Bonjour made to his superiors in Lausanne, MCBA, Bonjour, "Copies de lettres," II, 1907, pp. 302f., and MCBA, GA 1026 and GA 1027.
1172. I found no record that Grasset undertook the task, nor has the report on the value and condition of the collection been found.
1173. Lausanne, MCBA, GA 1026.
1174. See ibid., decree n° 760.
1175. The inventory of the sale is in Lausanne, MCBA, GA 1027.
1176. The basic documentation on the gift, as well as the inventory of its contents, is in Lausanne, MCBA, GA 1017. Mathilde's intention to donate some works in her collection is noted in a letter to Bonjour of 5 September 1911.

gift consisted of nine works, including three oil studies and a copy of Gleyre's self-portrait of 1841; Mathilde could not send the original self-portrait because it was willed to the Louvre, and she therefore had a copy executed at her own expense. The canton sent Mathilde an official letter of gratitude on 7 October 1911. On 1 December, these works were crated in her apartment at 16 rue de Moscou.

Five years later, Mathilde, gravely ill, was forced to leave her apartment, entering the Couvent des Espérances in Versailles. Through her companion and secretary, Mlle. Pape-Carpentier, she indicated her desire to donate another five works to the museum, including Cornu's youthful portrait of Gleyre.[1177] These works were sent in a Swiss diplomatic pouch because of the war, arriving first in Neuchâtel, from where they were sent on to Lausanne on 28 January 1917. One month later, Mathilde died in the convent in Versailles. There were various legal questions concerning her estate — she had never married — but it was clear that her intention, although not directly stated, was to donate the rest of her inheritance from her uncle, including the letters, to Lausanne.[1178] The legal questions were not wholly resolved until the fall and the crating and shipment of works to Lausanne did not begin until 3 January 1918. The crate containing the rest of her holdings arrived in Lausanne three weeks later: it contained forty works as well as Gleyre's letters and the two diaries from the Italian and Egyptian trips. By the end of World War I, the collection of Gleyre's works in Lausanne amounted to almost 450 items.

## CLÉMENT'S BIOGRAPHY AND CATALOGUE

The growth of Gleyre's celebrity after his death was substantially aided by two publications. In 1875, at the urging of Clément, the photographic firm of Braun issued a portfolio of reproductions of Gleyre's major works in public and private collections that made these paintings accessible to the critics and public alike for the first time. Clément recognized the importance of this publication, especially in respect to Gleyre's works executed after 1849 when so few of his paintings were exhibited.[1179] He predicted that the public would recognize Gleyre's artistic achievement as connoisseurs and respected collectors already had.

The second publication was Clément's own monograph, published in its first edition in 1878 in Paris and Switzerland simultaneously. As early as August 1874 Fritz Berthoud noted that Clément wanted to devote his fullest efforts to his monograph.[1180] Almost immediately after Gleyre's death he began to enlist the help of friends and associates in gathering letters, information, recollections, and other details. He even asked Olivier to contribute to the sections devoted to the histories of Davel and the second Vaudois commission, as well as to write his own personal memories of the special relationship he had with Gleyre for almost thity years.[1181] Within three years, Clément collected primary documents, ma-

1177. See the letter from Mlle. Pape-Carpentier to Bonjour of 6 December 1917, recorded in Lausanne, MCBA, Bonjour, "Copies de lettres," IV, 1917, unpaginated.
1178. Much of the information on this donation is in Lausanne, MCBA, GA, 1020.
1179. Clément 1876, pp. 332f. Clément's negotiations with Braun are contained in a dossier in Fleurier, CFC. Of particular interest are Braun's letters to Clément delineating the difficulties in locating some of Gleyre's works Clément wished to photograph.
1180. In Lausanne, BCU/DM, Tallichet, "Correspondance," IS 193. The implication in the letter is that Tallichet wanted an article on Gleyre by Clément.
1181. Olivier recounted this to Berthoud in a letter of November 1874 in Fleurier, CFC. It might be added that Olivier was reluctant to comply because of his age and failing health; it is not known whether he in fact provided Clément with the information he requested, either in written form or orally, although he must have discussed it at various times during the course of Clément's efforts.

jor salon reviews, a myriad of recollections from Olivier, Mme. Cornu, Mathilde, Nanteuil, and dozens of other friends.[1182] He also used and often quoted at length from the letters and diaries in Mathilde's collection. Of major importance was Clément's persistence in establishing a catalogue raisonné of the work, which he divided into six categories. Through his friends, he assembled data on dates and measurements, especially for works he could not see.[1183] While there are errors and clear omissions in the catalogue section — these are noted in the catalogue that follows — Clément's work was an astonishing enterprise. His catalogue of 683 items, including thirty Braun illustrations, remains the basis of our knowledge of Gleyre's œuvre. A second edition, slightly revised, appeared in 1886, but without the Braun illustrations.

But even though the public had prints and photographs of Gleyre's work available, as well as a detailed biography, they could not easily see his paintings first hand. After the memorial exhibition in Lausanne in 1874, no major retrospective of his work was planned or mounted until the centenary of his death. In Paris, where Gleyre spent his active years and taught an entire generation of students, there has never been an exhibition of his works, except in a special exhibit mounted at the Ecole des Beaux-Arts in 1884 where sixteen works were shown.[1184] By the end of World War I, the Musée Cantonal des Beaux-Arts in Lausanne displayed a large number of the Gleyre's works acquired through the Clément sale in the newly created Salle Gleyre, but that was disbanded some two decades later in favor of exhibiting other works that had subsequently entered the collection. Most of the drawings and watercolors were never seen by the public because of the difficulty of framing and showing them. A small exhibition in the Château of La Sarraz in 1958 showed a selection of Gleyre's drawings in relation to his important students — it was here that the Geneva sketchbooks were shown for the only time in public — but the exhibition had only a checklist of the works mounted and no historical examination of their importance.[1185] The only exhibition of Gleyre's works in America was in 1980, when a selection of the watercolors executed for his American patron, John Lowell, was mounted; these were never seen in Europe.

## BURIAL SITES

Finally, the matter of Gleyre's burial site must be mentioned here. After the funeral ceremony in Chevilly on 17 May 1874, it was thought that a permanent monument to the painter should be erected there to honor his contributions, but neither the cantonal nor village authorities acted at the time. Moreover, both Clément and Mathilde Gleyre felt that the isolated situation of the village would prevent the official recognition for which they had hoped.[1186] No action was taken until the summer of 1894, when Gleyre's nieces sent a collective request to the canton to have Gleyre's remains transferred to a more suitable site.[1187] In May 1895, the

1182. These letters are scattered in various dossiers in Fleurier, CFC. Clément, however, as has been noted, did not use all the information given to him.
1183. In many instances, Clément asked friends to trace works for him, relying, sometimes entirely, on the descriptions provided, as is seen in the letters he received, now in Fleurier, CFC. Often, too, there were questions from his friends as to how works should be measured. Thus in some instances, the page of the drawing is used as the basis for the measurements, while other times, the drawing itself is measured at its highest and widest points. Sometimes Clément only took approximate dimensions without indicating them as such.
1184. *Catalogue des dessins* 1884, n° 335–50.
1185. *Dessins d'il y a cent ans*, 1958.
1186. Olivier recounted this to Caroline after a discussion with Clément, in a letter of 21 May 1874; see Lausanne, BCU/DM, Fonds Olivier, IS 1905/47.
1187. B[achelin] 1898, p. 305, and Bonjour 1896, p. 177.

authorities approved the motion to transfer the body to the cemetery of La Sallaz in the northern section of Lausanne — precisely, as it happened, to the site that had been recommended in 1874.[1188] The administrative officials of Chevilly balked at the idea of losing their most celebrated site, but they were overruled by the canton who wished to accede to the nieces' requests.

Gleyre's body was thus transferred to a plot in Lausanne between the philosopher Charles Secrétan and the British Major-General Atlay, who had died in Lausanne. The formal ceremony at the grave took place on 21 September 1895, with speeches by Dr. Larguier, whose portrait Gleyre had executed twice in 1871, Cérésole, and the syndic Cuénod; only a few friends and admirers attended. The municipality had commissioned a small grave marker from the firm Imperali, consisting of a gray marble tablet resting on four supports; another white tablet was inscribed with the artist's name, his birth and death dates, and the words "Le beau est la splendeur du vrai."[1189] Meanwhile in Chevilly, the local sculptor Raphaël Lugeon made a commemorative plaque to Gleyre containing a relief of his figure for *The Charmer* on the north wall of the church.[1190]

Yet, the issue of where Gleyre's remains should rest was not resolved here. During the 1920s, the cemetery at La Sallaz was abandoned by the municipality in favor of a more spacious site in Montoie. Toward the end of the decade, most of the graves had been already transferred there, but no decision was reached on what to do with Gleyre's tomb until almost twenty years later. Finally, in May 1947, his body was again exhumed and relocated in the plot at the north wall of the church in Chevilly. Thus, for the fourth time in seven decades, Gleyre's grave was disturbed in this curious odyssey which led from Paris to Chevilly to Lausanne and back to Chevilly. The final burial ceremony took place on 12 September 1947 in the presence of only a few cantonal officials.[1191]

fig. 251

251. Anonymous, Burial of Gleyre in Chevilly, 12 September 1947. Chevilly, Private collection

1188. *Nouvelliste vaudois*, 1896, p. 1.
1189. Bonjour 1896, pp. 177–78.
1190. B[achelin] 1898, p. 305.
1191. M., J., *Journal de Cossonay*, 23 May, and 19 September 1947. The photographs of the last burial were provided by an anonymous witness to the ceremony in Chevilly.

## GLEYRE'S TEACHING STUDIO

252. George Du Maurier, *The Gleyre Studio*. From Moscheles [1896], p. 18

All histories of nineteenth-century French art agree that one of Gleyre's most significant roles in the art of his times was his substantial teaching activities in the studio he formed for the purpose in 1843.[1192] From this point onward, Gleyre never ceased to maintain his interest in pedagogy until his forced absence from Paris at the outbreak of the Franco-Prussian war. Gleyre provided primary instruction to more than five hundred students, ranging from rank amateurs unrecorded in standard biographical dictionaries to the luminaries of the Impressionist movement. During its peak years, Gleyre's studio was recognized as the most desirable and progressive in Paris, but Gleyre never wrote about his teaching practices, nor, apparently, did he ever discuss them with friends or colleagues. However, on the basis of students' accounts it is possible to reconstruct the general elements that made Gleyre's studio unique as an instructional institution.

1192. Hauptman 1985(e) discusses the material upon which this chapter is based.

327

Before elaborating on the nature of Gleyre's teaching and the social structure of the studio, it is important first to situate private studios in the context of nineteenth-century instruction in art. Until the decisive reforms of 1863, the prospective student could enter the Ecole des Beaux-Arts under the eye of an acknowledged master, but formal programs of instruction, including perspective, anatomy, and elementary art history, were not generally provided.[1193] The skills necessary to the profession were acquired haphazardly or through experience without a prescribed, tested curriculum; more often than not, the student was free to use the facilities of the Ecole and benefited from corrections and advice, but hardly more. Entrance to the Ecole was assured only after passing examinations which were meant to provide proof of existing talent and basic training, as indeed was the case when Gleyre passed these examinations in 1825. The private studios, formed by celebrated painters outside of their usual activities, were meant to fill in the gaps and thus provide the elementary student the essential preparation in drawing and other areas that would help him pass the examinations. In a very real sense, the private studios served as the backbone of the art educational system; the Ecole then honed and refined the student's skills to conform to specific standards and artistic tastes.

In the flush of Gleyre's celebrity after the triumph of his *Le Soir*, he was asked by Delaroche's students to form an independent teaching studio. Up to that time, Delaroche's studio was considered one of the most important in the period of the July Monarchy, as much, it was said, for the fame of the master as for his teaching practices.[1194] Delaroche was successful in imparting his views and gaining the respect of his students — Gérôme and Couture revered him — and equally adept at training them to do well in the Prix de Rome competitions. Moreover, his studio, like that of Gleyre later, had a reputation as a training ground for students of differing artistic views, easily accommodating traditionalists such as Hamon, Jalabert, and Hébert, as well as vanguard painters such as Millet, Daubigny, and Monticelli. Delaroche had inherited Gros's studio at the Institut de France and continued the tradition ostensibly befitting the location. The studio space was divided into two sections, one for working with the collection of plaster casts, the *bosses*, the other, a larger space for working with the live model.[1195] Delaroche, as was customary in all the private studios, came twice a week for criticism and correction, at times assigning specific compositions or themes; sometimes he lectured only. When he criticized students' work, he was inclined to be impatient and sometimes embarrassed an individual student in front of the others, particularly because of his loud, harsh voice. Millet complained once that Delaroche was adept at criticizing but rarely explained his basic ideals.[1196]

Delaroche, like his contemporaries, almost never provided individual instruction. His teaching was geared to the group in general terms rather than focused on specific problems or directed toward the individual student. This was perhaps because at times the studio was overcrowded — in 1839 there were 85 students enrolled[1197] — but it is also a reflection

1193. The basic text on instruction in art during this period is still Boime 1971, pp. 22–23. On the reforms in general, see pp. 181–84, but see also the actual text of the reform as discussed in Chesneau 1864.

1194. Soubiès 1904–15, II, pp. 169f.

1195. Ribeyre 1884, pp. 59–60; Reinaud 1903, pp. 1–2.

1196. Sensier 1881, pp. 59–60; see also Cartwright 1910, pp. 54–55.

1197. Reinaud 1903, p. 11, citing a letter from Jalabert to his mother in which this figure is noted.

of Delaroche's own reserve and the accepted social structure of the teaching studios, which forbade even the use of the familiar form of address when speaking to the master. Nevertheless, on occasion Delaroche was known to help favored students with their assignments and, later, in the advancement of their careers. He was also known sometimes to waive the fees for deserving but underprivileged students, as he did for Millet on the condition that he never mention it to the others so as to avoid the possibility of jealousy.[1198] In general, Delaroche's teaching was based on traditional values and methods that most students could have acquired elsewhere.

Delaroche abandoned the studio in 1843 because of a series of pranks, or *blagues*, which ended tragically and thus severely compromised the reputation of the studio. Normally a new student was subject to hazing as part of the rite of initiation into the studio.[1199] The hazing was meant to embarrass the newcomer slightly and to provide a form of amusement for the regulars, but also indirectly to allude to the social difference between the beginners and the established members. An example of hazing common in Delaroche's studio involved the impersonation of the master, often played by Cham, the future caricaturist. When a new student arrived, Cham, playing his part perfectly since he resembled Delaroche physically, asked the newcomer to disrobe in front of the others so as to point out blatant flaws in anatomy.[1200] Afterwards, when the charade was revealed, the newcomer was expected to purchase refreshment for the whole group, the traditional *bienvenue*, as a sign of his acceptance. Failure to do so, or even resistance, could result in ridicule or expulsion from the group. Whistler recalled that when he was in Gleyre's studio an unpopular student was forced to leave after an open coffin was placed near his easel.[1201]

The incident that persuaded Delaroche to close the studio is known in several versions, all involving the gregarious Cham. One version has it that Cham had challenged a new student to a mock duel over a trumped-up argument, and the student was either killed or died of fright.[1202] Another version notes that a student was hung upside down on a ladder — a favorite hazing prank in the studios — and died as a result of a blood clot, while a third version relates that a student was held too close to a burning stove and died several days later.[1203] Whatever the true story, Delaroche was furious when he heard of the student's death and, on advice from the police chief, closed the studio to avoid further scandal.[1204] The students protested vigorously but to no avail; by 12 July 1843, Delaroche noted in a letter that he had already abandoned his teaching activities and was preparing to leave for Italy. Many students had already left for their annual summer holidays and were surprised to find the studio closed upon their return. Gérôme wrote to his father on 11 October that the studio was indeed closed for good and that "une vingtaine d'élèves se sont mis sous la direction de M. Glaire [sic]; c'est le noyau d'un nouvel atelier qui va se former."[1205]

As we noted earlier, it is not certain how well Delaroche and Gleyre actually knew each other or how the former aided the latter when he

1198. Sensier 1881, p. 64.
1199. Chaud-Aigues 1841–42, I, pp. 53–54.
1200. Moreau-Vauthier 1906, p. 25, but the incident is understandably not mentioned in Ribeyre's biography of Cham.
1201. Pennell 1911, I, p. 49. Whistler noted that these *blagues* were often foolish pranks that had to be shrugged off as necessary evils in the studio system.
1202. Dubosc n.d., pp. 147–48. Gustave Crauk (1827–1905) was a sculptor who had worked with Pradier; the memoirs he edited were of the model Dubosc who was extremely well known in the studios.
1203. See Ribeyre 1884, pp. 66–71, and Prinsep 1904, p. 338.
1204. Ribeyre 1884, p. 75. The police inspector, Gabriel Delessert, had already been called numerous times because of student disturbances.
1205. Moreau-Vauthier 1906, p. 52. See also Ziff 1977, p. 207.

253. Auguste Bachelin, *Entrance to Gleyre's Studio.*
From a letter to Edouard Perrochet, 5 May 1850.
Neuchâtel, Bibliothèque de la Ville

returned to France in 1838 after his voyage with Lowell. It is probable that Gleyre sought his aid through Vernet, Delaroche's father-in-law, and received several commissions through Delaroche's intervention, including the *Plutarque français* and Dampierre commissions. But it was certainly Gleyre's success in the salon of 1843 that most impressed Delaroche, precisely because *Le Soir* showed an independent path between academic and romantic sensibilities in accord with Delaroche's own precepts. Despite his reputation as a staunch Academician, Delaroche had a liberal mind and was given to expressing his distaste for the official line. After 1837 he refused to exhibit in the salons; in 1836 and again in 1843 he refused to participate in jury decisions as a protest again the favoritism that prevailed.[1206] He no doubt recognized a kindred spirit in Gleyre and thus must have suggested to his students that they seek him out. Even though Gleyre had no experience in teaching, preferred his own self-absorbed artistic world, and did not seek to augment his reputation, he nevertheless launched a pedagogical enterprise that would last almost a quarter of a century.

Gleyre could not occupy Delaroche's old quarters at the Institute since that privilege was strictly reserved for members of the Academy. He therefore told these twenty-some students mentioned by Gérôme to rent a studio as a group with each student paying a proportional share of the rent. The location of the studio in the winter of 1843 was on the rue d'Erfurth, although the exact address seems not to have been recorded.[1207] By 1850, for unknown reasons, the studio was moved to 36 rue de l'Ouest, where it was registered under the name of the studio head, the *massier* charged with the running of the day-to-day affairs, who then was Louis Schuller.[1208] In 1859, the teaching studio again was moved, this time to 69 rue de Vaugirard where the student head was François Ehrmann.[1209] It was here that the major Impressionists studied in the early 1860s.

1206. Ibid., pp. 165–66. On his refusal to serve in 1843, see Paris, AL, Rapport, KK⁶⁰.
1207. The street is known from a letter addressed to Gleyre on 31 July 1849 from a Mr. Beauvais: "M. Gleyre, peintre/rue d'Erfurth." The letter is in Lausanne, MCBA, GA 996.
1208. Godet 1893, p. 21.
1209. The exact date of the third atelier comes from the unpublished diary of John Pradier, a student of Gleyre's and the son of the famous sculptor, who noted on 17 February 1874, "l'atelier des élèves de M. Gleyre, 69, rue Vaugirard." This information was given me by Mr. Douglas Siler, who is preparing the Pradier letters and journals for publication.

No descriptions of the first studio have survived, but the second one was vividly evoked by Gleyre's Swiss student Auguste Bachelin, who arrived there on 7 May 1850.[1210] The building itself, recently constructed, housed various other studios, those of Tabar, Mathout, Ottin, and the sculptor Duseigneur; Bonvin occupied one later. Gleyre's studio, containing a large uninterrupted space, was on the ground floor. The entrance was covered by a large curtain that had to be lifted to permit

fig. 253    access, a detail Bachelin illustrated in a letter.[1211] A large window about fifteen feet from the ground provided the main source of light, although apparently it was rarely cleaned and therefore the lighting in the interior was often less than ideal. Opposite the door and curtain was a large wall where the model stand was placed, with a stove nearby, always lit, to heat the area. A skeleton was suspended alongside the stand to allow study and comparison. A series of casts after antique sculpture hung on the main wall, which itself was frequently covered with graffiti, paint rubbings, and various caricatures. Low stools were placed in a semicircle around the model stand, with easels arranged in graduated heights so as not to hinder the view of the pose.

Another, slightly disguised, description of the studio exists in George Du Maurier's novel of bohemian artistic life, *Trilby*, published in 1894. While many of the incidents and events represented here are fictional, some of the anecdotes derive from Du Maurier's stay in the Gleyre studio in 1856, as well as from those he heard from other English students there. In the novel, Gleyre is the model for the character Carrel, while the physical descriptions of the studio interior accord with Bachelin's memory, including the polychromed wall that Du Maurier thought not disagreeable, and the arrangement of the low stools.[1212] Du Maurier's illustrations of his student days with Gleyre were done almost forty years later and are no doubt influenced by his imagination. However, one drawing by Du Maurier in a letter to his friend Felix Moscheles, the son of the famous composer and pianist Ignaz Moscheles and a previously unrecorded student of Gleyre, provides a reliable picture of the everyday task

fig. 252    of working from the model.[1213]

The daily routine in Gleyre's studio followed that of most of the other private studios in Paris. Work began in the morning when light was best and continued until about noon. Albert de Meuron, writing about the first studio on the rue d'Erfurth which he entered 26 October 1845, noted that most students arrived before eight and stayed until well after one. Bachelin wrote that it was customary for students to continue their studies in the afternoon in their own studios or to go to the Louvre for copying exercises. These practices continued well into the 1860s, as noted by Albert Darier, a student from Geneva. In some instances, students were permitted to return to the studio in the evening to reexamine drawings made in the morning, while many preferred to make additional studies at the Ecole de Médecine where special courses and cadavers were prepared for the purpose. This routine continued six days a week with the traditional holiday periods free; in late 1863, when the studio was in difficult financial straits, it functioned only Monday through Thursday.[1214]

1210. The description is in Bachelin 1889, pp. 543–44, in regard to the entry of Frédéric Simon into Gleyre's studio. On Bachelin's entry into the studio, see his letters in Neuchâtel, AE, Fonds Bachelin, Ms. 1747.
1211. The drawing is in a letter from Bachelin to Edouard Perrochet, Neuchâtel, AE, Fonds Bachelin, Ms. 1791ᴬ, dossier 1.
1212. Du Maurier 1895, pp. 75–76. George du Maurier's English friends included Armstrong, Poynter, Lamont, Prinsep, and others. Whistler originally appeared as the character Joe Sibley in the serialized version of the novel in *Harper's Monthly Magazine*, but Whistler was so incensed at the unflattering portrait that the character was changed for the book, and is now known as Anthony. On the importance of the novel, see Ormond 1969, pp. 34–35.
1213. The drawing remains untraced but is reproduced in Moscheles.
1214. Neuchâtel, AE, Fonds de Pury, VI, dossier 11, letter of 9–14 December, 1863. Edmond de Pury, who entered Gleyre's studio in late 1863, noted at this time that Fridays and Saturdays were left free for students to pursue their own interests. On the routine in Gleyre's studio discussed above, see also a letter of 23 May 1850, in Neuchâtel, AE, Fonds Bachelin, Ms. 1747; Milliet 1915, p. 237; letters of 26 October and 2 November 1845, from Alfred de Meuron to his father in Neuchâtel, AE, Fonds de Meuron, dossier 68¹; and other letters from this period by de Pury in the Fonds de Pury.

Certain practices in Gleyre's teaching studio were highly unusual. Gleyre never charged a fee for his teaching services at a time when these studios provided a firm financial base for dozens of established painters.[1215] Gleyre's decision to conduct a free studio was, curiously, one of his stipulations in accepting Delaroche's students and was certainly prompted by memories of his own student years when he had to pay Hersent thirty francs a month for his services. The savings accrued by a student in Gleyre's studio could be considerable: Anker wrote to his aunt in 1858 that his annual rent for lodging in Paris amounted to fifty francs, which was the equivalent of only two months of training in most studios.[1216] The only fee Gleyre expected of his students was an equitable share in the rental of the studio and the model. The money was always collected by the student head and never by the master, reflecting Gleyre's uneasiness about financial matters.[1217] Since there were normally between twenty-five and thirty students in the studio at one time — although that figure could double in the period preceding the Ecole examinations — the expenses remained constant and predictable. When Bazille entered the studio in late 1862, he itemized his expenses in a letter to his parents: thirty francs were paid as a one-time entrance fee giving the student the right to use the materials, ten francs for the monthly rent, and an additional fifteen francs for beer and punch for the *bienvenue*.[1218]

Gleyre insisted that each student concentrate at first on acquiring a firm foundation in ancient art, but not necessarily in the dry form often practiced by the traditional academicians. De Meuron noted that Gleyre stressed the essentials of Classical antiquity as rooted in nature and Greek art rather than its reinterpretation by the Davidian school. Similarly, when Bachelin had his first meeting with Gleyre in 1850, before his formal entry into the studio, Gleyre advised him not to copy immediately from the masters in the Louvre, but rather to draw from nature first; thus, he would better know and appreciate the true spirit of the antique.[1219] One cannot help but think of Gleyre's own reactions when he first saw the great ruins of Classical antiquity in Athens, which were nothing less than a revelation for him after years of knowing them only through artistic interpretations in the manner of David or Ingres.

With the ideological emphasis firmly placed on studies after nature, the role of the live model became especially important in the teaching process. To be sure, Gleyre stressed accurate depictions of the model and particularly the anatomy since this training was the basis for further interpretation. Gleyre noted that since all students draw from the model, the very act could become banal; the student should consider anew each model, who ultimately offers different challenges and possibilities. De Meuron, who had already worked in Düsseldorf before coming to Paris, remarked that Gleyre's attitude toward drawing from the model differed from that of his German teachers: the latter emphasized clinically memorizing the parts of anatomy that could later be reconstructed at will, while Gleyre stressed the significance of studying each model for its individuality.[1220] If the student should need particular help in difficult poses or further information on anatomical configuration, the skeleton hung

1215. Boime 1971, pp. 52–53, provides examples of typical studio fees. It seems that only the sculptor David d'Angers did not charge a teaching fee; see Péladan 1908, p. 624.

1216. Quinche-Anker 1924, p. 46. Breton 1890, p. 197, noted that his first studio cost him 350 francs which would have amounted to about a year's instruction.

1217. See letter of 5 May 1850, in Neuchâtel, AE, Fonds Bachelin, Ms. 1791^A, dossier 1.

1218. Poulain 1932, p. 18; these figures are confirmed in Milliet 1915, p. 237.

1219. See Godet 1893, pp. 20–21; see also a letter of 19 May 1847, in Neuchâtel, AE, Fonds de Meuron, dossier 68^1, cited in part in Godet 1901, p. 127.

1220. See letters of 11 February 1846 and 10 December 1845 in Neuchâtel, AE, Fonds de Meuron, dossier 68^1. De Meuron noted on 7 June 1846 that Gleyre disliked German painting and therefore German instruction as well.

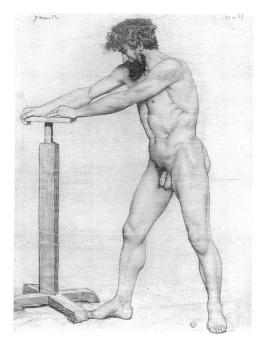
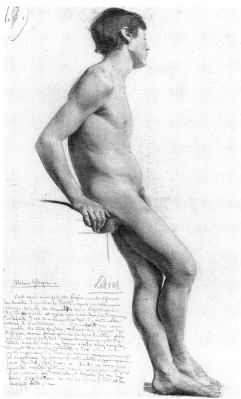

254. Frédéric Bazille, *Study of a Model*, 1863. Montpellier, Musée Fabre
255. Friedrich Walthard, *Study of a Model*, 1845. Bern, Private collection

nearby. In effect, the skeleton provided the essential foundation for the pose, while the model provided the stimulus for individual expression.

fig. 254 There are, however, relatively few examples of these model studies extant. A drawing by Bazille of 7 March 1863 provides a case in point.[1221] While the pose of the model is standard, the drawing clearly attempts to go beyond the purely academic exercise often seen in contemporary works by other students. The drawing also shows the care with which Bazille interpreted the pose and includes the various erasures to insure accuracy and fluidity of the line. An even more instructive drawing is one of 1845 of the model Lebras by Friedrich Walthard, one of Gleyre's first Swiss students. Walthard noted at the left, in his imperfect French, some of the salient points of Gleyre's criticism, especially the fact that the harmony between the mass and the detail was less successful than hoped for. Walthard added, however, that the drawing was still admired by Gleyre, who agreed that he was ready to begin working in color, thus advancing in the training process.[1222]

Both male and female models were used, depending on the required exercises. Du Maurier noted in *Trilby* that it was customary in Carrel's studio to alternate male and female models each week,[1223] although it is more likely, as in other studios, that each model stayed for two-week periods. The models were generally chosen by the student head, but it is known that Gleyre was timid about permitting male models to pose when female students were present. Renoir recalled one incident in which a young Englishwoman, one of three in the studio at the time, was drawing from the nude model when Gleyre came for his consultations. He

1221. Daulte 1952, pp. 15, 193; and Marandel 1978, pp. 34–35, cat. n° 1–2.
1222. The transcription of Walthard's notes at the left of the drawing is in Staiger-Gayler 1974, p. 135. The basic study of Friedrich Walthard, including many of his letters, is Walthard 1966, pp. 11f. He first studied with Menn, and then with Gleyre after November 1844. My thanks to Bernard Walthard who shared his family documents with me.
1223. Du Maurier 1895, pp. 75–76.

immediately ordered the model to put on his underwear, to the conster-
nation of the student. She told Gleyre in private that she had a French
lover and therefore was hardly offended by the nudity. Gleyre, however,
insisted since, he said, he had to protect the other students as well as his
reputation in the neighborhood.[1224]

Female models, on the other hand, were frequently subject to sport or
even abuse when Gleyre was not present. Paul Milliet, who had pronounced liberal tendencies, wrote to his friend Jules Nicole that female
models were often degraded with insults or obscene jokes, especially those
of the lower classes who were forced to earn their income in the insecure
trade of the studio model.[1225] Sisley was guilty of abusing the models on
numerous occasions. He was known to inspect the intimate parts of the
female body closely, claiming it was essential to the truth of his artistic
expression: once he was discovered by Gleyre applying red paint to the
model's nipples.[1226] Milliet noted as well that the student head sometimes hired adolescent girls, much to his disgust, since he thought this a
blatant exploitation of the poor.[1227] But Milliet noted also that Gleyre
himself never sanctioned this practice.

All sources remark that Gleyre's fashion of conducting the teaching
studio was distinctly unconventional. His studio structure was conceived
in accord with his political philosophy, on a republican basis which eliminated the formal and artificial protocol that existed elsewhere, as in Ary
Scheffer's studio where students were expected to rise when the master
came in for corrections and remain standing until told to be seated.[1228]
In Gleyre's studio, students were responsible through appointed committees for the day-to-day matters, including vacation time and the actual hours the studio functioned.[1229] Gleyre was regarded as a member of
the group but was treated with respect and always addressed as "le patron." Students themselves were often called by adopted nicknames such
as "le Cayenne," after the penal colony where one student's father was an
official; "Veronese," a sarcastic title given to another student because his
colors were always the opposite of those used by the Venetian painter; or
"Sucredolski," a corruption of sucre d'orge, given to a Polish student whose
real name was thought unpronounceable.[1230]

Gleyre came to the studio twice a week, usually on Monday and Thursday, to inspect the students' work. He always entered unannounced and
spoke in a soft voice so as not to disturb the students at work. He made it
a point to inspect each work individually, a rarity in the teaching system,
giving his personal advice on each exercise.[1231] His comments could be
severe but they were never considered unjust. His special encouragement
went to students who were disciplined and worked honestly, even if the
results were not always the best.[1232] On rare occasions he praised individual initiative in front of the other students, as he did when Bazille had
the idea of drawing the model life-size on a huge sheet of paper,[1233] but
most often counsel was given privately in methodical consultations. De
Meuron remembered that Gleyre's advice was presented calmly and simply, always approaching the essentials of the problem.[1234] Jean-Louis
Hamon remarked that Gleyre exhibited great patience in never refusing

1224. Renoir 1962, p. 102.
1225. Milliet 1915, p. 241.
1226. Renoir 1962, p. 108. Monet too was known
to have inspected the model's skin closely. In a letter to George Moore in 1922, William Mark Fisher,
an American student who came to Gleyre's studio
in 1863, said that most Americans went to Couture,
but an unnamed German-American student suggested Gleyre instead. On Sisley, Fisher noted: "I
never saw him doing any work there [in Gleyre's
studio]." On Fisher, see Weinberg 1991, p. 62.
Lines 1966, p. 19, cites Fisher's memoirs regarding
Sisley's working habits.
1227. Milliet 1915, p. 241. Milliet recounted in a
letter of 10 September 1863 that the model they had
a week earlier was only eleven years old and forced
to pose to earn her living.
1228. Armstrong 1912, p. 4.
1229. See a letter of 17 August 1850, in Neuchâtel,
AE, Fonds Bachelin, Ms. 1791A.
1230. Perdicaris 1867, p. 648.
1231. Virtually every memoir of the Gleyre's atelier stresses this as a distinct trait of Gleyre's teaching method.
1232. Milliet 1915, p. 236, in a letter from Albert
Darier to Milliet of 22 March 1863.
1233. Marandel 1978, p. 191, cites the entire letter in which the drawing is discussed; Poulain 1932,
p. 29, provides only an excerpt, omitting Gleyre's
praise for Bazille's initiative.
1234. See a letter of 10 December 1845 in which
he lauded Gleyre's methods of corrections in the
studio; Neuchâtel, AE, Fonds de Meuron, dossier
68¹. This is repeated later in another letter of
28 January 1846.

to explain difficult points.[1235] An Alsatian student, Henri Zuber, who entered the studio just before it closed, commented that Gleyre's recommendations were pointed and profound, providing substantial food for thought afterwards: "On ne sortait jamais de chez lui sans que la pensée eût été remuée par la parole bienveillante et incisive."[1236]

Beside providing a firm foundation in drawing in the studio, Gleyre also advocated a program of work outside the confines of daily studio exercises. This could encompass copying from select examples in the Louvre or sketching out of doors, fully in accord with Gleyre's insistence on using nature as the basic artistic dictionary. Moreover, Gleyre recommended drawing from memory exercises already completed in the studio, a practice not unique to Gleyre, but one that was hardly followed elsewhere with regularity.[1237] Hamon frequently drew from models and from memory in his room, bringing these efforts for Gleyre's inspection later. Gleyre often remarked that these drawings were superior to those executed in the studio, showing a greater invention and freshness.[1238] Hamon remarked that it was common for students to draw together in their own rooms after classes, with some students taking the role of the model while others criticized.[1239]

Gleyre's teaching also stressed the importance of composition and proportion.[1240] To aid in these crucial areas of instruction, Gleyre assigned recommended subjects or themes as exercises, generally to be sketched in a two-week period, although these, in the liberal spirit of the studio, were not required; the student was free to select other themes more appropriate to his needs or desires.[1241] If problems persisted in the execution of these, Gleyre encouraged the student to make changes. In this way, Gleyre assured each student that the progress made was indeed his own, a practice that contrasted with many other teaching studios where the corrections were made by the master in charge or an advanced student.[1242]

Since the program was founded on drawing, students were permitted to take up brushes only when Gleyre felt they were ready to do so. The time spent wholly in drawing varied depending on the student's progress in acquiring the necessary technique. Bachelin noted that he spent at least seven months following Gleyre's program of drawing from the model before he could begin working in color; Bazille wrote that he drew five months before working in oils.[1243] As de Meuron wrote to his father, Gleyre never mentioned color or painting technique until he felt the student prepared to absorb this aspect of his education.[1244]

But when this stage was reached, Gleyre introduced the student to the philosophy of color with special emphasis on the importance of realizing the rough sketch as a crucial step toward the final product. Gleyre would compliment the student if he was able to visualize his artistic idea adequately in the initial rough sketch, no matter how hasty or crude this might be. To help students realize their painterly ideas, Gleyre stressed preparing the palette before each stage of development. Anker explained that the basic tones were assembled in small packets of color; for the figure, these would be the general flesh tones and an amber base. The question of color, in other words, would be partially resolved before the

1235. Hoffman 1903, p. 55.
1236. In a letter to his mother, dated 11 May 1874, Zuber, having heard of Gleyre's death, related his experience with him. The letter was kindly transmitted to me by Claude Zuber from his family archives.
1237. Gleyre was known to follow the ideas of Lecoq de Boisbaudran, whose treatise on memory drawing was published in 1848.
1238. Hoffman 1903, p. 54.
1239. Menaud cites Hamon's experiences working with Walthard as described here, but I found no corroboration in the Walthard papers in Bern. However, the Walthard collection contains his portrait of Hamon of 1845 with an inscription noting their close relationship.
1240. Milliet 1915, pp. 236f.
1241. In a letter of 22 March 1863, Albert Darier told Milliet that some of the suggested themes were "The Banquet of Plato," "Joseph and Potiphar," and "Ruth and Boaz"; see Milliet 1915, p. 236.
1242. Lethève 1972, p. 16; on Couture's corrections, see Boime 1980, p. 449.
1243. See Marandel 1978, p. 192: the letter is not dated here, but Wildenstein 1974, I, p. 23, note 116, cites the same letter, dating it 1 March 1863, thus at least five months after Bazille's entry into the studio. See also Neuchâtel, AE, Fonds Bachelin, Ms. 1791A, dossier 1.
1244. De Meuron noted in a letter of 2 November 1845 that of the twenty students in the studio at the time, only six actually worked with color; see Neuchâtel, AE, Fonds de Meuron, dossier 68¹.

256. Albert de Meuron, *David*, 1846–47. Neuchâtel, Musée d'Art et d'Histoire

1245. Clément, pp. 175–76; Quinche-Anker 1924, p. 36.
1246. See Armstrong 1912, p. 190; Pennell 1911, II, pp. 49–50. Both note Whistler's erratic attendance.
1247. All of the following material comes from de Meuron's letters in Neuchâtel, AE, Fonds de Meuron, doss. 44¹, 68¹, and 72¹¹, which also include comments from de Meuron's father to him.

student actually began his work, so that the prepared colors on the palette would allow him to concentrate on his composition.[1245] Anker added that Gleyre preached the importance of ivory black as the base of all tones. Whistler, who studied with Gleyre irregularly and often denied the influence of Gleyre in his formation, nevertheless followed this practice throughout his career in the preparation of his palette and in the use of black tones.[1246]

A good example of how Gleyre advised and encouraged students in painting can be seen in de Meuron's letters describing the development of his first Parisian oil, *David*. Since de Meuron had already had some experience in Düsseldorf, he was permitted to advance to painting earlier than others. By spring 1846, de Meuron had already completed an oil study of the work and had shown it to Gleyre for comment. Gleyre told de Meuron not to rush the work, to follow a prescribed plan in bringing it to completion so as to insure that the results were intended rather than accidental. He noted the importance of first having a finished nude for the main figure, of transferring it *aux carreaux*, of rendering the rough study after the drawing so that the idea of the composition is fully expressed, and then completing it by relying on direct observation of the model.[1247] Gleyre even told de Meuron that he preferred to inspect each stage of this process, and if necessary, he would come to de Meuron's private studio to supervise.

fig. 256

De Meuron began in fact to develop the composition according to Gleyre's system and was ready to ask Gleyre's advice by 23 April. Further sessions continued on 9 May and again on 23 May. However, on 7 June, de Meuron wrote that in spite of this previous advice Gleyre had misgivings about the result and thought the study should be redone. Again Gleyre told de Meuron not to rush, noting that it was not uncommon to devote weeks to achieving the proper relationships between forms and colors. Presumably de Meuron followed this advice, but there are no further comments about the progress of the work in his correspondence with his father. But on 14 January 1847, de Meuron wrote to Léon Berthoud, himself a prominent landscapist, that there were indeed many difficulties in developing the painting, due in fact to his German training, which he now found inadequate. It seems apparent that Gleyre's insistence stemmed from his belief that de Meuron's German instruction had to be undone before he could truly advance. De Meuron informed Berthoud that if he were to have any success as a painter, it would be thanks to Gleyre and his ideal of liberating creativity by thought and method. De Meuron did not finish the work until spring of 1847.[1248] Gleyre continued to aid de Meuron in his next painting, *Nymphs Surprised by a Fawn*, begun in May 1847, through bi-monthly meetings until 1848.

One of Gleyre's most distinctive qualities as a teacher was his refusal to impose blindly any specific stylistic system on his students once they had developed their base in drawing. As a result, Gleyre's students were noted for their individuality, a trait that substantially differentiated their work from that of other studios. Bachelin actually claimed that he could distinguish the work of Gleyre's students precisely because it hardly mirrored the master's style. Hamon went further in noting that throughout the teaching process, Gleyre instilled a true horror of imitation; great art, he taught, was a result of experience and imagination, not stylistic mimicry. Gleyre told Bachelin that the artist should in fact strive to have the widest possible experience so that his artistic personality could be better expressed, meaning a wide education in travel, literature, and all aspects of culture. It is no wonder that Renoir could so easily praise Gleyre's initiative in instilling these notions in his students. Furthermore, as if to emphasize Gleyre's own liberal attitudes, Renoir wrote that while Gleyre did not actually profess the basic creed of *plein air* painting, he nevertheless encouraged these experiments and had the good sense not to interfere with those who practiced it.[1249]

The artistic freedom that was the core of the studio philosophy attracted a wide variety of students. The measure of its liberalism can be seen in the fact that the studio could accommodate painters of different artistic persuasions ranging from the purely academic students interested only in drawing instruction or a base in decorative art to the most outspoken experimentalists. Of the latter group, particularly in the early 1860s, painters such as Sisley and Renoir, to name but two prominent examples, proudly proclaimed themselves "élèves de Gleyre" when they exhibited; Renoir pronounced himself such in salon livrets well into the

1248. The painting was sold to the Société des Amis des Arts, Neuchâtel, for 500 Swiss francs; see de Meuron's own record book of his sales in Neuchâtel, AE, Fonds de Meuron, dossier 66ᵛ. Unfortunately, Berthoud's letters from this period are missing, but from de Meuron's letters, it is known that Berthoud wrote at various times apparently to encourage his efforts.
1249. Vollard 1920, p. 25: "Il [Gleyre] avait le mérite de leur [the Impressionists] laisser toute liberté." On Gleyre's encouragements of individuality in his students, see Perdicaris 1867, p. 646; Claretie 1882, I, p. 64; Godet 1893, pp. 21, 23; Hoffman 1903, p. 55; Milliet 1915, pp. 236–37f., letter of 12 December 1850.

1890s.[1250] In this light, it should also be noted that not only did Gleyre's students exhibit regularly in the salons, but no fewer than a dozen of them also exhibited in the notorious Salon des Refusés in 1863, a further indication of the diverse paths Gleyre's students selected.[1251] At no time did these students voice displeasure with Gleyre's teaching or repudiate their initial experiences in the studio, contrary to opinions often expressed in the literature.[1252]

Another reason why the studio attracted such a diverse group of students was the reputation it maintained as a politically liberal social fraternity in which opinions could be expressed openly. The English painter Val Prinsep, one of the so-called "English Gang" described so vividly in *Trilby*, remarked that at times discussions centered more on current political events than on artistic matters. When the singing of the *Marseillaise* in public was banned in the Second Empire, the anthem could be heard coming from the studio in a particularly loud and defiant way.[1253] It is fully comprehensible that the regime of the Second Empire suspected the private studios of harboring subversive political and artistic radicals. This may be one of the indirect reasons why it pushed through the reforms of 1863 which ultimately diminished the *raison d'être* for private instruction, providing instead a platform of control whereby the government could better supervise this radicalism.

Beside the liberalism that distinguished Gleyre's studio, it also had a reputation for its social activities. Students were particularly fond of creating theatrical productions, designing and making costumes and scenery in their spare time. Bazille wrote to his mother in January 1863 that the studio was preparing at the moment a ludicrous version of Dumas's play, *La Tour de Nesle*, in which even former students were taking part, including Gérôme, who would shortly be named professor at the Ecole.[1254] Invitations were sent out to friends and critics; the entrance fee was designated as one candle per seat. The production achieved a certain notoriety in Parisian circles and was even the subject of a caricature in the press showing the towering figure of Bazille at the left in the role of Sire de Pierrefonds.[1255] Later that year, Bazille informed his family that the students planned another production, this time a highly original version of *Macbeth* in which he had not planned to participate, but in which he was finally persuaded to take the role of a "danseuse," complete with a farcical tutu.[1256] At the end of the performance, songs especially written by the students were sung for the audience. Among the notables said to have been present were Baudelaire, Duranty, Champfleury, Fantin-Latour, Manet, Whistler, and Gérôme.[1257]

Since Gleyre's studio was generally free from artistic rivalry or social pressures, the traditional hazing was more humorous than malicious and at no time did it create substantial difficulties or cause police intervention. Whistler noted that one had only to be a good sport and be able to accept little jokes to be included in the group.[1258] Gleyre himself intervened when he suspected that a joke might turn nasty, as in the late 1850s when an unnamed American student was so insulted that he swore vengence by traditional American means, the six-shooter. Gleyre sent him

fig. 257

1250. As early as 1863, Sisley signed his name as an "élève de Gleyre" in a protest letter to the administration; see Paris, AN, Beaux-Arts, F²¹, 616. In the salon of 1866, Sisley also noted his affiliation, as did Renoir in 1869 and later. On Renoir's pride in being associated with Gleyre, see White 1984, pp. 13–14.

1251. The salon livret notes eleven students identifying themselves as students of Gleyre, although not all of the participants provided studio affiliation.

1252. It is common to play down the academic training of many of the Impressionists, as Daulte 1952, p. 18, who notes only that Bazille, Renoir, and Sisley passed through the studio; but see Boime 1971, p. 63. It should be noted that the admiration these artists had for Gleyre was real and intense. As Bazille noted, Gleyre was "aimé de tous ceux qui l'approchent"; see Marandel 1978, p. 195.

1253. Prinsep 1904, p. 340.

1254. Marandel 1978, p. 195; Poulain 1932, p. 21, cites the same letter but with variations in the text.

1255. The illustration, by Félix Régamey, was published in the 8 February 1863 issue and illustrates scene IX of the play.

1256. Marandel 1978, p. 183, clearly does not follow the chronological order presented here. The actual performance of the play took place around Christmas 1863, as noted in a letter from Edmond de Pury to his parents, dated 9–10 December 1863 in Neuchâtel, AE, Fonds de Pury, V, dossier 11: "Les élèves de l'atelier montent une pièce, les sorciers de Macbet [sic], qu'ils comptent donner en présence d'amis et de connaisseurs dans 3 ou 4 semaines." See also Marandel 1978, p. 193, for another letter from Bazille, clearly datable, as a result of de Pury's letter, to January 1864, noting his role in the production.

1257. Rewald 1961, p. 73.

1258. Pennell 1911, I, p. 50. Whistler wrote that he was not subject to this initiation, but this is contradicted by Prinsep 1904, p. 338.

257. Félix Régamey, *Performance in Gleyre's Studio.*
From *Le Boulevard*, 8 February 1863

to a former student, also an American, perhaps Whistler himself, who convinced him instead to buy wine for everyone in the studio to demonstrate the generosity of *les Américains à Paris*. A typical example of the harmless jokes played in Gleyre's studio was an impersonation of the *patron* who, with the Vaudois accent Gleyre must have had, would ask the newly arrived student to go to the Louvre to demand the return of the missing arms of the *Venus of Milo* so as to complete the plaster model the students normally used.[1259]

Since Gleyre himself was held in such high esteem as a member of the atelier as well as its director, students sometimes felt free to play certain jokes on him, an unimaginable practice in other teaching studios. The most outrageous practical joke was recounted by Renoir. It seems that the Dutch ambassador and his family paid a visit to the studio to determine whether it was proper for his daughter's art education. After noticing a group of drawings tacked to the wall where the sexual parts of the male models were highly exaggerated, Gleyre guided his visitors discreetly toward a private room reached by a small staircase. One of the students was in the habit of leaving on the stair a faience sculpture that looked exactly like human excrement and had done so again that day, much to Gleyre's embarrassment. Gleyre explained to his horrified guests that it was no more than a joke, reaching for the object to demonstrate that it was but a clever imitation. This time, however, "par un mystère qui ne devait jamais être éclairci," it was the real thing.[1260] It is difficult to imagine any other teacher of a private studio whose relationship with his students would have permitted such an act.

1259. These incidents are recounted in Perdicaris 1867, pp. 647–49.
1260. Renoir 1962, p. 106.

258. Louis-Mathieu Cochereau, *David's Studio at the Collège des Quatre-Nations*, 1814. Paris, Musée du Louvre

## THE STUDIO SELF-PORTRAIT

There are dozens of paintings from the nineteenth century that depict studio routines and provide portraits of students. They often have similar iconographic features and generally reflect the character of the studio's patron. Cochereau's painting representing David's studio in 1814, typical for the period, shows a small group of students actively engaged in drawing and painting from the model.[1261] The image is surely meant to characterize the overall dignity of the studio itself, befitting the reputation and seriousness of David's teaching. This work contrasts sharply with Horace Vernet's painting of his studio in 1820, which while maintaining its respectability, already shows the freer attitudes that developed among the more bohemian climate.[1262] To be sure, painting is still the central activity — as seen at the left in the group around Robert Fleury at the easel — but a clear sense of the studio as a social fraternity is also projected. Vernet himself is seen in the center smoking a cigarette while nonchalantly fencing with his student Ledieu, thus showing himself a member of the studio group even while acting as its director. The two figures with boxing gloves, incidentally, are Montfort and Lehoux, who nursed Gleyre in Beirut years later. The fact that sporting and musical activities are depicted, not to

fig. 258

fig. 259

1261. The work is in the Louvre, Inv. n° 3280, and was first exhibited in the salon of 1814. The iconography of studio scenes is discussed in Georgel and Lecoq 1982, pp. 130–58.
1262. *Horace Vernet* 1980, p. 68, provides the history of the work and the essential bibliography.

259. Horace Vernet, *The Studio*, 1820–21. Paris, Private collection

341

260. Louis-Léopold Boilly, *The Students of Baron Gros in 1820*, c. 1820. Paris, Musée Carnavalet
261. Armand Colin, *Girodet's Studio*, 1820. Paris, Bibliothèque Nationale, Cabinet des Estampes
262. Gleyre's students, *Collective Portraits*, c. 1862–63. Paris, Musée du Petit Palais

1263. For the Boilly group, see Delafond 1984, pp. 93–94; for the Girodet group, see Adhémar 1933, pp. 274–75.
1264. Ribeyre 1884, pp. 77–78.

mention an assortment of animals including a monkey at the left, underscores the camaraderie in Vernet's studio which was often described and which Gleyre too encouraged in his own two decades later.

There also appears to have been a tradition in the private studios of group portraits, much like high school yearbooks. A few examples of these have survived, like Boilly's portraits of the students in Gros's studio in 1820, showing among others such notable figures as Bonington (n° 17) and Delaroche (n° 9), who later inherited Gros's students; or Armand Colin's depiction of the Girodet group showing twenty-eight students, with the master seen in the center at the top.[1263] It is probable that all of the private studios had at one time similar pictorial keepsakes which were generally executed, as in the examples by Boilly and Colin, by a single hand.

This tradition extended as well to Gleyre's studio, but in a different form. The history of this group portrait is more complex and is related to another canvas depicting Delaroche's students which clearly precedes it. The two canvases together contain eighty-eight portraits, many of them painted by different artists over a long period of time. Delaroche's group portrait is mentioned only once in the literature, by Cham's biographer, Ribeyre, who remembered seeing it in Delaroche's studio.[1264] He described it as being about two meters long and containing about fifty or sixty portraits painted by the students themselves. When he traced the actual canvas in 1884 to the collection of Paul Baudouin, he noted that many of the portraits he had originally noticed on the canvas had disappeared. Similarly, there is only one description of the Gleyre group portrait —

fig. 260

fig. 261

fig. 262
fig. 263

263. Delaroche's students, *Collective Portraits*, before 1843. Paris, Musée du Petit Palais

264. Jean-François Millet, *Self-Portrait*, c. 1845. Paris, Musée du Louvre, Cabinet des Dessins

by Bachelin, who saw it in the second studio at the rue de l'Ouest in 1850.[1265] Bachelin wrote that it was hung opposite the large window and contained about thirty portraits; inclusion in the group, he noted, was considered an honor reserved for especially hard-working or distinguished alumni. Bachelin does not mention the canvas depicting the Delaroche students, nor does Ribeyre note the existence of a canvas showing Gleyre's students. In fact, the two canvases were no doubt in Delaroche's time a single work that after 1843 was cut apart to distinguish the Gleyre group.

This fact is underscored by the identification of some of the portraits in the Delaroche group which can be made as a result of inscriptions or comparative portraits.[1266] The painter Jean-François Millet is seen as the fully bearded figure at the left in the third tier from the bottom; his features correspond to his own self-portrait of around 1845. As was noted before, Millet was given free tuition by Delaroche and was never associated with Gleyre, as is also true of Cham, the perpetrator of the notorious jokes, who is seen here as the second figure from the left in the second tier from the top; the inscription on the back of the canvas notes that the portrait was painted by Adolphe Yvon, also a student of Delaroche who had no affiliation with Gleyre. One of the figures, however, bridges the gap between the two studios, namely Gérôme, who we know studied with both masters. He is portrayed — with the inscription on the back as "Jérôme" — full face at the center of the top tier, as can be verified by comparing his self-portrait of around 1845.[1267] Conversely, some of the students here are known to have been associated only with Gleyre and not with Delaroche, as for example Auguste Toulmouche, who is por-

fig. 264

fig. 265

1265. Bachelin 1889, p. 545. The work was seen by Milliet before 1915 in the collection of Paul Baudouin, whom he knew from Gleyre's studio. It is not known how Baudouin acquired both works, but they remained in his collection until they entered the Petit Palais on 9 July 1931, Inv. n° 899 and 900. The only known exhibition of the works was in *Un siècle d'art français* 1953, n° 33 and 34.
1266. Many of the inscriptions are in different hands, although on the portrait of the Gleyre group, there is clearly a series by one hand, no doubt Paul Baudouin, written as a reminder of the identity of the students he knew from the atelier. There are several inscriptions as well directly on the canvas, evidently made at the time the portraits were painted.
1267. The authorship of the portrait has been disputed by Cugnier 1981, p. 6, who attributes it to Gérôme's friend Daméry who accompanied him to Rome when Delaroche closed the studio. The description of the portrait Daméry is known to have made of Gérôme in Moreau-Vauthier 1906, p. 156, does not accord with the image here. All agree, however, that the figure is Gérôme.

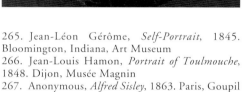

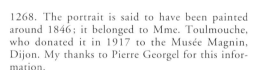

265. Jean-Léon Gérôme, *Self-Portrait*, 1845. Bloomington, Indiana, Art Museum
266. Jean-Louis Hamon, *Portrait of Toulmouche*, 1848. Dijon, Musée Magnin
267. Anonymous, *Alfred Sisley*, 1863. Paris, Goupil collection

1268. The portrait is said to have been painted around 1846; it belonged to Mme. Toulmouche, who donated it in 1917 to the Musée Magnin, Dijon. My thanks to Pierre Georgel for this information.
1269. Daulte 1959, p. 33, reproduces this photograph, but ascribes the date to 1882, which is clearly an error. The correct date is given in Daulte 1992(b), p. 12, although there is no indication from where the information comes; the photograph is from the Goupil collection.
1270. The letter is to Alfred Tavernier and dated 19 January 1892, and is deposited in Paris, Fondation Custodia, Institut néerlandais, 1973–A1: "J'entrais à l'atelier Gleyre en 1860. J'y restais deux ans." The full letter is reproduced in Shone 1992, p. 216. But see Geoffroy 1927, pp. 9–10; Venturi 1939, I, p. 28; Daulte 1959, p. 27.
1271. Lines 1966, p. 19.
1272. See Daulte 1959 for the early works.
1273. The letter is dated 8 November 1861 and is in Paris, BN, Cabinet des estampes, Y° 118, t1.

trayed second from the left in the topmost tier; his portrait can be compared with Hamon's portrait of him of 1848.[1268] Toulmouche listed himself as a student of Gleyre in the livret of the salon of 1852 and was instrumental in recommending Gleyre's studio to Monet years later. fig. 266

The Gleyre group contains forty-three portraits, thirty-four of which can be identified through various inscriptions — in different hands — on the back of the canvas. None of these is known to have worked with Delaroche, thus underlining the fact that the canvas was cut to recognize the new studio under Gleyre's leadership. The specific identification of these figures has already been published, but it is perhaps worthwhile to point out the portraits of two major Impressionists so as to stress once more their integration into the studio structure. Alfred Sisley is seen in full face, the third figure from the left in the third tier from the top. The likeness can be verified by comparing a photograph of him taken on 10 March 1863 when he was still following Gleyre's instruction.[1269] There is some doubt as to the precise date Sisley entered the studio: some biographers give the date as October or November 1862, but Sisley himself said in a letter that he enrolled in 1860, spending two years in the studio.[1270] If his assertion is correct, then he was the first of the Impressionists to associate himself with Gleyre and may have had an indirect role in recruiting the others. Sisley's activities in Gleyre's studio are not recorded except in passing in the memoirs of an American friend, William Mark Fisher, who noted that he, like Whistler, was lazy and worked only irregularly.[1271] Nor can Gleyre's influence on Sisley be readily determined since little of his correspondence of the period is extant and much of his painting before the 1870s has been destroyed.[1272] fig. 267

Of the Impressionists particularly attached to Gleyre and his instruction, Renoir must be singled out. He entered the studio in the fall of 1861 and in November Gleyre signed a letter on his behalf requesting permission for him to copy works in the Louvre.[1273] While Renoir is re-

corded as having minor differences with Gleyre over how to paint a model, he still followed the basic program and proclaimed later that it was Gleyre who taught him the fundamentals of his art.[1274] Renoir advanced quickly under Gleyre's tutelage; on 1 April 1862 he took the Ecole examinations and placed sixty-eighth out of the eighty allotted places; this performance improved later in other examinations in perspective and in figure drawing and painting.[1275] In the studio canvas, Renoir is seen in profile, the third from the left in the second tier from the bottom, an unusual likeness that can be compared to a photograph of him taken at about the same time. The portrait of Renoir was painted by his friend Henri-Emile Laporte, whose profile faces Renoir immediately to his right, painted by Renoir himself in an academic manner, more restrained than another portrait of Laporte painted slightly later.

It is curious, however, that of the group that surrounded Sisley and Renoir, Bazille, known by his very distinct features, is noticeably absent. Bazille's letters reveal that he particularly appreciated Gleyre's teaching and felt genuine concern when the master's health problems seriously menaced studio functions.[1276] Moreover, Bazille was well liked and wholly integrated into the social life of the studio; therefore one would expect to find his portrait included in the group. It is possible that his portrait was in fact painted but later effaced, perhaps after his untimely death in 1870, as portraits were altered at various times and in some cases actually cut from the canvas. A section at the bottom right corner, depicting John Pradier, the famous sculptor's son, was sewn into the canvas apparently after a section was removed.

Monet's absence from the portrait is more complex. While all sources agree that Monet was a student of Gleyre, the data concerning the length of time is contradictory and still uncertain. Monet first presented himself in 1859 to Troyon, who suggested he seek more formal training, advising him to go to Couture.[1277] Monet, however, was refused by Cou-

fig. 268

fig. 269

fig. 270

268. Anonymous, *Pierre-Auguste Renoir*, c. 1860. Paris, Bibliothèque Nationale, Cabinet des Estampes
269. Pierre-Auguste Renoir, *Portrait of Emile Laporte*, 1864. Paris, Private collection
270. Anonymous, *Frédéric Bazille*, c. 1860. Paris, Bibliothèque Nationale, Cabinet des Estampes

1274. André 1928, p. 8, notes that Gleyre desired a greater sense of the antique in contrast to the unsparing realism Renoir portrayed. But in Vollard 1920, p. 26, Renoir noted that he owed a great debt to Gleyre for having taught him the technique of painting.
1275. For Renoir's stay at the Ecole, see Rey 1926, pp. 33–37.
1276. Poulain 1932, p. 35; Marandel 1978, p. 195; Clément, pp. 283–84, notes Gleyre's illness at this time.
1277. Rewald 1961, p. 41.

345

ture and went instead to the free Académie Suisse, where in 1861 his studies were interrupted by his military obligations. When he returned to Paris in the fall of 1862, it has been thought that upon the advice of Toulmouche — actually his cousin as well as his tutor — Monet enrolled in Gleyre's studio.[1278] Yet, on 5 March 1863, Monet applied for permission to copy in the Louvre, citing himself as a student of Amand Gautier, not Gleyre.[1279]

However, it is certain that by Easter of that year, which fell during the first week of April, Monet was working in Gleyre's studio and had already met his comrades in the Impressionist movement. During the Easter recess, Monet, Sisley, Bazille, and Renoir went to Chailly-en-Bière near Fontainebleau, intending to remain only for the two weeks allotted for the holiday period. When his compatriots returned to Paris, Monet stayed on alone, causing Toulmouche to reproach him for having abandoned his studies despite Monet's assurance that this was not the case.[1280] Monet apparently tried to rejoin the studio in June but found it closed for the summer and thereupon went to Le Havre, returning to Paris only in October. It has been assumed that he continued his studies with Gleyre at this time, remaining until summer 1864,[1281] thus under Gleyre's tutelage for a total period of about a year.

Monet himself contradicted this version of events when he was eighty-one years old, noting that his training under Gleyre amounted to no more than about two weeks after which he left the studio.[1282] This comment has always been discounted by scholars as another example of Monet's desire to minimize his academic instruction and augment the myth that his art developed from his own natural instincts. But the chronological sequence outlined here suggests that Monet's memory regarding the time he spent with Gleyre was correct. If in early March Monet considered himself to be a student of Amand Gautier, then it is likely that he sought out Gleyre shortly afterwards, but left with his comrades for the Easter holidays two weeks later. There is no documentation to suggest that he went back to Gleyre's studio after his return from Le Havre. Except for brief references to Monet in Gleyre's studio found in the correspondence of Bazille — all of them dating from March 1863 — Monet is never mentioned as an habitué of the studio. It is therefore not surprising that Monet was the only member of the Gleyre Impressionist group who never cited himself in exhibitions as an "élève de Gleyre".

1278. Daulte 1959, p. 27; Rewald 1961, p. 71; Wildenstein 1974, I, p. 121.
1279. The inscription in the Louvre is noted in Adhémar 1980, p. 45. Monet's correspondence at this time with Gautier is in Wildenstein 1974, I, pp. 420–21; on Gautier, see Weisberg 1980.
1280. See Régamey 1927, p. 68; Wildenstein 1974, I, p. 420, letter 6.
1281. Venturi 1939, I, p. 20; Champa 1973, p. 22; Levine 1976, p. 5, among others.
1282. Monet related this in an interview with Marcel Pays; see Pays 1921. Monet's disagreement with Gleyre is often mentioned, but see especially Thiébault-Sisson 1900.

ADDENDUM

Since Gleyre's studio was a free forum in which students, like Monet, could come and go, it is unlikely that a complete count of all who studied there can be compiled. There were no registers and it was not uncommon for students to work with two masters at a time. Staiger-Gayler's list, which she noted is not complete, identifies more than 500 names taken from various sources, including salon records, permissions to copy, dictionaries, and correspondence. In the course of the present research, I have encountered various artists who studied with Gleyre but whose names escaped Staiger-Gayler. These are briefly noted below along with the sources that delineate an affiliation with Gleyre. The abbreviations employed are to the standard editions of Bénézit (Bén); Thieme and Becker (T-H); and Bellier de la Chavignerie (B-A); all other citations refer to works in the general bibliography.

1. Emile Avon (1847–1914) came to Paris around 1862 from Avignon. He is noted as an "élève de Gleyre" in two sources: the Salon des Refusés of 1863 where he showed one painting (n° 14), and a previously unpublished letter of 23 April 1863 from Gleyre, now in Paris, Fondation Custodia, Institut néerlandais, 1973-A 767, which reads as follows:

> Monsieur le directeur
> Je vous prie de vouloir accorder l'entrée des galeries du Louvre, pour les jours d'étude, à Monsieur Avon Emile l'un de mes élèves.                                                    C. Gleyre

There is little information on his activities; see Bén, I, p. 336, which provides only a few words on his art.

2. Jean-Baptiste Blanc (1835–80?) is one of three students named Blanc who studied with Gleyre; Staiger-Gayler 1974 lists only one, Célestin. Jean-Baptiste Blanc also studied with Meissonier and Hesse; he entered the Ecole des Beaux-Arts on 5 April 1860, having no doubt worked with Gleyre somewhat earlier. See Bén, II, p. 65; T-B, IV, p. 90; and B-A, I, pp. 95–96.

3. Paul-Emile Blanc (?), of whom nothing is known, is noted as a student of Gleyre in Bén, II, p. 65.

4. William Mark Fisher (1841–1923) was an American student who must have particularly interested Gleyre since he had first studied at the Lowell Institute in Boston, which Lowell first conceived when he was in Egypt with Gleyre. Fisher also knew George Inness well, having come to Paris in 1863 on his advice. He maintained a long relationship with Sisley whom he met in Gleyre's studio. See Bén, IV, p. 384, and the general biographical material in Lines 1966. The influence of Gleyre on his art is noted in Weinberg 1991, p. 62.

5. Henri Johnson Fusino (?) was listed as a student of Gleyre in the Salon des Refusés of 1863 where he showed two paintings on the Faust theme (n° 179 and 180).

6. François Guillon (1840–?) came to Paris from Nantes in 1861 to work in Gleyre's studio on the advice of Auguste Coutan, who was also a student there. He entered the Ecole des Beaux-Arts in 1862 but returned to Nantes where he made his career. He should not be confused with Adolphe Guillon (1829–96) who also studied with Gleyre, as noted in Staiger-Gayler 1974. See Bén, V, p. 133, and E. Maillard 1888, p. 220.

7. Edward Lamson Henry (1841–1919) was a contemporary of Fisher and was in the studio for a time with him. He returned to the United States in 1863; it is not certain how long he stayed in the studio. He is listed as a student of Gleyre in T-B, XVI, p. 422, but not in Bén, V, p. 493, where he is affiliated with Robert-Fleury, Benjamin Constant, and Courbet. On Gleyre's influence on his work, see Weinberg 1991, p. 62.

8. Louis Jacottet (1843–?) showed in the Salon des Refusés (n° 237) and later made a reputation in painting Swiss landscapes. There is some confusion concerning him since several painters bore the same surname, including two named Louis-Julien. See B-A, II, p. 810.

9. Paul-Claude Jance (1840–?) trained first in Lyons between 1855 and 1861 before coming to Paris to work with Gleyre. He exhibited in the salon of 1864 (n° 996) as a student of Gleyre but then made his career in Lyons. See Bén, VI, p. 29; B-A, II, p. 820.

10. C. Kergrohen (?), about whom little is known, is mentioned as Gleyre's student in an unpublished letter written by Gleyre in late 1843, just when he formed the studio, on Kergrohen's behalf. The letter is in Paris, AN, F²¹, 38, and reads as follows:

> Je certifie que M. Cle. Kergrohen, mon élève, est parfaitement capable par son talent et ses études d'exécuter une bonne copie d'après les anciens maîtres.       C. Gleyre

Kergrohen received a commission on 20 December 1843 for a copy of an *Ascension* for a church in the Pas-de-Calais, which he completed on 4 July 1844; he was paid 800 francs for the commission.

11. Daniel Ridgway Knight (1839–1924) was another American who worked in the studio in the early 1860s with Fisher and Henry. Knight left Paris in 1863 but returned in 1871 or 1872 to work further with Meissonier. See Bén, VI, p. 254, and T-B, XX, pp. 594–95, where Knight is listed as Ridgway rather than Daniel. Gleyre's influence on his style is discussed in Weinberg 1991, pp. 63–66.

12. L. de Lajolais (?), about whom nothing is known, is mentioned by Zola 1959, p. 58, as Gleyre's student when he showed in the salon of 1866.

13. Alphonse-François Le Hénaff (1821–1900?) worked first with Delaroche before studying with Gleyre after 1843. Bén, VI, p. 548, however, notes his master only as Devéria while T-B, XVI, p. 372 — listing him under Hénaff — notes Delaroche and Gleyre along with Devéria; B-A, III, p. 981, provides no affiliation. His most important work is a huge mural for Notre-Dame in Nantes which contains no fewer than 140 figures. See E. Maillard 1888, p. 239.

14. Célestin Longbray (?), about whom nothing is known, is recorded as a student of Gleyre in the register of the Ecole des Beaux-Arts, AN, AJ[52], 235, when he entered on 9 October 1856.

15. Felix Stone Moscheles (1833–1917) was the son of the composer and pianist Ignaz Moscheles. He opted for studies in art rather than in music and is listed in Bén, VII, p. 561, and T-B, XXV, p. 176, as a student of Van Lerias, but in his own autobiography, p. 17, he remarked that he studied with Gleyre when Whistler was a member of the studio.

16. Arthur Murch (?) is mentioned by Prinsep 1904, p. 339, as one of the "English Gang" in the studio. He was a friend of Lord Leighton, who advised him to study in Paris rather than in London.

17. Charles Nanteuil (1811–?), who met Gleyre in Italy, was one of Gleyre's most intimate friends. Nanteuil is known to have studied with Ingres, but T-B, XXV, p. 340, also lists Gleyre as his master.

18. Adrien-Jean Nargeot (1837–?), who was chiefly known for his engravings, studied drawing and painting with Gleyre in the 1850s. See Bén, VII, p. 653, and B-A, III, p. 149.

19. Willie O'Connor (?) is mentioned as one of the "English Gang" in Gleyre's studio in Armstrong 1912, p. 139; he was befriended by Edward Poynter in the studio. Perhaps he is the W. H. O'Connor noted in Bén, VIII, p. 779, and T-B, p. 558.

20. Francesco Oller Y Cestero (1833–1917) was from Puerto Rico and came to Paris to work with Couture in whose studio he met Manet. He seems to have worked with Gleyre afterwards for a time as noted in Monneret, II, p. 108.

21. August Van Vreckom (1820–?) was a Belgian painter about whom little is known. He is cited in Bén, X, p. 582, and T-B, XXXIV, p. 568, but no information is provided. He is, however, listed as a student of Gleyre in "Demandes de cartes d'entrée pour les galeries du Louvre et du

Luxembourg," in Archives du Louvre, dossier Gleyre, P[30], where a letter by Gleyre, dated 26 August 1845, makes the request for him, noting that Vreckom is his student.

# EXHIBITIONS

## PARIS 1833

*Explication des ouvrages de peinture, sculpture, architecture, gravure et lithographies des artistes vivans [sic] exposés au Musée Royal,* Louvre, Paris, 1833, n° 1077 (three unidentified watercolor portraits under the same catalogue number).

## LYONS 1839

*Livret explicatif des ouvrages de peinture, sculpture, dessin, gravure,… admis à l'exposition de la Société des amis des arts de Lyon,* Musée des Beaux-Arts, Lyons, 1839, n° 176 (*Saint John on the Isle of Patmos,* exhibited under the title *Saint Jean inspiré par la vision apocalyptique*).

## PARIS 1840

*Explication des ouvrages de peinture, sculpture…,* Louvre, Paris, 1840, n° 714 (*Saint John,* exhibited under the title *Saint Jean inspiré par la vision apocalyptique*).

## PARIS 1843

*Explication des ouvrages de peinture, sculpture…,* Louvre, Paris, 1843, n° 512 (*Le Soir*).

## PARIS 1845

*Explication des ouvrages de peinture, sculpture…,* Louvre, Paris, 1845, n° 729 (*Mission of the Apostles,* exhibited under the title *Départ des apôtres allant prêcher l'Evangile*).

## PARIS 1849

*Explication des ouvrages de peinture, sculpture,… exposés au Palais des Tuileries,* Palais des Tuileries, Paris, 1849, n° 914 (*The Dance of the Bacchantes*).

## LAUSANNE 1850

*Exposition des ouvrages de peinture, dessin, sculpture et gravure des artistes vivants exposés dans les salles du Musée Arlaud,* Musée Arlaud, Lausanne, September 1850, n° 83 (*Major Davel,* exhibited under the title *La Mort du Major Davel*).

## GENEVA 1854

*Exposition des Beaux-arts,* Musée Rath, Geneva, September 1854, no catalogue (*Venus Pandemos;* and *Ruth and Boaz*).

## LAUSANNE 1858

*Exposition des ouvrages de peinture…,* Musée Arlaud, Lausanne, September 1858, no catalogue n° (*The Romans Passing under the Yoke*).

## LAUSANNE 1862

*Exposition suisse de peintures, dessins, sculpture, émaux… d'artistes vivants,* Musée Arlaud, Lausanne, 18 May–15 June 1862, n° 53 (*The Romans Passing under the Yoke*).

## LONDON 1862

*Universelle Exposition of 1862. French Section. Official Catalogue,* South Kensington Museum, London, 1 May–15 November 1862, n° 90 (*Le Soir*).

## PARIS 1862

*Exposition,* Goupil Galleries, Paris, December 1862, no catalogue (*Hercules and Omphale*).

## PARIS 1865

*Notice des peintures et sculptures exposées dans les galeries du Corps législatif,* Corps législatif, Paris, 1866, n° 15 (*Le Soir* was exhibited here from December 1865 to April 1867 before its transfer to the Louvre).

## GENEVA 1866

*Exposition des Beaux-Arts de la Société des amis des arts,* Musée Rath, Geneva, July 1866; *Exposition des Beaux-Arts,* Musée Arlaud, Lausanne, August 1866, no catalogue (*Minerva and the Three Graces*).

## BASEL 1869

*Verzeichniss der Kunst-Gegenstände aus der Schweizerischen Kunst-Ausstellung in Basel im Jahre 1869,* Kunsthalle, Basel, 1869, n° 142 (*The Charmer*).

## VIENNA 1873

*Welt-Ausstellung 1873. Wien. Officieller Kunst-Katalog,* Prater, Vienna, 1 May–2 November 1873, Swiss Section, n° 76 (*The Charmer*).

## LAUSANNE 1874

*Exposition d'œuvres de Charles Gleyre,* Musée Arlaud, Lausanne, 15 August–15 September 1874, no catalogue (10 works indicated plus "portraits divers").

## BASEL 1874

*Ausstellung* (?), Kunsthalle, Basel, exact date unknown, no catalogue (Study for *Pentheus*).

**PARIS 1875**

*Œuvres d'art exposées par la Ville de Paris*, Ecole des Beaux-Arts, Paris, July 1875, n° 27 (*The Pentecost*).

**LAUSANNE 1876**

*Exposition,* Galerie Wenger, Lausanne, Summer 1876, no catalogue (*Manfred Invoking the Spirit of the Mountains;* and *Raphael Leaving His Father's House*).

**ZÜRICH 1883**

*Schweizerische Landesausstellung,* Zürich, 1 May-2 October 1883, n° 632 (Study for *Pentheus*).

**PARIS 1884**

*Association des artistes. Catalogue des dessins de l'Ecole moderne exposés à l'Ecole nationale des Beaux-Arts au profit de la caisse de secours de l'association,* Ecole des Beaux-Arts, Paris, February 1884, n° 335–50 (various studies and portraits).

**PARIS 1885(A)**

*Portraits du siècle, ouvert au profit de l'œuvre à l'Ecole des Beaux-Arts,* Société philanthropique, Paris, April-May 1885, n° 102 (*Madame Raffalovich*).

**PARIS 1885(B)**

*Exposition de tableaux, statues et objets d'art au profit de l'œuvre des orphelins d'Alsace-Lorraine.* Salle des Etats, Louvre, no dates, 1885, n° 230 (*Venus Pandemos*).

**ZÜRICH 1904**

*Ausstellung Gottfried Keller-Stiftung,* Zürich, Summer 1904, no catalogue (*The Return of the Prodigal Son*).

**LAUSANNE 1921**

*Exposition des portraits anciens de la Suisse romande,* Mon Repos, Lausanne, 17 September–15 October 1921, n° 199–200, and 338 (Study of *Jean-Jacques Mercier; Jean-Jacques Mercier;* and *Fellahin*).

**PARIS 1923**

*L'art et la vie romantique,* private exhibition, Hôtel de M. Jean Charpentier, Paris, 25 February–25 March 1923, n° 212 (*Léon Vaudoyer*).

**LAUSANNE 1923**

*Le Major Davel,* Musée historiographique, Lausanne, Spring–Summer 1923, no catalogue (various studies for the *Major Davel*).

**PARIS 1924**

*Exposition de l'art suisse du XVᵉ au XIXᵉ siècle. De Holbein à Hodler,* Musée du Jeu de Paume, Paris, June-July 1924, n° 47–50, and 270–71 (*The Charmer; Pentheus; Souvenir of Smyrna;* Study for *The Bath; Sappho; Hercules and Omphale*).

**LA SARRAZ 1936**

*Exposition,* Château de La Sarraz, La Sarraz, no dates indicated, 1936, n° 56–59 (*Charles Knébel; Louis Knébel; Alexander Knébel [?];* and *A. Speranza de Montepagano*).

**LAUSANNE 1937**

*Sainte-Beuve. Le Lausanne de 1837,* Bibliothèque cantonale et universitaire, Lausanne, 31 October–14 November 1937, n° 130, 135–36 (*Urbain Olivier; Juste Olivier; Caroline Olivier*).

**ZÜRICH 1939**

*Schweizerische Landesausstellung 1939. Zeichnen Malen Formen. I. Die Grundlagen,* Kunsthaus, Zürich, 20 May–6 August 1939, n° 571–575 (*Self-Portrait,* 1827; *Study of Davel; Turks and Arabs; Daphnis and Chloe; The Bath*).

**BERN 1942**

*50 Jahre Gottfried Keller-Stiftung,* Kunstmuseum, Bern, 13 June-1 November 1942, n° 393–94 (*The Return of the Prodigal Son; Sappho*).

**GENEVA 1943**

*L'art suisse des origines à nos jours,* Musée d'art et d'histoire, Geneva, no precise dates indicated [1943], n° 946–49. (*Self-Portrait,* 1827; *Turks and Arabs; Amour and the Fates; Mme François Gleyre*).

**LAUSANNE 1953**

*Artistes vaudois du XVIIᵉ siècle à aujourd'hui,* Musée cantonal des Beaux-Arts, Lausanne, 28 March–1 November 1953, no catalogue (15 works by Gleyre).

**PARIS 1957**

*Henri Heine, 1797–1856,* Bibliothèque nationale, Paris, Summer, 1957, n° 147 (*Heinrich Heine*).

**SCHAFFHAUSEN 1957**

*Kunst und Kultur der Kelten,* Museum zu Aller-heiligen, Schaffhausen, 1 August–3 November 1957, n° 42 and 103 (Studies for *The Romans Passing under the Yoke*).

**LA SARRAZ 1958**

*Dessins d'il y cent ans. Charles Gleyre et son atelier,* Château de La Sarraz, La Sarraz, 22 June–31 August, 1958 n° 1–36; 37–42 (no titles are given in the checklist, but the author possesses a copy with several handwritten notes of works exhibited, including studies for *Major Davel,* and *The Romans Passing under the Yoke*).

**BALTIMORE 1965**

*The George A. Lucas Collection,* Baltimore Museum of Art, Baltimore, 12 October–21 November 1965, n° 15 (Oil study for *The Return of the Prodigal Son*).

**COPPET 1967**

*Grandes heures de l'amitié franco-suisse,* Château de Coppet, Coppet, July–October, 1967, n° 15 and 638 (Study for *The Romans Passing under the Yoke; Jomini*).

**WINTERTHUR 1968**

*Von Toepffer bis Hodler. Die Schweizer Zeichnung im 19. Jahrhundert.* Kunstmuseum, Winterthur, 14 January–25 February 1968; Kunsthaus, Chur, 3 March–15 April; Kunstmuseum, Lucerne, 28 April–3 June; Kunstmuseum, Basel, 8 June–21 July; Museo di belle arti, Lugano, 17 August–8 September; Musée cantonal des Beaux-Arts, Lausanne, 20 September–31 October; Kunstmuseum, Bern, 9 November–15 December, n° 63-65 (*View of Corfu; Mother of Tobias;* Study for *Sappho*).

**PARIS 1968-69**

*Baudelaire,* Petit Palais, Paris, 23 november 1968–17 May 1969, n° 143 (*Mission of the Apostles*).

**LAUSANNE 1969**

*Du Léman aux sources du Nil,* Musée de l'Ancien-Evêché, Lausanne, 18 July–31 August 1969, no catalogue (26 works).

**PAYERNE, 1969**

*Général Antoine-Henri Jomini, 1779–1869,* Musée de Payerne, Payerne, March–June 1969, n° 1 (*Jomini*).

**PULLY 1972**

*Hommage à C. F. Ramuz*, Musée de Pully, Pully, 28 October–23 December 1972 (Study for *Major Davel*, not in catalogue).

**PARIS 1973**

*"Equivoques", Peintures françaises du XIXᵉ siècle*, Musée des arts décoratifs, Paris, 9 March–14 May 1974, no catalogue n° (*Le Soir*).

**PARIS 1974**

*Le Musée du Luxembourg en 1874*, Grand Palais, Paris, 31 May–18 November 1974, n° 106 (*Le Soir*).

**HEMPSTEAD 1974**

*Art Pompier: Anti Impressionism*, Emily Lowe Gallery, Hofstra University, Hempstead, New York, 22 October–15 December 1974, n° 52–53 (*The Bath*; Study for *The Return of the Prodigal Son*).

**WINTERTHUR 1974–75**

*Charles Gleyre ou les illusions perdues*, Kunstmuseum, Winterthur; Musée Cantini, Marseille; Städtische Galerie im Lehnbachhaus, Munich; Kunsthalle, Kiel; Aargauer Kunsthaus, Aarau; Musée cantonal des Beaux-Arts, Lausanne, no precise dates indicated, 1974–75 (184 works).

**BALTIMORE 1975**

*Selections from the Lucas Collection*, Downtown Gallery, Baltimore, 21 July–22 August 1975, no catalogue (Oil study for *The Return of the Prodigal Son*).

**LAUSANNE 1977**

*L'identité et ses visages,* Musée cantonal des Beaux-Arts, Lausanne, 4 March–1 May 1977, n° 99 (*Self-Portrait*, 1827).

**BOSTON 1978**

*Visions of Vesuvius*, Museum of Fine Arts, Boston, 15 April–16 July 1978 (*Bay of Naples*; *Temple of Jupiter, Pompeii*).

**CHICAGO 1978**

*Frédéric Bazille and Early Impressionism*, Art Institute of Chicago, Chicago, 4 March–30 April 1978 (Study for *The Dance of the Bacchantes*).

**PHILADELPHIA 1978–79**

*The Second Empire 1852–1870: Art in France Under Napoleon III*, Philadelphia Museum of Art, Philadelphia, 1 October–26 November 1978; The Detroit Institute of Arts, Detroit, 15 January–18 March 1979; Grand Palais, Paris, 24 April–1 July 1979, Paris, n° VI–62 (*The Bath*).

**NEW YORK 1980**

*Charles Gleyre 1806–1874*, Grey Art Gallery and Study Center, New York University, New York, 6 February–22 March 1980; The University of Maryland Art Gallery, College Park, 3 April–2 May 1980 (114 works).

**BERN 1981–82**

*Anker in seiner Zeit*, Kunstmuseum, Bern, 19 September–15 November 1981; Kunstmuseum, Winterthur, 16 January–7 March 1982, n° 46 (*Hercules*).

**LAUSANNE 1982**

*Fantaisie équestre*, Musée cantonal des Beaux-Arts, Lausanne, 23 July–12 September 1982, n° 143–47 (*Egyptian Modesty*; *Turks and Arabs*; *Rape of Deianeira*; *Glory*; *The Centaurs*).

**ROCHESTER 1982**

*Orientalism: The Near East in French Painting, 1800–1900*, Memorial Art Gallery of the University of Rochester, Rochester, New York, 27 August–17 October 1982; Neuberger Museum, State University of New York at Purchase, Purchase, New York, 11 November–23 December, 1982, n° 46–48 (*Turkish Lady, Angelica; Jewish Woman of Smyrna; Interior of the Palace, Karnak*).

**ATLANTA 1983**

*French Salon Paintings from Southern Collections*, High Museum of Art, Atlanta, 21 January–23 October 1983; Chrysler Museum, Norfolk, 4 April–15 May 1983; North Carolina Museum of Art, Raleigh, 25 June–21 August 1983; The John and Mable Ringling Museum of Art, Sarasota, Florida, 15 September–23 October 1883, n° 40 (*The Bath*).

**LONDON 1984**

*The Orientalists: Delacroix to Matisse. European Painters in North Africa and the Near East*, The Royal Academy of Arts, London, 24 March–27 May 1984, n° 43–62 (Egyptian watercolors).

**LAUSANNE 1985**

*L'autoportrait à l'âge de la photographie. Peintres et photographes en dialogue avec leur propre image*, Musée cantonal des Beaux-Arts, Lausanne, 18 January–24 March 1985, n° 1 (*Self-Portrait*, 1827).

**NYON 1985**

*Gleyre et l'Orient*, Château, Nyon, 10 May–16 September 1985, no catalogue.

**LUCERNE 1985**

*"Ich male für fromme Gemüter". Zur religiösen Schweizer Malerei im 19. Jahrhundert*, Kunstmuseum, Lucerne, July–September 1985, n° IV/7–IV/13.

**NORFOLK 1986–87**

*French Paintings from the Chrysler Museum*, The Chrysler Museum, Norfolk, Virginia, 31 May–14 September 1987; Birmingham Museum of Art, Birmingham, Alabama, 6 November 1986–18 January 1987, n° 21 (*The Bath*).

**LAUSANNE 1986–87**

*Dessins et travaux sur papier*, Musée cantonal des Beaux-Arts, Lausanne, Winter 1986–87, no catalogue.

**NEW YORK 1987**

*French Nineteenth Century Drawings, Watercolors, Paintings and Sculpture*, Shepherd Gallery, New York, Spring 1987, n° 94 (Study of *Omphale*).

**STUTTGART 1987**

*Exotische Welten. Europäische Phantasien*, Instituts für Auslandsbeziehungen und des Württembergischen Kunstvereins, Stuttgart, 2 September–29 November 1987, n° 3.57 (*Queen of Sheba*) and 3.58 (*Egyptian Modesty*).

**ATLANTA 1988**

*From Liotard to Le Corbusier: 200 Years of Swiss Painting 1730–1930*, High Museum of Art, Atlanta, 9 February–10 April 1988, n° 25–27 (*Turks and Arabs; Sappho;* Study for *The Bath*).

**ZÜRICH 1988**

*Triumph und Tod des Helden/Triomphe et mort du héros*, Kunsthaus, Zürich, 3 March–24 April 1988; Musée des Beaux-Arts, Lyons, 19 May–17 July 1988, n° 36 (*The Romans Passing under the Yoke*). N.B. The exhibition was seen at the

Wallraf-Richartz Museum, Cologne, 30 October 1987–10 January 1988, without Gleyre's canvas.

**BERLIN 1989**

*Europa und der Orient, 800–1900*, Martin-Gropius-Bau, Berlin, 28 May–27 August 1989, n° 1/251 (*Queen of Sheba*) and 15/4 (*Egyptian Modesty*).

**BERN 1991**

*Emblèmes de la liberté. L'image de la république dans l'art du XVI<sup>e</sup> au XX<sup>e</sup> siècle*, Kunstmuseum, Bern, 1 June–15 September 1991, n° 421–28.

**PARIS 1991–92**

*Les Vaudoyer: une dynastie d'architectes*, Musée d'Orsay, Paris, 22 October 1991–12 January 1992, n° 5 (*Léon Vaudoyer*)

**LAUSANNE 1994**

*Charles Gleyre et la Suisse romande*, Musée historique de Lausanne, 23 September–31 December 1994 (55 works).

**LUCERNE 1994**

*Gemälde alter und moderner Meister*, Galerie Fischer, Lucerne, 27 August–17 September 1994 (*The Dance of the Bacchantes*).

**LAUSANNE 1995(A)**

*La genèse des formes. Œuvres sur papier de la collection*, Musée cantonal des Beaux-Arts, 17 March–28 May 1995 (30 works).

**LAUSANNE 1995(B)**

*Charles Gleyre: La Danse des Bacchantes*, Musée cantonal des Beaux-Arts, 17 March–28 May 1995 (*The Dance of the Bacchantes* and six works).

**NANTES 1995–96**

*Les années romantiques. La peinture française de 1815 à 1850*, Nantes, Musée des Beaux-Arts, 4 December 1995–17 March 1996; Paris, Grand-Palais, 16 April–15 July 1996; Piacenza, Palazzo Gotico, 6 September–17 November 1996, n° 104–105 (*Le Soir*, and *The Mission of the Apostles*).

**LAUSANNE 1996**

*Entre Rome et Paris. Œuvres inédites du XIV<sup>e</sup> au XIX<sup>e</sup> siècle*, Musée cantonal des Beaux-Arts, 17 February–28 March 1996 (*The Dance of the Bacchantes* and nine works).

**ROMA 1996**

*Dei e eroi. Classicità e mito fra '800 e '900*, Roma, Palazzo delle Esposizioni, 15 March–30 May 1996, n° 18 (*Pentheus*).

# ABBREVIATIONS

| | |
|---|---|
| Clément | The citation Clément, followed only by a page or catalogue number, is a reference to the first edition of his text and catalogue : CLÉMENT, Charles. *Gleyre. Étude biographique et critique avec le catalogue raisonné de l'œuvre du maître*, Geneva / Neuchâtel / Paris, 1878. All other references to Clément's publications follow the standard form of citation. |
| ACE | Lausanne, Archives du Conseil d'Etat |
| AE | Neuchâtel, Archives de l'Etat |
| AL | Paris, Archives du Louvre |
| AM | Montpellier, Archives Municipales |
| AN | Paris, Archives Nationales |
| AS | Paris, Archives de la Seine |
| ASBA | Geneva, Archives de la Société des Beaux-Arts |
| ACV | Lausanne, Archives Cantonales Vaudoises |
| AVL | Lausanne, Archives de la Ville de Lausanne |
| BCU/DM | Lausanne, Bibliothèque Cantonale et Universitaire, Département des Manuscrits |
| BL | London, British Library |
| BM | Lyons, Bibliothèque Municipale |
| BMFA | Boston, Museum of Fine Arts |
| BN | Paris, Bibliothèque Nationale, Département des Manuscrits |
| BV | Neuchâtel, Bibliothèque de la Ville |
| CFC | Fleurier, Clément Familly Collection |
| GA | Lausanne, Musée Cantonal des Beaux-Arts, Gleyre Archives |
| IF | Paris, Institut de France |
| KB | Basel, Kunstmuseum, Bibliothek |
| MAH | Geneva, Musée d'Art et d'Histoire |
| MCAH | Lausanne, Musée Cantonal d'Archéologie et d'Histoire |
| MCBA | Lausanne, Musée Cantonal des Beaux-Arts |
| MH/AVL | Lausanne, Musée Historique de Lausanne, Collection de l'Association du Vieux-Lausanne |
| SKB | Basel, Staatsarchiv des Kantons Basel-Stadt |

**BASEL**

Kunstmuseum, Bibliothek (KB)
 Kommission am Museum. Protokoll, I. March 1842–November 1881.

Staatsarchiv des Kantons Basel-Stadt (SKB)
 Erziehungsakten. Ausstellungskorrespondenz. DD/7ᵇ.
 Erziehungsakten. Kunstsammlung-Kunstkommission 1841–1908. DD/7.


**BERN**

Bürgerbibliothek
 Gleyre. Letter to Christian Bühler, 1863. Hist. Helv. XI, 178B.

Kunstmuseum
 Bernische Kunstgesellschaft. Protokolle. 1864–65.

Private collection
 Walthard, Friedrich. Papers.


**BOSTON**

Museum of Fine Arts (BMFA)
 Lowell Family Collection.

 Lowell, John. *Diaries*, 1834–35, 8 handwritten volumes (on deposit in the Egyptian Department).

 Everett, E. "A Memoir of Mr. John Lowell, Jr., Delivered as the Introduction to the Lectures of His Foundation", typescript, Boston, 31 December 1839.


**CHAMPS-SUR-MARNE**

Albert Ehrmann Collection
 Ehrmann, François. Correspondence.


**CHEXBRES**

Jean-Charles Biaudet Collection
 Biaudet Family. Correspondence


**FLEURIER**

Private collection
 Clément Family Collection (CFC). Correspondence to and from Charles Clément.

 Nanteuil, Charles. "Notes concernant Gleyre" (after 1874).


**FRANCE**

Private collection
 Clément, Charles. *Journal*, fragment, c. 1864–73.

 Clément, Charles. Scattered correspondence in various dossiers.

 Portfolio "Charles Gleyre", signed "LG", handwritten transcriptions of press clippings and notes.


**GENEVA**

Archives de la Société des Beaux-Arts (ASBA)
 Commission pour l'Exposition des Beaux-Arts du Musée Rath. Procès-verbaux, 1854.

 Société des Beaux-Arts. Procès-verbaux des séances, 1862.

 Société des Beaux-Arts. Procès-verbaux des séances, 1874.

Musée d'Art et d'Histoire (MAH)
 Comité du musée. Procès-verbaux.

**LA SARRAZ**

Private collection
Knébel Family. Correspondence.


**LAUSANNE**

Archives du Conseil d'Etat (ACE)
Conseil d'Etat. Lettres à l'intérieur du canton.

Conseil d'Etat. Lettres à l'extérieur du canton.

Copies de lettres.

Archives Cantonales Vaudoises (ACV)
Campiche, F.-Raoul. "Généalogie Olivier, 1500–1923", Campiche/92.

Commission des musées, des antiquités et des Beaux-Arts. Procès-verbaux, 1873–74. K XIII/66.

Commission des musées et de la bibliothèque. Copies de lettres, 1849–63, K XIII/55.

Commission des musées et de la bibliothèque. Procès-verbaux, 1849–73. K XIII/54[1-2].

Conseil d'Etat. Lettres, K XIII/68.

Conseil d'Etat. Registres des délibérations.

Département de l'Instruction publique. Lettres. K XIII/63.

Département des Travaux publics. Service des bâtiments, 1861–68. Cathédrale: vitraux, K IX, 1217/9.

Musée Arlaud. Séances et lettres. 1840-1849. K XIII/65.

Naeff, Hans. "L'église de Chevilly et sa restauration. Rapport. 24 septembre 1897", AMH, A 37/2.

Registres paroissiaux. Cuarnens. EB 41/8–10.

Registres paroissiaux. La Sarraz. EB 70/5.

Registres pour l'instruction des dons faits aux musées cantonaux. K XIII/56.

Testaments. K XIX, dossier, 1845, n° 57.

Archives de la Ville de Lausanne (AVL)
Livre des étrangers de l'Hôtel Gibbon à Lausanne, c. 1865.

Permis de séjour des Vaudois à Lausanne.

Recensement, 1850f.

Bibliothèque Cantonale et Universitaire, Département des Manuscrits (BCU/DM)
Budry, Paul. "Charles Gleyre", IS 2134/14.

Courvoisier, James. "Conférence. Juste Olivier d'après sa correspondance", [1903], IS 1905/54.

David, Emile. "Correspondance", IS 4540 (photocopy).

Delhorbe, Cécile. "Un poète chez nous. Juste Olivier", [1939], manuscript of a radio play, IS 1905/51.

Dossier Antoine Baron, F[18].

Dossier Aloys Olivier, IS 1905/59.

Faure, Jocelyne and Anne Ramelet. "Index des personnages littéraires et politiques cités dans les chroniques de la Revue suisse dans les années 1843 à 1853", typescript, 1975.

Fonds Bridel, IS 2070.

Fonds Louis-Henri Delarageaz, IS 3681.

Fonds Develey, B[15].

Fonds Henri Druey, IS 3442.

Fonds Eusèbe-Henri Gaullieur, IS 142.

Fonds Jean-Jacques Larguier des Bancels, IS 1907/201.

Fonds Olivier, IS 1905.

Fonds Louis Ruchonnet, IS 1922.

Godet, Antoinette. "Bibliographie des œuvres de Juste Olivier", typescript, 1943.

Olivier, Edouard. "Ma maison, 1600–1924", IS 1905/136.

Olivier, Gustave. "Chronique de Givrins, 1824–1915", IS 1905/117.

–. "Souvenirs. 10 mai 1838–21 avril 1924", IS 1905/117.

Olivier, Jean. "Histoire, correspondance, souvenirs de la famille Juste Olivier-Ruchet. 1815–68", IS 1905/60.

Olivier, Juste. "Correspondance à Jacques Adert". IS 40.

–. "Correspondance à Charles Eynard", IS 1905/81–82.

–. "Notes pour une conférence sur Gleyre", [after 1874], IS 1088.

Olivier, Urbain. "Extraits d'histoire de ma vie", IS 1905/60.

–. "La mort de Jean-Louis Olivier", IS 1905/60.

–. "Souvenirs", transcribed ms, 1927, IS 1905/73.

–. Correspondence, IS 1905/112.

–. Letters to Eynard, IS 1905/81.

Olivier, Mme. Urbain. Letters (1867–71), IS 1905/119.

Perrenoud, Marianne and Olivier Pavillon. "Inventaire des archives de Louis-Henry Delarageaz", typescript, IS 3681.

Tallichet, Edouard. "Correspondance", IS 193.

Fondation Mercier
Mercier-de Molin, Jean-Jacques. "Correspondance".

Institut Suisse pour l'Etude de l'Art
Archives de la Société vaudoise des Beaux-Arts. Procès-verbaux, ISEA 101.

Musée Cantonal d'Archéologie et d'Histoire (MCAH)
Troyon, Frédéric. "Albums", 3 vols.

Musée Cantonal des Beaux-Arts (MCBA)
Bonjour, Emile. "Copies de lettres, 1895–1936", 8 vols.

Dessins et travaux sur papier de la collection du musée, 1986–87.

Entrées et sorties des tableaux au Musée des Beaux-Arts, 1926.

Gleyre Archives (GA), various unclassified dossiers.

Gleyre Archives, letters to his aunt and uncle, 1825–32, dossier, 985.

Gleyre Archives, letters to his brother Henry, 1825–43, dossier, 986.

Gleyre Archives, letters to his niece Mathilde, 1862–72, dossier, 987.

Gleyre Archives, letters to Sébastien Cornu, 1840–48, dossier, 988.

Gleyre Archives, letters to unknown correspondents, 1841–67, dossier, 989.

Gleyre Archives, letters to the Canton de Vaud and the Musée Arlaud, 1850–62, dossier, 990.

Gleyre Archives, "Journal", Italian trip, 1826–34, dossier 998.

Gleyre Archives, "Journal", Egyptian trip, 1834–37, dossier, 999.

Grand livre de l'Exposition fédérale, 1862.

Letters addressed to Gleyre, 1845-1874, doss. 996.

Livre d'acquisition, (undated), 2 vols.

Museum Archives, A series, 1820 to the present.

Société des artistes. Dépenses et recettes.

Vuillermet, Joseph. "Nomenclature des peintres du Musée des Beaux-Arts", 1912.

Musée Historique, Collection de l'Association du Vieux-Lausanne (MH/AVL)
Fonds Georges Bridel.

Private collection
David, Emile. Correspondence.

Gaudin, Jean-Daniel. "Journal", 1825–56, 3 vols.

Olivier, Juste. Various letters of 1859–65.

Olivier, Juste, "Notes sur Gleyre", 1874.

## LONDON

British Library (BL)
Egerton Papers, Add. Ms. 3166, ff. 91–93 and Add. Ms. 3168, ff. 36-64.

Lane, William. "Papers", Add. Ms. 34080–8.

## LYONS

Bibliothèque Municipale (BM)
Comptes rendus [dossier of reviews from local newspapers].

Fleury-Richard. "Biographie artistique de Fleury-Richard, peintre lyonnais, par lui-même", n° 1647.

Société des Amis des arts. Procès-verbaux. Série R².

Private collection
Fleury-Richard. "Mes souvenirs", undated manuscript.

## MARSEILLE

Archives de la Ville de Marseille
Série ID, 94.

## MONTPELLIER

Archives Municipales (AM)
Séries R 2/3, dossier 6, 1902.

## NEUCHÂTEL

Archives de l'Etat (AE)
Fonds Albert de Meuron.

Fonds Auguste Bachelin.

Fonds Jules Jacot-Guillarmod.

Fonds Edmond de Pury.

Bibliothèque de la Ville (BV)
Collection Lidia Brefin, Ms 2124

Musée d'Art et d'Histoire (MAH)
Catalogue par ordre de date des sculptures, dessins… du musée de peinture de la Ville de Neuchâtel, n. d.

Procès-verbaux. Séances. Musée d'art et d'histoire.

Rapport de la Commission des Beaux-Arts, 1874.

## ORLEANS

Musée des Beaux-Arts
Dossiers (without inventory numbers).

## PARIS

Archives du Louvre (AL)
Dossier Gleyre, P³⁰.

Dossier X. Salon de 1840.

Dossier X. Salon de 1843.

Dossier X. Salon de 1845.

Dossier X. Salon de 1849.

Enregistrement des ouvrages. Exposition de 1833. KK²⁷.

Enregistrement des ouvrages, Exposition de 1840. KK³⁴.

Enregistrement des ouvrages. Exposition de 1843. KK³⁷.

Enregistrement des ouvrages. Exposition de 1845. KK³⁹.

Enregistrement des ouvrages. Exposition de 1849. KK⁴³.

Pape-Carpentier, Mme. "Correspondance", dossier V⁸, 1917.

Procès-verbaux du jury. 1844–45. KK⁶¹.

Rapport à Monsieur l'Intendant général de la Liste civile sur l'exposition de 1843. KK⁶⁰.

Registre des copies, 1893–1914.

Archives Nationales (AN)
Beaux-Arts, series F²¹.

Concours pour le Grand Prix, le 1 avril 1824, AJ⁵², 17.

Concours pour les places pendant le semestre d'hyver [sic] de la salle de modèles, 6 octobre 1825, AJ⁵², 7.

Concours pour les places pendant le semestre d'hiver à la salle de la bosse, 19 novembre 1825, AJ⁵², 7.

Concours pour les places pendant le semestre d'été à la salle du modèle, 6 mars 1826, AJ⁵², 7.

Demandes d'achat d'objets d'art par les artistes, 1840, F²¹, 485.

Elèves. Peintures. XII. Gigou-Guasco AJ⁵², 261.

Enregistrement de MM. les élèves. Ecole spéciale de peinture et sculpture de Paris, AJ⁵², 234.

Inventaire après le décès de M. Gleyre, 8 juin 1874, Minutier central des notaires parisiens, XXXVI.

Maître Bezanson. Minutier central des notaires parisiens. Various dossiers.

Mandats de paiements, Series O⁴.

Musée Campana. "Etat des mémoires des travaux exécutés pour l'installation de l'exposition au Palais de l'Industrie", 1863, F²¹, 486, dossier V.

Note des tableaux expédiés depuis le 1ᵉʳ août jusqu'au 10 décembre 1840, F²¹, 500.

Répertoire des actes. 28 septembre 1868 au 6 octobre 1874. Minutier central des notaires parisiens.

Archives de la Seine (AS)
Direction générale de l'enregistrement. Table alphabétique des successions et des absences. Partie n° 52/3.

Registre de recette. Déclarations des mutations par décès. Livre 305, n° 6.

Bibliothèque Nationale, Département des Manuscrits (BN)
Chenavard, Paul. "Correspondance", Nouv. Acq. Fr. 11955.

Montfort, A. A. "Journal d'un voyage en Orient, 18 mars 1837–14 février 1838", Nouv. Acq. Fr. 11551.

Quinet, Edgar. "Correspondance", Nouv. Acq. Fr. 20789.

Quinet, Mme Edgar. "Journal des dernières années", Nouv. Acq. Fr. 11844.

–. "Mémorial de Madame Quinet", Nouv. Acq. Fr. 11825–11846.

Bibliothèque Nationale, Cabinet des Estampes
Letters and Prints, Yᵉ series

Series AA⁴.

Dossier Gleyre, DC 306.

Fondation Custodia, Institut néerlandais
Gleyre. Letters. 1973-A767.
Sisley, Alfred. Letters. 1973-A1.

Institut de France (IF)
Bibliothèque Spoelberg de Lovenjoul, Fonds Franklin-Grout, B III.

Mme Raffalovich. "Lettres", Dossier XIII-XVIII, mss. 2653–3658.

Mairie, VIIᵉ arrondissement
Registre des actes de décès, 1874, 1D. Gleyre, 42–649.

Private collection
Zuber, Henri. Correspondence.


**SAINT-PREX**

Private collection
Larguier des Bancels, Jacques. Correspondence and private papers.


**SCHAFFHAUSEN**

Stadtbibliotek
Moser, Henri. Papers, Gs 73.453.


**VEVEY**

Private collection
Ormond Family Collection.

# B. PUBLISHED ARTICLES AND BOOKS

ACKERMAN, Gerald M. "Gérôme's 'A Chat by the Fireside'", *The Register of the Museum of Arts, University of Kansas*, IV, n° 4-5, March, 1971, pp. 21–33.

–. "Drawings of a Famous Teacher : Charles Gleyre", *Master Drawings*, XIII, n° 2, Summer, 1975, pp. 161–69.

–. *La vie et l'œuvre de Jean-Léon Gérôme*, Paris, 1986.

–. "The Néo-Grecs : A Chink in the Wall of Neoclassicism", in June Hargrove, ed., *The French Academy. Classicism and Its Antagonists,* Newark/London/Toronto, 1990, pp. 168–95.

ACQUIER, Hippolyte. "Salon de 1849. Deuxième visite", *La Liberté,* n° 192, 9 July 1849, unpaginated.

ADAM, Juliette. *Nos amitiés politiques avant l'abandon de la revanche*, Paris, 1908.

ADAMINA, Jacques. "Le Major Davel au théâtre", *Bibliothèque universelle et Revue suisse*, CVIII, 1922, pp. 3-22 and 208-230.

–. "Jeanne d'Arc et le Major Davel", *La Famille*, n° 1, 5 January 1923(a), pp. 2–7.

–. "Davel après sa mort", *La Revue,* 4 March–22 April 1923(b), unpaginated.

ADHÉMAR, Jean. "L'enseignement académique en 1820 : Girodet et son atelier", *Bulletin de la Société de l'histoire de l'art français*, 1933, pp. 274–75.

AGASSIZ, Daisy. *A. L. Du Cros, peintre et graveur, 1748–1810. Etude biographique*, Lausanne, 1927.

–. "François Keisermann. Un paysagiste suisse à Rome, 1765-1833", *Revue historique vaudoise*, XXXVIII, 1930, pp. 65–89.

–. "Charles-François Knébel, 1810–1877. Un peintre suisse-romain", *Revue historique vaudoise*, XLIII, 1935, pp. 353–71.

ALANIC, Mathilde. *Le mariage de Hoche, ou le roman de l'amour conjugal*, Paris, 1928.

ALAZARD, Jean. *L'Orient et la peinture française au XIXᵉ siècle. D'Eugène Delacroix à Auguste Renoir*, Paris, 1930.

*Album de la Guêpe*, Lausanne, 1851.

ALEM, Jean-Pierre. *Enfantin. Le prophète aux sept visages*, Paris, 1963.

ALEXANDRE, Arsène. *Jean-François Raffaëlli. Peintre, graveur et sculpteur*, Paris, 1909.

*Almanach bottin du commerce de Paris*, Paris, 1851.

*Almanach de Lausanne pour l'année 1858*, Lausanne, 1858.

*Almanach du Major Davel pro 1896*, Lausanne, 1896.

*Almanach national pour 1874*, Paris, 1874.

*Almanach royal et national pour l'an MDCCCXLV*, Paris, 1845.

*Almanach de la Suisse illustrée et Almanach populaire de la Suisse romande*, Lausanne, 1874.

ALLMEN, Pierre von, ed. *Léo Châtelain, architecte, 1839–1913*, exh. cat., Musée d'art et d'histoire, Neuchâtel, 1985.

AL-SAYYID-MARSOT, Afaf Lutfi. *Egypt in the Reign of Muhammad Ali*, Cambridge, 1984.

ALTICK, Richard D. *Paintings From Books. Art and Literature in Britain, 1760–1900*, Columbus, 1985.

AMAURY-DUVAL, Eugène. *L'atelier d'Ingres,* Paris, 1924.

AMAYA, Mario. "Contrasts and Comparisons in French Nineteenth-Century Painting", *Apollo*, CVII, n° 194, April, 1978, pp. 254–63.

AMIEL, Henri-Frédéric. *Journal intime*, Bernard Gagnebin and Philippe M. Monnier, eds., Lausanne, 1976 et seq.

AMPRIMOZ, François-Xavier. "Un décor 'Fouriériste' à Florence", *Revue de l'art*, XLVIII, 1980, pp. 57–67.

ANDRÉ, Albert. *Renoir*, Paris, 1928.

ANDRÉE, Rolf. *Arnold Böcklin. Die Gemälde,* Basel/Munich, 1977.

ANDREWS, Keith. *The Nazarenes. A Brotherhood of German Painters in Rome*, Oxford, 1964.

ANDRIEU, L. "Un ami de Flaubert. Edmond Laporte (1832–1906)", *Les amis de Flaubert*, XLIX, 1970, pp. 20–28.

ANGRAND, Pierre. *Monsieur Ingres et son époque*, Paris, 1967.

ARCHINARD, Charles. *Histoire de l'instruction publique dans le canton de Vaud*, Lausanne, 1870.

ARLETTAZ, Gérard. *Libéralisme et société dans le canton de Vaud, 1814–1845,* Lausanne, 1980.

ARMANDI, Le Chevalier P. "Histoire des éléphans [sic]", *Le Voleur et le Cabinet de lecture réunis*, deuxième série, n° 50, 10 September 1845, pp. 217–20.

ARMSTRONG, Thomas, *Thomas Armstrong, C. B.: A Memoir*, L. M. Lamont, ed., London, 1912.

ARNASON, Hjoervardur Harvard. *The Sculptures of Houdon*, London, 1975.

ARNOULET, Docteur F. "La pénétration intellectuelle en Tunisie avant le Protectorat", *Revue africaine*, XCVIII, 1954, pp. 140–80.

ARSLAN, Edoardo. *I Bassano*, 2 vols., Milan, n. d. [1960](a).

–. *Le pittore del Duomo di Milano*, Milan, 1960(b).

*The Artist and the Studio in the 18th and 19th Centuries*, exh. cat., Cleveland Museum of Art, Cleveland, 1978.

*L'art et la vie romantique*, exh. cat., Hôtel de Jean Charpentier, Paris, 1923.

ATHANASSOGLOU-SOUYOUDJOGLOU, Nina. *French Images from the Greek War of Independence, 1821–1827*, Princeton, 1980.

ATKINSON, J. Beavinton. "International Exhibition, 1862. Pictures of the French, Belgian, Italian, and Spanish Schools", *The Art Journal*, I, 1862(a), pp. 165–68.

–. "International Exhibition, 1862. Pictures of the Dutch, Russian, Scandinavian, and Swiss Schools", *The Art Journal*, I, 1862(b), pp. 197–200.

AUBERT, Albert. "Lucrèce", *La Revue indépendante*, VII, 25 April 1843, pp. 560–82.

AUBERT-LECOULTRE, Béatrice. *François Bocion*, Lutry, 1977.

AUDEMARS, Georges. "Coup d'œil sur la Société artistique et littéraire de Lausanne pendant l'année sociétaire 1850–51", *La Revue suisse*, XIV, December, 1851, pp. 826–34.

AUDIN, Marius and Eugène VIAL. *Dictionnaire des artistes et ouvriers d'art du Lyonnais,* Paris, 1918.

AUDLEY, George. *Collection of Pictures*, Southport, 1923.

AUGUSTIN-THIERRY, A. "Souvenirs d'un peintre militaire: Adolphe Yvon", *Revue des Deux-Mondes*, VIII, n° 17, 15 October 1933, pp. 844–49.

AULANIER, Christian. *Les trois salles des Etats*, Paris, 1952.

AVENEL, Henri. *Histoire de la presse française depuis 1789 jusqu'à nos jours*, Paris, 1900.

AVERY, Samuel P. *The Diaries of Samuel P. Avery, Art Dealer, 1871–1882*, Madeleine Fidell-Beaufort, H. L. Kleinfeld, and Jeanne Welcher, eds., New York, 1979.

[AVERY, Samuel P.]. "Letter", *New York Evening Post*, 18 May 1874, unpaginated.

B., E. "Les 'Gleyre' du Château de La Sarraz", *Bulletin d'information. Société des amis du Château de La Sarraz*, n° 3, May, 1976, unpaginated.

B., F. "Lettre sur l'exposition de peinture à Paris", *La Revue suisse*, XII, July, 1849, pp. 422–28.

BL., Jules. "Les Secrétan", *Journal bourgeoisial*, IV, n° 36, 25 August 1925, pp. 1–2.

BACH, Eugène, Louis BLONDEL, and Adrien BOVY. *Les monuments d'art et d'histoire du canton de Vaud, II: La cathédrale de Lausanne*, Basel, 1944.

BACHELIN, Auguste. "Exposition nationale au profit des incendiés de Travers", *Musée neuchâtelois*, II, 1865, pp. 303–305 and 325–29.

–. *Iconographie neuchâteloise, ou catalogue raisonné des tableaux, dessins, gravures, statues, médailles, cartes et plans relatifs au canton de Neuchâtel*, Neuchâtel, 1878.

–. "Frédéric Simon", *Bibliothèque universelle et Revue suisse*, XLIII, n° 3, 1889, pp. 538–60.

B[ACHELIN], A[uguste]. "En souvenir du peintre Gleyre", *La Patrie suisse*, 21 December 1898, pp. 305–307.

BAETJER, Katharine. "Extracts from the Paris Journal of John Taylor Johnston, First President of The Metropolitan Museum", *Apollo*, CXIV, n° 238, December, 1981, pp. 410–17.

BAILBÉ, Joseph. "Le voyage en Egypte de Flaubert. Illusion et poésie", in *Flaubert et Maupassant. Ecrivains normands*, Paris, 1981.

BAILLY-HERZBERG, Janine. *L'eau-forte de peintre au dix-neuvième siècle. La Société des aquafortistes 1862–1867,* 2 vols., Paris, 1972.

BALLARIN, Andreina. *Pinacoteca di Vicenza,* Vicenza, 1982.

BALSIGER, Roger Nicholas and Ernst KLÄY. *Bei Schah, Emir und Khan: Henri Moser Charlottenfels, 1844–1923*, Schaffhausen, 1992.

BALTEAU, Jules et al. *Dictionnaire de biographie française*, Paris, 1929 et seq.

BANVILLE, Théodore de. *Les exilés*, Paris, 1875.

BARATIER, Edouard, ed. *Documents de l'histoire de la Provence*, Toulouse, 1971.

BARBAULT, Jean. *Les plus beaux monuments de Rome ancienne*, Rome, 1761.

BARBEY, Frédéric. "Le peintre Gleyre à Sainte-Marguerite de Paris", *Gazette de Lausanne*, 1 August 1946, p. 4.

BARBEY, Gilles and Jacques GUBLER. "La 'Cité des villas' Dubochet à Clarens, paysage architectural total", *Nos monuments d'art et d'histoire*, XXIX, n° 4, 1978, pp. 391–401.

BARBEY, Maurice. "L'iconographie de Davel", in *Le Major Davel, 1670–1723. Etude historique*, Lausanne, 1923, pp. 259–75.

BARBIERI, Franco. *Il museo civico di Vicenza*, Vicenza, 1962.

BARNUM, Emily Keene. "Romance and Legends of the Builders of Switzerland: Divico and Orgetorix", *The Swiss Monthly*, II, n° 2, November, 1923, pp. 23–26.

BARRON, Louis. *Paris pittoresque. 1800–1900*, Paris, n. d.

BART, Benjamin. *Flaubert*, Syracuse, 1967.

BARZUN, Jacques. *Berlioz and the Romantic Century*, 2 vols., New York/London, 1969.

BASCHET, Robert. *E.-J. Delécluze, témoin de son temps, 1781–1863*, Paris, 1942.

BÄTSCHMANN, Oskar. *La peinture de l'époque moderne* (Ars Helvetica, VI), Disentis, 1989.

BAUD-BOVY, Daniel. *Peintres genevois*, Geneva, 1903.

–. "A l'ombre parisienne d'un phalanstère d'artistes genevois", *Formes et couleurs*, n° 1, 1942, unpaginated.

BAUDELAIRE, Charles. "Salon de 1845", in *Œuvres complètes*, Jacques Crépet, ed., Paris, 1923, I, pp. 3-78.

BÉDOLLIÈRE, E. de la. "Le modèle", in *Les Français peints par eux-mêmes*, Paris, 1858, I, pp. 367–71.

BEENKEN, Hermann. "Masaccios und Masolinos Fresken von San Clemente in Rom", *Belvedere*, XI, 1932, pp. 7–13.

*Belles-Lettres de Lausanne. Livre d'or du 150ᵉ anniversaire. 1806–1956*, Lausanne, 1956.

BELLIER DE LA CHAVIGNERIE, Emile and Louis AUVRAY, *Dictionnaire général des artistes de l'Ecole française*, Paris, 1882–87.

BELZONI, Giovanni. *Narrative of the Operations and Recent Discoveries with the Pyramids...*, London, 1820 (revised 1827).

–. *Travels of Belzoni in Egypt and Nubia*, London, 1822 (reed. 1979).

[BENAÏD, Le général]. *Notice sur le général Benaïd, sa famille et son administration à Tunis*, Paris, 1853.

BENASSIS, A. "Charles-Augustin Sainte-Beuve. Ses médecins et ses maladies", *Revue thérapeutique des alcaloïdes*, n° 82, July, 1929, pp. 7–14.

BÉNÉDITE, Léonce. *La peinture au XIXᵉ siècle*, Paris, n. d. [1909].

–. *Thédore Chassériau. Sa vie et son œuvre*, Paris, n. d. [1931].

BÉNÉZIT, Emmanuel. *Dictionnaire critique et documentaire des peintres, sculpteurs, etc.*, Paris, 1911–23.

BENISOVICH, Michel. "Lettres inédites de Courbet", *Les amis de Gustave Courbet, Bulletin*, n° 4, 1948, pp. 21–24.

BENNASSUTI, Giueseppe. *Guida e compendio. Storico della città di Verona*, Verona, 1831.

BENOIST, Luc. *Musée des Beaux-Arts, Nantes. Catalogue et guide*. Nantes, 1953.

BÉRARD, Claude and Jacques-Pierre VERNANT, eds. *La cité des images. Religion et société en Grèce antique*, Lausanne/Paris, 1984.

BERGDOLL, Barry. *Les Vaudoyer: une dynastie d'architectes*, exh. cat., Musée d'Orsay, Paris, 1991.

BERGER, Jacques-Edouard. "Gleyre et l'Orient", in *Charles Gleyre ou les illusions perdues*, exh. cat., Kunstmuseum, Winterthur, 1974, pp. 50–69.

B[ERGER], Ric. "Les quatre sépultures d'un artiste vaudois", *Feuille d'avis de Lausanne*, 28 August 1961, p. 32.

BERGERAT, Emile. "Hamon", *Galerie contemporaine*, July-December, 1877, unpaginated.

BERGOUNIOUX, Edouard. "Le salon de 1845. Peinture religieuse et historique", *Revue de Paris*, III, 1 April 1845, pp. 478–80.

BERLIOZ, Hector. *Correspondance inédite, 1819–1868*, Paris, 1879.

–. *Mémoires*, Pierre Citron, ed., Paris, 1969.

*Berlioz and the Romantic Imagination*, exh. cat., Victoria and Albert Museum, London, 1969.

BERNABEI, Franco. *Pietro Selvatico nella critica e nella Storia dell'arti figurative dell'Ottocento*, Vicenza, 1974.

BERNARD. "Le Salon de Genève", *Journal de Genève*, 1 September 1854, pp. 1–2; 3 September 1854, p. 2; 7 September 1854, pp. 1–2; 14 September 1854, pp. 1–2; and 16 September 1854, pp. 1–2.

BERNARD, Claude. *Lettres à Madame R.*, Saint-Julien-en-Beaujolais, 1974.

–. *Lettres parisiennes*, Paris, 1978.

BERNHARD, Marianne. *Deutsche Romantik Handzeichnungen*, Munich, 1973.

BERTELLI, Carlo, Vittorio GREGOTTI, and Simonetta BEDONI. *Raffaello e Brera*, exh. cat., Pinacoteca di Brera, Milan, 1984.

BERTHOUD, Charles. "Charles Gleyre", in *Galerie suisse*, III, Lausanne, 1880(a), pp. 536–54.

–. *Juste Olivier*, Lausanne, 1880(b).

BERTHOUD, Dorette. "Le refuge en Suisse des enfants d'Orléans", *Revue de la Société suisse des amis de Versailles*, V, 1960, pp. 19–20 and VI, pp. 15–18.

BERTHOUD, Fritz. "Charles Gleyre", *Bibliothèque universelle et Revue suisse*, L, 1874, pp. 454–76 and 604–27.

–. "Juste Olivier", *Gazette de Lausanne*, 31 January 1876, pp. 1–2; 1 February 1876, pp. 1–2; and 2 February 1876, pp. 1–2.

–. "Charles Clément", *Le rameau de sapin*, 1 February 1888, pp. 5–6 and 1 March 1888, pp. 9–10.

–. "Un souvenir de Gleyre", *Bibliothèque universelle et Revue suisse*, CIII, n° 9, 1898, pp. 449–83 and n° 10, 1898, pp. 102–28.

BERTI, Luciano and Umberto BALDINI. *Filippino Lippi*, Florence, 1957.

BERTRAND, Alexis. "Art et sociologie d'après des lettres inédites de P. Chenavard", *Archives d'anthropologie criminelle de médecine légale et de psychologie normale et pathologie*, XXVI, 1911, pp. 525–49.

BESSIS, Henriette. *Marcello sculpteur*, exh. cat., Musée d'Art et d'Histoire, Fribourg, 1980.

BIAUDET, Jean-Charles. "Henri Monod et le Major Davel", *Etudes de Lettres*, III, July/September, 1960, pp. 120–27.

–, ed. *Histoire de Lausanne*, Lausanne, 1982.

BILLETER, Erika, ed. *Chefs-d'œuvre du Musée cantonal des Beaux-Arts, Lausanne*, Bern, 1989.

BILLY, André. *Sainte-Beuve. Sa vie et son temps*, Paris, 1952.

BLANC, Charles. *Histoire des peintres de toutes les écoles depuis la Renaissance*, III, Paris, 1865.

–. *Grammaire des arts du dessin*, Paris, 1867.

–. *Les artistes de mon temps*, Paris, 1876.

–. *Une famille d'artistes. Les trois Vernet, Joseph, Carle, Horace*, Paris, n. d. [1889].

BLANC, Henri. *Dr Jacques Larguier, professeur à l'Université de Lausanne, 1844–1904*, Lucerne, 1905.

–. "Le Musée zoologique de Lausanne", *Bulletin de la Société vaudoise des sciences naturelles*, XLVIII, n° 175, 1912, pp. 71–123.

BLANCHET, Rodolphe. *Notice sur le Major Davel, mort le 24 avril 1723*, Lausanne, 1850.

[–]. *Histoire glorieuse du Major Davel de Cully, mort le 24 avril 1723, avec le dessin du tableau de M. Gleyre*, Payerne, 1851.

–. *Lausanne dès les temps anciens*, Lausanne, 1863.

BLETON, Auguste. "Sociétés des Beaux-Arts", in *Lyon et la région lyonnaise en 1906*, Lyons, 1906, pp. 505–508.

BLOCH, Ferdinand and A. MERCKLEIN. *Les rues de Paris*, Paris, 1894.

BLUNDEN, Maria and Godrey. *Journal de l'impressionnisme*, Geneva, 1970.

BLUNT, Anthony, *The Paintings of Nicolas Poussin. A Critical Catalogue*, London, 1966(a).

–. *Nicolas Poussin*, London, 1966(b).

BLUNT, Wilfrid. *On Wings of Song. A Biography of Felix Mendelssohn*, London, 1974.

BOIME, Albert. "Le Musée des copies", *Gazette des Beaux-Arts*, LXIV, October, 1964, pp. 237–47.

–. *The Academy and French Painting in the Nineteenth Century*, London, 1971.

–. "The Instruction of Charles Gleyre and the Evolution of Painting in the Nineteenth Century", in *Charles Gleyre ou les illusions perdues*, exh. cat., Kunstmuseum, Winterthur, 1974, pp. 102–24.

–. "The Teaching Reforms of 1863 and the Origins of Modernism in France", *The Art Quarterly*, I, n° 1, 1977, pp. 1–39.

–. *Thomas Couture and the Eclectic Vision*, New Haven/London, 1980.

BOINET, Amédée. *Les églises parisiennes, III : XVIIᵉ et XVIIIᵉ siècles*, Paris, 1964.

BOISSARD, Fernand. "Les ateliers d'élèves en peinture", *La Liberté, Journal des arts*, I, 1832, pp. 104–108.

BOITEL, Léon. "Exposition de 1839–49", *Revue du Lyonnais*, XI, 1840, pp. 77–91.

BOLLI, Laurent, *Chronique de l'Asile des aveugles de Lausanne, 1843–1943*, Lausanne, 1944.

*Bonaparte en Egypte*, exh. cat., Musée de l'Orangerie, Paris, 1938.

BONJOUR, Emile. *Catalogue du musée de Lausanne*, Lausanne, 1887.

–. "Sur la tombe de Charles Gleyre", *La Revue du dimanche*, 7 June 1896, pp. 177–78.

–. *Le Musée Arlaud (1804–1904)*, Lausanne, 1905.

–. "Gleyre et le canton de Vaud", *La Revue du dimanche*, 7 April 1907, pp. 106–108, and 14 April 1907, pp. 113–14.

BONJOUR, Félix. *Louis Ruchonnet. Sa vie, son œuvre*, Lausanne, 1936.

BONNARD, Albert. "Davel à la scène", in *Notice-souvenir de la représentation de Davel, poème dramatique de Virgile Rossel*, Lausanne, 1898, pp. 32–40.

BONNAT, Léon. "Comment je suis devenu collectionneur", *La Revue de Paris*, 15 February 1926, pp. 757–64.

BONS, Charles de. "Divicon ou la Suisse primitive", *Petit journal suisse*, n° 7, 25 November 1865, pp. 1–2.

BOREL, Gustave. "Strophes écrites après une visite à la tombe de Charles-Gabriel Gleyre, à Chevilly", *Au foyer romand*, IV, 1890, pp. 34–36.

BORGEAUD, Charles. "Ce que l'on sut à Genève de l'entreprise et de la mort du Major Davel", *Revue historique vaudoise*, XXXVIII, 1930, pp. 273–85.

BORGEAUD, Eugène. *Lausanne en images. Essai d'iconographie*, Lausanne, 1912–13.

BOSSAGLIA, Rosana and Mia CINOTTI. *Tesoro e Museo del Duomo*, Milan, 1978.

BOTHMER, Bernard V. "Ptolemaic Reliefs I. A Granite Block of Philip Arridaeus", *Bulletin of the Museum of Fine Arts* (Boston), L, June, 1952, pp. 19–27.

BOUGHTON, G. H. "A Few of the Whistlers I Have Known", *The Studio*, XXX, 1903, pp. 208–18.

BOUILHET, Louis. *Lettres à Louise Colet*, Paris, 1973.

BOUIN, Philippe and Christian-Philippe CHANUT, *Histoire française des foires et des expositions universelles*, Paris, 1980.

BOVET-DAVID, Marie. *Emile David, 1824–1891*. Lausanne, 1943.

BOVY, Adrien. *La peinture suisse de 1600 à 1900*, Basel, 1948.

BOY DE LA TOUR, Maurice. *Le Musée des Beaux-Arts de Neuchâtel*, Neuchâtel, 1922.

BRANDOLESE, Pietro. *Pitture, sculture, architettura ed altre cose notabili di Padova*, Padova, 1795.

BRAS, Sœur Mary Benvenuta. *Gustave Planche (1808–1857). Sa vie, son œuvre de critique d'art, son œuvre de critique dramatique*, Paris, 1936.

BREGUET, Elizabeth. *100 ans de photographie chez les Vaudois, 1839–1939*, Lausanne, 1981.

BREJON DE LAVERGNÉE, Arnauld. *L'inventaire Le Brun de 1683. La collection des tableaux de Louis XIV*, Paris, 1987.

– and Dominique THIÉBAULT, eds. *Catalogue sommaire illustré des peintures du Musée du Louvre*, Paris, 1981.

BREM, Anne-Marie de. *Louis Hersent, 1777–1860. Peintre d'histoire et portraitiste*, exh. cat., Musée de la vie romantique, Paris, 1993–94.

BRETON, Jules. *La vie d'un artiste. Art et nature*, Paris, 1890.

–. *Nos peintres du siècle*, Paris, n. d. [1901?].

BREVANS, Alfred de. "Genève. Exposition des Beaux-Arts", *L'Illustration*, XXIV, n° 604, 23 September 1854, pp. 221–22.

BRIDEL, Georges-Antoine, ed. *Album Vinet. Collection iconographique relative à Alexandre Vinet*, Lausanne, 1902.

–. "A propos de Davel et de trois portraits donnés récemment au Musée du Vieux-Lausanne", *Revue historique vaudoise*, XXIX, 1921, pp. 97–107.

– and Eugène BACH. *Lausanne. Promenades historiques et archéologiques*, Lausanne, 1931.

BRILLI, Attilio. *Il viaggio in Italia. Storia di una grande tradizione culturale dal XVI al XIX secolo*, Milan, 1987.

BRONSTEIN, Leo. *Altichiero. L'artiste et son œuvre*, Paris, 1932.

BROWN, Leon Carl. *The Tunisia of Ahmad Bey, 1837–1855*, Princeton, 1974.

BRUGNOLI, Pierpaolo. *Maestri della pittura veronese*, Verona, 1974.

BRUN, Carl. *Bericht der Gottfried Keller-Stiftung*, Zürich, 1895.

–. *Bericht der Gottfried Keller-Stiftung*, Zürich, 1909.

–, ed. *Schweizerisches Künstler-Lexikon*, Frauenfeld, 1905–17.

BRUN, Georges. "Lettre à Monsieur Marquis, au Châtelard, près Clarens", *Journal de Genève*, 4 January 1863, pp. 1–2.

BRUNE, L'Abbé Paul. *Dictionnaire des artistes et ouvriers d'art de la Franche-Comté*, Paris, 1912.

BRUNEAU, Jean and Jean A. DUCOURNEAU, eds. *Album Flaubert*, Paris, 1972.

BRÜSCHWEILER, Jura. *Barthélemy Menn, 1815–1893. Etude critique et biographique*, Zürich, 1960.

BUCHE, Joseph. *L'Ecole mystique de Lyon, 1776–1847*, Paris, 1935.

BUCHON, Max. "Henri Heine", *La Revue suisse*, XIX, June, 1856, pp. 396–410.

BUCHOWIECKI, Walther. *Handbuch der Kirchen Roms*, Vienna, 1967–74.

BUDGE, Ernest Alfred Wallis. *The Egyptian Sudan. Its History and Monuments*, London, 1907(a).

–. *Travels in Nubia*, London, 1907(b).

–. *A History of Ethiopia, Nubia and Abbyssinia*, London, 1928.

BUDRY, Paul. "L'art romantique", in Daniel BAUD-BOVY, Paul BESSIRE, Philippe BRIDEL, et al., *La vie romantique au Pays romand*, Paul Budry, ed., Lausanne/Geneva, n. d. [1930], pp. 257–91.

BUFFENOIR, Hippolyte. *Les portraits de Jean-Jacques Rousseau*, Paris, 1913.

BUGLER, Caroline. "Innocents Abroad: Nineteenth Century Artists and Travellers in the Near East and North Africa", in Mary Anne Stevens, ed. *The Orientalists: Delacroix to Matisse*, exh. cat., The Royal Academy of Art, London, 1984, pp. 27–31.

BUGAHIR, Mario. *The Iconography of the Maltese Islands 1400–1900. Paintings*, Valletta, 1987.

BÜHLER, Winfried. *Europa. Ein Überblick über die Zeugnisse des Mythos in der antiken Literatur und Kunst*, Munich, 1968.

BURCKHARDT, Jakob. *Der Cicerone*, in *Gesammelte Werke*, X, Basel/Stuttgart, 1978.

BURCKHARDT, John Lewis. *Travels in Nubia*, London, 1819.

BURETTE, Théodose. "Salon de 1840", *Revue de Paris*, April, 1840, pp. 123–43.

BURNAND, René. *Eugène Burnand. L'homme, l'artiste et son œuvre*, Paris/Lausanne, 1926.

–. *L'étonnante histoire des Girardet, artistes suisses*, Neuchâtel, 1940.

–. *Jeunesse de peintres. Eugène Burnand et ses amis*, Lausanne, 1949.

BURNIER, Charles. "Correspondance entre J. Olivier et Ls. Vulliemin", *Revue historique vaudoise*, XV, 1907, pp. 65–75.

–. "Le ménage Olivier à Paris", *Le Conteur vaudois*, n° 27, 2 July 1910, p. 2.

BURTY, Philippe. "La gravure au Salon de 1870", *Gazette des Beaux-Arts*, 1 August 1870, pp. 135–46.

BURY, John Bagnell. *The Cambridge Medieval History*, V, Cambridge, 1929.

BURY, John Patrick Tuer. *Gambetta and the Making of the Third Republic*, London, 1973.

BUSONI, Philippe. "Courrier de Paris", *L'Illustration*, XXI, n° 526, 26 March 1853, p. 194.

–. "Courrier de Paris", *L'Illustration*, XXVII, n° 679, 1 March 1856, pp. 134–35.

BUTLER, Eliza Marian. *Heinrich Heine. A Biography*, London, 1956.

C., Alf. [CÉRÉSOLE, Alfred]. "Cérésole. Branche vaudoise", *Recueil de généalogies vaudoises*, Lausanne, 1923, I, pp. 297 ff.

C., Dr. de. "Nécrologie. Le Dr. Larguier-des-Bancels", *Revue médicale de la Suisse romande*, XXIV, 1904, pp. 384–86.

C., J. "L'exposition en faveur des Alsaciens-Lorrains", *L'Illustration*, LXIII, 2 May 1874, p. 278.

C., L. "L'Enfant prodigue de Gleyre", *Le Chrétien évangélique*, XVII, 1874, pp. 419–20.

CAHN, Théophile. *La vie et l'œuvre d'Etienne Geoffroy Saint-Hilaire*, Paris, 1962.

CAILLIAUD, Frédéric. *Voyage à Méroë, au fleuve blanc au-delà de Fâzoql*, Paris, 4 vols., 1823–27.

[CALLCOTT, Lady]. *Description of the Chapel of the Annunziata dell'Arena; or Giotto's Chapel in Padua by Mrs Callcott*, London, 1835.

CALONNE, Alphonse de. "Salon de 1845", *Le Voleur et le Cabinet de lecteur réunis*, n° 19, 5 April 1845, pp. 312–13 and n° 22, 20 April 1845, pp. 358–59.

CARNE, John. *Syria, the Holy Land, Asia Minor*, London/Paris, 1836–38.

CARRÉ, Jean-Marie. *Voyageurs et écrivains français en Egypte*, Cairo, 1956.

CART, Jacques. *Histoire du mouvement religieux et ecclésiastique dans le canton de Vaud pendant la première moitié du XIXe siècle*, 6 vols., Lausanne, 1870–80.

CARTWRIGHT, Julia. *Jean François Millet. His Life and Letters*, London, 1910.

CASELLI, C. *Nuovo ritratto di Milano in riguardo alle Belle Arti*, Milan, 1827.

CASSINA, Fernandino. *Le fabbriche più cospicue di Milano*, Milan, 1840.

CASTAGNARY, Jules Antoine. *Salons, 1857–1870*, Paris, 1892.

CASTELNUOVO, Enrico et al. *La pittura in Italia. Il Duecento e il Trecento*, 2 vols., Milan, 1985.

*Catalogue. The Collection of Paintings, Drawings, and Statuary. The Property of John Taylor Johnston, Esq.*, New York, 1876.

*Catalogue des dessins de l'Ecole moderne…*, exh. cat., Ecole des Beaux-Arts, Paris, 1884.

*Catalogue des dessins… provenant de la Collection His de La Salle*, Paris, 1883.

*Catalogue de l'Exposition fédérale des Beaux-Arts à Lausanne du 3 mai au 24 mai 1874*, cat. exh., Musée Arlaud, Lausanne, 1874.

*Catalogue de l'exposition Sainte-Beuve. Le Lausanne de 1837*, cat. exh., Lausanne, 1937.

*Catalogue de l'exposition Vieux-Lausanne*, exh. cat., Musée du Vieux-Lausanne, Lausanne, 1902.

*Catalogue officiel de l'Exposition nationale suisse*, exh. cat., Zürich, 1883.

*Catalogue des ouvrages de peinture…*, exh. cat., Musée Arlaud, Lausanne, 1850.

*Catalogue des œuvres d'art appartenant à la Ville de Neuchâtel*, Neuchâtel, 1928.

CATTAUI, René. *Le règne de Mohamed Aly d'après les Archives russes en Egypte*, 4 vols., Cairo, 1931–36.

*Cent ans de peinture genevoise*, exh. cat., Musée d'art et d'histoire, Geneva, 1937.

*Centenaire de l'impressionnisme*, exh. cat., Grand Palais, Paris, 1974.

CHAMPA, Kermit Swiler. *Studies in Early Impressionism*, New Haven/London, 1973.

CHAMPFLEURY [Jules Husson]. *Œuvres posthumes*, Paris, 1894.

CHAPONNIÈRE, Paul. "J.-E. Chaponnière, sculpteur", *L'Art en Suisse*, January 1927, pp. 1–16 and February 1927, pp. 31–45.

CHARAVAY, Etienne. *Lettres autographes composant la collection de M. Alfred Bovet*, Paris, 1885.

CHARLÉTY, Sébastien. *Histoire du saint-simonisme, 1825–1864*, Paris, 1931.

CHARRIÈRE, Frédéric de. "Une vue sur Davel", *La Revue suisse*, XIII, November, 1850, pp. 776–77.

CHASTEL, André. "La redécouverte de Giorgione", in Rodolfo Pallucchini, ed., *Giorgione e l'umanesimo veneziano*, Florence, 1981, II, pp. 565–82.

CHASTELLAIN, Henri. "L'entreprise de Davel", in *Le Major Davel, 1670–1723*, Lausanne, 1923, pp. 78–219.

CHASTENET, Geneviève. *Marie-Louise: L'impératrice oubliée*, Paris, 1983.

CHATELANAT, Charles. *Souvenirs de Henri Euler*, Lausanne, 1871.

–. "Un héros chrétien au XVIIIᵉ siècle", *La Famille*, XXXI, 1890, pp. 268–75.

CHAUD-AIGUES. "Le Rapin", in *Les Français peints par eux-mêmes*, I, Paris, 1841–42.

CHAUDONNERET, Marie-Claude. *Fleury Richard et Pierre Révoil. La peinture troubadour*, Paris, 1980.

–. *La figure de la République. Le concours de 1848*, Paris, 1987.

CHAVANNES, Daniel-Alexandre. "Le Musée cantonal. Ducroz [sic]. Kayserman. Muellener et Brandoin", *Journal de la Société vaudoise d'utilité publique*, XXI, 1835, pp. 3–4.

CHENNEVIÈRES, Philippe de. *Souvenirs d'un directeur des Beaux-Arts*, Paris, 1883–1889, reprint, Paris, 1979.

CHESNEAU, Ernest. *Le décret du 13 novembre et l'Académie des Beaux-Arts*, Paris, 1864.

–. *Les chefs d'Ecole. La peinture au XIXᵉ siècle*, 2nd ed., Paris, 1883.

CHESSEX, Pierre. *Images of the Grand Tour. Louis Ducros 1748–1810*, exh. cat., Kenwood House, London, 1985.

CHIARA, Piero, Gian Alberto DELL'ACQUA, Germano MULAZZANI, et al. *Sacro e profano nella pittura di Bernardino Luini*, exh. cat., Luino, 1975.

CHIROL, Elisabeth. "Trois grands collectionneurs du XIXᵉ siècle", in *Dieux et héros de la Grèce*, exh. cat., Musée des Beaux-Arts, Rouen, 1982–83.

*Un choix de dessins de Géricault, Gleyre, Fromentin*, Braun et Cie., ed., Paris, 1927.

CHOMER, Gilles. "Le séjour en Italie (1822–1830) de Victor Orsel", in *Lyon et l'Italie. Six études d'histoire de l'art*, Gilles Chomer and Marie-Félix Pérez, eds., Lyons, 1984, pp. 181–211.

*Christian Imagery in French Nineteenth-Century Art, 1789–1906*, exh. cat., Shepherd Gallery, New York, 1980.

CHRISTIN, Marc. *Lausanne. Les parrains de ses rues*, Renens, 1910.

CHRISTOPHE, Louis-A. *Abou-Simbel et l'épopée de sa découverte*, Brussels, 1965.

CHUARD, J.-L. "Le 'Davel' de l845", *Gazette de Lausanne*, 10 February 1898, p. 1.

CHUARD, Jean-Pierre. *L'histoire d'un tableau. Le portrait du général Jomini par Charles Gleyre*, Payerne, 1979.

–. "'Le Major Davel' de Charles Gleyre", *24 Heures*, 2 September 1980, p. 44.

–. "Le Vaudois qui inventa la presse illustrée", *24 Heures*, 28 March 1983, p. 56.

CLANET, Louis. "Gleyre", *La Plume*, 1892, p. 483.

CLAPARÈDE, Jean. "Le séjour de Courbet à la Tour de Farges", *Les amis de Gustave Courbet. Bulletin*, n° 7, 1950, pp. 1–12.

CLARETIE, Jules. *Peintres et sculpteurs contemporains*, 2 vols., Paris, 1882–84.

CLAYTON, Peter A. *The Rediscovery of Ancient Egypt. Artists and Travellers in the 19th Century*, London, 1982.

CLÉMENT, Charles. "Hercules aux pieds d'Omphale. Tableau de M. Charles Gleyre", *Revue des Deux-Mondes*, XXXIII, 15 February 1863, pp. 1008–16.

–. "La jeunesse de Michelangelo", *Journal des débats*, April-May, 1864.

–. "Exposition de 1865", *Journal des débats*, 24 April 1865(a), pp. 1–2.

–. "M. Gleyre, à propos du tableau *Hercule aux pieds d'Omphale*", in *Etudes sur les Beaux-Arts en France*, Paris, 1865(b), pp. 213–35.

–. *Géricault. Etude biographique et critique avec le catalogue raisonné de l'œuvre du maître*, Paris, 1868.

–. *Prud'hon. Sa vie, ses œuvres et sa correspondance*, Paris, 1872.

–. *Léopold Robert, d'après sa correspondance inédite*, Paris, 1875.

–. *Artistes anciens et modernes*, Paris, 1876.

–. *Gleyre. Etude biographique et critique avec le catalogue raisonné de l'œuvre du maître*, Geneva/Neuchâtel/Paris, 1878 (2nd ed., 1886).

–. *Le genre cyclamen*, Paris, n. d. [1888?].

CLEMENT, Clara Erskine and Laurence HUTTON. *Artists of the Nineteenth Century and Their Works*, Boston/New York, 1879.

CLÉMENT-GRANDCOURT, Michel. "Charles Gleyre et Charles Clément", in William Hauptman, *Charles Gleyre et la Suisse romande*, exh. cat., Lausanne, 1994, pp. 17–19.

CLÉMENT DE RIS, Louis. "Le Musée du Luxembourg", *L'Artiste*, 9 April 1848, pp. 72–74.

CLOSSMAN, A. de. "A Schaffhausen", *Le Touriste*, n° 20, August, 1866, pp. 237–38.

COGLIATI ARANO, Luisa. *Leonardo all'Ambrosiana: Il Codice Atlantico. Disegni di Leonardo e sua cerchia*, exh. cat., Ambrosiana, Milan, 1982.

COLIN, Nelly. "Jean-Claude Bonnefond et l'Italie", in *Lyon et l'Italie. Six études d'histoire de l'art*, Gilles Chomer and Marie-Félix Pérez, eds., Lyons, 1984, pp. 213–35.

COMTE, Philippe. "Judith et Holopherne ou la naissance d'une tragédie", *La Revue du Louvre*, n° 3, 1977, pp. 137–39.

*Concours pour le monument Davel. Rapport du jury.* Lausanne, 1895.

CONSTANÇON, Maurice. *Davel. Drame historique en six actes et un épilogue*, Lausanne, 1923.

CONSTANS, Claire. *Musée national du château de Versailles. Les peintures.* I, Paris, 1995.

COOK, Clarence. *Art and Artists of Our Time*, 2 vols., New York, 1888.

CORNAZ-VULLIET, Emma. "Souvenirs du Major Davel à l'exposition", in *Journal officiel illustré de l'Exposition suisse, Genève 1896*, n° 38, 9 October 1896, p. 455.

–. *Le Major Davel. Chrétien, soldat, patriote et martyr. Dédié à la jeunesse*, Geneva, 1898.

COURTOIS. "Beaux-Arts. Salon de 1849. Peinture", *Le Corsaire*, 30 June 1849, unpaginated.

COURVOISIER, James. "Fritz Berthoud", *Musée neuchâtelois*, XXVIII, 1891, pp. 137–44; 167–73; 193–201; and 242–51.

–. "Lettres inédites de Juste Olivier à Fritz Berthoud", *Au foyer romand*, XVIII, 1905, pp. 33–102.

COUTURE, Thomas. *Méthodes et entretiens d'atelier*, Paris, 1867.

COZIC, Henri. "Jacques Dubochet", *L'Illustration*, LII, 19 September 1868, pp. 191–92.

CRANE, Sylvia. *White Silence: Greenough, Powers, and Crawford. American Sculptors in Nineteenth Century Italy*, Coral Gables, 1972.

CRESPELLE, Jean-Paul. *Les maîtres de la Belle Epoque*, Paris, 1966.

CRESSON, André. *Hippolyte Taine. Sa vie, son œuvre*, Paris, 1951.

CROSNIER, Jules. *La Société des arts et ses collections*, Geneva, 1910.

CROTTET, Alexandre César. *Histoire et annales de la Ville d'Yverdon*, Geneva, 1859.

CROUZET, Marcel. *Un méconnu du réalisme. Duranty (1833–1880). L'homme, le critique, le romancier*, Paris, 1964.

CROWE, Joseph and Giovanni Battista CAVACASELLE. *A History of Painting in Northern Italy*, London, 1871.

[CUÉNOD, Victor]. *Au foyer romand, 1887–1912. Table alphabétique des noms d'auteurs*, Vevey, 1936.

CUGNIER, Gilles, ed. *Jean-Léon Gérôme, 1824–1904*, Vesoul, 1981.

CURTIUS, Ludwig. *Pentheus*, Berlin/Leipzig, 1929.

CURTO, Silvio. *Storia del Museo Egizio di Torino*, Turin, 1976.

CUZIN, Jean-Pierre, ed. *Raphaël et l'art français*, Paris, 1983.

D. "Divico. Drame représenté à Bevaix", *La Patrie suisse*, 5 August 1908, p. 190–91.

Dˣˣˣ. [Untitled], *Le Démocrate*, n° 83, 19 October 1858, p. 3.

D., M. "L'Omphale de M. Gleyre", *Journal de Genève*, 23 November 1865, p. 3.

–. "Charles Gleyre", *Journal de Genève*, 7 May 1874, pp. 2–3.

–. "L'exposition de Gleyre", *Journal de Genève*, 16 August 1874, pp. 2–3.

D., P. "Caroline Juste-Olivier", *Gazette de Lausanne*, 15 January 1935, p. 3.

DACOS, Nicole. *Le Loggie di Raffaello*, Rome, 1977.

D'ALBENAS, Georges. *Montpellier. Catalogue de peinture et sculpture*, Montpellier, 1910.

DAULTE, François. *Frédéric Bazille et son temps*, Geneva, 1952.

–. *Alfred Sisley. Catalogue raisonné de l'œuvre peint*, Lausanne, 1959.

–. *Auguste Renoir. Catalogue raisonné de l'œuvre peint*, I, Lausanne, 1971.

–. "A True Friendship: Edmond Maître and Frédéric Bazille", in *Frédéric Bazille and Early Impressionism*, J. Patrice Marandel, ed., exh. cat., Chicago, 1978, pp. 23–30.

–. *Frédéric Bazille et les débuts de l'impressionnisme. Catalogue raisonné de l'œuvre peint*, Paris, 1992(a).

–. *Sisley. Les saisons*, Lausanne/Paris, 1992(b).

*Davel. Essai littéraire par un Vaudois*, Vevey, 1881.

DAWSON, Warren and Eric UPHILL. *Who Was Who in Egyptology*, London, 1972.

DAX, Pierre. "Chronique", *L'Artiste*, 24 October 1858, pp. 126–27.

–. "Chronique", *L'Artiste*, 1 June 1860, p. 239.

–. "Chronique", *L'Artiste*, 1 February 1863, p. 68.

–. "Chronique", *L'Artiste*, 15 December 1865, p. 282.

–. "Chronique", *L'Artiste*, 1 April 1866, p. 167.

–. "Chronique", *L'Artiste*, 1 December 1867, pp. 427–31.

–. "Chronique", *L'Artiste*, 1 February 1874, p. 137.

DÉDÉYAN, Charles. "Giorgione dans les lettres françaises", in *Giorgione e l'umanesimo veneziano*, Rodolfo Pallucchini, ed., Florence, 1981, pp. 659–746.

DELABORDE, Henri. "La Séparation des Apôtres", *Revue des Deux-Mondes*, X, 1 June 1851, pp. 981–83.

–. *Etudes sur les Beaux-Arts*, II, Paris, 1864.

–. *L'Académie des Beaux-Arts depuis la fondation de l'Institut de France*, Paris, 1891.

DELACROIX, Eugène. *Journal d'Eugène Delacroix*, André Joubin, ed., Paris, 1932.

–. *Correspondance générale*, André Joubin, ed., Paris, 1936–38.

DELAFOND, Marianne et al. *Louis Boilly. 1761–1845*, exh. cat., Musée Marmottan, Paris, 1984.

DELAROCHE-VERNET, H. "Lettres à Paul Delaroche", *La Revue de Paris*, XVI, 1 December 1910, pp. 498–528.

DELAUNAY, A.-H. "Actualités-Souvenirs", *L'Artiste*, 24 September 1843, p. 206.

DELÉCLUZE, Etienne. "Salon de 1840", *Journal des débats*, 5 March 1840, pp. 1–2; 7 March 1840, pp. 1–2; 12 March 1840, pp. 1–3; and 19 March 1840, pp. 1–3.

–. "Salon de 1843", *Journal des débats*, 20 April 1843, unpaginated.

–. "Salon de 1845", *Journal des débats*, 9 April 1845, unpaginated.

–. "Exposition des ouvrages d'art aux Tuileries en 1849", *Journal des débats*, 17 July 1849, unpaginated.

DELÉDEVANT, Henri and Marc HENRIOUD, eds. *Le livre d'or des familles vaudoises*, Lausanne, 1923.

DELESSERT, Camille. "Rapport de la commission exécutive au grand comité des monuments Davel", *Revue historique vaudoise*, VIII, 1900, pp. 202–17.

DELHORBE, Cécile. *Juste et Caroline Olivier*, Neuchâtel/Paris, n.d. [1937].

DELLA CHIESA, Angela Ottino. *San Maurizio al Monastero Maggiore*, Milan, 1982.

DELVAU, Alfred. *Histoire anecdotique des cafés et cabarets de Paris*, Paris, 1862.

DENVIR, Bernard, ed. *The Impressionists at First Hand*, London, 1987.

DEONNA, Waldemar. *L'art suisse des origines à nos jours*, exh. cat., Musée d'art et d'histoire, Geneva, 1943.

DESBARROLLES, Adolphe. "Lettre sur le Salon de 1845", *Bulletin des amis des arts*, III, n° 10, 1845, pp. 344–402.

DESCHARMES, René and René DUMESNIL. *Autour de Flaubert*, Paris, 1922.

*Dessins d'il y a cent ans. Charles Gleyre et son atelier*, exh. cat., Château de La Sarraz, La Sarraz, 1958.

DEUCHLER, Florens, Marcel RÖTHLISBERGER, and Hans A. LÜTHY. *La peinture suisse du moyen âge à l'aube du XXᵉ siècle*, Geneva, 1975.

*Dictionnaire de l'Académie des Beaux-Arts*, IV, Paris, 1858.

*Dictionnaire géographique de la Suisse*, Charles Knapp, Maurice Borel, and Victor Attinger, eds., 6 vols., Neuchâtel, 1902–10.

*Dictionnaire historique et biographique de la Suisse*, Victor Attinger, Marcel Godet, and Henri Türler, eds., 8 vols., Neuchâtel, 1921–34.

*Dictionnaire historique, géographique et statistique du canton de Vaud*, Eugène Mottaz, ed., Lausanne, 1921.

*Dictionnaire des localités de la Suisse*, Bern, 1967.

DIEPOLDER, Hans. *Der Penthesilea-Maler*, Leipzig, 1936.

DIMIER, Louis. *Histoire de la peinture française au XIXᵉ siècle*, Paris, 1914

DISSARD, Paul. *Le Musée de Lyon. Les peintures*, Paris, 1912.

*Les donateurs du Louvre*, exh. cat., Louvre, Paris, 1989.

DONOP, L. von. *Die Wandgemälde der Casa Bartholdy in der Nationalgalerie*, Berlin, 1889.

DOUCET, Jérôme. *Les peintres français*, Paris, 1905.

DOUIN, Georges. *L'Egypte de 1828 à 1930*, Rome, 1935.

DRACOULIDES, Nicolas N. "Interprétation psycho-analytique des 'Bacchantes' d'Euripide", *Acta psychotherapeutica*, II, 1963, pp. 14–27.

DRISKELL, Michael Paul. "Icon and Narrative in the Art of Ingres", *Arts Magazine*, LVI, December, 1981, pp. 100–07.

–. *Representing Belief. Religion, Art, and Society in Nineteenth Century France*, University Park, 1992.

DRUEY, Henri. *Correspondance*, Michel Steiner and André Lasserre, eds, II, Lausanne, 1978.

DUBOIS, Frédéric-Théodore. "Promenade héraldique à la cathédrale de Lausanne", *Archives héraldiques suisses*, XLIV, 1930, pp. 201–06.

DUBOSC, C. *Soixante ans dans les ateliers des artistes. Dubosc modèle*, G. Crauk, ed., Paris, n. d.

DUBOSC DE PESQUIDOUX. "Gleyre", *L'Artiste*, 1 September 1874, pp. 158–62.

DUBUISSON, A. *Bonington*, Paris, 1927.

DU CAMP, Maxime. "Exposition universelle. Beaux-Arts", *Revue de Paris*, XXVI, 1 June 1855, pp. 5–21 and 15 June 1855, pp. 172–207.

–. *Souvenirs littéraires*, Paris, 1883.

–. *Souvenirs d'un demi-siècle*, 2 vols., 24th ed., Paris, 1949.

–. *Lettres inédites à Gustave Flaubert*, G. Bonaccorso and R. M. di Stepfano, eds., Messina, 1978.

DUCOURAU, Vincent and Arlette SÉRULLAZ, eds. *Dessins français du Musée Bonnat à Bayonne*, Paris, 1979.

DUFOUR, A. "Minerve et les Grâces", *Gazette de Lausanne*, 6 September 1874, pp. 489–90.

DUFOURNET, Paul. *Hector Horeau précurseur*, Paris, n. d.

DU MAURIER, George. *Trilby*, London, 1895.

DUMESNIL, René. *Flaubert. Documents iconographiques*, Vésenaz/Geneva, 1948.

DUNHAM, Dows. *The Egyptian Department and Its Excavations*, Boston, 1958.

–. *The Barkal Temples*, Boston, 1970.

– and Jozef Maria Antoon JANSSEN. *Second Cataract Forts, I. Semma, Kumma*, Boston, 1960.

DU PASQUIER, Marcel. *Edgar Quinet en Suisse. Douze années d'exil*, Neuchâtel, 1959.

DU PAYS, Augustin-Joseph. "Les Romains passant sous le joug. Tableau de M. Gleyre", *L'Illustration*, XXXII, n° 816, 16 October 1858, pp. 241–42.

–. "Salon de 1865", *L'Illustration*, XLV, n° 1159, 13 May 1865, pp. 298–99.

D[U PAYS], A[ugustin]-J[oseph]. "Salon de 1849", *L'Illustration*, XIII, 28 July 1849, pp. 339–42.

DUPLAIN, Georges. "Une belle exposition au Château de La Sarraz", *Journal de Cossonay*, 18 July 1958, p. 2.

DUPLOMB, Charles. *La rue du Bac*, Paris, 1894.

DUPRAZ, Louis. "Histoire du Major Jean-Abraham-Daniel Davel du 31 mars au samedi 24 avril 1723", *La Revue*, n° 272, 19 November 1898, p. 2.

DURAND, Louis. *Le Major Davel. Poésie, musique, dessins*, Lausanne, 1879.

DURANDE, Amédée. *Joseph, Carle et Horace Vernet. Correspondance et biographie*, Paris, n. d. [1864].

DURET, Théodore. *Histoire d'Edouard Manet et de son œuvre*, Paris, 1902.

–. *Histoire des peintres impressionnistes*, Paris, 1906.

–. *Histoire de J. M$^c$. N. Whistler et de son œuvre*, Paris, 1914.

DUREY, Philippe. *Le Musée des Beaux-Arts de Lyon*, Paris, 1988.

DUSSAUD, René. "Le peintre Montfort en Syrie (1837–1838)", *Syria*, I, 1920, pp. 58–71 and 155–64; and II, 1920, pp. 63–72.

DUSSIEUX, Louis. *Les artistes français à l'étranger*, 3rd ed., Paris/Lyons, 1876.

EASTON, Malcolm. *Artists and Writers in Paris. The Bohemian Idea, 1803–1867*, London, 1964.

EATON, Daniel Cady. *A Handbook of Modern French Painting*, New York, 1909.

EDEL, Leon and Lyall H. POWERS. *The Complete Notebooks of Henry James*, New York and Oxford, 1978.

EDWARDS, Stewart. *The Paris Commune 1871*, New York, 1977.

EGBERT, Donald Drew. *Social Radicalism and the Arts: Western Europe*, New York, 1970.

EGLI, Marie-Françoise. *L'orientalisme chez Charles Gleyre*, Zürich, 1978.

*Egypte-France*. exh. cat., Musée des arts décoratifs, Paris, 1949.

*Egyptomania. L'Egypte dans l'art occidental, 1730–1930*, exh. cat., Louvre, Paris, 1994.

*Ein griechischer Traum. Leo von Klenze, der Archeologue*. exh. cat., Munich, 1985–86.

EITNER, Lorenz. *Géricault's "Raft of the Medusa"*, London, 1972.

–. *Géricault. His Life and Work*, London, 1983.

*The Elegant Academics. Chroniclers of Nineteenth-Century Parisian Life*, exh. cat., The Sterling and Francine Clark Art Institute, Williamstown, 1974.

EMERIT, Marcel. "L'égérie de Napoléon III. Madame Cornu", *Revue de Paris*, 1 June 1937, pp. 550–75 and 15 June 1937(a), pp. 794–825.

–. *Madame Cornu et Napoléon III. D'après les lettres de l'Empereur conservées à la Bibliothèque nationale et d'autres documents inédits*, Paris, 1937(b).

ENAULT, Louis. *Paris et les Parisiens*, Paris, 1856.

*Encyclopédie illustrée du Pays de Vaud*, VII, *Les arts de 1800 à nos jours*, Claude Reymond, ed., Lausanne, 1978.

ENKIRI, Gabriel. *Ibrahim Pacha, 1781–1848*, Cairo, 1948.

ERNST, Fritz. *Wilhelm Tell, als Freiheitssymbol Europas*, Zürich, 1979.

ESQUIROS, Alphonse. "Critique. Un tableau du Salon", *Revue de Paris*, XVI, n° 160, 10 May 1845, pp. 61–63.

ETEX, Antoine. *James Pradier. Etude sur sa vie et ses ouvrages*, Paris, 1859.

–. *Les souvenirs d'un artiste*, Paris, n. d. [1877].

E[ULER], H[enri]. "Canton de Vaud. Exposition de Lausanne", *Le Courrier suisse*, 11 September 1850, p. 2; 13 September 1850, pp. 1–3; 22 September 1850, pp. 2–3; 2 October 1850, pp. 2–3; and 6 October 1850, pp. 1–2.

*Exotische Welten. Europäische Phantasien*. exh. cat., Institut für Auslandsbeziehungen, Stuttgart, 1987.

*Explication des ouvrages de peinture exposés au profit de la colonisation de l'Algérie par les Alsaciens-Lorrains*, Paris, 1874.

*Explication des ouvrages de peinture, sculpture, architecture, gravure et lithographie des artistes vivants*, Paris, 1864.

*Explication des ouvrages…*, Paris, 1865.

*Explication des ouvrages…*, Paris, 1866.

*Explication des ouvrages…*, Paris, 1867.

*Explication des ouvrages…*, Paris, 1868.

*Explication des ouvrages…*, Paris, 1869.

*Exposition des œuvres d'Edmond de Pury*. exh. cat., Musée d'art et d'histoire, Neuchâtel, 1912.

*Exposition universelle de 1867 à Paris. Catalogue général… Première partie contenant les œuvres d'art*, Paris, 1867.

F., P. [FEVAL, Paul?] "Salon de 1843", *Le Voleur et le Cabinet de lecteur réunis*, 30 March 1843, pp. 326–27.

F., V. "Un parent du Major Davel", *La Revue du dimanche*, IV, n° 36, 4 September 1892, p. 277.

–. "Notre plus grand peintre", *Le Conteur vaudois*, n° 31, 30 July 1910, p. 1.

FABRE, Marc-André. *Hoche. L'enfant de la victoire, 1768-1797*, Paris, 1947.

FASOLO, Giulio. *Guida del Museo civico di Vicenza*, Vicenza, 1940.

FAURE, Elie. "Renoir", *La Revue hebdomadaire*, XXIX, April, 1920, pp. 350–68.

FAVRE, Louis. "Notre Musée des Beaux-Arts", *Musée Neuchâtelois*, XXX, September, 1893, pp. 197–207 and 227–38.

FELS, Marthe de. *La vie de Claude Monet*, Paris, 1929.

FERRAN, André. *Le Salon de 1845 de Charles Baudelaire*, Toulouse, 1933.

FERRETI, Giovanni. *Luigi Amadeo Melegari a Losanna*, Rome, 1941.

–. *Melegari à l'Académie de Lausanne*, Lausanne, 1949.

'FEU DIDEROT'. "Salon de 1849", *L'Artiste*, 1 July 1849, pp. 97–99.

FIDELL-BEAUFORT, Madeleine and Jeanne WELCHER. "Some Views of Art Buying in New York in the 1870's and 1880's", *Oxford Art Journal*, V, n° 1, March, 1982, pp. 48–55.

FINK, Lois Marie. "American Artists in France, 1850–1870", *American Art Journal*, V, November, 1973, pp. 32–49.

–. "French Art in the United States, 1850–1870. Three Dealers and Collectors", *Gazette des Beaux-Arts*, XCII, September, 1978, pp. 87–100.

– and Joshua C. TAYLOR. *Academy: The Academic Tradition in American Art*, Washington, 1975.

FINKE, Ulrich. *German Painting From Romanticism to Expressionism*, London, 1974.

FINLAY, Nancy A. "Fourierist Art Criticism and the *Rêve de Bonheur* of Dominique Papety", *Art History*, II, September, 1979, pp. 327–38.

FIORO, Maria Teresa and Mercedes GARBERI. *La pinacoteca del Castello Sforzesco*, Milan, 1987.

FISCHER, Beat de. *Contributions à la connaissance des relations suisses-égyptiennes*, Lisbon, 1956.

FITZLYON, April. *The Price of Genius. A Biography of Pauline Viardot*, London, 1964.

FLANARY, David A. *Champfleury: The Realist Writer as Art Critic*, Ann Arbor, 1980.

FLANDIN, Eugène. *Histoire des chevaliers de Rhodes*, Tours, 1873.

FLANDRIN, Louis. *Hippolyte Flandrin. Sa vie et son œuvre*, Paris, 1902.

FLANDRIN, Marthe and Madeleine FROIDEVEAUX-FLANDRIN. *Les frères Flandrin. Leur correspondance. Le journal inédit d'Hippolyte Flandrin en Italie*, Paris, 1984.

FLAUBERT, Gustave. *Correspondance*, René Descharmes, ed., Paris, 1922 et seq.

–. *Correspondance*, Louis Conard, ed., Paris, 1926–33.

–. *Œuvres complètes*, Bernard Masson, ed., Paris, 1964.

–. *Correspondance*, Jean Bruneau, ed., Paris, 1973–91.

–. *Flaubert in Egypt: A Sensibility on Tour*, Francis Steegmuller, ed., Boston/Toronto, 1972.

FLEMING, Gordon. *The Young Whistler 1834–1866*, London, 1978.

FOCILLON, Henri. *La peinture au XIX° siècle*, Paris, 1907.

–. *La peinture au XIX° siècle. Le retour à l'antiquité. Le romantisme*, Paris, 1927.

FONTAINAS, André. *Histoire de la peinture française au XIX° siècle*, Paris, 1906.

FONTANA, Gian Jacopo. *Venezia Monumentale. I palazzi*, Venice, 1845–63.

FORBIN, Auguste, Comte de. *Voyage dans le Levant en 1817–1818*, Paris, 1819.

FOSCA, François [pseudonym of Georges DE TRAZ]. "Gleyre et Vallotton", *Vie, Art, Cité*, I, 1949, pp. 21–23.

–. *Renoir. L'homme et son œuvre*, Paris, 1961.

FOUCART, Bruno. *Le renouveau de la peinture religieuse en France (1800–1860)*, Paris, 1987.

FOUCART, Jacques and Bruno, eds. *Hippolyte, Auguste and Paul Flandrin. Une fraternité picturale au XIX° siècle*, exh. cat., Musée du Luxembourg, Paris, 1984.

FOURNEL, Victor. *Les artistes français contemporains. Peintres-sculpteurs*, Tours, 1884.

*Les Français peints par eux-mêmes*, Paris, 1840.

*French Nineteenth Century Drawings, Watercolors, Paintings, and Sculpture*, exh. cat., Shepherd Gallery, New York, 1987.

FREY, Lina. *Conrad Ferdinand Meyer's Gedichte und Novellen*, Leipzig, 1892.

FRITH, Francis. *Egypt and Palestine*, New York, n. d.

FROMENTIN, Eugène. *Lettres de jeunesse*, Paris, 1909.

–. *Voyage en Egypte*, Paris, n. d.

FROMMEL, Gaston. *Esquisses contemporaines. Edmond Scherer*, Lausanne/Paris, 1891.

FUSIL, Casimir-Alexandre. *La poésie scientifique de 1750 à nos jours*, Paris, 1917.

GABET, Charles. *Dictionnaire des artistes de l'Ecole française au XIX° siècle*, Paris, 1831.

GABEREL, Jean. "Notice biographique sur John-Etienne Chaponnière de Genève, statuaire", *Bibliothèque universelle de Genève*, XVII, 1838, pp. 49–67.

GALIFFE, James Auguste. *Italy and Its Inhabitants. An Account of a Tour in that Country in 1816 and 1817*, London, 1820.

GALIMARD, Auguste. *Examen du Salon de 1849*, Paris, 1849.

GAMBETTA, Léon. *Lettres de Gambetta*, D. Halévy and E. Pillias, eds., Paris, 1938.

GAMBONI, Dario. "Religion und Malerei in der Westschweiz von der Helvetik zum Ersten Weltkrieg", in *"Ich male für fromme Gemüter". Zur religiösen Schweizer Malerei im 19. Jahrhundert*, exh. cat., Kunstmuseum, Lucerne, 1985, pp. 157–67.

–. *Louis Rivier (1885–1963) et la peinture religieuse en Suisse romande*, exh. cat., Musée cantonal des Beaux-Arts, Lausanne, 1985.

–. *La géographie artistique* (Ars Helvetica, I), Disentis, 1987.

GANDY, Adolf. *Die Kirchlichen Baudenkmäler der Schweiz*, Berlin/Zürich, 1921.

GANIAGE, Jean. *Les origines du protectorat français en Tunisie (1861–1881)*, Paris, 1959.

GANTNER, Joseph. "Die bilder der 'Ernte'", *Die Ernter. Schweizer Jahrbuch*, Zürich, 1923, pp. 188–90.

GANTNER, Joseph and Adolf REINLE. *Kunstgeschichte der Schweiz*, IV, *Die Kunst des 19. Jahrhunderts*, Frauenfeld, 1962.

GANZ, Paul. *Les dessins de Hans Holbein le Jeune*, Geneva, 1921.

GANZ, Paul Leonhard. *Die Malerei der Schweiz in Farben*, Olten, 1953.

GARCIN DE TASSY. "Mémoire sur les noms propres et sur les titres musulmans", *Journal asiatique*, III, May-June, 1854, pp. 422–510.

GASSIER, Pierre. *Léopold Robert*, Neuchâtel, 1983.

GAULLIEUR, Eusèbe-Henri. "Exposition de peinture à Genève", *Revue suisse*, XVII, 1854, pp. 579–83.

G[AULLIEUR], E[usèbe]-H[enri]. "Chronique des arts et de la littérature", *Le Musée suisse*, II, 1855, pp. 127–28.

GAUTHIEZ, Pierre. *Bernardino Luini*, Paris, 1905.

GAUTIER, Léopold, ed. *Un bouquet de lettres de Rodolphe Töpffer*, Lausanne, 1974.

GAUTIER, Théophile. "Salon de 1845", *La Presse*, 20 March 1845, unpaginated.

–. "Salon de 1849", *La Presse*, 3 August 1849, unpaginated.

–. "A travers les ateliers", *L'Artiste*, IV, 16 May 1858, pp. 17–20.

–. *Histoire du romantisme*, Paris, 1874.

–. *Portraits et souvenirs littéraires*, Paris, 1881.

GEELHAAR, Christian. *Kunstmuseum Basel. Die Geschichte der Gemäldesammlung und eine Auswahl von 250 Meisterwerken*, (Schriften des Vereins der Freunde des Kunstmuseums Basel, VII), Zürich/Basel, 1992.

GEFFROY, Gustave. *Claude Monet. Sa vie, son œuvre*, Paris, 1924.

–. *Sisley*, Paris, 1927.

*Le Général Jomini et les mémoires du Baron de Marbot*, Paris, 1893.

GENEQUAND, Jean-Etienne et al. *La République à Saint-Pierre*, Geneva, 1981.

GEORGEL, Pierre. "Les transformations de la peinture vers 1848, 1855, 1863", *Revue de l'art*, XXVII, 1975, pp. 62–77.

– and Anne-Marie LECOQ. *La peinture dans la peinture*, exh. cat., Musée des Beaux-Arts, Dijon, 1982.

GÉRÔME, Jean-Léon. "Notes autobiographiques", *Bulletin de la Société d'agriculture, lettres, sciences et arts de la Haute-Saône*, XIV, 1980, pp. 1–23.

GIELLY, Louis. *Catalogue des peintures et sculptures*, Geneva, 1928.

GIGOUX, Jean. *Causeries sur les artistes de mon temps*, Paris, 1885.

GILLARD, Charles. "Notice historique sur la Société", in *Centenaire de la Société d'histoire de la Suisse romande (1837–1937)*, Lausanne, 1937.

GINANNI, Marc'Antonio. *L'arte del Blasone…*, Venice, 1756.

GIORGINI, Michela Schiff. *Soleb*, Florence, 1965.

GIRARD, Georges. *La vie de Lazare Hoche*, Paris, 1926.

GIRARDET, Lucien. *Le Major Davel ou la joie parfaite*, Lausanne, n. d. [1973].

GIRONI, R. and M. BISI. *Pinacoteca del Palazzo Reale delle Scienze e delle Arti di Milano*, Milan, 1812.

GLEYRE, Céline. "Adrien à Charles Gleyre, le peintre de mon village", *Journal du district de Cossonay*, 8 August 1947, p. 2.

GLEYRE, Charles. "Rapport sur la participation de la Suisse à l'Exposition universelle de 1867", *Feuille fédérale suisse*, XX, 7 March 1868, pp. 293–300.

GODET, Philippe. *Art et patrie. Auguste Bachelin d'après son œuvre et sa correspondance*, Neuchâtel, 1893.

–. *Charles Berthoud d'après ses lettres à sa famille et à ses amis, 1813–1894*, Neuchâtel, 1895.

–. "Les arts plastiques dans la Suisse française", in *La Suisse au dix-neuvième siècle*, Lausanne/Bern, II, 1900, pp. 427–81.

–. *Le peintre Albert de Meuron d'après sa correspondance avec sa famille et ses amis*, Neuchâtel, 1901.

–. "Lettres de Juste Olivier et Caroline Olivier à Sainte-Beuve", *Bibliothèque universelle et Revue suisse*, XXXIV, 1904, pp. 59–95 and 258–87.

–. "Correspondance inédite de Juste Olivier et d'Eugène Rambert", *Au foyer romand*, XIX, 1906, pp. 33–130.

GONCOURT, Edmond de. *Catalogue raisonné de l'œuvre peint, dessiné et gravé de P. P. Prud'hon*, Paris, 1876.

– and Jules de. *Journal. Mémoires de la vie littéraire*, Monaco, 1956.

GOUIRAND, André. *Les peintres provençaux*, Paris, 1901.

GOUPIL-FESQUET, Frédéric. *Voyage d'Horace Vernet en Orient*, Paris, n. d. [1843].

GOURDAULT, Jules. *La Suisse. Etudes et voyages*, Paris, 1879.

GOUY, Isabelle. "La Société des Amis des arts à Lyon au XIXᵉ siècle", Mémoire de maîtrise, University of Lyons, 1984.

GRANDCHAMP, Pierre and Béchir MOKADDEM. "Une mission tunisienne à Paris", *Revue africaine*, XC, 1946, pp. 58–98.

GRANDJEAN, Marcel. *Les monuments d'art et d'histoire du canton de Vaud*, 1: *La ville de Lausanne, I*; and *III*: *La ville de Lausanne, II*, Basel, 1965 and 1979.

GRAPPE, Georges. *Jules Claretie*, Paris, 1906.

GRATE, Pontus. "Art Historians and Art Critics. V. Gustave Planche", *The Burlington Magazine*, CI, n° 676/7, July/August, 1959(a), pp. 277–81.

–. *Deux critiques d'art de l'époque romantique: Gustave Planche et Théophile Thoré*, Stockholm, 1959(b).

GRÉARD, Octave. *Edmond Scherer*, Paris, 1890.

–. *Jean-Louis-Ernest Meissonier. Ses souvenirs, ses entretiens*, Paris, 1897.

GREENSLET, F. *The Lowells and Their Seven Worlds*, Boston, 1946.

GRELLET, Francis. *Madame Vinet et ses amis*, Lausanne, 1980.

GRELLET, Marc. *Nos peintres romands du XVIIIᵉ et du XIXᵉ siècle*, Lausanne, 1920.

GRÉNIER, Edouard. "Charles Gleyre", *Revue bleu*, 12 August 1893, unpaginated.

GRIENER, Pascal. "Charles Gleyre et Léopold Robert. Le bon usage de Dionysos", in *Entre Rome et Paris. Œuvres inédites du XIVᵉ au XIXᵉ siècle*, Lausanne, 1996, pp. 49-56.

GRIFFITH, Francis L. "Scenes From a Destroyed Temple at Napata", *The Journal of Egyptian Archeology*, XIV, 1929, pp. 26–28.

GRIFFITHS, David Albert. *Jean Reynaud. Encyclopédiste de l'époque romantique*, Paris, 1965.

GRIMMER, Georges. "Courbet et Chenavard", *Les amis de Gustave Courbet. Bulletin*, n° 9, 1951, pp. 1–9.

GRUNCHEC, Philippe. *Géricault. Tout l'œuvre peint*, Paris, 1978.

–. *Géricault*, exh. cat., Villa Medici, Rome 1979.

–. *Géricault. Dessins et aquarelles de chevaux*, Lausanne/Paris, 1982.

–. *Le Grand Prix de peinture. Le concours des Prix de Rome de 1797 à 1863*, exh. cat., Ecole nationale supérieure des Beaux-Arts, Paris, 1983.

GRUNEWALD, Marie-Antoinette. *Paul Chenavard et la décoration du Panthéon de Paris en 1848*, Lyons, 1977.

–. "Paul Chenavard (1807–1895): La palingénésie sociale ou la philosophie de l'histoire, 1830-1852", *Bulletin des musées et monuments lyonnais*, VI, n° 1, 1980, pp. 317–43.

GSELL-FELS, Theodor. *Die Schweiz*, Munich/Berlin, n. d. [1876–77].

GUBLER, Jacques et al. *Les 'Villas Dubochet' à Clarens. Ensemble résidentiel de la riviera lémanique*, Lausanne, 1981.

GUERLE, Charles de. "Exposition de Lyon", *L'Artiste*, V, 1840, pp. 107–109.

*Guida per l'I. R. Pinacoteca di Brera*, Milan, 1838.

*Guide de Lausanne et de ses environs*, Lausanne, 1886.

GUIFFREY, Jean. *L'œuvre de Pierre-Paul Prud'hon*, Paris, 1924.

GUILLAUME, Germaine. "Influence de l'atelier de Gleyre sur les impressionnistes français", in *Résumés du XIVᵉ Congrès international d'histoire de l'art*, I, Basel, 1936, pp. 11–12.

GUILLON, Edouard and Gustave BETTEX, *Le Léman dans la littérature et dans l'art*, Montreux/Paris, 1912.

GUILLOT, Arthur. "Salon de 1845", *La Revue indépendante*, XX, 10 May 1845, pp. 53–81.

GUIZOT, M. *Etudes sur les Beaux-Arts en général*, Paris, 1860.

GUIZOT, François-Pierre-Guillaume. *Mémoires pour servir à l'histoire de mon temps*, Paris, 1858–66.

*Gustave Flaubert. Exposition du centenaire*, exh. cat., Bibliothèque nationale, Paris, 1980(a).

*Gustave Flaubert. Des livres et des amis*, exh. cat., Bibliothèque municipale and Musée des Beaux-Arts, Rouen, 1980(b).

GUYOT DE FÈRE. *Statistique des Beaux-Arts en France*, Paris, 1835.

H. "Exposition universelle. Section des Beaux-Arts", *Le Journal illustré*, 21-28 April 1867, p. 121.

H., E. "Le Major Davel à l'échafaud", *La Suisse*, IX, 1 September 1863, pp. 286–87.

HAGER, Werner. "Vier Historienbilder", in *Beiträge zum Problem des Stilpluralismus*, Werner Hager and Norbert Knopp, eds., Munich, 1977, pp. 134–40.

HAKEM, Ahmed M. Ali. "A History of Archeological Research in Nubia and Sudan", *Africa in Antiquity*, I, New York, 1978, pp. 37–45.

HALBERT D'ANGERS, Arthur. *Description de l'extérieur et de l'intérieur de la nouvelle église de Saint-Vincent-de-Paul*, Paris, 1844.

HALPERN, Bernard. "Claude Bernard", in Claude Bernard, *Lettres à Madame R.*, Saint-Julien-en-Beaujolais, 1974, pp. 175–82.

HALLOPEAU, Marie-Laure. "Les Gaulois et la peinture au XIXᵉ siècle", in *Nos ancêtres les Gaulois*, M.-L. Hallopeau and Antoinette Ehrard, eds., exh. cat., Musée des Beaux-Arts, Clermont-Ferrand, 1980, pp. 5–33.

HAMERTON, Philip Gilbert. "Art-Education in France", *London Student*, October, 1868(a), pp. 259–68.

–. *Contemporary French Painting*, London, 1868(b).

HAMMER, Karl. *Jacob Ignaz Hittorff. Ein Pariser Baumeister, 1792-1867*, Stuttgart, 1968.

HARDING, James. *Les peintres pompiers. La peinture académique en France de 1830 à 1880*, Paris, 1980.

HARDOUIN-FUGIER, Elisabeth. *Le poème de l'âme par Janmot. Etude iconographique*, Lyons, 1977.

–. *Louis Janmot (1814–1892)*, Lyons, 1981.

HARRISON, Jefferson C. *French Painting from the Chrysler Museum*, Norfolk, 1986.

HASKELL, Francis. "The Old Masters in Nineteenth Century French Painting", *The Art Quarterly*, XXXIV, n° 1, Spring, 1971, pp. 55–85.

–. *Rediscoveries in Art. Some Aspects of Taste, Fashion and Collecting in England and France*, Ithaca, 1980.

– and Nicholas PENNY. *Taste and the Antique: The Lure of Classical Sculpture 1500–1900*, New Haven/London, 1981.

HAUPTMAN, William. "The Persistence of Melancholy in Nineteenth Century Art: The Iconography of a Motif", Ph. D. diss., The Pennsylvania State University, 1975.

–. "Allusions and Illusions in Gleyre's *Le Soir*", *The Art Bulletin*, LX, n° 2, June, 1978, pp. 321–30.

–. "Charles Gleyre: Tradition and Innovation", in *Charles Gleyre 1806–1874*, William Hauptman and Nancy Scott Newhouse, eds., exh. cat., Grey Art Gallery, New York University, New York, 1980, pp. 11–71.

–. "Gleyre, Vernet, and the Revenge of the *Brigands Romains*", *The Bulletin of the Cleveland Museum of Art*, January, 1981(a), pp. 17–34.

–. "Ingres and *Les docteurs*", *Perceptions. Indiana Museum of Art Bulletin*, I, 1981(b), pp. 55–59.

–. "Charles Gleyre et la famille Gaudin. Leurs rencontres peu connues à Lausanne et à Paris", *Revue historique vaudoise*, XCI, 1983, pp. 93–118.

–. "Juries, Protests, and Counter-Exhibitions Before 1850", *The Art Bulletin*, CXVII, March, 1985(a), pp. 95–109.

–. "Grosclaude and Courbet's 'L'après-dînée à Ornans de 1849'", *Gazette des Beaux-Arts*, CV, March, 1985(b), pp. 117–21.

–. "La note historique 'perdue' de Gleyre sur *Les Romains passant sous le joug*", *Revue historique vaudoise*, XCIII, 1985(c), pp. 97–105.

–. "Il maestro di Renoir", *FMR*, XXXVI, October, 1985(d), pp. 135–52.

–. "Delaroche's and Gleyre's Teaching Ateliers and Their Group Portraits", *Studies in the History of Art* (The National Gallery of Art, Washington), XVIII, November, 1985(e), pp. 79–119.

–. "Deux œuvres de Charles Gleyre dans les collections de l'AVL", *Bulletin d'information. Association du Vieux-Lausanne*, 1986(a), pp. 11–12.

–. "Charles Gleyre's *Penthée* and the Creative Imagination", *Zeitschrift für Schweizerische Archäologie und Kunstgeschichte*, XLIII, n° 2, 1986(b), pp. 215–28.

–. "Charles Gleyre and the Swiss Fine Arts Section of the Exposition Universelle of 1867", *Zeitschrift für Schweizerische Archäologie und Kunstgeschichte*, XLIII, n° 4, 1986(c), pp. 368–70.

–. "Les autoportraits de Gleyre. Un peintre se cache", *Nos monuments d'art et d'histoire*, XLI, n° 3, 1990, pp. 310–17.

–. "Gleyre, Troyon et les *Romains* en 1858", *Archäologie der Schweiz*, XIV, n° 1, 1991, pp. 29–36.

–. "Some New Nineteenth-Century References to Giorgione's *Tempesta*", *The Burlington Magazine*, CXXXVI, February, 1994(a), pp. 78–82.

–. *Charles Gleyre et la Suisse romande*, exh. cat., Musée historique de Lausanne, Lausanne, 1994(b).

–. "Un chef-d'œuvre méconnu de Charles Gleyre", in *Charles Gleyre, La Danse des Bacchantes*, Lausanne, 1995(a), pp. 3-16.

–. "Gleyre's *Manfred*: An Early Esquisse Rediscovered", *Florilegium: Scritti di storia dell'arte in onore di Carlo Bertelli*, Milan, 1995(b), pp. 184-88.

HAUSSARD, Prosper. "Beaux-Arts. Salon de 1840", *Le Temps*, 12 April 1840, unpaginated.

–. "Beaux-Arts. Salon de 1843", *Le National*, 29 March 1843, unpaginated.

–. "Salon de 1845", *Le National*, 6 and 13 April 1845, unpaginated.

HAUTECŒUR, Louis. *Littérature et peinture en France du XVIIᵉ au XXᵉ siècle*, Paris, 1942.

–. *Catalogue de la galerie des Beaux-Arts. Musée d'art et d'histoire*, Geneva, 1948.

–. *Histoire de l'architecture classique en France*, V, Paris, 1955.

HAVERKAMP-BEGEMANN, Egbert and Carolyn LOGAN. *Creative Copies: Interpretative Drawings from Michelangelo to Picasso*, New York, 1988.

HAZLITT, William. *Notes of a Journey through France and Italy*, London, 1826.

HEDENBORG, Johann. *Resa i Egypten och det ihre Afrika, aven 1834 och 1835*, Stockholm, 1843.

HEINE, Heinrich. *Lutèce. Lettres sur la vie politique, artistique et sociale de la France*, Paris, 1855.

–. *Correspondance inédite*, III, Paris, 1877.

–. *Heinrich Heine. Sein Leben in Bildern*, Stuttgart, 1956.

–. *Briefe: 1840–1856*, Fritz H. Eisner, ed., XXIII, Berlin/Paris, 1972.

–. *Briefe an Heine: 1842–1851*, Christa Stöcker, ed., XXVI, Berlin/Paris, 1975.

HEINEMANN, Fritz. *Trésors d'art suisse,* Lausanne, 1922.

HELD, Julius. *Rembrandt and the Book of Tobit*, Northhampton, 1964.

HELLER, Geneviève. *"Propre en ordre". Habitation et vie domestique, 1850–1930. L'exemple vaudois*, Lausanne, 1979.

HERBERT, Robert L. *David, Voltaire, «Brutus» and the French Revolution: An Essay in Art and Politics*, New York, 1975(a).

–. *Jean-François Millet (1814–1875)*, exh. cat., Grand Palais, Paris, 1975(b).

HEROLD, Jean Christopher. *Bonaparte in Egypt*, New York, 1962.

HEWISON, Robert. *Ruskin and Venice*, London, 1978.

HILLAIRET, Jacques. *Dictionnaire historique des rues de Paris*, Paris, 1964.

HILMY, Prince Ibrahim. *The Literature of Egypt and the Sudan: A Bibliography*, London, 1886–87.

*Hippolyte Taine. 150ᵉ anniversaire d'un Vouzirois illustre, 1828–1978*, Vouziers, 1978.

HOFER, Paul. *Die Kunstdenkmäler des Kantons Bern, III: Die Staatsbauten der Stadt Bern*, Basel, 1947.

HOFFMAN, Eugène. *Jean-Louis Hamon. Peintre (1821–1874),* Paris, 1903.

HOFMANN, Werner. *Das Irdische Paradis. Motive und Ideen des 19. Jahrhunderts*, Munich, 1960.

HOFMEISTER, Rudolph Heinrich. "Das Leben des Kunstmalers J. J. Wolfenberger", in *Neujahrsblatt der Künstlergesellschaft*, Zürich, 1854.

–. "Das Leben des Kunstmalers Karl Gleyre", in *Neujahrsblatt der Künstlergesellschaft*, Zürich, 1879.

HOLLAND, Clive. "Lady Art Student's Life in Paris", *The Studio*, XXX, 1903, pp. 225–33.

HOLT, Elizabeth Gilmore. *The Art of All Nations 1850–1873. The Emerging Role of Exhibitions and Critics*, New York, 1981.

*Hommage à Monet, 1840–1926*, exh. cat., Grand Palais, Paris, 1980.

*Hommage à C. F. Ramuz*, exh. cat., Musée de Pully, Pully, 1973.

HONEGGER, Suzanne. "Un poète vaudois. Juste Olivier (1807–1876)", *La Patrie suisse*, n° 987, 10 April 1929, p. 179.

HONOUR, Hugh. *L'image du Noir dans l'art occidental. De la révolution américaine à la Première Guerre mondiale*, Paris, 1989.

*Horace Vernet (1789–1863)*, exh. cat., Ecole nationale supérieure des Beaux-Arts, Paris, 1980.

HOREAU, Hector. *Panorama de l'Egypte et de la Nubie*, Paris, 1841–42.

HOSKINS, G. A. *Travels in Ethiopia*, London, 1835.

HOUBEN, Heinrich Hubert. *Henri Heine par ses contemporains*, Paris, 1929.

HOUSSAYE, Arsène. "Le Salon de 1843", *Revue de Paris*, XV, 26 March 1843, pp. 284–95 and XVI, 9 April 1843, pp. 32–46 and 107–26.

–. *Voyage à Venise*, Paris, 1850.

–. *Voyage à ma fenêtre*, Paris, 1851.

–. "Lettre", *L'Artiste*, XIII, 1870, pp. 319–20.

–. *Les poésies*, Paris, n. d. [1877].

–. *Les confessions. Souvenirs d'un demi-siècle, 1830–1880*, Paris, 1885.

–. *Souvenirs de jeunesse. 1830–1850*, Paris, n. d.

[HOUSSAYE, Edouard]. "Nouvelles d'art", *L'Artiste*, II, 1858, pp. 31–32.

HOUTSMA, Martijn Theodoor, ed. *Encyclopédie de l'Islam*, Leyden/Paris, 1913–38.

HUARD, Lucien. *Les musées chez soi*, II, Paris, n. d.

HUBER, Jörg. *Schweizer Malerei von den Anfängen bis ins 20. Jahrhundert, II, Zwischen Harmonie und Aufbruch*, Zürich, 1984.

HUGGLER, Max, ed. *Albert Anker. Katalog der Gemälde und Ölstudien*, Bern, 1962.

– and Anna Maria CETTO. *La peinture suisse au dix-neuvième siècle*, Basel, 1943.

HUGLI, Jean. "Histoire et préhistoire d'une école d'art", in *Cette école d'art*, Lausanne, 1983, pp 7–114.

HUMPHRY, Peter. *Cima da Conegliano*, Cambridge, 1983.

HUNGERFORD, Constance. "The Art of Jean-Louis-Ernest Meissonier: A Study of the Critical Years 1834 to 1855", Ph. D. diss., University of California at Berkeley, 1977.

HUNT, Herbert James. *The Epic in Nineteenth Century France*, Oxford, 1941.

HÜRLIMANN, Martin, ed. *La Suisse vue à travers l'Exposition nationale 1939. L'Art en Suisse*, Zürich, 1940.

HURT-BINET, Oscar and Eusèbe-Henri GAULLIEUR. *Le Major Davel. Drame historique*, Lausanne, 1864.

I., J. [DURANTY, Louis-Emile-Edmond]. "Gleyre", *La vie parisienne*, XIII, 10 April 1875, pp. 205–206.

*Indicateur commercial et industriel du canton de Vaud pour 1874*, Lausanne, 1874.

*Indicateur général du canton de Vaud, ou Guide statistique et commercial. 1850–1856,* Lausanne, 1857.

*Indicateur vaudois*, Lausanne, 1901.

INGAMELLS, John. *Richard Parkes Bonington*, New York, 1979.

*Ingres and Delacroix through Degas and Puvis de Chavannes: The Figure in French Art, 1800–1870*, exh. cat., Shepherd Gallery, New York, 1975.

*Inventaire général des œuvres d'art appartenant à la Ville de Paris. Edifices religieux*, III, Paris, 1884.

*Inventaire général des œuvres d'art décorant les édifices du département de la Seine*, Paris 1880.

*Inventaire général des richesses d'art de la France. Paris. Monuments religieux*, Paris, I-II, 1877–88.

*Inventaire général des richesses d'art de la France. Province. Monuments religieux*, Paris, I-III, 1886–1901.

JACCARD, Paul-André. "Turnus, Expositions nationales suisses des Beaux-Arts, SPSAS, SSFPD, Expositions nationales suisses: Listes des expositions et des catalogues", *Zeitschrift für Schweizerische Archäologie und Kunstgeschichte*, XLIII, n° 4, 1986, pp. 436–59.

JAFFE, Irma B. "Flaubert: The Novelist as Art Critic", *Gazette des Beaux-Arts*, LXXV, May-June, 1970, pp. 355–70.

JAMESON, Mrs. Anna. *Memoirs of the Early Italian Painters*, London, 1845.

JANIN, Jules. "Le Salon de 1840", *L'Artiste*, V, 1840, n° 12, pp. 201–208.

–. *L'été à Paris*, Paris, 1844.

JANZEN, Reinhild. *Albrecht Altdorfer. Four Centuries of Criticism*, Ann Arbor, 1980.

JATON, Nicole. "Correspondance entre le Colonel Ferdinand Lecomte et Edgar Quinet", Mémoire de licence, University of Lausanne, 1970.

JAUBERT, Caroline. *Souvenirs de Madame C. Jaubert: Lettres et correspondances*, 3rd ed., Paris, n. d.

JEANNERET, Maurice. *Un siècle d'art à Neuchâtel. Histoire de la Société des amis des arts (1842–1942)*, Neuchâtel, n. d. [1943].

JEANRON, Philippe-Auguste. "Beaux-Arts. Peinture. Salon de 1845", *Le Pandore*, I, n° 13, 15 April 1845, pp. 201–205 and n° 17, 15 June 1845, p. 265–67.

JÉQUIER, Hugues. *La famille de Pury*, Neuchâtel, 1972.

JOANNIDES, Paul. "Towards the Dating of Géricault's Lithographs, *The Burlington Magazine*, CXV, n° 847, October, 1973, pp. 666–71.

–. *The Drawings of Raphael. With a Complete Catalogue*, Oxford, 1983.

JOHNSTON, William R. *The Nineteenth-Century Paintings in the Walters Art Gallery*, Baltimore, 1982.

JONES, Owen and Jules GOURY. *Views on the Nile from Cairo to the Second Cataract*, London, 1843.

JOUBIN, André. *Catalogue des peintures et sculptures exposées dans les galeries du Musée Fabre de la Ville de Montpellier*, Paris, 1926.

JOURDAIN, Aleth, ed. *Charles-François Jalabert, 1819–1901*, Nîmes, 1981.

JULLIAN, Philippe. *Les orientalistes. La vision de l'Orient par les peintres européens au XIX<sup>e</sup> siècle*, Fribourg, 1977.

JUNOD, Philippe and Philippe KAENEL, eds. *Critiques d'art de Suisse romande. De Töpffer à Budry*, Lausanne, 1993.

KAENEL, Gilbert. "L'archéologie vaudoise a 150 ans. Frédéric Troyon et le Musée des Antiquités", *Perspectives*, II, March, 1988, pp. 24–26.

KAENEL, Philippe. "Le mythe de la reine Berthe aux XIX<sup>e</sup> siècle en Suisse romande", *Nos monuments d'art et d'histoire*, XXXIII, n° 4, 1982, pp. 404–10.

KARL, Charles-A. "L'Athénée à Genève", *Le Touriste*, n° 1, 1866(a), pp. 12–14.

–. "L'exposition nationale de Neuchâtel au profit des incendies de Travers", *Le Touriste*, n° 3, 1866(b), pp. 39–41.

KAUFFMANN, Claus Michael. *The Victoria and Albert Museum. Catalogue of Foreign Paintings*, II, London, 1973.

KEMP, Wolfgang. "Perspektive als Problem der Malerei des 19. Jahrhunderts", in *Kunst als Bedeutungsträger*, Berlin, 1978, pp. 405–16.

KERN, Johann Conrad. *Souvenirs politiques*, Bern/Paris, 1887.

KJELLBERG, Pierre, ed. *Le guide des églises de Paris*, Paris, 1970.

KLUCK, Frederck, J. "Charles Gleyre and the French Romantics", *Nineteenth Century French Studies*, X, Spring/Summer, 1982, pp. 228–43.

KNAB, Eckhart, Erwin MITSCH, and Konrad OBERHUBER. *Raphael. Die Zeichnungen*, Stuttgart, 1983.

KNEPLER, Henry, ed. *Man About Paris: The Confessions of Arsène Houssaye*, New York, 1970.

KOELLA, Rudolf. "Charles Gleyre, Maler der verlorenen Illusionen", in *Charles Gleyre ou les illusions perdues*, exh. cat., Kunstmuseum, Winterthur, 1974, pp. 8–21.

KOLB, Marthe. *Ary Scheffer et son temps. 1795–1858*, Paris, 1937.

KUHNE, E. "Le peintre Gleyre", *Noël suisse*, IV, 1901, pp. 36–40.

KUTHY, Sandor. *Anker in seiner Zeit*, exh. cat., Kunstmuseum, Bern, 1981.

– and Hans A. LÜTHY. *Albert Anker. Deux portraits d'un artiste*, Lausanne, 1980.

L., St. [LECLERC, Louis-Stéphane?]. "Exposition 1840", *Le National*, 19 March and 4 April, 1840, unpaginated.

LACAMBRE, Geneviève, ed. *Le Musée du Luxembourg en 1874*, exh. cat., Grand Palais, Paris, 1974.

LACROIX (fils). *Réflexions sur l'ophthalmie d'Egypte ou asiatique,* Paris, 1827.

LACROIX, Paul. *Annuaire des artistes et des amateurs*, Paris, 1860–62.

LAFENESTRE, Georges. "Jean-Louis Hamon", *L'Art*, I, 1875, pp. 394–99.

–. *La tradition dans la peinture française*, Paris, 1897.

LAFFON, Juliette. *Catalogue sommaire illustré des peintures. Musée du Petit-Palais*, Paris, n.d. [1982].

LA FONTAINE, Jean de. *Fables*, E. Pillon and F. Dauphin, eds. Paris, n. d.

LAGENEVAIS, Frédéric de. "Le Salon de 1849", *Revue des Deux-Mondes*, III, 15 August 1849, pp. 559–93.

LAMEIRE, Charles. "Alexandre Denuelle", *Gazette des Beaux-Arts*, XXI, 1880, pp. 193–95.

LAMI, Stanislas. *Dictionnaire des sculpteurs de l'Ecole française au dix-neuvième siècle*, Paris, 1914–21.

LANCE, Adolphe. *Dictionnaire des architectes français*, Paris, 1872.

LANDOLT, Hanspeter, ed. *Gottfried Keller-Stiftung. Sammeln für die Schweizer Museen, 1890–1990*, Bern, 1990.

LANE, Edward William. *Account of the Manners and Customs of the Modern Egyptians*, London, 1836.

LANE, Laura. *The Life and Writings of Alexander Vinet*, Edinburgh, 1890.

LANE-POOLE, Stanley. *Life of Edward William Lane*, London, 1877.

LAPAIRE, Claude and Jean-René GABORIT. *Statues de chair. Sculptures de James Pradier (1790–1852)*, exh. cat., Musée d'art et d'histoire, Geneva, 1985–86.

LAPAUZE, Henry. *Catalogue sommaire des collections municipales*, Paris, 1904–06.

–. *Ingres. Sa vie et son œuvre (1780–1867), d'après des documents inédits*, Paris, 1911.

–. *Histoire de l'Académie de France à Rome*, II, Paris, 1924.

[LARDY, Charles]. *Catalogue des objets d'art exposés dans le Musée Arlaud*, Lausanne, 1846.

LAROUSSE, Pierre, ed. *Grand dictionnaire universel du XIX<sup>e</sup> siècle*, Paris, 1866–90.

LASSERRE, André. *Henri Druey*, Lausanne, 1970.

–. *La classe ouvrière dans la société vaudoise, 1845 à 1914*, Lausanne, 1973.

LASTEYRIE, Ferdinand. *La peinture à l'Exposition universelle de 1862*, Paris, 1863.

LATOUCHE, Henri de. *Œuvre de Canova*, Paris, 1825.

LAURENS, Jules. *La légende des ateliers*, Paris, 1901.

LAVANCHY, Charles. *Les médailles du canton de Vaud*, Lausanne, 1975.

LAVERDANT, D. *De la mission de l'art et du rôle des artistes. Salon de 1845*, Paris, 1845.

LAVERGNE, Claudius. *Exposition universelle de 1855*, Paris, 1855.

LÈBRE, Adolphe. "Le Major Davel", *La Revue suisse*, VIII, 1845, pp. 294–314.

LECOMTE, Ferdinand. *Le général Jomini. Sa vie et ses écrits*, Paris, 1860.

LECOMTE, Frédéric. *Le Major Davel. Notice historique*, Lausanne, 1850.

LECOMTE, Georges. "Les Goncourt critiques d'art", *Revue de Paris*, IV, 1894, pp. 201–24.

LECOMTE, Jules-François. *Venise, ou coup d'œil littéraire, historique, poétique et pittoresque sur les monuments et les curiosités de cette ville*, Paris, 1844.

LECOY DE LA MARCHE, Albert. *L'Académie de France à Rome*, Paris, 1874.

LEDUC-ADINE, Jean-Pierre. *Jules Sandeau*, exh. cat., Mairie, VIe arrondissement, Paris, 1983.

LEIRIS, Alain de. *From Delacroix to Cézanne. French Watercolor Landscapes of the Nineteenth Century*, exh. cat., University of Maryland Art Gallery, College Park, 1977.

LEMAISTRE, Alexis. *L'Ecole des Beaux-Arts, dessinée et racontée par un élève*, Paris, 1889.

LEMAÎTRE, E, ed.. *Arsène Houssaye. Notes et souvenirs*, Rheims, 1897.

LEPDOR, Catherine, Patrick SCHAEFER, and Jörg ZUTTER. *La collection du Musée cantonal des Beaux-Arts*, Bern, 1994.

LEPDOR, Catherine, "Charles Gleyre 1806-1874", in *La genèse des formes. Œuvres sur papier de la collection*, exh. cat., Musée cantonal des Beaux-Arts, Lausanne, 1995, pp. 6–9.

LE PICHON, Yann. *L'érotisme des chers maîtres*, Paris, 1986.

LÉPINE, Olivier. *"Équivoques". Peinture française du XIXe siècle*, exh. cat., Musée des Arts décoratifs, Paris, 1973.

LEPSIUS, Karl Richard. *Denkmäler aus Aegyptien und Aethiopen, 1842–1845*, Berlin, 1849.

LEROY, Louis. *Artistes et rapins*, Paris, 1868.

*Les années romantiques. La peinture française de 1815 à 1850*, Paris, 1995.

LETHÈVE, Jacques. "Le public du Cabinet des estampes au dix-neuvième siècle", in *Humanisme actif. Mélanges d'art et de littérature offerts à Julien Cain*, Paris, 1968, II, pp. 101–11.

–. *Daily Life of French Artists in the Nineteenth Century*, Hilary E. Paddon, tr., London, 1972.

LEUBA, Pierre. *Familles de la région de Cossonay*, Cossonay, 1953–55.

LEVI, C. A. *Le collezioni veneziane d'arte e antichità del secolo XIV ai giorni nostri*, Venice, 1900.

LEVINE, Neil. "The Competition for the Grand Prix in 1824", in *The Beaux-Arts and Nineteenth-Century French Architecture*, Robin Middleton, ed., London, 1982, pp. 66–123.

LEVINE, Steven Zalman. *Monet and His Critics*, New York/London, 1976.

LEVINSON, Arthur. *Le Major Davel. Sa vie et sa mort. Notes biographiques et historiques*, Lausanne, 1896.

LEVITINE, George. "Girodet-Trioson: An Iconographic Study", Ph. D. diss., Harvard, 1952.

LEWALD, Fanny. *Sommer und Winter am Genfersee*, Berlin, 1872.

LEYMARIE, Jean. *La peinture française. Le dix-neuvième siècle*, Geneva, 1962.

LIEB, Norbert. *Leo von Klenze. Gemälde und Zeichnungen*, Munich, 1979.

LIECHTI, Samuel. "Die Schlacht am Leman", in *Die Schweizergeschichte im Spiegel der neuesten Dichtung*, Bern, 1857.

LINES, Vincent. *Mark Fisher and Margaret Fisher Prout. Father and Daughter*, London, 1966.

LINKS, L. "La saison des ventes publiques", *L'Art*, X, 1877, pp. 213–15.

LISCA, Alessandro da. *Studie e richerche originali sulle chiesa di San Fermo di Verona*, Verona, 1909.

*Livret explicatif des ouvrages de peinture, sculpture, dessin, gravure, etc. à l'exposition de la Société des amis des arts de Lyon*, Lyons, 1839.

LLEWELLYN, Briony. *The Orient Observed: Images of the Middle East from the Searight Collection*, exh. cat., Victoria and Albert Museum, London, 1989.

LOËS, Alexis de. "M. et Mme de Rumine", *La Revue du dimanche*, n° 44, 4 November 1906, pp. 346–49.

LONGCHAMPS, Frédéric-Charles. *Bibliographie générale des ouvrages publiés ou illustrés en Suisse et à l'étranger de 1475 à 1914 par des écrivains et des artistes suisses*, Paris/Lausanne, 1923.

LONGHI, Roberto. "Fatti di Masolino e di Masaccio", in *Edizione delle opere complete di Roberto Longhi*, Florence, 1975, VIII/1, pp. 3–65.

LOSTÈVE, E. and Léo DE BERNARD. "Visite au Salon de Paris", *La Suisse*, VI, 1 June 1863, pp. 177–78.

LOYRETTE, Henri and Gary TINTEROW, eds. *Impressionnisme. Les origines, 1859–1869*, exh. cat., Grand Palais, Paris, 1994.

LUCAS, George A. *The Diary of George A. Lucas: An American Art Agent in Paris, 1857–1909*, Lilian M. C. Randall, ed., Princeton, 1979.

LUGEON, Raphaël. *Charles Gleyre. Le peintre et l'homme*, Lausanne, 1940.

LUGT, Fritz. *Répértoire des catalogues de ventes publiques*, The Hague, 1938–64.

LUNA, Juan. J. "Charles Gleyre: 'La Danza de Bacantes' de 1849", in *Miscelanea de arte*, Madrid, 1982, pp. 244–51.

LUNARDI, Roberto. *Arte e Storia in Santa Maria Novella*, Florence, 1983.

LÜTHY, Hans A. "Charles Clément (1821–1888), der Biograph Gleyres", *Neue Zürcher Zeitung*, n° 404, 1 September 1974, p. 50.

–. "Charles Clément. Biographer of Géricault and Gleyre", *Source*, III, Fall, 1983, pp. 28–30.

–. "Charles Clément and French Landscape", in *The Documented Image. Visions in Art History*, Gabriel P. Weisberg and L. S. Dixon, eds., Syracuse, 1987, pp. 309–18.

LUTZ, Marc. *Dictionnaire géographique-statistique de la Suisse*, Lausanne, 1836.

LUZ, Christiane. *Das Exotische Tier in der europäischen Kunst*, exh. cat., Zoologisch-botanischer Garten Wilhelma, Wurttemburg, 1987.

M. "Juste Olivier", *La Suisse illustrée*, 21 October 1876, pp. 505–507.

M., B. "Visages d'artistes. Charles Gleyre", *Journal du district de Cossonay*, 20 June 1958, p. 1.

M., G.-B. "General Jomini", *The Galaxy*, June, 1869, pp. 874–88.

M., J. "Les restes du peintre Gleyre reviendront à Chevilly", *Journal du district de Cossonay*, 23 May 1947(a), p. 1.

–. "Retour des restes de Gleyre à Chevilly", *Journal du district de Cossonay*, 19 September 1947(b), p. 1.

M., M. "Le général Mohamoud Ben Aiad", *L'Illustration*, LII, 12 September 1868, p. 165.

M., M. *Une vie. Henri Moser, Charlottenfels*, Lausanne, 1929.

MAAS, Jeremy. *Victorian Painters*, New York, 1969.

MAFFEI, Scipione. *Verona illustrata*, Verona, 1731–32.

MAILLEFER, Paul, ed. *Géographie illustrée du canton de Vaud*, Lausanne/Neuchâtel, n. d. [1927–28].

– and Raphaël Lugeon. "L'emplacement de la statue du Major Davel à Lausanne. Rapport présenté au comité central des monuments Davel", *Revue historique vaudoise*, I, August, 1893, pp. 225–32.

Maillard, Emile. *L'art à Nantes au XIXᵉ siècle*, Paris, n. d. [1888].

Maillard, Frédéric. "M. Louis Vulliemin", *La Suisse illustrée*, n° 19, 9 May 1874, pp. 218–20.

–. "Charles Gleyre", *La Suisse illustrée*, n° 23, 6 June 1875, pp. 265–68.

–. "Charles Gleyre", *Almanach de la Suisse illustrée et Almanach populaire illustré de la Suisse romande*, Lausanne, 1875, pp. 39–45.

Mainardi, Patricia. *Art and Politics of the Second Empire*, New Haven/London, 1989.

Mallé, Luigi. *Incontri con Gaudenzio. Raccolta di studi e note su problemi gaudenziani*, Turin, 1969.

Mallon, Jean. *L'influence française dans la Régence de Tunis avant l'établissement du Protectorat*, Paris, 1931.

Mandach, Conrad de. "L'art en Suisse", in *Le Musée d'art*, Paris, n. d., pp. 325–32.

Manganel, Ernest. *Artistes vaudois du XVIIIᵉ siècle à aujourd'hui*, Lausanne, 1953.

Mantz, Paul. "Le Musée du Luxembourg", *L'Artiste*, V, 1844, p. 238.

–. "Salon de 1845. Les peintures religieuses", *L'Artiste*, III, 1845, pp. 193–96.

–. "Ecole des Beaux-Arts. Les concours. Les envois de Rome", *L'Artiste*, II, 1857, pp. 75–78.

–. "Charles Gleyre", *Gazette des Beaux-Arts*, XI, 1 March 1875, pp. 233–44 and 1 May 1875, pp. 404–14.

–. "Les dessins de l'Ecole moderne", *Le Temps*, 9 March 1884, unpaginated.

*Manuel des voyageurs dans le canton de Vaud*, Lausanne, 1857.

Manuel, Frank E. *The New World of Henri Saint-Simon*, Cambridge, 1956.

–. *The Prophets of Paris*, Cambridge, 1962.

– and Fritzie P. Manuel. *Utopian Thought in the Western World*, Oxford, 1979.

Marandel, J. Patrice. *Frédéric Bazille and Early Impressionism*, exh. cat., The Art Institute, Chicago, 1978.

Marcel, Henry. *La peinture française au XIXᵉ siècle*, Paris, 1905.

Marconi, Sandra M. *Gallerie dell'Academia di Venezia*, Rome, 1955.

Mariéton, Paul. "Jasmin", in *La grande encyclopédie*, XXI, Paris, n. d., pp. 55–56.

–. "Souvenirs et anecdotes sur Chenavard", *Le Figaro*, 16 April 1895, unpaginated.

Marks, Henry Stacy. *Pen and Pencil Sketches*, London, 1894.

Marlowe, John. *Spoiling the Egyptians*, London, 1974.

Martens, F. *Souvenir de Lausanne et de ses environs*, Lausanne, n. d. [c.1850–60].

Martin, Henri. *Histoire de France*, Paris, 1855.

Martignier, David and Aymon de Crousaz. *Dictionnaire historique, géographique et statistique du canton de Vaud*, Lausanne, 1867.

Marx, Roger, ed. *Exposition centennale de l'art français 1800–1900*, Paris, 1900.

Matteson, Lynn R. "John Martin's 'The Deluge'. A Study in Romantic Catastrophe", *Pantheon*, XXXIX, July-September, 1981, pp. 220–28.

Mazade, Charles de. "Jasmin et la poésie populaire méridionale", *Revue des Deux-Mondes*, V, 1 January 1854, pp. 101–24.

Meier, Philipp, "Von Jan van Goyen bis Charles Gleyre. Verkaufsausstellung von Fischer und Meissner in Luzern", *Neue Zürcher Zeitung*, 10/11 September 1994.

Meissner, Alfred. *Heinrich Heine. Erinnerungen*, Hamburg, 1856.

Meister, Robert. *Albert Anker und seine Welt*, Bern, 1981.

Mellini, Gian Lorenzo. *Altichiero e Jacopo Avanzi*, Milan, 1965.

–. *Scultori veronesi del Trecento*, Milan, n. d. [1971].

Ménard, René. "Exposition de Vienne", *Gazette des Beaux-Arts*, VIII, September 1873, pp. 185–214.

–. *Les curiosités artistiques à Paris. Guide du promeneur dans les musées, les collections et les édifices*, Paris, 1878.

– and Louis Ménard. *Musée de peinture et de sculpture*, Paris, 1874–75.

Ménault, Ernest. "La jeunesse d'Hamon", *Le XIXᵉ siècle*, 5, 6, 8 and 9 July 1874, unpaginated.

Mende, Fritz. *Heinrich Heine. Chronik seines Lebens und Werkes*, Berlin, 1970.

Mendelssohn, Félix. *Lettres inédites de Mendelssohn*, A. A. Rolland, ed., Paris, n. d. [1864].

–. *Voyage de jeunesse. Lettres européennes (1830–1832)*, Paris, 1980.

Mennechet, Edouard, ed. *Le Plutarque français. Vie des hommes et des femmes illustres de la France*, 6 vols., Paris, 1844–47.

Mensuelli, Guido. *Galleria degli Uffizi. Le sculture*, I, Rome, 1958.

Mercey, M. F. "Les arts depuis le dernier Salon", *Revue des Deux-Mondes*, III, 1852, pp. 129–35.

Mercier-Campiche, Marianne. *Le théâtre de Lausanne de 1871 à 1914*, Lausanne, 1944.

–. *L'affaire Davel*, Lausanne, 1970.

Mérimée, Prosper. *Etudes sur l'histoire romaine*, Paris, 1844.

–. *Correspondance générale*, M. Parturier, ed., III, Paris, 1943.

Merson, Olivier. *La peinture en France*, Paris, 1861.

Meyer, Julius. *Geschichte der modernen französischen Malerei seit 1789*, Leipzig, 1867.

Meylan, Henri. "Trois lettres écrites de Vevey (avril 1723) sur l'affaire du Major Davel", *Revue historique vaudoise*, LXXVIII, 1970, pp. 69–79.

Meystre, Edith. "Charles Eynard, Madame de Krudener et la Contesse d'Edling", *Revue historique vaudoise*, LXVII, 1959 pp. 134–48.

Michaud, Joseph and J.-J. Poujoulat. *Correspondance d'Orient*, Paris, 1833–35.

Michel, Serge. *Chemins de fer en Lyonnais*, Lyons, 1986.

Michelet, Jules. *Journal*, 4 vols., Paris, 1959–76.

–. *Œuvres*, XXXVI, Paris, 1885–88.

Michetti-Prod'hom, Chantal. "Origine et naissance du Musée Arlaud", *Revue historique vaudoise*, XCVI, 1988, pp. 97–120.

Michod, Alexandre. "Une représentation historique par la Vigie de Lausanne", *Le Conteur vaudois*, 5 January 1867, p. 1.

Migne, Jacques-Paul, ed. *Patrologiae Cursus Completus. Ser. Latina*, Paris, 1844–65.

Milliet, Paul. "Une famille de républicains fouriéristes, les Milliet", *Cahiers de la Quinzaine*, Paris, 1913.

–. *Une famille de républicains fouriéristes. Les Milliet*, 2nd ed., Paris, 1915.

Milner, John. *The Studios of Paris: The Capital of Art in the Late Nineteenth Century*, New Haven/London, 1988.

MINUTOLI, La Baronne de. *Mes souvenirs d'Egypte*, Paris, 1826.

MIRECOURT, Eugène de. *Les contemporains : Ponsard*, Brussels, 1855.

–. *Les contemporains : Paul Delaroche*, Brussels, 1856.

MIREUR, Hippolyte. *Dictionnaire des ventes d'art faites en France et à l'étranger pendant les XVIIIᵉ [et] XIXᵉ siècles*, III, Paris, 1911–12.

MIRIMONDE, Albert-Pomme de. "Un document inédit sur l'Age d'or", *Bulletin du Musée Ingres*, V, December, 1958, p. 4.

–. *Catalogue du Musée Baron Martin à Gray*, Gray, 1959.

MOLINS, Auguste de. "Minerve et les Grâces par M. Gleyre", *Gazette de Lausanne*, 14 September 1866, pp. 1–2; 15 September 1866, pp. 1–2; 19 September 1866, pp. 1–2; and 20 September 1866, pp. 1–2.

MOMMSEN, Theodor. *Römische Geschichte*, II, Berlin, 1889.

MONNARD, Charles. "Le Major Davel", *Album de la Suisse romane*, IV, 1846, pp. 5–8 and 22–25.

MONNERET, Sophie. *L'impressionnisme et son époque. Dictionnaire international illustré*, 4 vols., Paris, 1978-1981.

MONTAIGLON, Anatole de, ed. *Correspondance des directeurs de l'Académie de France à Rome*, Paris, 1887 et seq.

MONTÉGUT, Emile. "Thomas Carlyle et John Sterling", *Revue des Deux-Mondes*, XV, July, 1852, pp. 133–64.

–. "Ecrivains modernes de la France : Gustave Planche", *Revue des Deux-Mondes*, XXVIII, June, 1858, pp. 642–70.

–. "Charles Gleyre", *Revue des Deux-Mondes*, XLVIII, September, 1878, pp. 395–426.

–. *Nos morts contemporains*, Paris, 1884.

MONTET, Albert de. *Dictionnaire biographique des Genevois et des Vaudois*, Lausanne, 1877–78.

[MONTET, Louis]. "Charles Gleyre", *Le Conteur vaudois*, IV, 9 December 1865, pp. 1–2.

MONTFAUCON, Bernard de. *L'Antiquité expliquée et représentée en figure*, Paris, 1719–24.

MONTROSIER, Eugène. *Les artistes modernes*, II, Paris, 1882.

MOR, Carlo Guido et al. *Il palazzo della Ragione*, Venice, 1963.

MORAX, René. *Davel. Drame en cinq actes*, Lausanne, 1923.

MOREAU-VAUTHIER, Charles. *Gérôme peintre et sculpteur. L'homme et l'artiste*, Paris, 1906.

MORIN, Georges. "Un médecin, ami de Raspail et de Sainte-Beuve. Le docteur Veyne (1815–1875)", *La Chronique médicale*, XXXIV, n° 9, 1 September 1927, pp. 259–64.

MORRIS, Edward and Amanda MCKAY. "British Painters in Paris 1814–1825 : Demand and Supply", *Apollo*, CXXXV, February 1992, pp. 78–84.

MOSBY, Dewey F. *Alexandre-Gabriel Decamps 1803–1860*, New York/London, 1977.

MOSCHELES, Félix. *In Bohemia with Du Maurier*, London, n. d. [1896]

MOSCHINI, Giovanni. *Guida per la città di Venezia all'amico delle belle arti*, Venice, 1815.

–. *Guida per la città di Padova*, Venice, 1817.

MOTTAZ, Eugène. "Le Major Davel", *Bibliothèque universelle et Revue suisse*, CX, n° 328, April 1923, pp. 62–73.

MULLER, F. *Centenaire de la Compagnie du gaz et du coke, S. A., 1861–1961*, Vevey, 1962.

MÜNTZ, Eugène. *Guide de l'Ecole nationale des Beaux-Arts*, Paris, n. d. [1889].

MURET, Ernest. "La légende de la reine Berthe", *Archives suisses des traditions populaires*, I, 1897, pp. 284–317.

MURPHY, Alexandra R. *Visions of Vesuvius*, exh. cat., Museum of Fine Arts, Boston, 1978.

MURRAY, John. *Hand-Book for Travellers in Northern Italy*, London, 1842.

*Musée Claude Bernard*, Saint-Julien-en-Beaujolais, n. d. [1968].

MUSSET, Paul de. *Biographie d'Alfred de Musset. Sa vie et ses œuvres*, Paris, 1877.

MUTHER, Richard. *The History of Modern Painting*, rev. ed., New York, 1907.

N. "Le portrait de Davel", *Le Conteur vaudois*, XXIX, 10 July 1891, pp. 1–2.

N., F. "Minerve et les Grâces. Tableau de M. Gleyre", *Le Conteur vaudois*, IV, 1 Sept. 1866, pp. 1–2.

–. "Une seconde visite à Minerve", *Le Conteur vaudois*, IV, 8 September 1866, pp. 2–3.

NAAMAN, Antoine Youssef. *Les lettres d'Egypte de Gustave Flaubert, d'après les manuscrits autographes*, Paris, 1965.

NAEF, Hans. "Ingres und das Familie Hittorff", *Pantheon*, July-August 1964, pp. 258–64.

–. *Die Bildniszeichnungen von J.-A.-D. Ingres*, III Bern, 1979.

NATALE, Mauro. *Le goût et les collections d'art italien à Genève du XVIIIᵉ au XXᵉ siècle*, Geneva, 1980.

–, ed. *Zenale e Leonardo. Tradizione e rinnovamento della pittura lombarda*, Milan, 1982.

NERVAL, Gérard de. "Voyage en Orient", in *Œuvres complètes*, Paris, 1961.

NEUWEILER, Arnold. *La peinture à Genève de 1700 à 1900*, Geneva, 1945.

NEWHOUSE, Nancy Scott. "From Rome to Khartoum : Gleyre, Lowell, and the Evidence of the Boston Watercolors and Drawings", in *Charles Gleyre 1806–1874*, William Hauptman and Nancy Scott Newhouse, eds., exh. cat., Grey Art Gallery, New York, 1980, pp. 79–117.

NOLOT, A. "Ecole nationale des Beaux-Arts et écoles municipales de dessin. Esquisse historique", in *Lyon et la région lyonnaise en 1906*, Lyons, 1906, I, pp. 319–47.

NOON, Patrick. *Richard Parkes Bonington. 'On the Pleasure of Painting'*, exh. cat., Yale Center for British Art, New Haven, 1991.

*Notice des peintures et sculptures exposées dans la galerie du Corps législatif*, Paris, 1866.

*Notes biographiques sur J.-J. Dubochet*, Paris, 1869.

*Nouveau guide de l'étranger à Lausanne et dans ses environs*, Lausanne, 1848.

OCKMAN, Carol. "The Restoration of the Château de Dampierre : Ingres, the Duc de Luynes and the Unrealized Vision of History", Ph. D. diss., Yale, 1982.

–. "Gleyre's 'Destroyed' Staircase Decorations at Dampierre : A Glaring Error", *Gazette des Beaux-Arts*, CIII, March, 1984, pp. 111–14.

OLIVARI, Maria T. B. *La Pinacothèque de Brera*, Florence, 1983.

OLIVIER, Frank. "La carrière d'Urbain Olivier", *Etudes de Lettres*, XVIII, n° 3, July 1944, pp. 120–50.

OLIVIER, Jean. "Olivier de La Sarraz et Eysins", *Recueil de généalogies vaudoises*, Lausanne, 1935, II, pp. 221–71.

–. *Cergnemin, Gryon et les Olivier*, Geneva, 1955.

OLIVIER, Juste. *Le canton de Vaud*, Lausanne, 1837.

–. *Le Major Davel. Etudes d'histoire nationale*, Lausanne, 1842.

–. *Les chansons lointaines, poèmes et poésies*, 2nd. ed., Paris/Geneva/Lausanne, 1855.

–. [Untitled description of Gleyre's *Romains*], *Gazette de Lausanne*, 23 July 1857, p. 4.

–. "Sainte-Beuve à Lausanne et dans sa jeunesse", *Bibliothèque universelle et Revue suisse*, LVI, 1876, pp. 5–37, 391–414, and 571–592.

–. *Œuvres choisies*, Lausanne, 1879.

–. *Paris en 1830. Journal*, André Delattre and Marc Denkinger, eds., Lausanne, 1951.

[OLIVIER, Juste]. "Chronique", *La Revue suisse*, XII, July 1849, p. 415.

[–]. "Chronique", *La Revue suisse*, XX, July 1857, pp. 474–75.

OLLIVIER, Emile. *L'empire libéral. Etudes, récits, souvenirs*, V, Paris, 1895.

OLMSTED, James M. D. and E. Harris OLMSTED. *Claude Bernard and the Experimental Method in Medicine*, New York, 1952.

ORMOND, Léonée. *George Du Maurier*, London, 1969.

ORY, Pascal. *Les expositions universelles de Paris*, Paris, 1982.

OWEN, Edward Roger John. *Cotton and Egyptian Economy*, London, 1969.

P. "Nécrologie", *L'Illustration*, XXXIII, 1 January 1859, p. 16.

P., A. "Chronique des arts et de la littérature", *Le Musée suisse*, II, 1855, pp. 141–47.

PAILLERON, Marie-Louise. *François Buloz et ses amis. Les écrivains du Second Empire*, Paris, 1924.

–. *Le ruisseau de la rue du Bac*, Paris, 1930(a).

–. *La vie littéraire sous Louis-Philippe*, Paris, 1930(b).

–. *Le paradis perdu. Souvenirs d'enfance*, Paris, 1947.

PALLUCCHINI, Rodolfo, ed. *Giorgione. Atti del convegno internazionale di studio per il 5° centenario della nascita*, Venice, 1979.

–. *Giorgione e l'umanesimo veneziano*, Florence, 1981.

PANNIER, Jacques. "Un libraire protestant à Paris il y a cent ans. J.-J. Dubochet", *Bulletin de la Société de l'histoire du protestantisme français*, XC, January-March 1941, pp. 46–51.

PANOFSKY, Erwin. *Problems in Titian, Mostly Iconographic*, New York, 1969.

PANOFSKY, Erwin and Dora. *Pandora's Box. The Changing Aspect of a Mythical Symbol*, New York, 1962.

PAOLETTI, Ermolao. *Il fiore di Venezia*, Venice, 1840.

PAPADOPOULOS, Stelios A. *Liberated Greece and the Morea Scientific Expedition. The Peytier Album in the Stephan Vagliano Collection*, Athens, 1971.

PAREDI, Angelo, ed. *L'Ambrosiana*, Milan, 1967.

*Paris guide par les principaux écrivains et artistes de la France*, Paris, 1867.

PARMÉNIE, Antoine and Catherine BONNIER DE LA CHAPELLE. *Histoire d'un éditeur et de ses auteurs. P.-J. Hetzel*, Paris, 1953.

PASCHOUD, François. "Les Romains sont-ils passés sous le joug à Montreux ? A propos d'un célèbre tableau de Charles Gleyre", *Museum Helveticum. Schweizerische Zeitschrift für klassische Altertumswissenschaft*, LII, 1995, pp. 49–62.

PAYS, Marcel. "Une visite à M. Claude Monet dans son ermitage de Giverny", *Excelsior*, 26 January 1921, unpaginated.

PEACOCK, Carlos. *Richard Parkes Bonington*, New York, 1980.

PEISSE, Louis. "Le Salon", *Revue des Deux-Mondes*, III, 1 April 1843, pp. 85–109 and 15 April 1843, pp. 255–87.

–. "Salon de 1849", *Le Constitutionel*, 1 July 1849, unpaginated.

PÉLADAN, Joséphin. "Notes sur Hébert", *Revue de Paris*, XVI, December, 1908, pp. 621–57.

PELET, Joseph. "L'industrie et les transports", in *Cent cinquante ans d'histoire vaudoise. 1803–1953*, Lausanne, 1953, pp. 131–50.

PELLETAN, Eugène. "Salon de 1845", *La Démocratie pacifique*, 31 March 1845, unpaginated.

PELLOQUET, Théodore. *Guide dans les musées de peinture et de sculpture du Louvre et du Luxembourg*, Paris, 1856.

–. *Dictionnaire de poche des artistes contemporains*, Paris, 1858.

PENNELL, Elizabeth and Joseph. *The Life of James McNeill Whistler*, London, 1911.

–. *The Whistler Journal*, Philadelphia, 1921.

PERDICARIS, Ion. "Reminiscences of a Parisian Atélier [sic]", *The Galaxy*, III, 15 March 1867, pp. 644–52.

PERROCHON, Henri. "Un oublié: Charles Eynard", *Gazette de Lausanne*, 27 September 1931, p. 1.

–. *Artistes vaudois à Rome. La Maison des Bourguignons, 1798–1909*, Lausanne, 1943.

–. "Le peintre Gleyre et le Pays de Vaud", *Semeur vaudois*, n° 41, 11 October 1947, pp. 1–2.

–. "De Juste Olivier à Charles Gleyre", *Revue historique vaudois*, LVI, 1948, pp. 202–206.

–. *Portraits et silhouettes du passé vaudois, 1706–1897*, Lausanne, 1969.

–, ed. *Le Général Antoine-Henri Jomini, 1779–1869*, exh. cat., Musée de Payerne, Payerne, 1969.

PETROZ, Pierre. *L'art et la critique en France depuis 1822*, Paris, 1875.

PIANTONI, Gianna and Stefano SUSINNO. *I Nazareni a Roma*, Rome, 1981.

PIERRE. "L'anniversaire de la mort du Major Davel", *Feuille d'avis de Lausanne*, 24 April 1903, p. 4.

–. "Juste Olivier, nouveau Davel", *Feuille d'avis de Lausanne*, 17 December 1906, p. 4.

PIGLER, Andar. *Barockthemen*, Budapest, 1974.

PIGNATTI, Terisio. *Veronese*, Venice, 1976.

P[ILLET], Fab[ien]. "Beaux-Arts. Salon de 1843", *Le Moniteur universel*, 19 April 1843, p. 806–807.

–. "Beaux-Arts. Salon de 1845", *Le Moniteur universel*, 31 March 1845, pp. 776–77.

–. "Exposition des Beaux-Arts aux Tuileries", *Le Moniteur universel*, 4 July 1849, p. 2235.

PINELLI, B. *Raccolta di cinquanta costumi pittoreschi*, Rome, 1809.

PLANCHE, Gustave. "Salon de 1840", *Revue des Deux-Mondes*, XXII, 1 April 1840, pp. 100–21.

–. "Peintres et sculpteurs modernes de la France. M. Charles Gleyre", *Revue des Deux-Mondes*, XII, 1 November 1851, pp. 489–505.

–. *Portraits d'artistes. Peintres et sculpteurs*, Paris, 1853.

PLANISCIG, Leo. *Venezianische Bildhauer der Renaissance*, Vienna, 1921.

POESCHEL, Erwin. *Die Kunstdenkmäler der Kantons Graubünden, VII: Chur und der Kreis fünf Dörfer*, Basel, 1948.

POINTON, Marcia. "The Italian Tour of William Hilton, R. A., in 1825", *Journal of the Warburg and Courtauld Institutes*, XXXV, 1972, pp. 339–58.

POLI, Annarosa, ed. *Voyageurs français à Vérone*, Geneva, 1984.

POLLA, Louis. *Rues de Lausanne*, Lausanne, 1981.

POLLIG, Hermann. "Exotische Welten. Europäische Phantasien", in *Exotische Welten. Europäische Phantasien*, exh. cat., Stuttgart, 1987, pp. 16–25.

PONTMARTIN, Armand A. de. *Les jeudis de Madame Charbonneau*, Paris, 1889.

POPE-HENNESSY, John. *The Complete Work of Paolo Uccello*, London, 1950.

–. *Fra Angelico*, New York, 1952.

PORRET, Alfred. "Juste Olivier–Gaudin–Gleyre", *Gazette de Lausanne*, 27 December 1904, p. 1.

PORRET, Edith. "Une bourgeoisie d'honneur de la ville de Lausanne", *Journal bourgeoisial*, XXV, n° 291, 1946, p. 9.

POTTIER, Edmond. *Vases antiques du Louvre*, III, Paris, 1922.

POULAIN, Gaston. *Bazille et ses amis*, Paris, 1932.

–. "Une œuvre inconnue de Frédéric Bazille", *Arts de France*, n° 16–17, 1947, pp. 122–23.

PRADIER, James. *Correspondance*, Douglas Siler, ed., Geneva, 1984.

PREVITALI, Giovanni. *La fortuna dei primitivi. Dal Vasari ai neoclassici*, Turin, 1964.

PRINSEP, Val C. "A Student's Life in Paris in 1859", *Magazine of Art*, II, May 1904, pp. 338–42.

*Programme officiel des représentations de Davel*, Lausanne, 1923.

PROUST, Antonin. *Edouard Manet. Souvenirs*, Paris, 1913.

QUADRI, Antoine. *Huit jours à Venise*, 4th ed., Venice, 1828.

QUARTIER-LA-TENTE, Edouard. *Les familles bourgeoises de Neuchâtel. Essais généalogiques*, Neuchâtel, 1903.

QUATREMÈRE DE QUINCY, Antoine-Chrysostome. *Histoire de la vie et des ouvrages de Raphaël*, Paris, 1824.

*Quelques renseignements sur Lausanne et le canton de Vaud*, Lausanne, 1858.

QUESTEL, C. *Notice sur M. Duban*, Paris, 1872.

QUINCHE-ANKER, Marie. *Le peintre Albert Anker, 1831–1910, d'après sa correspondance*, Bern, 1924.

QUINET, Edgar. *Œuvres complètes*, Paris, 1857.

–. *Lettres d'exil*, Paris, 1885–86.

QUINET, Madame Edgar. *Mémoires d'exil*, Paris, 1869–70.

R. "Le Musée Arlaud", *L'Estafette*, 25 November 1885, p. 2.

R., G. "La tombe de Gleyre", *La Patrie suisse*, 15 September 1897, pp. 219–20.

RAITT, Alan William. *Prosper Mérimée*, London, 1970.

[RAMBERT, Charles]. *50 ans de la Société vaudoise des Beaux-Arts*, Lausanne, 1912.

RAMBERT, Eugène. "La bataille du Léman. Tableau de M. Gleyre", *Gazette de Lausanne*, 14 September 1858, pp. 3–4.

–. "Souvenirs de Vienne", *Bibliothèque universelle et Revue suisse*, XLIX, 1873, pp. 260–300.

–. "Juste Olivier. Notice biographique et littéraire", in Juste Olivier, *Œuvres choisies*, Lausanne, 1879, I, pp. iii-ccxxiv.

–. "Charles Gleyre. Etudes et souvenirs", in *Mélanges*, Lausanne, 1890, pp. 291–364.

–. *Alexandre Vinet. Histoire de sa vie et ses ouvrages*, Lausanne, 1912.

– et al. *Montreux*, Bern, 1877.

RAPIN, André. "Un grand archéologue du siècle dernier: Frédéric-Louis Troyon (1815–1866)", *Revue historique vaudoise*, LXXIV, 1966, pp. 141–49.

RATCLIFF, Carter. "Illusions of an Academic: Charles Gleyre", *Art in America*, LXX, September 1980, pp. 116–18.

RECHT, Roland. *La cathédrale de Strasbourg*, Stuttgart, 1971.

*Recueil de généalogies vaudoises*, 3 vols., Lausanne, 1912–50.

REFF, Theodore. *Degas. The Artist's Mind*, London, 1976.

–. *The Notebooks of Edgar Degas*, Oxford, 1976.

RÉGAMEY, Félix. *Horace Lecoq de Boisbaudran et ses élèves. Notes et souvenirs*, Paris, 1903.

RÉGAMEY, Raymond. "La formation de Claude Monet", *Gazette des Beaux-Arts*, XV, February, 1927, pp. 65–84.

REGARD, Maurice. *Gustave Planche, 1808–1857*, Paris, 1955.

REINAUD, Emile. *Charles Jalabert. L'homme et l'artiste d'après sa correspondance*, Paris, 1903.

RENAN, Ernest. "Madame Hortense Cornu", in *Œuvres complètes*, II, Paris, 1948, pp. 1113–22.

–. *Œuvres complètes. Correspondance 1845–1892*, X, Paris, 1961.

[RENAUD, Paul]. *Collection d'un amateur*, Paris, 1984.

RENOIR, Jean. *Renoir*, Paris, 1962.

RENOU, Henri. "Vers au sujet du dernier tableau de M. Gleyre", *Nouvelliste vaudois et Journal national suisse*, n° 241, 13 October 1858, pp. 3–4.

*Répertoire des noms de famille suisses*, Zürich, 1968.

REWALD, John. *The History of Impressionism*, New York, 1961.

–. *Post-Impressionism. From Van Gogh to Gauguin*, New York, 1962.

REY, Robert. "Renoir à l'Ecole des Beaux-Arts", *Bulletin de la Société de l'histoire de l'art français*, 1926, pp. 33–37.

REYMOND, William. "Peintre suisse: Charles Gleyre", *Feuille populaire de la Suisse romande*, I, n° 7, 1853, pp. 9–14.

–. "Chronique", *Journal de Genève*, 8 August 1857(a), unpaginated.

–. "J. C. Kern", *L'Illustration*, XIX, n° 732, 7 March 1857(b), pp. 163–65.

–. "Le Divicon de M. Gleyre", *Feuille populaire de la Suisse romande*, III, n° 16, 1858(a), pp. 123–26.

–. *La peinture alpestre*, Geneva, 1858(b).

–. "La colonie suisse", in *Paris guide*, Paris, 1867, pp. 1047–51.

–. "Les Beaux-Arts à Lausanne. Le Musée Arlaud", *La Suisse*, n° 21, 20 May 1871, pp. 176–77; n° 23, 3 June 1871, pp. 194–95; and n° 30, 22 July 1871, pp. 247–49.

R[EYMOND], W[illiam]. "Exposition de tableaux au Musée Arlaud", *La Revue suisse*, XIII, October 1850, pp. 692–99.

[–]. "Le Major Davel. Drame historique et romantique en 5 actes", *La Guêpe*, II, 27 November 1852, p. 7.

[–]. "Exposition universelle de Vienne. Catalogue de l'Exposition suisse des Beaux-Arts", *La Suisse illustrée*, 1 November 1873, pp. 518–28.

RIBAUX, Alfred. *Divico. Drame en cinq actes, en prose*, Neuchâtel/Paris, 1908.

RIBEYRE, Félix. *Cham. Sa vie et son œuvre*, Paris, 1884.

RIEBEN, Henri. "Les artisans de la prospérité", in *Encyclopédie illustrée du Pays de Vaud*, Claude Reymond, ed., III, Lausanne, 1972.

RIGASSI, Georges. "Exposition de portraits anciens de la Suisse romande, Mon Repos, Lausanne", *Pages d'art*, VII, 1921, pp. 257–60.

RIGAUD, Jean-Jacques. *Renseignements sur les Beaux-Arts à Genève*, Geneva, 1876.

RIOUX DE MAILLOU, Pedro. *Souvenirs des centres*, Paris, 1917.

*La riscoperta dell'Egitto nel secolo XIX. I primi fotografi.* exh. cat., Museo Egizio di Torino, Turin, 1981.

RISHEL, Joseph, ed. *The Second Empire. Art in France Under Napoleon III*, exh. cat., Philadelphia Museum of Art, Philadelphia, 1978.

RITSCHARD, Claude. "Autoportrait", in *L'identité et ses visages*, exh. cat., Musée Cantonal des Beaux-Arts, Lausanne, 1977, pp. 39–45.

RITTER, William. *Edmond de Pury*, Geneva, 1913.

[RIVE, William de La]. *William Haldimand*, Geneva, 1863.

RIVERA, Diego. *Cincuenta años de su labor artistica*, Mexico City, 1951.

RIVIER, Louis. *Le peintre Paul Robert*, Neuchâtel/Paris, 1930.

RIVIÈRE, Georges. *Renoir et ses amis*, Paris, 1921.

ROBERTS, David. *Egypt and Nubia*, London, 1846–50.

ROBERTS, Keith. "A Gleyre Anniversary Exhibition", *The Burlington Magazine*, CXVI, December 1974, pp. 773–74.

ROBINSON, Lilien F. "Marc-Charles-Gabriel Gleyre", Ph. D. diss., Johns Hopkins University, 1978.

ROCHEGUDE, Marquis de. *Promenades dans toutes les rues de Paris*, Paris, 1910.

ROCHER-JAUNEAU, Madeleine, ed. *Les peintres de l'âme. Art lyonnais du XIXᵉ siècle*, exh. cat., Musée des Beaux-Arts, Lyons, 1981.

ROD, Edouard. *Les idées morales du temps présent*, Paris, 1911.

ROEDER, G. and W. RÜPPEL. *Der Tempel von Dakke*, Cairo, 1913–30.

ROMANELLI, Giandomenico. *Museo Correr*, Milan, 1984.

ROSELLINI, Ippolito. *I monumenti dell'Egitto e della Nubia*, Pisa, 1832–44.

ROSENBLUM, Robert. *Jean-Auguste-Dominique Ingres*, New York, 1967(a).

–. *Transformations in Late Eighteenth Century Art*, Princeton, 1967(b).

– and Horst Woldemar JANSON. *Nineteenth Century Art*, New York, 1984.

ROSENTHAL, Donald A. *Orientalism: The Near East in French Painting 1800–1880*, exh. cat., Memorial Art Gallery of the University of Rochester, Rochester, 1982.

ROSENTHAL, Léon. *La peinture romantique*, Paris, 1900.

–. *Du romantisme au réalisme*, Paris, 1914.

ROSSEL, Virgile. *Davel. Poème dramatique*, Lausanne, 1898.

–. *Histoire littéraire de la Suisse romande*, Neuchâtel, 1903.

–. *Eugène Rambert. Sa vie, son temps et son œuvre*, Lausanne, 1917.

[ROSSIER, Edmond]. *Au peuple vaudois, 1803–1903*, Lausanne, 1903.

ROSSIGNOL, F. *Notice sur Jacques-Julien Dubochet*, Paris, 1868.

ROUCHÈS, Gabriel. *L'Ecole des Beaux-Arts*, Paris, 1924.

RÜPPEL, Wilhelm. *Atlas zu der Reise in nördlichen Afrika*, Frankfurt, 1826.

–. *Reisen in Nubien*, Frankfurt, 1829.

RUSKIN, John. *Ruskin in Italy. Letters to His Parents, 1845*, Harold I. Shapiro, ed., Oxford, 1972.

S., A. "Exposition d'Alsace-Lorraine au Palais Bourbon", *Journal de Genève*, 10 May 1874, pp. 2–3.

SAINT-RENÉ TAILLANDIER, Madeleine. *Mon oncle Taine*, Paris, n.d. [1942].

SAINT-RENÉ TAILLANDIER, René G. "Poètes contemporains de l'Allemagne. Henri Heine. Sa vie et ses écrits", *Revue des Deux-Mondes*, XIV, 1 April 1852, pp. 5–36.

SAINT-VICTOR, Paul de. *D'après nature par Gavarni*, Paris, 1858.

–. "Le Musée du Luxembourg", in *Paris guide*, Paris, 1867, I, pp. 416–58.

SAINTE-BEUVE, Charles-Augustin. "Horace Vernet", in *Nouveaux lundis*, V, Paris, 1872, pp. 42–149.

–. *Chroniques parisiennes (1843–1845)*, Jules Troubat, ed., Paris, 1876.

–. *Correspondance inédite de Sainte-Beuve avec M. et Mme Juste Olivier*, Léon Séché, ed., Paris, 1914.

–. *Correspondance générale*, Jean Bonnerot, ed., Paris, 1935.

SALMI, Mario. *Masaccio*, 2nd ed., Milan, 1948.

–, ed. *Raffaello. L'opera, le fonti, la fortuna*, Novarra, 1968.

SALMSON, Jules. *Entre deux coups de ciseaux. Souvenirs d'un sculpteur*, Geneva/Paris, 1892.

*Salon Bollag* [Sale Catalogue], Zürich, 1916.

SALVISBERG, Paul, ed., *Offizieller Katalog der Schweizerischen Landesausstellung*, Zürich, 1883.

SANDEAU, Jules. "Critique dramatique: *Lucrèce*, par M. Ponsard", *Revue de Paris*, XVI, 30 April 1843(a), pp. 371–78.

–. "Karl Henry", *La Mode*, IV, 5 August 1843(b), pp. 178–92.

–. "Le Château de Montsabrey", *Musées des familles*, XIX, July 1852, pp. 289–301 and August 1852, pp. 338–50.

–. *Fernand. Vaillance. Richard*, Paris, 1868.

SANDOZ, Marc. *Théodore Chassèriau, 1819–1856. Catalogue raisonné des peintures et des estampes*, Paris, 1974.

SAUNERON, Serge and Henri STIERLIN. *Edfou et Philae. Derniers temples d'Egypte*, Lausanne, 1975.

SAUNIER, Charles. *La peinture au XIXᵉ siècle*, Paris, n. d.

SAUSSURE, Le ministre de. *Discours prononcé avant l'exécution du Major Davel (en présence du peuple assemblé pour son exécution à Vidy, le 24 avril 1723)*, Lausanne, 1846.

SAYED, Raouf Abdel el. *Documents relatifs à Saïs et ses divinités*, Cairo, 1975.

SCHAPIRO, Meyer. "Fromentin as Critic", *Partisan Review*, January 1949, pp. 25–51.

SCHEYER, Ernest. "Jean Frédéric Bazille. The Beginnings of Impressionism, 1862–1870", *The Art Quarterly*, V, n° 2, Spring, 1942, pp. 115–34.

SCHLENOFF, Norman. *Les sources littéraires de Jean-Auguste-Dominique Ingres*, Paris, 1956.

SCHNEIDER, Donald David. *The Works and Doctrine of Jacques Ignace Hittorff 1792–1867*, New York, 1977.

SCHOOP, Albert. *Johann Konrad Kern*, Frauenfeld/Stuttgart, 1968.

SCHUBRING, Paul. *Altichiero und seine Schule*, Berlin, 1898.

SCHULMAN, Michel. *Frédéric Bazille 1841-1870. Catalogue raisonné*, Paris, 1995.

SECRÉTAN, Louise. *Charles Secrétan. Sa vie et son œuvre*, Lausanne, 1911.

SÉGAL, Georges Berthold. *Der Maler Louis Léopold Robert, 1794–1835*, Basel, 1973.

*Seizième rapport du comité de la Société des amis des arts de Neuchâtel*, Neuchâtel, 1874.

SELVATICO, Pietro. *Sulla capellina degli Scrovegni nell'Arena di Padova*, Padua, 1836.

–. *Sull'architettura e sulla scultura in Venezia*, Venice, 1847.

SENSIER, Alfred. *La vie et l'œuvre de J.-F. Millet*, Paris, 1881.

SEREX, Victor. *Davel. Le martyr de Vidy*, Morges, 1923.

SEROUX D'AGINCOURT, Jean-Baptiste-Louis-Georges. *Storia dell'arte col mezzo dei monumenti*, Mantua, 1841.

SÉRULLAZ, Arlette and Régis MICHEL. *L'aquarelle en France au XIXᵉ siècle. Dessins du Musée du Louvre*, Paris, 1983.

SÉRULLAZ, Maurice. *Encyclopédie de l'impressionnisme*, Paris, 1974.

–. *Dessins d'Eugène Delacroix, 1798–1863*, Paris, 1984.

SERVIER, E. "Le gaz à Paris", in *Paris guide*, Paris, 1867, II, pp. 1632–37.

SÉVERY, William de. "William Haldimand et le Denantou", *Gazette de Lausanne*, 21 October 1928, p. 1 and 25 October 1928, p. 3.

SEZNEC, Jean. "Flaubert and the Graphic Arts", *Journal of the Warburg and Courtauld Institutes*, VIII, 1945, pp. 175–90.

SHEDD, Meredith. "Phidias at the Universal Exposition of 1855: The Duc de Luynes and the 'Athena Parthenos'", *Gazette des Beaux-Arts*, CVIII, October 1986, pp. 123–34.

SHEON, Aaron. *Monticelli. His Contemporaries. His Influence*, exh. cat., Pittsburgh, 1979.

SHINE, Hill. *Carlyle and the Saint-Simonians. The Concept of Historical Periodicity*, Baltimore, 1941.

SHONE, Richard. *Sisley*, London, 1992.

SHINN, Earl. [Obituary Notice of Charles Gleyre], *The Nation*, n° 464, 21 May 1874, p. 332.

SIEBENHÜNER, Herbert. *Der Palazzo Barbarigo della Terrazza in Venedig und seine Tizian-Sammlung*, Berlin, 1981.

*Un siècle d'art français, 1850–1950*, exh. cat., Petit-Palais, Paris, 1953.

SIEVERNICH, Gereon and Hendrik BUDDE, eds. *Europa und der Orient, 800–1900*, exh. cat., Martin-Gropius-Bau, Berlin, 1989.

SILVER, Mabel. *Jules Sandeau. L'homme et la vie*, Paris, 1936.

SILVESTRE, Théophile. *Les artistes français, II: Eclectiques et réalistes*, Paris, 1926.

SIM, Katherine. *David Roberts, R. A. 1796–1864*, London, 1984.

SIMOND, Charles, ed. *La vie parisienne à travers le XIXᵉ siècle*, Paris, 1900.

SIMOND, Louis. *Voyage en Italie et en Sicile*, 2nd ed., Paris, 1828.

SIRET, Adolphe. *Dictionnaire historique et raisonné des peintres de toutes les écoles...*, 3rd ed., Berlin, 1924.

SITZMANN, Edouard. *Dictionnaire biographique des hommes célèbres de l'Alsace*, Rixheim, 1909–10.

SLOANE, Joseph C. "The Tradition of Figure Painting and Concepts of Modern Art in France from 1845 to 1870", *The Journal of Aesthetics and Art Criticism*, VII, 1948, pp. 1–29.

–. *French Painting Between the Past and the Present. Artists, Critics, and Traditions, From 1848 to 1870*, Princeton, 1951.

–. *Paul Marc Joseph Chenavard. Artist of 1848*, Chapel Hill, 1962.

*Société des Belles-Lettres. Neuchâtel. Livre d'or, 1832–1907*, Neuchâtel, 1907.

SONOLET, Jacqueline. "Le Musée Claude Bernard à Saint-Julien-en-Beaujolais", *L'Œil*, n° 407, June 1989, pp. 68–69.

SOUBIÈS, Albert. *Les membres de l'Académie des Beaux-Arts*, II, Paris, 1904–15.

SOULLIÉ, Louis. *Bibliographie des ventes du XIXᵉ siècle*, Paris, 1896.

–. *Livre d'or des collectionneurs*, Paris, 1903.

*Souvenir du cinquantième anniversaire de la fondation de l'Eglise évangélique libre de Montreux*, Lausanne, 1897.

SPECTOR, Jack J. *The Murals of Eugène Delacroix at Saint-Sulpice*, New York, 1967.

SPENCER, Michael Clifford. *The Art Criticism of Théophile Gautier*, Geneva, 1969.

SPIAZZI, Anna Maria. "Giotto a Padova", *Bolletino d'Arte*, LXIII, 1982, pp. 13–58.

STACKELBERG, Baron Otto de. *Costumes et usages des peuples de la Grèce moderne, gravés d'après les dessins exécutés sur les lieux en 1811*, Rome, 1825.

STAIGER-GAYLER, Brigit. "Gleyre und seine Schweizer Schüler", in *Charles Gleyre ou les illusions perdues*, exh. cat., Kunstmuseum, Winterthur, 1974, pp. 126–49.

STARKIE, Enid. *Flaubert: The Making of the Master*, London, 1967.

–. *Flaubert: The Master*, London, 1971.

STERLING, Charles and Hélène ADHÉMAR. *Musée national du Louvre. Peintures. Ecole française. XIXᵉ siècle*, Paris, 1958–61.

STEVENS, Mary Anne, ed. *The Orientalists: Delacroix to Matisse, European Painters in North Africa and the Near East*, exh. cat., The Royal Academy of Arts, London, 1984.

STRAHAN, Edward [Earl Shinn]. *The Art Treasures of America. Being the Choiced Works of Art in the Public and Private Collections of North America*, Philadelphia, 1879–82.

–. *Etudes in Modern French Art*, New York, 1882.

STRANAHAN, C. H. *A History of French Painting. From its Earliest to Its Present Practice*, New York, 1888.

STRAUSS, Walter, ed. *The Complete Engravings, Etchings and Drypoints of Albrecht Dürer*, New York, 1972.

STRYIENSKI, Casimir. *Une carrière d'artiste au XIXᵉ siècle. Charles Landelle, 1821–1908*, Paris, 1911.

STUNZI, Lilly, ed. *Quel Tell?*, Lausanne, 1973.

*Le style Troubadour*, exh. cat., Musée de l'Ain, Bourg-en-Bresse, 1971.

*La Suisse historique et pittoresque*, Paris, 1858.

SUSINNO, Stefano. "Gli affreschi del Casino Massimo in Roma. Apunti per un quadro Riperimento nell'ambiente Romano", in *I Nazareni a Roma*, Rome, 1981, pp. 369–81.

SUTTON, Denys. *James McNeill Whistler. Paintings, Etchings, Pastels and Watercolours*, London, 1966.

–. "Giorgione and Pater", in *Giorgione. Atti del convegno internazionale di studio per il 5° centenario della nascite*, Rodolfo Pallucchini, ed., Venice, 1979, pp. 339–42.

SWEETMAN, John. *The Oriental Obsession. Islamic Inspiration in British and American Art and Architecture 1500–1920*, Cambridge, 1988.

SYMMONS, Sarah. "Flaxman and the Continent", in *John Flaxman*, David Bindman, ed., exh. cat., The Royal Academy of Arts, London, 1974, pp. 152–68.

SZRAMKIEWICZ, Romuald. *Les régents et censeurs de la Banque de France nommés sous le Consulat et l'Empire*, Geneva, 1974.

TABARANT, Adolphe. *La vie artistique au temps de Baudelaire*, Paris, 1942.

–. *Manet et ses œuvres*, Paris, 1947.

*Tableaux de la population de la Suisse, dressé d'après les résultats du dernier recensement fédéral (18–23 mars 1850)*, Bern, 1851.

TAILLENS, Jules. "A propos du cinquantenaire de la faculté de médecine à Lausanne," *Revue historique vaudoise*, LII, 1944, pp. 65–78.

TAINE, Hippolyte. [Obituary Notice of Gleyre]. *Journal des débats*, 6 May 1874, unpaginated.

–. *Sa vie et sa correspondance*, Paris, 1902.

–. *Derniers essais de critique et d'histoire*, 3rd ed., Paris, 1903.

TAVEL, Hans Christoph von. *Un siècle d'art suisse. Peinture et sculpture de Böcklin à Giacometti*, Lausanne, 1969.

–. *L'iconographie nationale* (Ars Helvetica, X), Disentis, 1992.

TAVERNIER, R. "Etudes sur les transports à Lyon", in *Lyon et la région lyonnaise en 1906*, II, Lyons, 1906, pp. 575–636.

TAVIGNOT, Le docteur. "Kyste hydatique de l'orbite. Opération. Ses résultats", *Gazette médico-chirurgicale*, IV, 24 January 1846, unpaginated.

TERNOIS, Daniel. *Ingres*, Paris, 1980(a).

–. "La peinture lyonnaise du XIXᵉ siècle. Etat des travaux et bibliographie", *Revue de l'art*, XLVII, 1980(b), pp. 98–112.

TERRAPON, Michel. *François Bonnet, 1811–1894. Rome, Lausanne, Fribourg*, Fribourg, 1969.

THÉVOZ, Michel. "Peinture et idéologie", in *Charles Gleyre ou les illusions perdues*, exh. cat., Kunstmuseum, Winterthur, 1974, pp. 70–85.

–. *L'académisme et ses fantasmes. Le réalisme imaginaire de Charles Gleyre*, Paris, 1980.

THIÉBAULT-SISSON. "Claude Monet. Les années d'épreuves", *Le Temps*, 26 Nov. 1900, unpaginated.

THIEME, Hugo. *Bibliographie de la littérature française de 1800 à 1930*, Paris, 1933.

THIEME, Ulrich and Felix BECKER. *Allgemeines Lexikon der Bildenden Künstler von der Antike bis zur Gegenwart*, Leipzig, 1907–50.

THORÉ, Théophile. *Le Salon de 1845, précédé d'une lettre à Béranger*, Paris, 1845.

–. *Salons de T. Thoré*, Paris, 1868.

THORNTON, Lynne. *Les orientalistes. Peintres voyageurs, 1828–1908*, Paris, 1983.

THUILLIER, Jacques. *Peut-on parler d'une peinture 'pompier'?*, Paris, 1984.

TIMBAL, Charles. *Notes et causeries sur l'art et les artistes*, Paris, 1851.

–. "L'exposition de peinture du Palais Bourbon au profit des Alsaciens-Lorrains", *Revue des Deux-Mondes*, 15 May 1874, pp. 444–64.

TÖPFFER, Rodolphe. *Réflexions et menus propos d'un peintre genevois*, Paris, 1853.

TOUSSAINT, Hélène. *Les portraits d'Ingres. Peintures des musées nationaux*, exh. cat., Louvre, Paris, 1985.

TRAUNECKER, Claude and Jean-Claude GOLVIN. *Karnak. Résurrection d'un site*, Fribourg, 1984.

TRAVERSARI, Gustavo. *Sculture del V–VI secolo a. C. del Museo archeologico di Venezia*, Venice, 1973.

–. *La statuaria ellenistica del Museo archeologico di Venezia*, Rome, 1986.

TRAVLOS, John. *Pictorial Dictionary of Ancient Athens*, New York, 1980.

TROYON, Frédéric. *Description des tombeaux de Bel-Air près Cheseaux-sur-Lausanne*, Lausanne, 1841.

–. "Antiquités helvétiennes de la forêt de Vernand de Blonay, près de Lausanne", *Le Pays*, n° 183, 5 August 1856, pp. 1–2.

–. *Habitations lacustres des temps anciens et modernes*, Lausanne, 1860.

TSCHARNER, Beat von. *Rapport annuel de la Société cantonale des Beaux-Arts de Berne*, Bern, 1875.

–. *Die bildenen Künste in der Schweiz in den Jahren 1886–1888*, Bern, 1889.

TSIGAKOU, Fani-Maria. *The Rediscovery of Greece: Travellers and Painters of the Romantic Era*, London, 1981.

TUCKER, Judith E. *Women in Nineteenth-Century Egypt*, Cambridge, 1985.

V., R. "Le Duc de Luynes", *L'Illustration*, 4 January 1868, pp. 2–3.

VADIER, Berthe. *Pierre-Jules Hetzel*, Geneva, 1889.

VAISSE, Pierre. "François Ehrmann", *Bulletin de la Société de l'histoire de l'art français*, 1976, pp. 341–61.

VALÉRY, M. *Venise et ses environs*, Brussels, 1842.

VALÈS, Albert. *Edgar Quinet. Sa vie et son œuvre*, Carrière-sous-Poisy, 1936.

VALLEIX, François-Louis-Isidore. *Guide du médecin praticien…*, 5th ed., Paris, 1866.

VALLETTE, Gaspard. "Le sculpteur J.-E. Chaponnière d'après des lettres inédites", *Nos anciens et leurs œuvres*, 1911, pp. 3–60.

VAN DEN HEUVEL, Jacques. *Album Voltaire*, Paris, 1983.

VAN GOGH, Vincent. *Correspondance complète de Vincent van Gogh*, Georges Charensol, ed., Paris, 1960.

VAN MUYDEN, Berthold, ed. *Lausanne à travers les âges*, Lausanne, 1906.

–. *Pages d'histoire lausannoise*, Lausanne, 1911.

VAN MUYDEN, Georges. *Les années d'apprentissage du peintre Alfred van Muyden*, Lausanne, 1950(a).

–. "Le premier voyage d'Alfred van Muyden en Italie (1844)", *Revue historique vaudoise*, LVIII, 1950(b), pp. 113–52.

VAN ZANTEN, David. *Designing Paris. The Architecture of Duban, Labrouste, Duc, and Vaudoyer*, Cambridge, 1987.

VAPEREAU, Gustave. *Dictionnaire universel des contemporains…*, 4th ed., Paris/London/Leipzig, 1870.

V[ARINSKI], C[arle] de. "Récompenses décernées à l'issue du Salon", *Journal des artistes*, XXXIII, 1843, pp. 401–403.

VASARI, Giorgio. *The Lives of the Painters, Sculptors, and Architects*, William Gaunt, ed., London, 1963.

VAUDOYER, Jean-Louis. "Méconnu et oublié. Charles Gleyre", *Echo de Paris*, 20 July 1922, unpaginated.

VAUDREMER, E. *Notice sur Louis Joseph Duc*, Paris, 1881.

VAVALA, Evelyn Sandburg. *La pittura veronese del Trecento e del primo Quattrocento*, Verona, 1926.

VÉGA. *Henri Heine peint par lui-même et par les autres*, Paris, 1936.

VENTO, Claude. *Les peintres de la femme*, Paris, 1888.

VENTURI, Lionello. *Les archives de l'impressionnisme*, 2 vols., Paris/New York, 1939.

VERDI, Richard. "Poussin's 'Deluge': The Aftermath", *The Burlington Magazine*, CXXIII, July 1981, pp. 389–400.

VÉRON, Le docteur. *Mémoires d'un bourgeois de Paris*, Paris, 1853.

VEY, Horst. *Die Zeichnungen Anton Van Dycks*, Brussels, 1962.

VEYNE, François. *Mort apparente et mort réelle*, Paris, 1874.

VIAL, Eugène. "Chenavard et Soulary", *Mémoires de l'Académie des sciences, belles-lettres et arts de Lyon*, XVII, 1921, pp. 95–125.

VIARDOT, Louis. *Les musées d'Italie*, Paris, 1859.

VIGÉE-LEBRUN, Marie-Louise. *Souvenirs*, Paris, 1835–37.

VILLARCEAUX, Xavier de. "Gabriel Gleyre", *L'Artiste*, 1 June 1874, pp. 447–48.

*La ville de Lausanne en l'an 1850*, Lausanne, n. d. [1851?].

VINET, Alexandre. "'Le Major Davel' par Juste Olivier", *Le Semeur*, 6 April 1842, p. 303.

–. *Lettres*, Lausanne, 1947–49.

VITET, Louis. "Beaux-Arts. Les peintures de Saint-Vincent-de-Paul et de l'Hôtel de Ville", *Revue des Deux-Mondes*, IV, 1853, pp. 1002–15.

VOGÜÉ, Melchior de. *Le Duc de Luynes*, Paris, 1868.

VOGÜÉ, Comte Eugène-Melchior de. *Nouvelles orientales*, Paris, 1901.

VOILQUIN, Suzanne. *Souvenirs d'une fille du peuple, ou la Saint-Simonienne en Egypte*, Paris, 1978.

VOLLARD, Ambroise. *La vie et l'œuvre de Pierre-Auguste Renoir*, Paris, 1920.

VUILLE, Albert. *Fritz Berthoud*, Geneva, 1894.

VUILLEUMIER, Henri. "Encore quelques bribes d'histoire à propos du Major Davel", *Revue historique vaudoise*, III, 1895, pp. 321–29.

–. *Le Major Davel. Etude d'histoire religieuse*, Lausanne, 1923.

VULLIEMIN, Charles, *Louis Vulliemin d'après sa correspondance et ses écrits*, Lausanne, 1892.

VULLIEMIN, Louis. *Aimé Steinlen. Notice*, Lausanne, 1864.

–. "La Reine Berthe", in *Galerie suisse*, Lausanne, 1873, I, pp. 14–27.

W. "William Haldimand", *Feuille d'avis de Lausanne*, 20 September 1962, p. 13.

W., G. "Figures disparues", *Gazette de Lausanne*, 11 November 1942, p. 1.

WADDINGTON, George and B. HANBURY, *Journal of a Visit to Some Parts of Ethiopia*, London, 1822.

WAGNIÈRE, Georges. *Dix-huit ans à Rome. Guerre mondiale et fascisme, 1918–1936*, Geneva, 1944.

WALDEGG, J. Heusinga von. "Jean-Léon Gérômes 'Phryné vor dem Richtern'", *Jahrbuch der Hamburger Kunstsammlungen*, XVII, 1972, pp. 122–42.

WALKER, Mark Steven and Louise D'ARGENCOURT, eds. *William Bouguereau, 1825–1905*, exh. cat., Petit-Palais, Paris, 1984.

WALLACE, Richard W. *The Etchings of Salvator Rosa*, Princeton, 1979.

WALTHARD, Bernard. "Der Kunstmaler Walthard, 1818–70", *Burgdorfer Jahrbuch*, 1966, pp. 11–153.

WARD, Roger. *Baccio Bandinelli, 1493–1560. Drawings from British Collections*, Cambridge, 1988.

WARNERY, Henri. "Devant le tableau de Gleyre", *La Revue du dimanche*, X, n° 46, 13 November 1898, pp. 363–64.

WESCHER, Paul. *Die Romantik in der Schweizer Malerei*, Frauenfeld, 1947.

WEEKS, Edward. *The Lowells and Their Institute*, Boston, 1966.

WEINBERG, H. Barbara. "American Impressionism in Cosmopolitan Context", *Arts Magazine*, LV, November, 1980, pp. 160–66.

–. *The Lure of Paris. Nineteenth Century American Painters and Their French Teachers*, New York, 1991.

WEINSTEIN, Leo. *Hippolyte Taine*, New York, 1972.

WEINSTOCK, Herbert. *Rossini: A Biography*, London, 1968.

WEISBERG, Gabriel P. [Review of *Charles Gleyre ou les illusions perdues*], *The Art Bulletin*, LVIII, n° 3, September 1976, p. 464–67.

–, ed. *The Realist Tradition: French Painting and Drawing, 1830–1900*, exh. cat., Cleveland Museum of Art, Cleveland, 1980.

WELLEK, René. *A History of Modern Criticism: 1750–1950*, IV, New Haven/London, 1965.

WENIG, Steffan. *Africa in Antiquity. The Arts of Ancient Nubia and the Sudan*, Brooklyn, 1978.

WENTWORTH, Michael. *James Tissot*, Oxford, 1984.

WETHEY, Harold. *The Paintings of Titian*, 3 vols., London, 1969–75.

WEY, Francis. "Salon de 1843", *Le Globe*, 23 March 1843, unpaginated.

WHITE, Barbara Ehrlich. *Renoir. His Life, Art, and Letters*, New York, 1984.

WHITE, Christopher and Karl G. BOON. *Rembrandt's Etchings*, Amsterdam/London/New York, 1969.

WHITE, Harrison C. and Cynthia. *Canvases and Careers*, New York, 1965.

WIDEN, G. *Luigi Lablache*, Göteborg, 1897.

WILDENSTEIN, Daniel. *Claude Monet. Biographie et catalogue raisonné, I: 1840–1881. Peintures*, Lausanne/Paris, 1974.

WILKINSON, A. *Typography of Thebes*, London, 1835.

WILSON, David Alec. *Carlyle At His Zenith (1848–1853)*, London/New York, 1927.

WISDOM, John Minor. *French Nineteenth Century Oil Sketches: David to Degas*, exh. cat., Duke University Art Gallery, Chapel Hill, 1978.

WISSOWA, Georg, ed. *Real-Encyclopädie der Classischen Altertumswissenschaft*, Stuttgart, 1894 et seq.

WOILLEZ, Docteur. "Notice sur Valleix", in F. L. I. Valleix, *Guide du médecin praticien…*, 5th ed., Paris, 1866, pp. xviii-xxiv.

WUHRMANN, Sylvie. "Le Déluge. Emergence et évolution d'un thème iconographique aux XVIIIᵉ et XIXᵉ siècles", Mémoire de licence, University of Lausanne, 1991.

X. "Salon de 1845", *L'Artiste*, 13 April 1845, pp. 225–28 and 27 April 1845, pp. 257–61.

–. "Exposition d'œuvres de Gleyre", *Gazette de Lausanne*, 3 September 1874, p. 2.

–. "Nouvelles et correspondance. Vaud", *Le Chrétien évangélique*, XIX, 1876, pp. 488–89.

YVON, Adolphe. "Souvenirs", *Revue des Deux-Mondes*, XVII, 15 October 1933, pp. 849–73.

Z., T. "Tableau", *Journal de Genève*, 11 May 1919, p. 1.

ZAFRAN, Eric M. *French Salon Paintings From Southern Collections*, exh. cat., The High Museum of Art, Atlanta, 1983.

ZAKON, Ronnie L. *The Artist and the Studio in the Eighteenth and Nineteenth Centuries*, Cleveland, 1978.

ZELGER, Franz. *Heldenstreit und Heldentod. Schweizerische Historienmalerei im 19. Jahrhundert*, Zürich, 1973.

–. "Zu Gleyres Historienbildern", in *Charles Gleyre ou les illusions perdues*, exh. cat., Kunstmuseum, Winterthur, 1974, pp. 86–101.

–, ed. *"Ich male für fromme Gemüter". Zur religiösen Schweizer Malerei im 19. Jahrhundert*, exh. cat., Kunstmuseum, Lucerne, 1985.

ZERI, Federico, ed. *Pinacoteca di Brera. Scuole lombarda e piemontese 1300–1535*, Milan, 1988.

ZIFF, Norman. *Paul Delaroche: A Study in Nineteenth Century French History Painting*, New York, 1977.

–. "Jeanne d'Arc et l'art de la Restauration française", in *Images de Jeanne d'Arc*, Paris, 1979.

ZOLA, Emile. *Salons*, F. W. J. Hemmings and Robert J. Niess, eds., Geneva/Paris, 1959.

ZWICKY VON GAUEN, Johann-Paul. *Almanach généalogique suisse*, VIII, Zürich, 1951.

## C. ANONYMOUS ARTICLES IN PERIODICALS

*Album de la Suisse romande.*
"Portrait de Chaponnière, par D'Albert-Durade", I, 1843, pp. 143–44.

*Album de la Suisse romane.*
"Le Château de Chatelard", III, 1845, pp. 192–94.

*Apollo.*
"Art Across North America. Outstanding Exhibitions. With Lowell to Khartoum", CXI, June 1980, p. 469.

*Archives héraldiques suisses.*
"La famille Larguier des Bancels", XXVI, 1913, pp. 94–95.

*L'Art.*
"Chronique française", VII, 1876, p. 95.

*L'Art et les artistes.*
[Untitled]. CI, August 1913, p. 196.

*L'Artiste.*
"Beaux-Arts", 2nd ser., VI, 1840, p. 166.

"Beaux-Arts", 2nd ser., VII, 1841, p. 298.

"Salon de 1843", 3rd ser., III, 21 May 1843, pp. 321–25.

«Revue de la Semaine», 4th ser., IV, 5 October 1845, p. 23.

"Gravures du numéro. Les Bacchantes", 5th ser., III, 15 October 1849, p. 220.

"Gravures du numéro. Cléonis et Cydippe", 8th ser., II, 15 August 1862, p. 96.

*Basler Nachrichten.*
[Untitled], LX, 11 March 1865, unpaginated.

*Les Beaux-Arts.*
"Salon de 1843", I, n° 3, 1843, pp. 41–47.

*Bibliothèque universelle de Genève.*
"Concours Haldimand. Du rapport présenté sur le concours", XIV, 1850, pp. 39–50.

*Le Carillon.*
[Untitled], 1 December 1877, unpaginated.

*Le Charivari.*
"Salon de 1843. II. Une heure d'élégie", 23 March 1843, p. 1.

"Choses et autres", 10 November 1865, p. 2.

*La Chronique des arts et de la curiosité.*
"Chronique", 1855, pp. 451–52.

"Gleyre", 8 May 1874, p. 187.

"Chronique", 19 May 1874, p. 187.

"Chronique", 30 May 1874, p. 216.

"Le buste de Gleyre", 2 December 1876, p. 339.

*Le Conteur vaudois.*
"Chronique", 22 December 1866, p. 1.

"A propos de Davel. Les deux glaives. Le bourreau de Moudon", 18 December 1897, pp. 1–2.

"Le bourreau de Moudon. Le portrait de Davel. La représentation du centenaire", 1 January 1898, p. 3.

"Le véritable nom du bourreau de Davel", 21 January 1899, p. 3.

"Réponses à la 'question intéressante'", 24 May 1902, p. 2.

"Les Jean-Jacques Mercier", 31 October 1904, pp. 1–2.

*Courrier de Lyon.*
"Exposition", 31 December 1839, unpaginated.

*Le Courrier suisse.*
"Notice", 3 May 1844, pp. 3–4.

"Exposition. Genève", 9 September 1845, p. 4.

*Du.*
"Charles Gleyre", March 1954, pp. 6–14.

*L'Estafette.*
"Chronique", 9 May 1874, p. 6.

"Chronique", 14 May 1874, p. 6.

"Chronique", 16 May 1874, p. 6.

"Chronique", 18 May 1874, p. 3.

"Chronique", 11 July 1876, p. 4.

*Feuille d'avis de Lausanne.*
"Musée des Beaux-Arts", 23 July 1910, p. 19.

"Louis Ormond (1828–1901)", 16 February 1962, p. 11.

*Le Figaro.*
"La mort subite du peintre Gleyre", 7 May 1874, unpaginated.

*Gazette des Beaux-Arts.*
"Chronique des arts", XCVIII, September 1981, p. 22.

*Gazette de Lausanne.*
"Exposition de peinture à Lausanne", 19 September 1850, p. 3; 24 September 1850, p. 4; 28 September 1850, pp. 3–4; 3 October 1850, pp. 3–4; 8 October 1850, p. 3; and 15 October 1850, pp. 3–4.

[Untitled], 23 July 1857, p. 2.

[Untitled], 10 September 1858, p. 4.

[Untitled], 16 October 1858, p. 2.

[Untitled], 10-11 and 13 October 1865.

[Untitled], 2 January 1867, p. 3.

"Gleyre", 8 May 1874 pp. 1–2.

[Untitled], 19 May 1874, p. 3.

"Exposition des œuvres de Charles Gleyre", 9 September 1874, p. 2.

"Une soirée chez Juste Olivier", 24 January 1876, p. 1.

"Correspondance, par un bibliophile", 29 January 1876, p. 3.

[Untitled], 5 July 1876, p. 2.

"L'inauguration du buste de Gleyre", 22 November 1876.

"Dubochet", 26 October 1877, p. 2–3.

[Edouard Fehr], 26 September 1894, p. 1.

"Gleyre au Musée Arlaud", 31 January 1898, p. 3.

"Le 'Davel' de 1845", 5 February 1898, p. 2.

"Louis Ormond", 26 April 1901, pp. 2–3.

"Juste Olivier. Gaudin. Gleyre", 27 December 1904, p. 1.

"M. Adrien Mercier", 10 March 1908, p. 1.

"Achat de la collection Clément", 5 May 1908, p. 3.

"Melegari à Lausanne", 13 January 1942, p. 2.

*Gazette universelle des Beaux-Arts.*
"Musée du Louvre. Exposition de 1845. Tableaux religieux", II, n° 95, 23 March 1845, unpaginated.

*Gazette vaudoise.*
[Untitled], 6 September 1858, p. 2.

[Untitled], 1 October 1858, p. 4.

*Harvard Alumni Bulletin.*
"John Lowell, World Traveler", 1949, p. 636.

*L'Illustration.*
"Salon de 1843", I, 22 April 1843, p. 120–21.

"Chronique. Cours scientifique", I, 29 April 1843, pp. 130–31.

"Achmed-Pacha. Bey de Tunis", I, 12 August 1843, pp. 369–70.

"Fête de Saint-Louis, à Tunis", II, 23 September 1843, p. 55.

"Une visite au poëte Jasmin", II, 4 November 1843, pp. 145–46.

"Salon de 1845", V, 19 April 1845, pp. 120–22 and 26 April 1845, pp. 135–38.

"Tunis", V, 19 July 1845, pp. 327–30 and 2 August, pp. 363–66.

"Voyage du Bey de Tunis en France", VIII, 7 November 1846, pp. 152–54.

"Arrivée du Bey de Tunis à Toulon", VIII, 21 November 1846, p. 192.

[Untitled], XXVI, 15 December 1855, p. 397.

*L'Illustré.*
"Compte rendu", 14 April 1923, p. 170.

*Journal des débats.*
[Untitled], 23 November 1846, unpaginated.

[Untitled], 16 December, 1846 unpaginated.

"Salon de 1865", 30 March 1865, p. 1f.

*Journal du district de Cossonay.*
"Succès d'une exposition", 15 August 1958, p. 2.

*Journal de Genève.*
"Exposition de tableaux à Lausanne", 8 October 1850, pp. 1–2 and 12 October 1850, pp. 1–2.

"Chronique", 5 September 1858, p. 2.

"Chronique", 18 September 1858, p. 2.

"Chronique", 30 September 1858, pp. 2–3.

"William Haldimand", 8 September 1863, p. 1 and 10 September 1863, p. 1.

"Exposition", 16 and 21 November 1865, p. 2.

"Exposition", 31 July 1866, p. 3.

"Chronique", 7 May 1874, p. 2.

*Journal de Lyon.*
"Gleyre", 10 May 1874, unpaginated.

*Magasin pittoresque.*
"Salon de 1845. Peinture. Le Départ des Apôtres, par M. Gleyre", XIII, June 1845, pp. 187–88.

"Ruth et Booz", XXVI, April, 1858, pp. 129–30.

"Sébastien Cornu", XLII, June, 1874, pp. 81–82.

"Le Major Davel", XLVIII, June, 1880, pp. 185–86.

*Le Messager des Alpes.*
"Retour de l'exposition artistique à Lausanne", 27 May 1874, p. 3.

*Le Moniteur universel.*
[Untitled], 17 November 1846, unpaginated.

[Untitled], 23 November 1846, unpaginated.

[Untitled], 2 December 1846, unpaginated.

"Salon de 1866", 15 August 1866, unpaginated.

*Musée des familles.*
"Une éruption de l'Etna", XI, January, 1844, p. 126.

"Le Salon de 1852", XIX, June, 1852, pp. 273–75.

*Le National.*
"Salon de 1840", 1840, unpaginated.

*Nouvelliste vaudois.*
"L'Exposition", 3 September 1850, p. 2.

"Sur l'exposition de peinture à Lausanne", 7 September 1850, p. 1; 14 September 1850, p. 1; and 28 September 1850, p. 1.

"Chronique", 28 August 1858, p. 3.

"Chronique", 4 September 1858, p. 2.

"Chronique", 6 September 1858, pp. 2–3.

"Chronique", 13 October 1858, pp. 3–4.

"Chronique", 14 October 1858, p. 4.

"Chronique", 16 October 1858, pp. 3–4.

"Chronique", 11 October 1865, p. 3.

"Exposition", 7 August 1866, p. 2.

"Chronique", 17 August 1866, p. 3.

"Chronique", 25 August 1866, p.3.

"Chronique", 18 May 1874, p. 3.

"Chronique", 19 May 1874, pp. 2–3.

"Chronique", 21 May 1874, p. 3.

"Chronique", 13 October 1876, p. 3.

"Le peintre Charles Gleyre", 22 September 1896, p. 1.

"Au Musée des Beaux-Arts", 26 July 1910, p. 1.

*La Patrie.*
[Untitled], 10 October 1863, p. 2.

*Petit journal suisse.*
"Le Major Davel", November, 1865, pp. 1–3.

"L'Athénée de Genève", 10 February 1866, unpaginated.

*La Petite presse.*
"Mort de Gleyre", 7 May 1874, unpaginated.

*Putnam's Magazine.*
"Pictures in the Private Galleries of New York. II. Gallery of John Taylor Johnston", July 1870, pp. 81–86.

*Recueil de généalogie vaudoise.*
"Fatio. Branche de Vevey et rameau de Genève", I, 1923, pp. 589–625.

*La Revue.*
"Achat de la collection Clément", 5 May 1908, pp. 1–2.

"Le Docteur Combe", 16 March 1917, p. 2.

*La Revue des Beaux Mondes.*
"Les héros helvétiques, XII, 1 November 1845. pp. 520–22.

*La Revue du dimanche.*
"Le monument de Gleyre à Chevilly", X, 27 November 1898, p. 378.

"A propos de Gleyre", X, n° 49, 4 December 1898, pp. 385–86.

*Revue historique vaudoise.*
"Chronique", II, 1894, p. 189.

*La Revue indépendante.*
"Salon de 1843", VII, 10 April 1843, pp. 402–15.

"Revue théâtrale. Lucrèce jugée en Allemagne", X, October 1843, pp. 420–23.

*La Revue du Louvre et des musées de France.*
"Les récentes acquisitions des musées nationaux", XXVII, 1977, p. 366.

*La Revue suisse.*
"Chronique", VIII, April 1845, pp. 246–47.

"Exposition de peinture à Lausanne", XIII, November 1850, pp. 777–79.

"Chronique", XIV, February 1851, p. 127.

"Chronique", XVI, March 1853, pp. 264–65.

"Chronique", XVIII, June 1855, pp. 446–54.

"Chronique", XX, July 1857, pp. 474–75.

"Chronique", XXI, August 1858, pp. 558–59.

"Chronique", XXXI, October 1858, pp. 701–702.

*Die Schweiz.*
"Im Wald", VII, 1903, pp. 320–21.

*La Suisse.*
"Le Général Jomini", 6 July 1867, pp. 63–65.

*La Suisse illustrée.*
"Penthée poursuivi par les Bacchantes", 1 March 1873, pp. 102–103 and 106.

"Divico, ou la bataille du Léman", 20 September 1873, pp. 455–56 and 27 September 1873, pp. 474–77.

"Exposition Gleyre", 6 September 1874, pp. 426–29.

*Le Touriste.*
"Hercule aux pieds d'Omphale", September 1866, pp. 280–82.

*La Tribune de Genève,*
"L'Exposition", 31 July 1866, unpaginated.

*La Tribune de Lausanne et l'Estafette.*
"Le monument de Charles Gleyre", 22 September 1896, p. 1.

*Le XIX<sup>e</sup> siècle.*
[Untitled], 7 May 1874, unpaginated.

# LIST OF ILLUSTRATIONS

171. Study for *The Romans Passing under the Yoke*, 1856–58. Oil on canvas, 46 x 37.5 cm. Lausanne, Musée Cantonal des Beaux-Arts (cat. n° 681)
172. Léopold Robert, *The Return of the Pilgrims*, 1827. Oil on canvas, 142 x 212.5 cm. Paris, Musée du Louvre
173. Léopold Robert, *The Arrival of the Harvesters*, 1830. Oil on canvas, 141.7 x 212 cm. Paris, Musée du Louvre
174. *Chimera*, c. 350 B.C. Bronze. Florence, Museo Archeologico
175. Anonymous, *Frédéric-Louis Troyon*, c. 1855. Photograph. Lausanne, Musée Historique de Lausanne
176. Frédéric-Louis Troyon, *Archeological Studies*, 1847. Watercolor on paper. Lausanne, Musée Cantonal d'Archéologie et d'Histoire
177. Roman Shield from Avenches, c. 100 B.C. Lausanne, Musée Cantonal d'Archéologie et d'Histoire
178. Studies after Troyon's *Albums*, c. 1856. Pencil on paper, 10 x 16 cm. France, Private collection (cat. n° 744, folio 15ʳ)
179. Samuel Heer-Tschudi, *Charles Gleyre*, 1858. Photograph. Lausanne, Musée Historique de Lausanne
180. Performance of Adolphe Ribaux's *Divico* at Bevaix, 25 July 1908. From *La Patrie Suisse*, 5 August 1908, p. 191
181. Edward Poynter, *Israel in Egypt*, 1867. Oil on canvas, 137.2 x 317.5 cm. London, Guildhall Art Gallery
182. Anton Aloys Brandenberg, *The Romans Passing under the Yoke*, 1891. Plaster, 133 x 200 cm. Chur, Bünder Kunstmuseum
183. Vaudois government session note, 12 October 1858. Lausanne, Archives Cantonales vaudoises
184. "La Bataille du Léman", Brochure. Imprimerie Corbaz et Rouiller Fils, Lausanne, [1858]. Lausanne, Bibliothèque Cantonale et Universitaire, Département des Manuscrits, Dossier Antoine Baron, F¹⁸, II, n° 183

CHAPTER 9

185. *The Mother of Tobias*, 1860. Detail of ill. 203
186. *Portrait of Antoine-Henri Jomini*, 1859. Oil on canvas, 89 x 72 cm. Lausanne, Musée Cantonal des Beaux-Arts, on deposit in Payerne, Musée de Payerne et de l'Abbatiale, Salle Jomini (cat. n° 749)
187. Anonymous, *Antoine-Henri Jomini*, c. 1858. Photograph. Lausanne, Musée Historique de Lausanne
188. *Portrait of William Haldimand*, 1859. Oil on canvas, 130 x 105 cm. Lausanne, Musée Cantonal des Beaux-Arts (cat. n° 751)
189. Friedrich von Martens, *Le Denantou*, c. 1850. Lithograph. Lausanne, Musée Historique de Lausanne
190. Anonymous, *William Haldimand*, 1862. Photograph. Lausanne, Musée Historique de Lausanne
191. *Portrait of Louis Vulliemin*, 1859. Oil on canvas, 73 x 59.5 cm. Lausanne, Musée Cantonal des Beaux-Arts (cat. n° 753)

192. Study for the *Portrait of Louis Vulliemin*, 1859. Pencil on paper, 22.2 x 29 cm. Lausanne, Musée Cantonal des Beaux-Arts (cat. n° 755)
193. Samuel Heer-Tschudi, *Louis Vulliemin*, c. 1860. Photograph. Lausanne, Musée Historique de Lausanne
194. *Phryne before the Judges*, 1859–61. Oil on wood panel, 66 x 36 cm. Lausanne, Musée Cantonal des Beaux-Arts (cat. n° 785)
195. Study for *Phryne before the Judges*, 1859–61. Charcoal and crayon on canvas, 39.2 x 31.5 cm. Lausanne, Musée Cantonal des Beaux-Arts (cat. n° 786)
196. Victor-Louis Mottez, *Phryne*, 1859. Oil on canvas, 80 x 100 cm. Dijon, Musée des Beaux-Arts
197. *Portrait of Thérèse Olivier*, 1860. Pencil on paper, 43 x 33 cm. Geneva, Collection René des Gouttes (cat. n° 757)
198. *Amor and the Fates*, c. 1860. Oil on canvas, 37 x 28 cm. Lausanne, Musée Cantonal des Beaux-Arts (cat. n° 762)
199. *The Bathers*, c. 1860. Oil on canvas, diameter 27.4 cm. Lausanne, Musée Cantonal des Beaux-Arts (cat. n° 768)
200. *Innocence*, 1860. Oil on canvas, 32.5 x 40.5 cm. Lausanne, Musée Cantonal des Beaux-Arts (cat. n° 759)
201. *Young Woman Reading*, c. 1860. Oil on canvas, 32.5 x 24.5 cm. Lausanne, Musée Cantonal des Beaux-Arts (cat. n° 772)
202. *Daphnis and Chloe*, 1860–62. Oil on canvas, 80 x 62.2 cm. New York, Private collection (cat. n° 793)
203. *The Mother of Tobias*, 1860. Pencil and crayon on paper, 36.7 x 62.7 cm. Lausanne, Musée Cantonal des Beaux-Arts (cat. n° 761)
204. *Raphael, Leonardo, Michelangelo*, 1860. Engraving. From *Clément, Michel-Ange, Léonard de Vinci, Raphaël*, 1860, frontispiece (see catalogue n° 760)
205. *Joan of Arc*, c. 1860. Pencil and crayon on paper, 60.3 x 33.8 cm. Lausanne, Musée Cantonal des Beaux-Arts (cat. n° 778)
206. *Hercules and Omphale*, 1862. Oil on canvas, 145 x 111 cm. Neuchâtel, Musée d'Art et d'Histoire (cat. n° 808)
207. *Hercules and Iphitus*, 1858–65. Crayon on paper, 37.6 x 29.5 cm. Lausanne, Musée Cantonal des Beaux-Arts (cat. n° 845)
208. Diego Rivera, *Study of Omphale*, 1898. Pencil on paper, 36.2 x 28.3 cm. Mexico City, Universidad Nacional Autónoma de Mexico, Escuela Nacional de Bellas Artes
209. *Pentheus Pursued by the Maenads*, 1865. Oil on canvas, 121.1 x 200.7 cm. Basel, Öffentliche Kunstsammlung Basel, Kunstmuseum (cat. n° 850)
210. *Pentheus Surprising the Maenads*, 1859 (?). Crayon and wash on paper, 27 x 45.7 cm. Lausanne, Musée Cantonal des Beaux-Arts (cat. n° 867)
211. John Flaxman, *Ulysses Terrified by the Ghosts*, 1805. Engraving. New Haven, Yale Center for British Art
212. Raphael, Detail of *The Expulsion of Heliodoros*, 1512. Fresco. Rome, Vatican, Stanza d'Eliodoro

213. William Bouguereau, *The Remorse of Orestes*, 1862. Oil on canvas, 227.3 x 278.2 cm. Norfolk, The Chrysler Museum of Art, Gift of Walter P. Chrysler, Jr., 1971

CHAPTER 10

214. Study of Animals for *Minerva and the Three Graces*, 1865. Oil on canvas, 36.5 x 27 cm. Lausanne, Musée Cantonal des Beaux-Arts (cat. n° 875)
215. The Château des Crêtes, near Vevey. Photograph. Bern, Eidgenössisches Archiv für Denkmalpflege
216. *Minerva and the Three Graces*, 1866. Oil on canvas, 226.5 x 139 cm. Lausanne, Musée Cantonal des Beaux-Arts (cat. n° 872)
217. *Portrait of Madame Audiffred*, 1867. Oil on canvas, 125 x 85 cm. Troyes, Musée d'Art et d'Archéologie (cat. n° 900)
218. *Portrait of Madame Eulalie Carrié*, 1867 (?). Oil on canvas, 65 x 54.5 cm. Montpellier, Musée Fabre (cat. n° 906)
219. *Sappho*, 1867. Oil on canvas, 108 x 72 cm. Lausanne, Musée Cantonal des Beaux-Arts (cat. n° 908)
220. *The Charmer*, 1868. Oil on canvas, 82.3 x 50.6 cm. Basel, Öffentliche Kunstsammlung Basel, Kunstmuseum (cat. n° 914)
221. *The Bath*, 1868. Oil on canvas, 91.4 x 53.4 cm. Norfolk, The Chrysler Museum of Art, Gift of Walter P. Chrysler, Jr., 1971 (cat. n° 920)
222. *The Bath*, 1868. Detail of ill. 221
223. *Portrait of Jacques-Julien Dubochet*, 1869. Oil on canvas, 120 x 77 cm. Vevey, Musée Jenisch (cat. n° 937)
224. Franck (Pseudonym of François Gobinet de Villecholle), *Jacques-Julien Dubochet*, c. 1862. Photograph. Lausanne, Musée de l'Elysée
225. *Portrait of Madame Raffalovich*, 1868–69. Oil on canvas, 76 x 55 cm. London, Private collection (cat. n° 941)

CHAPTER 11

226. *Double Portrait of Louis-Francis Ormond*, 1870. Pencil on paper, 26.7 x 20.4 cm. London, Collection of Richard Ormond (cat. n° 952)
227. *Portrait of Frédéric Clément*, 1870. Pencil on paper, 24.8 x 30.2 cm. Switzerland, Private collection (cat. n° 947)
228. *Portrait of Madame Ormond*, 1870–71. Oil on canvas, 93 x 63 cm. Vevey, Musée Jenisch (cat. n° 950)
229. *Portrait of Louis Ormond*, 1870–71. Oil on canvas, 93 x 63 cm. Vevey, Musée Jenisch (cat. n° 948)
230. *Portrait of Victor Ruffy*, 1871. Oil on canvas, 63.5 x 50 cm. Lausanne, Musée Cantonal des Beaux-Arts (cat. n° 953)
231. Frédéric Gorgerat, *Victor Ruffy*, c. 1868. Photograph. Lausanne, Musée de l'Elysée

# PHOTO CREDITS